REAL WAGES
IN SOVIET RUSSIA
SINCE 1928

REAL WAGES
IN SOVIET RUSSIA
SINCE 1928

JANET G. CHAPMAN

HARVARD UNIVERSITY PRESS

Cambridge, Massachusetts

1963

Copyright © 1963, by The RAND Corporation
All rights reserved

•

Distributed in Great Britain by Oxford University Press, London

Library of Congress Catalog Card Number: 63–13809

•

Printed in the United States of America

For
J. W. C. and H. P. C.

PREFACE

The living standard of the Russian people is one of the grand criteria on which the performance of the Soviet economy will be judged. This study provides significant evidence on this momentous matter. My objective is not to add to the impressionistic accounts of the hardships to which the Russian people have been subjected in the course of forced industrialization. Rather, it is to present and analyze the statistical data on the real wages of the Soviet worker. The transformation of these data into a portrait of the quality of life under the Soviet regime is left to the reader.

In May 1954, preliminary results of this study were published in the *Review of Economics and Statistics*. At that time I promised that complete documentation would be made at a later date. The present volume represents more than this and something rather different. The revisions and improvements, as well as the regrettably long delay in publication of the final study, are due largely to the increase in information released by the Soviet government since 1954. In the first place, it has been possible to extend the investigation to cover certain additional years — 1940, 1944, 1954, and, in less detail, the years since 1954. Secondly, the publication by the Soviet government in 1956 of fairly detailed data on the structure of Soviet retail sales provided a basis for the computation of weights for the cost-of-living index number for each of the years studied, and for revisions of the 1937 weights previously presented. Beyond this, other information released by the Soviet government at about the same time made it advisable to check and revise some of the price comparisons and certain other aspects of my calculations.

I have, I believe, taken into account the new Soviet information most important to my study, but it was not possible to cover systematically all Soviet materials that have appeared in the last few years. The basic computations of the cost of living and of real wages through 1954 were completed in 1958, and some elements of the computations were completed even earlier. Subsequently, the 1944 figures were revised. Otherwise, more recent information indicates some errors were made at various points (I point these out in the footnotes, where possible). These do not appear to be serious enough to justify extensive recalculations or to affect the results significantly. For various other aspects of the study, and especially for developments since 1954, I have made use of materials that became available through 1960. The first Soviet monograph on Soviet real wages to appear since the 1920's, published in 1960, came into my hands only late in the summer of 1961. The manuscript was then too far advanced to treat this fully, but I have inserted a small section on it in my final chapter. I make frequent use of data from the studies of Soviet national income by Abram Bergson, Hans Heymann, Jr., Oleg Hoeffding, and Nancy Nimitz. Although they generously kept me informed of revisions as their studies progressed, in some cases I still use preliminary figures that differ somewhat from their final published figures.

This study is both a dissertation under the auspices of the Department of Economics of Columbia University and part of a research program conducted by The RAND Corporation for the United States Air Force. It is, so far as the retail price computations are concerned, one of a series of studies of Soviet prices undertaken in connection with the RAND studies of Soviet national income under the direction of Abram Bergson, formerly of Columbia University and now of Harvard University, who served also as my dissertation adviser. I am deeply grateful to him for inspiration, aid, and encouragement. I am also indebted to him for having had the forethought to acquire, on a 1937 visit to Russia, the series of 1936 Soviet retail price handbooks so important to this study. I am pleased to express my appreciation to Joseph Kershaw of The RAND Corporation, who with generosity and patience facilitated the research in many ways. The study has also benefited from the assistance of other colleagues at RAND — in particular, Hans Heymann, Jr., Oleg Hoeffding, Norman Kaplan, and Nancy Nimitz.

I also wish to thank James Blackman of the University of North Carolina; Warren Eason of Princeton University; Holland Hunter of Haverford College; Naum Jasny of the Soviet Economics Study Group, Washington, D.C.; Alec Nove of the London School of Economics; Francis Seton of Nuffield College, Oxford; Caroline Recht Shilling, formerly at the Harvard University Russian Research Center; Lynn Turgeon of Hofstra College; and Eugène Zaleski of the Conseil National de la Recherche Scientifique, Paris, for aid on various aspects of this study; and Alexander Erlich, Gary S. Becker, and Julius Rubin, all of Columbia University, for helpful comments on the manuscript. Special thanks are due to the many persons who have observed and reported on prices in Moscow shops.

The study owes much to my training in the Russian Institute and the Department of Economics of Columbia University. My graduate work during the period 1946 to 1949 was aided by the Hannah Leedom Fellowship awarded by Swarthmore College, the Garth Fellowship awarded by Columbia University, a Russian Institute Student Aid Grant, and an American Association of University Women fellowship. My husband has cheerfully shared family responsibilities so that I might have more time at my desk.

Except where otherwise noted, the translations from the Russian are
my own. The method of transliteration from the Russian is based on the
Library of Congress system, but is simplified in some respects, most no-
ticeably perhaps by the omission of the tie marks which in that system
are used to connect two Latin letters representing a single Cyrillic letter.
All ruble values are given in terms of the "old" Soviet currency used
before the monetary revaluation of January 1961.

Pittsburgh, Pennsylvania   Janet G. Chapman
March 1962

CONTENTS

APPENDIXES

TABLES

TEXT TABLES

APPENDIX TABLES

FIGURES

I ·

INTRODUCTION

THE object of this study is the measurement of the changes in the cost of living and in real wages of Soviet workers since the introduction of the First Five Year Plan in 1928. Reliable data on changes in real wages are indispensable to an understanding of the nature of the Soviet policy of industrialization, of the effectiveness of Soviet planning, and of Soviet domestic politics. They should be illuminating, too, as the record of the course of real wages in one country going through a recent and rapid industrial development. How the worker has fared under Soviet Communism is a question of great interest throughout the world, and one on which the success and appeal of the Soviet system will undoubtedly be judged in many quarters. Welfare, of course, is more than real wages, but real wages are an essential aspect of welfare. Although my study is limited to the change in real wages in a fairly restricted sense, I also consider the "social wage." In the Soviet case — though this would not be true of countries with less restrictive information policies — the measurement of real wages is a formidable enough task in itself, and it is one of the areas about which very little has been known.

The need for a study of this sort has to be understood in light of the Soviet information policy on this vital question. The question of the cost of living and real wages in the Soviet Union is one on which officially published information runs the widest gamut from raw data of complete reliability to propaganda statements very close to outright lies. It provides, too, one of the clearest examples of the withholding of information. When real wages are rising, information to that effect is widely publicized, but when real wages are falling, the facts are withheld. During most of the period the Soviet government has released serial data on money wages. These, particularly in the prewar years, showed a phenomenal increase, and the government did not hesitate to cite them in claiming large increases in the material well-being of the working class. But from 1930 to 1954 the government systematically withheld measures of the cost of living necessary to translate the money wage figures into real terms. It was not until 1954 that the Soviet government resumed publication of index numbers of the cost of living and of real wages. In 1956 they began publication of an index number of retail prices in state and cooperative shops and an index number of prices on the collective farm, or free market. These various index numbers compare the 1950's with 1940, but there are still no official index numbers for the period 1930–40. Moreover, few details concerning the computation of the cost-of-living and real wage index numbers have been published and an independent inquiry still seemed in order. The official index number of retail prices in state and cooperative shops is supported by considerable detail in the Soviet sources and, my own study permits me to conclude, is reliable.

While the Soviet government has withheld measures of the cost of living, it has published a good deal of data on the retail prices of individual commodities. These publications take the form of price handbooks, price decrees, and the like issued for purposes of controlling the retail market. Beyond this some price data are available from other sources, especially from visitors to the USSR. These data provide the basis for an independent computation of the changes in the Soviet cost of living. Taken together with the available data on average money wages, they provide the basis for the measurement of real wages made in this study.

Some of the available price statistics have been used by other students of the Soviet economy, and this is not the first independent investigation in this area. Calculations for the prewar period by S. N. Prokopovicz were the only significant ones which had been made at the time my study was initially undertaken in late 1949. Since then, however, some additional studies have been completed — most notably those of Naum Jasny and Eugène Zaleski.[1] While the present study, as will be seen, tends to corroborate the striking results obtained by Prokopovicz, Jasny, and Zaleski, there were several reasons for undertaking and carrying through this independent inquiry. Prokopovicz deflated money wages by an average of the prices of only eleven foodstuffs, and he admittedly had little information on the comparability of the foods priced. Jasny has not published the full details of his computations. His measure of the cost of living includes prices of some manufactured goods and services, but apparently his sample is still limited to a very few commodities. Zaleski's study is based on fairly extensive price data for the postwar years, but his data for the prewar years are rather limited, and again there are questions

---

[1] S. N. Prokopovicz (ed.), *Quarterly Bulletin of Soviet-Russian Economics,* Geneva, nos. 1–2, November 1939, and no. 8, May 1941; Naum Jasny, *The Soviet Economy During the Plan Era* (Stanford, 1951); Eugène Zaleski, "Les fluctuations des prix de détail en Union Soviétique," *Études et Conjoncture,* no. 4, April 1955, pp. 329–384. Mention should also be made of the following: Irving B. Kravis and Joseph Mintzes, "Food Prices in the Soviet Union, 1936–50," *Review of Economics and Statistics,* 32:164–168 (May 1950); Edmund Nash, "Purchasing Power of Soviet Workers, 1953," *Monthly Labor Review,* 76:705–708 (July 1953); M. Allais, "L'Économie Soviétique est-elle efficiente?" *Nouvelle Revue de L'Économie Contemporaine,* no. 10, October 1950, pp. 4–12; and P. J. D. Wiles, "Retail Trade, Retail Prices and Real Wages in USSR," *Bulletin of the Oxford University Institute of Statistics,* 16:373–392 (1954). This latter study is based in part on my own preliminary results in "Real Wages in the Soviet Union, 1928–52," *Review of Economics and Statistics,* 36:134–156 (May 1954).

concerning comparability of the quotations. The present study makes use of more data than any previous study, and the question of comparability has been a major concern. Also, a systematic attempt is made for the first time to apply the economic theory of index numbers and to compute Soviet cost-of-living index numbers on the basis of alternative sets of weights.[2]

In choosing the methods to employ in measuring the change in real wages, I take as my point of departure the economic theory of index numbers. According to this theory, there is not one measure of the change in real wages between any two years, but two — one in which the quantities consumed are valued at the prices prevailing in the first year, and one in which they are valued at the prices prevailing in the second year. Correspondingly, in the case of the cost of living (and it is measures of the cost of living that I compute in detail), there are two measures — one each from the standpoint of the consumption pattern of both of the two years. Depending upon the extent of the changes in price structure and in the pattern of consumption, the two measures may diverge significantly. This familiar index number problem arises in acute form in the present case. The period of the five year plans witnessed major changes in both price structure and consumption patterns, particularly during the prewar period. Under the circumstances it seemed in order to compute alternative index numbers based on weights drawn from the consumption patterns of each year studied.

As might have been expected, the alternative measures diverge considerably. The divergence is great for the period 1928 to 1937 when the greatest changes in price structure and pattern of consumption took place. From 1937 on, such changes were more moderate and there is fairly close agreement between the alternative index numbers; but the wide divergence for the 1928–37 period shows up in any comparisons between 1928 and later years. Index number theory unfortunately provides no basis for choice between the divergent results. The alternative measures should, nevertheless, tend to limit the range of conjecture on this important subject.

Perhaps, too, this study may contribute to a further understanding of the index number problem. The Paasche and Laspeyres index numbers have been applied in the measurement of industrial output and in international comparisons of living standards and national products,[3] but this

[2] Zaleski makes some use of alternative weighting systems, it should be said, but his 1951 weights represent only slight modifications of his 1925/26 weights and his index number formulas do not appear to be entirely appropriate for the purpose. Kravis and Mintzes also experiment with different sets of weights, but their study is limited to food prices and to a period when weighting makes relatively little difference.

[3] Most notably, Alexander Gerschenkron's index numbers of machinery output in the United States in his *A Dollar Index of Soviet Machinery Output, 1927/28 to 1937*, The RAND Corporation, R-197, April 6, 1951, pp. 51–55, appendix VI; and Milton Gilbert

study, it is believed, represents the first systematic attempt to measure changes in real wages within a given country on the basis of the appropriate alternative weighting systems.

The cost-of-living index numbers are intended to measure the changes in average prices paid by workers in all retail markets in the urban USSR. The detailed computations are based in the first instance on official prices prevailing in Moscow. I then estimate and take into account the movement of prices in urban areas outside Moscow and of prices on the free market. The weights employed in computing the index numbers of the cost of living are intended to reflect the expenditure pattern of urban workers in each of the years studied. On the basis of the same price data, I compute also index numbers of average prices in all retail markets in the entire Soviet Union. In this computation the weights reflect the structure of total retail sales.

The Soviet hired labor categories are *rabochie* and *sluzhashchie*, translated here as "wage earners" and "salaried employees." In Soviet usage, *rabochie* are ordinary workers up to the rank of foreman, including apprentices. *Sluzhashchie* are supervisory or administrative personnel of the rank of foreman or over, up to and including the director of the factory; engineers and other technical personnel; doctors, economists, teachers, and other hired professional workers; and office workers generally.[4] I do not consider the wages of wage earners and salaried employees in agriculture in this study, nor am I concerned with the income of the independent peasants and collective farmers who constituted the bulk of the Soviet working population on the eve of the five year plans and who still number about 40 percent of the total. Among nonagricultural workers, I study only the so-called "free" workers. Hence, no account is taken of prisoners engaged in forced labor, who, at least until recently, must have numbered in the millions. Finally, the cost-of-living index numbers could be calculated with most assurance for urban workers, particularly for the early years. While the money wage figures cover rural wage earners and salaried employees outside agriculture, the resulting figures on real wages are best viewed as referring to urban wage earners and salaried employees alone. These constitute the major part, but by no means all, of the hired labor force. The calculations, then, fall far short of measuring the material lot of Soviet consumers generally. But they refer to a class of prime political and economic importance in the USSR, whose material status is of outstanding interest in itself. Wage earners and salaried employees in the USSR, exclusive of prisoners but inclusive of those in rural localities and in agriculture, numbered 10.8 million in 1928, 26.7 million in 1937, 31.2

---

and Irving B. Kravis, *An International Comparison of National Products and the Purchasing Power of Currencies: A Study of the United States, the United Kingdom, France, Germany and Italy*, OEEC (Paris, 1954).

[4] Abram Bergson, *The Structure of Soviet Wages* (Cambridge, Mass., 1946), pp. 213–214.

million in 1940, 27.3 million in 1945, 34.2 million in 1948, 42.2 million in 1952, and 47.3 million in 1954.[5]

Wages, as understood in this study, are average earnings. I deal only with the average earnings of all nonagricultural wage earners and salaried employees, and hence do not consider changes in the distribution of income within this class. I compute, first, measures of gross real wages by deflating average gross money earnings by the cost-of-living index numbers. Secondly, I compute in a similar manner measures of net real wages after the deduction of direct taxes and the tax-like purchases of government bonds. The basic computations are made in terms of average annual earnings, but I consider also changes in the length of the work-year and present approximate measures of real hourly earnings. Finally, I attempt to estimate the real value of the various benefits provided by the government in cash or in the form of free services and present measures of net real wages including benefits. Conceptually and statistically such benefits are difficult to evaluate, but I have nevertheless made the attempt in view of the particular interest attaching to the "social wage" in the Soviet case. Needless to say, the results are not nearly so reliable as the measures of gross or net real wages excluding benefits.

The "social wage" includes social insurance, various cash benefits such as mothers' subsidies, and the free education and health services provided by the government and other institutions. In the case of social insurance, there is the difficulty that the benefits for the most part are not current but are either contingent upon accident or illness, or, in the case of old age pensions, are deferred until old age. Ideally, one would wish to measure the current value to the worker of these contingent and future benefits and the security they provide. In practice, however, this is hardly measurable, and I have adopted the expedient of taking the total social insurance grants and pensions paid during a given year as a percentage of total earnings of wage earners and salaried employees in the same year to approximate the value to the worker of his social insurance, expressed as a percentage of the average wage. In the case of free educational and health services, the knotty question of what the value of these services really is to the consumer is bypassed, and I value them at the cost to the government of providing them. For deflation, special index numbers of the change in the cost of providing the services are constructed, but they are rather crude. There are additional difficulties in attempting to determine the

[5] TSU, *Narodnoe khoziaistvo SSSR* (Moscow, 1956), p. 189. The 1948 figure is an estimate from Warren Eason's "Population and Labor Force," in A. Bergson (ed.), *Soviet Economic Growth* (Evanston, 1953), p. 110. For 1928, earlier sources give a figure for all wage earners and salaried employees of 11.6 million, of which 9.9 million were outside agriculture. See TSUNKHU, *Trud v SSSR* (Moscow, 1936), pp. 10–20; TSUNKHU, *Narodnoe khoziaistvo SSSR* (Moscow, 1932), p. 414. In 1937, the total outside agriculture was 24.5 million, of which some 5 million may have been employed in rural localities. See Gosplan, *Tretii piatiletnii plan razvitiia narodnogo khoziaistva Soiuza SSR (1938–42 gg.) (proekt)* (Moscow, 1939), p. 228.

share of total government expenditures on these free services and also on some of the cash benefits enjoyed by the wage-earner and salaried-employee class. Beyond this, it will be evident that the meaning of the word *wages* is somewhat stretched in the term *social wage* and in the designation of my final measure as *net real wages including benefits*. While social insurance can properly be considered as (in some sense) part of wages, neither mothers' subsidies nor free education and health services can, though all contribute to real income. The measure of net real wages including benefits is close in concept to *real consumable income* (or, since the free services must be consumed to be enjoyed, to *real consumed and consumable income*). My measure, however, falls somewhat short of total real consumable income of wage earners and salaried employees, for I consider only their earnings and the benefits received by them and their families. Total real consumable income of the family of a wage earner or salaried employee might include such items as earnings of members of the family who are not wage earners or salaried employees, income from a private garden plot, payment for odd jobs performed on a private basis, or sales of hand-made objects or personal belongings. Such additional sources of income may be important in individual cases, but on the average for all wage-earner and salaried-employee families they constitute a rather small addition to income.

It would have been an impossible task to compute index numbers for every year of this period, and the investigation is limited to the years 1928, 1937, 1940, 1944, 1948, 1952, and 1954. The choice of years was in the first instance determined largely by the years covered in the RAND studies of Soviet national income, of which my own study forms a related part; but the basic considerations underlying the choice of these years are also applicable to the study of real wages.

By 1928 the Soviet economy generally had recovered from the disruption of the years of war and revolution. The 1913 levels of physical output had on the whole been regained, and the hired labor force for the first time numbered as many as in 1913. The standard of living had probably recovered and possibly risen somewhat above the prewar level. Soviet figures, which may not be very reliable, indicate that real wages in industry exceeded the 1913 level by something over 10 percent, or by over 20 percent when benefits are taken into account.[6] The year 1928 is also of great interest as the last year preceding the First Five Year Plan. The Soviet

[6] The purchasing power of average weekly earnings of industrial wage earners in 1927/28 was 111 percent of the 1913 level, according to *Ekonomicheskoe obozrenie*, March 1929, p. 125, cited by Solomon Schwarz, *Labor in the Soviet Union* (New York, 1951), p. 131. Including social insurance and other benefits, real wages of wage earners in industry in 1927/28 were 122.5 percent of the 1913 level, according to Gosplan, *The Soviet Union Looks Ahead: The Five Year Plan for Economic Construction* (New York, 1929), pp. 152, 242; according to a more recent source, *Planovoe khoziaistvo*, no. 10, 1957, pp. 76–77, counting benefits, real wages of wage earners in state industry at the end of 1927 were 128.4 percent of the 1913 level.

economy had become increasingly a planned one even before 1928, but the First Five Year Plan introduced planning on a full scale and, more important, launched the forced drive for industrialization. Although the First Five Year Plan provided for a substantial increase in real wages, its actual impact on Soviet consumption levels was drastic. The high rate of investment and the very rapid increase in the urban labor force would undoubtedly have created difficulties in any case, and there were errors in forecasting and planning; but the major factor was the catastrophic decline in agricultural output and in livestock, mainly the unanticipated result of forced collectivization. Unfortunately, I am unable to present a measure of the extent to which Soviet real wages declined during the First Five Year Plan.[7] The entire period 1929 into early 1936 was characterized by rationing and a multiple price system, and it is doubtful that any meaningful measure of real wages could be computed for these years.

The year 1937 was the terminal year of the Second Five Year Plan, during which a substantial recovery in agriculture was achieved and per capita output of consumer goods was increased beyond the 1928 level. An open market for consumer goods again prevailed after many years of rationing, and the consumer market was more or less in equilibrium. Soviet workers were relatively better off than they had been in the earlier 1930's. Although 1938 or 1939 was probably as good or better from these points of view, the 1937 information is more complete. The last full prewar year was 1940, and it has the important advantage for our purposes that it is the prewar year with which virtually all postwar official Soviet data are compared. Although real wages almost certainly continued to increase after 1937, by 1940 military preparations and the Finnish war had already begun to depress living standards. Thus, I unfortunately do not cover the prewar year in which real wages reached their highest peak after 1928. The open market for consumer goods was maintained through 1940 until after the Nazi attack in June 1941, when rationing began to be introduced. The rationing, multiple prices, and extreme shortages of the war years mean that a measure of real wages for these years is of dubious value. I have, nevertheless, made a rough attempt to quantify the wartime privations of the Soviet worker in 1944. My calculations for 1944 are presented then with the warning that they are not very reliable. By 1944, most of the territory lost to the Germans had been regained. Military output was high; production generally had begun to recover from the enormous devastation of the war but was still well below the prewar level, particularly in consumer goods.

The year 1948 was the first postwar year during which an open market for consumer goods prevailed. It was also, when this study was begun, a very recent year. Output of consumer goods, which had fallen much more than production generally during the war, was still well below the prewar

[7] Rough estimates of Schwarz and Jasny are given in chapter IX.

level, though very rapid recovery had taken place in the rest of the economy. Roughly speaking, 1950 might be taken as the year marking virtually complete recovery from the war. As time passed, the study was extended to cover the post-recovery years 1952 and 1954. In 1954 the last of the series of annual retail price reductions begun in 1949 was effected, and there has been little change to date in the cost of living. Thus, although my formal calculations stop at 1954, it is an easy matter to bring the story up to the eve of the new Seven Year Plan. This is facilitated by the resumed publication of certain official Soviet index numbers.

Anyone embarking upon a serious investigation of any aspect of the Soviet economy thereby admits, at least tacitly, a belief that some confidence can be placed in at least some types of Soviet information. My study is based almost entirely on Soviet sources, although I have also been able to make use of the observations of visitors to the USSR. Brief comment may be in order, therefore, on the reliability of Soviet information. In the first place, we cannot forget that statistics — and good statistics — are of crucial importance in a planned economy, and we can be sure that efforts are continuously being made to improve the collection and collation of statistics in the Soviet Union for the planners' own use. So far as published statistics are concerned, I agree with the view, which I believe is held by most who have worked with Soviet figures, that the statistics published by the Soviet government are not falsified in the sense of being freely invented. But it is also true that the manner in which the facts are cited or (no less significantly) omitted in Soviet publications is often designed to deceive, and even when there seems to be no intent to deceive, the figures are not presented in a manner that inspires confidence. They are usually presented without any kind of explanation, much less the full documentation required by scholarly standards. To be sure, definitions and methodological explanations for many Soviet statistical series have been published, and these are certainly useful to the specialist who can search them out, but they are usually to be found only in textbooks on statistics and rarely accompany the figures themselves. For the core of truth in Soviet statistics, we must indeed search diligently and proceed with great caution. The dangers and inadequacies of Soviet statistics generally, as well as the arguments for believing that they are not falsified, have been adequately discussed elsewhere,[8] and I shall limit my further

[8] Abram Bergson, *Soviet National Income and Product in 1937* (New York, 1953), pp. 6–9; Seymour Harris, Colin Clark, A. Gerschenkron, Paul Baran, Abram Bergson, and A. Yugov, "Appraisals of Russian Economic Statistics," *Review of Economic Statistics,* 29:213–246 (1947); Harry Schwartz and Maurice Dobb, "Further Appraisals of Russian Economic Statistics," *Review of Economics and Statistics,* 30:34–41 (1948); Lynn Turgeon, "On the Reliability of Soviet Statistics," *Review of Economics and Statistics,* 34:75–76 (1952); Stuart Rice, Harry Schwartz, Frank Lorimer, A. Gerschenkron, Lazar Volin, and Abram Bergson, "Reliability and Usability of Soviet Statistics," *The American Statistician,* April-May 1953, pp. 8–21, and June-July 1953, pp. 8–16. Naum Jasny, though demonstrating great ability to discover the truth in Soviet statistics, appears to take the view that they are falsified; see his *The Socialized Agriculture of the*

discussion to the varying reliability of the kinds of information relevant
to my own study.

I am fortunate in that the data for much of my study are among the
most reliable of all types of Soviet information. I refer here to official
retail prices of individual commodities. The retail prices set by the Soviet
government are intended to be put into effect, and publication of the
prices is a means of ensuring this. The retail price handbooks are issued for
the use of store managers and the like rather than for the general public
or for foreigners (though sometimes it is possible to obtain copies), but
decrees concerning prices are often published in the Soviet press to inform
the Soviet public as well as the store managers of the correct retail prices.
In the case of output figures, it would be possible for the government to
provide a set of false figures for public consumption (though it seems im-
probable that the government actually does so), but in the case of current
retail prices of individual commodities the publication of false figures
would be manifestly absurd. Retail prices are common knowledge of the
entire Soviet population. Beyond this, they can be checked by foreigners
in the shops themselves. All this is not to say that there are not great difficulties in working with the raw price data and great gaps in the available
price information. It should be mentioned, too, that in the case of prices
on the free market, Soviet statistics are quite inadequate — in large part
because the Soviet statisticians themselves lack full information.

Questions have been raised concerning the adequacy of the Soviet wage
statistics, but the inadequacies were found to be explicable on grounds
other than falsification.[9] Furthermore, the deficiencies appear to be fairly
serious so far as the size of the total wage bill is concerned, but relatively
minor when it is the average wage which is at issue, as in this study.

Because of the many gaps, pitfalls, and deficiencies in Soviet statistics,
the investigator must exercise judgment and extreme caution at every step
of his investigation. He is also obligated to reveal his every step to the
reader. At relevant points in this study I comment at some length on the
nature and reliability of the more important source material. In addition,
all details concerning the sources and nature of specific price quotations
and other data, the gaps in the data, and the steps in my own computations are set forth either in the text or in the appendixes so that the reader
may judge for himself the extent to which my computations and conclusions based on Soviet data may be relied upon.

In view of the central role of Soviet retail prices in this analysis, chap-

USSR (Stanford, 1949), pp. 8–15; "Soviet Statistics," *Review of Economics and Statistics,* 32:92–99 (1950); *The Soviet Economy During the Plan Era* (Stanford, 1951);
The Soviet 1956 Statistical Handbook: A Commentary (East Lansing, 1957). But see
also A. Gerschenkron, "Comments on Naum Jasny's 'Soviet Statistics,'" *Review of
Economics and Statistics,* 32:250–251 (1950).
    [9] Abram Bergson, "A Problem in Soviet Statistics," *Review of Economic Statistics,*
29:234–242 (November 1947).

ter II is devoted to a brief description of the Soviet retail market and the Soviet retail price system. I also discuss here Soviet retail price policies and the effectiveness of the operation of the Soviet retail market in the years covered in the study. In chapter III, the economic theory of index numbers, which provides the basis for the choice of index number formulas, is outlined, and the formulas employed in computing the index numbers are described, with a discussion of their proper interpretation and their limitations. Also discussed are some special problems limiting the applicability of the theory to the Soviet case — including the question of the meaningfulness of Soviet retail prices — and my methods of attempting to handle them.

In chapters IV and V, I describe the computation of the index numbers of official retail prices in Moscow which form the basis for the cost-of-living index numbers. Chapter IV is concerned with the price data and chapter V with the weights. In chapter VI, I make the step from the index numbers of official retail prices in Moscow to the final cost-of-living index numbers, which take account of official prices outside Moscow and of prices on the free market. It should be mentioned here that because the calculations for 1944 are so rough, they are described separately in appendix D.

The money wage figures are presented and described in chapter VII. Here I also explain my estimates of direct taxes and bond subscriptions which must be deducted from gross earnings if changes in real take-home pay are to be measured as well as changes in gross real wages. The "social wage" is the subject of chapter VIII, where I describe the main features of the Soviet social insurance system, mothers' subsidies, and education and health services, and the trends in such benefits over the period, in addition to explaining my methods of attempting to quantify the value of these benefits. I also compare my estimates with Soviet statements concerning benefits. My measures of real wages are presented in chapter IX with an appraisal of the significance of the alternative results. I also compare my findings with the results of other non-Soviet calculations and with Soviet claims relating to retail prices, the cost of living, and real wages. In chapter X, I attempt to fit my findings into the broader picture of Soviet economic development. I compare my measures of real wages with various indicators of changes in real per capita consumption and consider why, over much of the period, real wages decreased more, or increased less, than real per capita consumption, and why the Soviet record on real wages has been so poor. A brief comparison is made of the trend in Soviet real wages with that of other countries. Various factors affecting the welfare of the Soviet worker family not taken into account in statistical measures of real wages are pointed out. Finally, I comment on the course of Soviet real wages since 1954 and on the prospects for future improvement in the Soviet worker's welfare.

II·

THE RETAIL MARKET AND RETAIL
PRICES IN THE SOVIET UNION

As a background for the discussion of this and subsequent chapters, I describe very briefly the organization of the Soviet retail market in section 1 and the Soviet retail price system in section 2; in section 3, I discuss in somewhat more detail, but in rather general terms, Soviet retail price policy. The effectiveness of the operation of the Soviet retail market is the subject of section 4. Here I consider the question of the extent to which Soviet retail prices have been set so as to balance demand with the supplies made available in the government shops, and the relationship between the government-fixed prices in these shops and prices on the free market during the years covered in the present study.

I. ORGANIZATION OF THE SOVIET RETAIL MARKET

Throughout the period under review, the bulk of retail sales was made in the shops and restaurants of the state and cooperative retail trade systems.[1] Although there are various differences in administrative organization and other matters between the state and cooperative trade systems, for present purposes they are essentially similar in that supplies for these systems are for the most part directly planned by the government, and sales in the retail shops and restaurants of both systems are made at prices fixed by the government. I shall at times refer to both state and cooperative shops and restaurants as *official outlets,* and to the prices charged in them as *official prices* or *state shop prices.* The term retail sales as I use it includes sales in restaurants as well as in shops, unless otherwise noted. Side by side with the official retail shops, there has also existed a free market, in which prices are not controlled but are allowed to find their own level in response to the conditions of demand and supply. Since 1932, the free market has been called the *collective farm market.*

[1] For a more detailed description of the organization of the Soviet retail market, see M. M. Lifits, *Sovetskaia torgovlia* (Moscow, 1948); G. L. Rubinshtein, *et al., Ekonomika sovetskoi torgovli* (Moscow, 1950); S. V. Serebriakov, *Organizatsiia i tekhnika sovetskoi torgovli* (Moscow, 1949); V. I. Vinogradov and Ia. A. Kaminskii, *Organizatsiia i tekhnika sovetskoi torgovli* (Moscow, 1954); L. E. Hubbard, *Soviet Trade and Distribution* (London, 1938); Harry Schwartz, *Russia's Soviet Economy* (2d ed., New York, 1954), pp. 430–439.

The state trade system includes the retail shops of the Ministry of Trade, the Departments of Workers Supply or ORS shops run by industrial enterprises for their employees, and the specialized retail shops of various industrial ministries and other government organizations. During periods of rationing, the state trade system operated both ration shops, where goods could be purchased only with ration coupons, and "commercial shops," where goods could be purchased without ration coupons but at much higher prices. Such commercial shops were in existence between 1932 and 1935 or early 1936 and again between April 1944 and December 1947. They are of interest to us only in connection with the year 1944. Since 1935, the state trade system has accounted for most of the urban retail trade.

Of the cooperative trade, the bulk represents sales by the consumer cooperative shops and restaurants. The share of the consumer cooperatives in total cooperative sales was about 80 percent in 1928 and around 90 percent in 1937 and most years since.[2] The remainder represents sales in the retail shops of various producers' cooperatives. In 1928, cooperative trade was the predominant form and accounted for 79 percent of the retail sales of the state and cooperative systems. At that time, the cooperative system operated shops in both urban and rural areas. By a decree of October 1935, the consumer cooperative system was confined to the country, and urban consumer cooperatives were transferred to the state trading system. Since then the cooperatives have accounted for only 25 to 30 percent of all state and cooperative retail sales, and even less during the war years. After the war, in November 1946, in an effort to increase the supply of food available to urban workers, consumer cooperative trade was again permitted and, in fact, encouraged in the cities, but the privilege was apparently withdrawn during 1949. Inasmuch as a certain leeway in price fixing was granted to such urban cooperative trade, this is of some interest for the study of 1948. It is discussed in more detail below. In 1953, a new form of retail trade, *commission trade,* in which the consumer cooperatives play a part, was begun in the cities. Commission shops are organized and operated by the consumer cooperative system in cities. In these shops, the cooperatives sell surplus agricultural produce for the account of collective farms — and individual members of collective farms — on a commission basis at prices determined more or less by the free play of the market. In Soviet statistics this trade is sometimes classified as cooperative trade and sometimes as collective farm market trade. So far this is essentially collective farm market trade conducted through shops run by the cooperative system, and for this reason I classify it as collective farm market trade. Commission sales amounted to less than 0.1 billion rubles in 1953, to 2.2

[2] TSUNKHU, *Socialist Construction in the USSR* (Moscow, 1936), p. 609; TSU, *Sovetskaia torgovlia; Statisticheskii sbornik* (Moscow, 1956), pp. 24, 27.

billion rubles in 1954, and to 4.9 billion rubles in 1955 — a very small share of total retail sales.[3]

In 1928, the last year of the New Economic Policy, private retail trade was still permitted. Although the private traders were rapidly being squeezed out of existence, private trade must have accounted for well over a quarter of total retail sales.[4] Owners of private stores were generally free to set their own prices, though for some products (including bread, cigarettes, alcoholic beverages) the official prices were obligatory for private as well as for state and cooperative shops.[5] Prices on the peasant market were completely uncontrolled.

Shortly after the introduction of the First Five Year Plan, all private trade was made illegal; but a few years later, in 1932, the peasant market, now called the collective farm market, was revived. On this market, collective farms, individual members of collective farms, independent peasants, and other citizens with gardens, after meeting their obligations to the government, are permitted to sell their produce directly to the consumer at uncontrolled prices. This is still the one free market in the Soviet Union. The bulk of sales on the urban collective farm market is of food, but there is a small volume of sales of livestock, feed, and the products of peasant handicraft. The relative importance of the collective farm market in total Soviet retail sales in the years covered in this study is shown in Table 1. The figures relate to sales on the urban collective farm markets; intrarural sales on the village markets are not covered in official Soviet statistics.[6]

A question might be raised as to the rationale of the persistence of the free market. The collective farm market is tolerated primarily, it appears, as a source of food supplies for urban workers above and beyond the amounts the government is able to extract directly from the farms. It introduces some flexibility into the system and may serve to soften the ef-

[3] TSU, *Sovetskaia torgovlia; Statisticheskii sbornik*, p. 19.

[4] The official Soviet figures indicate that private trade conducted by "intermediaries" in "stationary" shops accounted for 23 percent of total retail sales. See TSUNKHU, *Narodnoe khoziaistvo SSSR* (Moscow, 1932), pp. 316–317; TSU, *Sovetskaia torgovlia; Statisticheskii sbornik*, p. 14. Both sources agree that sales in private shops were 3.6 billion rubles; the 1932 source puts sales in state and cooperative shops at 12.3 billion rubles, while the 1956 source puts this at 11.8 billion rubles. The reason for this discrepancy is not known. But these official figures do not take account of sales in the peasant markets or of other direct producer-consumer sales by private individuals, which were of considerable importance. See Oleg Hoeffding, *Soviet National Income and Product in 1928* (New York, 1954), pp. 9, 31.

[5] Rubinshtein, *et al.*, *Ekonomika sovetskoi torgovli*, p. 475.

[6] In 1940, collective farm market sales on urban markets were 29.1 billion rubles and on all markets, including the village markets, 41.2 billion rubles. This latter figure is cited in Lifits, *Sovetskaia torgovlia*, p. 33, without explanation of its coverage. The coverage of the two figures is made clear in a letter from the Chief of the USSR Central Statistical Administration (TSU), Professor V. Starovskii, to Abram Bergson, August 29, 1956.

TABLE 1

Retail Sales in State and Cooperative Shops and on the Collective Farm Market,
USSR, 1937–54

	Retail sales (billion rubles)			Retail sales (percent of total)		
Year	State and cooperative shops	Collective farm market	Total	State and cooperative shops	Collective farm market	Total
1937	125.9	17.8	143.7	87.6	12.4	100.0
1940	175.1	29.1	204.2	85.7	14.3	100.0
1944	119.3	33	152.3	78.3	21.7	100.0
1948	310.2	38	348.2	89.1	10.9	100.0
1952	393.6	53.7	447.3	88.0	12.0	100.0
1954	479.7[a]	51.2[a]	530.9	90.4	9.6	100.0

[a] Commission sales amounting to 2.2 billion rubles are classified here as sales on the collective farm market. Sources: TSU, *Sovetskaia torgovlia; Statisticheskii sbornik* (Moscow, 1956), pp. 19–20. The 1937 collective farm market figure is from N. S. Margolin, *Voprosy balansa denezhnykh dokhodov i raskhodov naseleniia* (Moscow, 1939), p. 8. The 1944 and 1948 figures for collective farm market sales are from Abram Bergson, Hans Heymann, Jr., and Oleg Hoeffding, *Soviet National Income and Product, 1928–1948: Revised Data*, The RAND Corporation, RM-2544, November 15, 1960, p. 62. The figures for sales in state and cooperative shops include sales in restaurants.

fects of errors in distribution and in price fixing in the controlled market. A drawback, however, is that the operation of the free market may interfere with the planned distribution of income, particularly as between workers and peasants.

2. THE SOVIET RETAIL PRICE SYSTEM

The retail prices charged in state and cooperative shops are fixed by the government. The specific agency that fixes prices depends on the importance of the commodity and the importance of the producer. Retail prices of the most important commodities are established or at least approved by the Council of Ministers or the USSR Ministry of Trade. As early as 1930, three-quarters of total retail sales in state and cooperative shops were made at such centrally fixed prices, and in the early 1950's centrally fixed prices applied to 80 to 90 percent of all state and cooperative retail sales. Prices of less important products, or in some cases of important products produced from locally procured raw materials or factory waste, are established by the Councils of Ministers of the various republics or the Executive Committees of the oblast, krai, or city Soviets, in accord with regulations and limits established centrally.[7]

Generally speaking, the official prices provide a single system of prices applicable throughout the USSR. Some retail prices are uniform for the entire country, some are differentiated by regions or price zones, and some by urban and rural areas.[8] But in any one location there is, as a rule, only

[7] Rubinshtein, *et al.*, *Ekonomika sovetskoi torgovli*, pp. 477, 480–481; N. Riauzov and N. Titel'baum, *Kurs torgovoi statistiki* (Moscow, 1947), p. 134.

[8] See Janet G. Chapman, *The Regional Structure of Soviet Retail Prices*, The RAND Corporation, RM-425, July 20, 1950 (also on file as Master's essay at Columbia University).

one official price for each commodity. This is not entirely true of the system in effect during 1928. At that time, although there were many commodities with prices which were uniform for the entire country, the official prices usually took the form of ceiling prices. In some cases the ceiling price was differentiated by region and in others, apparently, a single ceiling price was fixed. The trade organizations played a significant role in determining the actual price for a given locality within the legal limit. The specific maximum price for a given locality, it is believed, was often determined by the state trade organization for state shops under its jurisdiction and by the local union of consumer cooperatives for cooperative shops under its jurisdiction. Thus, the price of a given item might vary among cities in the same region; and within the city, the state shop price might differ somewhat from the price in cooperative shops. In 1937, the trade organizations had some discretion in setting the trade margin and hence in determining the final retail price in the case of some of the less important commodities, but this was of minor significance. In 1937 and later years (except during periods of rationing), it is largely true that a single price prevailed in a given locality. There have been certain exceptions, of which the most important are commercial shop prices during periods of rationing, special cooperative prices during 1948, and prices in commission trade since 1953.

The government exercises no direct control over prices on the collective farm market, which are free to fluctuate in accord with demand and supply. This was true also of prices on the peasant market in 1928 and, with certain exceptions, of prices in the private shops at that time. For obvious reasons, the free market prices tend to be about at the level of official prices at times when the supply of goods in state and cooperative shops is adequate to meet demand at the official prices, and to rise above official prices when supplies at official prices are inadequate. Thus, the relationship between the official and the free market prices provides important evidence on the correctness of the official prices, and on the effectiveness of the Soviet official market.

Various factors, however, tend to complicate the relationship between official and free market prices, and to make it difficult to reach any simple conclusions. Probably the most important of these factors is the very local character of most of the collective farm markets. For most collective farms and farm members the nearest town is the only feasible free market for their produce. Local conditions of demand and supply often predominate in the determination of the local market price. Thus, even during a period when a particular commodity is generally scarce in the country as a whole, the supply in a particular locality may be plentiful in relation to local demand, with the result that the free market price may be at or even below the official price; or, the local supply may be particularly short when the commodity is in easy supply in the rest of the country, resulting in a local free market price above the official price. Also, it is apparently Soviet practice in some cases not to make any supply of a commodity available in the state shops of a given town when there is a local supply on the free market. In this case, the listed state shop price is inoperative, and one can hardly speak of the relationship between the official and market prices. Other factors affecting the relationship between official and free market prices are differences in the quality of the commodities and services offered, the relative convenience of the market and the state shops, and seasonal variations in supply. The free market prices fluctuate continually in response to changes in supply and demand. The official prices remain the same for considerable periods, and although official prices of seasonal products are adjusted seasonally, the adjustments are not closely correlated with market conditions.

3. SOVIET RETAIL PRICE POLICY

The Soviet government reserves to itself the decision as to the allocation of total resources between consumption on the one hand and investment and defense on the other. Within the total resources allocated to consumption, the government also decides what kinds of goods to produce. While the government is interested in providing what consumers need and want and studies the action of consumers in the market, it is not willing to allow the allocation of resources to be determined by the preferences of consumers as expressed in the retail market. The consumer is by no means sovereign in the USSR. For the distribution among the consumers of goods that the government does make available for consumption, the Soviet government prefers to rely on an open market with free consumer choice rather than on direct distribution by rationing. Rationing has been resorted to for two rather long periods — from the end of 1928 until the beginning of 1936, and from mid-1941 until December 1947. But the fact that an open market was re-established when supply conditions made this feasible would seem proof that this is the preferred method. An open market for consumer goods is much less of an administrative burden than rationing. Furthermore, if the money wage differentials which the Soviet government relies on as incentives are to be effective in real terms, freedom of consumer choice is necessary. In Soviet terms, an open market is necessary to assure the socialist principle of "to each according to his work."

If such an open market is to be an effective means of distributing consumer goods, it is clear that retail prices must be set so as just to clear the market of each and every good that the government makes available for consumption. Soviet economists are clearly aware of this, and it can be said, with qualifications, that this is the basic principle of retail price fixing in the Soviet Union.[9] It might be noted that the fact that the retail

---

[9] On Soviet price policy, see I. Veitzer, "Sovetskaia politika tsen," *Pravda*, August 7, 1937, pp. 2–3; L. Maizenberg, "Voprosy tsenoobrazovaniia," *Planovoe khoziaistvo*, no.

price of vodka is set high to discourage consumption, and the prices of some other goods that the government would, for social or other reasons, like to see consumed in larger quantities are set low, is no violation of this principle as long as the prices reflect the supplies of these goods that the government does make available.

Soviet retail price practice and policy have shown many departures from this principle. The very nature of the problem of planning, at the center, the retail prices of thousands of different goods would seem to mean there would inevitably be imperfections in the retail price system, and perhaps more than in an actual capitalist retail market. This is so even though in practice there is, of course, much participation in the actual determination of specific retail prices all the way down the administrative hierarchy to the producing factory.[10] One would expect a certain amount of arbitrariness in price fixing and greater price rigidity than in a competitive market. It is easier to fix and enforce food prices for only three price zones in the entire Soviet Union (as has been done since December 1947) than to effect more precise regional price differentials. Once a price schedule is drawn up, it is easier to stick to it for a period and wait to make any necessary adjustments in the structure of prices until an over-all change in the price level becomes necessary, than constantly to keep an eye on the market and make continuous adjustments. But imperfections of this nature are relatively unimportant and do not seem to concern the Soviet planners very much.

More important, the high rate of investment and other nonconsumption expenditures has meant that there has always been a large gap between the value at cost of the consumer goods made available and the money income of the population. The Soviet tool for bridging this gap is the turnover tax, a sales tax with rates varying for different kinds of commodities. This is a flexible tool which permits adjustments of relative prices as well as a balance between the general retail price level and total consumer income. In view of the size of the gap, it can readily be understood that Soviet economists have on the whole been less concerned with fine adjustments of relative retail prices than with the total gap. But even here for various reasons they have not been very successful. More often than not during Soviet planning history, consumers have had more money in their pockets than they could spend on the goods in the shops at the official

---

5, 1939, pp. 18–37; L. Maizenberg, "O tsenoobrazovanii v sovetskoi ekonomike," *Planovoe khoziaistvo*, no. 6, 1945, pp. 57–69; L. Maizenberg, *Tsenoobrazovanie v narodnom khoziaistve SSSR* (Moscow, 1953); Rubinshtein, *et al., Ekonomika sovetskoi torgovli;* Lifits, *Sovetskaia torgovlia;* Henry H. Ware, "The Function and Formation of Commodity Prices in the USSR," *Bulletins on Soviet Economic Development*, no. 4, September 1950, pp. 21–31.

[10] The degree of centralization in price fixing has recently been found excessive and a decree ordering more decentralization in retail price fixing was promulgated in March 1957. See *Voprosy ekonomiki*, no. 4, 1957, pp. 114–118.

prices. This is essentially the result of the failure through most of the period to control the rise in money wages, or, granting this, to anticipate the rise in money wages and to make appropriate retail price changes. This was particularly true of the prewar and war years.

Although in theory the government could set prices as high as necessary to absorb all excess purchasing power, this method is necessarily limited in practice. In particular, prices of absolute necessities cannot be set so high as to exclude any groups of consumers from the market for these necessities. In the early 1930's and during World War II and its aftermath, this consideration must have been the reason for choosing to ration consumer goods rather than raise retail prices to the high levels necessary to balance demand with the small supplies of goods then available.

Aside from the ration periods, it seems that the failure to close the gap between demand and supply has to some extent been the result of an official doctrine that "demand should outstrip supply." [11] It is claimed that this stimulates increased output of consumer goods, but it is difficult to see just how, when output is centrally planned and factory managers have little leeway to adapt their output to demand. This doctrine may have been largely window dressing for a situation that had gotten out of hand. Nevertheless, it has certain practical advantages for an economy straining its resources at every point.[12] As consumers with extra cash in their pockets are not so choosy, "too low" prices make it easier to ensure that everything produced will be sold.[13] Errors in the fixing of relative prices will not have serious consequences, and no resources will be "wasted" on the shelves of the shops. "Too low" prices also permit economies in inventories — of some importance in a tight supply situation — though they result in queues and waste the consumers' time.

[11] For example, the following statement from Stalin's report to the Sixteenth Party Congress in late 1930: "Here in the USSR the growth of consumption (purchasing power) of the masses always runs ahead of the growth of production, pushing it forward, but in the capitalist countries the growth of consumption (purchasing power) never catches up with the growth of production and always lags behind it." See J. V. Stalin, *Sochineniia*, vol. XII (Moscow, 1949), pp. 322–323. See also Ware, *Bulletins on Soviet Economic Development*, no. 4, September 1950, p. 22.

[12] Now that the supply situation is easier, it appears that this doctrine is being repudiated and current discussions evidence concern for a more exact balance between demand and supply and for the proper fixing of relative retail prices. See, for example, Mikoyan in *Izvestiia*, February 18, 1956; S. Partigul in *Voprosy ekonomiki*, no. 10, 1959 (trans. in *Problems of Economics*, 2:11 (February 1960)).

[13] An amusing illustration of this was reported in *Trud*, September 20, 1956, p. 2 (trans. in *Current Digest of the Soviet Press*, 8:21 (November 7, 1956)):

"There's a lot of money around and there isn't always anything to spend it on. The demand for manufactured goods exceeds the supply. People want worthwhile, costly articles —pianos, for instance. It's absurd how few pianos we get for sale."

"Yet I've seen pianos in miners' homes here that no one plays. The miner and his wife don't know how to play and there's nobody to teach the children."

"That's true, too. But our miners are willing to buy pianos for future use. Don't we sell television sets, even though the Stalinogorsk Television Center isn't finished yet?"

Political factors have also played a role. While private trade was still permitted, low official prices in the state and cooperative shops were a tool in squeezing the private shop out of existence.[14] Later, low official prices were seen as exerting a downward influence on collective farm market prices. More generally, it is always impolitic to raise retail prices while great political advantage can be made of price reductions.[15]

4. EFFECTIVENESS OF THE SOVIET RETAIL MARKET

Here I shall discuss briefly the effectiveness of the Soviet retail market and the meaningfulness of the official prices during each of the years covered in the present investigation. During each of the years studied, except 1944, the market for consumer goods was open in that individuals were free to purchase what they chose in unlimited quantities at the official prices. This is not to say that unlimited quantities were always available — and indeed, there were often shortages of goods at the official prices — but there was no formal system of rationing such as prevailed in 1944. In 1928, supplies of many commodities in the state and cooperative shops were low in relation to the official prices, and there was a gap between official prices and those in private shops that averaged almost 40 percent.[16] The gap increased during the year, quite markedly in the case of grain products. The situation had become so tight by the end of the year that bread rationing was introduced in a few cities, and rationing was rather generally adopted during 1929.

Rationing was replaced by an open market during 1935 and early 1936, and the new official prices were set considerably above the former low ration level. It is believed that by 1937 an equilibrium had been largely attained in the market for consumer goods, and there was little if any spread between prices in state shops and those on the collective farm market. According to Prokopovicz' calculations based on a small number of food products, state shop prices of foods in 1937 were about 375 percent of the level in 1932, and 210 percent of the level in 1934.[17] At the same time, prices on the collective farm market had fallen greatly and

---

[14] Kommunisticheskaia akademiia, Institut ekonomiki, *Ekonomika sovetskoi torgovli* (Moscow, 1933), p. 318; Maizenberg, *Tsenoobrazovanie v narodnom khoziaistve SSSR,* pp. 37–41; Maizenberg, *Planovoe khoziaistvo,* no. 5, 1939, p. 18.

[15] The systematic reduction of retail prices is set forth as a prime policy of the Soviet government and as a law of socialist development. Interestingly, however, this law is proclaimed only during periods when retail prices are in fact being reduced. Compare Maizenberg's article in *Planovoe khoziaistvo,* no. 5, 1939, written at a time when retail prices were being raised, with his *Tsenoobrazovanie v narodnom khoziaistve SSSR,* written in 1953 during the period of annual postwar price reductions.

[16] See chapter VI.

[17] S. N. Prokopovicz (ed.), *Quarterly Bulletin of Soviet-Russian Economics,* nos. 1 and 2, November 1939, p. 25. Prokopovicz' calculations have been revised since the publication of this bulletin, but his later figures do not cover the year 1937; I accordingly cite his original figures.

in 1937 were only some 42 percent of the level in 1933.[18] Data for 1935 indicate that official prices and prices on the collective farm market did not diverge significantly, and in fact show some market prices lower than the official prices, though some also still higher.[19] By 1936, it was claimed that the gap between official and collective farm market prices had been eliminated.[20] Money wages continued to increase, though at a slower rate. But the increase in supplies in the state and cooperative shops and on the collective farm market which took place over these years, coupled with the raising of official prices, undoubtedly brought supply and demand into a reasonable equilibrium in 1937.

Many outstanding students of the Soviet economy have believed that the consumer goods market was operating fairly effectively in the Soviet Union during 1937, but the absence of any information on market prices during 1937 itself led them to qualify their supposition.[21] Recently J. F. Karcz has located a number of collective farm market price quotations for 1937. These data are still too limited to provide absolute certainty, but they tend strongly to confirm the impression that the retail market was operating quite effectively during 1937. Of forty-eight free market quotations for meat in several cities during the period April through December 1937, most are within the range of the official prices for the same type of meat in the corresponding price zone. Precise comparisons cannot be made as the quality of the meat is not specified in the case of the free market quotations. All nine of the located collective farm market prices for various specified grades of flour are below the corresponding official price. For other products the data are less conclusive as there was no uniform centrally established price or set of zonal prices for state and cooperative trade. Official prices of such perishable, seasonal products as milk, eggs, vegetables, and fruit were set locally at that time. For milk, twenty market quotations located by Karcz ranged from 0.55 ruble to 1.70 rubles per liter in various cities during the period April through December. The state shop price in Moscow was 1.60 rubles per liter all year. In two cases, the market price could be compared with the official price in the same city on the same date. In one of these cases, the market price was the same as the official price, and in the other case, the market

[18] This can be computed from the figures on collective farm market sales in current and in constant prices for the period 1933 to 1939 in A. P. Dadugin and P. G. Kagarlitskii, *Organizatsiia i tekhnika kolkhoznoi-bazarnoi torgovli* (Moscow, 1949), p. 5. The calculation should result in the official Soviet index number of collective farm market prices. The Soviet index number for this period was particularly subject to shortcomings and cannot be relied on very heavily.

[19] TSUNKHU, *Kolkhoznaia i individual'no-krestianskaia torgovlia* (Moscow, 1936).

[20] Gosplan, *Narodno-khoziaistvennyi plan na 1936 god* (2d ed., Moscow, 1936), pp. 334–335.

[21] For example, Abram Bergson, *Soviet National Income and Product in 1937* (New York, 1953), pp. 63–65; Alexander Baykov, *The Development of the Soviet Economic System* (New York, 1947), p. 260; Naum Jasny, *The Soviet Price System* (Stanford, 1951), p. 33.

price was below the official price. Seven quotations for eggs on the Moscow market seem in line with the Moscow official prices. Twenty-seven market quotations for potatoes in several cities ranged from 0.09 ruble to 1.50 rubles per kilogram. Of these, five relate to Moscow and ranged from 0.14 ruble to 0.45 ruble per kilogram during the period October through December, when the Moscow state shop price was 0.40 ruble per kilogram. Seventeen quotations for cabbage on the markets of various cities between June and October ranged from 0.10 ruble to 1.50 rubles per kilogram. The latter is a price for early cabbage. During the same period, the state shop price of cabbage in Moscow declined from 2.00 rubles in June to 0.30 ruble per kilogram at the end of August, where it remained through the rest of the year.[22]

Many of the available market quotations appear to be below the official prices. To some extent this is only because in the above summary the state shop price in Moscow is compared with the collective farm market prices in other cities. Moscow state shop prices of perishable products were generally higher than prices in cities in agricultural producing regions and in smaller towns, and presumably this was true also of Moscow collective farm market prices. Other factors are differences in the quality of the product and in the relative convenience of the market and the state shops in the different cities. As has been said, the collective farm markets are very sensitive to local conditions of demand and supply, which may of course differ from conditions in the country as a whole. It is also possible that there is some downward bias in the sample of market quotations located in the Soviet press. Many of the quotations are of prices prevailing during preholiday trade or during special fairs when prices usually decline for the duration of the fair. On the whole, though, the weight of the evidence of the free market quotations, of observers' reports that marketing was fairly orderly with only occasional queues for particular commodities, and of information on conditions in the economy as a whole does seem to show that the consumer goods market was operating relatively effectively during 1937.

The equilibrium attained in the consumer goods market in 1936 or 1937 apparently lasted through 1938 and part of 1939, but by 1940 the market was no longer in balance. Partly as a result of military preparations and the Finnish war, there was an acute shortage of consumer goods, particularly during the early part of 1940. The official prices at the begin-

[22] The collective farm market quotations, except for cabbage, are from J. F. Karcz, *Soviet Agricultural Marketings and Prices, 1928–1954*, The RAND Corporation, RM-1930, July 2, 1957, Tables E-6, E-10, E-12, E-16, and E-18. His source for most of these quotations and the source for the collective farm market quotations for cabbage was the daily *Sovetskaia torgovlia* for 1937. The official price quotations cited in comparison are from appendix A of this volume; G. I. Kuznetsov (ed.), *Sbornik otpusknykh i roznichnykh tsen i torgovykh nakidok na prodovol'stvennye tovary* (Moscow, 1936); Moskovskii oblastnoi otdel vnutrennei torgovli, *Spravochnik roznichnykh tsen na prodovol'stvennye tovary po Moskovskoi oblasti* (Moscow, 1936); the daily *Sovetskaia torgovlia*.

ning of 1940 were generally still at about the 1937 level or only slightly higher. At these prices many goods were unavailable, and others were on sale only irregularly. As early as January 24, 1940, some official food prices were raised, but it was not until later in the year that there was a general increase.

Insofar as foods were short in the official outlets, prices on the collective farm market were far higher than official prices. Data for Moscow on January 1, 1940, show a very wide gap between the official and free market prices. The Moscow official and free market prices in effect on January 1, 1940, and also Moscow official prices in July 1940 and January 1941 are shown in Table 2. By July, judging on the basis of data

TABLE 2

Official and Collective Farm Market Prices of Selected Foods, Moscow, 1940

Commodity	Unit	Collective farm market price (rubles) January 1940	Official price (rubles)		
			January 1940	July 1940	January 1941
Beef steak	kg	20.00	14.00	20.80	20.80
Beef roast	kg	17.00	10.50	18.00	18.00
Beef, second quality	kg	14.00	9.00	14.00	14.00
Mutton	kg	17.00	8.00	18.00[a]	14.00
Milk	liter	5.00	2.10	2.10	2.30
Sour cream	kg	16.00	6.80	10.00	11.00
Eggs	ten	12.00	8.50	8.50	7.50
Potatoes	kg	6.00	0.50	8.00	0.90
Onions	kg	2.50	1.50	—	3.00
Beets	kg	1.50	0.50	—	1.00
Carrots	kg	2.00	0.50	9.00	1.50
Cabbage	kg	10.00	—	10.00	—

[a] Price established April 10, 1940; item not available July 1, 1940.
Note: The dash (—) indicates that the item was not available.
Sources: *Monthly Labor Review*, May 1940, pp. 1273–1274; August 1940, p. 501; February 1941, p. 476; May 1941, pp. 1294–1295.

for Moscow, a shift toward a market balance for foods had begun, a result partly of seasonal increases in the supply of foods in both markets and partly of sharp increases in the official food prices. For the rest of the year food supplies continued to increase both in the state shops and on the free market, and there was some further seasonal price decline on both markets. In October, the official price of potatoes was reduced, but the official prices of the most commonly consumed types of bread were raised, this being the first increase since the abolition of bread rationing in 1935. For the year as a whole, my calculations suggest that collective farm market prices exceeded official prices by something like 60 percent.[23]

Clothing and textiles were especially scarce during the early part of 1940. American visitors in Moscow reported that almost no clothing items

[23] See chapter VI.

could be found in Moscow shops in January. In early July, clothing and textile prices were raised. The stores selling these items were closed for two weeks but reopened in mid-July with larger stocks than had been seen earlier in the year. In spite of the price increases, these stocks began to run low within a month. Later, the high prices apparently began to cut demand down toward the available supplies. By the end of the year, most types of clothing were fairly easily obtainable and fewer customers were seen in the Moscow shops than during the preceding months.[24]

With the outbreak of war, rationing was introduced. In July 1941, rationing was begun in a few cities and later was extended to the entire urban population.[25] Rationing was differential, as was the case also of the earlier ration period, with the highest rations going to wage earners and salaried employees in key defense industries and the lowest rations to adults not engaged in productive work outside the house. In addition, food beyond the usual ration was supplied in the factory canteens to workers meeting or surpassing output goals. Most consumer goods were distributed on a ration basis through the state and cooperative shops and restaurants. Ration prices were maintained about at the level prevailing just prior to the introduction of rationing until September 1946 when there was the first of a series of increases in ration prices. In April 1944, the state began to operate commercial shops in which goods could be purchased without ration coupons but at prices greatly exceeding the ration prices.[26] During 1944, sales in commercial shops amounted to 6 billion rubles,[27] or only 5 percent of total retail sales in state and cooperative shops, including the commercial shops. The share of commercial shops increased after this.

As a result of the wartime shortage of all kinds of consumer goods, prices on the collective farm market in 1944 soared to astronomical heights — roughly 11 times the level of market prices in 1940 and 22 times the level of market prices in 1937. Prices in the commercial shops were supposedly set somewhat lower than the free market prices in an effort to exert a downward pressure on the market prices. There was indeed some decline in free market prices after the opening of the commercial shops, followed by some reductions in commercial shop prices. But on the whole,

[24] The foregoing description of the Moscow retail market during 1940 is based on reports in the *Monthly Labor Review,* May and August 1940, and February and May 1941.

[25] Formal rationing apparently was not extended to the rural population except that ration coupons for bread were distributed to persons in rural areas who were not connected with agriculture. See N. Riauzov and N. Titel'baum, *Kurs torgovoi statistiki,* pp. 85–86. Some form of controlling the distribution of consumer goods in rural areas was undoubtedly practiced.

[26] A third set of official prices, between the low ration prices and the high commercial shop prices, was in effect for retail sales of some manufactured consumer goods in rural areas. See the discussion under "special rural prices" in appendix E of this volume.

[27] *Sovetskaia torgovlia za tridtsat' let* (Moscow, 1947), p. 129.

commercial shop prices of foods seem to have been about the same as the free market prices during 1944. Roughly, prices on the free market and in the commercial shops were 15 times the ration prices.[28]

In December 1947, rationing was abolished, the commercial shops lost their special character, and an open market at a single set of official prices was again introduced.[29] In preparation for this, ration prices had been raised rather considerably and there had been some reductions in the prices in commercial shops so that the gap between the two sets of official prices had been much reduced. The abolition of rationing was accompanied by the Currency Reform of December 1947, in which cash holdings were exchanged at the rate of ten old rubles for one new ruble and savings deposits and bonds were exchanged at more favorable rates. This served to reduce the inflationary pressure represented by large hoards of cash accumulated during the war, mainly by peasants. The cash that urban workers and employees couldn't spend in state shops mostly found its way to the collective farm market and hence to the peasants' mattresses.[30]

The new official retail prices seem on the whole to have been more or less correctly set in relation to conditions of demand and supply. It seems quite clear that there was a period of adjustment to the new system during which the market was not operating very effectively, and, in some respects, was not even really free. Although ration coupons were no longer in use, legal limitations were established on the amount of any one commodity which could be sold to one customer at a time (for example, two kilograms of bread, meat, fish; 500 grams of butter or sugar; one liter of milk; five eggs).[31] Such regulations were presumably designed to prevent a rush on supplies in the early days of the new consumer freedom. It is believed that they were not generally enforced after the first few weeks except in cases where a particular commodity was in short supply in a given locality. Supplies in state and cooperative shops generally were, it is believed, adequate at the new official prices during the year 1948 taken as a whole, although a few commodities remained in short supply through-

[28] For a more complete description of the wartime rationing and the Soviet retail price system during the war, see Alexander Baykov, "Internal Trade During the War and Its Postwar Development," *Bulletins on Soviet Economic Development*, no. 4, September 1950, pp. 1–2; Harry Schwartz, "Prices in the Soviet War Economy," *American Economic Review*, 36:872–882 (December 1946); Irving B. Kravis and Joseph Mintzes, "The Soviet Union: Trends in Prices, Rations, and Wages," *Monthly Labor Review*, 65:28–35 (July 1947).

[29] *Pravda*, December 15, 1947.

[30] The text of the currency reform decree was published in *Pravda*, December 15, 1947. For a more complete description of the provisions of the decree and an analysis of the intents and effects of the currency reform, see Franklyn D. Holzman, *Soviet Taxation* (Cambridge, Mass., 1955), pp. 232–239; Paul Baran, "Currency Reform in the USSR," *Harvard Business Review*, 26:194–200 (March 1948).

[31] These limits were established by laws and regulations of the Ministry of Trade in November and December 1947 and March 1948. *Spravochnik direktora prodovol'stvennogo magazina* (Moscow, 1949), pp. 179–190.

out the year. Collective farm market prices had been falling since 1943. Although they were still considerably higher than state shop prices immediately after the abolition of rationing, they apparently declined quite rapidly toward the level of state prices. For the year as a whole, it is estimated, collective farm market prices exceeded the official prices by something under 15 percent.[32]

It should be mentioned here that during 1948 some consumer cooperative trade was not subject to the official retail prices. The official prices applied to sales in cooperative shops of consumer goods procured from centrally controlled sources of supply, the bulk of goods. In the case of agricultural products procured by the cooperatives directly from collective farms and collective farmers, and consumer goods produced by the cooperatives from raw materials so procured, the regional unions of consumer cooperatives were allowed to establish the retail prices at which such goods could be sold. By central regulation, these cooperative prices were to be at least 10 percent below the collective farm market prices, and every effort was to be made to reduce these prices to the level of the official prices in state shops, or even below them.[33] The aim of reducing prices in the cooperative shops to the level of state shop prices appears to have been substantially fulfilled by mid-1948.[34]

Between 1948 and 1952, prices on the collective farm market seem to have fallen about as much as official prices so that the gap between the official and free market prices was rather moderate and roughly the same as in 1948. But in 1954, collective farm market prices, beginning to rise while state prices had been further reduced, were roughly some 35 percent higher than official prices.[35]

Special mention should be made of the market for housing. Throughout the period under review (including 1937) housing was extremely tight. The volume of urban housing, inadequate in 1928, by no means kept up with the increase in the urban population. The basic housing law sets forth the right of each tenant to 9 square meters of dwelling space per person, but the actual dwelling space available has never come near this

---

[32] See chapter VI.

[33] Lifits, *Sovetskaia torgovlia*, pp. 92–93. This is the situation roughly as it existed in 1948. The privilege was initially granted in November 1946. The upper limit for the special cooperative shop prices from November 1946 until the abolition of rationing in December 1947 was the level of the commercial shop prices. The relevant portions of the November 1946 decree are in *Postavka tovarov v sisteme sovetskoi torgovli; sbornik vazhneishikh postanovlenii, instruktsii i prikazov* (Moscow, 1947), p. 62. See also Z. I. Shkundin, *Obiazatel'stvo postavki tovarov v sovetskom prave* (Moscow, 1948), pp. 201–202; F. Aliutin, "Rol' potrebitel'skoi kooperatsii . . . ," *Izvestiia Akademii nauk SSSR, otdelenie ekonomiki i prava*, no. 1, 1949, pp. 13–31; A. P. Klimov, *Sovetskaia potrebitel'skaia kooperatsiia* (Moscow, 1948), pp. 15 ff.

[34] S. Gurevitch, "Soviet Rural Stores," *USSR Information Bulletin* (Soviet Embassy, Washington, July 1948), p. 451; Klimov, *Sovetskaia potrebitel'skaia kooperatsiia*, p. 16; *Pravda*, June 25 and August 10, 1948; and unpublished materials.

[35] See chapter VI.

norm. Urban per capita dwelling space was 5.8 square meters in 1928, 4.6 square meters in 1937, 4.5 square meters in 1940, under 4.0 square meters in 1944, 5.2 square meters in 1948, 4.9 square meters in 1952, and 5.0 square meters in 1954.[36] At the same time the government rental rates are extremely low. The rental formula for determining rent has remained virtually unchanged since its establishment in 1928. Rent is based in part on the earnings of the tenant, so as money wages have increased there has been some rise in rents, but at a much slower rate; and there is a legal maximum rent of 1.32 rubles per square meter per month.[37] Sometime between 1944 and 1948 the average wage of all wage earners and salaried employees reached a level at which the maximum rent applied; since then the only increases in rent can have been for persons earning less than the average wage. These low rental rates clearly greatly undervalue housing space in view of the great shortage of housing. Urban housing is, in effect, distributed on a rationed basis. The indications are that this has been true also in varying degrees of electricity and some other utilities.

While it seems clear that it is Soviet policy to attempt to set retail prices so as to balance demand with the supplies made available, it is evident from the foregoing discussion that the Soviet planners have rarely achieved this balance in practice. Of the years covered in this study, only 1937 can be considered as a year in which the retail market was operating reasonably effectively. But even in 1937 there were certainly some imperfections in the market, and the market for housing and some other services was out of balance. The imbalance in the retail market was relatively moderate in 1948 and 1952 but substantial in 1928, 1940, and 1954. And in 1944, rationing existed, accompanied by extremely high prices in the commercial shops and on the collective farm market with serious shortages in all markets. The existence of multiple prices over most of the period raises some questions regarding the meaningfulness of a cost-of-living index number under Soviet conditions. The theoretical problems raised and my general approach to them are discussed in chapter III. The details of the estimates of the gap between the official and free market prices prevailing during the various years, and the procedures for taking account of the free market prices in the cost-of-living index number are explained in chapter VI.

[36] See Table 27.
[37] The official formula for determining rent is described in appendix A.

III·

INDEX NUMBER THEORY AND ITS
APPLICATION TO THE SOVIET CASE

THE ultimate interest in an index number of Soviet real wages lies in
the light it may throw on changes in the welfare of the Soviet worker.
With this in mind, in deciding on methods of measuring the change in
the cost of living and in the real wages of Soviet workers, I have taken
as a point of departure the economic theory of index numbers.[1] The theory
is distinctly abstract, and inevitably in attempting to adhere to it one
meets many difficulties. Some of these arise from inadequacies in the
available data, others from the nature of the underlying economic facts.
The difficulties of the former kind are, understandably, particularly
troublesome when working with limited Soviet data. These difficulties
will dog our steps through most of this study but need not detain us here.
More basically, the question must be raised as to how applicable the
theory is under Soviet conditions; or, put in another way, how meaningful
in theoretic terms can an index number of real wages be for the Soviet
Union over a period during which so many fundamental changes in institutions and ways of life took place and the market for consumer goods
was more often than not out of equilibrium.

In section 1 of this chapter, I give a brief presentation of the economic
theory of index numbers. Section 2 describes the methods used in applying
the theory to the Soviet case, including the formulas used for computing
the cost-of-living and real-wages index numbers, with a discussion of their
proper interpretation and limitations. I also discuss some special problems
in the Soviet Union limiting the application of the theory — in particular,
changes in taste and environment, the introduction of new goods, and the
meaningfulness of Soviet retail prices — and my methods of attempting

---

[1] The essentials of the theory are presented briefly in J. R. Hicks, "The Valuation of
Social Income," *Economica*, n.s., 7:105-124 (May 1940); and R. G. D. Allen, "The
Economic Theory of Index Numbers," *Economica*, n.s., 16:197–203 (August 1949). See
also Paul A. Samuelson, *Foundations of Economic Analysis* (Cambridge, Mass., 1947),
pp. 146–163; Ragnar Frisch, "Annual Survey of General Economic Theory: The Prob-
lem of Index Numbers," *Econometrica*, 4:1–38 (January 1936); Melville J. Ulmer, *The
Economic Theory of Cost-of-Living Index Numbers* (New York, 1949); and Bruce D.
Mudgett, *Index Numbers* (New York, 1951).

to handle these problems. Finally, I add a cautionary note regarding the calculations for the war year 1944.

I. THE ECONOMIC THEORY OF INDEX NUMBERS OF THE COST OF LIVING AND OF REAL WAGES

The purpose of constructing index numbers of real wages is to measure one very important aspect of the change in the welfare of the Soviet worker. In the theoretical literature, an index number of real wages is generally taken as a measure of the change in welfare or utility derived from consumption. Most proponents of the theory adhere to the view that utility can only be measured in an ordinal sense and that, therefore, the most one is entitled to conclude from an index number of real wages is whether one situation provides more or less satisfaction than another. The numerical values of the index numbers computed have, from this point of view, no other significance. However, even if one agrees that utility can only be measured ordinally, it is still very useful to consider real wages as having the properties of a composite commodity and, accordingly, as being measurable in a cardinal sense. If the consumption of all commodities doubled, I think everyone would agree that real wages had doubled, and no one would argue that it would be all right to speak of them as having possibly tripled instead. One need not, of course, hold that a doubling of real wages in the composite-commodity sense implies that the satisfaction derived from the real wages has precisely, or even approximately, doubled. In this study I shall treat real wages as a composite commodity and shall regard the numerical values of the index numbers compiled as meaningful in indicating changes in real wages in this sense. I do not claim to measure changes in welfare in the same way; but I hope the index numbers of real wages will ultimately shed light on changes in welfare.

The economic theory of index numbers teaches that there are two index numbers of the change in the cost of living between any two years; that is, for each pair of years, there is one cost-of-living index number from the standpoint of the level and pattern of consumption of the first year, and another from the standpoint of the level and pattern of consumption of the second year. Similarly, in the case of the change in real wages between any two years there are two measures, one in which the quantities consumed in each year are valued at the prices prevailing in the first year, one in which they are valued at the prices prevailing in the second year.

The reason the theory insists upon these two index numbers of the cost of living and the two corresponding index numbers of real wages is to make use of the information on consumer preferences revealed by the behavior of the consumer in each of the two actual situations being compared. So long as the concern is with welfare, it is the bundle of commodities chosen by the consumer himself and the relative value he places on each that are relevant. The problem with which the economic theory of index numbers is concerned is whether it can be determined from price and quantity data alone which of two situations yields a higher level of satisfaction. In practice, price and quantity data, no matter how imperfect, are generally available, but information on consumers' preference maps almost never is. However, under certain conditions, the price and quantity data for a given situation do give us some information about consumer preferences in that same situation. Given rational consumer behavior and an open market in each of two years o and i, we know that the collection of goods actually purchased in year o is the best collection; that is, it provides more satisfaction than any other collection of goods that could have been purchased with the money income of year o at the prices prevailing in year o. Furthermore, at this point the relative prices tend to correspond to the relative marginal utilities of the various goods to the consumer. In year i also, provided the same assumptions hold, the actual quantities of the various goods purchased and the structure of prices are indicative of consumer preferences in that year.

The two relevant cost-of-living index numbers that can be computed from the available price and quantity data are the Laspeyres and the Paasche index numbers. Using base-year quantity weights, the Laspeyres cost-of-living index number measures the change in the cost of living from the point of view of the level and pattern of consumption of the base year. Measuring the change from year o to year i, the Laspeyres cost-of-living index number is

$$C_o{}^{o,i} = \frac{\Sigma P_i Q_o}{\Sigma P_o Q_o}. \tag{1}$$

In the formulas, Q_o is the quantity of any particular commodity consumed in the base year, P_o is the price of that commodity in the base year, and the summation is taken over the various commodities. Q_i and P_i refer to the quantities consumed and the prices prevailing in the given year. C is the cost-of-living index number, with the subscript indicating the year from which the quantity weights are drawn. The superscripts indicate the direction in which the change is measured, in this case, from the base year o to the given year i. The Paasche cost-of-living index number uses given-year weights and measures the change in the cost of living from the point of view of the level and pattern of consumption of the given year. It is

$$C_i{}^{o,i} = \frac{\Sigma P_i Q_i}{\Sigma P_o Q_i}. \tag{2}$$

It follows from what has already been said that (leaving savings and direct taxes out of account) the money wage I of the base year is $I_o = \Sigma P_o Q_o$, and the money wage of the given year is $I_i = \Sigma P_i Q_i$, where the summation is taken over all commodities consumed. If there were no changes in the prices of the commodities from one year to the other, the index number of money wages I_i/I_o would, of course, measure the change in real wages during the period. Where price changes occur, the real-wage index number W is obtained by deflating the index number of money wages by a cost-of-living index number. Using the Laspeyres index number for this deflation, the resulting index number of the change in real wages between year o and year i is

$$W_i{}^{o,i} = \frac{I_i}{I_o} \cdot \frac{1}{C_o{}^{o,i}} = \frac{\Sigma P_i Q_i}{\Sigma P_o Q_o} \cdot \frac{\Sigma P_o Q_o}{\Sigma P_i Q_o} = \frac{\Sigma P_i Q_i}{\Sigma P_i Q_o}. \tag{3}$$

Deflating money wages by the Paasche cost-of-living index number results in the following index number of real wages:

$$W_o{}^{o,i} = \frac{I_i}{I_o} \cdot \frac{1}{C_i{}^{o,i}} = \frac{\Sigma P_i Q_i}{\Sigma P_o Q_o} \cdot \frac{\Sigma P_o Q_i}{\Sigma P_i Q_i} = \frac{\Sigma P_o Q_i}{\Sigma P_o Q_o}. \tag{4}$$

Note that when money wages are deflated by a cost-of-living index number using base-year quantity weights, the result is an index number of real wages in which the quantities of each commodity consumed are weighted by, or valued in terms of, the structure of prices of the given year. This fact is reflected in the notation by the subscript to W indicating the year to which the price weights refer. Similarly, deflation by a cost-of-living index number using given-year quantity weights yields an index number of real wages valued in terms of the price structure of the base year. This point, which is perhaps still not generally appreciated, is of considerable importance in the present study. The full significance will emerge in the subsequent discussion.

If there are no changes in price structure, or if there are no changes in the pattern of consumption, the Laspeyres and the Paasche cost-of-living index numbers will be equal, and the two index numbers of real wages will be equal. But in the more usual case there are changes in price structure and in patterns of consumption. Here the two cost-of-living index numbers will differ and so will the two index numbers of real wages; moreover, none of the index numbers that can be computed will equal its corresponding "true" index number. The "true" change in the cost of living from the viewpoint of the base-year budget position is defined as the ratio of (a) the cost of the cheapest basket of goods at year-i prices that will leave the consumer at the year-o level of satisfaction to (b) the cost of the year-o basket of goods at year-o prices. However, the Laspeyres cost-of-living index number, given in formula (1), measures the ratio of (a) the cost of the year-o basket of goods at year-i prices to (b) the cost of the year-o basket of goods at year-o prices. If relative prices change between the two years, there should be a basket of goods (denoted by the quantities $\tilde{Q}_o$) that would provide the same satisfaction as the actual year-o

basket of goods but, because of the possibility of substitution of cheaper for dearer goods, would cost less at year-i prices; that is $\Sigma P_i \tilde{Q}_o$ would be less than $\Sigma P_i Q_o$, the numerator of the Laspeyres cost-of-living index number. For this reason the Laspeyres cost-of-living index number is said to be the upper limit to the "true" change in the cost of living from the viewpoint of the year-o budget position. From the viewpoint of the year-i budget position, the Paasche cost-of-living index number provides the lower limit to the "true" change in the cost of living. It is the lower limit because if there are changes in relative prices, the denominator $\Sigma P_o Q_i$ in the Paasche formula is greater than $\Sigma P_o \tilde{Q}_i$, the cost of the cheapest basket of goods at year-o prices that would provide the year-i level of satisfaction. As we have no way of knowing what the various quantities $\tilde{Q}_o$ and $\tilde{Q}_i$ are, the two "true" index numbers cannot themselves be computed. Similarly, there are two "true" index numbers of real wages, one relating to the price structure of the base year and the other relating to the price structure of the given year. If there are changes in relative prices, formula (3) is a lower limit to the "true" change in real wages as valued at year-i prices because the denominator $\Sigma P_i Q_o$ is greater than the income necessary if expended optimally to obtain the year-i level of satisfaction at year-o prices. Formula (4) is the upper limit to the "true" change in real wages as valued at year-o prices because the numerator $\Sigma P_o Q_i$ is greater than the income necessary if expended optimally to obtain the year-i level of satisfaction at year-o prices.

Differences between the Laspeyres and the Paasche cost-of-living index numbers and differences between the two corresponding index numbers of real wages arise from changes in the price structure and changes in the pattern of consumption. In reality, of course, numerous changes in conditions or environment take place over time and are likely to result in changes in price structure and in patterns of consumption. The greater the changes the less reliable the index numbers that we can compute are as approximations to the "true" measures. When such changes are great, the two index numbers may diverge widely, and in some cases they may even give conflicting results. The two "true" index numbers of the cost of living might in some cases disagree, as each index number depends only on the level of satisfaction attained in one of the two situations. In the case of real wages, however, so long as tastes remain constant the two "true" index numbers must agree as to the direction of change because we are here comparing the level of satisfaction obtained in two situations in terms of an unchanged preference scale.[2] This does not, of course, ensure that even if tastes remain constant the two index numbers of real wages that we can compute will always agree. Unfortunately, the theory provides no basis for choice between the two measures of the change in the

[2] See Allen, *Economica*, n.s., 16:198–200 (August 1949).

cost of living or between the two measures of the change in real wages.

The theory presupposes ideally that tastes remain constant, for when tastes change the awkward consequence is that real income in the two situations is valued in terms of two different scales of values. The economist has no basis for choosing between such value scales. When tastes change, the alternative index numbers are no longer observations on the change in real wages of people with the same tastes, but they are still of interest. Each measure tells what the change was for a given set of tastes. Ivan-28 and Ivan-54 may each think his own real income is greater than that of the other. In this case there is no one answer as to the course of Soviet real wages, but the two answers are by no means devoid of interest. It is also possible that both Ivan-28 and Ivan-54 see the same situation as preferable. If two groups with different tastes both agree that situation B is preferable to situation A, we may, I think, quite safely agree that real income has risen. In such a case the two index numbers of real wages will agree as to the direction of change, although if tastes have changed much, the measures will very likely diverge significantly in magnitude and hence still may provide little clue as to whether real income has risen a great deal or only a little.

Strictly speaking, the theory focuses on the real wages of one individual. But the analysis may be extended to a group if we think in terms of an index number of average real wages. Preferably the individuals in the group should have similar tastes, and the more homogeneous the group is, in this sense, the better the index numbers will be. When dealing with a group, however, the welfare inferences that may be drawn from index numbers of real wages are complicated if there are changes in the distribution of income. Undoubtedly there have been changes in the distribution of income in the Soviet Union during the period of the five year plans, but this aspect must be left to a separate inquiry.

A further limitation of the theory lies in the fact that cost-of-living index numbers can take account only of goods that are available in both of the two situations compared. This is tantamount to assuming that welfare is unaffected by any goods that are available in only one of the two situations. In the present case, the problem of new goods is not nearly so important as might be supposed, but it is necessary to consider it nevertheless. The introduction of new types and varieties of goods is an important factor in long-run changes in real income. If the period since the base year is long enough, new goods are likely to predominate in the consumer's basket in year i. Clearly in such a case a comparison of the prices of only those goods consumed in both years would not give a very meaningful measure of the change in the cost of living between the two years.

The introduction of new goods between year o and year i does not affect the Laspeyres cost-of-living index number weighted by the quantities of the various goods consumed in year o, as the quantities Q_o are zero for goods newly available in year i. This is not to say, of course, that the Laspeyres cost-of-living index number will provide a meaningful basis for deflating money wages if new goods are of great importance. In the Paasche cost-of-living index number, on the other hand, the quantities Q_i are positive for the new goods while there are no corresponding prices P_o at which to value them. The appropriate price for a new good would be the price that in year o would have just made the demand for the good zero; but of course we cannot estimate such a price. Still, it can usually be assumed that the (hypothetical) price of such a new commodity will have fallen in relation to the prices of other commodities between year o and year i. This means that the Paasche index number computed only on the basis of goods actually available in both situations will somewhat overstate the rise in the cost of living by an amount that depends largely on the importance of new goods in the second situation.[3] This argument regarding the introduction of new goods can be adapted to the case of the wartime disappearance from the market of commodities that consumers still desire.

In short, meaningful comparisons of the cost of living and of real wages can only be made between situations in which the bulk of the goods consumed are common to both periods. There is no really satisfactory way of handling the problem of new goods, but various procedures for taking some account of them can be adopted, and direct comparisons of real wages can be limited to periods over which new goods are not of too great importance.

The assumptions of the theory regarding prices must also be made explicit here as they pose some very real problems in the Soviet case. In measuring changes in real income, the appropriate prices to use in valuing the quantities of the various goods consumed are those that reflect the relative marginal utilities of the various goods to the consumers. In a free market where the consumer can buy as many units of a commodity as he likes at the market price, retail prices will more or less closely represent relative marginal utilities. But if there is any restriction on the number of units that can be purchased — any form of rationing of any of the commodities — then the consumer will not be able to buy enough of the rationed commodity to reach the point where its marginal utility is measured by its price. Since in this case relative prices do not correspond to relative marginal utilities, we do not have the kind of information required for the application of the index-number tests as to whether real income has risen or fallen. We do know that the ration price understates the marginal utility of the rationed good in relation to the marginal utilities of other goods and that the price representing relative marginal utility would be the price that would just limit demand for the rationed

[3] See Hicks, *Economica*, n.s., 7:114 (May 1940).

good to the amount of the ration. Some adjustment along these lines may be made to take rationed goods into account, though of necessity it would be very rough. Where prices are fixed by the state, this kind of situation may arise even without formal rationing when the prices are fixed too low in relation to demand, as has often been the case in the Soviet Union.

2. APPLICATION TO THE SOVIET CASE

In the actual Soviet case we meet difficult problems in the application of the theory and in the interpretation of the index numbers of the cost of living and of real wages. In the period studied there have been extraordinary changes in environment and, probably, marked changes in tastes. New goods have been introduced and old ones have disappeared, and though this has not occurred on a very great scale, some consideration must be given to these changes. Prices set by the government have often been too low in relation to demand, and a multiple price system has prevailed during most of the period; there is therefore the problem of how to handle such multiple prices in constructing the index numbers. Also the question must be raised as to the meaningfulness of an index number of real wages based on Soviet prices.

The formulas. If an attempt is to be made to measure the change in real wages for a period during which tastes and environment have changed significantly, clearly both index numbers of real wages must be computed. The two index numbers together may provide only an ambiguous answer, but one index number alone would probably give an even more erroneous impression. Accordingly, I have computed both the Laspeyres and the Paasche index numbers of the cost of living and the two corresponding index numbers of real wages. This is done, however, only for the comparisons between 1937 and each given year. All index numbers are linked at the year 1937; this has several advantages and seems the best way of attempting to handle the main departures from theoretical conditions inherent in a dynamic society such as that of the Soviet Union.

Using 1937 as base year in all comparisons has an additional important practical advantage. As price data are available in larger volume for 1937 than for any other year, use of 1937 as base year ensures maximum coverage of commodities and a maximum degree of comparability of the particular items priced as between 1937 and any other year. The importance of assuring comparability in the price quotations used in the cost-of-living index numbers is obviously paramount, and the attempt to achieve physical comparability between items has been a primary concern of this study. As no theoretical issues are involved for comparability understood in this sense, the discussion of this problem is deferred to chapter IV and appendix A.

For each year (except 1944) I have computed two alternative cost-of-living index numbers and the two corresponding index numbers of real wages. One cost-of-living index number is based on weights drawn from the consumption pattern of 1937; the other is based on weights drawn from the consumption pattern of the given year. The formulas defining the two cost-of-living index numbers are

$$C_{37}{}^{37,i} = \frac{\Sigma P_i Q_{37}}{\Sigma P_{37} Q_{37}} = \frac{\Sigma (P_i/P_{37})(P_{37} Q_{37})}{\Sigma P_{37} Q_{37}} \tag{5}$$

and

$$C_i{}^{37,i} = \frac{\Sigma P_i Q_i}{\Sigma P_{37} Q_i} = \frac{\Sigma P_i Q_i}{\Sigma (P_{37}/P_i)(P_i Q_i)}. \tag{6}$$

Formula (5) is the Laspeyres formula (1) with 1937 as the base year, and formula (6) is the Paasche formula (2) with 1937 as the base year.

In the actual computations, the cost-of-living index numbers are computed as value-weighted averages of price relatives. Each of the price relatives, P_i/P_{37} in formula (5) and P_{37}/P_i in formula (6), represents for a particular commodity the ratio of the prices in effect in the two years. They are computed as percentages. The value weights corresponding to each price relative are, for formula (5), $(P_{37} Q_{37})/(\Sigma P_{37} Q_{37})$, and for formula (6), $(P_i Q_i)/(\Sigma P_i Q_i)$. They represent the share of total expenditure devoted to the particular commodity in the year in question; and they too are computed as percentages.

The two alternative index numbers of real wages are computed by deflating the index number of money wages by each of these cost-of-living index numbers. From formula (5) we obtain an index number of real wages in which the quantities consumed in each year are valued in terms of the structure of prices of the given year i, as follows:

$$W_i{}^{37,i} = \frac{\Sigma P_i Q_i}{\Sigma P_i Q_{37}}. \tag{7}$$

Formula (7) is equivalent to formula (3) rewritten with 1937 as the base year. From formula (6), we obtain an index number of real wages valued in terms of the structure of prices in 1937,

$$W_{37}{}^{37,i} = \frac{\Sigma P_{37} Q_i}{\Sigma P_{37} Q_{37}}, \tag{8}$$

which is equivalent to formula (4) rewritten with 1937 as the base year.

The index numbers from formulas (5) through (8) are the ones actually computed in detail. However, they provide only for a comparison between the given year and 1937. For purposes of comparing two years other than 1937, it is necessary to link the index numbers. For instance, to compare 1940 with 1954, the index number for 1937 to 1954 is divided by that for 1937 to 1940. One set of linked cost-of-living index numbers is obtained from the 1937-weighted links computed according to formula (5), and a second set is obtained from the given-year weighted links computed according to formula (6). The formulas of the resulting linked index numbers of the cost of living and of real wages are

$$C_{37}{}^{i,k} = \frac{C_{37}{}^{37,k}}{C_{37}{}^{37,i}} = \frac{(\Sigma P_k Q_{37})/(\Sigma P_{37} Q_{37})}{(\Sigma P_i Q_{37})/(\Sigma P_{37} Q_{37})} = \frac{\Sigma P_k Q_{37}}{\Sigma P_i Q_{37}}, \tag{9}$$

$$C_{ik}{}^{i,k} = \frac{C_k{}^{37,k}}{C_i{}^{37,i}} = \frac{(\Sigma P_k Q_k)/(\Sigma P_{37} Q_k)}{(\Sigma P_i Q_i)/(\Sigma P_{37} Q_i)}, \tag{10}$$

$$W_{ik}{}^{i,k} = \frac{W_k{}^{37,k}}{W_i{}^{37,i}} = \frac{(\Sigma P_k Q_k)/(\Sigma P_k Q_{37})}{(\Sigma P_i Q_i)/(\Sigma P_i Q_{37})}, \tag{11}$$

$$W_{37}{}^{i,k} = \frac{W_{37}{}^{37,k}}{W_{37}{}^{37,i}} = \frac{(\Sigma P_{37} Q_k)/(\Sigma P_{37} Q_{37})}{(\Sigma P_{37} Q_i)/(\Sigma P_{37} Q_{37})} = \frac{\Sigma P_{37} Q_k}{\Sigma P_{37} Q_i}. \tag{12}$$

In formulas (9) to (12), i stands (as before) for a given year and k stands for a later given year. The subscript ik used in formula (10) indicates that the quantities of both years i and k enter the calculation and the formula cannot be reduced to refer to the basket of goods of a single year as can formula (9). The subscript ik in formula (11) indicates that prices of both years i and k affect the results and the formula cannot be reduced to refer to the price structure of a single year, as can formula (12).

What meaning can be attributed to these various linked formulas? As a cost-of-living index number, formula (9), though difficult to interpret from the point of view of the economic theory of index numbers, makes a good deal of pragmatic sense. It reduces to $(\Sigma P_k Q_{37})/(\Sigma P_i Q_{37})$, which compares the costs in years i and k of the basket of goods consumed in 1937. This is the familiar "Laspeyres-type" formula with constant weights most frequently used in practice, as in the U.S. Bureau of Labor Statistics Consumers' Price Index. The measure may be of some additional economic significance if the 1937 basket of goods is in some sense "typical." It can be said that 1937 was as "normal" as any year during this period of Soviet history,[4] and it was also in some sense a midpoint in terms of the long-run changes in tastes and environment that occurred in the Soviet Union during the period. However, because of the low level of real wages in 1937, it might be argued that the selection of goods consumed was not representative of years of higher real wages. By using formula (9) to deflate the index number of money wages for year i to year k, we obtain formula (11). This index number of real wages is more difficult to interpret. It reflects changes in relative prices as well as changes in quantities. It can be said to show the change in the "real" wage that would have oc-

[4] The "normality" of the base year has traditionally been accorded much weight though, as Bruce D. Mudgett argues, without much justification. Any comparison, of course, involves data from the other less "normal" year as well as from the "normal" year; if the quantity weights for the price index are taken from the consumption pattern of the "normal" year, the deflated index number of real wages will value the quantities consumed at the price structure of the "abnormal" year. See Mudgett, *Index Numbers*, pp. 65–66.

curred if either the year-i or the year-k pattern of consumption had been the same as that of 1937. For example, if the year-k pattern of consumption were the same as that of 1937, we could substitute Q_k for Q_{37} in formula (11) and obtain $(\Sigma P_i Q_k)/(\Sigma P_i Q_i) = W_i^{i,k}$.

The cost-of-living index number formula (10) has no clear theoretic meaning. It shows the change in the cost of living that would have occurred had the prices in either year k or year i been the same as the prices in 1937. However, formula (12), obtained by deflating the index number of money wages by use of formula (10), is meaningful. It reduces to $(\Sigma P_{37} Q_k)/(\Sigma P_{37} Q_i)$, which compares the quantities of goods consumed in year i and year k in terms of 1937 prices. It will be observed that the prices of 1937 are not related to the quantities consumed and do not reflect relative marginal utilities in either year i or year k. This is indeed a shortcoming from the theoretical point of view. Nevertheless, formula (12) has considerable value in that it permits us to compare real wages in all of the years studied in terms of the same — 1937 — price structure.

For purposes of measuring recent changes in real wages some doubt may be felt about the appropriateness of valuing real wages during the postwar years in terms of the prewar, 1937 price structure. In an attempt to resolve this question, alternative computations are made in which changes in real wages during the years 1948 to 1954 are measured in terms of the price structure of 1948. For 1952 and 1954, cost-of-living index numbers using given-year weights and 1948-based price relatives are computed according to the following formula:

$$C_i^{48,i} = \frac{\Sigma P_i Q_i}{\Sigma (P_{48}/P_i)(P_i Q_i)}. \tag{13}$$

The corresponding index number of real wages is

$$W_{48}^{48,i} = \frac{\Sigma P_{48} Q_i}{\Sigma P_{48} Q_{48}}. \tag{14}$$

The results differ very little from those obtained with formulas (9) to (12). For the years 1948 to 1954, weighting apparently makes relatively little difference.[5]

It will be noted that all of the linked index numbers based on formulas (9) to (12) are affected by either the prices or the quantities of 1937 as well as by the prices and/or the quantities of the two years being compared. The sets of linked index numbers of the cost of living cannot, therefore, be identified as Laspeyres or Paasche index numbers, though each link is one or the other. Hence, the alternative results obtained from the two sets of linked index numbers cannot be considered as limits to the "true" measures as can (in the rather strict sense defined earlier) the unlinked Laspeyres and Paasche cost-of-living index num-

[5] See the figures given at the end of chapter V, fn. 19.

bers and the real-wage index numbers derived from them. Formula (9) may nevertheless approximate in some degree the Laspeyres cost-of-living index number as each link is a Laspeyres index number, and formula (10) may approximate in some degree the Paasche cost-of-living index number as each link is a Paasche index number. However, this is true only with respect to comparisons among years following 1937. Although in a formal algebraic sense — that is, considering 1937 as base year — the 1928–37 link in formula (9) is a Laspeyres index number, in historical terms the 1937 weights are end-year weights, and the link is a Paasche index number. Similarly, in historical terms the 1928–37 link in formula (10) is a Laspeyres index number. That is, for comparisons between pre-1937 and post-1937 years, the links are of a mixed nature.

We can, of course, define historically "consistent" (chronologically unidirectional) Laspeyres and Paasche linked cost-of-living index numbers that relate pre-1937 years to post-1937 years by means of a linkage to 1937. The linked Laspeyres index number would be consistent in the sense that each of its links would be a Laspeyres index number; and each of the links of the linked Paasche index number would be a Paasche index number. An index number for the pair of years o to i is the reciprocal of that for i to o (C for 1937–28 is the reciprocal of C for 1928–37), and the "consistently" linked Laspeyres cost-of-living index for the years 1928–54 is therefore in the form of the product:

$$(C_{28}{}^{28,37})(C_{37}{}^{37,54}) = \frac{\Sigma P_{37} Q_{28}}{\Sigma P_{28} Q_{28}} \cdot \frac{\Sigma P_{54} Q_{37}}{\Sigma P_{37} Q_{37}}. \tag{15}$$

The corresponding expression from formula (9) would be

$$\frac{C_{37}{}^{37,54}}{C_{37}{}^{37,28}} = \frac{(\Sigma P_{54} Q_{37})/(\Sigma P_{37} Q_{37})}{(\Sigma P_{28} Q_{37})/(\Sigma P_{37} Q_{37})} = \frac{\Sigma P_{54} Q_{37}}{\Sigma P_{28} Q_{37}}.$$

Similarly, for these years we can write the "consistently" linked Paasche cost-of-living index in the following form:

$$(C_{37}{}^{28,37})(C_{54}{}^{37,54}) = \frac{\Sigma P_{37} Q_{37}}{\Sigma P_{28} Q_{37}} \cdot \frac{\Sigma P_{54} Q_{54}}{\Sigma P_{37} Q_{54}}. \tag{16}$$

The corresponding expression from formula (10) would be

$$\frac{C_{54}{}^{37,54}}{C_{28}{}^{37,28}} = \frac{(\Sigma P_{54} Q_{54})/(\Sigma P_{37} Q_{54})}{(\Sigma P_{28} Q_{28})/(\Sigma P_{37} Q_{28})} = \frac{\Sigma P_{37} Q_{28}}{\Sigma P_{28} Q_{28}} \cdot \frac{\Sigma P_{54} Q_{54}}{\Sigma P_{37} Q_{54}}.$$

Formulas (15) and (16) and the corresponding "consistently" linked index numbers of real wages are computed for the comparison of 1928 with 1954. This is done for the purpose of providing what is presumably a theoretically better approximation to the limits of the "true" changes in real wages over the full period. The results are given in chapter IX, fn. 2. These limits diverge from each other somewhat more than those obtained from formulas (9) and (10), which I generally employ in my calculations. But neither formula (15) nor (16) leads to a measure of real wages that is un-affected by changes in relative prices, as is formula (12).

Changes in tastes and environment. The period 1928 to 1954 covers the introduction of full-scale planning, the industrial revolution, the revolution in agriculture, and the second World War. Political and economic institutions in the Soviet Union were fundamentally altered. The conditions of work and of consumption changed. Psychological attitudes to the state, to the family, to work and leisure, to personal and collective achievement have all changed. There have been mass migrations — from the farms to the cities and, on a lesser scale, from West to East. The very tempo of life has changed. Among the more specific developments affecting the pattern of consumption is the reduction in the supply of animal products resulting from losses of livestock during collectivization — losses which have only in the past few years been regained. Rapid industrialization, coupled with a low standard of living, has meant that many women have moved from the kitchen to the factory, with a resulting shift from baking at home to buying bread in a shop or at the factory canteen. There have been some changes in the types of goods offered to customers, a question that will be taken up below. These developments have clearly led to ex-traordinary changes in both price structure and in patterns of consumption.[6] No doubt there were significant changes in tastes in the theoretical sense. So we must face the fact that there may be no unambiguous answer to the question of real wage changes in the Soviet Union.

Nevertheless, linking the index numbers at an intermediate year such as 1937 seems the best way of handling the problem of changes in environ-ment and tastes. Strictly speaking, one can make theoretically valid com-parisons of real wages only between the two years to which the price and quantity data belong — in this case only between the given year and 1937. But the validity of direct comparisons diminishes the longer the period compared or the greater the changes in taste and environment that take place within the period. Thus comparisons of points distant in time made through a link with an intermediate point can be justified as a practical expedient and may well provide a more realistic measure than would a direct comparison. So far as changes in tastes occurred, the resultant dif-ficulties cannot, of course, be escaped; and it remains true of a linked index number no less than of a direct one that the index number becomes less reliable the farther apart or the more different are the two periods compared. Linked index numbers must be interpreted with caution.

By 1937 many of the more important long-run changes outlined above had already occurred. Collectivization of agriculture had been achieved and full-scale planning had been in effect for almost ten years. The year

[6] An impression of the changes that have occurred in price structure may be obtained from Figures 1, 2, 3, 4, and 5 (chapter V), which show the frequency distributions of the price relatives between 1937 and each of the other years studied.

1937 was really very different from 1928. But in broad outline the Soviet economic and institutional arrangements of today are not very different from those of 1937. Thus it will not be too surprising to find greater divergence between the two index numbers of real wages for the period 1928–37 than for the years since 1937. In the earlier period the changes in environment were so great that a large divergence between the two index numbers might have occurred even had tastes remained constant, but undoubtedly the difference is compounded by changes in tastes.

New goods. As with changes in tastes, there is no finally satisfactory way of dealing with new goods, but linking at the year 1937 provides a means of taking some account of their introduction. For the comparison of 1928 with 1937 I price a list of commodities which differs somewhat from the list of commodities priced for the comparison of 1937 with later years.[7] The differences between the 1928–37 list and the 1937–54 list reflect differences in the types of goods available in the two years 1928 and 1937. The freedom of selection of items to be priced was limited by the availability of price quotations, and I cannot claim to have been able to make a very fine adjustment for the introduction of new goods and the disappearance of old even between the two years 1928 and 1937. The list of goods priced for the comparison of 1937 with each of the years 1948, 1952, and 1954 is, with two minor exceptions, the same. For 1940, the list of goods that could be priced is so limited that in this case I make no claim to handle the problem of new goods. For so short a period as 1937 to 1940 new goods can perhaps be safely ignored; however, the scarcities of consumer goods during much of 1940 mean there is a problem of the disappearance of goods from the market. This is even more acute in the war year 1944.

The procedure of linking at the year 1937 does not permit taking into account goods that have entered or disappeared from the market since 1937. It means also that the comparison between 1928 and post-1937 years is based on different baskets of goods. Because the different baskets of specific goods will, for the most part, serve to meet the same basic wants, they may, nevertheless, provide a fairly realistic basis for comparison.

On the whole, new goods do not seem to have been of very great significance for the Soviet consumer, at least until very recently. Mainly as a consequence of the emphasis on heavy industry, a quarter century of rapid industrialization had surprisingly little effect on the kinds of goods available to the Soviet consumer. Among food products, the only significant development is canned foods. These are excluded from the index number for 1928 but included for later years. Frozen vegetables, vitamin-enriched foods, and baby foods are among the other new food products, but they are still of minor significance. Synthetic fabrics, leather sub-

[7] The items priced in the cost-of-living index numbers for each year are shown in Table 3.

stitutes, and plastics have been considerably developed, and it is possible to take some account of them in the cost-of-living index numbers for 1937 and the later years of the period studied. Kerosene lamps have probably been supplanted by electric lights in the cities. I price a kerosene lamp and chimney for the 1928–37 comparison and an electric light bulb for later years (except 1940). The primus stove is still seen about as frequently as the electric hot plate in Soviet kitchens;[8] I price only the primus stove for 1928 but both the primus stove and the electric hot plate for later years (except 1940). The foot treadle sewing machine, which Tom Whitney thinks has probably not changed even slightly since the revolution,[9] and the hand-crank phonograph are still standard. Both items are priced for 1937, 1948, 1952, and 1954 but, unfortunately, I could not locate quotations for 1928 or 1940.

Probably the most significant new good that I was unable to price is the radio. Virtually all Soviet citizens by now (and this was probably largely true also of 1937) have a radio or some means for receiving radio broadcasts. Recently many other new types of electrical appliances and other consumer durables have been appearing in Soviet shops. Production of refrigerators, washing machines, vacuum cleaners, electric phonographs, television sets, and automobiles has recently been increasing very rapidly; but for the most part total production is still very limited. Even so, the fact that such goods are now on the market, while previously many of them were not even offered for sale to private individuals, must have some positive effect on consumer welfare, even though the prices of such goods are still prohibitive for most Soviet workers. This must be kept in mind in interpreting the index numbers for 1952 and 1954 which omit these products.

Strictly speaking, changes in the quality of a given "commodity" sometimes mean in effect the introduction of a new good. This is true, for example, if there are improvements over time in the quality of a particular commodity or a long-run deterioration in quality. For the most part, price relatives are computed only for articles of a quite specific quality, and considerable time and attention have been devoted to ensuring comparability of the quotations. This, I hope, enables me to avoid most of the errors that might arise from quality changes over time. Also, linking at the intermediate year 1937 serves to minimize the extent of errors on this score. But some quality changes inevitably escape detection; and some quality changes, even though we know of them, cannot really be handled in constructing price relatives.[10] In the index numbers, the cost of living

[8] Statement by a former Soviet citizen to the author.

[9] *New York Times,* September 29, 1953, p. 6. In fact, an 1886 model sewing machine is still being produced in the Podolsk plant, according to *Pravda,* November 13, 1958.

[10] For instance, I have had to treat as the same commodity bread made of flour of the same type and extraction rate, though over much of the period there was a deterioration in quality resulting from an increased water content (see appendix A). Also,

will be overstated to the extent that improvement in quality is ignored, and understated to the extent that deterioration in quality is ignored. Fluctuations in quality, with improvements in relatively good years and deterioration in poor years, have been fairly characteristic of the Soviet Union, but these cannot be taken into account in any systematic way. On balance, quality improvements probably outweighed deteriorations over the full period 1928 to 1954, but in some of the intervening years, particularly the war years, quality deterioration was probably significant.

The problem of Soviet retail prices. As was said above, in measuring changes in real income, retail prices are employed on the grounds that they represent the relative marginal utilities of the various goods to the consumers. This is usually assumed to be more or less true of retail prices in a free market and presumably is also approximated in some measure by the official prices in the Soviet retail market at times when that market is in equilibrium. Evidence was presented that in 1937 the market was operating more or less effectively. For 1937, then, the official retail prices can be taken as meaningful in the sense that they at least roughly reflect relative marginal utilities. During the other years covered in this study, this was not the case and a multiple-price system prevailed. It will be recalled that there was a large gap between the official prices and prices on the free market in 1928, 1940, and 1954, and a somewhat more moderate gap in 1948 and 1952. In 1944 there was rationing, there were extreme shortages, and an enormous gap existed between ration prices and those on the free market and in the state-run commercial shops.

Insofar as multiple prices have prevailed in the Soviet retail market, it is necessary to take them into account in the cost-of-living index numbers. I have attempted to do this. In principle, the procedure adopted is to use an average of the official price and the price on the free market, weighted by the quantity sold in each market. In practice, the procedure is first to construct cost-of-living index numbers based on official retail prices and then to adjust these to take into account the average divergence between official prices and those on the free market. The final cost-of-living index numbers are intended to represent the change in the level of the average prices actually paid in all urban retail markets of the USSR.

It should be mentioned that using average prices actually paid in all markets does not permit me to take into account in even the roughest way any divergence of the official prices from relative marginal utilities that may at times have occurred in the case of goods for which there is no free market. For manufactured consumer goods there has not been a market alternative to the state and cooperative shops, except in 1928, when manufactured goods were sold in private shops, and in 1944, when

---

I have treated the magazine *Ogonek* as the same commodity throughout the period although the illustrations in 1928 were sparse and only in black and white, while the postwar issues are full of colored illustrations (see appendix A).

manufactured goods were sold in the commercial shops. For some years, then, the official prices used in the calculations may understate the relative marginal utilities of various manufactured consumer goods. In view of the continuous shortage of housing, electricity, and perhaps some other utilities at the low government rates, the official rental and service rates, which are taken at face value in my calculations, must have been well below the relative marginal utilities of the services in question in all years, including 1937.

It will readily be seen that from a theoretical standpoint my procedure is something of an expedient and leaves much to be desired even where there is a free market price for the commodity in question. On the average for all prices, of course, the correct price level must fall somewhere between the official price level and the level prevailing on the free market, so there is some justification for basing the cost-of-living index numbers on weighted averages of the prices prevailing in the two markets. Clearly though, there is no reason to suppose that such weighted-average prices would correspond exactly to relative marginal utilities. As a practical matter, no attempt can be made to achieve a closer approximation to prices corresponding to relative marginal utilities for years when there was a gap between the official prices and those on the free market.

Even a theoretical formulation of the ideal procedure for handling this problem seems difficult except under special circumstances. One special case may be suggested here, in which the correct price ratios would be those prevailing on the free market. This would be the case if all consumers had identical preferences, all were able to purchase the same quantities of each commodity at the official price, and all bought additional quantities on the free market. In this case, the prices corresponding to relative marginal utilities are those prevailing on the free market. If a single market were to be created, the total supply of each commodity would remain the same and, on our assumptions, the quantity of each commodity purchased by each consumer would remain the same, and therefore no change in relative prices should occur. The appropriate prices to establish would be proportionate to the price ratios formerly prevailing on the free market. The absolute level of prices would, of course, be lower than the former free market prices. This special case seems too unrealistic to provide a basis for taking account of multiple prices that would be preferable to the procedure I have adopted.

The divergence of the weighted-average prices from relative marginal utilities is of concern whenever I value the real volume of consumption in terms of the prices of a year in which multiple prices actually prevailed. This is the case for each year but 1937. Accordingly, the index numbers of real wages using given-year prices, that is, formulas (7) and (11), are subject to this limitation. For the real-wage index-number formulas (8) and (12), however, only 1937 prices are involved. From my account of the retail market in 1937 it seems clear that, except in the case of housing and some services, these prices can be taken as at least approximately corresponding to relative marginal utilities in that year. Thus, these formulas permit us to compare the real volume of consumption between any two years in terms of the (relatively) meaningful price structure of 1937.

The 1944 index numbers. The wartime conditions of 1944 were such as to make very dubious any index numbers of the cost of living or real wages. The main fact about real wages in 1944 is that, regardless of how high his money wages were, the Soviet worker could find very little in the shops to spend them on. However, it may be of some interest to attempt to quantify, if only in the broadest terms, the wartime privation of the Soviet worker. Accordingly, I have made some calculations for 1944 and present the results along with the more reliable results for other years. The index numbers for 1944 are put in parentheses in the text tables as a reminder to the reader of their questionable nature.

In addition to problems of interpretation arising from the conditions of this war year, various limitations of data mean that the index numbers for 1944 could not be computed in the same way as those for other years. First, the 1944 cost-of-living index number is not computed on the basis of detailed price quotations for 1944 but rather by linking an estimate of the average change in prices between 1940 and 1944 to the cost-of-living index number for 1937–40. Second, only one 1944 cost-of-living index number is computed. This is computed by linking to the 1937–40 cost-of-living index number using 1937 weights. It is more akin to a Laspeyres than to a Paasche cost-of-living index number, but because it is linked it is not a true Laspeyres index number. It seems unlikely, however, that the true Laspeyres index number would differ much from the one computed by linking at the year 1940, as the structure of ration prices in 1944 was very similar to the structure of official prices in 1940. Adjustments for prices of unrationed goods are made after the index number of ration prices is computed. Finally, the index number of real wages for 1944 obtained by deflating with a cost-of-living index number using 1937 weights is one in which the volume of consumption is valued in principle at 1944 prices. From what has been said about the condition of the market in 1944 it will be evident that the meaning of an index number of real wages based on 1944 prices is questionable. Because of the somewhat different nature of the data and computations for 1944, the 1944 estimates are explained in appendix D. Chapters IV and V deal with the price data and weights used in computing the index numbers of official prices for the other years covered in the study.

IV·

INDEX NUMBERS OF OFFICIAL RETAIL
PRICES IN MOSCOW: THE PRICE DATA

THE cost-of-living index numbers are based on a detailed computation of index numbers of retail prices prevailing in state and cooperative shops in Moscow. The index numbers so computed are subsequently adjusted to take into account prices on the free market and in other urban areas of the USSR. This chapter discusses the price data underlying the index numbers of official prices in Moscow, including (a) the nature of the sources of the price quotations, (b) the basis for selection and the representativeness of the commodities priced in the index number, and (c) the question of the comparability of the commodities priced for the various years. The discussion here is of necessity general, designed to give the reader an impression of the nature and reliability of the price data. Detailed notes on the source and nature of each price quotation, the commodity designation, and the degree of comparability achieved in each price comparison are presented in appendix A. As the cost-of-living index number for 1944 is not computed directly from price quotations for that year, I do not deal with the year 1944 in this chapter or the next. The method of estimating the cost-of-living index number for 1944 was outlined briefly in chapter III and is described in more detail in appendix D.

I. SOURCES OF THE PRICE QUOTATIONS

Official Soviet publications are the main sources of retail prices in the Soviet Union. The most important types of official sources are decrees establishing or changing retail prices and detailed price handbooks issued for the use of store managers and salesmen. Scattered additional quotations are found in newspaper advertisements for consumer goods, in announcements in the press of the current local official prices of seasonal fruits and vegetables, and in discussions of price fixing and related subjects in the specialized trade journals and in monographs.

As for the reliability of these Soviet sources, there seems no reason to doubt that the prices published in the price decrees, the price handbooks, and the press were the ones legally in force at the time of their publication. These materials are published primarily (and the price handbooks exclusively) for internal use to disseminate information on the legal prices and changes in them, and to control prices. As appears to be the practice regarding many other types of economic information, the dissemination of which is essential to the internal operation of the economy, the Soviet practice seems to be to withhold price information rather than to falsify it.

The practice of withholding information makes my task difficult enough for any period, but especially for 1940. Generally, it seems safe to say that the Russians publicize price reductions with great fanfare, but remain quite silent during periods when prices are being raised. During 1939 and 1940 there was a general change in the retail price schedule for manufactured consumer goods which, it is believed, involved price increases. Some of the details regarding changes in the turnover tax rates and trade margins were published in the collections of laws; although later Soviet writers have referred to new retail price lists established at the time, these were not published in the daily press or in the collections of laws. The only official 1940 retail price lists I have been able to find are in a source published in 1947.

Given this practice, one must regard with some suspicion the series of price cuts announced annually from 1949 through 1954. There is always the possibility that some prices were raised without any announcement of this fact. On the whole, it is my impression that this has occurred on a very limited scale. However, as Eugène Zaleski has raised a serious question on this point, it will be discussed in more detail below.

Another source of doubt regarding the quotations in the official Soviet sources is the extent to which the legal prices are actually enforced. Complaints in the Soviet press throughout the period under review indicate there is some evasion of the legal prices.[1] Reports of visitors to the USSR suggest that this practice is probably rather limited. In any case, there is no basis for making any quantitative estimate of the extent of illegal deviation from the established prices, and it is assumed for purposes of this study that such deviations were relatively insignificant.

Accounts containing information on prices actually observed in Soviet shops by former Soviet citizens, Western correspondents, and other visitors to the USSR are used extensively for the period 1937 on. These are, in fact, virtually the only source of price data for 1940. As such accounts differ widely in quality, detail, coverage, and reliability, it is necessary to use them with discretion. Taken all together, however, they provide a valuable body of material, serve to fill some of the many gaps in the available Soviet data, and provide some check on the Soviet data. Both published and unpublished materials of this nature are used.[2] Price data

---

[1] Reference is to evasion by the store manager or clerks. Prices charged by private individuals, called "speculators" in Soviet jargon, for the resale of commodities they have purchased at the legal prices cannot be taken into account in the price index but must be considered among the aspects of the imperfection of the market.

[2] Inasmuch as the sources of some of these unpublished visitors' and former Soviet citizens' reports wish to remain anonymous, all such unpublished materials are cited simply as "unpublished materials."

compiled from various sources by other Western students of Soviet retail prices and related subjects have also been consulted.

Generally, in terms of quantity and reliability, the price data for 1937 are good, the price data for 1928 and the postwar years are quite adequate, and those for 1940 are very limited. The more important sources for each of the years covered are described below:

1928. The main source of food price quotations and an important source also for prices of manufactured consumer goods is a Moscow monthly statistical bulletin: Statisticheskii otdel Moskovskogo soveta, *Ezhemesia-chnyi statisticheskii biulleten' po gorodu Moskve i Moskovskoi gubernii* for 1928 and January 1929. This source reports monthly on retail prices actually charged in state, cooperative, and private shops and on the peasant market in Moscow city and Moscow Province. The list of items priced is rather extensive and includes both foods and manufactured consumer goods. It changes somewhat during the year so that the series is not complete for all items. The commodity designations accompanying the price quotations are brief but often precise.

The other major source for 1928 is S. P. Sereda, *et al.* (eds.), *Universal'-nyi spravochnik tsen* (Moscow, 1928), a collection of official price lists and extracts from price legislation in effect at the time of publication. Price lists for many manufactured consumer goods are included. In most cases, these are wholesale price lists, but usually information on the maximum retail trade margin is included, thus making it possible to compute the maximum legal retail price and, in some cases, the Moscow price. The commodity designations are usually detailed and give the grade, type of material, processing method, size, article number, brand name, or other features necessary to identify a commodity and to distinguish it from similar commodities. Such data are given in abbreviated form and are often difficult or even impossible for a non-Russian layman to interpret. One particular difficulty in using this source is the absence of adequate explanations of the nature of some of the price lists in the collection.[3]

1937. The main Soviet sources for 1937 are a collection of detailed retail price handbooks for 1936. These include two price handbooks for foods — one for the USSR and one for Moscow oblast, and two price handbooks for manufactured consumer goods — one for the USSR and one for the city of Moscow.[4] In addition, handbooks of price lists for individual commodity groups — fish, confectionery, knitwear, garments, shoes — were

---

[3] See, for example, appendix A, item 159.

[4] Z. L. Nozhkina, *et al.* (comps.), *Sbornik otpusknykh i roznichnykh tsen i torgovykh nakidok na prodovol'stvennye tovary* (Moscow, 1936); Moskovskii oblastnoi otdel vnutrennei torgovli, *Spravochnik roznichnykh tsen na prodovol'stvennye tovary po Moskovskoi oblasti* (Moscow, 1936); Z. L. Nozhkina, *et al.* (comps.), *Otpusknye i roznichnye tseny i torgovye nakidki na promtovary* (Moscow, 1936); Moskovskii gorodskoi otdel vnutrennei torgovli, *Spravochnik roznichnykh tsen i torgovykh nakidok na promyshlennye tovary po g. Moskve* (2 vols., Moscow, 1936).

also consulted. These handbooks are collections of the price lists and other legislation and directives on retail (or wholesale and retail) prices in force at the time of publication. Usually the price lists are final retail prices; in some cases only the wholesale price is listed and the retail margin is specified as a percentage of the wholesale price. Notes on special additions to or deductions from the list price for such items as containers, quality differences, or transport charges accompany many of the price lists. The commodity designation is usually precise. Often it is very brief, but sometimes there are detailed supplementary descriptions.

These price handbooks were all published in 1936. Other information, however, permits the use of these sources for 1937. In the case of foods, there was very little change in prices between 1936 and 1937, and the quotations from the 1936 price handbooks can usually be used as 1937 quotations. There was a general reduction in the prices of manufactured consumer goods in mid-1937. The percentage price reductions for the various goods are specified in a published decree of the Council of Commissars of April 28, 1937 (no. 689).[5] Thus, average 1937 prices of these goods can be computed from the 1936 prices and the percentage reductions effected in 1937.

The daily press and the collections of laws provide information on the more important government decrees on prices. The major decree of this period has already been mentioned. In addition, the daily trade organ *Sovetskaia torgovlia* regularly published during 1937 the official Moscow prices of seasonal vegetables and fruits.

The major published non-Soviet sources of 1937 price quotations are the following: (a) U.S. Bureau of Labor Statistics, *Monthly Labor Review*, November 1939; May and August 1940; February and May 1941. This source contains retail prices of an extensive list of foods and manufactured consumer goods observed in Moscow shops at various dates between January 1936 and January 1941. Unfortunately, no quotations for 1937 are included, but the quotations for 1936 and 1938 are useful in connection with other data for 1937. (b) Vaso Trivanovitch, "Purchasing Power of Wages in the Soviet Union," National Industrial Conference Board, *Conference Board Bulletin*, 12:25–28 (March 7, 1938). This source contains Moscow retail prices of many consumer goods as of October 1935, April and July 1936, and April and July 1937. It is not clear whether the prices were observed by Trivanovitch himself or obtained from some other source. The list of items priced appears to be the same as that priced in the *Monthly Labor Review* series. The commodity designations in both these sources are brief.

1940. The available price data for 1940 are extremely limited and of rather doubtful reliability. The only official Soviet quotations located are

---

[5] Published in the Soviet press, April 28, 1937, and in *Biulleten' finansovogo i khoziaistvennogo zakonodatel'stva*, no. 13, 1937, pp. 19–20.

some utility and other service rates, a partial shoe retail price list, and a 1939 price list for made-to-order clothing.[6] Main reliance is placed on the quotations observed by visitors to the Soviet Union as reported in the *Monthly Labor Review* and unpublished materials. Quotations in these sources are accompanied only by the briefest descriptions. With the scarcity of consumer goods prevailing during 1940, it must have been more difficult than usual to obtain quotations for identical commodities at different dates. The "best" quality of a product on sale in July may not have been the same grade as that priced as "best" in January, but this might not be apparent to a foreigner who priced the article but did not consume it. The quotations in the visitors' accounts for 1939–42 in many cases show more up-and-down fluctuation than is usual in the pattern of Soviet prices, and this undoubtedly reflects differences in the qualities of the product priced at different dates as well as actual price changes. For foods, price quotations are available for January 1 and July 1, 1940, and for January 1, 1941; and in some cases for other dates as well. Some of the food price quotations cannot be used because of doubts concerning comparability with 1937 and during 1940. For the most part, however, the quotations for foods are reasonably adequate on the score of comparability and there are enough of them to provide a fairly clear picture of the movement of food prices between 1937 and 1940. The same is true of the quotations for soap, kerosene, and matches, which are available for the same dates.

The data are much less adequate for other types of manufactured consumer goods, and some commodity groups (haberdashery and notions, housewares, cultural and sports goods) could not be priced at all. There are data for the most important groups of manufactured consumer goods, but these have numerous shortcomings. No price quotations for textiles, garments, knitwear, or shoes are available for the first half of 1940.[7] However, it is believed there was little if any change in the prices of these goods between July 1939 and July 1940, and it is possible to use quotations for July 1939 to represent the prices of these commodities prevailing during the first half of 1940 without danger of any significant error. Prices of textiles, garments, knitwear, and shoes were raised on July 1, 1940. Unfortunately, the available quotations do not permit a very firm estimate of the extent of this price rise. Moscow quotations for a number of textiles, garments, knitwear items, and shoes are available for July 15, 1940, and January 1, 1941, and quotations for many of the same items in Kuibyshev in January 1942 are also available in an unpublished visitor's account. Not

[6] These latter two lists are contained in Ministerstvo torgovli SSSR, Sektor torgovykh kadrov i zarabotnoi platy, *Sbornik normativov i spravochnykh materialov dlia shveinykh i obuvnykh predpriiatii dlia predpriiatii sistemy Glavvoentorg* (Moscow, 1947).

[7] The *Monthly Labor Review*, May 1941, contains a table in which prices of manufactured goods are listed as having been in effect on January 1, 1940; but it is believed an error was made in the column heading, and that the listed quotations actually refer to July 1939. See the discussion under 1940 in appendix A.

all commodities are priced for all of these dates, and there are many gaps in the data. The 1940–41 Moscow price quotations show an erratic price pattern suggesting that they reflect differences in the articles priced at different dates, as well as changes in prices. Also, they seem on the whole to overstate the price rise that actually took place. The 1942 Kuibyshev prices of many items are lower than the 1940–41 Moscow prices (taking into account possible Moscow-Kuibyshev price differentials), yet it is almost certain that prices were not reduced between 1940 and 1942. The available price data for these goods for the latter half of 1940, then, permit a fairly wide range of results, depending on the selection of price quotations to use in the price index number as well as on the weights for the individual items.[8]

1948, 1952, 1954. The main official sources for the postwar years are a series of price decrees. The first is that promulgated in connection with the abolition of rationing and the elimination of the double system of official prices on December 14, 1947.[9] This decree sets forth the new official retail prices of a fairly extensive list of foods and manufactured consumer goods, effective December 16, 1947. The prices in this decree are in absolute ruble terms. The commodity designations are precise in that grade, type, material, brand, article number, or other distinguishing features of the commodity, are indicated. Following this was a series of annual price decrees of the Council of Ministers and the Central Committee of the Communist Party on April 10, 1948; March 1, 1949; March 1, 1950; March 1, 1951; April 1, 1952; April 1, 1953; and April 1, 1954.[10] Each of these decrees specifies price reductions for a variety of consumer goods, expressed in percentage terms. Finally, there is the decree of August 14, 1954, which sets forth new seasonal price schedules for vegetables and fruit in absolute

---

[8] An early computation in which the prices of textiles, garments, knitwear, and shoes in the second half of 1940 were based entirely on the Moscow quotations for July 1940 and January 1941 resulted in an index number of manufactured goods prices that seemed too high in light of various other information. I then re-examined the price data and took into account the 1942 Kuibyshev prices and also shoe prices from the partial official Soviet shoe price list for 1940. In selecting quotations from all these sources to use in a revised index number, I kept the firm comparisons used in the earlier calculation, excluded the most doubtful comparisons (and some of the largest price rises were shown in the more doubtful cases), and in the remaining cases resolved reasonable doubts as to comparability in favor of the lower price rise in each case. The group price index numbers for textiles, garments, knitwear, and shoes computed on this basis are considerably lower than the original ones, and the net effect on the index numbers of prices of all manufactured consumer goods is a reduction of 10 to 20 percent, depending upon the weighting system. Clearly, then, alternative results are possible. I have manipulated the data to force the price index of manufactured consumer goods in 1940 down below my original estimates; perhaps I have gone too far in this, and the resulting price index numbers may be on the low side. The underlying price comparisons are believed, nevertheless, to be more reliable than those used in the first computation. On the erratic nature of the 1940 quotations, see chapter X, section 4.

[9] *Pravda,* December 15, 1947.

[10] These are published in *Pravda* and *Izvestiia* of the dates of the decrees.

terms. This also specifies percentage reductions in the prices of vegetable oil and canned vegetables.[11]

Many of the 1952 and 1954 quotations used in the index numbers are computed from the absolute prices set forth in the December 1947 decree and the annual percentage price reductions. Similarly, given an absolute price for any date between December 1947 and the present, the corresponding price in effect in any of the years 1948, 1952, and 1954 can be computed with the aid of the annual price reduction decrees. This process is subject to a certain amount of error. In many cases, the price reduction is stated as an average percentage reduction for a broad category of commodities, and it is possible that the reduction for any given item falling within that category differed from the average; it is assumed in such cases that the average reduction applies to the particular item falling within the category that is priced in the index number. In some cases it is not clear whether an item priced in the index number is included in one or another of the categories for which a price reduction is announced.

Two other important Soviet sources are the 1949 and 1953 editions of L. Kh. Gurvits, *Torgovye vychisleniia*.[12] This textbook on the mathematics of trade cites a great many examples of actual retail prices in the exercises following each chapter. The retail prices in the 1949 edition are from official price lists in effect following the price reduction of March 1, 1949; those in the 1953 edition are from official price lists in effect following the price reduction of April 1, 1952. The commodity designations vary greatly in precision and completeness.

Two works by V. P. Maslakov on housing and municipal services provide most of the quotations for services for the postwar years.[13] Scattered actual price quotations and occasional advertisements for consumer goods that can be ordered by mail are found in the daily press. The local Moscow papers carry occasional announcements of seasonal price reductions.

Extensive use is made also of accounts of foreign visitors to the USSR, both published and unpublished, for the postwar years.[14] Mention should

[11] *Pravda*, August 14, 1954.

[12] I am indebted to Eugène Zaleski, not only for bringing these sources to my attention, but also for providing me with a copy of the lists of retail prices he compiled from them.

[13] V. P. Maslakov, et al., *Finansirovanie zhilishchno-kommunal'nogo khoziaistva* (Moscow, 1948); V. P. Maslakov, *Kommunal'nye tarify v SSSR* (Moscow, 1951).

[14] Among the published accounts, the following should be specially mentioned: Edmund Stevens' series of articles in the *Christian Science Monitor*, October 18, 1949, through February 9, 1950; Walter Bedell Smith, *My Three Years in Moscow* (Philadelphia, 1950); Michel Gordey's series of articles in the Paris *France-Soir*, July 1950; Frank Rounds, Jr., *A Window on Red Square* (Cambridge, Mass., 1953); P. J. D. Wiles and T. Schulz, "Earnings and Living Standards in Moscow," *Bulletin of the Oxford University Institute of Statistics*, 14:309–326 (September and October 1952), and 15:315–326 (September 1953), and the comment by G. H. Elvin in the same 1953 issue, "Earnings and Living Standards in Moscow: A Comment"; Charles Madge, "Notes on the Standard of Living in Moscow, April 1952," *Soviet Studies*, 4:229–236 (January

be made also of Kravis and Mintzes' study of Soviet food prices from
1936 to 1950 in the *Review of Economics and Statistics,* May 1950, and of
Eugène Zaleski's study of Soviet retail prices from 1913 to 1954.[15] In his
appendix, Zaleski quotes many prices observed over the period 1948
through 1954 from various visitors' reports, both published and unpublished.

Some of the above-mentioned postwar sources became available only
after the price comparisons had been made and the price relatives originally computed. The 1937–52 price comparisons were originally completed
during 1953 and were published in the *Review of Economics and Statistics*
in May 1954; the 1937–54 price comparisons were originally completed
before the end of 1954. The publication in 1956 of the official Soviet index
number of retail prices in TSU, *Narodnoe khoziaistvo SSSR,* suggested
that my index numbers for 1948, 1952, and 1954 were somewhat on the low
side, particularly for manufactured consumer goods. I then reviewed my
price comparisons with the aid of certain sources that had not been available earlier. They proved very valuable in checking on the computed prices
and the question of the comparability of the postwar quotations with
those for 1937. In the case of certain commodity groups — confectionery,
textiles, garments, and shoes — I found I had made some fairly serious
errors in comparability, all tending to understate the true price rise. In
these cases, revisions were made in the price comparisons. With regard to
the other commodity groups, these new sources tend to confirm the price
comparisons as originally made. Although errors are indicated in some
individual cases, they do not appear serious enough to justify the labor
of revision and recomputation. The sources referred to include the two
editions of Gurvits, *Torgovye vychisleniia;* Zaleski's study; and some unpublished materials.

As mentioned above, Zaleski expresses serious doubts about the correspondence of the prices actually charged in the Soviet state shops with
those that can be computed from the officially announced price cuts.
He cites a number of commodities for which he finds observed quotations
that are higher than the price computed on the basis of the annual price
reductions.[16] Observed quotations above the official price computed from
the announced price cuts would be clear evidence that the price cuts had
not been put into effect if the observed quotations were clearly for the
same type and quality of the commodity in question. For the most part,
the observed quotations are not accompanied by enough descriptive detail

---

1953); Marshall MacDuffie, "Russia Uncensored," *Collier's,* March 5, 1954; Emmet
Hughes, "A Perceptive Reporter in a Changing Russia," *Life,* February 8, 1954.

[15] Eugène Zaleski, "Les fluctuations des prix de détail en Union Soviétique," *Études et
Conjoncture,* no. 4, April 1955, and "Les fluctuations des prix de détail en Union
Soviétique; Annexe méthodologique et statistique," *Conjoncture et Études économiques,
Études spéciales,* no. 3, 1955.

[16] Zaleski, *Études et Conjoncture,* no. 4, April 1955, pp. 331–334.

to judge comparability. In cases where an observed quotation for a given commodity is described precisely enough to identify it as identical to a commodity for which an official price can be computed, I have found that the observed quotations usually agree with the computed prices.[17] On the whole, I am fairly well satisfied that the announced price reductions were actually put into effect. The bulk of the available evidence — both Soviet and non-Soviet — tends, I think, to support this conclusion. This is not to deny the possibility brought out by Zaleski that in some cases the cheaper varieties of a particular good are unavailable so that the consumer must buy a higher priced item than he would wish to.

2. COMMODITIES INCLUDED IN THE INDEX NUMBERS

The cost-of-living index number is a representative index. Each item priced is assumed to represent the prices of similar items, and all items priced are assumed to represent the movement of all retail prices of consumer goods. I do not, however, attempt to represent the movement of prices of building materials and other producer goods sold at retail.

Prices of restaurant meals are not directly represented in the price index, but it is believed they are fairly well represented by the movement of retail prices of foods. Sales in restaurants as a percentage of total retail sales in state and cooperative shops and restaurants were as follows: 4 percent in 1928, 8 percent in 1937, 13 percent in 1940, 24 percent in 1944, 14 percent in 1952, and 12 percent in 1954.[18] The prices of restaurant meals are calculated on the basis of the cost of the materials used and a percentage markup to cover costs of preparation and profits. This markup is fixed centrally and differentiated according to the type of dish and also according to three classes of restaurants.[19] The cost of the materials used in determining the price of the meal is the retail price.[20] Thus restaurant prices are closely linked to retail food prices and presumably move as retail food prices generally, except as the trade markup for restaurant meals varies. A rough calculation suggests that the restaurant trade markup averaged about 10.5 percent of the total value of sales in state

[17] In this sense, quotations are available that confirm the computed prices for 7 of the 14 food items and for 1 of the 5 manufactured goods Zaleski classifies as not in conformity with the official price cuts, and for 2 of the 11 foods he cites as not verified. There is, however, evidence that the top of the seasonal price range for eggs and milk was charged even during the "low-price" season during 1948, though not in later years. See appendix A, items 70 and 76.

[18] TSU, Sovetskaia torgovlia; Statisticheskii sbornik (Moscow, 1956), p. 20.

[19] G. L. Rubinshtein, et al., Ekonomika sovetskoi torgovli (Moscow, 1950), pp. 487–488.

[20] Lief Björk, Wages, Prices and Social Legislation in the Soviet Union (London, 1953), p. 150. Reference in this source is to the period since November 1947. While there is no specific information for earlier years on the system of fixing prices of restaurant meals, it was probably essentially similar. A 1935 source indicates that prices of restaurant meals were somewhat higher than the cost of the materials if purchased in the retail shops. A. I. Malkis, Potreblenie i spros v SSSR (Moscow, 1935), pp. 94–95.

and cooperative restaurants in 1928, about 17 percent in 1937, about 20.5 percent in 1940, and about 11.5 percent in 1954.[21] Thus there has been some variance in the restaurant trade margin, and if this calculation is correct, restaurant prices rose somewhat more than retail food prices up to 1940 and rose somewhat less than retail food prices between 1940 and 1954. Since 1948, restaurant prices have moved very closely with retail food prices, as each retail price decree has directed that restaurant prices be reduced correspondingly.

The items priced in the cost-of-living index numbers for the various years are listed with their absolute prices in Table A-1. Table 3 shows the corresponding price relatives, with 1937 as 100. It was not possible to price every commodity for all years; dashes in Table 3 and Table A-1 indicate that the particular item is not priced for that year. Often the commodity priced for the 1928–37 period is similar but not identical to the commodity priced for the post-1937 period. In the case of wheat flour, for instance, the comparison between 1928 and 1937 is based on the prices of *whole wheat flour* and *wheat flour, 30%*;[22] the comparison between 1937 and 1940 is based on the prices of *wheat flour, 72%* and *wheat flour, 30%*; and the comparison of 1937 with 1948, 1952, and 1954 is based on the prices of *wheat flour, 85%* and *wheat flour, 72%*. In some cases, the precise difference between two similar commodities listed separately is less clear than in the case of flour, or is too complicated to be indicated in the necessarily brief designations given in Table 3 and Table A-1. Full details on each commodity are given in appendix A.

The prices shown are official prices charged in state and cooperative shops or for services provided by state or municipally run enterprises. These are prices prevailing in the city of Moscow. The prices shown are intended to represent annual average prices. The year in question is the calendar year, except in the case of 1952 — for which the year is from April 1, 1952, to March 31, 1953; and 1954 — for which the year is April 1, 1954, to March 31, 1955. These periods correspond to the dates of the annual price decrees. The index numbers for 1952 and 1954 are adjusted to a calendar-year basis after the basic computations are made. The general principle on which the average annual prices are computed is to weight each price by the length of time it was in effect. Data are not available that would permit any attempt to take into account variations in the volume sold during a given year. An exception is made in the case of vegeta-

---

[21] This is computed from the figures on total sales in state and cooperative restaurants and the figures on the restaurant trade margin (*natsenka obshchestvennogo pitaniia*) shown in the breakdown by commodity group of total retail sales in state and cooperative shops and restaurants in TSU, *Sovetskaia torgovlia; Statisticheskii sbornik*, pp. 20, 41.

[22] The percentage figures in the flour designations refer to the rate of extraction of the flour from the whole grain.

TABLE 3

Retail Prices of Goods and Services, Official Prices, Moscow, 1928–54, Price Relatives

	Price relative[a] (1937 = 100)					
Commodity	1928	1937	1940	1948	1952	1954
Grain products and legumes						
1. Rye flour	6.9	100	—	300	150	131
2. Rye bread	9.4	100	104	353	176	147
3. Whole wheat flour	10.0	100	—	—	—	—
4. Wheat flour, 85%	—	100	—	258	125	108
5. Wheat flour, 72%	—	100	100	276	126	109
6. Wheat flour, 30%	4.8	100	100	—	—	—
7. Wheat bread, 96%	—	100	103	—	—	—
8. Wheat bread, 80 to 85%	14.1	100	100	259	118	100
9. Wheat bread, 72%	—	100	—	250	114	98
10. French loaf, 72%	—	100	—	222	101	88
11. French loaf, 30%	—	100	105	—	—	—
12. Macaroni, 72%	—	100	—	286	140	119
13. Macaroni, 40%	10.5	100	—	—	—	—
14. Buckwheat grits	4.7	100	105	279	145	130
15. Millet grits	8.1	100	143	286	159	143
16. Rice	8.5	100	—	—	—	—
17. Rice, grade 1	—	100	100	263	151	135
18. Wheat meal	—	100	100	—	—	—
19. Dried peas	15.1	100	—	—	—	—
20. Dried beans	—	100	—	268	139	125
21. Oats	18.3	100	—	417	192	158
Meat and poultry						
22. Beef, average fed, grade 1	11.1	100	174	387	191	163
23. Pork	9.2	100	183	462	228	206
24. Mutton, average fed, grade 1	10.5	100	—	395	185	157
25. Mutton	.	100	188	—	—	—
26. Mutton, above average fed, grade 1	—	100	—	354	166	147
27. Chicken, grade 1	—	100	127	318	157	134
28. Chicken, grade 2	—	100	147	413	204	173
29. Goose, grade 2	—	100	149	339	158	134
30. Duck, grade 1	—	100	168	—	—	—
31. Duck, grade 2	—	100	—	400	186	159
32. Turkey, grade 1	—	100	138	346	161	137
33. Turkey, grade 2	—	100	—	371	173	147
34. Rabbit	—	100	—	600	321	273
35. Bacon	—	100	156	369	175	149
36. Ham, smoked	—	100	143	—	—	—
37. Ham, smoked, average	—	100	—	393	187	159
38. Sausage, ordinary	—	100	163	—	—	—
39. Sausage, hamburger	—	100	142	—	—	—
40. Sausage, Moscow	—	100	—	349	172	146
Fish						
41. Pike-perch, fresh, frozen, or salted	14.4	100	—	—	—	—
42. Pike-perch, frozen	—	100	—	366	265	239
43. Perch, frozen	—	100	235	—	—	—
44. Sturgeon, fresh or frozen	—	100	188	363	264	238
45. Herring, salted, ordinary	9.2	100	—	—	—	—
46. Herring, salted, large	—	100	—	250	182	164
47. Herring, salted	—	100	128	—	—	—
48. Sturgeon, cured	—	100	213	489	277	249
49. Caviar, black, granular	—	100	203	753	414	373

[a] The absolute ruble prices from which these price relatives were computed are found in Table A-1.
Note: The dash (—) indicates that the item was not priced for that year.

TABLE 3 (Continued)

Retail Prices of Goods and Services, Official Prices, Moscow, 1928–54, Price Relatives

	Price relative[a] (1937 = 100)					
Commodity	1928	1937	1940	1948	1952	1954
Sugar and confectionery						
50. Sugar, lump	17.1	100	132	—	—	—
51. Sugar, small lump	—	100	—	375	297	269
52. Sugar, granulated	16.3	100	129	355	272	245
53. Cocoa	—	100	131	312	221	150
54. Chocolate candy, best	—	100	182	—	—	—
55. Bonbons	—	100	214	—	—	—
56. Honey	—	100	144	—	—	—
57. Hard candy	—	100	—	360	298	269
58. Soft candies	—	100	—	314	226	203
59. Caramels, "Theatre"	—	100	—	300	240	216
Fats						
60. Butter, sweet	14.2	100	—	—	—	—
61. Butter, rendered	11.2	100	—	—	—	—
62. Butter, grade 1	—	100	140	—	—	—
63. Butter, grade 2	—	100	135	—	—	—
64. Butter (average of 7 kinds)	—	100	—	384	175	158
65. Sunflower oil	3.6	100	105	202	146	123
66. Beef fat, rendered	9.2	100	—	—	—	—
67. Lard	8.2	100	—	—	—	—
68. Salt pork, fat	—	100	159	—	—	—
69. Margarine	—	100	—	314	156	141
Milk and milk products						
70. Milk, fresh	13.1	100	134	250	182	182
71. Sour cream (spring)	17.7	100	—	—	—	—
72. Sour cream	—	100	122	343	222	222
73. Cheese, Swiss-type	—	100	120	290	134	134
74. Cheese, Holland-type	—	100	170	—	—	—
75. Cheese, American-type	—	100	133	—	—	—
Eggs						
76. Eggs	8.8	100	135	261	170	153
Vegetables and fruit						
77. Potatoes	20.0	100	253	250	225	133
78. Cabbage, fresh (fall)	30.0	100	—	333	283	267
79. Cabbage, fresh (July)	—	100	625	—	—	—
80. Sauerkraut	26.7	100	333	—	—	—
81. Cucumbers, fresh (August)	—	100	—	222	200	100
82. Cucumbers, fresh (July)	—	100	200	—	—	—
83. Cucumbers, pickled	—	100	124	—	—	—
84. Cucumbers, salted	—	100	—	318	273	136
85. Onions	22.9	100	161	—	—	—
86. Green onions	—	100	166	—	—	—
87. Green onions (summer)	—	100	—	400	360	180
88. Beets (April)	20.0	100	—	—	—	—
89. Beets (January)	—	100	227	—	—	—
90. Beets (fall)	—	100	—	346	312	254
91. Carrots	—	100	256	—	—	—
92. Turnips	—	100	—	409	367	182
93. Tomatoes	—	100	—	250	225	113
94. Pumpkin	—	100	—	280	252	140
95. Mushrooms, dried	—	100	100	—	—	—

[a] The absolute ruble prices from which these price relatives were computed are found in Table A-1.
Note: The dash (—) indicates that the item was not priced for that year.

TABLE 3 (Continued)
Retail Prices of Goods and Services, Official Prices, Moscow, 1928–54, Price Relatives

	Price relative[a] (1937 = 100)					
Commodity	1928	1937	1940	1948	1952	1954
96. Mushrooms, pickled	—	100	172	—	—	—
97. Peas, canned	—	100	—	268	172	160
98. Apples, fresh	—	100	—	380	243	124
99. Apples, fresh (January)	—	100	114	—	—	—
100. Grapes, fresh	—	100	129	—	—	—
101. Apricots, canned	—	100	—	196	123	93
102. Apples, dried	—	100	—	374	239	192
103. Prunes, dried	—	100	104	286	183	146
104. Raisins	—	100	—	373	239	191
105. Mixed dried fruit	—	100	—	391	250	200
Salt						
106. Salt, ground	45.5	100	100	1364	318	200
Tea and coffee						
107. Tea	7.9	100	100	200	130	94
108. Coffee	—	100	—	147	113	76
Alcoholic beverages						
109. Vodka, 40°	13.4	100	137	653	330	294
110. Vodka, 50°	—	100	—	729	360	321
111. Champagne, Soviet	—	100	105	205	160	136
112. Red wine, "Kagor"	—	100	136	—	—	—
113. White wine, "Naporeuli"	—	100	118	—	—	—
114. Port wine, Soviet	—	100	129	—	—	—
Textiles						
115. Calico, no. 6	11.1	100	—	294	251	181
116. Calico	—	100	157	—	—	—
117. Sateen	11.8	100	—	—	—	—
118. Sateen, mercerized	—	100	—	392	333	241
119. Satinette	—	100	139	—	—	—
120. Sheeting, cotton, no. 49	12.3	100	—	—	—	—
121. Sheeting, cotton	—	100	—	356	303	219
122. Madapolam	11.7	100	—	—	—	—
123. Moleskin	13.4	100	—	—	—	—
124. Woolen, part wool broadcloth	8.6	100	—	—	—	—
125. Woolen, pure wool plush velour	5.6	100	—	—	—	—
126. Woolen, pure wool "Boston"	—	100	—	375	297	282
127. Worsted, part wool	13.1	100	—	—	—	—
128. Worsted, pure wool	6.8	100	—	—	—	—
129. Wool and cotton mixture	—	100	125	—	—	—
130. Coarse wool baize, solid color	18.8	100	—	—	—	—
131. Coarse wool baize, mixture	—	100	—	296	203	192
132. Sheeting, linen	15.4	100	—	—	—	—
133. Sheeting, part linen	15.2	100	—	291	245	227
134. Rayon crepe de Chine	—	100	—	278	220	220
135. Silk crepe de Chine no. 5	—	100	—	251	227	173
136. Silk crepe de Chine	—	100	154	—	—	—
Garments						
137. Shirt, cotton	—	100	179	—	—	—
138. Shirt, cotton zephyr	—	100	—	207	181	140
139. Cotton dress	—	100	—	265	230	177
140. Cotton blouse	—	100	—	271	236	178

[a] The absolute ruble prices from which these price relatives were computed are found in Table A-1.
Note: The dash (—) indicates that the item was not priced for that year.

TABLE 3 (Continued)

Retail Prices of Goods and Services, Official Prices, Moscow, 1928–54, Price Relatives

Commodity	Price relative[a] (1937 = 100)					
	1928	1937	1940	1948	1952	1954
141. Trousers, part wool	9.9	100	—	—	—	—
142. Suit, wool, fabric group 46	—	100	—	354	281	281
143. Suit, wool	—	100	150	—	—	—
144. Overcoat, common quality	—	100	145	—	—	—
145. Overcoat, women's	—	100	—	265	187	187
146. Overcoat, better	—	100	—	290	230	230
147. Blouse, silk	—	100	—	244	207	170
148. Necktie, rayon	—	100	131	—	—	—
149. Hat, felt	—	100	99	294	226	192
150. Hat, fur	—	100	100	242	196	182
Knitwear						
151. Stockings, cotton	—	100	—	398	338	216
152. Socks, cotton, plain	27.9	100	—	—	—	—
153. Socks, cotton	—	100	143	—	—	—
154. Socks, cotton, cheapest	—	100	—	366	312	201
155. Socks, rayon	—	100	114	—	—	—
156. Socks, rayon, no. 86	—	100	—	313	226	163
Shoes						
157. Cowhide boots, one-piece upper	9.9	100	—	—	—	—
158. Cowhide boots	—	100	112	—	—	—
159. Leather boots, black	9.2	100	—	—	—	—
160. Leather boots, welted	15.8	100	—	—	—	—
161. Leather boots, brown	—	100	—	242	206	176
162. Leather boots, composition soles	—	100	—	264	225	188
163. Leather oxfords, women's	14.5	100	—	—	—	—
164. Leather shoes, children's	19.3	100	—	—	—	—
165. Leather shoes, men's, no. 4004	—	100	145	—	—	—
166. Leather shoes, women's	—	100	121	—	—	—
167. Leather shoes, men's	—	100	—	259	220	189
168. Leather shoes, rubber soles	—	100	113	—	—	—
169. Sandals	10.4	100	—	—	—	—
170. Canvas shoes, leather soles	18.7	100	—	—	—	—
171. Cloth and leather shoes	—	100	—	274	186	120
172. Rubbers	17.7	100	117	224	202	151
173. Valenki	12.5	100	—	260	195	185
Haberdashery and notions						
174. Cotton thread, 6-strand	31.7	100	—	—	—	—
175. Cotton thread, 3-strand	—	100	—	610	417	317
176. Silk thread	—	100	—	242	163	126
177. Dress pattern	—	100	—	1221	1221	1035
178. Straightedge razor	—	100	—	441	338	304
179. Razor blades	—	100	—	154	115	108
Soap, drugs, etc.						
180. Household soap, 50% fat content	12.4	100	—	—	—	—
181. Household soap, 60% fat content	—	100	100	419	214	155
182. Glycerine soap	—	100	118	—	—	—
183. Toilet soap, "Family"	—	100	—	464	194	125
184. Toothpaste, "Sanit"	—	100	—	154	81	65
185. Toothbrush	—	100	—	397	298	213
186. Absorbent cotton	—	100	—	288	288	205
187. Gauze bandage	—	100	—	347	347	250

[a] The absolute ruble prices from which these price relatives were computed are found in Table A-1.
Note: The dash (—) indicates that the item was not priced for that year.

TABLE 3 (Continued)

Retail Prices of Goods and Services, Official Prices, Moscow, 1928–54, Price Relatives

	Price relative[a] (1937 = 100)					
Commodity	1928	1937	1940	1948	1952	1954
188. Thermometer	—	100	—	129	129	93
189. Castor oil capsules	—	100	—	100	100	72
Housewares						
190. Tea kettle, brass, 3.5-liter	14.8	100	—	—	—	—
191. Tea kettle, brass	—	100	—	260	221	199
192. Pan, aluminum, 22-cm	13.0	100	—	—	—	—
193. Pan, aluminum, 18-cm	—	100	—	229	178	160
194. Wash basin, aluminum	—	100	—	160	124	112
195. Wash basin, enameled iron	20.0	100	—	—	—	—
196. Cast-iron pot	22.1	100	—	—	—	—
197. Frying pan, enameled iron	26.2	100	—	—	—	—
198. Tea cup, enameled iron	40.0	100	—	—	—	—
199. Pail, galvanized iron	18.9	100	—	—	—	—
200. Primus stove	26.4	100	—	382	267	240
201. Samovar	18.7	100	—	324	259	233
202. Samovar, 711-mm	—	100	—	367	293	264
203. Kerosene lamp	40.0	100	—	—	—	—
204. Lamp chimney	54.5	100	—	—	—	—
205. Electric light bulb	—	100	—	217	174	117
206. Electric hot plate	—	100	—	147	103	87
207. Electric iron	—	100	—	391	264	225
208. Sewing machine	—	100	—	505	353	317
Reading matter						
209. *Pravda*	50.0	100	100	200	200	200
210. *Bol'shevik*	80.0	100	100	250	250	250
211. *Ogonek*	20.0	100	100	600	600	600
212. *Planovoe khoziaistvo*	66.7	100	100	100	100	100
213. *Lenin Collection*	86.7	100	160	160	131	131
214. *Pushkin Works*	—	100	167	233	191	191
215. Book on Turgenev	76.7	100	—	—	—	—
216. Novel	43.1	100	—	—	—	—
217. *The Quiet Don*	—	100	100	144	118	118
218. Pamphlet, 32 pages	40.0	100	—	240	200	200
219. Pamphlet, 48 pages	—	100	100	—	—	—
Cultural and sports goods						
220. Phonograph PT-3	—	100	—	218	107	107
221. Baian accordion	—	100	—	261	152	137
222. Piano	—	100	—	406	293	263
223. Bicycle	—	100	—	479	258	232
224. Camera, FED	—	100	—	139	100	90
225. Pencil, "Union"	42.9	100	—	—	—	—
226. Pencil	—	100	—	500	500	367
227. Pen holder	—	100	—	385	385	285
228. Pen point	—	100	—	250	250	150
229. Paint set	82.2	100	—	—	—	—
Kerosene and matches						
230. Kerosene	21.3	100	138	426	298	138
231. Matches	—	100	179	833	500	333
232. Matches	75.0	100	—	—	—	—

[a] The absolute ruble prices from which these price relatives were computed are found in Table A-1.
Note: The dash (—) indicates that the item was not priced for that year.

TABLE 3 (Continued)

Retail Prices of Goods and Services, Official Prices, Moscow, 1928–54, Price Relatives

Commodity	Price relative[a] (1937 = 100)					
	1928	1937	1940	1948	1952	1954
Tobacco products						
233. Cigarettes, grade 3	40.0	100	—	—	—	—
234. Cigarettes, "Metro"	—	100	—	198	123	119
235. Cigarettes, "Pushki"	—	100	96	—	—	—
236. Cigarettes, "Deli"	—	100	95	—	—	—
237. Cigarettes, "Kazbek"	—	100	—	184	118	106
238. Cigarettes, "Allegro"	—	100	96	—	—	—
239. Tobacco, grade 2	13.0	100	100	—	—	—
240. Tobacco, grade 1	—	100	—	200	130	123
241. Makhorka	17.3	100	—	307	187	167
242. Makhorka, highest grade	—	100	125	—	—	—
Services						
243. Rent	33.8	100	142	186	186	186
244. Electricity	90.0	100	120	155	200	200
245. Water	100.0	100	328	328	328	328
246. Tram ride	73.3	100	100	147	200	200
247. Railroad fare, Moscow-Leningrad	34.3	100	—	228	248	248
248. Railroad fare	—	100	153	—	—	—
249. Movie	30.0	100	—	300	300	200
250. Trousers made to order	—	100	229	—	—	—
251. Coat made to order	—	100	—	335	228	228
252. Haircut	—	100	—	—	125	94
253. Shave	—	100	—	—	300	225
254. Average hourly wage	24.0	100	122	195	223	233

[a] The absolute ruble prices from which these price relatives were computed are found in Table A-1.
Note: The dash (—) indicates that the item was not priced for that year.

bles and fruit subject to seasonal price fluctuations. In these cases, the quotations generally relate only to a short period, sometimes a single date, within the year. For each of these seasonal items, the quotations compared as between 1937 and one of the other years relate to approximately the same week or month in each year.

3. REPRESENTATIVENESS OF THE COMMODITIES PRICED

The selection of the items to be included in the cost-of-living index numbers was of necessity determined largely by the availability of price quotations that were reasonably comparable in the various years. Nevertheless, the list of commodities which it was possible to price is, it is believed, quite representative of the average Soviet consumption pattern. The cost-of-living index numbers for 1928–37 are based on the prices of 34 foods and beverages, 51 manufactured consumer goods, and 7 services — a total of 92 items. The 1937–40 cost-of-living index numbers are based on quotations for 64 foods and beverages, 34 manufactured consumer goods, and 7 services — a total of 105 items. The index numbers for 1948, 1952, and 1954 are based on quotations for 67 foods and beverages and 71 manufactured consumer goods. In addition, 8 services are priced in the index numbers for 1948 and 10 services in the index numbers for 1952 and 1954. This makes a total of 146 items covered in the index numbers for 1948 and 148 items covered in the index numbers for 1952 and 1954. The main consumption categories not represented in any way in these indexes are soft drinks and mineral waters, fuel (other than kerosene), and furniture. Certain categories represented in the index numbers for other years could not be represented in the 1940 index numbers; these are "haberdashery and notions," "housewares," and "cultural and sports goods." The index number for 1928–37 includes fewer commodities than the index numbers for the postwar years and is weak with respect to garments and durable consumer goods, but otherwise it seems almost as representative as the indexes for the postwar years. Altogether, the items covered in the cost-of-living index numbers represent, it is believed, somewhat under 90 percent of the purchases of goods and services by Soviet workers in the case of 1940 and somewhat over 90 percent in each of the other years studied.

Foods are well represented in all years. Each of the main groups is represented by at least one item, and most groups are represented by several items, though some groups are better represented than others. The *grain products and legumes* group, the most important single group,[23] is well represented both in terms of the number of items and in the representativeness of each item of what is actually most commonly consumed. The *meat and poultry* group is well represented. For 1928 the major fresh meats are included but sausage and poultry are not. Sausage is important in the Soviet diet but poultry is insignificant. For the postwar years, poultry is overrepresented; and the sausage and smoked meat items included are among the higher priced products in this group and are perhaps not entirely representative. The *fish* and *fats* groups are both rather well represented. *Sugar and confectionery* is well represented except for 1928, for which no confectionery items could be included. The *milk and milk products* group is rather well represented. *Vegetables and fruits* are very well represented for the postwar years. For 1940 also, many vegetables and fruits are included, but for several of these it was necessary to use an off-season price and the representativeness of the group is impaired on this score. The main vegetables are priced in the index number for 1928 but no fruits could be priced.

Among the *alcoholic beverages,* which account for a surprisingly high proportion of total sales, vodka, the single most important item, is represented in all years. The lighter alcoholic beverages, however, are not represented at all in the index numbers for 1928 and are represented only by wines in 1940 and only by domestic champagne in the postwar years, though beer is much more widely consumed. The price movement of wine

[23] It may be helpful at this point to refer to the table of group weights, Table 4.

(including champagne) may nevertheless have been quite similar to that of beer in that the prices of both reflect the Soviet policy of discouraging the consumption of hard liquor by setting relatively low prices for beverages of lower alcoholic content.

Canned foods, although not treated here as a separate group, are represented in the indexes for the postwar years by three items: caviar, canned peas, and canned apricots. They are represented in the 1940 index numbers only by caviar (hardly a representative item) and not at all in the index numbers for 1928. As canned goods accounted for only 1 percent or less of total retail sales of foods in 1928, 1937, and 1940,[24] this omission is hardly significant.

Among the manufactured goods, *textiles* are well represented. The cotton items included are among those produced in the largest quantities. Each of the major types of wool fabrics is represented in 1928, but only one wool could be priced for 1940 and the two wool items priced for the postwar years are not the most commonly consumed types. Linen or part-linen materials are represented for all years but 1940; silk is represented for 1940 and silk and rayon are both represented for the postwar years, but neither could be priced for 1928. *Garments* could be represented by only one item for 1928 but are rather well represented for the other years. The items priced include some of the cheaper grades probably sold in the largest volume, but some luxury garments (for example, the silk blouse) are also priced.

The *knitwear* group is represented only by hosiery items; hosiery has until recently been the most important kind of knitwear produced but knit underwear is also significant. For 1952 and 1954, however, the group index numbers computed on the basis of the prices of hosiery are adjusted to take into account changes in the prices of other knit goods. The adjustment is made on the basis of the annual price reductions. This is necessary because prices of hosiery fell considerably more than prices of other knitwear between 1948 and 1954. The *shoes* priced include representatives of the main types and materials, though for 1940 *valenki* (felt boots) could not be priced.

Haberdashery and notions is a miscellaneous group covering articles made of various materials and probably subject to different price patterns. Only thread could be priced in this group for 1928, and the group is not represented at all for 1940. Although several items are priced for postwar years, it is not known whether they are representative of the group price movement. The most important item in the *soap, drugs, etc.* group is soap; household soap is priced for all years and toilet soap for all years but 1928. Some additional items are priced for the postwar years.

The *housewares* group includes many of the items usually singled out as

[24] TSU, *Sovetskaia torgovlia; Statisticheskii sbornik*, p. 44.

important in Soviet statements, but the coverage is by no means complete. Glassware, china and pottery, and wooden utensils — all quite important in Soviet households — are not represented at all. Metal utensils are very well represented for 1928, but the particular metal utensils covered in the index numbers for postwar years are made of better materials (brass, aluminum) than the pots and pans sold in large quantities. The housewares group is not represented at all for 1940.

The main types of *reading matter* are represented for all years. *Pravda*, the daily organ of the Communist Party, along with *Izvestiia*, the daily organ of the Soviet Government (the price of which has always been the same as the price of *Pravda*) are, of course, the main dailies. *Bol'shevik* (*Kommunist*, since October 1952), a Party organ, is the major political journal. *Ogonek* is a popular illustrated weekly; and *Planovoe khoziaistvo*, published by the State Planning Commission, is one of the many specialized journals. The books include a Marx-Engels-Lenin-Stalin classic, a contemporary novel, and a Russian literary classic. The particular editions priced may in some cases be finer and more expensive than those usually purchased. The pamphlets priced are probably representative of the great number of pamphlets printed in the Soviet Union.

Cultural and sports goods are not represented in the 1940 index numbers and are represented only by two rather insignificant items in the 1928 index numbers. Many of the items included in this category for the postwar years are large, expensive consumer durables which are probably purchased mainly by the wealthy few and by clubs and similar organizations. The omission of radios here is unfortunate as they were probably quite commonly sold to workers in 1937 and have been of increasing importance in the postwar years. Smaller items such as toys, chess and checker sets, balls, notebooks and paper, which may well add up to the main share of the value of sales under this category, are represented only by the pencil, pen, and pen point. *Tobacco products* are well represented. Cigarettes, tobacco, and makhorka (a low grade tobacco) are all represented for each year, and for most years several brands of cigarettes are priced.

Among *services*, the most important items — rent, utilities, and transportation — are represented in all years. Entertainment is represented, probably fairly well, by the price of a movie ticket for all years but 1940. Clothing made to order is represented in the index numbers for 1940, 1948, 1952, and 1954; and barber services are represented in the index numbers for 1952 and 1954. The numerous other services are not directly represented at all; it is assumed that these are at least roughly represented by an index number of the average hourly wage. The average hourly wage also represents clothing made to order and barber services for years for which these services could not be priced.

4. COMPARABILITY OF THE COMMODITIES PRICED

A cost-of-living index number is obviously no more reliable than the price data on which it is based, and it is essential that the prices compared relate to the same quality product. The attempt to achieve reasonable comparability in the quotations used has been a prime concern of this study. In view of the importance of this aspect of the study, I present full details on the commodity designations and the reason for believing the quotations comparable or the area of doubtful comparability in the case of each comparison, as well as the sources and dates of each price quotation. Thus, the reader may form his own judgment on the question of comparability. In view of the bulk of the material and the scattered nature of the relevant data, these details are presented in appendix A. The total number of separate comparisons made comes to 639 (92 comparisons between 1928 and 1937, 105 comparisons between 1937 and 1940, 146 comparisons between 1937 and 1948, and 148 comparisons between 1937 and each of the years 1952 and 1954). Here I can do no more than attempt to give an idea of the procedures employed, of the kinds of problems met, and an impression of the accuracy of the comparisons taken as a whole.

The setting of the problem is the nature of the available price quotations, and particularly the adequacy of the accompanying descriptions of the products. More price quotations are available for 1937 than for any other year, and the commodity designations for 1937 are, on the whole, more complete from the point of view of descriptive detail. The procedure, then, was to start with a quotation for some other year, say 1928, or with all the available 1928 quotations for one kind of product and to search the 1936 price handbooks and 1937 visitors' accounts for products that could be considered comparable. This kind of matching process was carried on for each year. For 1952 and 1954, however, it was not necessary to make such a detailed study of commodity designations and comparability because most of the quotations for these years are computed from the quotations for 1948 and the annual price reductions.

For the purposes of this study, a commodity priced in a given year is considered to be comparable to one priced in 1937 if they are identical in those features that are, or might be expected to be, specified in the commodity descriptions appearing in the official Soviet price handbooks. For strict comparability, the price quotations must also be correct. The price handbook descriptions are generally detailed enough to identify a commodity and to distinguish it from similar products, but not necessarily so detailed as would be required if the purpose were to define the commodity completely or to describe how it is made. Quality changes of a kind that would not show up in such a designation or that would not generally be considered as having significantly changed the product are not considered. For instance, I cannot take into account the probable increase in the water content of bread nor the improvement in the appearance of the magazine *Ogonek*. Also, it was not always possible to determine whether changes were made in grading standards, and possibly there was undetected upgrading in the case of some products. In two cases — butter and cigarettes — evidence came to light that the system of classification and grading had changed between 1928 and 1937, and I made a systematic effort to track down and follow through the various changes.

The amount of descriptive detail required to identify a commodity sufficiently to determine comparability varies with the nature of the product, particularly with respect to such items as the number of grades, styles, or models, and with Soviet practice regarding grading, classification, and pricing. The 1936 price handbooks are an important source of information on the assortment produced of any commodity, the range of qualities, and on the kinds of features that are distinguished as relevant to price differentials. The 1928 price handbook, *Universal'nyi spravochnik tsen,* is useful in this respect for manufactured consumer goods in 1928. A number of commodity handbooks are available that provide details for the postwar years on the specifications of various commodities, the extent of the assortment produced, and data on the classification and grading systems, though unfortunately no price data.[25]

Food products, as a rule, are simpler and come in fewer grades than manufactured goods. Flour and the standard types of ordinary bread are classified according to the type grain from which the flour is produced and the extraction rate of the flour. Fresh meat is classified according to the type meat (beef, pork, et cetera), how well fed the animal is, and the part of the carcass from which the meat is cut; and poultry is classified only according to three grades. Sausage, smoked meats, and fish come in a wide variety of types and grades, and the classification system is not very clear. Salt and sugar are produced in only a few main types, and candy can usually be identified by brand name. Butter is classified according to several types and grades; in most cases it was possible to compare quotations for the same type and grade. Quotations for fresh vegetables and fruit generally are accompanied by no descriptive detail, though official quotations for these products are always for first grade products unless otherwise stated. The comparison of prices in effect at about the same period in each year should tend to make for comparability of the quality priced insofar as quality varies seasonally.

[25] For example, N. A. Arkhangel'skii (ed.), *Tovarovedenie promyshlennykh tovarov* (2 vols., Moscow, 1947); D. D. Bakzevich, *Tovarovedenie pishchevykh produktov* (Moscow, 1948); V. I. Petrov, *Tovarovedenie prodovol'stvennykh tovarov* (Moscow, 1947); G. B. Gubenko, *Kontrol' kachestva shveinykh tovarov* (Kiev, 1950); *Spravochnaia kniga po kul'ttovaram* (Moscow, 1954); F. V. Tsverevitinov, *Tovarovedenie pishchevykh produktov* (4 vols., Moscow, 1949)

Some of the simpler manufactured goods such as household soap, matches, and makhorka are produced in only one or a few grades; and some of the more complex items such as sewing machines are apparently made in only a few models. In most cases, however, manufactured goods present more of a problem than foods because of their greater complexity and the wide range of types, styles, models, sizes, and materials in which a single "product" may be made. For the more complex products the Soviet practices with respect to branding, classifying, and numbering products are sometimes extremely useful.

Brand names are used fairly commonly, particularly for consumer durables, where the brand is often the name or initials of the producing plant (the phonograph PT-3, the FED camera), and for small, standardized articles ("Theatre" caramels, "Family" toilet soap, "Sanit" toothpaste, "Union" pencils, the various brands of cigarettes). Such brand names serve to identify a product immediately and specifically (except possibly with respect to the package size).

For many products there are systems of model or article (*artikul*) numbers which are sometimes helpful. The numbering of shoes is highly systematized, and information on the system is available. From the article number of a shoe it is possible to determine the general style of shoe, the age and sex group for which it is intended, the material and method of attaching the sole, the material and color of the upper, the quality category ("standard," "special order," or "model"), and whether the shoe is handmade. Thus a postwar quotation for a shoe identified only by article number could be matched to a 1937 shoe with the same article number, or to a 1937 shoe with a description fitting the postwar article number even when the 1937 article number was not indicated. The 1928 shoe designations are not accompanied by article numbers, but the descriptions are usually detailed enough to be matched quite closely to those for 1937.

For some items in the textiles and knitwear groups, comparisons could be made for the same number article (calico no. 6, silk crepe de Chine no. 5, cotton sheeting no. 49, rayon socks no. 86). In each case, enough descriptive details were given to indicate that the comparison of article numbers was valid. Textile and knitwear article numbers could be used only when price quotations for the same number were available for two or more years, since the system used in numbering these products, if any, was not discovered by the investigator. However, the descriptive details accompanying many price quotations in these groups permitted additional fairly firm comparisons to be made without the aid of article numbers.

Garment article numbers include an indication of the relative price range of the fabric of which the garment is made and this fact proved useful in some cases (cotton zephyr shirt, cotton dress, wool suit of fabric group 46, silk blouse). Beyond this the garment numbers apparently indicate style, quality of workmanship, and other features, but unfortunately no details on the numbering system are available. The 1936 garment price handbook[26] describes such features but does not indicate the corresponding part of the article number. This makes it extremely difficult to compare quotations from this source with postwar official quotations, which generally include the complete article number but give barely any descriptive detail. Although the garment comparisons are less certain than for some other products, it is believed that at least some of them are quite close. They show a certain amount of internal consistency and are supported fairly well by price quotations available in non-Soviet sources. Although many of these quotations were accompanied by too little descriptive detail to be used individually, taken as a whole they provide a fairly clear idea of the range of prices for a given type of garment. However, as indicated, the data are very limited considering the complexity of clothing, and there is a possibility that errors of interpretation were made.

Reading material comparisons are quite firm, as books, periodicals, and newspapers are available in this country for inspection, and the prices are printed on each copy.

The accuracy of the comparisons made is believed close enough so that the index numbers can be used with some confidence. Where there are doubts as to comparability, these vary in degree and nature. In some cases there is a known but narrow range of error resulting, for instance, from lack of information as to whether the quotations are uniform with respect to the inclusion or exclusion of the container, as in the case of *sunflower oil* (item 65) or *vodka* (items 109 and 110). In some cases, midpoints of price ranges are compared; this inevitably involves some error, but where information on the price ranges is adequate and the range of prices prevailing in the different years is comparable, the error is likely to be small. There are cases, particularly among the more complex articles, where the comparison made is almost certainly correct, but if it is not, the error would be substantial. This is true, for example, of *pure wool "Boston"* (item 126), of several of the garment comparisons (items 138, 141, 142, 146), of one of the *samovars* (item 201), the *accordion* (item 221), and of *cigarettes, grade 3* (item 233). Also, there are a number of cases in which the lack of descriptive detail makes it virtually impossible to judge the degree of comparability. Many of the 1940 quotations fall in this group as do also such items as *margarine* (item 69), the *toothbrush* (item 185), and the *thermometer* (item 188). In still other cases — for example, *mutton, above average fed* (item 26) and *toilet soap, "Family"* (item 183) — the product is clearly comparable, but there is some doubt about the exact price. There does not seem to be any reason to think that

---

[26] NKVT, *Preiskurant roznichnykh tsen na shveinye izdeliia dlia vsekh magazinov vsekh torguiushchikh organizatsii gorodov: Moskva, Leningrad, Kiev, Minsk* (Moscow, 1936).

the errors are all in the same direction and, to a large extent, the numerous errors of comparability probably tend to offset each other. The nature of the problem is such that it would likely be misleading to attempt an estimate of the probable margin of error. I have classified the comparisons into four categories of comparability on a rather subjective basis: strictly comparable in the sense defined above, closely comparable, fairly comparable, of doubtful comparability. When all 639 comparisons between 1937 and all of the other years are considered, about 25 percent are strictly comparable, 35 percent are closely comparable, 33 percent are fairly comparable, and 7 percent are of doubtful comparability.

Among the commodity groups, the most reliable from the point of view of comparability are *grain products and legumes, sugar and confectionery, salt, tea and coffee, alcoholic beverages, shoes, reading matter, kerosene and matches, tobacco products, services,* and, for 1928, *textiles.* In these groups, 70 percent or more of the quotations are strictly or closely comparable. The *meat and poultry, fish, fats, textiles* (for years other than 1928), *knitwear,* and *soap, drugs, etc.* groups follow; although some of the comparisons within each of these groups are rather weak, the groups as a whole are rather reliable. The weakest groups are *vegetables and fruit, garments, haberdashery and notions,* and *cultural and sports goods,* although each contains some certain comparisons.

So far as the various years are concerned, 1940 is definitely the weakest from the point of view of comparability. Even so, about half the comparisons appear to be strictly or closely comparable. The year 1928 is probably the firmest from the point of view of comparability. Although somewhat less than 20 percent of the comparisons can be said to be strictly comparable, almost 70 percent of the comparisons are strictly or closely comparable and only one comparison is really doubtful. The year 1948 is also good from the point of view of comparability. About 25 percent of the quotations are strictly comparable and over 55 percent strictly or closely comparable, with about 6 percent rather doubtful. The years 1952 and 1954 are as firm as 1948, except for a few cases where there are doubts as to the application of the annual price cuts.

V ·

INDEX NUMBERS OF OFFICIAL RETAIL
PRICES IN MOSCOW: THE WEIGHTS

A SET of weights is required for each year considered in order to compute the alternative price index numbers. In accord with the formulas presented in chapter III, I compute for each year (except 1944) two alternative price index numbers, one in which the weights reflect the consumption pattern of 1937 and one in which they reflect the consumption pattern of the given year. The main task of the present chapter is to present the weights and to describe briefly the sources for and methods of estimating these weights. More complete details concerning the derivation of the weights are given in appendix B. I then show the resulting index numbers of official retail prices in Moscow which form the basis of the cost-of-living index numbers and discuss the significance of the alternative weighting systems.

I. THE WEIGHTS

The weights are intended to represent the percentage distribution of urban worker expenditures among the various goods and services represented in the cost-of-living index numbers. The major category and group weights for each year are shown in Table 4. Each weight here is expressed as a percentage of total expenditures on goods and services. The classification by commodity group follows, in the main, Soviet practice. The weight for the major category *foods* includes expenditures on restaurant meals and on alcoholic beverages. The weight assigned to each individual commodity priced in the index number is shown for each year in Table B-1. Here the weight for each item is expressed as a percentage of the weight for the commodity group within which it falls. Table B-1 also indicates the commodity group or subgroup represented by each commodity priced.

The weights discussed in this chapter are those employed in computing the urban cost-of-living index numbers. In addition to the cost-of-living index numbers, I compute parallel index numbers of average prices prevailing in all Soviet retail markets. The group and representative commodity weights are the same in each set of computations, but the major category weights differ. In the index number of average prices in all

TABLE 4

Category and Group Weights for the Cost-of-Living Index Numbers, USSR, 1928–54
(Percent of total)

Major category and commodity group	1928	1937	1940	1948	1952	1954
Foods						
Grain products and legumes	12.3	23.7	23.5	21.5	16.1	13.8
Meat and poultry	10.3	5.5	7.0	5.6	4.6	5.3
Fish	1.6	2.5	2.3	2.8	2.6	2.5
Sugar and confectionery	4.5	10.1	7.3	10.3	11.0	11.1
Fats (including butter)	3.5	3.7	3.8	5.2	4.6	4.6
Milk and milk products (excluding butter)	6.4	1.2	1.4	1.3	1.4	1.6
Eggs	1.4	0.4	0.7	0.5	0.4	0.4
Vegetables and fruit	6.4	3.5	3.7	3.1	3.3	2.4
Salt	0.1	0.2	0.2	0.6	0.4	0.2
Tea and coffee	0.6	0.7	0.6	0.8	0.7	0.6
Alcoholic beverages	3.6	9.2	10.2	11.4	11.1	11.7
Totals, all foods	50.7	60.7	60.7	63.2	56.3	54.3
Manufactured goods						
Textiles	6.4	5.6	6.8	7.9	9.0	9.2
Garments	7.8	4.9	7.0	4.6	6.0	7.3
Knitwear	2.1	1.6	2.2	1.6	2.4	2.4
Shoes	7.8	3.5	3.8	3.6	4.5	4.4
Haberdashery and notions	0.7	1.5	—	1.3	1.6	1.8
Soap, drugs, etc.	1.4	2.0	2.4	1.3	1.5	1.2
Housewares	3.2	1.7	—	1.0	1.3	1.5
Reading matter	1.3	1.0	1.2	0.6	0.7	0.8
Cultural and sports goods	0.9	2.3	—	1.4	1.9	2.2
Kerosene and matches	0.8	0.7	0.8	0.5	0.5	0.4
Tobacco products	1.6	2.5	3.1	2.0	2.3	2.0
Totals, all manufactured goods	33.8	27.3	27.3	25.8	31.7	33.2
Services						
Rent	3.9	1.6	2.0	1.4	1.4	1.4
Utilities	2.3	0.8	1.3	1.0	1.6	1.7
Transportation and communications	3.5	5.6	5.8	4.5	4.5	4.8
Entertainment	1.1	1.3	—	1.5	1.8	1.7
Clothing made and repaired	...	0.7	1.0	0.7	0.7	0.8
Personal services	...	0.5	...	...	0.5	0.5
Other services	4.7	1.5	1.9	1.9	1.5	1.6
Totals, all services	15.5	12.0	12.0	11.0	12.0	12.5
Totals, all goods and services	100.0	100.0	100.0	100.0	100.0	100.0

Note: Minor discrepancies in these data between calculated sums of items and indicated totals are due to round-ing. The dash (—) indicates that the group was not represented in the price index number for that year. Where one or more groups are not represented in the price index number for a given year, the sum of the given-year weights for the groups which are represented in a major category equals the total weight for that category. In computing the price index number for such a year, the 1937 weights are adapted to correspond to the groups represented in the index number for the given year. The sign (...) indicates that the item is represented under "Other services."
Sources and methods: See appendix B.

Soviet retail markets, the major category weights are based on the break-down between foods and manufactured goods of total retail sales in state and cooperative shops. For 1928, sales in private shops are also taken into account. These retail price index numbers are described in appendix E.

The 1928 weights. The 1928 weights are based on a Soviet study of the incomes and expenditures of urban wage earner families. This is the so-called "continuous" budget study. Records of daily expenditures were kept over the entire year by the families in the sample, with periodic visits by the investigators, and the results were collected and published quarterly. The weights used in computing the price index number are computed from budgets for the fourth quarter of 1927 and the first three quarters of 1928.[1] The results of the investigation for the final quarter of 1928 have not, to my knowledge, been published in detail.

The size of the sample was 585 households in the last quarter of 1927, and 672, 675, and 657 households in the first three quarters of 1928, respectively. The sample covers wage earner families in eight industrial regions of the USSR — Moscow, Leningrad, Ivanovo-Vosnesensk, Tula, Kharkov, the Urals, the Don Basin, and Kiev. The average for the USSR, it is believed, is computed by weighting the average for each of these cities or regions by the number of wage earners in that city or region. The so-called "November" budget study, carried on at the same time, was based on a larger sample — 2,000 to 3,000 households — but was limited to expenditures in the one month of November. The "continuous" budget study provides a more satisfactory basis for weights, even though the sample is smaller, as it covers expenditures during the entire year.

The expenditures of the families covered in the budget study are probably reasonably representative of expenditures of all urban worker families in the USSR, but there is relatively little information on this question. The average size of the families varied over the period covered from 4.16 to 4.36 persons, of which about 1.2 were employed. The annual wage of the chief breadwinner averaged 941 rubles, and earnings of other employed members of the families covered in the budget study averaged 520 rubles a year. The chief breadwinner's wage thus was some 20 percent higher than the national average annual wage of all nonagricultural wage earners and salaried employees, which was 775 rubles in 1928.[2] The income of the families covered in the budget study may then have been above the average for all wage-earner and salaried-employee families. One might, of course, expect the income of the chief wage earner to exceed the national average. On the other hand, the budget study was limited to wage earner families and did not cover families of salaried employees, whose average earnings probably exceeded those of wage earners. The wage earners covered in the budget inquiry may have been somewhat more skilled than the average wage earner. Also, inasmuch as detailed records of all expenditures had to be maintained, it seems likely that the families studied were more literate than the average. Their expenditure habits nevertheless should not have differed much on this account from those of the average Soviet worker family.

The budget study is undoubtedly subject to many shortcomings. One

[1] These are published in *Statistika truda,* no. 5–6, 1928, pp. 16–20; no. 1, 1929, pp. 18–19; no. 5–6, 1929, pp. 22–27.
[2] See Table 13.

wonders in particular how accurate the expenditure records could have been, broken down into such detail as they are. There seems, however, no ground for suspicion that the sample or the budget materials were deliberately manipulated for propaganda purposes as was true of some of the later publicized sketchy "budgets" of selected *stakhanovite* workers.

The budget study includes a breakdown by fairly broad categories of total income and expenditures per household.[3] This provides the basis for the weights for the three major categories — food, manufactured consumer goods, and services. Some of the outlay categories as given in the original study cover expenditures on both goods and services, and for such categories it was necessary to estimate, sometimes rather arbitrarily, the distribution of expenditures between goods and services. This may lead to some error in the major category weights, particularly for manufactured goods and for services, but the error is probably small. Also, no separate item of expenditures on transportation is given in the source and only a rough estimate of the weight for this could be made. As transportation is a fairly large share of the total weight for services, this is another possible source of error in the allocation of the total weight as between goods and services.

The budget study provides a very detailed breakdown of expenditures on food per person — or, more precisely, per conventional adult. Expenditures are shown for fifty separate foods or groups of foods. Both the group weights and the representative commodity weights for foods are based on these data. The weight for alcoholic beverages is derived from the breakdown of expenditures on alcoholic beverages and tobacco in the budget study.

Total expenditures on "clothing" are given in the budget study as a separate outlay category in the table that shows average household incomes and expenditures. The division of this large category into the separate component groups — *textiles, garments, knitwear, haberdashery and notions,* and *shoes* — is based on the fairly detailed breakdown of expenditures on clothing per person shown in a separate table in the budget study. This also provides the basis for the division of the textiles group into the subgroups — cotton, wool, linen. More detailed breakdowns within these subgroups are fairly arbitrary. The budget study provides at least a rough basis for dividing the weight for shoes into the subgroup and representative commodity weights. The budget study indicates also the proportion of total expenditures on clothing which was for repairs of clothing and clothing made to order; this is allocated to the weight for services.

The group weight for *housewares* and the group and representative commodity weights for *tobacco products* are taken directly from the budget study. The study includes a partial breakdown of expenditures on household articles. This enabled me to exclude furniture and bedding

[3] The breakdown of expenditures for 1927/28 is shown in Table B-2.

(which are not represented) and also repairs of furnishings (which are allocated to the weight for services) from the weight for the housewares group. The original breakdown, however, was not of much use in estimating the weights for the representative commodities within the housewares group, as the breakdown does not correspond with the items I price; the representative commodity weights had to be estimated on a rule-of-thumb basis.

The weight for the two groups *reading matter* and *cultural and sports goods* taken together is estimated rather arbitrarily to have amounted to about 70 percent of total expenditures on "culture and education," the remaining 30 percent of these expenditures being assumed to be for cultural and educational services. The division of the combined weight for these two groups into a separate weight for each as well as the representative commodity weights within these groups had to be made on a rule-of-thumb basis, with some help from budget studies for earlier years. The weight for *matches* is taken directly from the 1927/28 budget study and that for *kerosene* is estimated at 10 percent of total expenditures on "wood and kerosene" in 1927/28 on the basis of expenditures on "fuel and lighting" materials in the "continuous" budget study for 1926.

The weights for *rent* and *utilities* are estimated from the 1927/28 budget figure for total expenditures on "rent, utilities, construction and repair, and other expenditures on housing" and the breakdown of expenditures in this category in the 1926 budget study. The weight for *transportation and communications* is a rough estimate, based in part on railroad passenger revenue. The weight for *entertainment* is made up of 30 percent of expenditures on "culture and education" plus about 20 percent of expenditures on "rest homes, sanitoria, and other expenditures on vacations." The weight for *other services* is intended to cover services not included elsewhere in which labor accounts for a relatively large share of the cost. It includes expenditures on the making and repair of clothing; repairs of household articles; medical care; such personal services as baths, laundry, and barber services; payments for domestic help and various other household services; and 80 percent of expenditures on "rest homes, sanitoria, and vacations." [4]

The weights for 1937 and later years. For these years, the major category weights for the cost-of-living index numbers reflect the estimated distribution of urban worker expenditures among the three major categories — foods, manufactured consumer goods, and services. The further breakdowns of the weights for foods and manufactured consumer goods are intended to represent urban worker expenditures but are in fact based on the structure of total retail sales in state and cooperative shops and restaurants. Purchases by urban workers on the collective farm market

[4] Weights for some of these categories are shown in Table B-6; they are not shown in Table B-1 as no representative items could be priced.

are not taken into account in the weights used in computing the index numbers of official prices. They are taken into account at a later stage when the index numbers of official prices are adjusted for collective farm market prices.

The breakdown of total urban worker expenditures on commodities in state and cooperative shops between foods and manufactured consumer goods is estimated from data on the relative share of these two categories in sales in state and cooperative shops in each of the years studied. The share of food in urban sales in state and cooperative shops and restaurants was greater than the share of food in total (urban and rural) sales in state and cooperative shops and restaurants by a bit over 4 percent in 1937 and by about 5 percent in each of the years 1940, 1950, and 1954.[5] Purchases by the rural population in urban shops are fairly important and undoubtedly fall more heavily on manufactured consumer goods than on foods. Also, various institutions make some purchases in the urban retail shops and these, too, likely fall more heavily on manufactured goods than on foods. To take account of the rural and institutional purchases I assume that the share of foods in urban worker purchases in state and cooperative shops was about 10 percent greater than the share of foods in total retail sales in state and cooperative shops in each of the years studied. The constancy of the difference between the share of foods in total and in urban retail sales seems to justify a constant percentage here. Thus foods are estimated to have accounted for 69 percent of urban worker purchases in state and cooperative shops in 1937 and 1940, for 71 percent in 1948, 64 percent in 1952, and 62 percent in 1954.[6] As urban workers purchase additional quantities of food on the collective farm market, the share of food in the total expenditures of urban workers is, of course, higher than shown here for their purchases in state and cooperative shops and restaurants only.

The weight for *services* is the estimated ratio of expenditures on services to total urban worker expenditures for both services and goods in all markets. That is, in this case, purchases on the collective farm market are counted in the total weight for commodities. It is only the index numbers of official prices of commodities that are subsequently adjusted for prices on the collective farm market.

The 1937 weight for services is estimated on the basis of the data on

[5] The derivation of these figures is described in more detail in Table B-3 and in the explanation of that table.

[6] The share of foods in total retail sales in state and cooperative shops and restaurants is given as 57.3 percent in 1952 and 54.8 percent in 1954 in TSU, *Sovetskaia torgovlia; Statisticheskii sbornik* (Moscow, 1956), p. 39. But these figures are based on a definition of retail sales that differs from the definition underlying the figures for earlier years. According to the definition of retail trade in use up to 1951, the share of food in total sales in state and cooperative shops is estimated at 58.5 percent in 1952 and 56 percent in 1954. See Table B-3.

household outlays on goods and services in Abram Bergson's *Soviet National Income and Product in 1937*. Total household outlays on money rent, utilities, and miscellaneous services were 15.9 billion rubles in 1937. I assume 80 percent of this, or 12.7 billion rubles, represents expenditures by urban households. The urban share of expenditures on services must be even greater than their share of retail sales, though the exact share is not known. Total retail sales to urban households, including sales on the collective farm market, can be estimated at 92.9 billion rubles in 1937.[7] Thus services amounted to 12 percent and purchases of goods in all markets amounted to 88 percent of total retail sales to urban households plus urban household expenditures on services in 1937. Presumably the pattern of expenditures of all urban households is close enough to the pattern of urban worker household expenditures to be used.

The weights for services for the years 1940 through 1954 are crude guesses. There is very little information to permit an estimate of the value of services purchased by urban workers in these years. The weights are based in part on a comparison of (a) the change in the value of urban retail sales in state and cooperative shops and restaurants with (b) an approximate index number of the change in value of services consumed. This index number of the change in the value of services is extremely crude, being based on the estimated changes in price and volume of only six services. It is derived in the process of estimating the service group and representative commodity weights for these years.

The group weights for foods and manufactured goods shown in Table 4 are based on the breakdown by commodity group of total retail sales in state and cooperative shops and restaurants, given in TSU, *Sovetskaia torgovlia; Statisticheskii sbornik* (Moscow, 1956).[8] The data are given for 1937, 1940, 1950, and 1954. The weights for these years are computed directly from this breakdown. For 1948, the 1950 group and representative commodity weights are employed as if they were 1948 weights, though the major category weights for 1948 are based on 1948 figures. This likely leads to some error in the weights, as there may well have been changes in the structure of retail sales between 1948 and 1950 — a period when total retail sales increased fairly rapidly. But in broad outline, the 1950 pattern of consumption can represent that of 1948 reasonably well. The weights for 1952 are estimated from those for 1950 and 1954 and data on changes in the value of sales of the various commodity groups over the period 1950 to 1954. In cases of commodity groups for which no data on the change in value of sales were available, the average of the 1950

---

[7] Table 12 and Abram Bergson, *Soviet National Income and Product in 1937* (New York, 1953), p. 110.

[8] Pp. 44–47. The breakdown in percentage terms is reproduced in Table B-4. The absolute ruble figures are also given in the source.

and 1954 weights for the group was used. This procedure probably leads to only minor errors in the weights for 1952.[9]

Basing the group and subgroup weights — and in many cases the representative commodity weights also — on the structure of total retail sales in state and cooperative shops means the weights reflect purchases of the rural population and of institutions as well as the purchases of urban workers. There are, as one would expect, differences between the urban and rural expenditure patterns. For instance, among foods, the peasant spends relatively more than the urban worker on such processed foods as sugar, salt, and tea, and less on grain products and fresh produce. Thus sugar may be overweighted and grain products, meat, milk products, and vegetables and fruit somewhat underweighted in the index numbers. Among manufactured goods, the peasant buys relatively more cloth and fewer ready-made garments than the urban worker, and textiles are probably overweighted in relation to garments. Also, institutional purchases in the retail shops may fall relatively heavily on reading matter and cultural and sports goods; if so, then the weights for these groups are relatively too high. But the urban worker's consumption pattern must pretty well dominate the structure of retail sales[10] and the weights should approximate fairly well the pattern of urban worker expenditures in state and cooperative shops and restaurants.[11]

As has been said, purchases on the collective farm market are not taken into account in computing the weights for 1937 and later years. The collective farm market is an important source of food for the Soviet urban worker. Thus, food in general — and in particular meat, fats, dairy products, vegetables, and fruit — took a larger share of the worker's total expenditures in all markets than shown in the weights in Table 4 for

---

[9] This is confirmed by information on the 1952 structure of retail sales published in TSU, *Narodnoe khoziaistvo SSSR v 1958 g.* (Moscow, 1959), pp. 728–733.

[10] The urban share of sales in state and cooperative shops and restaurants was almost 70 percent in 1937 and has been over 70 percent since 1940. See TSU, *Sovetskaia torgovlia; Statisticheskii sbornik*, p. 21. Of course, not all sales in urban areas are to urban workers, and some are to rural households.

[11] In practice, fortunately, it does not seem to make much difference whether the weights are based on total retail sales or on urban worker expenditures. In an earlier calculation for the period 1928 to 1937, retail price index numbers using two sets of weights for each year, one based on total retail sales and one based on urban wage earner expenditures, were computed. The difference between the result using 1928 weights based on urban wage earner budgets and that using 1928 weights based on total retail sales is very small; similarly, the two sets of 1937 weights lead to very similar results. It should be said, however, that for lack of data on the structure of retail sales in 1928, the 1928 "all retail sales" weights had to be based largely on the urban wage earner budgets and only the more obvious and broader adaptations of the budget data could be made. And for lack of data on urban worker budgets in 1937, the 1937 "urban worker" weights were adapted roughly from the data on total retail sales. Had it been possible to employ weights based on more accurate and detailed data, the differences resulting from the different nature of the weights might have been larger.

state and cooperative shops only.[12] The subsequent adjustment of the index numbers of official prices to take purchases on the collective farm market into account is rough enough so that it may only partially compensate for this. This should be kept in mind in interpreting the results.

The breakdown of sales given in TSU, *Sovetskaia torgovlia; Statisticheskii sbornik* is on the whole arranged to suit my needs rather well, especially in the case of foods, and relatively little adaptation of the material was required. Such adaptations as were made are explained in appendix B, and I shall mention here only the cases in which there is some room for error. The weight for *alcoholic beverages* for each year had to be estimated as the source lumps alcoholic and nonalcoholic beverages together. For 1937, partial data indicate that alcoholic beverages amounted to something under three-quarters of sales of alcoholic and nonalcoholic beverages. Nonalcoholic beverages here apparently mean bottled drinks; tea, coffee, and fruit juices are accounted for in other categories. This same percentage distribution was used in computing the weight for alcoholic beverages from that for alcoholic and nonalcoholic beverages for all years. While the volume of sales of nonalcoholic beverages has probably risen much more than the volume of sales of alcoholic beverages, prices of alcoholic beverages have, it is believed, risen more than prices of nonalcoholic beverages. Nevertheless, this is a fairly arbitrary procedure and the weight for alcoholic beverages may be in error.

The weight for *housewares* is made up of the figures for sales of "metal utensils" and "glass and chinaware" given in the source plus a more or less arbitrary amount from "other non-foods" to allow for such items as electric light bulbs and appliances and sewing machines. I allow housewares other than metal utensils and glassware a steadily increasing proportion of the total weight for housewares. This is intended as a rough recognition of the increase in sales of appliances and such, particularly during the postwar years. As in the case of the 1928 weights, furniture is not included in the housewares group and is not directly represented in the price index number.

The further breakdowns of the group weights into subgroup and representative commodity weights shown in Table B-1 are in many cases based on the breakdown of retail sales in TSU, *Sovetskaia torgovlia; Statisticheskii sbornik*. For instance, *grain products and legumes* are broken down in the source into the following subgroups: "bread and bakery products," "flour," "grits and legumes," and "macaroni products." *Meat and poultry* is divided into the two subgroups: "(fresh) meat and poultry" and "sausage products." *Fats* are broken down into "butter,"

[12] Including purchases on the collective farm market, food accounted for around 65 percent and bread and other grain products for around 18 percent of total urban worker expenditures on goods and services in 1937.

"vegetable oil," and "other fats." Separate figures are given for "potatoes," "other vegetables," and "fruit." *Textiles* are divided into the subgroups "cotton," "wool," "silk," "linen." *Shoes* are divided into the subgroups "leather," "cloth or cloth and leather combined," "felt," and "rubber." Sales of *cultural and sports goods* are broken down in some detail.

The more detailed breakdowns had to be estimated on the basis of scattered Soviet data on consumption and production; sometimes the data
were fairly adequate, sometimes only of the roughest sort. And in some
cases the detailed breakdown had to be made on a rule-of-thumb basis.
In general, more detailed data are available for 1937 than for the other
years, and in some cases the breakdowns for all years are based on 1937
data. In such cases the representative commodity weights for the postwar years are adjusted to take into account at least the more obvious
changes in consumption patterns that have occurred since 1937. For instance, for 1948, 1952, and 1954 the weight for *wheat bread* is greater in
relation to that for *rye bread* than is the case for 1937 or 1940, for it
is believed that sales of wheat bread have increased more than sales of
rye bread. Also, sales of loaf bread have increased in relation to sales
of bread cut from large loaves and sold by weight; this is reflected in a
relative increase in the weight for the *French loaf* for the postwar years.
The representative commodity weights for the various types of garments
are of necessity rather arbitrary for all years; however, the weights for
the postwar years are intended to reflect the relatively greater increase
in the output of silk and wool than of cotton fabrics. Also, *rayon socks*
are given a larger share of the total *knitwear* weight in the postwar years
than in 1937. Among *housewares,* the postwar weights are greater for
electrical items and *sewing machines* and smaller for such items as the
primus stove and *samovar* than the 1937 weights.

In the case of *services,* the data from which weights might be estimated
are very limited and the estimates are very crude. The 1937 service weights
are based mainly on a Soviet study of the incomes and outlays of the
population in 1935.[13] The authors of this study are quite convincing in
their attempt to provide complete data but indicate there are many shortcomings and gaps in the information on expenditures on services. Probably expenditures on some services are omitted from their calculations,
so that even for 1935 the breakdown is not accurate. One wonders, in
particular, whether transportation and communications are overweighted.
Presumably, information available to the authors on the revenues of the
transportation system and post office were complete while there might
well be gaps in the data on municipally provided services, and an evaluation of expenditures on the many services provided by cooperatives and
individuals could hardly be more than an informed guess.

[13] U. Cherniavskii and S. Krivetskii, "Pokupatel'nye fondy naseleniia i roznichnyi
tovarooborot," *Planovoe khoziaistvo,* no. 6, 1936, pp. 111–112. See Table B-7.

Using this 1935 breakdown as the basis for weights for 1937 must involve further errors. Two indicators of changes in the value of services purchased — urban money rent and railroad passenger revenue — move closely enough over the period 1935 to 1937 to suggest that the relationship between these two important subgroups, at least, probably did not change much. In any case, several earlier computations of an index number of service prices suggest that within fairly wide limits differences in weighting do not make much difference in the results.

The Soviet study provides figures on the 1935 expenditures of the urban population on the following four categories of services: (a) rent and utilities, (b) transportation and communications, (c) cultural activities and recreation, and (d) personal services. I estimate in appendix B that rent amounted to about two-thirds and utilities to about one-third of expenditures on "rent and utilities" in 1935; I assume the same allocation for 1937. More detailed breakdowns of the 1937 weights for services are based on rather scattered data and in some cases are quite arbitrary.

For 1940, 1948, 1952, and 1954 the service weights are computed from those for 1937 and the estimated change in expenditures on the various services between 1937 and the year in question. A measure of the change in volume of the services provided can be estimated for the following six services — housing, electricity, water, railroad transportation, urban transportation, and entertainment. For housing, the index of volume is computed from total urban dwelling space. For electricity, the index of volume is based on the consumption of electric energy for municipal and household needs in urban areas. The index of the physical volume of water refers to urban average daily consumption of water. The index of the volume of railroad travel is based on the number of passenger-kilometers traveled. For urban transportation, the index of volume for 1937 to 1940 is based on the number of passengers carried in trams and trolley-busses, and for the postwar years autobus passengers are also taken into account. The index of the physical volume of entertainment refers only to motion pictures, though this is probably the most important form of entertainment. For 1937 to 1940 the number of motion picture theatres and projectors is the basis for the index of volume while for later years the index is based on the more satisfactory measure of motion picture attendance. The measures for railroad transport and entertainment relate to the entire USSR while those for the other services are for urban areas only.

To obtain an index number of the value of the service I multiply the index of volume of each of the six services by the price relative of the item representing that service in my price index numbers. I consider this index number of the value of the service as being an index number of money expenditures by urban workers for that service.[14]

The procedure in computing the service weights for 1940, 1948, 1952,

[14] The changes in volume, price, and value of these services are shown in Table B-8.

and 1954 is as follows: (a) The 1937 weight for each of the six service items for which there is an index number of the change in value is multiplied by the index number of the change in value of that service between 1937 and 1940 (or other given year). The results, divided through by the total, give the 1940 (or other year) percentage distribution among these six services.[15] (b) I assume arbitrarily, for all years, that these six services accounted for 77 percent of all urban worker expenditures on services, as was the case in 1937. (c) For lack of data on other services, the distribution of the remaining 23 percent of the total service weight among the various other services priced is in most cases also assumed to have been the same as in 1937.

2. SIGNIFICANCE OF ALTERNATIVE WEIGHTING SYSTEMS

The two alternative price index numbers for each year are shown by commodity group, by major category, for all commodities, and for all commodities and services in Table 5. The price index numbers shown in Table 5 are those based on urban worker expenditure patterns and used in deriving the cost-of-living index numbers.[16] The figures in Table 5 relate still to official prices in Moscow. To arrive at the corresponding index numbers of the cost of living, it is necessary to take into account prices on the unofficial markets and prices outside Moscow. This will be done in chapter VI. Here I shall briefly discuss the extent of agreement or divergence between the index numbers resulting from the use of alternative weights.

The two price index numbers for 1928 diverge widely. For all commodities and services, the index number for 1928 (1937 = 100) based on the 1928 expenditure pattern (13.6) is 5.9 percentage points or 43 percent lower than that based on the 1937 expenditure pattern (19.5); in other words, when 1928 weights are used, the price rise between 1928 and 1937 is 43 percent greater than when 1937 weights are used. With 1928 as 100, the 1928-weighted price index number for 1937 is 734 and the 1937-weighted price index number is 513. For foods, the 1928-weighted price index number (11.2) shows a price rise 19 percent greater than the 1937-weighted price index number (13.3); and for manufactured consumer goods the 1928-weighted price index number (14.3) shows a rise as much

---

[15] The weights so computed are, of course, rounded. In the case of the 1952 and 1954 weights, some adjustments are made in the weights computed from those for 1937 to take into account the results of a similar computation for 1952 based on the 1928 weights and the changes in value of the six services between 1928 and 1952.

[16] In computing the index numbers of prices in all retail sales in state and cooperative shops, the group price index numbers and the price index numbers for the major categories foods and manufactured consumer goods are the same as those shown in Table 5. The index numbers of prices of all commodities in all retail sales in state and cooperative shops, however, differ somewhat from those shown in Table 5 because of the different major category weights. These are shown in appendix E.

TABLE 5

Category and Group Price Index Numbers, Official Retail Prices, Moscow, 1928–54 (1937 = 100)

Major category and commodity group	1928 1937 weights[c]	1928 1928 weights[c]	1937 All weights[c]	1940 1937 weights[c]	1940 1940 weights[c]	1948 1937 weights[c]	1948 1948 weights[c]	1952[a] 1937 weights[c]	1952[a] 1952 weights[c]	1954[b] 1937 weights[c]	1954[b] 1954 weights[c]
Foods											
Grain products and legumes	11.7	8.5	100	103	103	281	270	134	127	112	109
Meat and poultry	10.1	10.5	100	164	164	390	381	190	188	165	165
Fish	13.0	11.9	100	190	167	357	333	247	229	223	200
Sugar and confectionery	16.7	16.7	100	149	147	343	339	265	262	233	226
Fats	9.8	8.5	100	133	128	327	308	164	161	146	142
Milk and milk products	13.9	13.5	100	133	133	270	268	181	173	181	173
Eggs	8.8	8.8	100	135	135	261	261	170	170	153	153
Vegetables and fruit	22.6	21.8	100	201	169	310	287	241	220	149	138
Salt	45.5	45.5	100	100	100	1364	1364	318	318	200	200
Tea and coffee	7.9	7.9	100	100	100	195	193	128	128	92	92
Alcoholic beverages	13.4	13.4	100	132	131	529	386	283	250	250	216
All foods	13.3	11.2	100	132	125	348	313	198	182	168	158
Manufactured goods											
Textiles	12.3	12.0	100	145	144	337	333	282	272	221	216
Garments	9.9	9.9	100	155	149	270	265	221	216	194	186
Knitwear	27.9	27.9	100	140	139	375	366	339	324	257	248
Shoes	14.5	13.3	100	122	121	251	249	210	207	172	169
Haberdashery and notions	31.7	31.7	100	106	105	428	305	313	226	259	195
Soap, drugs, etc.	28.5	25.2	100	—	—	321	269	196	165	140	121
Housewares	54.4	47.8	100	108	105	282	243	214	185	187	159
Reading matter	62.5	56.3	100	—	—	227	194	218	183	218	183
Cultural and sports goods	34.7	25.9	100	148	147	340	278	261	188	205	170
Kerosene and matches	35.8	31.4	100	100	99	528	546	349	359	187	178
Tobacco products	23.7	14.3	100	133	129	211	205	132	127	123	120
All manufactured goods	16.5	12.3	100	134	128	306	280	240	217	195	182
All commodities	16.5	12.3	100	132	126	335	302	211	193	176	166
Services	41.6	33.8	100	143	142	216	215	231	228	219	213
All commodities and services	19.5	13.6	100	133	128	321	289	213	196	181	171

[a] April 1, 1952, to March 31, 1953. [b] April 1, 1954, to March 31, 1955. [c] The 1937 weights refer to formula (5) given in chapter III; the given-year weights refer to formula (6).

Note: The dash (—) indicates that the item was not priced.

81

as 66 percent greater than the 1937-weighted price index number (23.7).

Two price index numbers will diverge the more, the greater the changes in price structure or the greater the changes in the pattern of consumption that occur between the two years compared. If both types of change take place, they may or may not tend to be mutually offsetting. As has been said, the entire period was characterized by great changes in both consumption pattern and price structure, but the greatest changes occurred between 1928 and 1937. The changes that occurred in the structure of prices between 1928 and 1937 are indeed striking. This is illustrated in Figure 1, which shows the frequency distribution of the price relatives

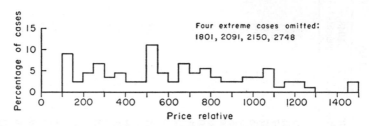

Figure 1. Frequency distribution of 1937 price relatives, 1928 = 100

for 1937 with 1928 as base year; these are computed from the absolute prices shown in Table A-1. The price relatives cover the extremely wide range of 100 (*water*) to 2748 (*sunflower oil*) and show no central tendency. It is not possible here to analyze in detail the nature of the changes in price structure which took place. One outstanding feature, however, is the relatively large rise in prices of animal products, both foods and the textiles, garments, and shoes for which animal products are the major raw materials. This reflects the scarcities of such products resulting from the losses of livestock during collectivization. Taken together with the very large rise in bread prices, it is apparent that the price rise was in general larger for basic necessities than for the less essential commodities.

Alternative weights may lead to very different results when the changes in price structure are so great. And it is clear that the consumption pattern also changed significantly between 1928 and 1937. While it is not surprising that the two index numbers differ greatly for this period, it is by no means easy to account satisfactorily for the nature and extent of the divergence. The index number for 1937 based on 1937 weights is lower than that based on 1928 weights partly because there was, as might be expected, a relative decrease in consumption of some of the products that rose most in price (meat, milk, eggs, textiles, garments, shoes) and a relative increase in the consumption of many goods that showed a smaller than average price increase (sugar and confectionery, haberdashery and notions, cultural and sports goods, reading matter, tobacco).[17] Other substitutions of this nature would be found to lie within rather than between commodity groups. Among grain products, there were shifts from those that rose most in price to those that rose less, most notably a shift from flour to bread. This is the main explanation of the large difference between the two 1928 price index numbers for grain products. Similarly, there was a shift from salt herring, which showed a large relative price rise, to other types of fish.

At the same time, however, there were some contrary movements of the "inferior goods" type. In particular, there was an increase in the relative importance of food in the budget while food prices rose more than other prices, and there was a relative increase in expenditures on grain products, although grain product prices rose more than the average and more than most other food prices.[18] Also, while the price of sunflower oil rose over

[17] Some of the difference between the two index numbers may arise from the different nature of the 1928 and 1937 weights. While the 1928 weights cover urban worker expenditures in all markets, the 1937 weights cover only purchases in state and cooperative shops and, except for the major category weights, are based on total sales in these shops. In terms of total urban worker expenditures in 1937, the 1937 weights understate the importance of meat in particular, food in general, and probably also garments, all of which showed relatively large price increases. Also, they overweight sugar and confectionery, (probably) reading matter and cultural and sports goods, and (possibly) alcoholic beverages and tobacco, all of which showed relatively small price increases. On these grounds, the 1937 weights would tend to minimize the average price rise. On the other hand, some of the divergences of the 1937 weights from the pattern of total urban worker expenditures are such as to exaggerate the price rise. Thus grain, which showed a very large price rise, is overweighted, and milk, vegetables, and fruit, which showed only moderate price rises, are underweighted in relation to total food purchases in all markets. These tendencies may be largely compensatory, and on the whole, errors in the 1937 weights (see fn. 11) apparently do not lead to any significant error in the resulting index numbers.

[18] Peter Wiles, commenting on my preliminary results published in the *Review of Economics and Statistics*, 36:134–156 (May 1954), raises some question as to whether the phenomenon of "inferior goods" actually took place. See P. J. D. Wiles, "Retail Trade, Retail Prices and Real Wages in USSR," *Bulletin of the Oxford University Institute of Statistics*, 16:383 (1954). It is indeed true that detailed data on either budget structure or the structure of retail sales which are comparable enough between 1928 and 1937 to provide firm evidence of this are not available. But there is enough information on output (unsatisfactory as this is in many ways) to show that consumption of animal products must have declined significantly for the entire population and no doubt also for urban workers between 1928 and 1937, while consumption of grain products was probably maintained or somewhat increased and consumption of potatoes increased. (See chapter X.) In light of this and of the fact that bread prices rose as much or more than prices of animal products between 1928 and 1937, there must have been an increase in the proportion of income spent on bread in relation to that spent on animal products.

Telling, if perhaps a bit indirect, evidence may be found also in the trend away from "inferior goods" which took place as real wages rose. Retail sales data which are comparable for the years from 1937 on indicate that in the postwar years foods, although they had become relatively cheaper than manufactured goods, accounted for a smaller share of retail sales than in 1937; similarly, bread, which had become relatively cheaper than meat, accounted for a smaller proportion of retail sales than in 1937. (See Table B-4.)

27 times — more than the price of any other product — expenditures on vegetable oil increased in relation to expenditures on butter and other fats. Presumably this was because sunflower oil was still cheaper than butter in 1937, though custom may also have played a role here.

For the years since 1937, the use of alternative weights does not lead to very great differences in results. The pattern of consumption as shown in the weights (Tables 4 and B-1) indeed changed during the period 1937 to 1954 but changes in the price structure have been much more moderate since 1937 than during the earlier period. The frequency distributions of the 1937-based price relatives for the years 1940, 1948, 1952, and 1954 are shown in Figures 2 through 5. In each case, the spread of price relatives is smaller than for 1928–37 and there is a marked central tendency.

For the years since 1937, the index number using 1937 weights — that is, the Laspeyres index number (formula (5), chapter III) — shows in each case a larger price rise than the given-year weighted or Paasche index number (formula (6)), but the difference is not great. The 1940 Laspeyres price index number of 133 for all commodities and services exceeds the corresponding Paasche price index number of 128 by 5 percentage points or about 4 percent. The 1948 Laspeyres price index number for all commodities and services (321) exceeds the corresponding Paasche price index number (289) by 12 percent. The 1952 Laspeyres price index number for all commodities and services (213) exceeds the corresponding Paasche price index number (196) by 9 percent. The 1954 Laspeyres price index

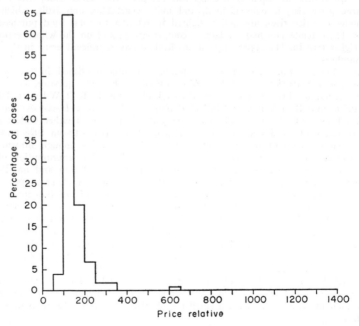

Figure 2. Frequency distribution of 1940 price relatives, 1937 = 100

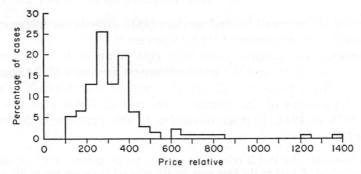

Figure 3. Frequency distribution of 1948 price relatives, 1937 = 100

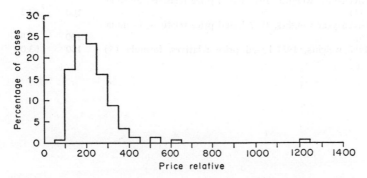

Figure 4. Frequency distribution of 1952 price relatives, 1937 = 100

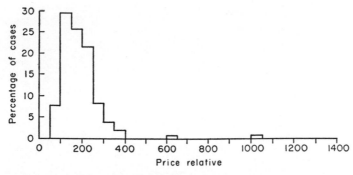

Figure 5. Frequency distribution of 1954 price relatives, 1937 = 100

number for all commodities and services (181) exceeds the corresponding Paasche price index number (171) by 6 percent.[19]

To compare the postwar years with 1928, however, it is necessary to link at the year 1937, and the widely divergent measures of the change in the cost of living between 1928 and 1937 will, of course, result in widely divergent measures of the change in the cost of living over the entire period 1928 to 1954. Further discussion of this problem is deferred to chapter IX.

---

[19] It is interesting also that if price index numbers for the postwar years are computed with 1948 instead of 1937 as the base year for the price relatives, the results are not very different from those shown in Table 5. Alternative computations using 1948 as base year for the price relatives and 1952 and 1954 given-year weights were made following formula (13) for $C_{52}^{48,52}$ and $C_{54}^{48,54}$. The resulting price index numbers for all commodities are compared below with those from Table 5. In all cases, 1948 is set equal to 100:

	1948	1952	1954
Retail price index number, all commodities			
(1) Given-year weights, 1948-based price relatives, formula (13)	100	62.2	53.5
(2) Given-year weights, 1937-based price relatives, formula (6)	100	63.9	55.0
(3) 1937 weights, 1937-based price relatives, formula (5)	100	63.0	52.5

VI·

INDEX NUMBERS OF THE COST OF LIVING IN THE ENTIRE URBAN USSR

THE index numbers of official prices in Moscow already described provide the basis for computing index numbers of average retail prices in all urban areas of the Soviet Union. I first adjust the index numbers of official Moscow prices for the difference in movement between Moscow official and average urban USSR official prices. I then take into account prices prevailing in private trade in 1928 and prices on the collective farm market in later years. The steps in the computation are shown in Table 6. The index numbers in lines 1 through 3 of Table 6 refer to the prices of commodities — foods and manufactured consumer goods. The adjustments are made in the index numbers of prices of commodities but not in the service

TABLE 6

Index Numbers of Urban Retail Prices,
Official Moscow, Official USSR, and Average USSR Prices, and
Cost-of-Living Index Numbers, 1928–54
(1937 = 100)

Index number[a]	1928	1937	1940	1944	1948	1952	1954
1. Official prices, commodities, Moscow							
a. 1937 weights	16.5	100	132	(143)[b]	335	214	178
b. Given-year weights	12.3	100	126	—	302	195	168
2. Official prices, commodities, urban USSR							
a. 1937 weights	15.6	100	132	(143)[b]	335	214	178
b. Given-year weights	11.4	100	126	—	302	195	168
3. Average prices all markets, commodities, urban USSR							
a. 1937 weights	18.1	100	142	(203)	342	218	184
b. Given-year weights	13.0	100	135	—	308	199	174
4. Cost of living; average prices all markets, commodities and services, urban USSR							
a. 1937 weights	20.9	100	142	(199)	327	220	188
b. Given-year weights	14.3	100	136	—	294	202	178

[a] The 1937 weights refer to formula (5) given in chapter III; the given-year weights refer to formula (6).
[b] Ration prices.
Note: The dash (—) indicates that data were not computed.
Sources and methods: For 1944 see appendix D; for other years see text.

price index numbers.[1] Once the index numbers of retail prices of commodities are adjusted, these are then combined with the index numbers of service prices (as shown in Table 5) to obtain the index numbers of average retail prices of all commodities and services in all markets in the entire urban USSR. These are the cost-of-living index numbers. They are shown in lines 4a and 4b of Table 6.

The Moscow price index numbers for 1952 and 1954 as well as those for other years shown in Table 6 refer to the calendar year. The 1952 and 1954 Moscow price index numbers shown in Table 5 were computed for the year April 1 of the given year to March 31 of the following year but are here adjusted to a calendar year basis.[2]

In section 1, I explain the adjustment for the difference between Moscow and average urban USSR official price movements. In section 2, I describe the adjustment for prices prevailing in private trade during 1928. Section 3 deals with prices on the collective farm market. There I present and describe an index number of collective farm market prices for the period 1937 to 1954. I explain my estimates of the gap between the official and free market prices and the method of taking this into account in the price index numbers. In section 4, I derive the final index numbers of the cost of living covering services as well as commodities.

I. MOSCOW AND AVERAGE URBAN USSR OFFICIAL PRICES

1928–37. Regional price data for 1928 are very limited and the estimate of the difference between the movement of Moscow official prices and average official prices in the entire USSR is of necessity rather rough. It was possible to obtain 1928 average USSR official prices as well as Moscow official prices for twenty consumer goods, and these prices can be compared with similar quotations for 1936. With regard to the 1928 average prices, in some cases the average is for all urban points in the USSR, in others the average is for 45 provincial capitals in the European part of the USSR, and in still others the average is for the district (*uezd*) towns. The 1936 average USSR official prices are computed from the zonal or urban-rural price differentials shown in the 1936 retail price handbooks. I cal-

---

[1] Similar adjustments are made in the index numbers of average prices prevailing in all Soviet markets, which take into account rural prices also. See appendix E.

[2] The adjustment was made on the basis of the following data: According to the retail price index numbers in TSU, *Sovetskaia torgovlia; Statisticheskii sbornik* (Moscow, 1956), p. 132, retail prices prior to the price reduction of April 1, 1952, were 6 percent higher than after this price reduction. The price index applicable to the first quarter of 1952 is then 6 percent higher than my price index number as computed for the period from April 1, 1952. Sales during the first quarter of 1952 were 23.7 percent of total annual sales in state and cooperative shops and restaurants; see M. M. Lifits (ed.), *Ekonomika sovetskoi torgovli* (Moscow, 1955), p. 239. In 1954, according to the same sources, retail prices in effect prior to the price reduction of April 1 exceeded by 4.7 percent those following the reduction, and first quarter sales were 22.8 percent of total sales for the year in state and cooperative shops and restaurants.

culate the price effective in each price zone and then weight the zonal prices according to the 1939 population of that zone. In the case of food products, the urban population is used in weighting as the bulk of foods are sold in urban areas. In the case of manufactured consumer goods, the total population of each zone is used in weighting for zonal price differentials and the estimated country-wide distribution of retail sales between urban and rural areas is used in weighting for the urban-rural price differential.[3] The Moscow and average USSR official prices for 1928 and 1936 are shown in Table 7.

TABLE 7

Moscow and Average USSR Official Retail Prices of Selected Commodities, 1928 and 1936

| Commodity | Unit | Price in rubles per unit | | | |
| | | 1928 | | 1936 | |
		Moscow	USSR	Moscow	USSR
Rye flour	kg	0 11	0.09	1.60	1.48
Rye bread	kg	0.08	0.09	0.85	0.82
Wheat bread, 80 to 85 percent	kg	0.24	0.18	1.70	1.62
Buckwheat grits	kg	0.20	0.20	4.30	4.20
Millet grits	kg	0.16	0.15	2.10	1.99
Beef	kg	0.86	0.66	7.60	7.45
Sugar, lump	kg	0.70	0.71	4.10	4.28
Sugar, granulated	kg	0.62	0.62	3.80	3.98
Butter, rendered	kg	2.26	2.26	18.50	18.12
Sunflower oil	kg	0.53	0.52	13.50	13.50
Salt	kg	0.05	0.04	0.11	0.12
Vodka 40°	½ liter	0.88	0.88	6.55	6.55
Calico	meter	0.31	0.32	3.15	3.23
Rubbers	pair	3.55	3.55	22.00	22.00
Household soap	kg	0.36	0.54	2.90	2.93
Book	one	2.30	2.30	3.00	3.00
Kerosene	liter	0.10	0.10	0.47	0.55
Matches	10 boxes	0.15	0.15	0.25	0.25
Makhorka	100 gm	0.13	0.13	0.75	0.75
Cigarettes	25	0.14	0.14	0.35	0.35

Sources and methods:
    1928, Moscow: Table A-1 and appendix A. The prices for millet grits and sunflower oil shown here differ from those in Table A-1 as they relate only to part of the year. The calico priced here is a different quality from that priced in Table A-1.
    1928, USSR: TSUNKHU, *Narodnoe khoziaistvo SSSR* (Moscow, 1932), pp. 348–349; *Sovetskaia torgovlia,* no. 8, 1928, p. 37, and no. 45–46, 1928, p. 70. The prices of the following products were uniform for the entire country and the Moscow quotations are accordingly used: vodka, rubbers, books, matches, makhorka, and cigarettes.
    1936, Moscow: Table A-1 and appendix A; Janet Chapman, *The Regional Structure of Soviet Retail Prices,* The RAND Corporation, RM-425, July 20, 1950; Z. L. Nozhkina, *et al.* (comps.), *Sbornik otpusknykh i roznichnykh tsen i torgovykh nakidok na prodovol'stvennye tovary* (Moscow, 1936), and *Otpusknye i roznichnye tseny i torgovye nakidki na promtovary* (Moscow, 1936).
    1936, USSR: Chapman, *The Regional Structure of Soviet Retail Prices.* Some additional average USSR prices not presented in that study are computed here in the same manner.

The 1928 average prices relate to urban areas only. The 1936 average prices are averages for the entire country, including rural as well as urban

[3] The procedure is described in more detail in Janet G. Chapman, *The Regional Structure of Soviet Retail Prices,* The RAND Corporation, RM-425, July 20, 1950. Most of the 1936 quotations used in the present computation are from that study.

areas. There was, however, so little difference at that time between urban and rural prices that the 1936 averages may be considered as urban averages and rather closely comparable with the 1928 urban averages. The 1936 relationship between Moscow official and average USSR official prices may be taken as representative of that prevailing in 1937 as there was no change in the regional structure of prices between 1936 and 1937.

Price index numbers computed from the Moscow and average USSR prices of this sample of twenty commodities indicate that average USSR prices rose somewhat more than Moscow prices between 1928 and 1937. When 1928 weights are used, the sample index numbers indicate an 8 percent greater rise in USSR average official prices than in Moscow official prices; when 1937 weights are used the difference is 6 percent. The two price index numbers for 1928 are adjusted accordingly. (See Table 6, lines 2a and 2b.) They then represent the change between 1928 and 1937 in average urban USSR official retail prices.

1937–54. For the years since 1937 the movement of Moscow official prices is taken as representative of the movement of average official prices in the entire USSR. The index numbers for these years in lines 2a and 2b of Table 6, therefore, are the same as those in lines 1a and 1b. For the years 1936 and 1948 a detailed study of regional pricing in the Soviet Union was made.[4] This study indicates that so far as official prices are concerned the change in Moscow prices can be considered as representative of the change in average prices in the USSR as a whole between 1937 and 1948. The evidence for this conclusion is summarized briefly here.

A comparison of the change between 1936 and 1948 in the Moscow and average USSR official prices of seventeen individual foods and seven manufactured consumer goods, the prices of which varied regionally in at least one of the two years, was made. The average USSR prices were computed from the zonal and urban-rural price differentials prevailing in each year weighted by the 1939 population of each zone or area as described briefly above and in more detail in my study, *The Regional Structure of Soviet Retail Prices.* In very few of the twenty-four price comparisons did the rise in the Moscow price between 1936 and 1948 differ from the rise in the average USSR price by more than 5 percent. Price index numbers for Moscow and for the entire USSR computed on the basis of the prices of the same twenty-four commodities differed by less than 3 percent.[5] Although the number of commodities included in these index numbers is small, the regional price pattern of an included item is in most cases representative of that of a group of similar commodities not included in the

[4] *Ibid.*

[5] These price index numbers are subject to numerous shortcomings, but the shortcomings affect the Moscow index number and the USSR index number about equally and the results seem reliable so far as the comparison of Moscow and average USSR price changes is concerned.

computations. The price index numbers cover only commodities of which the Moscow price differed from the average USSR price in at least one of the two years. The two price index numbers would be even closer if commodities with prices that were uniform for the entire country were represented.[6]

The foregoing study is based on average prices in the entire USSR including rural areas but the findings are approximately true also of average urban USSR prices. A few qualifying comments, however, should be made. (a) Prices of the major manufactured consumer goods — textiles, garments, knitwear, and shoes — were differentiated both zonally and between urban and rural areas in 1937, with Moscow always in the lowest price zone. In 1948, prices of these commodities, though still differing between urban and rural areas, were uniform for the entire urban USSR. Thus for these goods the Moscow price rise was somewhat greater than the average urban USSR price rise.[7] (b) It was not possible to take into account prices of perishable seasonal foods. The divergence between Moscow and average urban USSR movements in the prices of such products may have been a good deal greater than in the case of other products. The prices of these products were set locally in 1937 and, it is believed, exhibited wide local as well as regional variation.[8] Some prices of agricultural products are still fixed locally,[9] but there must be much more uni-

[6] Information on the geographic price patterns of commodities for which specific comparable price quotations for 1936 and 1948 are not available tends to confirm the results of the Moscow and USSR price index numbers. The nature of the changes that took place in regional price patterns between 1936 and 1948 was such as to suggest limits to the amount by which the movement of Moscow prices could have diverged from the movement of average USSR prices. Uniform prices were applicable in the entire USSR in the case of many commodities in both years. In 1948 there were fewer price zones and the zonal price differentials were generally smaller than in 1936. In the 1948 zonal price arrangements, Moscow was in the middle of three price zones for all foods for which data are available, excepting fish and fruit (for which it is in the highest of three price zones), and salt (for which it is in the lower of two price zones). In 1936, Moscow was in the third lowest of seven price zones for bread and other grain products, in the second of seven zones for salt, in the second of four zones for sugar and vegetable oil, and in the fourth of five zones for meat and fish. There were thus some definite changes in the relative position of Moscow prices. But since Moscow was rarely or never in either the highest or lowest price zone in 1936 and was usually in the middle price zone in 1948, it would seem that there could not have been very large divergences between the Moscow and average USSR changes in food prices.

[7] Taking urban and rural areas together, the increase in the urban-rural price differential was such as approximately to offset the effect of the change from zonal to uniform prices, and the difference between the rise in Moscow prices and the rise in average prices for the entire USSR was negligible in the case of these types of commodities.

[8] For example, in Moscow Oblast exclusive of Moscow city, the price of milk ranged from 0.80 rubles to 1.20 rubles per liter in 1936. See Moskovskii oblastnoi otdel vnutrennei torgovli, *Spravochnik roznichnykh tsen na prodovol'stvennye tovary po Moskovskoi oblasti* (Moscow, 1936), p. 72. At the same time, the price in Moscow city was 1.30 rubles per liter, according to the *Monthly Labor Review*, November 1939.

[9] L. Maizenberg, *Tsenoobrazovanie v narodnom khoziaistve SSSR* (Moscow, 1953), p. 166.

formity in the prices of such products than during 1937. The December 1947 price decree established zonal prices for some of the more important seasonal products, and the decree of August 14, 1954 greatly extended the list of seasonal products for which there are centrally established zonal prices. As the Moscow prices of seasonal products were, it is believed, generally higher than the prices in smaller cities and towns in 1937, this should mean that Moscow prices rose less than prices elsewhere in the urban USSR in the case of seasonal foods.[10] This may tend to offset the somewhat greater rise in Moscow than in average urban USSR prices of the major manufactured consumer goods.

Moscow price movements should also be representative of average urban USSR price movements for the period 1937 to 1940. No special investigation of regional price patterns prevailing in 1940 could be made. In 1939 there were some reductions in the number of price zones for zonally priced food products[11] but no details on these changes are available. As Moscow was generally in an intermediary zone prior to this change, the relationship between Moscow and average USSR prices may not have been much affected.

Between 1937 and 1944 Moscow price movements can also be taken as representative of average urban price movements. The ration prices prevailing during 1944 were, with only a few exceptions, the same as those in effect in late 1940.[12] So far as prices in the commercial shops are concerned, it is not known whether these varied locally or regionally; if prices on the free market were taken into account in fixing the commercial shop prices, there may have been some regional variation. In any case, sales in the commercial shops were so small a share of total sales in state and cooperative shops in 1944 that we may safely ignore the possibility that the relationship between Moscow and average USSR prices in the commercial shops differed from that prevailing in the ration shops.[13]

Since 1948, all announced retail price changes have applied uniformly to the entire USSR. Accordingly, Moscow price movements since 1948 are representative of average price movements in the entire USSR and in urban localities alone. As this was found to be true of the period 1937 to 1948, the price index numbers based on Moscow official prices for 1952 and 1954 can be considered as index numbers of average official prices in the entire USSR or in the urban areas of the USSR for the period 1937 to 1952 and 1954.

[10] This point was overlooked in Chapman, *The Regional Structure of Soviet Retail Prices.*

[11] Lifits (ed.), *Ekonomika sovetskoi torgovli,* p. 93.

[12] See appendix D.

[13] For some manufactured consumer goods, at this time a special set of rural prices was established, above the urban ration prices but below the prices charged in the urban commercial shops. See "Special Rural Prices" in appendix E. Thus Moscow price movements between 1937 and 1944 are not representative of rural price movements.

2. AVERAGE PRICES IN ALL MARKETS, 1928

In 1937, for reasons set forth in chapter II, it is believed the Soviet retail market was operating relatively effectively, and there was little or no gap between the official prices in state and cooperative shops and prices on the collective farm market. Accordingly, 1937 official prices are taken as representative of prices on the collective farm market in that year. In 1928, however, prices in private shops considerably exceeded prices in the state and cooperative shops, and this must be taken into account in the index numbers for 1928. My estimate of the gap in 1928 between the official prices and those in private trade, and also of the difference between official prices and average prices in all markets (that is, both private and official) is based on the retail price index numbers published by the Soviet Central Statistical Administration (TSU). Three retail price index numbers were computed and published by TSU at that time — an index number of official prices in state and cooperative shops, an index number of prices in private trade, and an index number of average weighted prices in both markets. As the base for the TSU index numbers was 1913 when a single open market existed, it can be assumed that the differences among the various TSU price index numbers for 1928 reflect the differences in 1928 between the price levels in the various markets. Soviet economists have used these index numbers in this way.[14] One Soviet source, however, points out that the difference between the index number of official prices and that of prices in private trade reflects differences in the commodities priced and in the commodity weights in the two index numbers as well as differences in the price levels in the two markets.[15]

The TSU retail price index numbers for the economic year 1927/28 (October 1, 1927 through September 30, 1928) and for the fourth quarter of 1928 are shown in Table 8. This table shows also the ratio between the prices in private trade and the official prices, and the ratio between the average prices in both markets and the official prices. The TSU retail price index numbers shown in Table 8 are described as "All-Union" index numbers but apparently they actually relate only to cities, and probably only to large cities.[16] They may not, then, be closely representative of the entire urban USSR. Prices prevailing on the free peasant market are, so far as can be determined, taken into account in the TSU retail price index number of average prices in all markets only beginning with the fourth

[14] M. Mudrik, "Kapitalisticheskaia torgovlia v gorodakh SSSR v 1927/28 g.," *Statisticheskoe obozrenie*, no. 11, 1929, p. 93.

[15] "Sistema detsentralizovannykh indeksov roznichnykh tsen TSU," *Statisticheskoe obozrenie*, no. 8, 1929, p. 119.

[16] According to *ibid.*, pp. 115 and 119, the index numbers for large cities covered 117 cities and the index numbers for medium-sized cities covered 257 cities and towns. But data collected for the medium-sized cities were not published. The sample may have been somewhat smaller in 1927 and 1928.

TABLE 8

Relation between Official, Private, and Average Retail Prices, USSR, 1927/28,
as Shown in the TSU Retail Price Index Numbers

Period and product category	TSU retail price index (1913 = 100)			Prices in private shops as percent of prices in official shops	Average prices in all shops as percent of prices in official shops
	Official shops	Private shops	All shops		
October 1927 through September 1928:					
Agricultural products	176	261	209	148.3	118.7
Industrial products	189	242	205	128.0	108.5
All products	184	250	207	135.9	112.5
October 1928 through December 1928:					
Agricultural products	181	308	227	170.2	125.4
Industrial products	188	259	210	137.8	111.7
All products	185	277	217	149.7	117.3
1928 calendar year:					
Agricultural products	—	—	—	153.8	120.4
Industrial products	—	—	—	130.5	109.3
All products	—	—	—	139.4	113.7

Note: The dash (—) indicates that data were not available.
Source: *Statisticheskoe obozrenie*, no. 10, 1928, p. 154; no. 1, 1929, p. 157. The 1928 calendar-year ratio is computed in each case by weighting the ratio for October 1927 through September 1928 by ¾ and the ratio for October 1928 through December 1928 by ¼.

quarter of 1928, but not in the index number for 1927/28. Too little is known about the peasant market to attempt to make any adjustment for this omission.

The weights used in computing the TSU retail price index numbers are based on the structure by commodity group of sales in the various markets.[17] The basic data from which the weights were computed relate, it is believed, to 1925/26, though there may have been some adjustments to take into account subsequent changes in the commodity structure of sales or in the relative share of the different markets. The share of private shops, and probably also of the peasant market, in total retail sales was declining over this period. If the market weights used in constructing the TSU index number of average prices in all markets were not adjusted for this, the index number would tend to overstate the gap between official prices and prices in all markets.

The TSU retail price index numbers have many shortcomings that are mainly the result of the inadequacies of the data available to the Soviet statisticians of the time. Data available to a Western economist of today

[17] *Ibid.*, p. 117. Weights for the TSU retail price index numbers for large cities are shown in this source. These are revised weights and were probably not used in computing the index numbers for 1927/28, but may have been used in the index numbers for the fourth quarter of 1928.

are much too limited to provide a basis for an independent computation, and the TSU retail price index numbers appear to provide the best available basis for estimating the differences between average prices in all markets and those in the state and cooperative shops. It can be said that the Soviet statisticians of the period were interested in obtaining a truthful picture of the relationships among the various markets. Furthermore, there seems to be a general agreement among the various studies of the period — a period in which research was characterized by considerably more independence and objectivity and less uniformity than in later years — as to the relationship between official prices and those on the private markets and between official prices and average prices in all markets.[18]

According to the TSU retail price index numbers as averaged for the calendar year 1928 and shown in Table 8, prices in private trade exceeded prices in state and cooperative shops by 54 percent in the case of agricultural products, by 30.5 percent in the case of industrial products,[19] and by an average of 39 percent for all products. And average retail prices in all markets (including the official) were almost 14 percent higher than prices in the official outlets only. Since the TSU weights among the various commodity groups are not entirely appropriate for my purposes, a recomputation of the gap between average prices in all markets and official prices is made on the basis of the TSU price index numbers for each commodity group[20] and my sets of 1928 and 1937 group weights. These computations indicate that when 1928 weights are used, average prices in all markets were about 14 percent above the official prices. The result is the same as that computed directly from the TSU index numbers for all commodities. The index number of average urban USSR official prices using 1928 weights in Table 6, line 2b, is accordingly multiplied by 1.14 to obtain the index number of average retail prices in all urban markets shown in Table 6, line 3b. When 1937 commodity group weights are used, the gap between official prices and average prices in all markets averages about 16 percent.[21] The 1928 index number of average urban official prices using 1937

[18] Compare the TSU retail price index numbers in Table 8 with the retail price index numbers computed by the Institute of Economic Trends of the Peoples' Commissariat of Finance and the cost-of-living index number computed by the USSR Central Bureau of Labor Statistics shown in Solomon Schwarz, *Labor in the Soviet Union* (New York, 1951), pp. 134–135. Maizenberg's statement in *Tsenoobrazovanie v narodnom khoziaistve SSSR,* p. 41, that in 1927/28 state and cooperative shops sold their goods at prices 33 percent cheaper than the private shopkeepers is also in accord with the TSU retail price index numbers.

[19] "Industrial products" include processed foods such as sugar, salt, tea, vegetable oil, and also fish and alcoholic beverages, according to the classification system of the period.

[20] The TSU retail price index numbers are presented for 18 separate commodity groups as well as for "agricultural products," "industrial products," and "all products" in *Statisticheskoe obozrenie,* no. 10, 1928, p. 154, and no. 1, 1929, p. 157.

[21] The 1937 weights used in this computation have since been revised. The revisions are such as would probably result in a somewhat smaller gap between official prices and those in all markets in 1928, but the resulting error in the cost-of-living index number is probably insignificant.

weights in Table 6, line 2a, is accordingly multiplied by 1.16 to obtain the index number of average urban USSR retail prices in all markets shown in Table 6, line 3a.

3. COLLECTIVE FARM MARKET PRICES, 1937–54

The paucity of data on the collective farm market and the wide variations in market conditions from town to town are such that it is impossible to make a reliable independent computation of the movement of prices on the collective farm market in the Soviet Union. I made various attempts to do this during the long period of Soviet silence on the collective farm market, but in view of the recent publication of an official Soviet index number, I now rely heavily on Soviet data. In particular, I use the official Soviet index number of collective farm market prices for the period 1940 on. But the information on the collective farm market available even to the Soviet statisticians is inadequate, and their statistics on the collective farm market are not very reliable. As John T. Whitman puts it: "The chief conclusion to be derived from an examination of statistical texts is that the market data are among the least reliable and least complete of the multitude of economic statistics available to the authorities. These deficiencies are the result of the diffuse, individualized, uncontrolled operations of the market and of the fact that, not being part of the plan, they command a low priority in the hierarchy of statistical tasks." [22] The Soviet methods of collecting and collating statistics on the collective farm market are described and the shortcomings of their collective farm market price index numbers and other data are discussed in appendix C. Here I shall briefly outline the main shortcomings of the Soviet data.

The raw price and quantity data are for the most part the estimates of recording clerks stationed at the market place. As trade at the markets is carried on by millions of individuals, it will be obvious that there is room for considerable error in the estimates of the volume of the various goods sold and of the average prices prevailing in a given market at a given time, no matter how expert the reporting officials may be. Too, there have been some complaints in the Soviet press about the lack of adequately trained officials for the job. Such data are collected only for a sample of products and only in a sample of cities. There have been changes in the size of the sample over the years, and this may introduce some bias in the index number. The sample, furthermore, is dominated by large cities and, by Soviet admission, it is not representative of collective farm market trade in all urban areas of the USSR. The data for the sample cities form the basis for the index numbers of prices, of volume of sales, and for the estimates of total sales in physical and value terms for all urban collective farm markets of the USSR. However, various adjustments of the results of the sample study are made on the basis of information on agricultural

[22] John T. Whitman, "The *Kolkhoz* Market," *Soviet Studies,* 7:385(1956).

output and procurements, farm consumption, incomes and expenditures of the population, et cetera. The nature of these adjustments is not described in the Soviet statistical texts. Undoubtedly they lead to results more applicable to the entire urban collective farm market than the results based only on the sample.[23] But it is clear that the official Soviet index numbers of collective farm market prices and sales, as well as their figures for total collective farm market sales valued at current market prices, are essentially rough estimates. Accordingly, my collective farm market price index numbers based on the Soviet data are subject to a wide margin of error.

Some price quotations for the Moscow collective farm market in various years are available, and I have made some computations on the basis of these. Recently published Soviet data make it clear that Moscow collective farm market prices and price movements are not typical of those on the collective farm markets in the rest of the country.[24] Hence my estimates of the movement of collective farm market prices based on the Moscow prices cannot be used. As they may be of some interest in themselves, however, the results for those years for which such computations were made will be briefly indicated in the discussion below.

The index numbers of prices on the collective farm market used in this study are shown in Table 9. These index numbers are probably best

TABLE 9

Index Numbers of Collective Farm Market Prices,
Urban USSR, 1937–54
(1937 = 100)

Year	Collective farm market price index number
1937	100
1940	200
1944	2200
1948	350
1952	208
1954	214

Sources and methods: See text.

considered as approximations to the Paasche type of index number. My own index number of collective farm market prices in 1940 is in principle equivalent to a Paasche index number. For the years from 1940 on, my index numbers are based on the official Soviet index number. As described in the statistical manuals, the Soviet index number of prices on the col-

[23] Some comparisons between the Soviet index numbers of prices and volume of sales on the collective farm market in the sample cities and those for the entire urban USSR are shown in appendix C, Tables C-1 through C-4.

[24] See appendix C, especially Table C-2, and L. Mazel', "Ob urovne tsen na gorodskikh kolkhoznykh rynkakh," *Sovetskaia torgovlia,* no. 9, 1956, pp. 11–17.

lective farm market is computed according to a given-year weighted aggregative formula.[25] The sources, although not entirely clear on this point, suggest that the index numbers are computed on a year-to-year basis, using weights of the second year in each case, and are then chained for comparisons of periods longer than a year. If this is true, the Soviet index numbers of collective farm market prices are not Paasche index numbers.[26] But since given-year weights are used in their computation, I assume the resulting index numbers are closer to the results that would be given by the Paasche than by the Laspeyres formula.

In 1937, as has been said, prices on the collective farm market are assumed to have been equal to the official prices in state and cooperative shops. Accordingly, no adjustment is required in the retail price index number for 1937.

The index number of collective farm market prices for 1937–40, shown in Table 9, is computed from data on the volume of sales of some of the most important products sold on the collective farm market in 1937 and 1940 and on 1937 collective farm market prices of these products. These data are estimates of J. F. Karcz, and are shown in Table 10. Valuing the

TABLE 10

Collective Farm Market Prices and Sales, Selected Products,
USSR: Prices 1937, Sales 1937 and 1940

Product	1937 Market price (rubles per ton)	Physical volume of sales (million tons)		Value of sales at 1937 prices (million rubles)	
		1937	1940	1937	1940
Grain products	1,000	2.5	0.7	2,500	700
Potatoes	600	2.8	2.2	1,680	1,320
Milk and milk products	1,200	2.2	2.3	2,640	2,760
Meat and livestock, live weight	3,400	1.1	1.2	3,740	4,080
Totals	—	—	—	10,560	8,860

Note: The dash (—) means not applicable.
Source: J. F. Karcz, *Soviet Agricultural Marketings and Prices, 1928–1954*, The RAND Corporation, RM-1930, July 2, 1957.

physical volume of sales in each year at the 1937 collective farm market prices, I compute an index number of the volume of sales in 1940 at about 84 percent of the volume of sales in 1937. At current prices, total sales on the urban collective farm market amounted to 17.8 billion rubles in 1937 and to 29.1 billion rubles in 1940,[27] or 163 percent of the value of sales in

[25] TSU, *Slovar'-spravochnik po sotsial'no-ekonomicheskoi statistike* (Moscow, 1944), p. 178; N. Riauzov and N. Titel'baum, *Kurs torgovoi statistiki* (Moscow, 1947), p. 150.
[26] Possibly the comparison between 1940 and 1950 is made directly rather than through links covering all the intervening years. If so, the index number for 1940–50 is a Paasche index number.
[27] See Table 1.

1937. An index number of the value of sales of 163 and a volume index number of 84 imply a price index number of 194. This is raised to a round 200. Inasmuch as the volume index number is weighted by base-year (1937) prices, the resulting price index number is equivalent to a given-year weighted or Paasche price index number.

Karcz feels his estimates of the 1940 physical volume of sales on the collective farm market are subject to a wide margin of error. The same, of course, is true of my index number of collective farm market prices in 1940, which is derived from his estimates. There is scattered evidence to support a 1940 index number of collective farm market prices of roughly the estimated magnitude, but the error might be as great as 50 percentage points. This is unfortunate, as the 1937–40 price index number is, of necessity, used as a link in computing the index numbers of collective farm market prices for later years.

Using very limited data on collective farm market prices in Moscow in 1940, two index numbers of the change in Moscow collective farm market prices between 1937 and 1940 were computed by the author. The extremely crude result was 266 when 1937 weights were used and 232 when 1940 weights were used; that is, some 16 to 33 percent higher than the index number shown above for the entire urban USSR.[28]

[28] The procedure in computing these Moscow price index numbers was first to estimate the gap prevailing in 1940 between the official prices and the Moscow collective farm market prices for four groups of commodities of major importance in collective farm market trade — meat, dairy products, vegetables and fruit, and eggs. For the first third of 1940 this gap is based on the free market prices prevailing in Moscow on January 1, 1940, shown in Table 2. No free market quotations were located for the other dates in 1940. On the basis of a single statement in an unpublished report that the gap between the free market and the official prices in Moscow in July 1940 averaged 20 to 40 percent, I assume that the gap averaged 30 percent for the remainder of 1940. Clearly the estimated average gap for the entire year is extremely tenuous. The next step was to obtain 1937–40 collective farm market group price index numbers for these four groups of commodities by multiplying the 1937–40 index numbers of official prices of each of these commodity groups by the estimated average gap between official and free market prices in 1940. Free market prices in 1937 can be assumed to be about the same as the official prices, and 1937 official prices can be used as a base for an index number of prices on the collective farm market in other years. This was done both for the group price index numbers of official prices using 1937 weights and those using 1940 weights, so that I obtained in this way both 1937-weighted and 1940-weighted group index numbers of 1940 collective farm market prices. The weights within each commodity group here refer to the structure of sales in state and cooperative shops. Finally, the 1937-weighted group price index numbers of collective farm market prices in 1940 were weighted according to the estimated relative importance of the four groups in collective farm market sales in 1937. Similarly, the 1940-weighted group price index numbers of collective farm market prices in 1940 were weighted according to the estimated relative importance of each group in sales on the collective farm market in 1940. These collective farm market weights, particularly for 1940, are also very rough estimates. Altogether the calculations are so tenuous at every step that they cannot be relied on even for collective farm market prices in Moscow, let alone the entire USSR. However, the results showing the rise in collective farm market prices between 1937 and 1940 as greater in Moscow than in the rest of the USSR seem generally consistent with what is known about the relationship between Moscow and average USSR free market prices.

The index number of collective farm market prices in 1944 is based on quarterly index numbers of prices on the urban collective farm market in 1944, published in a recent Soviet source. With average annual 1940 collective farm market prices as 100, these index numbers are as follows: January 1944, 1317; April 1944, 1488; July 1944, 1160; October 1944, 758; January 1945, 754.[29] The average for the entire year 1944 comes to about 1100 percent of 1940, or 2200 percent of 1937.

For 1944, account must also be taken of prices in the commercial shops. The 1944 index number of official prices shown in Table 6, lines 1a and 2a, is the index number of ration prices. Sales in the commercial shops are treated in the same manner as sales on the collective farm market. As explained in appendix D, scattered data suggest that prices in the commercial shops were at approximately the same level as prices on the collective farm market in 1944, though in later years commercial shop prices were probably somewhat lower than collective farm market prices. Thus I use the 1944 index number of collective farm market prices as indicative also of the degree to which prices in the commercial shops in 1944 exceeded the official prices prevailing in state and cooperative shops in 1937.

Scattered quotations for the Moscow collective farm market and commercial shops during the early part of 1944 seem generally higher than the estimated index number of collective farm market prices would indicate. But Moscow prices may well have been higher than in much of the rest of the country; and, as prices were declining during 1944, the quotations for the early part of the year would be higher than the average annual prices. The Soviet index numbers of collective farm market prices for the war years, on which I rely, must be even less reliable than for other years as the sample of cities for which collective farm market statistics were reported fell to only 36 during the war.[30] And again, my rather doubtful 1937–40 index number enters into the computation of that for 1944 with 1937 as base. Fortunately, however, even a very large error in the 1937–44 index number of collective farm market and commercial shop prices would have very little effect on the cost-of-living index number. At current market prices, sales to urban households on the collective farm market in 1944 were about 30 billion rubles, and sales in the commercial shops were 6 billion rubles, together amounting to about 30 percent of all retail sales to urban households. But because of the very large gap between prices in these markets and the ration prices, sales on the collective farm market and in the commercial shops amounted to less than 3 percent of total retail sales to urban households in real terms.[31]

For the period 1948 to 1954 my index numbers of collective farm market prices are based on the Soviet index number of collective farm market

[29] *Finansy i sotsialisticheskoe stroitel'stvo* (Moscow, 1957), p. 39.
[30] Whitman, *Soviet Studies*, 7:385(1956). See also appendix C.
[31] See Table 12.

prices for the years 1950 to 1954 with 1940 as base year, as published in TSU, *Sovetskaia torgovlia; Statisticheskii sbornik*. My index number of collective farm market prices for the period 1940 to 1948 is a fairly rough projection from the Soviet index number for 1940–50. The Soviet index number for 1950 is 105 percent of 1940. I assume the index number in 1948 was 175 percent of 1940. In 1949, prices on the collective farm market are reported to have been 29 percent lower than in 1948.[32] I assume a further fall in collective farm market prices between 1949 and 1950 of about 15 percent. This is an arbitrary estimate but seems reasonable in light of the "continued" price decline reported in the 1950 Annual Plan Fulfillment Report and the "considerable" price decline noted in another Soviet source.[33]

An index number computed on the basis of limited quotations of collective farm market prices in Moscow in 1948 comes close to 400 percent of 1937.[34] This is about 14 percent higher than the estimated price index number for all urban collective farm markets shown in Table 9. It is fairly certain that Moscow free market prices rose more than average urban USSR free market prices between 1940 and 1948,[35] and probably this was true also of the whole period 1937 to 1948. In light of this, the computations for Moscow seem broadly consistent with and lend some support to my estimate for the entire urban collective farm market.

[32] G. L. Rubinshtein, *et al.*, *Ekonomika sovetskoi torgovli* (Moscow, 1950), p. 364; *Bol'shaia sovetskaia entsiklopediia*, 2d ed., vol. 22, p. 76. I assume that this refers to average prices on all urban collective farm markets. It may be, however, that reference is only to the sample of cities for which free market statistics are regularly reported; the 1949 Annual Plan Fulfillment Report states only that free market prices "continued to decline." See *Pravda*, January 18, 1950.

[33] *Pravda*, January 26, 1951; Rubinshtein, *et al.*, *Ekonomika sovetskoi torgovli*, p. 363. A source that became available after these estimates were made indicates that prices on the collective farm markets in the sample of 71 large cities declined by 33 percent between 1948 and 1950. See I. D. Ignatov, "Razvitie kolkhoznoi torgovli," in B. I. Gogol' (ed.), *Sorok let sovetskoi torgovli* (Moscow, 1957), p. 116. This compares with my estimate that prices in all urban collective farm markets declined by about 40 percent between 1948 and 1950.

[34] The average relationship between the Moscow free market price and the official price prevailing during 1948 is estimated for nine representative commodities, with collective farm market prices given as a percentage of official prices, as follows: beef, 113; milk, 146; butter, 100; potatoes, 138; onions, 118; cabbage, 100; tomatoes, 100; beets, 100; and eggs, 145. These ratios are based on official quotations from appendix A and unpublished materials. For five of the nine commodities, the average 1948 collective farm market-official price ratio is based on Moscow quotations for nine to twelve months of 1948, and for the other commodities on quotations for one to six months. Thus the average gap for the year can be estimated with a fair degree of confidence. There are, however, doubts as to whether the official and free market quotations compared at any date are for precisely comparable commodities. The index number of collective farm market prices in Moscow is estimated from these ratios, the 1937–48 index numbers of official prices of the same commodity groups, and the estimated 1937 collective farm market weights. The procedure is similar to that employed in computing the 1937-weighted index number of collective farm market prices in 1940 described above.

[35] See Table C-2.

For 1952 and 1954 the index numbers of collective farm market prices shown in Table 9 are computed by linking the Soviet index numbers for these years, with 1940 as base, to my index number for 1940, with 1937 as base. The Soviet index number with 1940 = 100 is 104 in 1952 and 107 in 1954.[36] The Soviet index numbers of collective farm market prices cannot be relied on very heavily, but they are probably more accurate than any index number that could be computed independently on the basis of the very limited available data. It is not clear whether prices in commission trade are taken into account in the Soviet index number of free market prices in 1954, but commission sales were so small a part of total free market sales that this makes no difference. As in the computations for other years, my index number for 1937–40 provides a link in the index numbers of collective farm market prices for 1937–52 and 1937–54, and any errors in the 1940 index number will be reflected in the index numbers for 1952 and 1954.

A computation based on Moscow collective farm market prices in 1954 was made, following the same procedure as in the case of the similar computations for 1940 and 1948 already described. Both a 1937-weighted and a 1954-weighted index number were computed, but the results were very close. The body of observed quotations available for the Moscow market during 1954 is adequate to form some impression of the level of prices on the Moscow free market of twelve to fourteen commodities over a good part of 1954.[37] The resulting index number of collective farm market prices in Moscow comes to about 320 percent of the 1937 level. This is some 50 percent higher than the estimated price index number of 214 shown in Table 9 for all urban collective farm markets. While Moscow free market prices rose more than average urban USSR free market prices, one wonders whether the difference was as large as this. In any case, both the Moscow index number and the index number for all urban markets in the Soviet Union are subject to considerable error.

On the basis of the index numbers of prices on the collective farm market, the gap between the collective farm market and the official prices in each year can be computed. I estimate this for each year as the ratio of the index number of collective farm market prices to the index number of official prices of foods. I employ the index number of official prices of foods rather than of all commodities because the bulk of sales on the collective farm market is of foods. In this computation the index number of official prices of foods is used with given-year weights and computed ac-

[36] TSU, *Sovetskaia torgovlia; Statisticheskii sbornik*, p. 179.

[37] The main sources of these observed quotations are: *New York Times,* March 11, August 15, September 7, 1954, and February 6, 1955; *Washington Post,* December 29, 1953; Emmet Hughes, "A Perceptive Reporter in a Changing Russia," *Life,* February 8, 1954; Frank Rounds, Jr., *A Window on Red Square* (Cambridge, Mass., 1953), p. 187; Eugène Zaleski, "Les fluctuations des prix de détail en Union Soviétique," *Études et Conjoncture,* no. 4, April 1955, pp. 381–382; and unpublished materials.

cording to the Paasche formula. As has been said, the index number of collective farm market prices is equivalent to the Paasche index number for 1940. For subsequent years the index numbers are based on given-year weights, and, while not Paasche index numbers, they are more akin to the Paasche than to the Laspeyres index number. The procedure is somewhat different for 1944 for which no separate index number of official prices of foods is computed and the index number of collective farm market prices must be compared with the index number of official prices of all commodities. Also, the only 1944 index number of official prices computed, though not strictly a Laspeyres index number, is an approximation to a 1937-weighted index number. The index numbers of collective farm market prices and the given-year weighted index numbers of official food prices are shown in Table 11, together with the estimated relationship between prices on the collective farm market and those in the state and cooperative shops for each year. As previously said, I assume there was no gap between collective farm market and official prices in 1937.[38]

In order to take the collective farm market prices into account in the cost-of-living index numbers, it is necessary to estimate the relative share

[38] The relationship between official and free market prices shown in Table 11 and used in adjusting the index numbers of official prices appears to be confirmed for 1940 by a Soviet statement that average prices on the collective farm market in 1940 were 160 percent of the prices of the same commodities in state and cooperative shops. See M. Eidel'man, "O metodologii ischisleniia indeksa real'noi zarabotnoi platy," *Vestnik statistiki*, no. 3, 1956, p. 42. For 1948, the gap may be somewhat understated. The comparison made is between the free market prices and the official prices of all foods and alcoholic beverages. If the comparison were limited to the official prices of the kinds of food products that are sold in large quantities on the collective farm market — meat, vegetables and fruit, dairy products, eggs, and, to a lesser extent, grain products — the gap in 1948 would be larger than that shown in Table 11 because official prices of these products rose less between 1937 and 1948 than official prices of other foods, especially alcoholic beverages.

The gap of about 35 percent indicated for 1954 seems rather small in relation to my computations for Moscow. Also there is some Soviet evidence that suggests that the gap may have been considerably wider, though the evidence is by no means conclusive. TSU, *Sovetskaia torgovlia; Statisticheskii sbornik*, pp. 133–134, presents data for a sample of 102 cities on the relationship between prices in the commission shops and those in state shops and on the relationship between prices on the collective farm market and prices in commission shops. When a simple average is taken of the figures for the four quarters of 1954, prices in commission shops averaged 141 percent of prices in state shops. Again, taking a simple average of the figures for the four quarters of 1954, prices in commission shops averaged 81.5 percent of prices on the collective farm market. Dividing the former ratio by the latter, this would appear to indicate that prices on the collective farm market were about 173 percent of the official prices in state shops in these 102 cities. No explanation of how the figures were computed is given in the source, and my use of the figures may not be correct even for the 102 cities. It is not known whether the market relationships prevailing in this limited sample were typical of the entire urban USSR. But these data at least suggest that my estimate of the gap between free market and official prices in 1954 may err seriously on the low side. In any case, it must be kept in mind that, as is true of the index numbers of collective farm market prices, the estimates of the relationship between the free market and official prices shown in Table 11 are subject to a very wide margin of error. For new information bearing on possible errors in these computations see chapter X, section 4.

TABLE 11

Relationship between Collective Farm Market Prices
and Official Food Prices, USSR, 1937–54

Year	Collective farm market prices, index (1937 = 100)	Official food prices, index using given-year weights (1937 = 100)	Collective farm market prices in percent of official food prices
1937	100	100	100
1940	200	125	160
1944	2200	(143)[a]	1538
1948	350	313	112
1952	208	187	111
1954	214	158	135

[a] Index number of ration prices of foods and manufactured consumer goods, using 1937 weights.
Sources: Tables 5 and 9. The 1944 index number of official prices is from appendix D. The 1952 and 1954 figures here refer to the calendar year.

of the collective farm market in the total purchases of goods by urban workers. Lacking data on urban worker budgets, I base my computations on urban retail sales to households. Presumably this provides a reasonable approximation to the distribution of urban worker expenditures as between the state shops and the collective farm markets. Table 12 shows retail sales to households in urban state and cooperative shops, line 1, and on the collective farm market, line 2a, in current prices. In order to obtain a weight for the collective farm market in terms of the real volume of trade, sales on the collective farm market are revalued at the official prices. This is done by deflating collective farm market sales to households at market prices in each year by the ratio of collective farm market prices in that year to official prices in the same year — that is, by the ratios shown in Table 11. The resulting figures for collective farm market sales valued at official prices are shown in Table 12, line 2b. In Table 12, line 2c, collective farm market sales to households are shown as a percentage of total urban retail sales to households when all retail sales are valued at official prices. Sales in commercial shops in 1944 are included with sales on the collective farm market, and the figure shown for sales in state and cooperative shops covers only sales made at ration prices. The figures in Table 12, line 2c, are used as weights for the index numbers of collective farm market prices in computing the index number of average retail prices of commodities in all urban retail markets.

The data so far presented permit me to adjust the index numbers of official prices to cover average retail prices in all urban retail markets. Thus, in 1940, collective farm market prices exceeded official prices by 60 percent (Table 11), and collective farm market sales in real terms were 12.5 percent of all urban retail sales to households (Table 12, line 2c). Thus average prices in all urban retail markets were 7.5 percent (0.6 $\times$ 12.5 percent = 7.5 percent) higher than official retail prices in state and cooperative shops. The 1940 index numbers of official prices of commodities

TABLE 12

Share of Collective Farm Market Sales in Urban
Retail Sales to Households, USSR, 1937–54

Type of sale	1937	1940	1944	1948	1952	1954
1. Retail sales to households in urban state and cooperative shops, billion rubles	76.9	115.0	77.8ᵃ	229.5	267.6	321.8
2. Collective farm market sales to households						
a. At market prices, billion rubles	16.0	26.2	36ᵇ	34	51.0ᶜ	48.6ᶜ
b. At official prices, billion rubles	16.0	16.4	2.3	30.4	45.9	36.0
c. At official prices, percent of all urban retail sales	17.2	12.5	2.9	12.0	14.6	10.1

ᵃ Sales at ration prices.
ᵇ Including sales in commercial shops of 6 billion rubles.
ᶜ Including commission sales.
Sources and methods: Total retail sales to households in state and cooperative shops and sales to households on the collective farm market are from Abram Bergson, *Soviet National Income and Product in 1937* (New York, 1953), p. 18; Abram Bergson and Hans Heymann, Jr., *Soviet National Income and Product, 1940–1948* (New York, 1954), p. 21; preliminary figures from Abram Bergson, Hans Heymann, Jr., and Oleg Hoeffding, *Soviet National Income and Product, 1928–1948: Revised Data*, The RAND Corporation, RM-2544, November 15, 1960; preliminary figures from Oleg Hoeffding and Nancy Nimitz, *Soviet National Income and Product, 1949–1955*, The RAND Corporation, RM-2101, April 6, 1959. The 1944 figure for collective farm market sales is a rather crude estimate. The urban share of total retail sales to households in state and cooperative shops is based on the share which urban sales were of total retail sales in state and cooperative shops, as given in TSU, *Sovetskaia torgovlia; Statisticheskii sbornik* (Moscow, 1956), p. 21. For 1944, the 1945 percentage is used.
   The final retail sales figures in the above sources differ slightly in some cases from the preliminary figures used in this computation.

in the urban USSR in Table 6, lines 2a and 2b, are accordingly increased by 7.5 percent to obtain the 1940 index numbers of average prices of commodities in all markets in the urban USSR shown in Table 6, lines 3a and 3b. In 1944, prices on the collective farm market and in the commercial shops exceeded the official ration prices by 1,438 percent and sales on the collective farm market and in the commercial shops in real terms were 2.9 percent of all urban retail sales to households. Thus average prices in all markets in 1944 were about 42 percent higher than official ration prices. Following the same procedure, the adjustment factor computed for 1948 comes to 1.4 percent. I increase this to 2.0 percent to take account of the prices prevailing for some of the sales of consumer cooperatives, which at that time somewhat exceeded the official prices in state shops.[39] My computations indicate that average prices in all markets exceeded the official prices by 2.0 percent in 1952 and by 3.5 percent in 1954. The resulting index numbers of average USSR prices of commodities in all urban markets are shown in Table 6, lines 3a and 3b.

   The wide margin of error to which the index numbers of collective farm market prices are subject means that the adjustment for collective farm market prices is very crude. However, the urban worker makes a relatively small share of his purchases on the collective farm market in real terms. Because of this, large errors in the index numbers of collective farm market prices can have but little effect on the index numbers of average prices in all retail markets. For instance, if collective farm market prices were actually as much as 50 percent higher than estimated, the error in the

[39] See chapter II.

index number of average prices in all urban markets would be 5 percent in the case of 1952 and under 5 percent for the other years.

4. THE COST-OF-LIVING INDEX NUMBERS

The adjusted index numbers as described so far in this chapter refer only to the prices of commodities. To obtain the cost-of-living index numbers, it is necessary to include the index numbers of service prices shown in Table 5 and (for 1944) in appendix D. These are weighted according to the weight estimated for services in each year as shown in Table 4; the index numbers of average prices of commodities in all urban markets are given the weight for all purchases of commodities, also shown in Table 4. The resulting index numbers are the cost-of-living index numbers shown in Table 6, lines 4a and 4b.

The service price index numbers are based mainly on Moscow official prices. Limitations of data preclude any attempt to estimate the difference between Moscow and average USSR service price movements, and the Moscow service price index number is used as if it were applicable to the entire USSR. Moscow service price movements, however, may not be very typical of the country as a whole for the period 1928 until mid-1948. Service prices, with the major exceptions of rent and railroad fares, were established locally until mid-1948, and rather wide regional variations in rates have prevailed. In August 1948, uniform rates for the entire country were established for a number of services — electricity, gas, public baths, laundry, and urban transport. But even then, for some services, where the local rate already exceeded the new "uniform" rate, the former rate was maintained.[40] The possible error due to using the Moscow service price index as if it applied to the entire USSR should not be very significant. This is so because only a small weight is assigned to services in the cost-of-living index number covering all goods and services, and because among services a large weight is given to rent and railroad transportation, for which the rates have moved more or less uniformly for the country as a whole.

I am also unable to take into account prices of services rendered by private individuals, except insofar as some such services might be assumed to be represented by the hourly wage included in the service price index number. Services provided by private individuals were undoubtedly rather important in 1928, and there are still some private services, such as domestic service and services of doctors consulted privately outside the hours of their official duties. Among the services represented in the index number, there is some private renting of dwelling space. From 1928 through October 1937 there was apparently no limit on the rent that could be charged for privately owned dwelling space, but since October 1937

---

[40] V. P. Maslakov, *et al.*, *Finansirovanie zhilishchno-kommunal'nogo khoziaistva* (Moscow, 1948), pp. 89–90.

rent charged for privately owned dwelling space may legally exceed the official rental rate by only 20 percent.[41] Private individuals presumably also provide such services as the making and repairing of clothing, and they undoubtedly charge more than the official rates for such services. Very likely, the prices of such private services, which are omitted from the index number, rose more than the prices of the public services, which are represented in the index number. If so, the index numbers somewhat understate the rise in service prices since 1928. The effect on the cost-of-living index number covering all goods and services, however, should be very small.

[41] Timothy Sosnovy, *The Housing Problem in the Soviet Union* (New York, 1954), pp. 239, 254.

VII ·

MONEY WAGES, TAXES,
AND BOND PURCHASES

In the present chapter I first present and describe the series on average money wages of nonagricultural workers in the Soviet Union. The basic wage data are presented in terms of average annual earnings, but I attempt to allow for changes in the length of the work week and in vacation provisions so that comparisons can also be made of the amount earned per hour actually worked. The wages discussed in section 1 are gross earnings. In section 2, I estimate the deductions that must be made from the Soviet worker's gross earnings to obtain his net or take-home pay — namely, direct taxes and the purchase of government bonds. The reasons for considering purchases of government bonds as virtually equivalent to direct taxes in the Soviet case are indicated.

I. GROSS MONEY WAGES

Average annual money wages of wage earners and salaried employees in the Soviet Union in each of the years covered in the present investigation are shown in Table 13. Average wages are shown both for all wage earners and salaried employees and for nonagricultural wage earners and salaried employees. The average wage figures used in this study are those for nonagricultural wage earners and salaried employees. These figures are derived from the series for *all* wage earners and salaried employees; accordingly, I comment first on this series.

The figures in Table 13 for all wage earners and salaried employees are the official Soviet series on average annual earnings sometimes referred to, after Abram Bergson, as the TSUNKHU series.[1] Prior to the war these figures were published seriatim for most years. Generally, figures were published on the size of the labor force, the wage bill, and the average wage for separate branches of the economy as well as for all branches

[1] Abram Bergson, "A Problem in Soviet Statistics," *Review of Economic Statistics,* 29:234–242 (November 1947). TSUNKHU is the abbreviation of the name of the statistical agency responsible during the 1930's for the collection and compilation of the wage statistics — *Tsentral'noe upravlenie narodno-khoziaistvennogo ucheta* (Central Administration of National Economic Accounting). During the 1920's, the corresponding agency was known as *Tsentral'noe statisticheskoe upravlenie* (Central Statistical Administration), abbreviated as TSU. This name has been in use since 1939 also.

TABLE 13

Average Annual Money Wages, USSR, 1928–54

Year	All wage earners and salaried employees		Wage earners and salaried employees outside agriculture	
	Rubles per year	Index (1937 = 100)	Rubles per year	Index (1937 = 100)
1928	703	23.1	775	24.7
1937	3038	100	3140	100
1940	4054	133	4180	133
1944	5270	173	5430	173
1948	7000	230	7220	230
1952	7990	263	8250	263
1954	8350	275	8650	275

Sources:

All wage earners and salaried employees:
   1928: TSUNKHU, *Trud v SSSR* (Moscow, 1936), pp. 16–17.
   1937: Gosplan, *Tretii piatiletnii plan,* p. 228.
   1940: M. M. Lifits, *Sovetskaia torgovlia* (Moscow, 1948), p. 52. A figure of 4,069 rubles a year is implied by prewar Soviet data on the labor force and wage bill; see Abram Bergson, "A Problem in Soviet Statistics," *Review of Economic Statistics,* 29:236 (November 1947).
   1944: The average wage during the war years increased by 30 percent, according to *Finansy i sotsialisticheskoe stroitel'stvo* (Moscow, 1957), p. 224. Presumably the figure compares 1944 with 1940 and refers to average earnings of all wage earners and salaried employees in the economy, but the source is not explicit on these points. Average monthly wages of wage earners in industry increased 42 percent and average monthly wages of wage earners in "union industry" increased 53 percent between 1940 and 1944, according to N. Voznesenskii, *Voennaia ekonomika SSSR v period otechestvennoi voiny* (Moscow, 1948), pp. 117–118.
   1948: Abram Bergson, *The Real National Income of Soviet Russia Since 1928* (Cambridge, Mass., 1961), p. 422.
   1952: Money wages in 1953 were 2 percent higher than in 1952, according to the 1953 Plan Fulfillment Report (*Pravda,* January 31, 1954). In 1953, the average annual wage of all wage earners and salaried employees in the USSR was 201 percent of 1940 (see Akademiia nauk SSSR, Institut ekonomiki, *Politicheskaia ekonomiia* (Moscow, 1954), p. 462) or 8,149 rubles a year.
   1954: The average annual money wage of all wage earners and salaried employees in 1954 was 206 percent of 1940 (*ibid.,* 1955, p. 483).

Wage earners and salaried employees outside agriculture:
   1928: The figure is computed from the following data from TSUNKHU, *Trud v SSSR* (Moscow, 1936), pp. 10–11, 16–17, 20–21, and *Narodnoe khoziaistvo SSSR* (Moscow, 1932), p. 414:

	Labor force (thousands)	Wage bill (million rubles)	Average wage (rubles per year)
Total national economy	11,599	8,159	703
Agriculture and forestry	2,007	614	306
Forestry	331	150	450
Agriculture	1,676	464	277
Total national economy *less* agriculture	9,923	7,695	775

For forestry, the average wage and the wage bill are estimated by Oleg Hoeffding on the basis of the 1929 average wage of 493 rubles a year in forestry.
   1937: The figure is computed from the following data from Gosplan, *Tretii piatiletnii plan,* p. 228:

	Labor force (thousands)	Wage bill (million rubles)	Average wage (rubles per year)
Total national economy	26,990	82,247	3,038
Agriculture	2,483	5,266	2,121
National economy *less* agriculture	24,507	76,981	3,141

All years since 1937: It is assumed that the average wage of wage earners and salaried employees outside agriculture showed the same percentage increase as the average wage of all wage earners and salaried employees.

covered in the series. During the war and for several years after, no comparable wage figures were released. Finally, in 1954, the Russians began to publish figures on the average wage during the postwar years, but only as an index number with 1940 as base year. More recently, an index number of average wages in 1944 was published, but it is still necessary to estimate the 1948 average wage. There seems no doubt that the average wage index numbers released by the Soviet government since 1954 are a continuation of the prewar TSUNKHU series. The sources are fairly explicit as to the coverage of the average wage figure; that is, they indicate it is the average annual earnings of "wage earners and salaried employees in the national economy," which is the phrase used in connection with the prewar TSUNKHU series. Also, the official average wage figures are consistent with the estimates that could be made on the basis of data on the labor force, on the comprehensive wage bill, and scattered data on wage rates. These estimates had been accepted at least tentatively by most Western students of the subject.[2]

The TSUNKHU wage figures cover the earnings of the regular hired labor force in most branches of the national economy, including industry, construction, transportation and communications, trade, education and health, financial institutions, government, social institutions, forestry, and agriculture. Hired workers in agriculture are mainly the employees of the state farms and machine-tractor stations. Income of members of collective farms, the vast bulk of those engaged in agriculture, does not take the form of wages and is not included in the average wage figures.

The TSUNKHU average wage figures are based on monthly reports from the employing enterprises on the total wages paid and the average number of persons on the payroll during the month. Adjustments are made for plants in operation only part of the month, and in fields where double job-holding is significant (health, education, government, and social institutions), corrections are made for persons on more than one payroll.[3] The Soviet average wage appears to be very similar to the U.S. Department of Commerce concept of average earnings per full-time equivalent employee.[4]

As Abram Bergson was the first to point out, the TSUNKHU wage bill does not include all wages. He found that the TSUNKHU wage bill fell short of the comprehensive wage bill for the entire Soviet economy by something like 20 percent for the years for which both wage bill figures were available.[5] This discovery raised a certain amount of alarm among Western students of the Soviet economy as the TSUNKHU series had generally been presented in such terms as to suggest it was comprehensive.

---

[2] Murray Yanowitch, "Changes in the Soviet Money Wage Level Since 1940," *American Slavic and East European Review*, 14:195–223 (April 1955). In addition to presenting a considerable amount of previously unpublished material on the course of Soviet wage movements during the war and immediate postwar years, Yanowitch summarizes the estimates made by other Western economists prior to the Russians' release of their official figures.

[3] TSU, *Slovar'-spravochnik po sotsial'no-ekonomicheskoi statistike* (Moscow, 1944), pp. 213–214; A. M. Sukharev, *Kurs promyshlennoi statistiki* (Moscow, 1959), pp. 97–102, 162–165.

[4] See *Survey of Current Business*, June 1945, pp. 17–18.

[5] Bergson, *Review of Economic Statistics*, 29:234–242 (November 1947). See also Harry Schwartz, "A Critique of 'Appraisals of Russian Economic Statistics'," *Review of Economics and Statistics*, 30:38–41 (1948); P. J. D. Wiles, "Average Wages in USSR," *Bulletin of the Oxford University Institute of Statistics*, 15:327–339 (1953); Oleg Hoeffding, *Soviet National Income and Product in 1928* (New York, 1954), pp. 103–108.

The Soviet writers have not clearly defined the scope of either the TSUNKHU or the comprehensive wage bill and often neglect to specify which bill they are discussing. One must then be extremely careful in interpreting Soviet figures on the wage bill. There does, however, seem to be a reasonable explanation for the existence of the two wage bill concepts. And there is some evidence concerning the types of wage payments included in the larger but excluded in the smaller, though information on this point is by no means complete.

So far as can be made out, the comprehensive wage bill includes — while the TSUNKHU wage bill excludes — the following: earnings of members of producer cooperatives, the pay of the armed forces (and possibly of the police), wages paid to prison labor,[6] wages and salaries of paid officials of the Communist Party,[7] wages paid to workers hired by the collective farms,[8] probably wage payments by the state to members of collective farms for work in the machine-tractor stations,[9] earnings of domestic servants (since the war only),[10] wages paid to workers hired for less than five days for work in subsidiary operations of an enterprise, wage payments to students working for practical experience in connection with their courses of study,[11] and probably various other types of wage payments. In 1928 many of the above items were insignificant, but considerable amounts of farm wages and wages for nonagricultural work mainly on farms (especially construction) were unrecorded in the TSUNKHU statistics.[12] For

[6] TSU, *Slovar'-spravochnik po sotsial'no-ekonomicheskoi statistike*, p. 213, indicates that the comprehensive (*polnyi*) wage bill includes, in addition to the earnings of hired wage earners and salaried employees and cooperative artisans, the wages of military service personnel and other categories that are not voluntarily hired (*ne vol'nonaemnye*). This presumably includes prison labor. It might also include persons who are free but not hired, such as authors, as suggested by Wiles, *Bulletin of the Oxford University Institute of Statistics*, 15:335 (1953).

[7] TSUNKHU, *Trud v SSSR* (Moscow, 1936), p. 361; Alec Nove and Warren Eason report they were informed of this by Soviet officials.

[8] Abram Bergson, *Soviet National Income and Product in 1937* (New York, 1953), p. 103.

[9] Since about 1939, payments to collective farm members for their work in the machine-tractor stations have been made partly by the state and partly by the collective farms, under arrangements which have varied over the period. It would not make much sense to include in the TSUNKHU wage bill the partial payments made by the state in the form of wages; and it is known that labor-day payments made by collective farms to their members are not included. I am indebted to Alec Nove for this point.

According to a footnote in TSU, *Narodnoe khoziaistvo SSSR* (Moscow, 1956), p. 190, tractor brigade workers who had previously been recorded as in the labor force of the collective farms were in 1953 transferred to the machine-tractor stations and are now included in the figures on the number of wage earners and salaried employees — what we refer to as the TSUNKHU labor force. It does not necessarily follow, however, that their wages are now included in the official Soviet average wage figures.

[10] Domestic servants were included in the TSUNKHU series before the war (*Trud v SSSR* (1936), pp. 10–11) but have been excluded since the war. Warren Eason reports he was informed of this in conversation with Soviet officials.

[11] TSU, *Slovar'-spravochnik po sotsial'no-ekonomicheskoi statistike*, pp. 208–209.

[12] Hoeffding, *Soviet National Income and Product in 1928*, pp. 107–108.

the most part, the exclusions from the TSUNKHU wage bill mentioned above are wage payments to persons who would not be included in the TSUNKHU labor force. There is evidence also that part of the wages paid to persons in the TSUNKHU labor force are not included in the TSUNKHU wage bill but only in the comprehensive wage bill, though this probably accounts for only a small part of the difference between the two wage bills. The wages in kind of hired agricultural workers were probably not recorded in the TSUNKHU wage bill prior to 1934,[13] and some of the value of free goods and services provided as part of wages to non-agricultural workers may be excluded. Certain types of premium payments made to workers in the TSUNKHU labor force are not included in the TSUNKHU wage bill. These premiums — namely, from the fund for the encouragement of innovations and technical improvements, from special funds, and paid out of the profits of enterprises — apparently are of a one-time kind and on the whole are probably rather unimportant.[14] Premiums that are earned as part of the regular wage scale — for fulfill-ment or overfulfillment of plan, et cetera — are included in the TSUNKHU wage bill and these must be by far the most important form of premium payment.

The TSUNKHU series on the wage bill, labor force, and average wage are presented by Soviet writers, as Wiles has pointed out, in connection with measuring changes in average wages and related questions of the standard of living of the population. Figures on the comprehensive wage bill, on the other hand, are cited in the Soviet literature in connection with estimates of the total money income and outlay of the population and a concern about inflation. For this purpose, of course, it is necessary to in-clude all wages or wage-type income. For the purpose of measuring the change in the average wage, however, data based on a more restricted group may provide a better and more consistent measure.[15] The categories of labor excluded from the TSUNKHU labor force are, on the whole, ones we should wish to exclude in arriving at a figure for the average wage of the regular hired labor force. One does not think of the average wage as including military pay and subsistence or the earnings of prison labor. In the 1920's, when there was still a fair amount of private employment, it made sense to include domestic servants, but since they have become virtually the only remnant of private employment (and are a small group) it probably makes more sense to exclude them. Other exclusions from the TSUNKHU wage bill can probably be justified either on the grounds that the wage payments in question are not strictly wages and salaries or that they are too difficult to keep track of statistically. I am inclined to agree

[13] *Ibid.*, p. 107.

[14] TSU, *Slovar'-spravochnik po sotsial'no-ekonomicheskoi statistike*, p. 212. According to data for March 1935, premiums not recorded in the wage bill amounted to less than 0.3 percent of the wage bill. See TSUNKHU, *Trud v SSSR* (1936), p. 31.

[15] Wiles, *Bulletin of the Oxford University Institute of Statistics*, 15:334 (1953).

with Wiles that the TSUNKHU series represents an effort on the part of the Soviet statisticians to maintain a consistent series for purposes of measuring the change in the average wage.

There are, however, some shortcomings of the series that should be commented upon. In the first place, the figures are based on reports of the numerous enterprises and institutions that hire labor and pay wages. Undoubtedly these reports are subject to a certain amount of error and falsification.[16] So far as cheating is concerned, the pressure in the case of wage payments is to underreport; but Nove's "law of equal cheating" may operate here. There have also been changes in the definition of what types of labor and what types of wage payments are to be included in the TSUNKHU series. Such definitional changes might well be expected in a series maintained over a long period. Presumably they are intended to improve the series and to adapt it to changing conditions, though of course they introduce a certain amount of inconsistency in the series. The probable omission of farm wages in kind prior to 1934 makes for a fairly serious lack of comparability between 1928 and 1937 so far as agricultural wages are concerned but does not affect the average for nonfarm wages. The other changes in definition on which we have information — the change in treatment of domestic servants, the inclusion since 1953 of tractor brigade workers in the TSUNKHU labor force — could have only a very small effect on the average wage figure.[17] While the figures must be accepted with some reservations, I think the TSUNKHU average wage figures can be regarded as a reasonably reliable measure of the course of average wages, that is, average annual earnings of Soviet wage earners and salaried employees.

I use the average wage of wage earners and salaried employees outside agriculture for two reasons. First, the cost-of-living index number based mainly on urban prices and urban worker expenditures may not be applicable to agricultural workers. It is probably not too appropriate for rural hired workers outside agriculture either, but it is impossible to exclude their wages from the average wage figure. Secondly, the 1928 figure for the average wage of all wage earners and salaried employees including those in agriculture is much more significantly affected by the inclusion of low-paid farm labor than the figures for later years. In 1928, farm labor was a larger proportion of the total hired labor force than in later years and, more importantly, most of the agricultural labor force was made up of hired workers on private farms whose money wages were far below the average for the rest of the labor force and whose wages in kind were apparently not allowed for in the statistics. In 1937 and later years,

---

[16] Bergson cites numerous types of shortcomings in the reports from the Soviet literature in *Review of Economic Statistics*, 29:237–239 (November 1947).

[17] As indicated above, it is not clear whether the wages of tractor brigade workers have been included in computing the average wage figure since 1953.

the hired agricultural workers included in the wage statistics are all state employees on the state farms and in the machine-tractor stations, and there was a much smaller differential between their wages and the average wage outside agriculture. Also, their income in kind is apparently recorded in the statistics. Thus, in 1937 the average wage in agriculture as recorded in the statistics was 766 percent of that in 1928 while the average wage outside agriculture was only about 405 percent of that in 1928.[18] Use of the average wage of all wage earners and salaried employees would tend to overstate the rise between 1928 and 1937 in the money wages of the group of workers in which we are mainly interested, nonagricultural workers.[19]

For the years since 1937, breakdowns of the TSUNKHU labor force and payroll totals by branch of the economy, which would permit us to separate out workers in agriculture, are not available. Probably the average wage of agricultural workers has moved more or less as the average wage of nonagricultural workers; and in any case, hired agricultural workers are such a small proportion of the total labor force that inclusion of their wages would have a negligible effect on the movement of the average wage since 1937. Accordingly, I assume that the average wage of wage earners and salaried employees outside agriculture has shown the same percentage increase since 1937 as the average wage of all wage earners and salaried employees including those in agriculture.

The average money wage figures discussed so far refer to total annual earnings. The number of hours actually worked in a year has varied considerably over the period studied as a result of changes in the length of the work week, in provisions for vacations, in absenteeism and such. For some purposes, therefore, it is useful to consider also average hourly earnings. In 1928, the legal work day was 8 hours in most cases and the normal work-week 6 out of 7 days; allowing for shorter hours on the eves of Sundays and holidays, the normal work-week was 46.8 hours. In 1937 most workers were on a work schedule of 5 seven-hour days out of 6, which comes to 40.8 hours a calendar week. This same schedule was in effect during the first half of 1940, but in June 1940, a normal schedule of 6 eight-hour days out of 7, or 48 hours a week was established for most workers. The normal work-week averaged 44.4 hours during 1940 as a whole. The 48-hour week established in mid-1940 remained in effect through 1955, though during the war years there was a considerable amount of overtime work.[20] In addition to changes in the normal work-

[18] See the notes to Table 13 on the 1928 and 1937 figures for average wages outside agriculture.

[19] I am indebted to Oleg Hoeffding for bringing this point to my attention. See his *Soviet National Income and Product in 1928*, pp. 103–108.

[20] Abram Bergson, *The Real National Income of Soviet Russia Since 1928* (Cambridge, Mass., 1961), appendix H. Throughout the period, there were provisions for shorter working schedules for youths and for persons in dangerous or arduous occupations.

week, there have also been changes in the provisions for holidays and vacations and in the amount of overtime, work stoppages, absenteeism, et cetera, which affect the actual number of hours worked over an entire year. An index number of average hours actually worked per calendar week allowing for all of these factors has been estimated by Abram Bergson. His calculations refer to industrial wage earners only. They are probably reasonably applicable to all nonagricultural wage earners and salaried employees, except that in 1944 there was probably less overtime work outside of industry than in industry. The index number of average annual earnings of nonagricultural wage earners and salaried employees is divided by this index number of average hours worked to obtain an index number of average hourly earnings. These index numbers are shown in Table 14.

TABLE 14

Index Numbers of Average Annual and Hourly Money Wages of Nonagricultural
Wage Earners and Salaried Employees in the USSR, 1928–54
(1937 = 100)

Year	Average annual wage	Industrial working hours	Average hourly wage
1928	24.7	103	24
1937	100	100	100
1940	133	109	122
1944	173	144	120
1948	230	118	195
1952	263	118	223
1954	275	118	233

Sources: Average annual wage figures are from Table 13. Industrial working hours are from Abram Bergson, *The Real National Income of Soviet Russia Since 1928* (Cambridge, Mass., 1961), appendix H.

Because the work-week was shorter in 1937 than in the other years covered in this study, average hourly earnings in all other years are lower relative to those in 1937 than are average annual earnings. This is particularly the case of the war year 1944 when there was a large amount of overtime work and vacations were canceled.

One final comment should perhaps be made on the nature of the average wage figure used in the present study. As is evident from the coverage of the TSUNKHU average wage figures, the money wage figure is an average of the earnings of a wide range of workers — from charwoman to factory director, from messenger to Minister — though wage earners do in fact make up the bulk of the labor force covered.[21] Money wages vary widely in the Soviet Union with skill and training and by industry or branch of the economy. Thus, changes in the average money wage reflect changes in the composition of the labor force and changes in the struc-

[21] In industry, about 80 percent of the labor force are wage earners. *Bol'shaia sovetskaia entsiklopediia* (2d ed., Moscow, 1957), vol. 50 on USSR, p. 377.

ture of the economy as well as changes in the rate of pay for the same job. An increase in the proportion of the labor force in the higher occupational categories or a relative increase in employment in the higher paid industries would result in an increase in the average wage even if wage rates remained constant. Even in the absence of limitations on available wage data, one would choose to employ average earnings of all nonagricultural wage earners and salaried employees as a basis for measuring changes in the real income of the Soviet working class generally.

2. NET MONEY WAGES

The money wage figures discussed so far refer to gross earnings. When measuring changes in real income, take-home pay is of more interest than gross earnings. To obtain take-home pay it is necessary, of course, to deduct direct taxes.[22] Throughout the period studied, purchases of government bonds have been, to all intents and purposes, mainly compulsory, and I treat net purchases of government bonds as analogous to direct taxes. The figures for direct taxes and for the purchases of government bonds are given separately so that the effect of each may be determined.

Although nominally voluntary, subscriptions to Soviet government bonds exhibit many elements of compulsion and are more similar to direct taxes than to government bonds as we know them in the West. The reasons for considering Soviet bond subscriptions as virtually akin to taxes have been ably expounded elsewhere, and need not be outlined here.[23] The announcement of the Soviet government in April 1957 that no further interest would be paid on its bonds and that repayment of principal on the 260 billion rubles of mass-subscription loans outstanding would be postponed until 1977–1997 [24] seems to resolve any lingering doubts as to the tax-like character of the bonds.

I treat as taxes only net bond purchases, that is, purchases of bonds in excess of repayments of principal and interest receipts and lottery winnings on the bonds. Thus, income from the bonds is, in effect, taken into account as part of wages in the computations. The claim on the distribution of future income represented by current holdings of bonds is not considered as part of current income; it is taken into account only when actually realized, that is, as the bonds are actually repaid. Current holdings of bonds have represented very little real future benefit because of the inflation throughout most of the period, conversions of 1930, 1936,

[22] Indirect taxes are taken into account in the prices of goods and services entering into the cost-of-living index numbers.

[23] See, in particular, Franklyn D. Holzman, *Soviet Taxation* (Cambridge, Mass., 1955), pp. 200–208; and "An Estimate of the Tax Element in Soviet Bonds," *American Economic Review*, 47:390–396 (1957). For a discussion of the situation in 1928, when the degree of compulsion was somewhat less than in later years, see Hoeffding, *Soviet National Income and Product in 1928*, pp. 89–92.

[24] *Pravda*, April 20, 1957.

1938, and 1947 extending the maturity dates and reducing the face value of the bonds, and, finally, the 1957 postponement of any repayments for twenty years. The resulting measure of net real wages is one of currently consumable real wages.

If one were interested in measuring currently consumed real wages, it would be in order to deduct all net savings rather than just net bond purchases; however, I do not make this computation. Generally, savings other than bond purchases can be considered as voluntary in the Soviet Union and, in any case, they are (understandably) small for the Soviet worker. Two qualifying comments should be made concerning the measures for 1944 and 1954. In the war year 1944 there was an exceptionally large increment in savings deposits and in cash holdings of Soviet households,[25] and this must for the most part be considered as forced savings in the sense that consumers would have saved much less had there been more goods in the shops to buy. Also, some of the increase in savings deposits in that year was compulsory in that compensation for vacations not taken because of the wartime cancellation of all vacations was paid in the form of blocked deposits in savings banks.[26] Thus, it should be kept in mind that in 1944 the Soviet worker was not able to spend his entire net wage as I measure it. Between 1952 and 1954 the compulsory subscriptions to government bonds were cut in half, and this contributes to the increase in net wages between 1952 and 1954. But it should be pointed out that there was an increase in other forms of savings which partially compensated for the reduction in bond subscriptions.[27] In this period of improving living standards and falling retail prices, some of the increase in savings may well have been voluntary, but one suspects that a good share represented cash that the owners could not spend — or could not spend to their taste.

Estimates of the proportion of the average gross wage going to direct taxes and the purchase of government bonds in each of the years studied are shown in Table 15, lines 1 and 2. Taxes and purchases of bonds together (Table 15, line 3) amounted to about 2.5 percent of the average wage in 1928, to 4.0 percent in 1937, 7.6 percent in 1940, 28.4 percent in the war year 1944, 13.4 percent in 1948, 15.0 percent in 1952, and 10.7 percent in 1954. These estimates are explained below. Deducting tax payments and bond purchases from gross wages, net annual average wages were as shown in Table 15, line 5a. The index number of net annual aver-

[25] Abram Bergson and Hans Heymann, Jr., *Soviet National Income and Product, 1940–1948* (New York, 1954), pp. 21, 160–163.

[26] *Ibid.*, p. 160.

[27] For all Soviet households, bond purchases net of interest and principal repayments declined from 29.5 billion rubles in 1952 to 5.9 billion rubles in 1954, while net savings other than bond purchases increased from 5.5 billion rubles in 1952 to 10.8 billion rubles in 1954. See Oleg Hoeffding and Nancy Nimitz, *Soviet National Income and Product, 1949–1955*, The RAND Corporation, RM-2101, April 6, 1959, pp. 5, 84, 110.

TABLE 15

Average Money Wages Before and After Taxes and Bond Purchases,
Nonagricultural Wage Earners and Salaried Employees, USSR, 1928–54

	1928	1937	1940	1944	1948	1952	1954
1. Average direct taxes paid, percent of average wage	0.5	2.6	4.8	19.3	8.8	9.6	9.7
2. Average purchases of government bonds, percent of average wage	2.0	1.4	2.8	9.1	4.6	5.4	1.0
3. Direct taxes and bond purchases, percent of average wage	2.5	4.0	7.6	28.4	13.4	15.0	10.7
4. Average gross annual money wage, rubles per year	775	3,140	4,180	5,430	7,220	8,250	8,650
5. Average net annual money wage							
a. Rubles per year	755	3,015	3,860	3,890	6,250	7,010	7,720
b. Index, 1937 = 100	25.0	100	128	129	207	233	256
6. Average net hourly money wage, index, 1937 = 100	24.3	100	117	90	175	197	217

Sources and methods: See text.

age money wages with 1937 as 100 is shown in line 5b, and an index number of net average wages on an hourly basis in line 6. As taxes and the purchase of bonds have taken an increasing share of wages, the rise in net money wages has been more moderate than the rise in gross money wages over this period. While the gross annual average money wage increased over 11 times between 1928 and 1954, the increase in the net annual average money wage over this period was just over 10 times. The differences between the increase in gross and in net earnings are greater for the war year 1944 and the earlier postwar years.

For 1928, the estimates of the share of direct taxes and bond purchases in the average wage are based on a Soviet study of the incomes and outlays of the urban hired labor force in 1927/28 and 1928/29.[28] For the other years, the estimates of the share of wages going to direct taxes and bond purchases are based mainly on data on the money income of all Soviet households and their tax payments and purchases of government bonds, shown in Table 16. Purchases of government bonds as shown are net of receipts of interest and lottery winnings and repayment of principal. For the years 1937 through 1952, I assume that taxes and bonds took the same share of wages as they did of total household money income. I accordingly use the figures in Table 16 for these years. An examination of the Soviet household income accounts, of Soviet tax rate schedules, and of other scattered data suggest this is a fairly reasonable assumption.[29]

[28] Gosplan, *Kontrol'nye tsifry narodnogo khoziaistva SSSR na 1929/30 god* (Moscow, 1930), pp. 478–479.

[29] This would not be so of 1928, though in fact I made a similar assumption in my "Real Wages in the Soviet Union, 1928–52," *Review of Economics and Statistics,* 36:145–146 (May 1954). In 1928, for all nonfarm households, it can be computed from data in Hoeffding's *Soviet National Income and Product in 1928* that direct taxes amounted to 2.2 percent and purchases of bonds to 1 percent of all nonfarm household money income. This tax figure is in accord with that for the total urban population in Gosplan,

TABLE 16

Money Income, Tax Payments, and Bond Purchases of Soviet Households, 1937–54

	1937	1940	1944	1948	1952	1954
Money income of households (billion rubles)	152	229	254	421	547.2	614.8
Direct taxes paid by households (billion rubles)	4.0	11.0	49.0	37.0	52.8	52.5
Percent of money income	2.6	4.8	19.3	8.8	9.6	8.6
Bond purchases by households, net of interest and capital repayments (billion rubles)	2.1	6.5	23.2	19.6	29.5	5.9
Percent of money income	1.4	2.8	9.1	4.6	5.4	1.0
Taxes and bond purchases, percent of money income	4.0	7.6	28.4	13.4	15.0	9.6

Sources: Abram Bergson, *Soviet National Income and Product in 1937* (New York, 1953), p. 18; Abram Bergson and Hans Heymann, Jr., *Soviet National Income and Product, 1940–1948* (New York, 1954), pp. 20–21, 143; Abram Bergson, Hans Heymann, Jr., and Oleg Hoeffding, *Soviet National Income and Product, 1928–1948: Revised Data*, The RAND Corporation, RM-2544, November 15, 1960; Oleg Hoeffding and Nancy Nimitz, *Soviet National Income and Product, 1949–1955*, The RAND Corporation, RM-2101, April 6, 1959, pp. 4–5, 84.

The 1944 figure for direct taxes includes 3.3 billion rubles of cash contributions to patriotic funds "for defense" and for the Red Army and 4.6 billion rubles of net war lottery subscriptions. Although these contributions were allegedly voluntary, it is believed they are properly classified as direct taxes. See Bergson and Heymann, *Soviet National Income and Product, 1940–1948*, p. 162.

For 1954 I estimate that direct taxes took a slightly higher share of the average wage than in 1952 — 9.7 percent. While, as Table 16 shows, total direct taxes paid by all Soviet households declined from 9.6 percent of total household money income in 1952 to 8.6 percent in 1954, this reduction in taxes is apparently due entirely to a reduction in the agricultural tax which occurred in 1953. The agricultural tax was 9.6 billion rubles in 1952 and only 4.2 billion rubles in 1954. Direct taxes exclusive of the agricultural tax were then 43.2 billion rubles in 1952 and 48.3 billion rubles in 1954. This is an increase of about 12 percent, slightly greater than the increase of about 11 percent that took place between 1952 and 1954 in Soviet household money income exclusive of income from agriculture.[30] Thus, for nonfarm households, average taxes paid in 1954 were slightly higher than in 1952 as a percentage of money income. Apparently the income tax rates remained the same over this period, but the income tax rates are somewhat progressive so that the average tax paid rises as average income rises. The figure used for average bond purchases as a percentage of the average wage in 1954 shown in Table 15 is that based on total household bond purchases and total household money income shown in Table 16. This is very small — only 1 percent of household

Kontrol'nye tsifry narodnogo khoziaistva SSSR na 1928/29 god (Moscow, 1929), pp. 446–447, but it is much higher than that for urban hired workers only, as shown in this source and in Table 15. The 1928 tax rates discriminated sharply against persons in the private segment of the economy, of whom there were still a relatively large number. At the same time, bond purchases apparently took a larger share of workers' wages than of the income of other urban persons in 1928, probably because of the greater ease of collecting payment by wage-withholding in the case of hired workers.

[30] Hoeffding and Nimitz, *Soviet National Income and Product, 1949–1955*, pp. 4–5.

money income — because the mass subscription loan floated in 1954 was only half the size of that floated in 1952, and service on the debt had increased.

The figures shown in Table 15 and used in the calculations are intended to represent the taxes paid and the bonds purchased on the average by all wage earners and salaried employees, rather than the taxes paid and the bonds purchased by a worker earning the average wage. The former concept seems more appropriate for this study inasmuch as the average money wage figure used relates to the average earnings of all workers, not the earnings of an "average" worker.

Nevertheless, it may be of interest to compare the figures for average taxes paid with the tax that would have been payable by a person who earned the average wage in each of the years studied. In the following discussion I refer to the income tax and certain related taxes based on income. These form the bulk of all direct taxes on the Soviet worker, but there are various miscellaneous direct taxes which cannot be taken into account here. In 1928, a worker earning the average wage would have paid no income tax. The income tax rate applicable to a worker earning the average wage was 2.9 percent in 1937, about 4.3 percent in 1940, 14.0 to 19.5 percent in 1944, 6.0 to 12.0 percent in 1948, 6.5 to 12.5 percent in 1952, and 6.7 to 12.7 percent in 1954.[31] The income tax rate for a worker

[31] In all cases, the average wage on which the tax is computed is the average annual earnings of nonagricultural wage earners and salaried employees. The 1937 and 1940 tax rates include the "cultural and housing" tax, which, like the so-called "income tax," was based on income. The 1944 rate shown covers the "income tax" and the "war tax" (which was also based on income), but not the contributions to patriotic funds and subscriptions to the war lotteries. The tax rates shown for 1944, 1948, 1952, and 1954 include the tax on bachelors and small families. This tax differs according to the number of children in the family and is levied as a percentage of income. The higher rate shown for each of these years applies to persons with no children who pay the highest "bachelor" tax and the lower rate applies to persons with three or more children who are not liable for the "bachelor" tax. Throughout the period there have been reductions in the income tax for persons with four or more children. These reductions are not taken into account in the rates shown above.

The 1928 rate is computed from the schedule established December 14, 1927, in *Novyi zakon po podokhodnomu nalogu* (Moscow, 1928). The 1937 income tax rate is from Narodnyi komissariat finansov SSSR, *Instruktsiia Narodnogo komissariata finansov SSSR o poriadke provedeniia podokhodnogo naloga s chastnykh lits* (Moscow, 1936), p. 6. This source gives only the rates of the "income tax" proper; I assume that the "cultural and housing tax" rate was the same as the income tax rate at the level of income represented by the average wage. The 1940 tax is computed from the schedule of rates for the income tax and the cultural and housing tax established April 4, 1940, in *Shestaia sessiia verkhovnogo soveta SSSR, 29 marta-4 apreliia 1940 g.; Stenograficheskii otchet* (Moscow, 1940), pp. 505–519. The 1944 tax is estimated from data in K. N. Plotnikov, *Biudzhet sotsialisticheskogo gosudarstva* (Moscow, 1948), pp. 274–281. The average rates for 1948, 1952, and 1954 are computed from the schedule of income tax rates in D. V. Burmistrov (ed.), *Spravochnik nalogovogo rabotnika* (Moscow, 1951), pp. 86–97. The rates in this source are those established in April 1943 as amended through March 1951. The same rates are cited in Holzman, *Soviet Taxation*, p. 179, from a 1946 Soviet source, so apparently they were in effect in 1948. It is believed the same rates remained

earning the average wage was smaller than my estimate of average total direct taxes paid in 1928 and 1940 and somewhat larger in 1937. The computed average tax paid in 1944, excluding the contributions to patriotic funds and lottery subscriptions, falls within the range of income tax applicable to a worker earning the average wage. For the years 1948, 1952, and 1954, also, the computed average tax paid falls within the range of rates applicable to a worker earning the average wage.

---

in effect through 1954. Examples of tax rates cited in *Izvestiia*, July 24, 1960 (*Current Digest of the Soviet Press*, 12:33 (August 24, 1960)), suggest that these rates remained in effect through the first half of 1960 for persons earning over 5,400 rubles a year, though tax rates at lower income levels had been reduced in 1957.

VIII·

THE SOCIAL WAGE

BEYOND his money wage, the Soviet worker and his family receive various types of grants, pensions, and allowances from the government and consume free services provided by the government and other institutions. These cash benefits and free services constitute an addition to the worker's real income and must be taken into account. The main forms of benefits provided by the Soviet government and other institutions for the Soviet population — and the ones I shall consider — are health care, · education, social insurance, and, since 1936, subsidies to mothers of many children and to unmarried mothers. The task of this chapter is to determine the amounts of these various benefits received by the Soviet working class and to estimate their contribution to the average wage.

Section 1 deals with the cash benefits accruing to the Soviet worker. Here the most important item is social insurance together with similar payments disbursed under the social assistance program. I consider also the relatively unimportant mothers' allowances. Section 2 is concerned with health care and education. I estimate what part of the total of these services is enjoyed by the working class and attempt to evaluate the contribution of these services to the average wage. The value of these services is expressed first in current prices as a percentage of the average money wage. I then deflate the value of these services to obtain a measure in constant prices, which will enable me to evaluate them at a later stage as a contribution to real wages. In section 3 the various benefits are totaled, and Soviet statements regarding benefits are considered.

I. SOCIAL INSURANCE AND OTHER CASH BENEFITS

All Soviet wage earners and salaried employees are covered by the state social insurance system. This provides for compensation for loss of pay during temporary inability to work because of illness, accident, pregnancy, and childbirth; for pensions in case of prolonged or permanent disability and in old age; funeral benefits; pensions to the dependent survivors of deceased workers; and, until 1930, unemployment compensation.[1] The social insurance system has been in operation since the early years of the

[1] The end of unemployment was officially announced in October 1930, and unemployment compensation was abandoned at the same time. See Solomon Schwarz, *Labor in the Soviet Union* (New York, 1951), p. 50; *Izvestiia,* October 11, 1930.

Soviet regime though there have been numerous changes in provisions and rates of benefits. Some of the details regarding the various types of social insurance and the rates of benefit as changes occurred over the years are summarized in appendix F.

In general, the rates of benefit depend upon the level of earnings and the length of employment of the insured, but other factors such as the danger of the occupation and the importance of the occupation also enter into the determination of benefits. Grants (such as sickness and maternity grants) to compensate for loss of wages during temporary disability have generally been equal to the full amount of pay lost throughout the period, but eligibility requirements were stiffened and the length of maternity leave during which a woman is entitled to compensation was shortened during the period. Pension rates, on the other hand, though nominally a fixed percentage of the former earnings of the insured (a percentage which varies with the type of pension, length of employment, et cetera) have, in fact, amounted to a declining percentage of earnings over the period owing to a pension maximum established in 1932, which continued in force even as money wages were rapidly rising.[2] It should be mentioned also that in 1928, provision for old-age insurance had been made only for a very limited segment of the working class — only for wage earners in the textile industry. By 1932 old-age insurance had been extended to most wage earners and salaried employees and by 1937 to all.

Social insurance is financed entirely by the employing enterprises and institutions, which contribute to the social insurance fund an amount equal to a fixed percentage of their payrolls. This percentage varies from 3.7 percent to 10.7 percent but is fixed for any one industry.[3] The Soviet worker does not make any direct contribution to the system out of his earnings. Accordingly, all grants and pensions received from the social insurance system constitute a net addition to the Soviet worker's income.

The Soviet worker is entitled to social insurance by virtue of his position as a wage earner or salaried employee. Clearly, social insurance benefits are in some sense part of his wage. The nature of social insurance, however, is such as to make difficult an evaluation of social insurance benefits as part of the average wage, and perhaps there is no entirely satisfactory way of doing so. The problem is that the benefits to which the worker is entitled under social insurance are for the most part not current benefits but ones which will be received in the future; they are either contingent upon such factors as accident or illness, or are deferred until old age. In principle, what we want to know is the current value of the future security provided by social insurance as a percentage of the

[2] This limit was abolished in 1956 when the entire pension system was revised and rates substantially increased. See *Pravda*, July 12 and July 15, 1956.

[3] This scale of contribution rates has been in effect since 1937. See Schwarz, *Labor in the Soviet Union*, pp. 335–336; N. N. Rovinskii, *Gosudarstvennyi biudzhet SSSR* (Moscow, 1951), p. 297.

current average wage. The subjective valuation of this security by the worker cannot, of course, be measured, but one might reasonably argue that the current value of the future security provided by social insurance could be equated to the current actuarial cost of providing the insurance. Unfortunately, there seems no way of estimating the actuarially necessary cost of the Soviet social insurance system. In the case of old-age pensions, one might, alternatively, consider the amount which the worker would have to save each year in order to provide an income in old age equivalent to that provided by his pension. But this also seems too difficult to attempt to estimate. I must therefore adopt some practical expedient.

My procedure is to estimate the total social insurance grants and pensions received in a given year and to take this as a percentage of the wage bill for that year. I consider this percentage as an approximate measure of the addition to the worker's wage represented by his social insurance. Conceptually this is awkward in the case of pensions as it means in effect that the pensions received by those who in general are no longer working are taken as a percentage of the wages of those who are working. For several reasons this may differ from the average value of the pension which wage earners in a given year may expect to receive on retirement. These reasons would include changes in pension rates, in the purchasing power of a given money pension, in coverage of old-age insurance, and in the age composition of the population — in particular, changes in the ratio of those currently working to those retired on pensions. My procedure has the advantage, on the other hand, of relating social insurance benefits to currently consumable income. The other types of benefits received by the Soviet worker and his family have no direct connection with his wage and are best regarded as part of currently consumable income.

Some difficulties are involved in estimating the total grants and pensions paid which are properly considered as social insurance benefits. To understand my estimates it is necessary to be clear about the uses of the social insurance fund and about certain Soviet budgetary practices. (a) The social insurance system finances — in addition to grants and pensions — rest homes, resorts, and subsidized vacation trips, pioneer camps and other child care measures, and some educational measures; at times it has also financed some housing construction. While such measures contribute to the worker's real income, the appropriate place to take them into account is in evaluating health and education services; this is the method I follow. (b) Some of the payments which are properly considered as social insurance benefits — in fact, the bulk of social insurance pensions — are not disbursed directly by the social insurance system and are not included in the expenditures of the social insurance system as usually given in Soviet budget reports. Since 1937, pensions have been disbursed directly by the social insurance system only to pensioners who are still working while pensions to nonworking pensioners who were formerly wage earners or salaried employees or who are the dependents of deceased wage earners or salaried employees have apparently been disbursed by the social assistance authorities and are included under the budgetary heading "social assistance." These pensions were financed in 1937 from general funds of the state budget and since 1938 have been financed from funds of the social insurance system, which are transferred to the social assistance program for this purpose.

Thus, total social insurance grants and pensions to working and nonworking pensioners are the sum of (a) that part of the expenditure attributed to social insurance which actually goes to grants and pensions plus (b) that part of the expenditures of the social assistance program which is for pensions to retired wage earners and salaried employees and the dependents of deceased wage earners and salaried employees.[4] The available data are not always very clear on these matters and it is necessary to estimate the figures. Estimates of total expenditures on social insurance grants and pensions are shown in Table 17 and explained in appendix F. The figures shown are intended to cover compensation for sick, accident, and maternity leave, funeral grants, disability and old-age pensions to working and retired pensioners, and pensions to the dependent survivors of deceased wage earners and salaried employees. The 1928 figure includes also unemployment compensation of 0.12 billion rubles.

Social insurance benefits are taken as a percentage of the comprehensive civilian wage bill. This is the comprehensive wage bill discussed in chapter VII less military pay and subsistence. The earnings of cooperative artisans are also excluded as they have their own insurance schemes. The extent of coverage of the social insurance system is not entirely clear, so there is some doubt about which wage bill concept to use for comparison. The scope of the social insurance system appears to be broader than that of the TSUNKHU wage bill, and I assume it is at least roughly comparable in scope to the comprehensive civilian wage bill (excluding cooperative artisans). In principle, any person working in the capacity of wage

[4] Since the war the bulk of expenditures of the social assistance program has been for pensions to disabled veterans and the families of servicemen killed in action and for monthly allowances to the families of active military personnel in the lower ranks. The social assistance program also provides pensions and other forms of assistance to invalids and persons disabled by accident (other than wage earners and salaried employees covered by social insurance) or from birth. Certain special kinds of pensions to wage earners and salaried employees — namely, length of service pensions to scientific workers in higher educational institutions and "personal" pensions for outstanding service — are financed through the social assistance program. See Rovinskii, *Gosudarstvennyi biudzhet SSSR*, pp. 303–307. It is not clear whether these special pensions are included in my figures; in any case the total is probably not large enough to worry about.

TABLE 17

Social Insurance Grants and Pensions and the Wage Bill, USSR, 1928-54

Year	Comprehensive civilian wage bill,[a] billion rubles	Social insurance grants and pensions paid	
		Billion rubles	Percent of wage bill
1928	9.66	0.68[b]	7.0[b]
1937	103.7	4.5	4.3
1940	153	4.8[c]	3.1[c]
1944	146	5.2	3.6
1948	285	11.8	4.1
1952	372	17.4	4.7
1954	430	21.2	4.9

[a] Excluding earnings of cooperative artisans.
[b] Including unemployment compensation. Excluding unemployment compensation, the social insurance grants and pensions were 0.55 billion rubles or 5.7 percent of the wage bill.
[c] Information which became available after these computations were made indicate social insurance grants and pensions amounted to 5.2 billion rubles, or 3.4 percent of the wage bill in 1940. TSU, *Narodnoe khoziaistvo SSSR v 1958 g.* (Moscow, 1959), pp. 900, 906.
Sources: *Social insurance grants and pensions paid:* appendix F. *Comprehensive civilian wage bill:* Oleg Hoeffding, *Soviet National Income and Product in 1928* (New York, 1954), p. 14; Abram Bergson, *Soviet National Income and Product in 1937* (New York, 1953), p. 18; Abram Bergson and Hans Heymann, Jr., *Soviet National Income and Product, 1940–1948* (New York, 1954), p. 127; Abram Bergson, Hans Heymann, Jr., and Oleg Hoeffding, *Soviet National Income and Product, 1928–1948: Revised Data*, The RAND Corporation, RM-2544, November 15, 1960, p. 64; Oleg Hoeffding and Nancy Nimitz, *Soviet National Income and Product, 1949–1955*, The RAND Corporation, RM-2101, April 6, 1959, p. 68.

earner or salaried employee and receiving payment in the form of wages or salary, even for only a short time, is insured.[5]

Workers hired by the collective farms are probably not covered by the state social insurance system, and prisoners engaged in forced labor are certainly not covered. Probably, though, many of the other workers whose wages are included in the comprehensive but not the TSUNKHU wage bill are covered. Beyond this, certain students are covered by social insurance, as are certain groups that do not fall within the legal definition of wage earners or salaried employees, for example, lawyers working in consultation offices, and gold prospectors.[6] Use of the broader wage-bill concept may mean social insurance benefits are somewhat understated as a percentage of the average wage, but use of the TSUNKHU wage bill would almost certainly lead to an overstatement of such benefits.

The comprehensive civilian wage bill and total social insurance grants and pensions paid, in rubles and as a percentage of the comprehensive civilian wage bill, are shown in Table 17 for each year studied. As has been said, I interpret these percentage figures as approximations to the amount which social insurance contributes to the average gross wage. Thus, according to the data in Table 17, social insurance benefits amounted to an addition of 7 percent to the average wage in 1928,[7]

[5] A. S. Krasnopol'skii, *Osnovnye printsipy sovetskogo gosudarstvennogo sotsial'nogo strakhovaniia* (Moscow, 1951), chapter v.

[6] *Ibid.*, pp. 72, 97 (n. 1).

[7] This figure includes unemployment compensation. Inasmuch as both unemployment and unemployment compensation were officially ended in 1930, it may be of interest in some connections to consider the 1928 benefits other than unemployment compensation. When unemployment benefits are excluded, the social insurance grants and pensions

4.3 percent in 1937, 3.1 percent in 1940,[8] 3.6 percent in 1944, 4.1 percent in 1948, 4.7 percent in 1952, and 4.9 percent in 1954. Interestingly, after a decline from 1928 through 1944, there was an increase during the postwar years although the tendency over the period was for pension rates to decline when measured as a percentage of the average wage. Presumably, the explanation of the increase in total social insurance grants and pensions as a percentage of the wage bill in 1952 and 1954 is an increased number of pensioners. Undoubtedly, the ranks of pensioners have been swelled by former servicemen. In general, military pensions are financed by the social assistance program and, in some cases, by the Ministry of Defense. But servicemen who were wage earners and salaried employees before the war, or who entered the hired labor force on demobilization, are covered by social insurance, and their military service is counted as employment for purposes of determining their eligibility for a social insurance grant or pension and in computing the size of the pension.

Mothers' subsidies. Mothers' subsidies were introduced by a law of June 27, 1936, for families with seven or more children. According to this law, at the birth of the seventh child the mother was paid a lump sum of 2,000 rubles and then 2,000 rubles a year (in monthly payments) for the four years from the child's first to fifth birthdays. The same amounts were paid for the eighth, ninth, and tenth child. At the birth of the eleventh child, a lump sum of 5,000 rubles at birth was paid, and for four years thereafter monthly payments were made amounting to 3,000 rubles a year. In July 1944 such subsidies were extended to cover the third child and the benefit rates were increased. At the birth of the third child, a single lump sum of 400 rubles was paid. Beginning with the fourth child, a lump sum of 1,300 rubles was paid at birth, and in addition monthly payments were made for four years amounting to 960 rubles a year. The benefit rates ranged up to a maximum of an initial lump sum payment of 5,000 rubles plus monthly payments for four years amounting to 3,600 rubles a year for the eleventh and each succeeding child. These rates were cut in half by a law of November 27, 1947.[9]

---

amounted to 5.7 percent of the average wage in 1928. My figures for 1928 correspond reasonably well with the 1927/28 study of wage earner family incomes and expenditures. According to this study, in 1927/28 social insurance benefits received by the chief breadwinner averaged 5.5 percent of the wages of the chief breadwinner, and benefits received by the entire family from social insurance and social assistance averaged 7.8 percent of total family income from wages and salaries. See *Statistika truda,* no. 5–6, 1928, p. 16; no. 1, 1929, p. 18; no. 5–6, 1929, p. 22.

[8] More recent information shows the 1940 figure should be 3.4 percent. See the notes to Table 17.

[9] K. N. Plotnikov, *Biudzhet sotsialisticheskogo gosudarstva* (Moscow, 1948), p. 337; Rovinskii, *Gosudarstvennyi biudzhet SSSR,* p. 308; *Bol'shaia sovetskaia entsiklopediia: SSSR* (Moscow, 1948), cols. 1155–1156; Jean Romeuf, *Le Niveau de Vie en U.R.S.S.* (Paris, 1954), pp. 27–29, 129–131.

The July 1944 law provided also for subsidies to unmarried mothers. An unmarried mother with one child received 100 rubles a month, with two children 150 rubles a month, and with three or more children 200 rubles a month until the children reached the age of twelve. The subsidy rates were cut in half at the end of 1947. In addition, unmarried mothers are entitled to the same benefits for the third and each succeeding child as married mothers.[10]

Total payments of mothers' subsidies were almost 1 billion rubles in 1937, 1.2 billion rubles in 1940, 0.9 billion rubles in 1944, about 2.5 billion rubles in 1948, 4.2 billion rubles in 1952, and 4.7 billion rubles in 1954.[11] It seems reasonable to assume that the share of total mothers' subsidies received by the wage-earner and salaried-employee class is roughly proportional to their relative weight in the total population. Accordingly, it is estimated the wage-earner and salaried-employee class received 36 percent of the total mothers' subsidies or 0.34 billion rubles in 1937, 40 percent of the total or 0.54 billion rubles in 1940, 45 percent of the total or 0.40 billion rubles in 1944, 50 percent of the total or 1.3 billion rubles in 1948, 53 percent of the total or 2.2 billion rubles in 1952, and 57 percent of the total or 2.7 billion rubles in 1954.[12] This amounts to around 0.3 percent of the comprehensive civilian wage bill in 1937, 1940, and 1944, to almost 0.5 percent in 1948, and to 0.6 percent in 1952 and 1954.

Averaged over the entire wage-earner and salaried-employee class, the mothers' subsidies amount to very little, and only a relatively small share of the class receives such subsidies. But the subsidies can make a signifi-

[10] Rovinskii, *Gosudarstvennyi biudzhet SSSR,* p. 308; Romeuf, *Le Niveau de Vie en U.R.S.S.,* pp. 29, 130.

[11] The figures for 1937, 1940, and 1944 are from Plotnikov, *Biudzhet sotsialisticheskogo gosudarstva,* pp. 225, 329; that for 1948 is from Abram Bergson and Hans Heymann, Jr., *Soviet National Income and Product, 1940–1948* (New York, 1954), p. 140; those for 1952 and 1954 are from Oleg Hoeffding and Nancy Nimitz, *Soviet National Income and Product, 1949–1955,* The RAND Corporation, RM-2101, pp. 80, 212.

The number of mothers receiving monthly subsidies in selected years was as follows, in thousands:

Year	Mothers with four or more children	Single mothers with one or more children
1945	844	282
1950	3079	1952
1956	3323	3214
1958	3450	3286

The figures do not include mothers receiving a single lump sum payment at the birth of the third child, who numbered 691,000 in 1958. See TSU, *Narodnoe khoziaistvo SSSR v 1958 g.* (Moscow, 1959), p. 894.

The 1959 Soviet census indicates there were approximately 83.5 million women aged 16 or over, of whom 52 percent were married (*Pravda,* February 4, 1960).

[12] Wage earners, salaried employees, and their families made up 36 percent of the population in 1937 and 58 percent in 1955 (TSU, *Narodnoe khoziaistvo SSSR* (Moscow, 1956), p. 19). Crude interpolations are made for the intervening years in the absence of data on the class structure.

cant supplement to the earnings of large families and to the many families without a male head.[13]

2. EDUCATION AND HEALTH CARE

A free primary education has been provided the Soviet population throughout the period studied.[14] By 1932 a four-year primary education was virtually universal, and by 1939 most children received a free seven-year education, though it was not until 1952 that it was claimed that the seven-year schooling had been made universal.[15] The normal education was being extended to ten years in the larger cities during the postwar years, but until 1956 tuition was charged in the 8th, 9th, and 10th grades. The expansion in secondary education, vocational training, and higher education has been even more impressive. In 1954 the total number of pupils (including adults) in the general primary, seven-year, and secondary schools was 31.5 million or about 2.5 times that in 1928. The number of pupils in the first four grades increased by less than 25 percent over this period while in 1954 there were 8 times as many pupils in the fifth to seventh grades and 31 times as many pupils in the eighth to tenth grades as in 1928. Over the same period, the number of students in vocational secondary schools increased 8 times, from 0.2 million in 1928 to 1.6 million in 1954, and the number of students in universities and other higher educational institutions increased 6.5 times, from 177 thousand in 1928 to 1.1 million in 1954.[16] There has also been a great expansion in facilities for the day care and education of preschool children. The number of children in the permanent nurseries for children up to three years of age increased almost 14 times and the number of children in kindergartens for children of three to seven years increased about 12 times between 1928 and 1954.[17]

Ordinary or general secondary education was apparently free, at least to wage earners and salaried employees and their families, until 1940. According to a 1927 law, which apparently remained in effect until mid-

[13] See Franklyn D. Holzman, *Soviet Taxation* (Cambridge, Mass., 1955), p. 182, for a tabulation of the mothers' subsidies and tax concessions to families of various sizes in 1950.

[14] Free education in the Soviet Union does not include free textbooks, writing materials, or (where these are required) school uniforms, which are paid for by the parents. See U.S. Department of Health, Education and Welfare, *Education in the USSR,* Bulletin 1957, no. 14 (Washington, 1957), pp. 57–58.

[15] Gosplan, *Summary of the Fulfillment of the First Five Year Plan for the Development of the National Economy of the USSR* (Moscow, 1933), pp. 236–237, 296; *Pravda,* May 21, 1951; September 2, 1952.

[16] TSU, *Kul'turnoe stroitel'stvo SSSR; Statisticheskii sbornik* (Moscow, 1956), pp. 76, 122, 201–202. If students taking correspondence courses are included, the number of students receiving a secondary vocational education increased 9 times and the number of students receiving a higher education increased almost 10 times between 1928 and 1954.

[17] TSU, *Narodnoe khoziaistvo SSSR* (1956), p. 248. Expenditures on the nurseries are included with expenditures on health care rather than education.

1936, fees were charged in the vocational secondary schools and in the higher educational institutions. For workers and their families, however, the exemptions from fees based on income were such that probably very few were subject to fees in 1928, and some students received stipends.[18] The new Soviet Constitution of December 1936 abolished all tuition payments and stated that the majority of students in higher educational institutions should receive government stipends. Tuition was again introduced for ordinary secondary education (the 8th, 9th, and 10th grades), for vocational secondary education, and for the universities and other higher educational institutions at the beginning of the 1940/41 school year. At the same time, the criteria for receiving stipends were stiffened.[19] Even so, tuition payments remained very small on the whole and amounted to only a fraction of the stipends and scholarships received from the state.[20] For preschool children in the nurseries and kindergartens, fees which cover part of the cost and which vary with the income of the parent have been charged at least since 1940 and perhaps throughout the period studied.[21]

All Soviet citizens are entitled to free medical treatment and care, and there has been a great expansion in public health care and facilities under the Soviet regime. The number of doctors increased almost 5 times, from 63 thousand in 1928 to 310 thousand in 1955, and the total number of medical personnel increased about 6.6 times, from 399 thousand in 1928 to 2,627 thousand in 1955. The number of hospital beds also increased about 5 times, from 247 thousand in 1928 to 1,289 thousand in 1955.[22] There has also been a large expansion in the number of sanatoria and

[18] Abram Bergson, *The Structure of Soviet Wages* (Cambridge, Mass., 1946), pp. 27–29.

[19] The fee in secondary schools (both general and vocational) was 200 rubles a year in Moscow, Leningrad, and the Republic capitals and 150 rubles a year elsewhere. In the higher educational institutions, the fee was 500 rubles a year for higher education in art, music, and drama; for other types of higher education, the fee was 400 rubles a year in Moscow, Leningrad, and the Republic capitals and 300 rubles a year elsewhere. See Decree of the Council of Commissars of the USSR of October 2, 1940, *Sobranie postanovlenii i rasporiazhenii pravitel'stva SSSR*, no. 27, sec. 637, 1940, pp. 910ff. For an English translation of this decree, see Bergson, *The Structure of Soviet Wages*, pp. 234–235.

The fees did not apply to the schools established at the time to provide "state labor reserves" by drafting youths of 14 to 17 years of age for industrial training of six months' to two years' duration. These schools are free, and the students are maintained by the state during their training (*ibid.*, pp. 236–237).

The Sixth Five Year Plan provided for the abolition of all tuition payments beginning with the 1956/57 school year.

[20] Bergson and Heymann, *Soviet National Income and Product, 1940–1948*, pp. 142, 158.

[21] The scale of fees established in 1948 for urban areas ranged from 30 to 80 rubles a month in nurseries and from 40 to 100 rubles a month in kindergartens, depending on the parents' income. These fees are for a nine- or ten-hour day; for a longer period the fees are higher. Large families and single mothers are in certain circumstances subject to reduced fees. See Lief Björk, *Wages, Prices and Social Legislation in the Soviet Union* (London, 1953), pp. 128–129.

[22] TSU, *Narodnoe khoziaistvo SSSR* (1956), p. 244; TSU, *Narodnoe khoziaistvo SSSR v 1956 g.* (Moscow, 1957), p. 271. The figures exclude military medical personnel and hospital beds. The figures on hospital beds also exclude, it is believed, beds in sanatoria and rest homes.

rest homes for patients needing specialized treatment, for general con-
valescence, and also for vacations for the well. In some cases fees covering part of the cost of maintenance are charged those in sanatoria and rest
homes, while in other cases there is no charge or the fees are paid by
the workers' trade union from social insurance funds. Maternal and child
health centers have been widely developed, as have the nurseries for preschool children, already mentioned. General public health measures such
as the control of contagious diseases, inspection and control of sanitary
conditions in the manufacture and sale of food, and research on public
health and medicine have also been greatly extended.

Western medical observers during the 1930's were of the opinion that
the rapid expansion of medical facilities was made at the cost of a reduction in quality and find today that the quality of Soviet medical services
and personnel is still well below the United States level.[23] The evidence
suggests, nevertheless, that Soviet health services have accomplished a
great deal and have made a very substantial contribution to the health
and general well-being of the Soviet worker. Tuberculosis remains a serious problem, but beyond this there seems no evidence of frequent widespread epidemics or even of excessive loss of working time through illness
such as prevailed in Czarist Russia and in the industrial slums of nine-
teenth century England and America,[24] and this in spite of the increasingly congested Soviet housing conditions.[25] This must be attributed, of
course, to the general advance in medical knowledge as well as to the
medical care and health measures undertaken by the Soviet government.
Some indication of the effectiveness of Soviet health care may be provided
by the decline in death rates the Russians claim to have achieved over
the planning period, though various other factors such as the advance of
medical knowledge, the increased educational level of the population, and
the recent improvement in diet have also played a role. According to Soviet claims, average life expectancy increased from 44 years in 1926/27
to 67 years in 1955/56, and the crude death rate declined from 20 per
thousand inhabitants in 1926 to under 8 per thousand in 1956, 1957, and
1958.[26] On the face of it, these figures show striking advances and indeed

[23] Bergson, *The Structure of Soviet Wages*, pp. 31–32 and the sources cited there; U.S.
Department of Health, Education and Welfare, *Report of United States Public Health
Mission to the Union of Soviet Socialist Republics, August 13 to September 14, 1957*
(Washington, 1959).

[24] Frank Lorimer, *The Population of the Soviet Union* (Geneva, 1946), pp. 120–121;
U.S. Department of Health, Education and Welfare, *Report of United States Public
Health Mission to the Union of Soviet Socialist Republics, August 13 to September 14,
1957*, p. v.

[25] From this point of view, investment in public health has to some extent been a
substitute, and a fairly effective one, for investment in more adequate housing. Louis
Winnick, *American Housing and Its Use; The Demand for Shelter Space* (Census Monograph Series, New York, 1957), p. 2.

[26] TSU, *Narodnoe khoziaistvo SSSR v 1956 g.* (Moscow, 1957), pp. 269–270; TSU,
Narodnoe khoziaistvo SSSR v 1958 g. (Moscow, 1959), pp. 31, 35.

compare very favorably to current American rates.[27] But the crude rates reflect changes in the age distribution of the population which tend to overstate the Soviet advances and must be interpreted with caution.[28] These qualifications would not apply to the impressive reduction in infant mortality from 187 per thousand births in 1926/27 or 184 per thousand births as late as 1940 to 47 per thousand births in 1956 and 41 per thousand births in 1958.[29]

It is of considerable interest to attempt to evaluate the contribution of these free education and health services to the real income of the Soviet worker. There are several difficulties, however, and my estimates are, of necessity, rough. Such free services are part of real income but not, strictly speaking, part of real wages. For simplicity, I nevertheless express my measure of them as a percentage of the average wage. The education and health services outlined above are available to the entire Soviet population regardless of occupation.[30] It is necessary, therefore, to estimate the share of the total of such services which are consumed by the urban wage-earner and salaried-employee class. There is the further problem of valuing such services, a problem for which there is perhaps no entirely satisfactory solution. For present purposes, I assume that the value of the free services to the consumer is equal to the cost (to the government and other institutions) of providing them. The free services are accordingly valued first at the current cost of providing them. They are then revalued at constant prices, using a special price index number, so that the free services may be taken into account in the measures of real wages in chapter IX.

Total expenditures on education and on health care by the government

---

[27] In the United States in 1957 the average length of life was something over 69 years and the crude death rate was 9.6 per thousand. *Statistical Abstract of the United States: 1959* (Washington, 1959), pp. 59, 63.

[28] The Soviet crude death rate for recent years is affected by the relative decline of old people, who suffered most heavily from the wartime privations. Standardization for changes in age structure compared to the 1920's would have the effect of raising the current death rate and reducing life expectancy. In comparisons with the United States figures, it should be kept in mind that the United States has a higher proportion of old people than the Soviet Union. Warren Eason, "The Soviet Population Today," *Foreign Affairs*, July 1959, p. 604.

[29] Lorimer, *The Population of the Soviet Union*, p. 116; TSU, *Narodnoe khoziaistvo SSSR v 1958 g.*, p. 31. This decline in infant mortality, Eason estimates, accounts for about half the decline in the crude death rate. Eason, *Foreign Affairs*, July 1959, p. 604.

[30] This is true in general, but there are some benefits of this nature specifically for wage earners and salaried employees. These would include the services of the sanatoria, rest homes, and resorts, the children's nurseries and camps maintained by the social insurance system and those health, child care, and recreational facilities maintained by industrial enterprises or other institutions for their employees. Also, during the twenties and early thirties there was class discrimination in admissions to vocational schools and higher educational institutions and in the granting of stipends; the wage earner and, in some cases, the peasants were favored, while salaried employees were discriminated against, and children of persons living on unearned income and of the bourgeoisie generally were excluded from the vocational schools and universities. See Bergson, *The Structure of Soviet Wages*, pp. 109–115.

and other institutions in each of the years studied were as shown in Table 18, item 1. The total includes the government budget appropriations for education and health care (the major share of the total) and expenditures from the state social insurance fund. It also includes expenditures by

TABLE 18

The Soviet Worker's Health and Education Benefits, 1928–54

	1928	1937	1940	1944	1948	1952	1954
1. Total outlays by government and other institutions							
a. On education, billion rubles	1.09	20.6	27.0	24.8	64.5	68.8	77.2
b. On health, billion rubles	0.65	8.9	12.0	13.6	24.9	28.8	34.8
c. Total, billion rubles	1.74	29.5	39.0	38.4	89.4	97.6	112.0
2. Outlays benefiting urban population							
a. On education, billion rubles	0.49	9.7	13.0	11.9	32.3	37.2	44.0
b. On health, billion rubles	0.52	7.1	9.6	10.9	19.9	23.0	27.8
c. Total, billion rubles	1.01	16.8	22.6	22.8	52.2	60.2	71.8
3. Outlays on education and health benefiting urban workers							
a. Billion rubles	0.78	13.8	18.3	18.7	42.5	49.4	58.9
b. Percent of urban wage bill	11.0	17.5	15.8	16.9	21.1	17.5	18.0
c. Rubles per urban worker	85	550	660	918	1,523	1,444	1,557
4. Price index number for education and health services							
a. Using 1937 weights	19.8	100	127	132	265	219	206
b. Using given-year weights	17.7	100	124	—	249	209	201
5. Urban workers' education and health benefits at 1937 price level, rubles per worker							
a. Based on price index using 1937 weights	429	550	520	695	575	659	756
b. Based on price index using given-year weights	480	550	532	—	612	691	775

Note: The dash (—) indicates that data were not computed.
Sources and methods:
    Lines 1a, 1b, and 1c: 1928 through 1948: Abram Bergson, Hans Heymann, Jr., and Oleg Hoeffding, *Soviet National Income and Product, 1928–1948: Revised Data,* The RAND Corporation, RM-2544, November 15, 1960, pp. 82, 89. *1952, 1954:* Oleg Hoeffding and Nancy Nimitz, *Soviet National Income and Product, 1949–1955,* The RAND Corporation, RM-2101, April 6, 1959, pp. 163, 170.
    Lines 2a, 2b and 2c: See text.
    Line 3a: See text.
    Line 3b: The figures in line 3a are taken as a percentage of the urban comprehensive civilian wage bill. The comprehensive civilian wage bill in each year is shown in Table 17. The urban share of the comprehensive wage bill is estimated at 74 percent of the total in 1928 on the basis of some rough unpublished calculations. In 1937 the urban share of the comprehensive civilian wage bill is estimated to have been 76 percent on the basis of some unpublished computations of Abram Bergson and Faye Goldware. I assume the urban share of the comprehensive civilian wage bill in later years was the same as in 1937.
    Line 3c: Computed by applying the percentages in line 3b to the average annual wage of nonagricultural wage earners and salaried employees in Table 13.
    Lines 4a and 4b: See text.
    Lines 5a and 5b: Computed by dividing the figures in line 3c by the price index numbers in lines 4a and 4b.

economic enterprises, collective farms, trade unions, et cetera, on such items as education and training, health care (including physical training), sanitary inspection and control, and medical facilities. The figure for education includes payments of stipends and scholarships.[31] All expenditures on education and health are treated here as representing services to consumers, though it will be recognized that part, and perhaps a large

[31] In principle, tuition payments should be deducted from total expenditures on education, but these are so small as to make a negligible difference in the results.

part, of government expenditures of this nature might alternatively be viewed as investment. The figures include capital outlays on the construction of such buildings as schools and hospitals, which would be considered as investment from any point of view. The expenditures on education include, in addition to expenditures on schools and other educational institutions of all sorts and on-the-job training, the cost of political propaganda and expenditures on scientific research (including the budget of the Academy of Sciences, et cetera), which can hardly be considered as adding to the real income of workers. As shown in Table 19, breakdowns of the

TABLE 19

Expenditures on Education from the Soviet Government Budget,
1928/29, 1937, 1940, and 1954

	1928/29[a]		1937[b]		1940[b]		1954[b]	
	Million rubles	Percent of total	Billion rubles	Percent of total	Billion rubles	Percent of total	Billion rubles	Percent of total
1. Mass education								
a. General education of children and youths								
Schools	575	45.0	6.4	38.8	8.9	39.7	23.9	36.4
Children's homes and kindergartens	80	6.2	1.2	7.3	2.1	9.4	6.1	9.3
Other			0.6	3.6	0.6	2.7	2.7	4.1
Totals	655	51.2	8.2	49.7	11.6	51.8	32.7	49.8
b. General education and political enlightenment work among adults	185	14.5	1.1	6.7	1.0	4.4	2.3	3.5
c. Art and radio	8[e]	0.6	0.5	3.0	0.6	2.7	0.7	1.0
d. Printing	16	1.2	0.2	1.2	0.4	1.8	0.6	0.9
e. Totals	864	67.5	10.0	60.6	13.6	60.7	36.2	55.2
2. Higher education and vocational training								
a. Universities and other higher educational institutions	137	10.7	2.3[d]	13.9	2.9	12.9	9.7	14.8
b. Technikums and other secondary vocational schools	137	10.7	1.2	7.3	1.8	8.0	5.4	8.2
c. Other	66	5.2	2.1	12.7	3.0	13.4	7.4	11.3
d. Totals	340	26.6	5.6	33.9	7.7	34.3	22.6	34.4
3. Scientific institutes	75	5.9	0.9	5.5	1.1	5.0	6.8	10.4
Totals	1,279	100.0	16.5	100.0	22.5	100.0	65.6	100.0

[a] Gosplan, *Kontrol'nye tsifry narodnogo khoziaistva SSSR na 1929/30 god* (Moscow, 1930), p. 495. These figures include expenditures from outside the government budget. Note that these figures are given in millions of rubles while those for later years are in billions of rubles.
[b] TSU, *Kul'turnoe stroitel'stvo SSSR; Statisticheskii sbornik* (Moscow, 1956), p. 73.
[e] Cinema and radio.
[d] The further breakdown of expenditures in this category in 1937 was as follows:

	Million rubles
(1) Academies	72
(2) Higher educational institutions and clinics under medical institutions	1,982
(3) Communist higher educational institutions and Institutes of the Red Professoriat	42
(4) Higher Communist agricultural schools	131
(5) Candidates for degrees and scientific research in higher educational institutes	49
Total	2,276

(K. N. Plotnikov , *Biudzhet sotsialisticheskogo gosudarstva* (Moscow, 1948), p. 149.)

government expenditures on education in several years indicate that expenditures on scientific institutes rose from under 6 percent of the total in 1928/29 to almost 10.5 percent in 1954. Expenditures on museums, libraries, and parks, and subsidies to the press, radio, theatre, and cinema are also included in the totals for education. While such subsidies undoubtedly contribute to real income, my procedure may lead to some double-counting, inasmuch as the cost-of-living index numbers take account of the low, subsidized prices of books, newspapers, journals, and the movies. Some of the measures financed under the heading of health and education may not contribute anything to the Soviet worker's real income, some may even be onerous to him, and others may contribute only in an indirect general way. I point this out but can make no attempt to divide total expenditures into those which do and those which do not add to the worker's real income. Clearly, in taking total expenditures on "education," I overstate the contribution of educational services to real wages.

Of the total expenditures on education and health it is necessary to estimate the share that accrues to urban workers. Because the urban population receives more and better education and health services than the rural population, one cannot take a simple per capita expenditure. The first step is to estimate the share of total expenditures on education and health which accrues to the benefit of the urban population as a whole. The second is to estimate the amount of this which benefits urban wage earners and salaried employees and their families. These estimates are shown in Table 18, lines 2 and 3, and are explained below.

Taking education first, I estimate that, of total expenditures by the government and other institutions on education, the urban share was 45 percent in 1928, 47 percent in 1937, 48 percent in both 1940 and 1944, 50 percent in 1948, 54 percent in 1952, and 57 percent in 1954. The (necessarily very rough) estimates in terms of rubles are shown in Table 18, line 2a. They are based mainly on the urban-rural distribution of pupils.[32]

[32] The estimated urban share of total expenditures on "mass education" (see Table 19) is based on the urban-rural distribution of pupils in the elementary, seven-year and ordinary secondary schools, with an allowance for the higher cost per pupil in urban schools. Urban pupils were the following percentage of the total student body in these schools: 29 percent in 1928, 30 percent in 1937, 32 percent in 1940, 31 percent in 1945 (I use this figure for 1944), 35 percent in 1948, 40 percent in 1952, and 44 percent in 1954. TSU, *Kul'turnoe stroitel'stvo SSSR; Statisticheskii sbornik*, pp. 76–79. Undoubtedly the cost per pupil has been higher in urban than in rural areas, partly because of better facilities and higher paid teachers in urban schools (V. A. Shavrin, *Gosudarstvennyi biudzhet SSSR* (3d ed., Moscow, 1951), pp. 57–63) and partly, perhaps mainly, because of the larger proportion of urban pupils in the secondary schools. Rather arbitrarily I assume that the cost per pupil was about 40 percent higher in urban than in rural areas in 1928. At that time, the urban elementary, seven-year and ordinary secondary schools accounted for 37 percent of the teachers but for only 29 percent of the pupils; in later years the urban-rural ratio of teachers was about the same as that of pupils. (See TSU, *Kul'turnoe stroitel'stvo SSSR; Statisticheskii sbornik*, pp. 76–83.) In 1937 and later years I assume the cost per pupil was about 20 percent greater in urban than in rural schools. Allowing for this cost differential, the urban share of expenditures on mass

So far as health care is concerned, I assume that about 80 percent of total expenditures by the government and other institutions benefited the urban population in all years studied. The corresponding ruble figures are shown in Table 18, line 2b. The available data do not provide any very firm basis for estimating the urban-rural distribution of expenditures on health care, and this is a rough estimate.[33] It is based in part on data on the urban share of such items as hospital beds and doctors, which indicate that the amount of medical care of various sorts per capita must have been considerably greater in urban than in rural areas.[34] Undoubtedly, too, the quality of service and the cost of providing it per patient are higher in the cities than in the countryside. There are more highly trained doctors and specialists in urban areas while many rural

---

education is estimated at 37 percent in 1928, 34 percent in 1937, 36 percent in 1940, 35 percent in 1944, 39 percent in 1948, 44 percent in 1952, and 49 percent in 1954.

Of total expenditures on higher education and vocational training (see Table 19) I estimate, of necessity arbitrarily, that 80 percent accrued to members of urban families in 1928 and 70 percent in all other years. In the higher educational institutions only, wage earners and salaried employees and their families (who are mostly though not all urban) made up 82 percent of the student body in 1935 and 76 percent in 1938, according to Ia. A. Ioffe (comp.), *SSSR i kapitalisticheskie strany* (Moscow, 1939), p. 108, and E. N. Medynskii, *Narodnoe obrazovanie v SSSR* (Moscow, 1952), p. 164. The urban-rural distribution of expenditures derived from the calculations concerning expenditures on mass education and higher education and vocational training is assumed to apply to total expenditures on education.

[33] Some confirmation for this estimate appears to be provided in a source which became available after the computations were made. According to partial data on expenditures on health care from the government budget, expenditures on urban hospitals, dispensaries, and nurseries amounted to 81 percent in 1940, 78 percent in 1950, and 79 percent in 1956 of total expenditures on urban and rural hospitals, dispensaries and mobile clinics, and nurseries. See *Finansy i sotsialisticheskoe stroitel'stvo* (Moscow, 1957), p. 214. The above figures exclude medical health stations in the predominantly urban enterprises, the feldsher (subprofessional medical personnel) and midwife stations, which are probably largely rural, and perhaps other types of medical institutions. Thus, the figures cited above may not be typical of the urban-rural distribution of total expenditures on health care.

[34] The urban share of hospital beds has been around 75 percent of the total throughout the entire period, according to data in *Bol'shaia sovetskaia entsiklopediia: SSSR* (1948), col. 1163; *Bol'shaia sovetskaia entsiklopediia* (2d ed., Moscow, 1957), vol. 50 on USSR, pp. 392–394. The urban share of doctors has apparently been larger than this though the urban share of middle-ranking medical personnel — feldshers, midwives, and nurses — has been smaller. In 1937, 85 percent of the doctors were urban (TSUNKHU, *Sotsialisticheskoe stroitel'stvo SSSR, 1933–1938 gg.* (Moscow, 1939), p. 133) and in 1941, 84 percent of the doctors and 64 percent of the middle-ranking medical personnel were urban (*Bol'shaia sovetskaia entsiklopediia: SSSR* (1948), cols. 1178–1179). The urban share of places in permanent nurseries was 87 percent in 1928, 62 percent in 1938, 65 percent in 1940, 66 percent in 1950, and 68 percent in 1954 (TSU, *Narodnoe khoziaistvo SSSR* (1956), p. 248; *Bol'shaia sovetskaia entsiklopediia: SSSR* (1948), col. 1173). At the same time, the urban population was only 18 percent of the total in 1928 and had increased to 43 percent of the total in 1956. See Gosplan, *The Soviet Union Looks Ahead: The Five Year Plan for Economic Construction* (New York, 1929), p. 228; TSU, *Narodnoe khoziaistvo SSSR* (1956), p. 17.

areas are served only by feldshers or nurses,[35] and the hospitals and clinics are better equipped in the cities than in the country. Of course, some of the rural population must receive medical care in the cities. Finally, the wage-earner and salaried-employee class, predominantly urban, is the main recipient of the services of the various vacation facilities maintained by the government, by the social insurance system, and other institutions.

Clearly the bulk of expenditures on health care must have been spent on urban health facilities and services. At the same time, there has undoubtedly been an improvement in the relative position of the rural population with respect to health care over the entire period 1928 to 1954. Allowing the urban population a constant percentage of total expenditures on health care over the period while the urban population increased much faster than the rural population takes this into account, if only in the roughest way.

Of the total outlays on both education and health benefiting the urban population (Table 18, line 2c), urban workers and their families — urban wage earners and salaried employees and their families — received an estimated 77 percent in 1928 and 82 percent in later years. The amounts, shown in Table 18, line 3a, are rough estimates, based in part on the estimated ratio of urban wage and salary income to total urban income. Expenditures on urban worker education and health are shown as a percentage of the urban comprehensive civilian wage bill in Table 18, line 3b. I interpret these figures as the amount which the free education and health services add to the average gross money wage at current prices. Thus, according to the data in Table 18, the health and education services received by urban wage-earner and salaried-employee families amounted, at current prices, to 11 percent of the average wage in 1928, 17.5 percent in 1937, 15.8 percent in 1940, 16.9 percent in 1944, 21.1 percent in 1948, 17.5 percent in 1952, and 18.0 percent in 1954. Applying these percentages to the average annual wage of nonagricultural wage earners and salaried employees, the expenditure on education and health services in rubles per employed worker in current prices is computed. These figures are shown in Table 18, line 3c.

When the Soviet worker's income is measured in real terms, it will be necessary to express the value of the benefits received in real terms also. Cash benefits can be deflated by the cost-of-living index numbers, but these do not provide a very appropriate deflator for the free services. Accordingly, I compute special index numbers intended to represent, though

---

[35] Doctors' earnings were higher in urban than in rural areas in the 1930's, according to data in TSUNKHU, *Trud v SSSR* (Moscow, 1936), pp. 347–348. In recent years the salary scale for rural doctors has been higher than for urban doctors (Shavrin, *Gosudarstvennyi biudzhet SSSR*, pp. 84–85), but average earnings may still be higher in urban areas.

at best only roughly, the change in the cost to the government and other institutions of providing these services. In these computations I assume that payments for labor account for half of the cost of providing the services and purchases of commodities for the other half of the cost in all years.[36] To represent the change in the cost of labor, I use the index number of average nonagricultural money wages. Since it is the cost of the services which is of interest in this connection, I use the index number of average wages on an hourly basis (from Table 14). I assume that the index numbers of the official prices of commodities in the urban USSR (Table 6, lines 2a and 2b) are reasonably applicable to the prices of commodities purchased by the government and other institutions for use in education and health services. The price index number for education and health services computed from the index number of average hourly wages and the index number of official prices of commodities based on 1937 weights is shown in Table 18, line 4a; that computed from the index number of average hourly wages and the index number of official prices of commodities based on given-year weights is shown in Table 18, line 4b. The deflated value of the health and education benefits received per worker in each year, expressed in rubles at the 1937 price level, is shown in Table 18, lines 5a and 5b.

3. TOTAL BENEFITS

If we continue to consider, for the moment, the value at current prices, the various types of benefits in cash and in kind received by the Soviet worker in addition to his money wage amounted to about 18 percent of the average gross wage in 1928.[37] This compares with direct taxes and purchases of government bonds of 2.5 percent of the average gross wage. In 1937, benefits amounted to 22 percent of the average wage, and taxes and the purchase of government bonds took 4 percent of the average wage. In 1940, benefits added 19 percent to the average wage, and taxes and bonds took something over 7.5 percent of the average wage. In 1944, benefits amounted to almost 21 percent of the average wage, but taxes and bond purchases took over 28 percent of the average wage. In 1948, benefits amounted to almost 26 percent, and taxes and bond purchases to over 13 percent of the average wage. In 1952, benefits amounted to almost 23

---

[36] Abram Bergson found this ratio of expenditures to prevail in 1937; see his *Soviet National Income and Product in 1937* (New York, 1953), p. 134. Evidence that approximately this ratio of expenditures prevailed in 1940, 1950, and 1956 is to be found in *Finansy i sotsialisticheskoe stroitel'stvo*, pp. 210, 213–214. It is possible that in 1944 labor accounted for a somewhat higher percentage of total expenditures as teachers' salaries had been revised considerably and the wage scale for at least some medical personnel had been raised (Murray Yanowitch, "Changes in the Soviet Money Wage Level Since 1940," *American Slavic and East European Review*, 14:200–202 (April 1955)), while commodity prices paid by institutions on the whole remained at the prewar level.

[37] Including unemployment compensation. If unemployment compensation is excluded, the benefits amounted to not quite 17 percent of the average wage.

percent, and taxes and bond purchases to 15 percent of the average wage. In 1954, benefits amounted to 23.5 percent, and taxes and bond purchases to less than 11 percent of the average wage. In all but the war year 1944, benefits have been greater than taxes and bond purchases. Interestingly, when measured as a percentage of the average wage, the benefits received by the Soviet worker have varied much less over the period than their tax payments and purchases of government bonds.

In real terms, all benefits amounted to the following percentages of gross real wages, when wages and benefits are deflated by the 1937-weighted price index numbers: 1928, 18.6 percent; 1937, 22.1 percent; 1940, 21.0 percent; 1944, 29.4 percent; 1948, 30.8 percent; 1952, 22.8 percent; 1954, 22.0 percent. When the price index numbers using given-year weights are used, the results are: 1928, 15.8 percent; 1937, 22.1 percent; 1940, 20.7 percent; 1948, 29.6 percent; 1952, 22.2 percent; 1954, 21.5 percent.

It may be interesting at this point to consider the Soviet claims concerning the "social wage." Unfortunately, the available Soviet data concerning benefits are difficult to interpret and do not always seem consistent. Soviet statements concerning benefits fall into three main types. First, there is the total value of benefits accruing to the entire Soviet population.[38] Secondly, there are index numbers of the change in real income including benefits. Finally, there are statements regarding the value of the benefits received by workers, expressed as a percentage of the average wage or of average worker family income. I consider only this third type of statement here, and will take up the index numbers of real income including benefits in the next chapter.

Soviet claims concerning the value of benefits received by the working class as a percentage of wages or of income for various years during the period 1928 to 1956 are shown in Table 20. The figures for the various years are not always comparable. For one thing, the prewar and war figures relate to wage earners only and the postwar figures relate to wage earners and salaried employees. In the early years (prior to about 1937) manual workers received more favorable treatment under the social insurance system and in admission to higher education, and their benefits were undoubtedly greater than those enjoyed by nonmanual workers, both absolutely and as a percentage of earnings. Secondly, the figures in most cases are based largely on sample budget studies which may not be typical of all workers and may not be very comparable from one period to another. The budget studies provide the information on wages and cash benefits while the value of free services enjoyed is generally based on expenditure norms of the institutions supplying the services. Beyond this, the statements on benefits are often ambiguous on what is included

[38] The total benefits provided from the government budget and by enterprises for several years are given in TSU, *Narodnoe khoziaistvo SSSR* (1956), p. 38.

TABLE 20

Soviet Statements on Benefits
as a Contribution to Wages

Year	Benefits in percentage of wage or income
1927/28	27.9; 35.5
1928/29	28.4; 36.0
1929/30	27.9; 35.8
1930	31.0
1932	38.6
1935	34.5
1936	20 to 25
1944	38.0
1950–56	33.3

Sources and methods:
1927/28–1929/30: TSUNKHU, *Narodnoe khoziaistvo SSSR* (Moscow, 1932), p. 418. The data refer to wage earners in all branches of the economy. They are based on expenditures on benefits and on budget studies. The smaller figure in each case measures benefits (grants and pensions from social insurance and trade union funds, education, students' stipends, cultural benefits, medical aid, free living quarters at enterprises, and benefits from the "funds for improving the living conditions of workers" (FBUR)) as a percentage of earnings. The larger figure includes wages received during paid holidays and wages of students in the industrial training schools (FZU) with benefits, and excludes these items from earnings.
1930–1935: TSUNKHU, *Trud v SSSR* (Moscow, 1936), p. 342. The data refer to wage earners in large-scale industry and are based on budget studies. Benefits are expressed as a percentage of earnings.
1936: Bol'shaia sovetskaia entsiklopediia: SSSR (Moscow, 1948), col. 1140. The figure refers to wage earners and is based on budget studies. Benefits are expressed as a percentage of the family "budget," which probably means total family income.
1944: N. Voznesenskii, *Voennaia ekonomika SSSR v period otechestvennoi voiny* (Moscow, 1948), pp. 118–119. The figure refers to wage earners. Benefits include wages received for the usual paid vacations; as regular vacations were cancelled during the war, this presumably refers to compensation for leave not taken. Benefits are expressed as a percentage of average daily earnings. Average daily earnings exclude vacation pay and certain other payments which are included in average monthly earnings. See TSU, *Slovar'-spravochnik po sotsial'no-ekonomicheskoi statistike* (Moscow, 1944), pp. 212–213.
1950–1956: Bol'shaia sovetskaia entsiklopediia (2d ed., Moscow, 1957), vol. 50 on USSR, p. 384; Akademiia nauk SSSR, Institut ekonomiki, *Politicheskaia ekonomiia* (Moscow, 1954), p. 462; S. P. Figurnov, "Chto poluchaiut rabochie i sluzhashchie SSSR sverkh zarabotnoi platy," *V pomoshch' politicheskomu samoobrazovaniiu,* no. 9, 1959, p. 79. The figure refers to wage earners and salaried employees. Benefits are taken, it is believed, as a percentage of wages.

with benefits and what income concept is used. The benefits received by a family are generally taken as a percentage of the family's wages, it is believed, but the 1936 figure expresses benefits as a percentage of the family "budget." Probably benefits are taken as a percentage of wages (or income) gross of taxes, but none of the sources is explicit on this. Wages paid during paid holidays are counted as benefits and excluded from wages in the larger set of figures for 1927/28 to 1929/30 and in the figures for 1944 and 1950–56. The smaller set of figures for 1927/28 to 1929/30 count vacation pay with wages and not as benefits. It is not known how vacation pay is treated in the figures for 1930–36. The postwar figure also probably includes, while the prewar figures probably do not, a sort of housing subsidy based on the difference between rent paid and the cost to the government of maintaining the housing.[39]

[39] According to S. P. Figurnov, "Chto poluchaiut rabochie i sluzhashchie SSSR sverkh zarabotnoi platy," *V pomoshch' politicheskomu samoobrazovaniiu,* no. 9, 1959, pp. 78–79, government outlays on housing exceed rent by 2 to 3 rubles per square meter per month. (Maximum rent, which I assume to be the average rent paid in the postwar years, is 1.32 rubles per square meter per month.) The same source shows that benefits received by a sample of 200 Moscow wage earner families totaled 36.4 percent of family wages, of

The Soviet figures in Table 20 do not show any consistent rise in the contribution of benefits to wages. In view of the lack of comparability among the figures for the various years not much significance can be accorded this lack of trend. It is interesting that this is generally in accord with my own computations, yet the Russians claim that real income including benefits has increased more rapidly than gross real wages.[40] Of course, the Soviet figures in Table 20 are in current prices, and in real terms the trend might look different.

In comparison with my own computations, most of the Soviet figures in Table 20 are high. In some cases the difference can be largely explained by the different treatment of vacation pay. For 1954, I compute benefits at 23.5 percent of the average gross wage; deducting vacation pay from the average wage and adding it to benefits would bring my figure to about 30 percent — close to the Soviet "one-third." [41] For 1928 and 1944 the gap between the Soviet figures and my estimates is too large to be explained entirely by the different treatment of vacation pay. Part of the difference is probably explained by the fact that the Soviet figures refer only to wage earners who most certainly in 1928, and possibly during the war, received larger benefits than salaried employees. But there are undoubtedly other differences in coverage and definition. My figure for 1937 is close to the Soviet figure for 1936, but as the nature of this Soviet figure is not explained in any detail, this agreement may not be very significant. My own computations are admittedly very crude and may err, but the Soviet figures are not clear or consistent enough to provide a reasonable basis for checking my estimates against the Soviet claims.

---

which 2.9 percent represents the housing subsidy and 5.2 percent payments for paid vacations. The figures probably relate to 1957 or 1958.

The housing subsidy, Figurnov indicates, is not included in figures on total benefits provided the population from the government budget and by enterprises, although vacation pay is included. Reference to the housing subsidy is made also in a discussion of family budgets in Nauchno-issledovatel'skii institut truda Gosudarstvennogo komiteta Soveta ministrov SSSR po voprosam truda i zarabotnoi platy, *Voprosy truda v SSSR* (Moscow, 1958), pp. 390–393.

[40] See chapter IX.

[41] Payment during paid vacations, I assume here, amounted to about 5 percent of average annual earnings. Paid holidays averaged 16 working days in 1956 (TSU, *Dostizheniia sovetskoi vlasti za sorok let v tsifrakh* (Moscow, 1957), p. 334) which is about 5 percent of the total of 312 working days in a year (6 days a week for 52 weeks).

Adding the housing subsidy — 2.9 percent in (circa) 1958 according to a study of Moscow budgets (see fn. 39) — would bring my 1954 figure to almost exactly the Soviet figure.

IX ·

REAL WAGES

In this chapter I bring together the measures of the change in the cost of living and in money wages to arrive at the final measures of the change in the real wage of the Soviet worker over the period 1928 to 1954. In section 1, after a brief review of the major limitations of the calculations, I present and comment upon the results. I then compare my findings with those of other Western students of Soviet retail prices and real wages (section 2) and with the official Soviet claims concerning the course of retail prices and real wages (section 3).

I. REAL WAGES

As the reader will have noted, there are possibilities of error at almost every stage in the calculations. On the whole, I believe, the measures are quite reliable, but there are weak spots which it may be useful to review here. The cost-of-living index numbers are based on quite firm price comparisons so far as the official prices are concerned, and the weights are also well based. The fact that I rely rather heavily on total retail sales in state and cooperative shops rather than on urban retail sales or worker expenditures in compiling the weights for 1937 and later years does not appear to introduce significant error into the calculations. The price index numbers for both 1940 and 1944, however, are weak on the grounds of reliability and comparability of the price comparisons, and not all commodity groups could be represented for these two years. For 1944, also, it was not possible to compute 1944 weights, and I have only a single measure for that year. The index numbers of service prices for many reasons cannot be relied on very heavily for any year, but services account for such a small share of worker expenditures that even fairly large errors here would have relatively little effect on the cost-of-living index numbers.

While the index numbers of official retail prices in Moscow are, with the exceptions noted, quite reliable, the adjustments made in these in order to take into account prices outside of Moscow and prices on the free market are fairly crude. For 1928, the estimate of the gap between the official prices and prices in private trade is based on Soviet information which considers only prices in private shops but not prices on the peasant markets and is perhaps deficient in other respects as well. Also, the estimate of the difference between the movement of Moscow prices and average urban USSR prices between 1928 and 1937 is rather rough. Since 1937, Moscow and average urban USSR official prices have moved quite closely together, so there is little room for error here. The index number of collective farm market prices is subject to large error but, fortunately, even large errors in the index number of collective farm market prices can lead to only minor errors in the cost-of-living index numbers. This is partly because purchases on the collective farm market are, in real terms, a relatively small part of the Soviet worker's total expenditures and partly because my procedure is such that errors here tend to be compensatory. If, for example, I underestimate the gap between the official and the free market prices in a given year, at the same time I overstate the share of the free market valued at official prices in total worker purchases for that year.

The money wage figures are based on firm Soviet data, and the estimates of the burden of direct taxes and of subscriptions to government bonds are probably roughly correct as to order of magnitude and general trend. The estimates of the value of benefits received by the Soviet worker, however, are very rough and the measures of real wages including benefits should be treated with more caution than the measures of gross real wages or of real wages net of taxes and bond purchases.

In interpreting the results for any year, the reader will want to keep in mind the condition of the retail market. I have already pointed out the shortcomings involved in trying to evaluate real income in terms of the price structure of a year when multiple prices prevailed. Beyond this, it will be clear that the measures of real wages are somewhat spurious for years when there were real shortages in the consumer market. When the worker is left with cash in his pocket that he would prefer to spend, the measure of real wages overstates his real income. To some extent this is true of the index numbers for all years in comparison with 1937, more so in the case of 1928, 1940, and, particularly, 1944. The extreme wartime shortages of 1944 clearly meant the worker could not spend all he would have liked of his wages and on this ground the measure of real wages in 1944 overstates, perhaps grossly, the worker's real income in that year. My result shows real wages higher in the war year 1944 than in 1948, and this seems highly suspect. For the other years, with some reservations concerning 1940, I feel that my measures can be used with considerable confidence.

The results of my computations are shown in Table 21. The two index numbers of the change in the cost of living are shown in lines 1a and 1b. The index number of gross annual money wages is shown in line 2, and the index number of annual money wages net of taxes and bond purchases is shown in line 3. The index number of gross annual real wages obtained when money wages are deflated by the cost-of-living index number based

TABLE 21

Annual Real Wages of Nonagricultural Wage Earners and Salaried Employees,
USSR, 1928–54
(1937 = 100)

	1928	1937	1940	1944	1948	1952	1954
1. Cost-of-living index number							
a. Formula (5), 1937 weights	20.9	100	142	(199)	327	220	188
b. Formula (6), given-year weights	14.3	100	136	—	294	202	178
2. Annual money wages, gross	24.7	100	133	173	230	263	275
3. Annual money wages, net of taxes and bonds	25.0	100	128	129	207	233	256
4. Real wages, gross							
a. Formula (7), given-year prices	118.0	100	94	(87)	70	120	146
b. Formula (8), 1937 prices	173.0	100	98	—	78	130	154
5. Real wages, net of taxes and bonds							
a. Formula (7), given-year prices	120.0	100	90	(65)	63	106	136
b. Formula (8), 1937 prices	175.0	100	94	—	70	115	144
6. Real wages, net of taxes and bonds but including benefits							
a. Formula (7), given-year prices	116.0	100	90	(74)	69	109	138
b. Formula (8), 1937 prices	165.0	100	94	—	76	118	145

Note: The dash (—) indicates that data were not computed.
Sour e:
   Line 1· Table 6.
   Line 2· Table 13.
   Line 3: Table 15.
   Line 4a: Computed from data in lines 1a and 2.
   Line 4b: Computed from data in lines 1b and 2.
   Line 5a: Computed from data in lines 1a and 3.
   Line 5b: Computed from data in lines 1b and 3.
   Line 6: The value of cash benefits — social insurance grants and pensions, and mothers' subsidies, given in the text and Table 17 of chapter VIII — at current prices is added to net money wages before deflation. The value of free health and education services at the 1937 price level (Table 18) is added to the deflated figure for net money wages plus cash benefits.

on 1937 weights, as in formula (5) of chapter III, is shown in line 4a. This measure of real wages is equivalent to formula (7),

$$\frac{\Sigma P_i Q_i}{\Sigma P_i Q_{37}},$$

in which the physical quantities of the various goods consumed are valued in terms of the price structure of the given year, though at the 1937 level of prices. Deflating gross money wages by the cost-of-living index number based on given-year weights, as in formula (6), leads to the measure of gross annual real wages shown in line 4b. This index number of real wages is equivalent to formula (8),

$$\frac{\Sigma P_{37i} Q_i}{\Sigma P_{37} Q_{37}}.$$

Here the physical quantities consumed are valued in terms of the 1937 structure of prices as well as the 1937 level of prices. The two corresponding measures of real annual wages net of taxes and bond purchases are shown in lines 5a and 5b. Finally, in lines 6a and 6b are shown the two measures of the change in real annual wages net of taxes and bond purchases but including all benefits. These last measures are less reliable than the measures excluding benefits.

All index numbers in Table 21 are shown as they were originally computed with 1937 as base year. Table 22 shows the corresponding index

TABLE 22

Annual Real Wages of Nonagricultural Wage Earners and Salaried Employees, USSR, 1928–54
(1928 = 100)

	1928	1937	1940	1944	1948	1952	1954
1. Cost-of-living index number							
a. Formula (5) or (9)	100	478	679	(952)	1,565	1,053	900
b. Formula (6) or (10)	100	699	951	—	2,056	1,413	1,245
2. Annual money wages, gross	100	405	538	701	931	1,065	1,113
3. Annual money wages, net of taxes							
and bonds	100	400	512	516	828	932	1,024
4. Real wages, gross							
a. Formula (7) or (11)	100	85	80	(74)	59	102	124
b. Formula (8) or (12)	100	58	57	—	45	75	89
5. Real wages, net of taxes and bonds							
a. Formula (7) or (11)	100	83	75	(54)	53	88	113
b. Formula (8) or (12)	100	57	54	—	40	66	82
6. Real wages, net of taxes and bonds							
but including benefits							
a. Formula (7) or (11)	100	86	78	(64)	59	94	119
b. Formula (8) or (12)	100	61	57	—	46	72	88

Note: The dash (—) indicates that data were not computed.
Source: The figures in this table were computed from the index numbers in Table 21.

numbers with 1928 as base year. These are computed from the index numbers in Table 21 simply by shifting the base year. This means that the index numbers in Table 22 are linked index numbers. When money wages are deflated by the linked cost-of-living index number based on 1937 weights, as in formula (9), the resulting linked index number of real wages is equivalent to formula (11). With 1928 as year i and 1954 as year k, formula (11) is

$$\frac{(\Sigma P_{54} Q_{54})/(\Sigma P_{54} Q_{37})}{(\Sigma P_{28} Q_{28})/(\Sigma P_{28} Q_{37})}.$$

This formula, as has been been said, is rather difficult to interpret. The price structures of both 1928 and of 1954 (or other given year) enter into the computation so that the result is affected by changes in price structure as well as by changes in physical quantities between 1928 and 1954 (or other given year). The index number of real wages obtained when money wages are deflated by the cost-of-living index number based on weights of the given years, as in formula (10), is equivalent to the linked formula (12),

$$\frac{\Sigma P_{37} Q_k}{\Sigma P_{37} Q_i}.$$

When this formula is used, real wages in each of the years studied are valued in terms of the price structure of 1937. In the case of the comparison between 1928 and 1937, it should be noted, the index numbers in Table 22 are not linked index numbers but are simply the reciprocals of those shown in Table 21.

Between 1928 and 1937 the cost of living increased 4.8 times when 1937 weights are used as in formula (5), and almost 7 times when 1928 weights are used, as in formula (6). Table 22 is the more convenient of the two tables for the comparison between 1928 and 1937. Money wages increased only about 4 times so there was a clear decline in real wages. According to formula (7) — that is, when valued in terms of the 1928 price structure — gross real wages declined by 15 percent from 100 in 1928 to 85 in 1937. But according to formula (8) — that is, when valued in terms of the 1937 price structure — gross real wages declined by over 40 percent, from 100 in 1928 to 58 in 1937. Taxes and purchases of government bonds took a larger share of the average wage in 1937 than in 1928 so that the decline in real wages, net of taxes and bond purchases, is one or two percentage points greater than the decline in gross real wages, on the basis of either measure. On the other hand, benefits — social insurance and similar cash benefits, free education, and health services — contributed more in real terms to the average wage in 1937 than in 1928. Thus the decline in real wages net of taxes and bond purchases, but including benefits, was smaller by a few percentage points than the decline in gross real wages. In 1937 real wages net of taxes and bond purchases, but including benefits, were 86 percent of 1928 according to formula (7) and only 61 percent of 1928 according to formula (8). Both measures show a significant decline in real wages. The two measures, however, diverge widely, a problem to which we shall return subsequently. It should be mentioned here that the 1937 real wage, low as it was, represented a considerable recovery from a drastic decline in the early 1930's. Estimates of Solomon Schwarz and Naum Jasny put real wages in 1932 at roughly half the 1928 level and 20 to 25 percent below the 1937 level.[1]

Real wages undoubtedly rose during 1938 and 1939, but by 1940 the cost of living had risen somewhat more than money wages and there was a moderate decline in gross real wages. According to Table 21, gross real wages in 1940 were 94 percent of the 1937 level when valued in terms of the 1940 price structure, as in formula (7). When valued in terms of the

[1] Schwarz, *Labor in the Soviet Union* (New York, 1951), pp. 137–139, 163; Jasny, *The Soviet 1956 Statistical Handbook: A Commentary* (East Lansing, 1957), p. 41. Jasny's computations are based on a 1928-weighted cost-of-living index number and should thus be compared with my real wage figures for 1928 and 1937 computed according to formula (8). Prokopovicz calculates a decline in real wages between 1928 and 1932 of only about 15 percent, and a further decline to 1937; but he considers only official prices, and in 1932 the official ration prices were very much lower than prices in commercial shops and on the collective farm market. See S. N. Prokopovicz, *Russlands Volkswirtschaft unter den Sowjets* (Zurich, 1944), p. 306.

1937 price structure as in formula (8), gross real wages in 1940 were 98 percent of the 1937 level. By itself this is too small a difference to take into account as the error might very well exceed 2 percent; but since the alternative measure also shows a decline I conclude there was at least a moderate decline in gross real wages between 1937 and 1940. The burden of taxes and bond purchases had increased, and the real value of the various benefits showed some decline between 1937 and 1940. Thus real annual wages net of taxes and bond purchases and, in this case, either including or excluding benefits, declined by about 10 percent when valued at 1940 prices and by about 6 percent when valued at 1937 prices.

The single — and not very reliable — measure for the war year 1944 shows a further decline in real wages, as would be expected. Although ration prices were held at about the 1940 level, the very high prices in the commercial shops and on the collective farm market raised the cost of living considerably above that of 1940 and, according to my computations, to about double the 1937 level. Gross annual money wages continued to increase and, according to Table 21, were 173 percent of the 1937 level. Thus, on a gross basis, a decline in real wages of only 13 percent below 1937 is shown. But the very high wartime taxes and bond purchases meant that real take-home pay declined much more significantly to 65 percent of the 1937 level. To some extent, this decline was offset by an increase in the real value of the various benefits; real annual wages net of taxes and bond purchases but including benefits were 74 percent of the 1937 level. The calculations for 1944 are subject to very large errors and may overstate the level of real wages in that year. The lowest point in the wartime decline in real wages probably came before 1944.

By 1948, money wages had more than doubled in comparison with 1937 but the cost of living had more than tripled when measured on the basis of 1937 weights and almost tripled when 1948 weights are used. Thus gross annual real wages were 70 percent of the 1937 level when valued in terms of the 1948 price structure, as in formula (7), and 78 percent of the 1937 level when valued in terms of the 1937 price structure, as in formula (8). Taxes and bond purchases had fallen from the very high wartime level but were still above the 1937 level so that net annual real wages in 1948 were 63 or 70 percent of the 1937 level, according to the two alternative measures. The increase in taxes and bond purchases, however, was just about offset by an increase in the real value of benefits. Real wages in 1948 were considerably below the immediate prewar (1940) level on the basis of any of the measures. The data in Table 21 would seem to indicate that real annual wages in 1948 were even below those in 1944. This seems unlikely, though it is true that the recovery in the output of consumer goods proceeded very slowly in the immediate postwar years. As I have indicated, it is probable that my 1944 measure is in error.

By 1952, real annual wages had more than made up for the wartime losses and were higher than in 1937. The increase over 1937 in gross annual real wages was 20 percent when real wages are valued in terms of the 1952 price structure, as in formula (7), and 30 percent when valued in terms of the 1937 price structure, as in formula (8). Taxes and bond purchases, however, had increased over the period and more so than the real value of the benefits received by the Soviet worker. Thus the increase between 1937 and 1952 in real annual wages net of taxes and bond purchases, but including benefits, was 9 percent when valued in terms of the 1952 price structure and 18 percent when valued in terms of the 1937 price structure. This represents a striking recovery in real wages over the very low level of 1948. The annual retail price reductions reduced the cost of living by about one-third according to either cost-of-living index number while money wages increased by 14 percent, resulting in an increase in real annual wages net of taxes and bond purchases, but including benefits of almost 60 percent, between 1948 and 1952. Considering that this was seven years after the end of the war and that real wages were still not very much above the 1937 level, this rapid recovery between 1948 and 1952 is perhaps not so surprising.

There was a further improvement in real wages between 1952 and 1954. The continued annual price reductions cut the cost of living by 12 to 15 percent (depending upon which cost-of-living index number is used) and gross money wages increased by almost 5 percent. Thus in 1954 gross annual money wages were 275 percent of 1937, while the cost of living was well under 200 percent of 1937. Although bond purchases had been reduced since 1952, taxes and bond purchases together still took a larger share of the worker's wage in 1954 than in 1937. Net of taxes and bond purchases, real annual wages in 1954 were 136 percent of 1937 when valued in terms of the 1954 price structure, as in formula (7), and 144 percent of 1937 when valued at 1937 prices, as in formula (8). The real value of benefits received by the Soviet worker had not increased commensurately with the burden of taxes and bond purchases so that real annual wages, net of taxes and bond purchases but including benefits, were 138 or 145 percent of 1937, only one or two percentage points higher than the corresponding measures of real net wages excluding benefits.

The level of real wages attained in recent years may be compared with that existing at the beginning of the planning period in Table 22. As Table 22 shows, it was not until 1952 that Soviet real wages even began to approach the 1928 level, and that was certainly low compared with Western standards. The results, unfortunately, are ambiguous here. Gross annual real wages in 1952 slightly exceeded the 1928 level according to formula (11), but according to formula (12) they were still 25 percent below the 1928 level. Net of taxes and bond purchases, however, real wages were lower in 1952 than in 1928 on the basis of either measure; and this is true also when benefits are included. By 1954, the alternative measures give definitely conflicting results. When formula (11) is used, real wages are shown to have been higher in 1954 than in 1928; the increase according to this measure is 24 percent in the case of gross annual real wages, 13 percent in net annual real wages, and 19 percent in net annual real wages including benefits. Formula (12) indicates that real wages in 1954 were still lower than in 1928. According to this measure, the decline in gross annual real wages was 11 percent, the decline in net annual real wages was 18 percent, and the decline in net annual real wages including benefits was 12 percent.[2]

I shall take up the problem of the interpretation of these divergent results immediately after a brief discussion of the change in real wages on an hourly basis.

In some connections it is interesting to consider changes in real earnings per hour actually worked. Accordingly, I show in Table 23 the index

TABLE 23

Real Wages "Per Hour" of Nonagricultural Wage Earners and Salaried Employees,
USSR, 1928–54
(1937 = 100)

Wage	1928	1937	1940	1944	1948	1952	1954
1. Money wages "per hour," gross	24	100	122	120	195	223	233
2. Real hourly wage, gross							
a. Formula (7), given-year prices	115	100	86	(60)	60	102	124
b. Formula (8), 1937 prices	168	100	90	—	66	110	131
3. Real hourly wage, net of taxes and bonds							
a. Formula (7), given-year prices	116	100	82	(45)	54	85	115
b. Formula (8), 1937 prices	170	100	86	—	60	98	122
4. Real hourly wage, net of taxes and bonds but including benefits							
a. Formula (7), given-year prices	113	100	83	(51)	58	92	117
b. Formula (8), 1937 prices	160	100	86	—	64	100	123

Note: The dash (—) indicates that data were not computed.
Source: The figures in line 1 are from Table 14.

numbers of real wages on an hourly basis, with 1937 as base year. In interpreting these results it should be kept in mind that the hourly wage data are less reliable than the annual wage data. The Soviet worker worked on the average fewer hours during 1937 than during any other of the years studied. On an hourly basis, then, real wages in all other years are lower

[2] The alternative results here cannot be regarded as limits. An even wider divergence in results is obtained with a different set of index number formulas — the "consistent Laspeyres" and the "consistent Paasche" formulas. See the discussion in chapter III, section 2. With 1928 = 100, the "consistent Laspeyres" index number, formula (15), results in a 1954 cost of living of 1315 and a corresponding gross real wage of 85; the "consistent Paasche" index number, formula (16), results in a 1954 cost of living of 852 and a corresponding gross real wage of 131. It is not clear to what extent these figures, based also on linked index numbers, can properly be considered as limits. Direct comparisons between 1928 and 1954 might lead to a larger divergence.

relatively to those in 1937 than is the case of annual earnings. This is especially marked in the case of the year 1944 when there was extensive overtime work. Thus, while real take-home pay for the year 1944 was 65 percent of 1937, real take-home pay per hour worked was only 45 percent of 1937. And in 1952, net real wages on an hourly basis had barely reached the 1937 level on the basis of our most favorable measure, as in formula (8), or were still below the 1937 level on the alternative measure, as in formula (7), while on an annual basis both measures show net real wages higher in 1952 than in 1937. Interestingly, on an hourly basis, real wages in 1954 even on the most favorable measure barely exceeded the level of real wages in 1928. According to formula (11), gross hourly earnings in 1954 were 108 percent of 1928, net hourly earnings were 99 percent of 1928, and net hourly earnings including benefits were 104 percent of 1928. The 1954 index numbers of real wages computed according to formula (12) are, of course, well below the 1928 level on an hourly as well as on an annual basis.

The widely divergent measures of the extent of the decline in real wages since 1928 and the conflicting answers as to the level of real wages in 1954 in comparison with 1928 emphasize the difficulties of comparing standards of living in very different periods or places. The major difficulty in measurement falls within the period 1928 to 1937. From 1937 on, the two measures of real wages are quite close in each case. The great difference between the two measures of the change in real wages between 1928 and 1937 is, again, a reflection of the great changes in price structure and in patterns of consumption which took place during this very turbulent period of Soviet history. Both measures are valid and theory offers little basis for choice between them. Insofar as the retail market was more or less in equilibrium in 1937 and the 1937 prices are more meaningful in the sense that they reflected the relative marginal utilities of various goods to the 1937 consumer better than did the 1928 prices to the 1928 consumer, some preference might be accorded the measure valuing real wages in terms of the 1937 price structure — that is, formula (8).

The relative meaningfulness of the 1937 price structure provides some grounds also for preferring the linked index numbers of real wages which employ 1937 prices in valuing the change between 1928 and years following 1937, as in formula (12). A second important advantage of this measure is that the change in real wages between any two given years (including the change between 1928 and 1954) is valued in terms of the same (in this case, 1937) price structure. Only changes in physical quantities are shown in this measure, whereas the alternative measure is complicated by changes in price structure as well. The 1937 price structure, of course, reflects the particular supply and demand situation of that year. If the scarcities of 1937 had been unique to that year, or if tastes had changed greatly since then, one might hesitate to rely much on a measure which values real wages in all years in terms of the 1937 price structure. But we have already seen that the price structure of 1937 was not very different from that prevailing in more recent years. Thus, valuing real wages in all years in terms of the 1937 price structure should provide a measure reasonably in accord with the way the Soviet worker of today might evaluate the changes in real wages over the entire period, including the period from 1928 to 1937.

In interpreting the divergent results, one might also wish to consider the special character of the changes in the structure of consumption that occurred over the period. To an important degree, the period 1928 to 1937 witnessed a substitution of inferior goods for superior goods in the consumer's budget. More particularly, there was an increase in the importance of food and a shift from animal products to bread and potatoes. While such a substitution is to be expected in a period of declining real wages, all the indications are that in the Soviet Union it was on a notably large scale.[3] In addition to the pressure on food supplies of a rapidly expanding industrial labor force, there were the great losses of livestock during collectivization of agriculture. After 1937 there must have been still further substitutions of this nature, as the scarcity of animal products continued and, in fact, worsened during the war. In recent years there has been some improvement in supplies of animal products and the trend away from inferior goods has started. Shortages of animal products for clothing and shoes have been ameliorated by the development of synthetics. Food took a smaller share of the worker's budget in 1952 and 1954 than in 1937. Bread has become much cheaper relative to meat and many other products

---

[3] In the mid-1930's, among 31 countries studied, the Soviet Union ranked near the bottom, along with Yugoslavia and such rice-eating countries as China, Japan, and Korea, in terms of the small share of calories obtained from foods other than grains and potatoes, although the Soviet Union ranked near the top in terms of total calories consumed per capita. At this time (1934–38) grain and potatoes supplied an estimated 76 percent of the calories consumed in the Soviet Union. See M. K. Bennett, "International Disparities in Consumption Levels," *American Economic Review*, 41:646–647 (1951).

Data for 1925–27 cited by Lazar Volin, *A Survey of Soviet Russian Agriculture*, Agriculture Monograph 5, U.S. Department of Agriculture (Washington, 1951), p. 170, show that grain and potatoes provided about 76 percent of total calories consumed in the Soviet Union at that time also, although less for urban workers. The similarity of the share of grain and potatoes in the average Russian diet indicated by these studies for these two periods need not, I think, be taken as casting serious doubt on my point that the quality of the Soviet worker's diet declined between 1928 and 1937. In the first place, the two estimates are probably obtained by different methods (that for 1925–27 is based on budget data not available for the 1930's) and in any case must be fairly crude. Secondly, the figures are averages for the entire Soviet population and may not be representative of urban workers. Indeed, if grain and potatoes actually accounted for the same share of total calories consumed in both periods, this would probably imply an increase in the share of grain and potatoes in the urban worker's diet, for the urban worker's consumption of grain and potatoes was smaller than the peasant's in 1925–27, and the urban working class grew very rapidly between then and the mid-1930's.

than it was in 1937. There has undoubtedly been some improvement in diet. But even so, the proportion of meat to bread in the worker's diet seems to have been little better in 1954 than in 1937.[4] Under the circumstances, one is inevitably led to discount a measure of real wages which shows only a limited decline from 1928 to 1937 or to 1952 and which shows an increase from 1928 to 1954, and would be inclined to give somewhat more weight to the alternative calculations.

Several arguments which I find persuasive have been presented for giving more credence to the index number of real wages using 1937 prices and showing the larger decline in real wages. Nevertheless, it remains true that the magnitude of the change in real wages between 1928 and 1937 eludes precise measurement and the alternative possibility of a less drastic decline in real wages might be kept in mind. But even the most favorable measure shows that the Soviet worker's real wage in 1954 exceeded that of 1928 by less than 15 percent after taxes and bond subscriptions.

Before going on to discuss the wider implications of the findings, I shall compare my results with those of other students of the Soviet economy and with the Soviet claims concerning the course of real wages.

2. COMPARISON WITH OTHER STUDIES

In Table 24, I compare some of my findings with those of S. N. Prokopovicz, Naum Jasny, and Eugène Zaleski. Prokopovicz' study is of interest mainly as the first attempt to penetrate the Soviet propaganda screen on the question of real wages.[5] His index number of food prices is based on the prices of only eleven foodstuffs, and he admittedly had little information concerning the comparability of the price quotations for different dates. He uses his food price index number also to represent the

---

[4] The physical volume of sales of meat in the state and cooperative shops and restaurants doubled between 1937 and 1954, but the physical volume of sales of bread and other grain products also almost doubled. Sales of milk and butter showed a larger than two-fold increase, and sales of potatoes barely increased, suggesting some limited improvement in diet. These figures on the change in the physical volume of sales in state and cooperative shops and restaurants are computed from the data on the value of sales by commodity group in TSU, *Sovetskaia torgovlia; Statisticheskii sbornik* (Moscow, 1956), pp. 40–41, and my group price index numbers in Table 5. Inclusion of sales on the collective farm market would not substantially affect my conclusions, except in the case of potatoes. The physical volume of sales of potatoes on the collective farm market increased about 2.3 times between 1937 and 1954 while collective farm market sales of meat and of milk and milk products increased by about 20 percent and sales of grain declined by about 5 percent. These figures are rough. They are computed from the data on the physical volume of sales in 1937 and 1940 in Table 10 of this study and the Soviet index numbers of the change in volume of sales between 1940 and 1954 (TSU, *Sovetskaia torgovlia; Statisticheskii sbornik* (Moscow, 1956), p. 180).

[5] Prokopovicz' results were first published in "Standard of Life of Workers and Peasants," *Quarterly Bulletin of Soviet-Russian Economics*, no. 1–2, November 1939. The figures shown in Table 24 are from a later work and have been somewhat revised since his earlier study.

TABLE 24

Chapman and Other Western Findings on Retail Prices, Living Costs,
and Real Wages, USSR, 1928–54
(1928 = 100)

	1928	1937	1940	1948	1952	1954
Retail food prices, official Moscow						
Chapman, 1937 weights	100	752	993	2,617	1,484[a]	1,263[b]
Chapman, given-year weights	100	890	1,113	2,786	1,620[a]	1,406[b]
Prokopovicz, 1928 weights[c]	100	837	1,385[d]	—	—	—
Jasny, 1925/26 weights[e]	100	1,014	1,320	3,056	—	—
Zaleski, linked index[f]	100[g]	930[h]	1,442[i]	3,060	1,851[a]	1,591[b]
Cost of living, urban USSR						
Chapman, 1937 weights	100	478	679	1,565	1,053	900
Chapman, given-year weights	100	699	951	2,056	1,413	1,245
Jasny, 1925/26 weights[e]	100	750	1,100	2,200	—	—
Zaleski, linked index[f]	100[g]	801[h]	1,265[i]	2,435	1,658[a]	1,434[b]
Real annual wages, gross						
Chapman, formula (7) or (11)	100	85	80	59	102	124
Chapman, formula (8) or (12)	100	58	57	45	75	89
Prokopovicz[c]	100	43	36[d]	—	—	—
Jasny[e]	100	58	53	44	—	—

[a] April 1, 1952 to March 31, 1953.
[b] April 1, 1954 to March 31, 1955.
[c] S. N. Prokopovicz, *Russlands Volkswirtschaft unter den Sowjets* (Zurich, 1944), p. 306.
[d] April 1940.
[e] Naum Jasny, *The Soviet Economy During the Plan Era* (Stanford, 1951), pp. 58–59, 69. More recent computations of Dr. Jasny put gross real wages at 61 in 1937, 56 in 1940, 48 in 1948, 73 in 1952, and 80 in 1955 (1928 = 100). See his *The Soviet 1956 Statistical Handbook: A Commentary* (East Lansing, 1957), p. 41. His earlier figures are shown here as they were published prior to the publication of my own preliminary results while his later figures "largely follow" my results based on 1928 quantity weights.
[f] Eugène Zaleski, "Les fluctuations des prix de détail en Union Soviétique," *Études et Conjoncture*, no. 4, April 1955, pp. 337, 340, 342.
[g] 1927/28.
[h] July 1938.
[i] July 1940.
Note: The dash (—) indicates that data were not available.

change in the cost of living in general. His data are limited to official prices in Moscow. He employs weights based on Soviet worker expenditures in 1928.

Jasny's cost-of-living index number covers manufactured consumer goods and services as well as foods, though the number of commodities priced is nevertheless rather limited. His weights refer to the period 1925/26. His basic calculations rest on official Moscow prices, but he makes a rough adjustment to take into account prices on the free market and differences between Moscow and average USSR prices.

Zaleski's cost-of-living index number also covers foods, manufactured consumer goods, and services. The number of articles priced is rather limited and varies from period to period. His food price and cost-of-living index numbers shown in Table 24 consist of the following links: (a) 1922/23–1926/27, 33 articles, USSR prices in all markets, 1924 weights; (b) 1926/27–1928/29, 39 articles, USSR prices in all markets, 1927 weights; (c) 1938, 42 articles, Moscow official prices, 1928 weights; (d) 1939–1941 and 1947–1954, 83 articles, Moscow prices in all markets, 1951 weights. Links (a) and (b) are based on the official Soviet cost-of-living index number and Zaleski computes links (c) and (d). (Apparently 1938 is compared directly with the base year 1913 in link (c).) This linked index number is said to be computed according to the Laspeyres formula; apparently what this means is that in the computation of each link the weights are treated as if they were weights of the first year in the comparison. The weights refer in each case to Soviet worker expenditure patterns, but Zaleski points out that the 1951 weights are no more than rough modifications of the weights for the late 1920's. Because of the method of computation and the similarity of the postwar weights to those for the 1920's, the alternative computations do not lead to very different results.[6]

Considering the differences in commodities priced, in weights, in base year, and in methods, one would hardly expect these various calculations to lead to very close results. All of the studies, however, are similar in that they employ weights based on the consumption pattern of the late 1920's in computing the cost-of-living index number for the period 1928 to 1937. (Zaleski's linked cost-of-living index number for the period 1927 through 1938 is based on weights from the late 1920's; and my own given-year weights for this period are, of course, 1928 weights.) As Table 24 shows, whenever weights from the late 1920's are used, there is fairly close agreement as to the general magnitude of the rise in prices between 1928 and 1937. This agreement tends, I think, to confirm my own finding that the rise in the cost of living over this period was very great when 1928 weights are used. My food price and cost-of-living index numbers for this period based on 1937 weights are, as would be expected, considerably lower than any other calculation.

For the years following 1937, the various computations differ more so far as the weighting schemes are concerned. Jasny and Prokopovicz maintain their weights of the late 1920's and Zaleski employs 1951 weights from 1940 on. There is some disagreement as to the extent of the price rise between 1937 and 1940, partly because of these weighting differences

---

[6] For 1938 and later years, Zaleski makes alternative calculations of the cost-of-living index number and he computes also an index number of official retail prices. His alternative results for the comparison of 1913 with 1938 and of 1938 with 1954 are as follows:

	1938	1954
	(1913 = 100)	(1938 = 100)
(1) Cost-of-living index number:		
(a) Linked	1810	179
(b) 1928 weights, official prices, 42 articles	1810	171
(c) 1951 weights, official prices, 83 articles	1856	160
(d) 1951 weights, all prices, 83 articles	1866	164
(2) Retail-price index number, 1925/26 weights, official prices, 58 articles, weighted geometric average	1656	155

It is not clear why there is such a large difference between the retail-price index number and the cost-of-living index numbers.

and partly because of the unsatisfactory nature of the limited available price data for 1940. Prokopovicz and Zaleski both show a larger price rise between 1937 and 1940 than Jasny or than either of my measures, but then Zaleski shows a smaller rise in the cost of living after 1940 than either of my measures. All Western students are, however, in close agreement about the magnitude of the increase in the cost of living between 1937 and the postwar years.[7] This is perhaps not surprising in view of the rather limited changes in price structure that occurred over this period, but I find it, nonetheless, somewhat reassuring.

Turning now to the measures of real wages, it is obvious that Prokopovicz' figures are too low as his cost-of-living index number is based only on food prices, which rose more than the prices of manufactured consumer goods and services between 1928 and 1937 or 1940. Also, he uses a money wage figure which shows a considerably smaller rise than the average wage either of all wage earners and salaried employees or of all outside agriculture. Jasny's index number of real wages is based on annual average money earnings of all wage earners and salaried employees while my own is based on average earnings of wage earners and salaried employees outside agriculture. The former rose more between 1928 and 1937 than the latter. Also, the figure Jasny used in this computation for the average 1948 money wage has since been found to be on the low side. In light of these differences in the money wage figures, the agreement between Jasny's computations of real wages and my own is not quite so close as would appear in Table 24.

3. COMPARISON WITH SOVIET CLAIMS

Official Soviet measures of retail prices, of the cost of living, and of real wages are virtually nonexistent for the prewar period. When real wages began to decline in the late 1920's the Soviet government ceased publication of cost-of-living and real-wage index numbers and adopted the policy of withholding information, accompanied by deliberately misleading statements intended to convey the impression of a continuous and rapid improvement in living standards. With one somewhat questionable exception, no official index numbers of retail prices, of the cost of

---

[7] Setting 1937 = 100, the alternative index numbers of the cost of living in 1948 and 1954 are:

	1948	1954
Chapman, 1937 weights	327	188
Chapman, given-year weights	294	178
Jasny, 1925/26 weights	301	—
Zaleski, 1951 weights	329	171

Kravis and Mintzes' various measures of the change in Soviet retail food prices between 1936 and 1950 are also in close agreement with the other measures. Irving B. Kravis and Joseph Mintzes, "Food Prices in the Soviet Union, 1936–50," *Review of Economics and Statistics,* 32:167 (May 1950).

living, or of real wages were published during this period.[8] With the recent improvement in living standards, index numbers of retail prices, of the cost of living, and of real wages for the postwar years are again being published.

Information on the prewar period for the most part is not obtainable, but in 1957 an index number of the physical volume of retail sales in state and cooperative shops and restaurants, covering certain prewar as well as postwar years, was published. This, in conjunction with previously available information on the value of such sales in current prices, provides a basis for computing an official Soviet index number of retail prices in state and cooperative shops for the period 1928 to 1940. This official Soviet retail price index number is compared with my own index numbers of retail prices in all state and cooperative shops in Table 25. The Soviet official index number of retail prices in state and cooperative shops com-

---

[8] Thus, Gosplan, *Summary of the Fulfillment of the First Five Year Plan for the Development of the National Economy of the USSR* (Moscow, 1933), p. 32, claimed that "the task set by the Five Year Plan to improve the material condition of the toilers in town and country has been fulfilled, and as far as the decisive and fundamental indices are concerned, has been more than fulfilled." Now the First Five Year Plan provided, among other things, for an increase of 70 percent in the real wages of wage earners in industry and for a somewhat larger increase in the real per capita income of the nonagricultural working class (Gosplan, *The Soviet Union Looks Ahead: The Five Year Plan for Economic Construction* (New York, 1929), p. 242). One would think this certainly a "fundamental index," but it was clearly not fulfilled. Gosplan's *Summary of the Fulfillment of the First Five Year Plan* simply fails to mention real wages. It is said that wages more than doubled; but reference here is to money wages, and no information concerning the cost of living is given. It is further said that "the improvement" in living standards was influenced by the fact that more members of workers' families were working; that the living standards of peasants drawn into industry had increased 2.5 to 3 times. Beyond this, all statements concerning the improvement in the material and cultural standard of living relate to the elimination of unemployment, shortening of working hours, increased expenditures on social and cultural measures, and improvements in sanitary and safety conditions in the factories (*ibid.*, pp. 28–33, 192–204).

One specific statement regarding real wages was made during this period — that real wages of workers doubled during the Second Five Year Plan (1932–1937). (See V. Molotov, "The Third Five Year Plan," in *The Land of Socialism Today and Tomorrow* (Moscow, 1939), p. 107.) No information was given as to how this figure was computed and it does not correspond very well with other Soviet data. Even if it is correct, it is extremely misleading that no mention was made of the fact that any improvement in real wages between 1932 and 1937 represented a (partial) recovery from a drastic decline between 1928 and 1932.

The misleading conjunction of statements (a) that the material welfare of workers increased very rapidly during the First Five Year Plan and (b) that real wages of wage earners and salaried employees doubled during the Second Five Year Plan is made as late as 1948 in *Bol'shaia sovetskaia entsiklopediia: SSSR* (Moscow, 1948), cols. 1141–1142. Interestingly, this does not appear in the 1957 edition of this work. Instead, the highly suspect claim is made that the real income of wage earners, allowing for the elimination of unemployment, tripled between 1913 and 1940 (p. 382). This must be related to the claim made in Akademiia nauk SSSR, Institut ekonomiki, *Politicheskaia ekonomiia* (Moscow, 1954), p. 462 — a claim which has apparently since been abandoned — that real wages of wage earners and salaried employees in 1953 were about 6 times the 1913 level. See the discussion in the last part of this chapter.

TABLE 25

Chapman and Soviet Index Numbers of Retail Prices
in State and Cooperative Shops, USSR, 1928–40
(1928 = 100)

Index number	1928	1937	1940
Official Soviet index	100	536	637
Chapman index, formula (5) or (9)	100	621	820
Chapman index, formula (6) or (10)	100	870	1,096

Sources and methods: The official Soviet index numbers are computed from the index number of the physical volume of retail sales in state and cooperative shops and restaurants in *Sovetskaia torgovlia*, no. 11, 1957, p. 59, and the value of sales in current prices in TSU, *Narodnoe khoziaistvo SSSR* (Moscow, 1956), p. 201. Chapman index numbers are from Tables E-1 and E-3, and the 1928 price index numbers refer to urban prices.

puted in this way for 1937 is 85 percentage points or 14 percent below my lower price index number — that using 1937 weights; see formula (5). The gap widens by 1940 when the Soviet retail price index number is 183 percentage points or 22 percent below my index number based on 1937 weights; see formula (9). All computations based on 1928 weights show a very much larger price increase. As has already been seen, differences in weighting can lead to very large differences in results for the 1928–37 period. Offhand, differences of the magnitude involved between the Soviet price index and my own price index number using 1937 weights do not necessarily provide grounds for suspicion of either the Soviet or my own index numbers. Unfortunately there is no information at present as to how this Soviet retail price index number was computed, and it is impossible to evaluate its reliability. Taken at face value, the Soviet retail price index number implies a smaller decline in real wages between 1928 and 1940 than any other computations. It might be considered as the very lowest limit to the rise in retail prices.

In Table 26 the official Soviet retail-price, cost-of-living, and real-wage index numbers for the postwar years (with 1940 as base year) are compared with the corresponding index numbers computed by me. The Soviet index numbers of official retail prices in state and cooperative shops for this period appear to be reliable. They are supported by published price index numbers for groups of commodities[9] and by data on individual prices both in Soviet and non-Soviet sources, which I have looked into in detail. As described in the Soviet statistical texts, the index numbers of retail prices in state and cooperative shops are computed according to a given-year weighted formula[10] and apparently, though the sources are not en-

[9] TSU, *Sovetskaia torgovlia; Statisticheskii sbornik*, pp. 131–132.
[10] The formula is

$$C_i{}^{o,i} = \frac{\Sigma\, P_i Q_i}{\Sigma\, (1/m)(P_i Q_i)}.$$

where the quantities m are individual or group price index numbers of the form P_i/P_o. See TSU, *Slovar'-spravochnik po sotsial'no-ekonomicheskoi statistike* (Moscow, 1944), p. 178; N. Riauzov and N. Titel'baum, *Kurs torgovoi statistiki* (Moscow, 1947), pp. 147–149; and A. I. Gozulov, *Ekonomicheskaia statistika* (Moscow, 1953), p. 359.

TABLE 26

Chapman and Soviet Index Numbers of Retail Prices, Living Costs,
and Real Wages, USSR, 1940–54
(1940 = 100)

Index number	1940	1952	1953	1954
Retail prices in state and cooperative shops				
1. All commodities				
Soviet index[a]	100	161	146	138
Chapman, formula (9)[b]	100	164	—	136
Chapman, formula (10)[b]	100	157	—	135
2. Food				
Soviet index[a]	100	166	146	141
Chapman, formula (9)	100	150[c]	—	127[d]
Chapman, formula (10)	100	146[c]	—	126[d]
3. Manufactured consumer goods				
Soviet index[a]	100	156	145	134
Chapman, formula (9)	100	180[c]	—	149[d]
Chapman, formula (10)	100	168[c]	—	143[d]
Cost of living				
Soviet index[e]	100	—	122	118
Chapman, formula (9)	100	155	—	132
Chapman, formula (10)	100	149	—	131
Gross real wages				
Soviet index[e]	100	—	165	174
Chapman, formula (11)	100	128	—	155
Chapman, formula (12)	100	132	—	156

[a] TSU, *Sovetskaia torgovlia; Statisticheskii sbornik* (Moscow, 1956), p. 131.
[b] These price index numbers, like the Soviet index number with which they are compared, refer to retail prices in all state and cooperative shops and restaurants in the USSR. See Table E-1.
[c] April 1, 1952 to March 31, 1953.
[d] April 1, 1954 to March 31, 1955.
[e] *Bol'shaia sovetskaia entsiklopediia* (2d ed., Moscow, 1957), vol. 50 on USSR, p. 383; Akademiia nauk SSSR, Institut ekonomiki, *Politicheskaia ekonomiia* (Moscow, 1954), p. 462; (1955), p. 483. A later source reports the same real wage figure for 1954 but puts the cost of living at 121 percent of 1940 and average money wages at 210 percent of 1940 (S. P. Figurnov, "Osnovnye formy povysheniia real'noi zarabotnoi platy v SSSR," *Sotsialisticheskii trud*, no. 5, 1959, p. 51). The 1954 real wage figure shown in this table is based on a money wage of 206 percent of 1940.
Note: The dash (—) indicates that data were not computed.

tirely clear on this point, this is done on the basis of year-to-year links using weights of the second year in each case, which are then chained for purposes of comparisons over longer periods. It is possible, though, that the comparison between 1940 and 1950 is made directly rather than through year-to-year links. The Soviet formula thus is not comparable to either of my measures.

There is a close agreement between the Soviet and my own two measures of the change in average prices of all commodities in state and cooperative shops since 1940. In some ways this agreement is not very interesting for, it will be recalled, my own computations are not entirely independent of the official Soviet index numbers. But such adjustments as I made in my own computations to arrive at a closer agreement with the Soviet index numbers are well supported by specific individual price quotations and so, I think, the agreement can be taken to support the reliability of both my own and the Soviet measures. Although there is agreement in the over-all measure of retail prices, both of my food price index numbers are lower than the Soviet food price index number and both of my index numbers of prices of manufactured consumer goods are higher than the corresponding Soviet index number. This is somewhat puzzling. Some differences between my own and the Soviet index numbers are, of course, to be expected on the grounds of differences in the weighting formulas, in the commodities represented, and in the choice of base year. Beyond this, errors are possible in my computations. I believe that what appear to be compensating errors in my major category price index numbers for the period 1940–54 actually stem largely from errors in my 1937–40 price index numbers. My results for the postwar years appear to be quite reliable as originally computed with 1937 as base year, but when the base year is shifted to 1940 (as in Table 26) any errors in the 1937–40 price index numbers are carried through. And my 1937–40 price index numbers may be subject to large errors. In view of the evidence as to the reliability of the Soviet retail price index numbers for this period and considering also the more complete price data available to the Soviet statisticians than to an outsider, I would not hesitate to rely more heavily on the Soviet than on my own retail price index numbers for purposes of comparing the postwar years with 1940. (For the future, of course, one must continue to scrutinize the Soviet measures.) At the same time, for any comparisons between 1937 and the postwar years my own index numbers can, I think, be used with confidence.[11]

So far as the cost of living is concerned, the Soviet index number may be perfectly reliable, but we have very little information concerning it and should treat it with some reservations. The Soviet cost-of-living index number for 1954 (118) is some 20 percentage points or about 15 percent lower than their retail price index number for the same year (138), a larger difference than I obtain. Features of the Soviet cost-of-living index number which may explain much of this difference are discussed below.

(a) In the Soviet computation of the cost of living, index numbers of official retail prices by commodity groups are weighted according to the pattern of purchases by wage earners and salaried employees, and this may result in a smaller price rise. In my own computations, only the major category weights (foods, manufactured goods) are based on worker purchases, while within these major categories the weights are based on total retail sales in state and cooperative shops. As described in a Soviet source, the Soviet method of estimating the pattern of worker purchases is very crude, and the resulting cost-of-living index number cannot be so

[11] Actually, for all commodities, there is not much difference between the Soviet and my own measures of the change in official retail prices since 1937. If one links the Soviet index number of retail prices in state and cooperative shops for 1940–54 (Table 26) to their index number for 1937–40 (Table 25), the resulting price index number for 1954 (1937 = 100) is 164, compared with my results of 180 (using 1937 weights) or 170 (using 1954 weights).

firm as the price index number for all sales in state and cooperative shops.[12]

(b) The Soviet cost-of-living index number takes account, as does my own, of prices on the collective farm market, and these rose less than prices in state shops between 1940 and 1954. According to my calculations, the smaller rise in collective farm market prices could not reduce the index number of average prices of commodities by more than 5 percent because of the small share of the collective farm market in total worker purchases. In my computations I take account only of prices on the urban collective farm market. In the Soviet computation, however, prices paid by collective farmers in rural collective farm markets are taken to represent prices paid on the collective farm market by rural workers.[13] Prices on the rural collective farm markets are always lower than on the urban markets, but it is not known whether rural collective farm market prices increased less than urban collective farm market prices between 1940 and 1954. Possibly this means also that a larger weight is given to purchases on the collective farm market in the Soviet calculations than in my own.

(c) It seems quite possible that the Soviet index number of prices of services (which has not been published) shows a smaller increase than my own index numbers.[14]

[12] On the basis of data on peasant budgets, the purchases by peasants of the various commodities are estimated and then deducted from total retail sales to obtain the structure of purchases by wage earners and salaried employees in state and cooperative shops. See M. Eidel'man, "O metodologii ischisleniia indeksa real'noi zarabotnoi platy," *Vestnik statistiki,* no. 3, 1956, pp. 39–41.

In this connection, it is interesting to recall Mikoyan's announcement that, after the price cut of April 1954, prices of foods were 114 percent of the 1940 level, and prices of manufactured consumer goods were 127 percent of the 1940 level (*Pravda,* April 27, 1954). These figures are lower than the retail price index numbers subsequently published in TSU, *Narodnoe khoziaistvo SSSR* (Moscow, 1956) and shown in Table 26 of this study. I have assumed that the later figures represent revisions of preliminary figures released by Mikoyan, but an alternative possibility is that Mikoyan's figures are those used in the index number of the cost of living of wage earners and salaried employees. They appear more consistent with a cost-of-living index number of 118 than the more recent figures. Some support for this possibility is provided by the context in which Mikoyan presented his figures — that of reducing the cost of living and raising living standards. For a recent Soviet criticism of the official cost-of-living index number, see chapter X, section 4.

[13] Eidel'man, *Vestnik statistiki,* no. 3, 1956, p. 41.

[14] Some factors which might lead to a service price index lower than my own are: (a) It may be that service prices outside Moscow were higher than in Moscow in 1940, though in recent years service prices have been fairly uniform. If so, the rise in prices of services for the country as a whole was smaller than shown in my computations which are based largely on Moscow service prices. (b) The Soviet index number probably covers charges for such subsidized services as vacation accommodations, fees for children in nurseries, et cetera (not covered in my index number), which may well have risen less than prices of other services. (c) The Russians are currently claiming that rent has not increased since the prewar period (for example, see Akademiia nauk SSSR, Institut ekonomiki, *Sovetskaia sotsialisticheskaia ekonomika, 1917–1957 gg.* (Moscow, 1957), p. 599), and probably in computing the index number of service prices the Soviet

Turning now to the measures of real wages, the Soviet index number of gross real wages is a straightforward calculation obtained by dividing the index number of average annual money earnings of all wage earners and salaried employees by the official Soviet cost-of-living index number.[15] It is then entirely comparable in concept to my own measures of gross real wages. My index numbers refer to average annual earnings of non-agricultural wage earners and salaried employees, but I assume that the money earnings of this more limited group showed the same percentage increases after 1937 as the earnings of all wage earners and salaried employees. The Soviet index number of gross real wages in 1954 — 174 percent of 1940 — exceeds my own two measures (which differ by only one percentage point) by 18 or 19 percentage points or by about 12 percent. This difference is entirely the result of the lower Soviet cost-of-living index number. As I have previously said, there are reasons to think the official Soviet cost-of-living index number may be reliable, but there is not enough information about it to make a final judgment on this point.

In addition to — or more usually instead of — their index number of real wages (*real'naia zarabotnaia plata*), the Russians have published for various years an index number of average real income per wage earner and salaried employee. The phrase used is real income (*real'nye dokhody*), income in constant prices (*dokhody v sopostavimykh tsenakh*), or total income (*vse dokhody*) of wage earners and salaried employees per worker. Until recently, the sources of the average real income figures have given no description of the nature of the measure, and no details concerning the methods of computation or underlying data are available. Judging from the accounts of Soviet statisticians, in concept this is apparently a measure in constant prices of total income from all sources, less taxes and bond subscriptions, dues to social organizations, increases in savings deposits and cash holdings, plus benefits. Benefits, however, are treated in a peculiar manner. Cash benefits from the government and other institutions are included with other income. Free services are included only to the extent that they represent expenditures by the service institutions on material commodities consumed in the process of providing the services while wages paid doctors, teachers, et cetera, are not counted. Services for which the worker pays are treated in a similar manner; that is, expenditures by the service organizations on material commodities are included with

---

statisticians consider rent as unchanged since 1940. While it is true that the schedule of rents has not changed, this schedule is such that rent increases (up to a certain limit) as the income of the tenant increases; accordingly, the average rent actually paid must have increased over the 1940 level.

[15] For 1955 and 1956, the Russians have also published an index number of real wages of wage earners in industry. For 1955, the index number of gross real wages (1940 = 100) is 175 for all wage earners and salaried employees and 190 for wage earners in industry. For 1956, the corresponding index numbers are 182 for all wage earners and salaried employees and 195 for wage earners in industry. TSU, *Narodnoe khoziaistvo SSSR* (1956), p. 37; *Narodnoe khoziaistvo SSSR v 1956 g.*, p. 43.

workers' income and expenditures by workers on such services are deducted from income.[16]

The published index numbers of average real income per wage earner and salaried employee for years since 1956 are specifically said to be based on the income concept described above,[17] and this is probably true of that for 1955 also, but possibly the measures for earlier years are based on a different concept. In any case, the index numbers for the years 1948 to 1954 do not seem consistent with those for more recent years. The Soviet index numbers of average real income per wage earner and salaried employee, 1940 = 100, are as follows: 1948, 111; 1949, 124; 1951, 157; 1952, 168; 1953, 189; 1954, "over 200"; 1955, almost 178; 1956, almost 183; 1957, almost 196; 1958, almost 200; 1959, 200.[18] There is no other evidence to suggest that there was such a decline in real income after 1954 or that

---

[16] Reference is to a measure of income computed as part of the Soviet estimates of the share of the total national product which goes to private consumption. For all wage earners and salaried employees, total income is the sum of the following types of income: (a) Income from state and cooperative organizations — wages, premiums, travel allowances, and other wage-type income; pensions, grants, stipends; bond lottery winnings, insurance compensation, interest on savings deposits and other receipts from the financial system. (b) Net income from workers' own gardens and other private sources of income. (c) Expenditures by organizations and institutions on material goods consumed in the process of providing services (both free and paid for) to wage earners and salaried employees and their families, but not expenditures on wages paid in connection with the provision of services. From the sum of the above three items is deducted the sum of the following: (a) taxes and duties; (b) subscriptions to state loans; (c) dues to social organizations (for example, trade unions); (d) insurance premiums; (e) repayments of loans; (f) the increase in the savings deposits and cash holdings of wage earners and salaried employees; and (g) payments by wage earners and salaried employees for services. Total income per wage earner and salaried employee is computed by dividing the above sum by the number of wage earners and salaried employees. Real income is computed by dividing the total in current prices by index numbers of the prices of goods and services. See Eidel'man, *Vestnik statistiki*, no. 3, 1956, p. 35; and Gozulov, *Ekonomicheskaia statistika*, p. 466.

In a recent article, Figurnov argues that although services are not part of national income, they do add to the level of living of the population and should be counted as part of the real income of the population (S. P. Figurnov, "K voprosu o metodologii ischisleniia real'nykh dokhodov i real'noi zarabotnoi platy trudiashchikhsia SSSR," *Trud i zarabotnaia plata*, no. 12, 1959, pp. 44–46).

[17] TSU, *Narodnoe khoziaistvo SSSR v 1959 g.* (Moscow, 1960), pp. 829–830.

[18] The 1948 and 1949 figures are from the 1949 Plan Fulfillment Report, *Pravda*, January 18, 1950. (For 1950 no separate figure for wage earners and salaried employees was reported; the 1950 Plan Fulfillment Report stated that average real income of wage earners, salaried employees, and peasants was 19 percent greater than in 1949. See *Pravda*, January 26, 1951.) The 1951 figure is from Malenkov's speech to the 19th Party Congress (*Pravda*, October 6, 1952). The 1952 figure is computed from that for 1951 and the statement that in 1952 real income of wage earners and salaried employees per worker exceeded the 1951 level by 7 percent in the 1952 Plan Fulfillment Report, *Pravda*, January 23, 1953. All of these figures are repeated in Gozulov, *Ekonomicheskaia statistika*, pp. 465–466. The 1953 and 1954 figures are from Akademiia nauk SSSR, Institut ekonomiki, *Politicheskaia ekonomiia* (Moscow, 1954), p. 462; (Moscow, 1955), p. 483. The figures for 1955 through 1959 are from TSU, *Narodnoe khoziaistvo SSSR v 1958 g.* (Moscow, 1959), p. 100; *Narodnoe khoziaistvo SSSR v 1959 g.* (Moscow, 1960), p. 84.

real income in 1959 was no higher than in 1954. The series beginning in 1955 presumably represents either a revision downward of the entire postwar series or a change in method of computation. This suggests that the Soviet index numbers for 1948–54 should probably be regarded as an overstatement of the average real income per wage earner and salaried employee, even from the Soviet point of view. The Soviet index number showing real income in 1948 to be 11 percent greater than in 1940 seems incredibily high in relation to my finding that real wages in 1948 were still well below the 1940 level. The claimed increase in average real income between 1940 and 1954 of over 200 percent is high in relation to the increase of 74 percent shown by the official Soviet index number of real wages and is very high in relation to my own finding that net real wages including benefits rose by less than 55 percent over this period. My measure does not take into account income other than wages and differs in the treatment of services and in other respects from the Soviet concept so the results would not necessarily be very close to the Soviet results. Also, my own estimates of the real value of workers' benefits are admittedly crude and may be in error. But without more supporting data on the Soviet real income index numbers they cannot be taken very seriously, at least through 1954.[19]

Recently, in connection with the celebration of the fortieth year of Soviet power, the Soviet government announced that real wages in 1956 were 3.4 times the 1913 level. I should comment briefly on this, even though my own calculations do not go back to 1913, as this claim is by no means of the same order of reliability as the Soviet index numbers of real wages since 1940. It is, indeed, highly suspect. More specifically, the claim is that real wages of wage earners in industry and construction, after taxes and including benefits, were 3.4 times the 1913 level in 1956. Allowing for the elimination of unemployment, the 1956 figure is raised to 3.7 times the 1913 level, and allowing further for the reduction in the length of the working day, the figure is raised to 4.8 times the 1913 level.[20] This claim is inconsistent with such Soviet index numbers as have been published for intervening years and is in sharp conflict with my own find-

[19] The wage-earner and salaried-employee real income index numbers for the years since 1954 appear to be on a more reasonable level. Also, they are very close to the official Soviet index numbers of real wages for the two years 1955 and 1956 for which both the real income and real wage index numbers have been published. See TSU, *Narodnoe khoziaistvo SSSR v 1956 g.*, p. 43; *Narodnoe khoziaistvo SSSR v 1958 g.*, p. 100; *Narodnoe khoziaistvo SSSR v 1959 g.*, p. 84. The current series on real income may well be reliable but final judgment on this is withheld pending further explanations concerning it.

[20] TSU, *Dostizheniia sovetskoi vlasti za sorok let v tsifrakh* (Moscow, 1957), p. 329. Even so, this appears to be a substantial downward revision from the claim in Akademiia nauk SSSR, Institut ekonomiki, *Politicheskaia ekonomiia* (1954), p. 462; (1955), p. 483, that in 1953 and 1954 real wages of wage earners and salaried employees were about 6 times the 1913 level.

ings. Even without looking into the relevant materials for 1913, it is clear that the rise in real wages between 1913 and 1928 cannot have been large enough (considering the fall in real wages between 1928 and 1944 and the rise since 1944) to account for the very large rise between 1913 and 1956 claimed. If we accept the recent Soviet statement that real wages of wage earners in state industry, counting benefits, at the end of 1927 were 128.4 percent of the level of 1913,[21] the current claim implies that real wages in 1956 were 266 percent of the level at the end of 1927. Even allowing for the fact that money wages of wage earners in industry and construction probably increased more over the period than the average wage of all wage earners and salaried employees, this must be a gross exaggeration. It is certainly at odds with my findings that real wages of non-agricultural wage earners and salaried employees, after taxes and including benefits, were at best 119 percent of 1928 in 1954 and perhaps 5 percent higher than this in 1956.[22]

[21] *Planovoe khoziaistvo*, no. 10, 1957, pp. 76–77. This differs somewhat from the index number of real wages of wage earners in industry including social insurance and other benefits in 1927/28 of 122.5 percent of 1913 published in the First Five Year Plan (Gosplan, *The Soviet Union Looks Ahead: The Five Year Plan for Economic Construction*, pp. 152, 242).

[22] For a discussion of changes in real wages since 1954, see chapter X.

The official Soviet index number of gross real wages of wage earners in industry in 1956 is 195 percent of 1940 (TSU, *Narodnoe khoziaistvo SSSR v 1956 g.*, p. 43); including benefits this might come to as much as 225 percent of 1940. (For all wage earners and salaried employees, the 1953 and 1954 Soviet index numbers of real income including benefits are about 15 percent higher than the corresponding Soviet index numbers of gross real wages.) This would imply, in connection with the claim of a 3.4-fold increase between 1913 and 1956, that real wages of wage earners in industry in 1940 were around 50 percent higher than in 1913 or (assuming the 28 percent increase between 1913 and the end of 1927) some 18 percent higher than at the end of 1927. This, again, is in sharp conflict with my findings.

X ·

REAL WAGES, LIVING STANDARDS, AND WELFARE

Iɴ this chapter I attempt to fit my findings into the broader picture of Soviet economic development and consider some of the economic implications of the calculations. First, in section 1 I compare my measures of the change in Soviet real wages with various indicators of changes in per capita consumption of the working class and of the entire Soviet population. The very poor showing of the Soviet Union concerning the real wages of its workers is compared in section 2 with the records of other countries. I then comment briefly in section 3 on various factors not taken into account in a statistical measure of real wages which affect the welfare of the Soviet worker family in the broadest sense. Finally, in section 4 I bring the story of Soviet real wages up-to-date and comment on the prospects for future improvement in the Soviet worker's lot.

1. REAL WAGES AND PER CAPITA CONSUMPTION

The urban population. The index numbers of real wages are compared, in Table 27, with index numbers of the volume of urban per capita household purchases of commodities and with urban per capita housing space. These data on urban per capita consumption are presented as approximations to the per capita consumption of urban wage earners and salaried employees. Most of the urban population is made up of wage earners and salaried employees and their dependents, but it will be understood that this class and the urban population are not synonymous. The alternative index numbers of real wages net of taxes and bonds are shown in lines 1a and 1b of Table 27. Valued at the price structure of the given year, the changes in the real volume of urban per capita household purchases were as shown in line 2a of Table 27; valued at 1937 prices, real urban per capita household purchases were as shown in line 2b of Table 27. These index numbers are computed from the value at current prices of urban household purchases in state and cooperative shops and restaurants and on the urban collective farm market and from my alternative index numbers of average prices prevailing in all retail markets in the urban USSR. The distribution of total household purchases as between urban and rural households in 1928 is a rough estimate based on data on

TABLE 27

Real Wages, Real Per Capita Purchases, and Per Capita Output
of Consumer Goods, USSR, 1928–54
(1937 = 100)

	1928	1937	1940	1944	1948	1952	1954
1. Real wages, net of taxes and bonds							
a. At given-year prices	120	100	90	(65)	63	106	136
b. At 1937 prices	175	100	94	—	70	115	144
2. Urban per capita purchases of goods							
a. At given-year prices	76	100	85	(54)	65	99	127
b. At 1937 prices	106	100	90	—	72	108	134
3. Urban per capita housing space	126	100	98	85	113	107	109
4. USSR per capita purchases of goods							
a. At given-year prices	62	100	91	(53)	70	130	176
b. At 1937 prices	91	100	95	—	77	141	186
5. USSR per capita purchases of services	59	100	91	64	96	118	143
6. USSR per capita industrial output of consumer goods	67	100	92	43[a]	73	111	131

[a] 1945. According to the official Soviet index number of industrial output, total output of consumer goods in 1944 was 8 percent below that of 1945 (*Pravda*, October 6, 1952).
Note: The dash (—) indicates that data were not computed.
Sources and methods:
  Real wages: Table 21.
  Urban per capita purchases of goods: Computed from the data on retail sales to urban households in Tables 12, E-2, and E-4, the retail price index numbers in Table 6, lines 3a and 3b, and the urban population. The population figures are shown below.
  Urban per capita housing space: Based on urban population and the following figures on total urban housing space in terms of dwelling area, in million square meters: 163 in 1928, 225 in 1937, 280 in 1940, 215 in 1944, 323 in 1948, 383 in 1952, and 419 in 1954 (Abram Bergson, *The Real National Income of Soviet Russia Since 1928* (Cambridge, Mass., 1961), p. 316).
  USSR per capita purchases of goods: Computed from the data on retail sales to households in Table E-2, the retail price index numbers in Table E-1, and the total population.
  USSR per capita purchases of services: Based on a preliminary computation of an index number of the physical volume of utilities and other services (excluding housing) purchased by Soviet households by Bergson for *Real National Income*.
  USSR per capita industrial output of consumer goods: Computed from total population and N. M. Kaplan and R. H. Moorsteen's index number of the industrial output of consumer goods, a component of their index number of the output of final products of Soviet industry. See their "An Index of Soviet Industrial Output," *American Economic Review*, 50:312 (1960); *Indexes of Soviet Industrial Output*, The RAND Corporation, RM-2495, May 13, 1960, p. 260.
  The index numbers for 1948, 1952, and 1954 are based on fewer commodities than those for most other years and are obtained in part by interpolation from firmer index numbers for 1950 and 1955. The 1948 figures may be subject to appreciable error.
  The *population figures* used in the computations are as follows:

	USSR population, July 1 (millions)	
	Total	Urban
1928	151.5	28.2
1937	165.2	49.0
1940 (postwar area)	195.1	61.8
1944 (1945 figures)	175.0	55.0
1948	177.0	62.0
1952	188.0	77.7
1954	193.8	83.3

The total population figures are from the Foreign Manpower Research Office, U.S. Bureau of the Census. The urban population figures for all years but 1948 are approximate estimates kindly supplied by Mr. John F. Kantner of the Foreign Manpower Research Office, U.S. Bureau of the Census. The 1948 urban figure is based on a preliminary estimate of Warren Eason for "Soviet Manpower: The Population and Labor Force of the USSR" (unpublished Ph.D. dissertation, Department of Economics, Columbia University, 1959).

incomes and expenditures of urban and rural households.[1] For later years, the distribution of household purchases in state and cooperative shops as between urban and rural households is based on the distribution of total retail sales as between urban and rural areas. I am unable to take account of purchases by rural households in urban shops with the result

[1] See appendix E.

that urban household purchases are somewhat overstated. It can be assumed with only slight error that all household purchases on the urban collective farm market are made by urban households.

Interestingly, the course of urban per capita purchases has on the whole been more favorable than the course of real wages. Most of the disparity in movement arises in the 1928–37 period. At 1928 prices, urban per capita purchases of goods increased between 1928 and 1937 by 24 percentage points or 32 percent, while real wages declined by 20 percentage points or 17 percent. At 1937 prices, both measures show a decline between 1928 and 1937, but the decline in urban per capita purchases was only 6 percent while the decline in real wages was 43 percent (75 percentage points). Since 1937, real wages and urban per capita purchases have moved more closely together. The disparity of the earlier period persists, however, so that by 1954 real wages, even according to the more favorable measure, exceeded the 1928 level by only 13 percent, and according to the alternative measure were 18 percent below the 1928 level, while urban per capita purchases in 1954 were above the 1928 level by 67 percent according to the more favorable measure, and by 26 percent according to the less favorable measure.

The main factors explaining the better showing of urban per capita purchases than of real wages are the elimination of unemployment and the increase in the number of family members drawn into the labor force. In 1928, some 1.5 million persons were registered as unemployed[2] when the total employed (TSUNKHU) labor force was 11.6 million, but since 1930, according to official statements, there has been no unemployment in the Soviet Union. According to Soviet budget studies of urban wage earner families, the average number of breadwinners per family increased and the average size of the family decreased so that the number of dependents per wage earner fell from 2.46 to 1.59 between 1928 and 1935. More recent, and perhaps less reliable, Soviet wage earner budget data indicate the number of dependents per wage earner was 1.28 in 1940, 1.04 in 1952, and 1.07 in 1954.[3] How representative these figures are of the entire wage-earner and salaried-employee class is not known, but the general trend they indicate (though probably not the magnitude of the change) is sup-

[2] Gosplan, *Summary of the Fulfillment of the First Five Year Plan for the Development of the National Economy of the USSR* (Moscow, 1933), p. 28. For various reasons, this figure may not be very reliable. See also Oleg Hoeffding, *Soviet National Income and Product in 1928* (New York, 1954), pp. 69–70.

[3] The 1928 figure is from the 1927/28 budget studies used in deriving the 1928 weights for the cost-of-living index number — *Statistika truda*, no. 5–6, 1928, nos. 1, 5–6, 1929. Figures for 1930 through 1935 are in TSUNKHU, *Trud v SSSR* (Moscow, 1936), p. 342. The figures for 1940 to 1954 are computed from data on the family structure of a sample of wage earner families in leading branches in industry in TSU, *Narodnoe khoziaistvo SSSR v 1956 g.* (Moscow, 1957), p. 218. In the computation, nonworking pensioners and students receiving stipends are counted as dependents, as was probably done in the earlier studies.

ported by figures on the number of women in the hired labor force. The proportion of women in the labor force grew from 27 percent of the total number of wage earners and salaried employees in 1928 to 35 percent in 1937, 38 percent in 1940, and reached over 50 percent during the war (53 percent in 1942). Since the war there has been a decline, but women still make up a very high proportion of the hired labor force — 47 percent in 1947 and 1950; 45 percent in 1955 and 1956.[4]

Urban housing construction has never caught up with the increase in the urban population, as the index number of urban per capita housing space in line 3, Table 27, shows. The wartime losses appear to have been made good, but the urban inhabitant still has about 14 percent less space than he had in 1928.

The total population. For the entire Soviet population, the changes in the volume of average per capita household purchases of goods were as shown in Table 27. The index number in line 4a values per capita purchases in terms of the price structure of the given year and that in line 4b values per capita purchases in terms of the 1937 structure of prices. In obtaining these volume index numbers, the value of USSR household purchases is deflated by my alternative index numbers of average prices in all Soviet retail markets from appendix E. I show also an index number of the change in the physical volume of average USSR per capita purchases of services in line 5 of Table 27. This index number is computed by Abram Bergson, largely on the basis of the changes in the physical volume of six services — water, electricity, railroad passenger transport, urban passenger transport, and motion picture attendance.[5]

The period 1928 to 1937 presents a (by now perhaps fairly familiar) paradox. For the Soviet population as a whole, the figures in Table 27 show that per capita purchases of goods and services increased between 1928 and 1937, yet my study indicates a decline in real wages over the same period. This apparent conflict is largely explained by the great urbanization which took place over this period. Other factors are the elimination of unemployment and the decrease in the number of dependents among urban workers, already discussed. While the total population increased by 9 percent between 1928 and 1937, the urban population increased by 74 percent and the nonagricultural hired labor force increased by 150 percent. An urban life obviously requires more commodities and services — and, particularly, more highly processed goods and more purchased commodities — than a rural life, even to attain an equal standard

---

[4] TSU, *Narodnoe khoziaistvo SSSR v 1956 g.*, p. 206; Solomon Schwarz, *Labor in the Soviet Union* (New York, 1951), p. 72; N. Voznesenskii, *Voennaia ekonomika SSSR v period otechestvennoi voiny* (Moscow, 1948), p. 111; *Pravda*, March 8, 1949.

[5] Preliminary figures from Abram Bergson, *The Real National Income of Soviet Russia Since 1928* (Cambridge, Mass., 1961). The physical volume series underlying this computation for 1937 to 1954 are shown in Table B-8 of the present study, and some of the limitations of these series are discussed in the text of appendix B.

of living. Furthermore, the urban standard of living was superior to the rural standard in 1928. Real per capita income of urban households was roughly 1.7 times the real per capita income of rural households in 1928, according to calculations of Oleg Hoeffding.[6] Of course, a large part of peasant household consumption is produced at home and does not pass through the market. So far as household purchases of consumer goods are concerned, I estimate that urban per capita purchases were almost 5 times rural per capita purchases in 1928.[7]

To maintain the 1928 standard of living on the average, for the entire Soviet population, the real volume of consumption would have had to increase only commensurately with the increase in the total population, that is, by 9 percent. But so small an increase in consumption would have meant a decrease in the urban standard of living relative to its 1928 level. If, in 1928, urban household purchases per capita were in fact about 5 times rural household purchases per capita, then the main-tenance of the 1928 urban standard for the rapidly expanding urban popu-lation would have required much more than a 9 percent increase in house-hold purchases. Total household purchases (for the whole population, rural and urban combined) would have had to rise, in real terms, over 35 percent above 1928; and per capita household purchases for the popula-tion as a whole would have had to rise by about 25 percent above 1928. According to either of my measures, there was an increase in per capita household purchases between 1928 and 1937. When valued at 1928 prices, the increase in average USSR per capita household purchases was 61 per-cent (line 4a, Table 27), and this is large enough to have provided for an increase in per capita purchases for both the urban and rural popula-tions separately. But if consumption is valued at 1937 prices (in some respects a more reliable measure), per capita household purchases of

[6] Hoeffding, *Soviet National Income and Product in 1928*, pp. 63–70. According to Gosplan, *The Soviet Union Looks Ahead: The Five Year Plan for Economic Construc-tion* (New York, 1929), p. 242, per capita income of the nonagricultural population was 2.7 times the per capita income of the agricultural population in 1927/28. Naum Jasny, *The Soviet Economy During the Plan Era* (Stanford, 1951), pp. 66–67, computes from another Soviet source — Gosplan, *Kontrol'nye tsifry narodnogo khoziaistva SSSR na 1929/30 god* (Moscow, 1930) — that at that time urban per capita income was 3.7 times rural. These figures presumably do not take into account the lower cost of living in rural areas, and they likely also undervalue farm income in kind in relation to urban retail prices.

[7] Of the total household purchases in 1928 of 12.1 billion rubles, I estimate in ap-pendix E, urban households accounted for 60 percent or 7.3 billion rubles. This amounts to 257 rubles per head of the urban population. Rural household purchases amounted to 4.8 billion rubles at market prices. Revalued at urban retail prices, rural household pur-chases would amount to about 6.4 billion rubles, or to 52 rubles per head of the rural population. The rural price level in 1928 was about 75 percent of the urban price level, according to Gosplan, *Piatiletnii plan narodno-khoziaistvennogo stroitel'stva SSSR* (3 vols., Moscow, 1930), vol. II, part 2, pp. 12–13. I apply this price differential to all rural household purchases here, but this may be an overgenerous allowance as some rural household purchases were made in urban shops at urban prices.

goods increased by only 10 percent on the average for the entire population (line 4b, Table 27). This meant a decline of 6 percent in urban per capita household purchases and a significant decline also in rural per capita household purchases of goods between 1928 and 1937. This result seems more in line with my findings that real wages declined over this period and with indications that the real income of the farm population also declined over this period.[8]

To some extent, these factors continued to operate after 1937. Thus, in 1954, USSR average per capita household purchases of goods were 76 to 86 percent greater than in 1937 while real wages were only 36 to 44 percent greater than in 1937, according to the alternative measures. During this period, the urban population increased by some 70 percent while the rural population declined by 5 percent. Another factor in recent years appears to have been a rapid increase in peasant household purchases, which must have fallen to an extremely low level during the war years. The various measures taken, especially in 1953 and since, to provide monetary incentives to increase agricultural output and procurements as well as the actual increase in procurements have undoubtedly led to an increase in peasant money income and in peasant purchases.[9]

Finally, the real wage figures may be compared with an index number of the industrial output of consumer goods per capita. The index number shown in Table 27, line 6, is the consumer goods component of the index number of the output of final products of Soviet industry computed by Norman Kaplan and Richard Moorsteen, expressed on a per capita basis. In this measure, the index numbers of the volume of output of the various consumer commodities are weighted by the value of retail sales of that commodity in 1950. For some but not all commodities, the 1928 figures exclude the output of small-scale industry and on this score the increase in output since 1928 would tend to be overstated. But other features of the computations may lead to some understatement of the increase in output,[10] and it is not clear whether there is a definite bias one way or the other. Kaplan and Moorsteen use price weights of 1950 and one would expect their index number to show a smaller increase in output than if price weights from an early year were employed, but the difference in

[8] Jasny estimates that the real per capita income of the peasants declined by over 20 percent between 1928 and 1937. See Naum Jasny, *The Soviet 1956 Statistical Handbook: A Commentary* (East Lansing, 1957), p. 41. See also his *The Soviet Economy During the Plan Era*, p. 73, and *The Socialized Agriculture of the USSR* (Stanford, 1949), pp. 701ff.

[9] The ratio of per capita retail sales in urban areas (including sales on the urban collective farm market) to per capita retail sales in rural areas at current prices was about 9:1 in 1944, about 8:1 in 1948, about 5:1 in 1952, and something over 4:1 in 1954.

[10] In some cases, Kaplan and Moorsteen found it necessary to represent a more highly fabricated commodity (garments, bread and bakery products) by a less highly fabricated commodity (fabrics, flour), and this might have a depressing effect on the increase in total output shown.

this case might not be great.[11] It should be kept in mind that the index numbers shown in Table 27 represent only the output of industry and not total output of consumer goods. And it is, of course, understood that per capita consumption of industrial consumer goods may differ from per capita output because of industrial and military uses, stockpiling, exports or imports, waste, et cetera.

The output figures show, in general, the same picture as the USSR average per capita household purchase figures. Thus, when real wages fell between 1928 and 1937, there was an increase in the per capita output of industrial consumer goods as well as in per capita purchases. Almost all the measures in Table 27 show a decline of 5 to 10 percent between 1937 and 1940 and a further substantial decline to 1944.[12] Not revealed in these figures are the numbers who could not survive the wartime privations; their deaths meant that what was produced went further among those who managed to survive. By 1948, all measures indicate a substantial recovery from the war years, though the 1940 level had still not been regained. The index numbers of real wages, as an exception, indicate a further decline, but this must be due to the overstatement of the 1944 real wage.

The increase between 1948 and 1954 in the per capita industrial output of consumer goods, though substantial, does not appear to be sufficient to account for so great a rise in real wages or in average USSR per capita household purchases as is shown in Table 27. Real wages increased by over 100 percent between 1948 and 1954 (by 106 percent in terms of the prices of the given years and by 116 percent in terms of 1937 prices) and USSR per capita household purchases increased by 142 to 151 percent, according to the alternative measures. Yet the index number of per capita industrial output of consumer goods shows an increase of only 79 percent between 1948 and 1954. There is some evidence of a tightening of the consumer market in 1954, and if there were greater shortages in the shops at the lowered official prices in 1954 than in 1948, the measures of real wages and of per capita purchases would exaggerate the real increase between 1948 and 1954. There was, however, a significant increase in imports of consumer goods, and this factor may go far toward explaining the greater growth in real wages and per capita purchases than in per

[11] G. Warren Nutter computes two index numbers of industrial output, one based on 1928 price weights and one based on 1955 price weights, but the results do not differ much in the case of consumer goods, except for consumer durables. See his "Industrial Growth in the Soviet Union," *American Economic Review,* 48:404 (1958). In general, Nutter's results are rather similar to those of Kaplan and Moorsteen.

[12] The index numbers of industrial output of consumer goods per capita show a greater decline between 1940 and 1944 than the USSR per capita purchase figures. This seems a little puzzling, for the diversion of consumer goods to the armed forces and other military uses must have meant that civilian consumption of industrial consumer goods fell more than output. But in view of the inadequacies of the data for the war years, one cannot be too concerned here about such apparent discrepancies.

capita output of consumer goods. Valued in foreign trade rubles at current prices presumably close to world market prices, total Soviet imports of consumer goods increased 2.5 times and net imports of consumer goods increased over 30 times between 1950 and 1955.[13] There is evidence, too, that reserves were drawn upon to increase the supply of consumer goods made available during 1953 and 1954.[14]

The data in Table 27, although illuminating, do not adequately reflect total real per capita consumption, particularly in the case of foods. Neither the retail sales data nor the industrial output data cover farm consumption in kind. Unfortunately, there are no adequate measures of total per capita food consumption. The great losses of livestock meant a serious deterioration in the quality of the Soviet diet, and this must be kept in mind. Per capita consumption of meat, milk, and fats was considerably lower in 1937 than in 1928, per capita consumption of grain was probably little greater in 1937 than in 1928, and the only important foods of which per capita consumption increased over this period were potatoes, other vegetables, and sugar.[15] As recently as 1952, the per capita output of edible animal products is estimated by Jasny to have been at least 30 percent below the 1928 level and the grain crop was no larger on a per capita basis than in 1928, though human consumption of grain may, nevertheless, have been somewhat greater.[16] The available data

[13] Imports of consumer goods totaled 885 million rubles in 1950 and 2,240 million rubles in 1955. Exports of consumer goods totaled 840 million rubles in 1950 and 863 million rubles in 1955. Thus, net imports of consumer goods were 45 million rubles in 1950 and 1,377 million rubles in 1955. These figures are computed from data in TSU, *Narodnoe khoziaistvo SSSR v 1958 g.* (Moscow, 1959), pp. 798–801. Imports and exports here are valued at the prices actually paid or received in foreign currencies and then converted to rubles at the official Soviet exchange rates. It is believed that imports and exports in 1950 as well as in 1955 are valued in the source at four rubles per dollar, the official rate in force from March 1950 through 1960.

The effect on domestic consumption levels of net imports of consumer goods of less than 1.4 billion rubles will be more readily understood if it is kept in mind that there is an enormous spread between the prices at which imports are valued in the above figures and Soviet domestic retail prices. For instance, the 1955 import value of refined sugar was 0.39 rubles per kilogram (Ministerstvo vneshnei torgovli SSSR, *Vneshniaia torgovlia SSSR za 1956 god* (Moscow, 1958), p. 33) while the domestic retail price of refined sugar was 10.70 rubles per kilogram (Table A-1).

The above foreign trade figures refer to final consumer goods. They appear to be the relevant ones for comparison with the index number of Soviet industrial output of consumer goods. It should be mentioned, however, that grain and raw cotton were significant items in Soviet exports over this period. See TSU, *Narodnoe khoziaistvo SSSR v 1958 g.*, pp. 800–803.

[14] Malenkov was accused by Bulganin (*Pravda,* February 19, 1955) of using state reserves for current consumption, and Khrushchev revealed (*Pravda,* December 16, 1958) that grain reserves were drawn on during 1953.

[15] Jasny, *The Socialized Agriculture of the USSR,* pp. 84–96; Lazar Volin, *A Survey of Soviet Russian Agriculture,* Agriculture Monograph 5, U.S. Department of Agriculture (Washington, 1951), pp. 172–175.

[16] Naum Jasny, "Prospects for Soviet Farm Output and Labor," *Review of Economics and Statistics,* 36:212 (1954); Gregory Grossman, "Soviet Agriculture Since Stalin," *Annals of the American Academy of Political and Social Science,* 303:63–64 (January 1956).

suggest that the 1928 level of per capita output of meat and milk was finally regained in about 1955.[17]

With strong reservations on the score of animal foods and of housing, the figures in Table 27 can be taken as indicating that average per capita consumption of the Soviet population taken as a whole probably increased during the period 1928 to 1954, with the exception of the declines of the early 1930's and the war years. The austere urban consumption levels of the 1930's may still have meant a considerable improvement in living standards for those who moved out of agriculture, even though the increase in the output of consumer goods that was achieved was not sufficient to maintain the urban real wage at the 1928 level. Between 1952 and 1954, the more favorable measure shows, real wages finally regained the 1928 level, but the alternative measure shows them still below the 1928 level. When account is taken of the decrease in the number of dependents per worker, however, it appears that the 1928 urban standard of per capita consumption had probably been regained by 1954, and perhaps even by 1952, even on the basis of the less favorable measure.

An advance of at best 15 percent in real wages (as shown in my more favorable measure) is indeed a modest achievement over more than a quarter century for a state which proclaims itself the "workers' state." A consideration of the entire period since 1928 puts into proper perspective the rapid improvement in Soviet real wages of the past decade. The Soviet record in terms of per capita consumption for the entire population is not so dismal as its record on real wages, but the results of my study are nonetheless striking, especially when contrasted with the familiar Soviet claims and with their achievements in other lines. The Soviet achievements have indeed been impressive in the development of heavy industry and in the build-up of military strength; their achievements in atomic science and in the exploration of outer space are no less spectacular. But light industry has lagged,[18] housing has been neglected, and agricultural output has barely advanced. The share of total output devoted to consumption in the Soviet Union has declined more or less persistently throughout the

[17] D. Gale Johnson and Arcadius Kahan in Joint Economic Committee, U.S. Congress, *Comparisons of the United States and Soviet Economies* (Washington, 1959), part 1, pp. 234–235.

[18] According to the official Soviet index numbers of industrial output, total output in 1955 was 21 times as large as in 1928, the output of means of production (including military goods) in 1955 was almost 39 times as large as in 1928, but the output of consumer goods was less than 9 times as large as in 1928 (TSU, *Narodnoe khoziaistvo SSSR* (Moscow, 1956), p. 46). As is well known, the Soviet index number grossly exaggerates the increase in output. It is the difference between the increase claimed for producer goods and for consumer goods which I wish to point out here. The Kaplan-Moorsteen index number of Soviet industrial output shows 1955 total industrial output 5.8 times 1928 output, 1955 output of machinery 20 times 1928 output, 1955 output of other producer goods 7.5 times 1928 output, and 1955 output of consumer goods only a bit over 3 times 1928 output. See N. M. Kaplan and R. H. Moorsteen, "An Index of Soviet Industrial Output," *American Economic Review,* 50:296 (1960).

period, though this tendency is perhaps now being somewhat modified.[19]

What is the explanation of this disparity in achievements? A major factor has been the policy of the Soviet dictators. Their policies on the tempo of industrialization and on the direction of investment — heavy industry and military might — have meant that few of the gains of industrialization have gone into increasing consumption. Their aim has undoubtedly been to let consumer income rise as total output rises, though at a slower rate. This was achieved during the second half of the 1930's and has again been achieved since the end of the war. But when difficulties have arisen, it has been consumer needs which were neglected while all efforts were turned to meeting the plans for the higher priority goals of world political, economic, and military power. The difficulties have been of various kinds. Some stem from the relatively poor agricultural resources and climate. Others are more or less normal accompaniments of industrialization; I have in mind here the initial backwardness of agricultural techniques and of the agricultural population and institutions and the difficulties of adapting to a rapidly expanding urban labor force.[20] Some factors, such as the drought of the early 1930's and, particularly, World War II with its enormous devastation, are essentially "outside" factors or calamities. Others are the results of inadequacies of information, mistakes in planning, and errors in policy. The catastrophe in agriculture that resulted from collectivization has had drastic and long-lasting effects. It is extraneous in the sense that it is not a normal accompaniment of industrialization, although the problem which collectivization was intended to solve often does accompany industrialization. A catastrophe of this kind is not likely to be repeated. But the decision to collectivize as well

---

[19] The share of household consumption and communal services in the Soviet gross national product was as follows:

Year	At established prices	At "adjusted" prices
1928	73	70
1937	70	63
1940	69	61
1944	55	45
1948	66	55
1952	62	55
1954	67	61

(Hoeffding, *Soviet National Income and Product in 1928,* p. 80; Abram Bergson, *Soviet National Income and Product in 1937* (New York, 1953), p. 75; Abram Bergson and Hans Heymann, Jr., *Soviet National Income and Product, 1940–1948* (New York, 1954), p. 71; Bergson, *The Real National Income of Soviet Russia Since 1928,* pp. 237, 245; Oleg Hoeffding and Nancy Nimitz, *Soviet National Income and Product, 1949–1955,* The RAND Corporation, RM-2101, April 6, 1959, p. 16).

The "adjusted" prices are intended to approximate current factor costs and to correct for various peculiarities of the Soviet price system. See the sources cited, especially Bergson's study of 1937, chapter III.

[20] Some of the decline in real wages in the early years was undoubtedly the result of a faster inflow of would-be workers than could immediately be absorbed efficiently by industry and of the low caliber of many of the new workers just off the farm.

as the rapid and ruthless method of achieving collectivization were deliberate matters of policy, although the worst consequences of the policy were not foreseen.

2. SOME INTERNATIONAL COMPARISONS

The reader hardly needs to be reminded that the Soviet standard of living in 1928 was extremely low compared with American or Western European standards. But it may be startling to realize that, during the more than a quarter of a century in which the Russians have been engaged in full-scale socialist planning and have in other areas been gaining on the foremost capitalist countries, the material position of the Soviet worker has probably declined relative to that of workers in other countries. I cannot test this surmise carefully, as it is beyond the scope of this study to investigate the movement of real wages in other countries. But the data on the purchasing power of hourly earnings in terms of food in the Soviet Union and a number of other countries in 1928, the mid-1930's, and the early 1950's shown in Table 28 are suggestive. In interpreting them it must be kept in mind that for the Soviet Union this was a period of rapid industrialization, while most of the other countries listed in Table 28 were already highly industrialized in 1928. Also, the Soviet losses in World War II were greater than those of any other country, with the possible exception of Germany. The index numbers in Table 28 can be considered only as very rough approximations to the relative level of Soviet real wages and to changes in this relative level. In the first place, just food is taken into account in these comparisons. Food is, of course, only part of any worker's real wage, and in the Soviet case, when the decline in agricultural output and the loss of livestock which accompanied collectivization are considered, a measure based just on food may tend to exaggerate the relative decline in Soviet real wages. Beyond this, the method used by the International Labor Office in computing the index numbers for 1928 is not entirely comparable to that used by the U.S. Bureau of Labor Statistics in computing the index numbers for the other years. Furthermore, for any given date, the underlying data on wage rates and food prices are not strictly comparable among the various countries. These and other limitations of the computations mean that no precision can be attached to any individual index number (and some may be subject to very large error) but in broad outline the over-all picture shown is probably fairly realistic.[21]

According to Table 28, the Soviet Union was near but not at the bottom of the list of countries shown in terms of the food-purchasing power of hourly wages in 1928.[22] By 1936–38, the Soviet Union was at the bot-

[21] For additional comments on the index numbers shown in Table 28, see Schwarz, *Labor in the Soviet Union*, pp. 131–132; 175–178; 234–238.

[22] Belgium, Estonia, and Poland (not included in Table 28) also showed index numbers below the Soviet Union in 1928.

TABLE 28

Purchasing Power of Hourly Wages in Terms of Food, USSR and
Selected Other Countries, 1928, 1936–38, 1950–52
(USSR = 100)

Country	1928	1936–38	1950	1951–52
USSR	100	100	100	100
Austria	90	158	200	167
Czechoslovakia	94	142	329[a]	—
Hungary	—	121	193	—
Italy	86[b]–98[c]	108	171	144
France	112	283	221	200
Germany	142	213	271	233
Netherlands	170	188	271	217
Sweden	176	250	450	—
Finland	—	204	279	—
Norway	—	283	600	394
Denmark	216	304	521	344
Switzerland	—	204	329	267
Great Britain	200	192	443	361
Ireland	202	183	329	267
Israel	—	217	450	—
Australia	—	383	764	—
Chile	—	108	264	—
Canada	310	358	557	—
United States	370	417	714	556

[a] Based on ration prices and legal minimum wage rate in Prague.
[b] Rome.
[c] Milan.
Note: The dash (—) indicates that data were not available.
Sources and nature of data: These series are presented and compared in Solomon Schwarz, *Labor in the Soviet Union* (New York, 1951), pp. 131–132, 175–178, 234–238. They are based on the following studies:
1928: International Labour Review, July 1928, p. 117; October–November 1928, p. 660. The index numbers are intended to measure the relative amount of food a worker could buy with his hourly wage at the prices in his own country. For each country, six index numbers based on six different regional patterns of food consumption were computed and the arithmetic average of these six index numbers taken. The six sets of weights include an Eastern European pattern but not a Soviet pattern of consumption. An additional index number based on seven food baskets, including one for the USSR, was computed for Moscow and London; this showed British real wages to be 192 percent of Soviet real wages (in terms of food). The wage figures represent in each case an unweighted average of hourly earnings in a number of specified occupations. For the USSR the average wage in these occupations in Moscow used in the computations is considerably higher than average earnings of all nonagricultural wage earners and salaried employees at the time. This may mean that the purchasing power in terms of food of hourly earnings in other countries is understated in relation to the average for the USSR; but it is possible that for other countries also the wage figure used exceeded the national average. In all cases the data refer to April 1928. In each case, the data are for a particular city rather than for the entire country. The wage and price data are not entirely comparable as among the various countries.
1936–38, 1950, 1951–52: Monthly Labor Review, February 1951, p. 143; June 1952, p. 658. The index numbers are intended to measure the relative amount of food a worker could buy with his hourly wage at the prices in his own country. In each case, the comparison was made between the United States and another country. The index number shown for a given country is a geometric average of two index numbers — one using United States weights and one using weights drawn from the consumption pattern of the country being compared. The wage figures for the Soviet Union represent average hourly earnings of all wage earners and salaried employees — for the postwar years as estimated by the U.S. Bureau of Labor Statistics. For other countries, the hourly earnings are for the most part based on wage rates rather than actual earnings. The wage and price data are not entirely comparable among the various countries. For the USSR, the dates to which the data refer are July 1936, April 1950, and April 1952. So far as the comparison between the USSR and the United States is concerned, the data refer to the same date within each period, but for other countries the data (including the U.S. data compared) for the prewar period refer to various dates between 1936 and 1938, and for 1951–52 the data refer to the second half of 1951.

tom of the list, and the gap between the amount of food the Soviet worker could buy with his hourly wage and the amount workers in other countries could buy with their hourly wages had widened considerably in almost all cases. By 1950, this gap was further widened, often considerably, in all countries listed.[23] Between 1950 and 1952, when Soviet real wages

[23] France is an exception here, but might not be if family allowances, a very important part of the French worker's wage in postwar years, were taken into account. See the *Monthly Labor Review*, February 1951, p. 145.

were increasing so rapidly, the gap between the food-purchasing power of wages in the USSR and other countries tended to become narrower, and this trend probably continued at least through 1954.[24] But the position of the Soviet worker, relative to the workers in most of these countries, was still much worse than it was in 1928. Recent, more detailed studies indicate that in the mid-1950's the Soviet worker's real wage was probably less than half of the British or French worker's real wage and at best no more than one-quarter of the American worker's real wage.[25]

3. OTHER FACTORS IN THE WELFARE OF THE SOVIET WORKER'S FAMILY

Real wages, though extremely important, are, of course, not the whole of the real income of the Soviet worker and his family. In addition to wages proper, I have attempted to measure the benefits provided by the government and other institutions. The Soviet worker's family may receive additional income in cash or in kind from earnings of members of the family who are not wage earners or salaried employees, or from such

[24] Between 1952 and 1955 Soviet gross real wages increased by 19 percent to 23 percent, according to my alternative calculations and allowing for the 0.5 percent increase between 1954 and 1955 indicated by Soviet figures. During the same period, real wages increased by 12 percent in the United States, by 5 percent in Belgium, by 17 percent in both France and Germany, by 6 percent in Italy, by 10 percent in the Netherlands, by 9 percent in Sweden, and by 5 percent in the United Kingdom, according to calculations of J. Herbert Furth, "Indicators of Inflation in Western Europe, 1952–55," *Review of Economics and Statistics,* 38:337 (1956).

[25] For comparisons of British and Soviet real wages, see P. J. D. Wiles and T. Schulz, "Earnings and Living Standards in Moscow," *Bulletin of the Oxford University Institute of Statistics,* 14:309–325 (1952), and 15:315–326 (1953); A. Nove, "The Purchasing Power of the Soviet Ruble," *Bulletin of the Oxford University Institute of Statistics,* 20:187–204 (1958).

A French study concludes that French real hourly wages were 1.6 times Soviet real wages in 1928, and 2.4 times Soviet real wages in 1955; including benefits, French real hourly wages were 1.5 times Soviet real wages in 1928 and 2.8 times Soviet real wages in 1955. See M. Allais, "Productivités, niveaux de vie et rythmes de croissance comparés en Russie Soviétique, aux États-Unis et en France, 1880–1955," Communication devant L'Académie des Sciences Morales et Politiques, April 30, 1955 (photo offset), part I, pp. 28–34; part II, annexe D3b.

Norman Kaplan and Eleanor Wainstein find that in 1954 Soviet gross real wages were 16 percent to 22 percent of gross real wages in the United States. Their computations are based on a detailed comparison of Soviet and United States retail prices of foods and manufactured consumer commodities in 1950; the 1950 results are then moved to 1954 on the basis of the United States and the official Soviet retail price index numbers and changes in money wages in the two countries. The lower figure is that obtained when American quantity weights are used in the retail-price comparison and the higher figure is that obtained when Soviet quantity weights are used. N. M. Kaplan and Eleanor Wainstein, *A Comparison of Soviet and American Retail Prices in 1950,* The RAND Corporation, RM-1692-1, May 1, 1956, rev. October 3, 1956; and *An Addendum to Previous USSR-US Retail Price Comparisons,* The RAND Corporation, RM-1906, May 13, 1957.

For a more detailed comparison of Soviet and American living standards, see Janet G. Chapman, "Consumption," in Abram Bergson and Simon Kuznets (eds.), *Economic Trends in the Soviet Union* (Cambridge, Mass., 1963), pp. 235–282.

sources as payment for odd jobs performed on a private basis, income from a private garden plot, or sales of hand-made objects or personal belongings. I do not attempt to estimate the exact amount of such supplementary income, but it is clear it is quite small on the average. Thus my measures of net real wages including benefits fall a bit short of measuring total real income, as ordinarily understood. Beyond this, there are other elements in real income which are intangible and do not lend themselves to measurement. Here I can do little more than mention several factors which one might wish to consider in evaluating changes in the Soviet worker's welfare.

As has already been said, per capita real income for workers' families decreased less than the average real wage because families have grown smaller and more family members work. Another side of this coin is a decrease in family leisure and a reshaping of family life. The Soviet government has done much to free the woman of household duties by providing factory canteens and restaurants and by maintaining nurseries and other institutions for the care of children during working hours. But labor-saving devices are still practically unknown in Soviet kitchens. Because of shortages and inefficiencies in retailing, the working wife and mother must waste much time queueing at the shops after her day's work or on Sundays — unless there is a grandmother in the household to perform this function. One wonders how the Russians feel about the changed pattern of family life — mother at the factory or office and children in institutions all day. To some, this is undoubtedly welcomed as emancipation, but to many others it must be faced as a grim necessity.

The worker's security has increased in many respects under Soviet rule. There is no fear of unemployment. Social insurance, the pension system, and free medical care for all generally provide against the various misfortunes that may befall a family. The value of these benefits in terms of sense of security may not be the same as the value attributed to them in the measures of real wages, including benefits. On the other hand, there are the insecurities stemming from the fact that there is essentially but one employer — a very strict and often arbitrary one, enforcing obedience not only to the work regulations but also to its ideology. The fear of reprisals for failure to meet output goals or for political indiscretions must often be acute. To the rank and file worker the political insecurities may not be so important as the strict labor discipline, infraction of which has been a criminal offense until very recently.

Soviet labor legislation became increasingly strict from the start of the industrialization drive in the late 1920's until 1940. A law of June 26, 1940, made unjustifiable absence from work (interpreted to include being more than 20 minutes late or arriving at work drunk) a criminal offense punishable by corrective labor at the place of work up to six months, with a reduction in wages of up to 25 percent. Leaving a job without permission was subject to two to four months' imprisonment. A law of October 18, 1940, permitted the compulsory transfer of workers from one job to another.[26] These laws, purportedly emergency wartime measures, remained in effect into the 1950's. The criminal penalties for unjustified absenteeism were modified or abolished, except in extreme cases, in 1951.[27] From about that time the laws prohibiting the leaving of jobs without permission and permitting the compulsory direction of labor were apparently not generally enforced or were enforced leniently; and in April 1956, these laws were officially repealed. Currently, the Soviet authorities are relying more on social and economic pressures than on legal penalties to maintain labor discipline and to control the movement of labor.[28]

A great increase in equality of opportunity has been achieved under Soviet rule. The opening of education to all and the great expansion in educational facilities has, in a sense, been measured in the index numbers of real wages including benefits (and there educational benefits may be overvalued from some points of view). But the increased equality of opportunity resulting both from the education program and from the great expansion of the economy is hardly measurable and deserves separate mention. There have been some fluctuations so far as equality of opportunity is concerned. In the early days of Soviet power, the manual workers were most favored, and there was some discrimination against the nonmanual workers as well as sharp discrimination against former property owners and other dispossessed classes. As the economy settled into its present form, there has been a trend for an upper class to become fairly well established with a result that their children have an easier entrance to higher education and the better jobs.[29] But still the society remains fluid and the opportunities are wide for any industrious Soviet citizen.

So far as equality of income is concerned, the gross inequalities that can

---

[26] *Vedomosti Verkhovnogo soveta SSSR,* nos. 20 and 42, 1940. Translations of these laws are in Abram Bergson, *The Structure of Soviet Wages* (Cambridge, Mass., 1946), pp. 235–236, 238–239.

On the development of Soviet labor legislation, see Schwarz, *Labor in the Soviet Union,* chapter iii; Vladimir Gsovski, "Elements of Soviet Labor Law," *Monthly Labor Review,* March 1951, pp. 257–262, and April 1951, pp. 385–390.

[27] By a law of July 14, 1951, which was never published. See G. R. Barker, *Some Problems of Incentives and Labour Productivity in Soviet Industry* (Oxford, 1955), pp. 98–99; J. G. Gliksman, "Recent Trends in Soviet Labor Policy," *Monthly Labor Review,* July 1956, pp. 770–771.

[28] *Vedomosti Verkhovnogo soveta SSSR,* no. 10, May 8, 1956, pp. 246–248; Gliksman, *Monthly Labor Review,* July 1956, pp. 767–775; Emily C. Brown, "The Soviet Labor Market," *Industrial and Labor Relations Review,* 10:179–200 (1957).

[29] Official acknowledgment of this is to be found in Khrushchev's speeches on the reorganization of the educational system. "Every young man and woman, no matter what position the parents occupy, should prepare for useful labor under conditions equal to all. Sonny and daughter must realize that papa is papa but that they have to win the respect of others on their own and not live off their parents' records of achievement" (*Pravda,* April 19, 1958, as translated in *Current Digest of the Soviet Press,* 10:18 (April 9, 1958)).

prevail under capitalism were eliminated with the abolition of private ownership of the means of production. Beyond this, the first thing to be said is that equality of income — "from each according to his ability, to each according to his needs" — is not a currently operative principle in the Soviet Union but a distant goal for "full communism." The operative principle is "to each according to his work," and the Soviet planners rely heavily on wage differentials as incentives. Differentials in earnings are roughly similar to those prevailing under capitalism,[30] and there are many signs in Soviet daily life that different styles of life are led by different income groups. Wage differentials, it seems clear, were greater in 1937 than in 1928.[31] Thus, it was those in the lower paid jobs who suffered the greatest decline in real wages over this period. This may not have been true, however, for those of the lower paid workers who came from the farms during these years; many of these must have improved their real income by the move in spite of the decline in the average real wage.

The rather limited data available on wage differentials since the 1930's indicate that differentials in earnings continued to increase through the war. The cost-of-living wage increase granted to the lower paid workers in September 1946, in connection with the raising of ration prices in preparation for derationing, considerably reduced the wage differentials prevailing immediately before. Murray Yanowitch finds that, largely as a result of this, the postwar wage structure is characterized by narrower skill differentials in basic wage rates, and probably also in earnings, than prevailed in 1940. The narrowing of wage differentials effected in 1946, although viewed at the time as a temporary measure, has apparently been adopted as a more permanent policy.[32] There is, however, reason to think that the very lowest paid workers enjoyed a smaller than average increase in real wages between 1937 and 1954. This inequity was apparently remedied by the increase in the minimum wage in January 1957.[33]

[30] Bergson, *The Structure of Soviet Wages;* and "On Inequality of Incomes in the USSR," *American Slavic and East European Review,* 10:95–99 (1951).

[31] Bergson, *The Structure of Soviet Wages,* pp. 134–135.

[32] Murray Yanowitch, "Trends in Soviet Occupational Wage Differentials" (unpublished Ph.D. dissertation, Department of Economics, Columbia University, 1960); "Changes in the Soviet Money Wage Level Since 1940," *American Slavic and East European Review,* 14:222 (April 1955). See also Brown, "The Soviet Labor Market," *Industrial and Labor Relations Review,* 10:183–185 (1957).

[33] In January 1957, minimum wages for wage earners and salaried employees directly engaged in industry, construction, transport, and communications, and for other wage earners and salaried employees in urban areas, were set at 300 to 350 rubles a month; for other wage earners and salaried employees in rural areas, the minimum was set at 270 rubles a month. At the same time, earnings of this level (and up to 370 rubles a month) were exempt from the income and "bachelor" taxes. (*Bol'shaia sovetskaia entsiklopediia* (2d ed., Moscow, 1957), vol. 50 on USSR, p. 383.) This meant an increase over the 1937 legal minimum wage, which was 110 to 115 rubles a month, comparable to the increase between 1937 and 1957 in the average wage of all wage earners and salaried employees, net of taxes and bond purchases. But the January 1957 increase in the minimum wage was said to have raised the wages of low paid workers by 33

Taking the broadest view of welfare, one might wish to consider the psychological atmosphere. On the one hand, there are the enhanced status of the worker as a member of the leading class, the enthusiasm for progress, the satisfaction of working together on a definite program, and pride in the fact that the country has been transformed from a backward and mainly agricultural economy to an advanced industrial economy, from a third-rate power to the second power. On the other hand, we find the strains and hardships resulting from collectivization, from the rapid industrialization and militarization of the country, from the purges of the 1930's, and the constant failure to fulfill the promises to the consumer. After the great suffering of the prewar planning period, the further deprivations and hardships of the war must have been extreme. Many indeed did not survive them. Yet these hardships, for once, did not have to be attributed to their own regime but could be attributed to a genuine foreign enemy; the German attack as well as the Soviet victory no doubt served to justify to many Soviet citizens the harsh policies of the 1930's.[34] And since the war, real wages have advanced rapidly enough so that one would think the Soviet population's well-justified skepticism regarding the promises to the consumer may have been quieted. Even though the level of real wages in the middle 1950's was little if any higher than in 1928, it may well be that the continuous improvement in living standards experienced over the last ten years or so is foremost in the average Soviet worker's mind today, rather than the still very low standard.

4. INCREASE IN REAL WAGES SINCE 1954

By 1957, according to official Soviet index numbers, gross real wages of all wage earners and salaried employees had increased by 9 percent above the 1954 level.[35] In 1958, there was apparently a decline of about 1 percent, leaving gross real wages at about 108 percent of the 1954 level. Real wages net of taxes and bond purchases, however, are said to have increased by about 3 percent between 1957 and 1958, and by 15 percent between

---

percent! (*Ibid.*) The increase in the average wage between 1954 and 1957 was only about 9 percent.

The minimum wage established in November 1937 for wage earners and salaried employees in state industry, rail, and water transport was 115 rubles a month in the case of time workers and 110 rubles a month in the case of piece workers. (See *Sobranie zakonov i rasporiazhenii SSSR,* 1937, part I, no. 71, section 340, p. 743. The relevant sections of this decree are translated in Bergson, *The Structure of Soviet Wages,* pp. 239–240.) Wages of this level were not subject to the income tax according to the 1936 tax schedule, which remained in effect through 1937 (Narodnyi komissariat finansov SSSR, *Instruktsiia Narodnogo komissariata finansov SSSR o poriadke provedeniia podokhodnogo naloga s chastnykh lits* (Moscow, 1936), p. 6).

[34] See Boris Pasternak, *Doctor Zhivago* (New York, 1958), p. 507, for an interesting expression of this point.

[35] The official Soviet index numbers, 1940 = 100, are as follows: 1954, 174; 1955, 175; 1956, 182; 1957, "over 150 percent of 1950," which comes to over 189 percent of 1940 (*Bol'shaia sovetskaia entsiklopediia* (2d ed., 1957), vol. 50 on USSR, p. 383; TSU, *Narodnoe khoziaistvo SSSR v 1956 g.,* p. 43; *Pravda,* January 2, 1958).

1955 and 1958.[36] This would probably amount to a 16 percent increase in net real wages between 1954 and 1958.

Further information* on the course of Soviet real wages up to 1958 is presented in S. P. Figurnov, *Real'naia zarabotnaia plata i pod"em material'nogo blagosostoia-niia trudiashchikhsia v SSSR* (Moscow, 1960). This is the first serious and detailed Soviet work since the 1920's on real wages of which I am aware. Unfortunately, it came into my hands too late to be taken into account in this study, and I can only add here a brief note on the major aspects of Figurnov's work that bear on my findings. For the period since 1954, Figurnov estimates that the average gross real wage of all wage earners and salaried employees in 1958, though very slightly below 1957, was still in round terms 9 percent above the 1954 level. The average net real wage in 1958 was 16 percent above 1955 but 14 percent above 1954 because, according to Figurnov (pp. 192, 198), net wages declined by about 2 percent in 1955. He actually presents only money-wage figures (gross and net) for 1954, but it can be assumed that the cost of living was the same in 1954 as in 1955 (for which he gives a figure), as there were no changes between these two years in prices in state and cooperative shops or on the collective farm market. (See TSU, *Narodnoe khoziaistvo SSSR v 1956 g.*, pp. 232, 237; TSU, *Sovetskaia torgovlia; Statisticheskii sbornik*, 1956, p. 182.) Figurnov estimates the increase in gross money wages between 1950 and 1958 as 21 percent. This is lower than the 24 percent quoted by Mikoyan (*Pravda*, November 23, 1959).

In comparing the postwar years with 1940, Figurnov criticizes the official (TSU) real wage index number. He argues, first, that net rather than gross real wages should be measured. In this connection, he points out that gross wages increased faster than net wages from 1940 until 1957, with the exception of the years 1953 and 1954, but that net wages increased faster during 1953 and 1954 and have been increasing faster than gross wages since 1957 (pp. 191–192). He adds that in 1958, after the suspension of compulsory bond subscriptions and some income tax reduction, taxes took 8 to 9 percent of the average wage; and this, he says, is about the same percentage as taxes and bonds took of the average wage in 1940 (p. 191). This is higher than my estimate that 7.6 percent of the average wage went to taxes and bonds in 1940.

Secondly, Figurnov finds the official cost-of-living index number too low in relation to the index number of prices in state and cooperative shops and feels this is probably because the official cost-of-living index number does not correctly take into account collective farm market prices. Allowing for the increased share of the

---

[36] Most Soviet sources are silent on the change in real wages since 1957. The 1958 Annual Plan Fulfillment Report states that the average real income of wage earners, salaried employees, and peasants increased by 5 percent between 1957 and 1958, but gives no measure relating only to wage earners and salaried employees (*Pravda*, January 16, 1959). TSU, *Narodnoe khoziaistvo SSSR v 1958 g.*, does not present index numbers of gross real wages as did the 1956 and 1957 editions, but instead presents a measure of average real income of wage earners and salaried employees. This shows an increase of 2 percent between 1957 and 1958 (p. 100). The 1959 Annual Plan Fulfillment Report does not give figures for either real wages or real income (*Pravda*, January 22, 1960). The 1958 decline in gross real wages is indicated by S. P. Figurnov, "K voprosu o metodologii ischisleniia real'nykh dokhodov i real'noi zarabotnoi platy trudiashchikhsia SSSR," *Trud i zarabotnaia plata*, no. 12, 1959, p. 48. According to his figures, between 1955 and 1958, gross average money wages of wage earners and salaried employees increased by 8 percent, net money wages increased by 17 percent, gross real wages increased by 7 percent, and net real wages increased by 15 percent.

* This and the following paragraphs in small print refer to recent Soviet materials that became available too late to be taken account of fully in this study.

collective farm market in the volume of purchases of urban workers, he estimates that the cost of living rose between 1940 and 1953 by 39 percent, as compared with the official series showing an increase of only 22 percent. Thus, Figurnov's index number for 1953 (1940 = 100) is 143 for net real wages and about 145 for gross real wages (pp. 192–198). This makes Figurnov's real wage figures for 1940–54 very close to my own computations.

Figurnov presents, though without much explanation, some new information on collective farm market prices. In 1940, he says, collective farm market prices exceeded prices in state shops on the average by 75 percent (p. 197). This is a larger gap than I estimate. However, the official Soviet index number shows a smaller rise in prices in state and cooperative shops between 1937 and 1940 than I do, so the difference concerning the extent of the rise in collective farm market prices between 1937 and 1940 might not be much. Also, according to Figurnov, collective farm market prices in 1948 were 34 percent higher than in 1940 (p. 158), a considerably smaller rise than the 75 percent rise I estimate.

Figurnov incidentally throws some light on the erratic nature of the 1940 observed price quotations for manufactured consumer goods that I have discussed in chapter IV, section 1. He says that during 1940 certain quantities of the most important manufactured consumer goods were sold in special "deluxe" shops (*pokazatel'nye univermagi* or *"liuksy"*) at prices up to two or more times the regular price (p. 158). Figurnov's work does not treat the pre-1940 years in any detail but does contain a Soviet admission (fn., pp. 51–52) that the average real wage failed to rise between 1928 and 1940.

This admission, accompanied by somewhat more data, is to be found also in another source which only recently became available, B. P. Plyshevskii, *Raspredelenie natsional'nogo dokhoda v SSSR* (Moscow, 1960), p. 194. This work, it should be mentioned, includes an index number of prices in state and cooperative shops in 1945 showing prices over twice the 1940 level and 259 percent of the 1937 level (p. 183). This suggests that my 1944 retail price index number may well be too low.

The increase in real wages since 1954 is the result almost entirely of increases in money wages. An important factor here is the increase in the minimum wage effected in January 1957.[37] The greater gain in net than in gross real wages since 1954 reflects tax reductions and the discontinuance in 1958 of compulsory bond subscriptions. Monthly earnings of 370 rubles or less were exempted from the income and "bachelor" taxes in January 1957, and the tax rates on monthly earnings between 370 and 450 rubles were reduced in March 1957.[38] In January 1958 the "bachelor" tax on couples and single persons with one or two children and on childless single women was abolished, leaving a tax of this nature only for couples and single males with no children.[39] During the years 1955 through 1957 these tax gains were partially offset by compulsory subscriptions to government bonds, which were considerably higher than in 1954,[40] but, as has been said, the bond subscriptions were discontinued in 1958.

[37] See fn. 33.
[38] *Bol'shaia sovetskaia entsiklopediia* (2d ed., 1957), vol. 50 on USSR, p. 383.
[39] *Pravda,* December 21, 1957.
[40] *New York Times,* February 5, 1955; *Finansy i sotsialisticheskoe stroitel'stvo* (Moscow, 1957), p. 72.

The cost of living apparently remained virtually constant from 1954 through 1957 and then showed an increase of about 2.5 percent in 1958.[41] There were some selective changes in official retail prices[42] but the official index number of retail prices in state and cooperative shops remained at 74 percent of the 1950 level (138 percent of the 1940 level) from 1954 through 1957 and rose to 76 percent of the 1950 level in 1958. The rise was caused mainly by an increase in the prices of alcoholic beverages.[43] Prices on the collective farm market declined moderately from 1954 through 1957, and then they too showed an increase in 1958.[44]

Accepting the official Soviet index number of gross real wages in 1958 as 108 percent of 1954, and linking this to my index number of gross real wages valued at given-year prices, I can compute that Soviet gross real wages in 1958 were 134 percent of the 1928 level; but when I link the official index number to my index number valued at 1937 prices, I find that Soviet gross real wages as late as 1958 had still barely reached (were 96 percent of) the 1928 level. Following the same procedure, and assuming that the increase in net real wages between 1954 and 1958 was 16 percent, I can compute that the net real wages of Soviet workers in 1958, measured in terms of given-year prices, were 131 percent of the 1928 level, and in terms of 1937 prices were but 95 percent of the 1928 level.

The benefits received by the Soviet worker have probably shown some relative increase since 1954. The only development of importance here is the pension law of July 1956, which sharply increased pension rates.[45] As a result, government expenditures on pensions were almost to double between 1955 and 1957, the first full year at the new rates.[46] Another measure was the abolition at the beginning of the 1956/57 school year of tuition fees, which had been charged for secondary and higher education since 1940.[47] Tuition fees had not amounted to much so this would have little effect on real wages. The current official Soviet index number of average real income, including benefits, of wage earners and salaried employees shows an increase of 12 percent between 1955 and 1958.[48]

It should be mentioned also that the first steps toward the gradual

[41] As estimated by the Nauchno-issledovatel'skii institut truda, the cost-of-living index number (1950 = 100) was 79 in 1955, 78 in 1956 and 1957, and 80 in 1958. See Figurnov, Trud i zarabotnaia plata, no. 12, 1959, p. 48.

[42] See, for example, Welles Hangen in the New York Times, January 23, 1956; B. I. Gogol' (ed.), Sorok let sovetskoi torgovli (Moscow, 1957), p. 14; Sovetskaia Rossiia, October 10, 1956; Pravda, April 25, September 29, November 1, 1957; January 2, 1958; July 1, 1959; Trud, October 14, 1956; Izvestiia, September 15, 1957.

[43] TSU, Narodnoe khoziaistvo SSSR v 1956 g., p. 232; and Narodnoe khoziaistvo SSSR v 1958 g., p. 771.

[44] TSU, Sovetskaia torgovlia; Statisticheskii sbornik (Moscow, 1956), p. 182; Narodnoe khoziaistvo SSSR v 1958 g., p. 789.

[45] Pravda, July 15, 1956. See also appendix F.

[46] Finansy i sotsialisticheskoe stroitel'stvo, pp. 216–217.

[47] Pravda, January 15, 1956.

[48] TSU, Narodnoe khoziaistvo SSSR v 1958 g., p. 100.

reduction in working hours from the standard 8-hour day were taken during 1956 and 1957.[49] The number of workers affected through 1958 was small.

As for the future, the Soviet goals for the worker are outlined in the Seven Year Plan for 1959–65.[50] According to this plan, for wage earners and salaried employees, average real income per worker is to increase 40 percent by 1965. Reference is to total net income plus benefits. Gross money wages are to increase on the average by about 26 percent,[51] and net money wages will increase somewhat more than this, as it is proposed to abolish income taxes. Price reductions are promised for restaurant meals, but beyond this the only price reductions are to affect certain commodities whose prices are out of line with those of other commodities. These price cuts will apparently reduce the cost of living by 5 percent or less, and gross real wages are to increase by about one-third.[52] Roughly speaking, an increase of this magnitude is in accord with the planned increase of about 60 percent in both the total industrial output of consumer goods and in retail sales.[53] Average peasant real income, it might be noted, is to increase at the same rate as average worker real income.

The Soviet goal for real income includes benefits, and these are to increase. The most specific and probably most important measure here is a further significant increase in pension rates. Expenditures on other types of benefits are to continue to increase, though no significant specific improvements are mentioned.[54] Beyond this, hours of work are to be reduced from the 48-hour week, which was standard until March 1956, to 42 hours in 1960 and 40 hours in 1962; and between 1964 and 1968, a 35-hour week, with two days off, is to be introduced. It is not known whether the reduction in working hours is counted as part of the planned 40 percent increase in real income per worker. The housing program — a 60 percent increase in urban housing space — will relieve some of the worst crowding, though it will still fall far short of providing decent housing for the bulk of the Soviet worker families.

Interestingly, the plan calls for a revision of the wage structure which will result in a considerable equalization of wages. The minimum wage is to increase by 70 to 85 percent from the 1957 range of 270 to 350 rubles

[49] *Bol'shaia sovetskaia entsiklopediia* (2d ed., 1957), vol. 50 on USSR, p. 385; *Pravda,* January 2 and 27, 1958.

[50] *Pravda,* November 14, 1958; February 7 and 8, 1959.

[51] *Pravda,* November 25, 1958.

[52] S. P. Figurnov, "Chto poluchaiut rabochie i sluzhashchie SSSR sverkh zarabotnoi platy," *V pomoshch' politicheskomu samoobrazovaniiu,* no. 9, 1959, pp. 77, 80.

[53] This would amount to an average per capita increase of 33 to 40 percent, assuming a seven-year population increase of 15 to 20 percent.

[54] And, in fact, Khrushchev's proposed reorganization of the education system appears to represent a retreat from the former goal of providing a ten-year compulsory education for all. The reform appears to envision eight years of compulsory education for all, with further education available to most only through evening and correspondence courses taken while performing a regular job (*Pravda,* September 21 and November 14, 1958).

a month to a range of 500 to 600 rubles a month.[55] Adjustments are to be made in the wages of those currently at the middle of the wage scale, but apparently no general wage increases are planned for those in the upper pay brackets. This would appear to be a stride toward the egalitarian goal of full communism. One need not suppose, however, that the motivation is entirely idealistic. There are reasons to think that this ultimate goal coincides at the moment with the practical necessity to adapt the policy of incentive wage differentials to changed conditions of demand and supply of labor. The Soviet Union now faces a shortage of labor; but so far as skilled labor is concerned, the shortage must be less acute now than in earlier years, in view of the large body of skilled workers who have already been trained. The wage differentials needed to induce workers to acquire greater skills are presumably smaller than they formerly were. The existing wage schedules apparently provided larger differentials than were needed to call forth additional effort. In part, at least, this was the result of bonus and piece-rate systems based on work norms which had become obsolete. On the other hand, the new entrants to the labor force today are better educated and more familiar with modern industrial processes — and are, therefore, presumably "worth" more — than the peasants who entered the industrial labor force in such large numbers in the 1930's. Also, by now there is a well-established system for training youths for the jobs where they are most needed;[56] and the proposed educational reforms appear to be designed to improve this system. At the same time, the decline in births during and after the war means there will be a shortage of new entrants to the labor force.[57] The ambitious program in agriculture, combined with the difficulties of providing housing in the already crowded cities, seem to preclude much migration from the farms to the urban labor force, for the time being at least. In fact, the present plan does not appear to anticipate any significant rural-urban migration. Offering more attractive beginning wages may be seen as a means of speeding up recruitment of new members of the labor force from among youths and, especially, wives who might otherwise remain outside the labor force. The enormous propaganda value of a relatively high minimum wage and greater equality of income has surely been taken into consideration also.

The improvement in real income promised for the seven years 1959–65 is smaller than was provided in the previous seven years, but, if achieved,

---

[55] This is equivalent to 50 to 60 rubles a month in terms of the new, "heavy," rubles in use since January 1961.

[56] Walter Galenson, "Industrial Training in the Soviet Union," *Industrial and Labor Relations Review,* 9:562–576 (1956); Brown, *Industrial and Labor Relations Review,* 10:185–192 (1957).

[57] Illustrative of the decline in births is the decline in the number of children attending the first four grades of school from some 20 to 21 million in the years 1936 to 1941, to 12 to 13 million in the years 1952 to 1956 (TSU, *Kul'turnoe stroitel'stvo SSSR; Statisticheskii sbornik* (Moscow, 1956), p. 122).

it will nevertheless be a solid gain for the Soviet worker and will take real wages well beyond the 1928 level.

What are the prospects that the goals for living standards will be fulfilled? The plan generally calls for a continued growth of the economy at a rate which, though below that attained in the prewar and early postwar periods, is still very rapid. In agriculture, the planned rate of growth far exceeds anything previously attained. Through Khrushchev's efforts, agriculture appears to be emerging from its long-standing stagnation, and the prospects are for continued growth in agricultural output. But it seems highly doubtful that the 70 percent increase planned for 1965 can be achieved. In industry, the Russians are seeking to expand output by 80 percent. They will certainly encounter difficulties — among them, the shortage of labor already mentioned, and the growing need to replace worn-out and obsolete machinery. On the other hand, they now have available a large body of scientific and technical personnel. This factor, in addition to various measures being taken to increase efficiency in industry and the steady increase in the volume of capital investment planned, should serve to counteract some of the limiting factors and provide the basis for a continued high rate of industrial output. The plan, as usual, is ambitious and there are several competing goals. The emphasis on heavy industry is maintained. Expenditures on military output will no doubt be great. The housing program and the planned renovation of the transportation system require heavy investment which does not pay off directly in increased output. In addition to this, the Soviet leaders are committed to a policy of extending aid to other countries of the Communist bloc, and they have embarked on a small but growing program of aid to underdeveloped countries outside the bloc. (They may well benefit from imports of scarce raw materials and agricultural products from these countries.) And they have promised to raise living standards appreciably. Possibly all of these goals can be met, and it would be most unwise in light of past performance to underestimate the Soviet prospects. But possibly, too, the planners have been overly optimistic.

In the past, when plans have turned out to be overly ambitious, it has been the goals for living standards which have been sacrificed in the effort to meet as nearly as possible the goals for heavy industry and defense. One can hardly expect any basic change in this scheme of priorities, but perhaps the needs of the consumers will not be relegated to quite so residual a position. Khrushchev appears to be sensitive to the enormous importance to the Soviet Union's standing abroad of a good showing so far as the consumers are concerned. No one any longer doubts the Soviet capacity in industry, in war, or in science; but if they wish to extend Soviet influence abroad, the Soviet leaders must also, one would think, be able to demonstrate that the system can provide an increasing standard of living for its people. One might, then, expect them to make every effort to assure at least some visible gain in living standards during the coming years, though the gain may be less than promised if the plan as a whole cannot be fulfilled. Khrushchev's promise that in the 1970's the Soviet people will enjoy the highest standard of living in the world is not to be taken seriously, especially when one considers that the Soviet worker's real wage is still no more than a quarter of that of the American worker. But so long as the Soviet economy continues to expand, as it must be expected to, it should be able — even without reducing the share of total resources allocated to investment and defense — to provide a continuous (though perhaps moderate) increase in consumption.

APPENDIX A

NOTES TO TABLE 3: SOURCES AND DATES OF PRICE QUOTATIONS;
DESCRIPTIONS AND COMPARABILITY OF COMMODITIES

The absolute ruble prices from which the price relatives in Table 3 are computed are shown in Table A-1. The prices shown are those prevailing in the city of Moscow, except where otherwise indicated in this appendix, and are the official prices charged in state and cooperative shops. They are intended to represent annual average prices.

The year in question is the calendar year, except in the case of 1952 — for which the year is from April 1, 1952 to March 31, 1953 — and 1954 — for which the year is from April 1, 1954 to March 31, 1955. For vegetables and fruits subject to seasonal price fluctuations the quotations generally relate only to a short period, sometimes a single date, within the year. For each of these seasonal items, the quotations compared between 1937 and one of the other years relate to approximately the same week or month in each year.

The general principle on which the average annual prices of nonseasonal items are computed is to weight each quotation by the length of time it was in effect. Data are not available that would permit any attempt to take into account variations in the volume sold during a given year. The dates of the quotations available in the principal sources for each year are indicated below by year. I also comment on some special problems arising in the derivation of annual average prices and in the computation of postwar prices from the annual percentage price reductions.

1928: (1) The quotations in *ESBM** are monthly reports of the prices actually charged in Moscow shops. The list of items priced in this source changed somewhat during the year and the series is not complete for all items. Quotations are available for every month of 1928 except June, and for January 1929. The June price can often be inferred from the May and July quotations. In computing the annual average price, the quotations for January 1928 and January 1929 are each given a weight of one-half month and those for other months are each given a weight of one month. This source cites prices in both state and cooperative shops. Usually there was little or no difference between the prices charged in these two types of outlet. When there was a difference, the average is usually taken; but in some cases the series is more complete for cooperative shops and the average of the monthly cooperative shop quotations is taken.

(2) Prices in *SMG-28,* a collection of official price lists, were established at various dates up to the time of publication sometime in 1928. It is assumed that the quotations in this source remained in effect throughout 1928, except where there is evidence to the contrary. Several of the price lists in this source are wholesale price lists and it is necessary to estimate the Moscow retail price from the wholesale price and the maximum retail trade allowance.

1937: (1) Vaso Trivanovitch ("Purchasing Power of Wages in the Soviet Union," National Industrial Conference Board, *Conference Board Bulletin,* 12:25–28 (March 7, 1938)) reports observed prices of foods, soap, kerosene, matches, and cigarettes on April 1 and July 1, 1937. *UM* reports prices of the same products on these

* See the list of abbreviations at the end of this volume.

TABLE A-1

Retail Prices of Goods and Services, Official Prices, Moscow, 1928–54, Absolute Prices

Commodity	Unit	Price in rubles per unit					
		1928	1937	1940	1948	1952	1954
Grain products and legumes							
1. Rye flour	kg	0.11	1.60	—	4.80	2.40	2.10
2. Rye bread	kg	0.08	0.85	0.88	3.00	1.50	1.25
3. Whole wheat flour	kg	0.18	1.80	—	—	—	—
4. Wheat flour, 85%	kg	—	2.40	—	6.20	3.00	2.60
5. Wheat flour, 72%	kg	—	2.90	2.90	8.00	3.65	3.15
6. Wheat flour, 30%	kg	0.22	4.60	4.60	—	—	—
7. Wheat bread, 96%	kg	—	1.00	1.03	—	—	—
8. Wheat bread, 80 to 85%	kg	0.24	1.70	1.70	4.40	2.00	1.70
9. Wheat bread, 72%	kg	—	2.80	—	7.00	3.20	2.75
10. French loaf, 72%	kg	—	3.60	—	8.00	3.65	3.15
11. French loaf, 30%	kg	—	5.70	6.00	—	—	—
12. Macaroni, 72%	kg	—	3.50	—	10.00	4.90	4.15
13. Macaroni, 40%	kg	0.46	4.40	—	—	—	—
14. Buckwheat grits	kg	0.20	4.30	4.50	12.00	6.25	5.60
15. Millet grits	kg	0.17	2.10	3.00	6.00	3.35	3.00
16. Rice	kg	0.51	6.00	—	—	—	—
17. Rice, grade 1	kg	—	6.50	6.50	17.10	9.80	8.80
18. Wheat meal	kg	—	4.50	4.50	—	—	—
19. Dried peas	kg	0.34	2.25	—	—	—	—
20. Dried beans	kg	—	3.95	—	10.60	5.50	4.95
21. Oats	kg	0.11	0.60	—	2.50	1.15	0.95
Meat and poultry							
22. Beef, average fed, grade 1	kg	0.86	7.75	13.47	30.00	14.80	12.60
23. Pork	kg	0.96	10.38	19.00	48.00	23.70	21.40
24. Mutton, average fed, grade 1	kg	0.80	7.60	—	30.00	14.05	11.90
25. Mutton	kg	—	8.00	15.06	—	—	—
26. Mutton, above average fed, grade 1	kg	—	9.60	—	34.00	15.90	14.10
27. Chicken, grade 1	kg	—	11.00	14.00	35.00	17.30	14.70
28. Chicken, grade 2	kg	—	7.50	11.00	31.00	15.30	13.00
29. Goose, grade 2	kg	—	7.38	11.00	25.00	11.65	9.90
30. Duck, grade 1	kg	—	11.00	18.50	—	—	—
31. Duck, grade 2	kg	—	8.50	—	34.00	15.80	13.50
32. Turkey, grade 1	kg	—	13.00	18.00	45.00	20.95	17.80
33. Turkey, grade 2	kg	—	10.50	—	39.00	18.15	15.40
34. Rabbit	kg	—	4.00	—	24.00	12.85	10.90
35. Bacon	kg	—	16.00	25.00	59.00	28.00	23.80
36. Ham, smoked	kg	—	18.00	25.78	—	—	—
37. Ham, smoked, average	kg	—	15.00	—	59.00	28.00	23.80
38. Sausage, ordinary	kg	—	9.25	15.08	—	—	—
39. Sausage, hamburger	kg	—	16.00	22.66	—	—	—
40. Sausage, Moscow	kg	—	23.50	—	82.00	40.50	34.40
Fish							
41. Pike-perch, fresh, frozen, or salted	kg	0.49	3.40	—	—	—	—
42. Pike-perch, frozen	kg	—	3.28	—	12.00	8.70	7.85
43. Perch, frozen	kg	—	3.61	8.50	—	—	—
44. Sturgeon, fresh or frozen	kg	—	8.00	15.00	29.00	21.15	19.00
45. Herring, salted, ordinary	kg	0.55	6.00	—	—	—	—
46. Herring, salted, large	kg	—	8.00	—	20.00	14.55	13.10
47. Herring, salted	kg	—	7.03	9.00	—	—	—

Note: The dash (—) indicates that the item was not priced for that year.

TABLE A-1 (Continued)

Retail Prices of Goods and Services, Official Prices, Moscow, 1928–54, Absolute Prices

Commodity	Unit	Price in rubles per unit					
		1928	1937	1940	1948	1952	1954
48. Sturgeon, cured	kg	—	18.00	38.33	88.00	49.90	44.90
49. Caviar, black, granular	kg	—	49.25	100.00	371.00	204.00	183.70
Sugar and confectionery							
50. Sugar, lump	kg	0.70	4.10	5.41	—	—	—
51. Sugar, small lump	kg	—	4.00	—	15.00	11.90	10.70
52. Sugar, granulated	kg	0.62	3.80	4.92	13.50	10.35	9.30
53. Cocoa	kg	—	61.80	81.04	193.00	136.65	92.90
54. Chocolate candy, best	kg	—	44.40	80.65	—	—	—
55. Bonbons	kg	—	16.59	35.45	—	—	—
56. Honey	kg	—	7.34	10.60	—	—	—
57. Hard candy	kg	—	4.20	—	15.10	12.50	11.30
58. Soft candies	kg	—	6.05	—	19.00	13.70	12.30
59. Caramels, "Theatre"	kg	—	10.00	—	30.00	24.00	21.60
Fats							
60. Butter, sweet	kg	2.49	17.50	—	—	—	—
61. Butter, rendered	kg	2.26	20.25	—	—	—	—
62. Butter, grade 1	kg	—	20.00	28.00	—	—	—
63. Butter, grade 2	kg	—	17.50	23.66	—	—	—
64. Butter (average of 7 kinds)	kg	—	17.50	—	67.14	30.60	27.60
65. Sunflower oil	kg	0.54	14.84	15.65	30.00	21.60	18.23
66. Beef fat, rendered	kg	1.08	11.75	—	—	—	—
67. Lard	kg	1.73	21.00	—	—	—	—
68. Salt pork, fat	kg	—	22.00	35.00	—	—	—
69. Margarine	kg	—	10.50	—	33.00	16.40	14.80
Milk and milk products							
70. Milk, fresh	liter	0.21	1.60	2.15	4.00	2.90	2.90
71. Sour cream (spring)	kg	1.28	7.25	—	—	—	—
72. Sour cream	kg	—	7.73	9.45	26.50	17.20	17.20
73. Cheese, Swiss-type	kg	—	24.80	29.66	72.00	33.20	33.20
74. Cheese, Holland-type	kg	—	14.76	25.15	—	—	—
75. Cheese, American-type	kg	—	21.15	28.19	—	—	—
Eggs							
76. Eggs	ten	0.54	6.13	8.25	16.00	10.40	9.35
Vegetables and fruit							
77. Potatoes	kg	0.08	0.40	1.01	1.00	0.90	0.53
78. Cabbage, fresh (fall)	kg	0.09	0.30	—	1.00	0.85	0.80
79. Cabbage, fresh (July)	kg	—	1.60	10.00	—	—	—
80. Sauerkraut	kg	0.12	0.45	1.50	—	—	—
81. Cucumbers, fresh (August)	kg	—	0.90	—	2.00	1.80	0.90
82. Cucumbers, fresh (July)	ten	—	6.00	12.00	—	—	—
83. Cucumbers, pickled	kg	—	2.75	3.40	—	—	—
84. Cucumbers, salted	kg	—	1.10	—	3.50	3.00	1.50
85. Onions	kg	0.32	1.40	2.25	—	—	—
86. Green onions	kg	—	1.40	2.33	—	—	—
87. Green onions (summer)	kg	—	1.00	—	4.00	3.60	1.80
88. Beets (April)	kg	0.08	0.40	—	—	—	—
89. Beets (January)	kg	—	0.33	0.75	—	—	—
90. Beets (fall)	kg	—	0.26	—	0.90	0.81	0.66
91. Carrots	kg	—	0.39	1.00	—	—	—
92. Turnips	kg	—	0.33	—	1.35	1.21	0.60
93. Tomatoes	kg	—	1.60	—	4.00	3.60	1.80

Note: The dash (—) indicates that the item was not priced for that year.

TABLE A-1 (Continued)

Retail Prices of Goods and Services, Official Prices, Moscow, 1928–54, Absolute Prices

Commodity	Unit	Price in rubles per unit					
		1928	1937	1940	1948	1952	1954
94. Pumpkin	kg	—	0.25	—	0.70	0.63	0.35
95. Mushrooms, dried	kg	—	35.00	35.00	—	—	—
96. Mushrooms, pickled	kg	—	3.25	5.60	—	—	—
97. Peas, canned	500 gm	—	3.40	—	9.10	5.85	5.45
98. Apples, fresh	kg	—	5.40	—	20.50	13.15	6.70
99. Apples, fresh (January)	kg	—	7.20	8.20	—	—	—
100. Grapes, fresh	kg	—	7.00	9.00	—	—	—
101. Apricots, canned	kg	—	8.95	—	17.50	11.00	8.30
102. Apples, dried	kg	—	7.48	—	28.00	17.90	14.35
103. Prunes, dried	kg	—	14.00	14.50	40.00	25.60	20.50
104. Raisins	kg	—	8.31	—	31.00	19.85	15.90
105. Mixed dried fruit	kg	—	8.00	—	31.30	20.00	16.00
Salt							
106. Salt, ground	kg	0.05	0.11	0.11	1.50	0.35	0.22
Tea and coffee							
107. Tea	100 gm	0.63	8.00	8.00	16.00	10.40	7.50
108. Coffee	kg	—	51.00	—	75.00	57.40	39.00
Alcoholic beverages							
109. Vodka, 40°	½ liter	0.88	6.55	9.00	42.75	21.60	19.23
110. Vodka, 50°	½ liter	—	9.00	—	65.64	32.40	28.85
111. Champagne, Soviet	bottle	—	20.88	22.00	42.75	33.50	28.50
112. Red wine, "Kagor"	⅘ liter	—	14.00	19.00	—	—	—
113. White wine, "Naporeuli"	⅘ liter	—	9.63	11.40	—	—	—
114. Port wine, Soviet	⅘ liter	—	17.80	23.00	—	—	—
Textiles							
115. Calico, no. 6	meter	0.38	3.43	—	10.10	8.60	6.20
116. Calico	meter	—	3.50	5.50	—	—	—
117. Sateen	meter	0.61	5.15	—	—	—	—
118. Sateen, mercerized	meter	—	6.43	—	25.20	21.40	15.50
119. Satinette	meter	—	7.90	11.00	—	—	—
120. Sheeting, cotton, no. 49	meter	0.90	7.30	—	—	—	—
121. Sheeting, cotton	meter	—	9.71	—	34.60	29.40	21.25
122. Madapolam	meter	0.45	3.83	—	—	—	—
123. Moleskin	meter	0.65	4.85	—	—	—	—
124. Woolen, part wool broadcloth	meter	3.89	45.00	—	—	—	—
125. Woolen, pure wool plush velour	meter	16.65	300.00	—	—	—	—
126. Woolen, pure wool "Boston"	meter	—	120.00	—	450.00	356.00	338.00
127. Worsted, part wool	meter	2.22	17.00	—	—	—	—
128. Worsted, pure wool	meter	3.19	47.00	—	—	—	—
129. Wool and cotton mixture	meter	—	67.50	84.50	—	—	—
130. Coarse wool baize, solid color	meter	5.55	29.51	—	—	—	—
131. Coarse wool baize, mixture	meter	—	36.43	—	108.00	73.90	70.00
132. Sheeting, linen	meter	2.04	13.25	—	—	—	—
133. Sheeting, part linen	meter	1.67	11.00	—	32.00	27.00	25.00
134. Rayon crepe de Chine	meter	—	30.00	—	83.50	66.00	66.00

Note: The dash (—) indicates that the item was not priced for that year.

TABLE A-1 (Continued)

Retail Prices of Goods and Services, Official Prices, Moscow, 1928–54, Absolute Prices

		Price in rubles per unit					
Commodity	Unit	1928	1937	1940	1948	1952	1954
135. Silk crepe de Chine no. 5	meter	—	54.50	—	137.00	123.50	94.50
136. Silk crepe de Chine	meter	—	58.50	90.00	—	—	—
Garments							
137. Shirt, cotton	one	—	39.35	70.50	—	—	—
138. Shirt, cotton zephyr	one	—	42.90	—	89.00	77.50	60.00
139. Cotton dress	one	—	41.50	—	110.00	95.50	73.50
140. Cotton blouse	one	—	22.10	—	60.00	52.20	39.30
141. Trousers, part wool	pair	7.39	75.00	—	—	—	—
142. Suit, wool, fabric group 46	one	—	395.00	—	1,400.00	1,110.00	1,110.00
143. Suit, wool	one	—	600.00	900.00	—	—	—
144. Overcoat, common quality	one	—	317.00	460.00	—	—	—
145. Overcoat, women's	one	—	314.00	—	832.00	586.00	586.00
146. Overcoat, better	one	—	577.00	—	1,675.00	1,328.00	1,328.00
147. Blouse, silk	one	—	81.00	—	198.00	168.00	138.00
148. Necktie, rayon	one	—	14.55	19.00	—	—	—
149. Hat, felt	one	—	42.50	42.00	125.00	96.00	81.50
150. Hat, fur	one	—	300.00	300.00	725.00	587.00	546.00
Knitwear							
151. Stockings, cotton	pair	—	1.76	—	7.00	5.95	3.80
152. Socks, cotton, plain	pair	0.51	1.83	—	—	—	—
153. Socks, cotton	pair	—	2.58	3.68	—	—	—
154. Socks, cotton, cheapest	pair	—	1.49	—	5.45	4.65	3.00
155. Socks, rayon	pair	—	6.58	7.50	—	—	—
156. Socks, rayon, no. 86	pair	—	5.44	—	17.00	12.30	8.85
Shoes							
157. Cowhide boots, one-piece upper	pair	13.50	136.00	—	—	—	—
158. Cowhide boots	pair	—	107.00	120.00	—	—	—
159. Leather boots, black	pair	8.90	97.08	—	—	—	—
160. Leather boots, welted	pair	11.50	72.81	—	—	—	—
161. Leather boots, brown	pair	—	102.00	—	247.00	210.00	180.00
162. Leather boots, composition soles	pair	—	57.00	—	150.50	128.00	107.00
163. Leather oxfords, women's	pair	9.15	63.10	—	—	—	—
164. Leather shoes, children's	pair	4.60	23.83	—	—	—	—
165. Leather shoes, men's, no. 4004	pair	—	82.50	120.00	—	—	—
166. Leather shoes, women's	pair	—	68.00	82.50	—	—	—
167. Leather shoes, men's	pair	—	87.40	—	226.00	192.00	165.00
168. Leather shoes, rubber soles	pair	—	35.50	40.00	—	—	—
169. Sandals	pair	4.05	38.83	—	—	—	—
170. Canvas shoes, leather soles	pair	8.15	43.69	—	—	—	—
171. Cloth and leather shoes	pair	—	30.50	—	83.50	56.75	36.50
172. Rubbers	pair	3.55	20.08	23.58	45.00	40.50	30.30
173. Valenki	pair	9.40	75.00	—	195.00	146.00	139.00
Haberdashery and notions							
174. Cotton thread, 6-strand	200 yards	0.13	0.41	—	—	—	—
175. Cotton thread, 3-strand	200 meters	—	0.30	—	1.83	1.25	0.95

Note: The dash (—) indicates that the item was not priced for that year.

TABLE A-1 (Continued)

Retail Prices of Goods and Services, Official Prices, Moscow, 1928–54, Absolute Prices

Commodity	Unit	Price in rubles per unit					
		1928	1937	1940	1948	1952	1954
176. Silk thread	100 meters	—	0.95	—	2.30	1.55	1.20
177. Dress pattern	one	—	0.43	—	5.25	5.25	4.45
178. Straightedge razor	one	—	11.10	—	49.00	37.50	33.75
179. Razor blades	one	—	0.26	—	0.40	0.30	0.28
Soap, drugs, etc.							
180. Household soap, 50% fat content	kg	.36	2.90	—	—	—	—
181. Household soap, 60% fat content	kg	—	3.10	3.10	13.00	6.65	4.80
182. Glycerine soap	cake	—	1.61	1.90	—	—	—
183. Toilet soap, "Family"	100 gm	—	0.80	—	3.71	1.55	1.00
184. Toothpaste, "Sanit"	tube	—	2.71	—	4.17	2.20	1.75
185. Toothbrush	one	—	0.89	—	3.53	2.65	1.90
186. Absorbent cotton	50 gm	—	0.78	—	2.25	2.25	1.60
187. Gauze bandage	7 meters	—	0.98	—	3.40	3.40	2.45
188. Thermometer	one	—	3.50	—	4.50	4.50	3.25
189. Castor oil capsules	box	—	1.00	—	1.00	1.00	0.72
Housewares							
190. Tea kettle, brass, 3.5-liter	one	5.85	39.50	—	—	—	—
191. Tea kettle, brass	one	—	50.00	—	130.00	110.50	99.50
192. Pan, aluminum, 22-cm	one	2.45	18.80	—	—	—	—
193. Pan, aluminum, 18-cm	one	—	12.00	—	27.50	21.30	19.20
194. Wash basin, aluminum	one	—	20.00	—	32.00	24.80	22.30
195. Wash basin, enameled iron	one	1.30	6.50	—	—	—	—
196. Cast-iron pot	one	1.15	5.20	—	—	—	—
197. Frying pan, enameled iron	one	0.55	2.10	—	—	—	—
198. Tea cup, enameled iron	one	0.30	0.75	—	—	—	—
199. Pail, galvanized iron	one	1.08	5.70	—	—	—	—
200. Primus stove	one	7.67	29.00	—	110.80	77.40	69.70
201. Samovar	one	19.60	105.00	—	340.00	272.00	245.00
202. Samovar, 711-mm	one	—	120.00	—	440.00	352.00	317.00
203. Kerosene lamp	one	0.80	2.00	—	—	—	—
204. Lamp chimney	one	0.06	0.11	—	—	—	—
205. Electric light bulb	one	—	0.69	—	1.50	1.20	0.81
206. Electric hot plate	one	—	21.00	—	30.83	21.60	18.35
207. Electric iron	one	—	23.00	—	90.00	60.75	51.65
208. Sewing machine	one	—	183.80	—	927.50	648.00	583.00
Reading matter							
209. *Pravda*	1 copy	0.05	0.10	0.10	0.20	0.20	0.20
210. *Bol'shevik*	1 issue	0.40	0.50	0.50	1.25	1.25	1.25
211. *Ogonek*	1 issue	0.10	0.50	0.50	3.00	3.00	3.00
212. *Planovoe khoziaistvo*	1 issue	2.00	3.00	3.00	3.00	3.00	3.00
213. *Lenin Collection*	1 vol.	3.25	3.75	6.00	6.00	4.90	4.90
214. *Pushkin Works*	1 vol.	—	15.00	25.00	35.00	28.70	28.70
215. Book on Turgenev	one	2.30	3.00	—	—	—	—
216. Novel	one	2.80	6.50	—	—	—	—
217. *The Quiet Don*	one	—	9.00	9.00	13.00	10.70	10.70
218. Pamphlet, 32 pages	one	0.10	0.25	—	0.60	0.50	0.50
219. Pamphlet, 48 pages	one	—	0.30	0.30	—	—	—
Cultural and sports goods							
220. Phonograph PT-3	one	—	353.00	—	770.00	378.00	378.00
221. Baian accordion	one	—	1,505.00	—	3,929.00	2,288.00	2,059.00

Note: The dash (—) indicates that the item was not priced for that year.

TABLE A-1 (Continued)

Retail Prices of Goods and Services, Official Prices, Moscow, 1928–54, Absolute Prices

Commodity	Unit	Price in rubles per unit					
		1928	1937	1940	1948	1952	1954
222. Piano	one	—	2,000.00	—	8,125.00	5,850.00	5,265.00
223. Bicycle	one	—	250.00	—	1,197.00	645.00	580.50
224. Camera, FED	one	—	792.50	—	1,100.00	792.00	713.00
225. Pencil, "Union"	one	0.03	0.07	—			
226. Pencil	one	—	0.06	—	0.30	0.30	0.22
227. Pen holder	one	—	0.13	—	0.50	0.50	0.37
228. Pen point	one	—	0.02	—	0.05	0.05	0.03
229. Paint set	10 tubes	1.85	2.25	—	—	—	—
Kerosene and matches							
230. Kerosene	liter	0.10	0.47	0.65	2.00	1.40	0.65
231. Matches	box	—	0.024	0.043	0.20	0.12	0.08
232. Matches	10 boxes	0.15	0.20	—	—	—	—
Tobacco products							
233. Cigarettes, grade 3	25	0.14	0.35	—	—	—	—
234. Cigarettes, "Metro"	25	—	1.30	—	2.57	1.60	1.55
235. Cigarettes, "Pushki"	25	—	2.35	2.25	—	—	—
236. Cigarettes, "Deli"	25	—	2.83	2.70	—	—	—
237. Cigarettes, "Kazbek"	25	—	3.30	—	6.08	3.90	3.50
238. Cigarettes, "Allegro"	25	—	4.71	4.50	—	—	—
239. Tobacco, grade 2	100 gm	0.65	5.00	5.00	—	—	—
240. Tobacco, grade 1	100 gm	—	8.00	—	16.00	10.40	9.85
241. Makhorka	100 gm	0.13	0.75	—	2.30	1.40	1.25
242. Makhorka, highest grade	100 gm	—	0.80	1.00	—	—	—
Services							
243. Rent	square meter per month	0.24	0.71	1.01	1.32	1.32	1.32
244. Electricity	kw-hr	0.18	0.20	0.24	0.31	0.40	0.40
245. Water	cu. m.	0.122	0.122	0.40	0.40	0.40	0.40
246. Tram ride	ride	0.11	0.15	0.15	0.22	0.30	0.30
247. Railroad fare, Moscow-Leningrad	1 way	12.06	35.20	—	80.29	87.20	87.20
248. Railroad fare	km	—	0.031	0.047	—	—	—
249. Movie	ticket	0.30	1.00	—	3.00	3.00	2.00
250. Trousers made to order	pair	—	17.50	40.00	—	—	—
251. Coat made to order	one	—	77.50	—	260.00	177.00	177.00
252. Haircut	one	—	1.60	—	—	2.00	1.50
253. Shave	one	—	1.00	—	—	3.00	2.25
254. Average hourly wage	Index 1937 = 100	24.0	100	122	195	223	233

Note: The dash (—) indicates that the item was not priced for that year.

dates and also on January 1 and October 1, 1937 and January 1, 1938. In computing annual average prices from these quarterly quotations, the January 1937 and January 1938 quotations are each given a weight of 1½ months, and the other quotations are each given a weight of 3 months.

(2) The dates for which observed price quotations for most manufactured consumer goods are available in the same sources are January 1, April 1, and July 1,

1937. Account is taken of the price decree of April 28, 1937 ordering percentage price reductions for a wide range of manufactured goods, effective for some products on June 1, and for others on July 1, 1937. Inasmuch as the prices observed on July 1 should reflect the announced price reductions, it is assumed that the prices observed July 1 remained in effect for the remainder of the year, except where there is evidence to the contrary.

In computing the annual average price, the quotation for January 1, 1937 is given a weight of 1½ months. The July 1 quotation is given a weight of 7 months in the case of items for which a price reduction was effected on June 1, and a weight of 6 months in the case of items for which a price reduction was effected on July 1. For items not affected by the mid-1937 price decree, the July quotation is given a weight of 7½ months — the sum of the weights that would be assigned to quotations for July and October 1937 and January 1938 if quotations were available for the latter two dates. The remainder of the year — 3, 3½, or 4½ months, depending on the weight assigned to the July quotation — is assigned as weight to the quotation for April 1.

(3) Quotations for 1937 from Soviet price handbooks are for the most part from handbooks published in 1936, such as *SRTS-36, SRTS-M-36, RTS-36, RTS-M-36*. It is assumed that these 1936 quotations remained in effect through 1937, except where there is evidence to the contrary.

1940: (1)*MLR* and *UM* report observed prices for foods, soap, kerosene, matches, and cigarettes on January 1 and July 1, 1940, and January 1, 1941. In computing the annual average price, the quotations for these three dates are weighted equally. In some cases the dates of price changes are known, and I make use of this information in computing the average annual prices.

(2) For textiles, garments, and knitwear, quotations observed in July 1939, reported in *MLR* and *UM*, are taken to represent the prices prevailing during the first half of 1940. Quotations for early 1940 are not available for these types of commodities. (*MLR*, May 1941, lists prices of these goods for January 1940 in a table but in the text states that such goods could not be priced in January. It is believed from this statement, from the identity of the prices quoted for January 1940 with those quoted for July 1939 in *MLR*, February 1941, and from data in *UM*, that an error was made in the table heading in *MLR*, May 1941 and that the prices listed there as effective January 1, 1940 were actually those in effect in July 1939.) But there was, it is believed, little or no change in the prices of these consumer goods between July 1939 and July 1, 1940. Early in July 1940, prices of many manufactured consumer goods were raised. To represent the prices in effect after this rise, in some cases I rely on Moscow quotations for July 15, 1940 and January 1, 1941, from *MLR* and *UM*. In such cases, the July and January quotations are each given a weight of 3 months. There are reasons to believe that the prices observed in Moscow in July 1940 and January 1941 seriously overstate the rise in prices of some textiles, garments, and knitwear. In such cases, the price observed in Kuibyshev in January 1942, reported in *UM*, is taken to represent the price prevailing during the second half of 1940. Errors may have been made in the selection of quotations for the second half of 1940, and in general the prices of manufactured consumer goods used for 1940 are considerably less reliable than those for other years.

1948: (1) Prices established by the price decree of December 14, 1947 (*Pravda,* December 15, 1947) are assumed to have remained in effect throughout 1948, except when they were changed by the price decree of April 10, 1948 (*Pravda,* April 10, 1948) or where there is other evidence of price changes.

(2) Observed quotations, primarily in *UM*, are available for many dates for one

commodity or another. The date of such a quotation is indicated in the notes on individual commodities below.

1952, 1954: Most of the 1952 and 1954 prices are computed from the 1948 prices and the percentage price reductions contained in price decrees published in *Pravda* since 1948. The dates of these decrees are given below. They are cited in the notes on individual commodities only by month and year.

March 1, 1949, March 1, 1950, March 1, 1951, April 1, 1952, April 1, 1953, April 1, 1954, August 14, 1954: All of these decrees are general ones, effecting percentage reductions in the prices of a more or less wide variety of commodities, except that of August 14, 1954, which established new seasonal price schedules for fruits and vegetables and effected price reductions for a few other foods.

The *1952* prices are those established by the price decree of April 1, 1952. These presumably remained in effect until the decree of April 1, 1953. The *1954* prices are those established on April 1, 1954, with modifications to take into account the price changes of August 14, 1954. For the most part these prices were still in effect in September 1956.

The process of obtaining quotations for 1952 and 1954 by applying the annual percentage price reductions to the 1948 absolute prices is subject to a certain amount of error. In many cases the price reduction is stated as an average percentage reduction for a broad category of commodities, and it is possible that the reduction for any given item falling within such a category differed from the average; it is assumed in such cases that the average reduction applies to the particular item falling within the category priced in our index. In some cases it is not clear whether an item priced in the index is included in one of the categories for which a price reduction is announced.

Because of such doubts I do not present commodity designations for 1952 and 1954 in the notes below when the quotations for these years are computed from the 1948 price and the percentage reductions. Insofar as the percentage price reductions are correctly applied, the 1952 and 1954 designations are in each case the same as the 1948 designation, and the degree of comparability achieved between the 1937 and 1952 or 1954 quotations should be the same as that between the 1937 and 1948 quotations.

The 1937–52 price comparisons had been made and the price relatives originally completed during 1953, and those for 1937–54 were originally completed before the end of 1954. The limited body of observed quotations available at that time seemed generally to confirm the computed prices. Since then certain additional sources have become available which are very valuable in checking on the computed prices and on the question of comparability of the postwar quotations with those for 1937. In the case of certain commodity groups — confectionery, textiles, garments, and shoes — these new sources indicate that I made some fairly serious errors in comparability, all tending to understate the true price rise. In these cases revisions have been made in the price comparisons. With regard to the other commodity groups, these new sources tend to confirm the quotations as originally computed. Although errors are indicated in some individual cases, these do not appear to be serious enough to justify the labor of revision and recomputation. Whether or not these sources were consulted in arriving at the price comparison in question, data from these sources are included in the notes below where relevant either on the question of the correctness of a computed price or on the question of comparability. The sources referred to include L. Kh. Gurvits, *Torgovye vychisleniia* (Moscow, 1949) and the 2d ed. (1953); Zaleski's study; and some unpublished visitors' reports, cited as *UMA* (to distinguish them from unpublished materials consulted before the original computations were completed, cited as *UM*).

Notes on Individual Commodities

The following notes on the commodity designation, source, and date of each quotation are presented in the order in which the commodities are listed in Table 3. Where annual average prices were computed from quotations for several dates within the year, I cite the dates of all quotations used. The method of averaging is as described above. Under each item, reference is made first to 1937 — the year of comparison with each of the other years — and then to the other years in chronological order. A comment on the comparability of the quotations for the different years follows in each case.

1. Rye flour

1937: Muka rzhanaia oboinaia 95% pomola (rye flour, coarse milled, 95% extraction). The quotation is for 1936, from *SRTS-36*, p. 28. Prices of grain products for which 1937 quotations are available indicate that there were no changes in grain product prices during 1937.

1928: Rzhanaia muka oboinaia (rye flour, coarse milled). This price — 0.11 ruble per kg — is the price in effect in Moscow cooperative shops from January 1 to July 1, 1928, as reported in *ESBM*. The price in state shops was 0.10 ruble per kg until April 1, and 0.11 ruble from April to July, according to the same source. No quotations are available after July; I assume there was no price change during the rest of the year.

This flour is a *95% extraction flour,* according to decrees of August 10, 1927 and May 16, 1928 (*ZA,* no. 48, 1927, p. 4; *ZA,* no. 61, 1928, p. 2).

1948: Muka rzhanaia oboinaia (rye flour, coarse milled). The quotation is from *PD-14-12-47*. This flour is a *95% extraction flour,* according to F. V. Tsverevitinov, *Tovarovedenie pishchevykh produktov* (Moscow, 1949), I:21–22.

1952: This price is computed from the 1948 price and the following price reductions: March 1949, bread and flour, 10%; March 1950, coarse milled rye flour, 25%; March 1951, rye flour, 15%; April 1952, rye flour, 12%.

1954: This price is computed from the 1952 price and the following price reductions: April 1953, rye flour, 10%; April 1954, rye flour, 5%.

Comparability: The quotation for each year is for flour of the same type and extraction rate.

2. Rye bread

1937: Khleb iz rzhanoi muki 95% pomola (bread of 95% extraction rye flour) and *khleb iz rzhanoi muki prostogo pomola* (bread of simple grind rye flour) (*SRTS-36,* p. 43); *black bread, rye* (Trivanovitch; *UM*). This price was established in September 1935 (*SRTS-36,* pp. 37, 43) and remained in effect until October 1940 (Trivanovitch; *UM; MLR,* May 1941; *New York Times,* October 22, 1940).

1928: Rzhanoi pechenyi khleb kisl. (baked rye bread, sour). This price is that prevailing in cooperative shops throughout 1928, reported in *ESBM*. Presumably the price in state shops was the same.

Legislation specified that this bread be made of coarse milled (*oboinaia*) rye flour of 95% extraction or of simple grind (*prostaia*) rye flour of 97.5% extraction (*ZA,* no. 2, 1928, pp. 18–19).

1940: Bread, black, rye. This price is the average annual price, computed on the basis of the price of 0.85 ruble in effect until October 21, 1940 and the price of 1.00 ruble in effect for the rest of the year (*MLR,* May 1940; February and May 1941; S. N. Prokopovicz, *Quarterly Bulletin of Soviet-Russian Economics,* no. 6, December 1940, p. 81; *New York Times,* October 22, 1940).

1948: Khleb rzhanoi (rye bread). The quotation is from *PD-14-12-47*.

1952: This price is computed from the 1948 price and the following price reductions: March 1949, bread and flour, 10%; March 1950, rye loaf bread and other breads of rye and coarse wheat flour, 25.9%; March 1951, rye and wheat bread, rolls, and other bakery products, 15%; April 1952, rye bread, 12%. The computed price corresponds to that given in Gurvits (1953) for *khleb rzhanoi iz oboinoi muki* (rye bread of coarse milled flour), and is confirmed by visitors' observations in Moscow during 1952 and 1953 (Charles Madge, "Notes on the Standard of Living in Moscow, April 1952," *Soviet Studies*, 4:232 (January 1953); *UM*).

1954: This price is computed from the 1952 price and the following price reductions: April 1953, rye and wheat bread, rolls, and other bakery products, 10%; April 1954, rye bread, 8%. The computed price is confirmed by visitors' observations *(UMA)*.

Comparability: All quotations are for bread of the same type of flour. The 1940 designation does not mention the flour of which the bread is made, but the continuity of the price between 1937 and late 1940 indicates the same bread is priced in both years. The 1948 designation does not mention the flour of which the bread is made but the 1952 quotation and designation in Gurvits (1953) confirms that my postwar quotations are for the bread priced in 1937.

Some quality deterioration, which cannot be taken into account, probably occurred over this period. The water content of the bread was apparently higher, or — what amounts to the same thing — the flour content of the bread was lower in 1948 than in 1937. The minimum yield of bread per unit of flour for whole rye bread was 152% ("batch bread") and 156% ("tin bread"), according to a government order of 1939, which appears to have been in effect until 1946 or 1947 when the yield was raised to 160% or higher. (Naum Jasny, *The Socialized Agriculture of the USSR* (Stanford, 1949), p. 558, n. 39; V. P. Vankevich, *Khlebobulochnye tovary* (2d rev. ed., Moscow, 1948), pp. 6, 33; A. K. Suchkov, *Dokhody gosudarstvennogo biudzheta SSSR* (Moscow, 1945), p. 41, and his *Gosudarstvennye dokhody SSSR* (Moscow, 1949), p. 77.) The actual yield was 160.4% in 1940 and 163.7% in 1949, according to I. K. Sivolap, *Pod"em pishchevoi promyshlennosti SSSR v poslevoennoi Stalinskoi piatiletke* (Moscow, 1950), p. 20. This source implies that the higher 1949 yield was the result of improved mechanization of the baking industry. It may be that the increase in bread yield per unit of flour reflects in part a reduction of waste in processing, and in part an increase in the practice of "watering" the bread.

There likely was some deterioration in quality also between 1928 and 1937, but we do not have evidence regarding this period. Since 1948 there may have been some improvement in the quality of bread.

3. Whole wheat flour

1937: Muka pshenichnaia 96% pomola (wheat flour, 96% extraction). The quotation is for 1936, from *SRTS-36*, p. 28.

1928: Pshenichnaia muka prostogo pomola (wheat flour, simple grind). The price is that reported in cooperative shops on March 1, 1928 in *ESBM*. I assume that this price was in effect throughout 1928 in both state and cooperative shops. The quotation is for cities in Moscow Province, outside of Moscow city; probably the price was the same in Moscow city.

Standards established for this kind of flour in May 1928 specify an extraction rate of 95% (*ZA*, no. 61, 1928, pp. 2–4). Presumably the extraction rate was the same in March, the date of the price quotation.

Comparability: The quotation for each year is for a comparable flour; a difference of 1% in extraction rate is negligible.

4. Wheat flour, 85%

1937: Muka pshenichnaia 85% pomola (wheat flour, 85% extraction). The quotation is for 1936, from *SRTS-36*, p. 28.

1948: Muka pshenichnaia II sorta (wheat flour, grade 2). The quotation is from *PD-14-12-47*. *Grade 2 wheat flour* is extracted at a rate of 85%, according to V. I. Petrov, *Tovarovedenie prodovol'stvennykh tovarov* (Moscow, 1947), p. 61.

1952: This price is computed from the 1948 price and the following price reductions: March 1949, bread and flour, 10%; March 1950, first and second grade wheat flour, 30%; March 1951, rye, wheat, corn, and other flour, 15%; April 1952, graded wheat flour, 15%.

1954: This price is computed from the 1952 price and the following price reductions: April 1953, rye, wheat, corn, and other flour, 10%; April 1954, rye, wheat, corn, and other flour, 5%.

Comparability: The quotation for each year is for the same flour.

5. Wheat flour, 72%

1937: Muka pshenichnaia 75 i 72% pomola (wheat flour, 75% and 72% extraction) (*SRTS-36*, p. 29); *flour 72%* (Trivanovitch; *UM*). This price was in effect throughout 1936 and 1937 (*SRTS-36*, p. 29; Trivanovitch; *UM*).

1940: Flour, 72%. This price was observed on January 1, 1941 (*MLR*, May 1941). Since this is the same as the 1937 price, it was undoubtedly in effect throughout 1940.

1948: Muka pshenichnaia I sorta (wheat flour, grade 1). The quotation is from *PD-14-12-47*. *Grade 1 wheat flour* is extracted at a rate of 72%, according to Petrov, p. 61.

1952: This price is computed from the 1948 price and the following price reductions: March 1949, flour, 10%; March 1950, first and second grade wheat flour, 30%; March 1951, wheat flour, 15%; April 1952, graded wheat flour, 15%.

1954: This price is computed from the 1952 price and the following price reductions: April 1953, wheat flour, 10%; April 1954, wheat flour, 5%.

Comparability: The quotation for each year is for the same flour.

6. Wheat flour, 30%

1937: Pervyi sort dvukhsortnoi pshenichnoi muki s vykhodom 30% (first grade of two-grade wheat flour with a yield of 30%) (*SRTS-36*, p. 29); *flour, 30%* (Trivanovitch; *UM*). This price was in effect throughout 1937 (*SRTS-36*, p. 29; Trivanovitch; *UM*).

1928: Pshenichnaia muka krasnaia I sort (wheat flour, red label, grade 1). The price shown in Table A-1 — 0.22 ruble per kg — is that prevailing in cooperative shops from January 1 through July 1, 1928, as reported in *ESBM*. The price in state shops was slightly lower — 0.21 ruble per kg — from January until April 1, and then rose to the cooperative shop level. The only quotation for later than July is the cooperative shop price on November 1, which was 0.27 ruble per kg (*ibid.*). This higher, November price is not taken into account as it is believed that this high quality flour was probably on sale only briefly for the November 7 holidays; the use of this flour was restricted as of June 1, 1928 to the macaroni and confectionery industries and for dietetic purposes (*ZA*, no. 61, 1928, pp. 2–4).

Legislation of 1926 and late 1927 relating to standardization and branding of flour indicates that *red label* flour is made of soft wheat or a mixture of soft wheat and rye (up to 15%); and that *grade 1 red label flour* is the first (or finest) 30% of the flour extracted in a three-grade grinding, in which the total of all three grades extracted is 80% of the grain (*ZA*, no. 8, 1927, p. 7; no. 67, 1927, pp. 6–7).

1940: Flour, 30%. This price was in effect throughout 1940 (*MLR,* May 1940; February and May 1941).

Comparability: The 1928 and 1937 quotations are for products which appear to be essentially similar. There were apparently various changes in milling practices between 1928 and 1937, but they were probably minor. The 1937 and 1940 quotations are for the same product.

7. Wheat bread, 96%

1937: Khleb pechenyi iz muki pshenichnoi 96% pomola (baked bread of 96% extraction wheat flour). The quotation is from *SRTS-36,* p. 43.

1940: Wheat bread of 96% grinding. The price was raised from 1.00 ruble per kg to 1.15 rubles per kg on October 21, 1940, according to Prokopovicz, *Quarterly Bulletin of Soviet-Russian Economics,* no. 6, December 1940, p. 81.

Comparability: The quotations for each year are for the same product.

8. Wheat bread, 80 to 85%

1937: Khleb pechenyi prostoi iz pshenichnoi muki 85% pomola (plain baked bread of 85% extraction wheat flour) (*SRTS-36,* p. 44); *bread, white, wheat* (Trivanovitch; *UM*). This price was in effect throughout 1937 (*SRTS-36,* p. 44; Trivanovitch; *UM*).

1928: The commodity designation varies somewhat at different dates in *ESBM,* as follows: January 1 through April 1, 1928: *pshen. pechen. khleb belyi vesovoi I sort* (baked wheat bread, white, sold by weight, grade 1); April 1928 through July 1, 1928 and January 1929: *khleb pshenichnyi* (wheat bread); August 1 through December 1, 1928: *khleb pshenichnyi standartnyi* (wheat bread, standard). It is believed that these designations and the accompanying price quotations all relate to *wheat bread of 80% extraction flour.* (1) It is quite clear that the quotations from July 1 to the end of 1928 (with the possible exception of December, see (3)) relate to bread of 80% extraction flour. In June, 80% extraction wheat flour became the standard type wheat flour, when the production of higher quality flours was curtailed and limited to the needs of the macaroni and confectionery industries (*ZA,* no. 61, 1928, pp. 2–4). Also, it will be noted, the *ESBM* designation from August on was *standard* wheat bread.

(2) It is assumed that the quotations before July also relate to bread of 80% extraction wheat flour, but the designation of the bread as *first grade* from January to April 1 throws some doubt on this assumption. A decree of January 3, 1928, which established the types of bread to be produced in Moscow and Leningrad, defines *first grade wheat bread* as being made of a mixture of *first* and *second grade flours* in a 60:40 ratio (*ZA,* no. 2, 1928, pp. 18–19). The *first grade flour* here is the 30% extraction flour described above, it is believed, and the *second grade flour* is the second 30% of the flour extracted from the same grain. The flour from which the bread legally classified as *first grade* was made would thus be approximately equivalent to a 60% extraction flour, and the bread would presumably be somewhat finer and whiter than bread of 80% extraction flour. Bread made of 80% extraction flour is designated in the same decree as *prostoi sitnyi* (plain, made of sifted flour). It is possible, then, that the *ESBM* quotations for the first half of 1928 relate to the bread legally defined as *first grade,* a higher quality bread than was priced from July 1 on. If this were the case, however, the *ESBM* quotations would indicate that the price of bread of 80% extraction flour was set in June at a level higher than the former price of the higher quality bread defined in the decree as *first grade.* This seems unlikely in view of an order of June 8 directing that bread prices be revised downward in connection with the curtailment of the use of higher quality flours for bread. This order provides that the price of a

bread formerly produced of a 60:40 mixture of *first grade* and *second grade* flours, but henceforth to be produced of 80% extraction flour, was to be lowered in accord with the lower price of the 80% extraction flour (*ZA*, no. 37, 1928, p. 16).

(3) It is possible that the quotations for December 1, 1928 and January 1, 1929 relate to bread made of *85%* instead of *80% extraction flour*. A decree of November 10, 1928 on "measures to increase the food balance" directed that all centrally collected grain of the 1927/28 harvest (with certain exceptions) was to be milled at an extraction rate of 85% instead of the former 80% (*ZA*, no. 67, 1928, pp. 5–6). It is not known whether the change-over from 80% to 85% flour was completed early enough to have affected the bread sold at retail before the end of December 1928.

The price shown in Table A-1 — 0.24 ruble per kg — is the average of the prices prevailing in cooperative shops during 1928 reported in *ESBM*. The actual quotations are 0.22 ruble per kg from January through May 1928, and 0.26 ruble per kg from July 1, 1928 through January 1, 1929.

1940: Bread, white, wheat. This price was in effect throughout 1940, according to *MLR*, May 1940; February and May 1941.

1948: Khleb pshenichnyi iz muki II sorta (wheat bread of grade 2 flour). The quotation is from *PD-14-12-47*. As indicated above, in 1948 *grade 2 wheat flour* was *85% extraction flour*.

1952: This price is computed from the 1948 price and the following price reductions: March 1949, bread, 10%; March 1950, bread of graded wheat flour, 30%; March 1951, wheat bread, 15%; April 1952, bread of graded wheat flour, 15%. The price computed for 1952 is the same as that cited in Gurvits (1953).

1954: This price is computed from the 1952 price and the following price reductions: April 1953, wheat bread, 10%; April 1954, wheat bread, 5%. The price computed for the item after the 1953 price cut is confirmed by observations in Moscow (*UMA*).

Comparability: 1928–37. As indicated, the 1937 bread was made of 85% extraction flour, somewhat coarser than the 80% extraction flour of which the 1928 bread was made. The quality difference here is probably relatively minor; in fact, the 1936 retail prices of *80%* and *85% extraction flours* were the same (*SRTS-36*, p. 28). Nevertheless, the reduction in the quality of flour used means that the comparison understates the true price rise, though probably only slightly. There may, of course, have been quality changes in addition to the change in the extraction rate of the flour.

As was explained, there is some doubt about the quality of the bread priced in the first half of 1928. If, in fact, this bread was not made of *80% extraction flour* as assumed, but was the legally defined *first grade bread* made of flour of approximately 60% extraction, the calculation made here significantly understates the rise in the price of wheat bread. On the assumption made that the 1928 quotations are for *bread of 80% extraction wheat flour* throughout the year, the indicated price rise between 1928 and 1937 is about 7 times; on the alternative but less likely assumption, the price rise would probably be nearer 9 or 10 times.

1937–40–48–52–54. The 1937, 1940, and postwar quotations are all for the same bread. As in the case of rye bread, it is possible that the water content of this bread was raised between 1937 and 1948. The yield of this type of bread per unit of flour was 142.5% in 1940 and 147% in 1949, according to Sivolap, p. 20.

9. Wheat bread, 72%

1937: Khleb pechenyi prostoi iz pshenichnoi muki 75% pomola (plain baked bread of 75% extraction wheat flour). The quotation is from *SRTS-36*, p. 45.

1948: Khleb pshenichnyi iz muki I sorta (wheat bread of grade 1 flour). The quotation is from *PD-14-12-47*. As indicated above, *grade 1 flour* is *72% extraction flour.*

1952: This price is computed from the 1948 price and the following price reductions: March 1949, bread, 10%; March 1950, bread of graded wheat flour, 30%; March 1951, wheat bread, 15%; April 1952, bread of graded wheat flour, 15%.

1954: This price is computed from the 1952 price and the following price reductions: April 1953, wheat bread, 10%; April 1954, wheat bread, 5%.

Comparability: The 1937 bread is described as being made of *75% extraction flour* while the bread priced in the postwar years is of *72% extraction flour;* however, there was no retail price differential in 1936 between 72% and 75% extraction wheat flours and there would presumably have been no differential in the corresponding bread prices. Again, the water content of the bread was probably higher in 1948 than in 1937, though there may have been some improvement in quality since 1948.

10. French loaf, 72%

1937: Frantsuzskie bulki iz pshenichnoi muki 75% (French loaves of 75% extraction wheat flour). The quotation is from *SRTS-36*, p. 46.

1948: French loaf, 72%. The quotation is for January 1949, from *UM*. Presumably this price was in effect throughout 1948.

1952: This price is computed from the 1948 price and the following price reductions: March 1949, bread, 10%; March 1950, bread of graded wheat flour, 30%; March 1951, wheat bread, rolls, and other bakery products, 15%; April 1952, bread of graded wheat flour, rolls, and other bakery products, 15%.

1954: This price is computed from the 1952 price and the following price reductions: April 1953, wheat bread, rolls, and other bakery products, 10%; April 1954, wheat bread, rolls, buns, and other bakery products, 5%.

Comparability: The remarks made concerning item 9 are applicable here.

11. French loaf, 30%

1937: Frantsuzskie bulki iz pshenichnoi muki 30% pomola (French loaves of 30% extraction wheat flour). The 1936 price is listed at 5.40 rubles per kg in *SRTS-36*, p. 46. The same price was in effect for *French loaf* in April 1937 but had been raised to 6.00 rubles by July 1937, according to Trivanovitch. The annual average price is computed from these quotations.

1940: French loaf. The quotation is from *MLR*, May 1940; February and May 1941.

Comparability: It is clear from the continuity of the price quoted for 1937 and 1940 and also for the years between that the bread priced in both years is of 30% extraction flour.

12. Macaroni, 72%

1937: Makarony I sorta iz pshenichnoi muki 72 i 75% pomola (macaroni, grade 1, of 72% and 75% extraction wheat flour). The quotation is from *SRTS-36*, p. 32 and *SRTS-M-36*, p. 15. It is assumed that this price remained in effect throughout 1937. Trivanovitch's quotations for *macaroni* are higher for 1937 than for 1936, but he notes that the 1937 macaroni priced was made of better quality flour.

1948: Makaroni iz muki I sorta (macaroni of grade 1 flour). The quotation is from *PD-14-12-47*.

1952: This price is computed from the 1948 price and the following price reductions: March 1949, grits and macaroni, 10%; March 1950, macaroni products, 25%;

March 1951, macaroni, vermicelli, noodles, and food concentrates, 15%; April 1952, macaroni, noodles, and other macaroni products, 15%.

1954: This price is computed from the 1952 price and the following price reductions: April 1953, macaroni, vermicelli, noodles, and other macaroni products, 10%; April 1954, macaroni, vermicelli, noodles, and other macaroni products, 5%.

Comparability: The quotations for each year are for comparable macaroni.

13. Macaroni, 40%

1937: Macaroni of 40% extraction wheat flour. The price of macaroni of 40% extraction flour is estimated to fall midway between the price of *macaroni of 30% extraction wheat flour* and that of *macaroni of 50% extraction wheat flour.* The quotations for the latter two macaronis on which I base my estimate are given in *SRTS-36,* pp. 21–32.

1928: Makarony (macaroni). The quotation is for January 1929, from *ESBM.* It is assumed the price was the same throughout 1928.

The commodity priced, it is believed, is *macaroni of 40% extraction wheat flour.* The decree of November 10, 1928, mentioned in item 8, part (3), which ordered the change from 80% to 85% extraction flour as the general rule, states that a certain amount of the centralized grain stock was to be ground into a two-grade flour, of which the first grade would be 40% extraction flour; this 40% extraction flour was to be allocated to the macaroni industry and for certain other purposes (*ZA,* no. 67, 1928, pp. 5–6).

Comparability: As indicated, it is believed that the 1928 quotation is for macaroni of 40% extraction wheat flour. The 1937 price for macaroni of 40% extraction flour estimated on the basis of the prices of macaroni of 30% and 50% extraction flour (though perhaps fictitious) should be closely comparable.

14. Buckwheat grits

1937: Krupa grechnevaia iadritsa (hulled whole buckwheat). The quotation is from *SRTS-36,* p. 26. The same price was in effect throughout 1937 for *buckwheat grits,* according to Trivanovitch and *UM.*

1928: Grechnevaia krupa iadritsa (hulled whole buckwheat). This is the average of the monthly quotations for state and cooperative shops reported in *ESBM.*

1940: Buckwheat grits. The quotation is for January 1, 1941, from *MLR,* May 1941.

1948: Krupa grechnevaia iadritsa (hulled whole buckwheat). The quotation is from *PD-14-12-47.*

1952: This price is computed from the 1948 price and the following price reductions: March 1949, grits, 10%; March 1950, buckwheat grits, 15%; March 1951, buckwheat grits, 15%; April 1952, buckwheat grits, 15%. The computed price — 6.25 rubles per kg — is about the same as that cited for 1952 in Gurvits (1953) — 6.20 rubles per kg. The difference is probably due to rounding.

1954: This price is computed from the 1952 price and the following price reduction: April 1953, buckwheat grits, 10%.

Comparability: The quotation for each year is for the same commodity.

15. Millet grits

1937: Psheno tolchenoe, I sorta (millet grits, pounded, grade 1). The quotation is from *SRTS-36,* pp. 25–26. The same price was in effect for *shelled millet grits* throughout 1937 (Trivanovitch; *MLR,* November 1939).

1928: Psheno tolchenets (millet grits, pounded). This price is the annual average calculated from the monthly quotations for state and cooperative shops in *ESBM.*

1940: Shelled millet grits. The quotation is for January 1, 1941, from *MLR*, May 1941.

1948: Psheno tolchenoe I sorta (millet grits, pounded, grade 1). The quotation is from *PD-14-12-47*.

1952: This price is computed from the 1948 price and the following price reductions: March 1949, grits, 10%; March 1950, millet grits, 14.8%; March 1951, millet grits, 15%; April 1952, millet grits, 15%. The computed price is within 5 kopeks of that quoted for 1952 in Gurvits (1953).

1954: This price is computed from the 1952 price and the following price reduction: April 1953, millet grits, 10%.

Comparability: The 1928 commodity designation does not indicate the grade of millet grits although it was probably *grade 1* and comparable to the quotations for other years. The designation is the same for all other years.

16. Rice

1937: This price is an average of the price of *ris I sorta* (rice, grade 1) — 6.50 rubles per kg — and of *ris 2 sorta* (rice, grade 2) — 5.50 rubles per kg. The quotations are from *SRTS-36*, p. 26.

1928: Ris persidskii (rice, Persian). This price is an average of the prices in state and cooperative shops in August and November 1928, as reported in *ESBM*.

Comparability: There is some margin for error here as the 1928 designation indicates the origin of the rice but not the grade, while the 1937 designation indicates only the grade.

17. Rice, grade 1

1937: Ris, 1 sorta (rice, grade 1). The quotation is from *SRTS-36*, p. 26. The same price is reported for *rice* throughout 1937 in Trivanovitch; *MLR*, November 1939; *UM*.

1940: Rice. The quotation is for January 1, 1941, from *MLR*, May 1941.

1948: Rice. The quotation is from Irving B. Kravis and Joseph Mintzes, "Food Prices in the Soviet Union, 1936–50," *RES*, 32:166 (May 1950). It can be deduced from the correspondence of the price computed for 1952 with a price cited for 1952 in Gurvits (1953) that the 1948 quotation is for *grade 1 rice*.

1952: This price is computed from the 1948 price and the following price reductions: March 1949, grits, 10%; March 1950, rice, 12%; March 1951, rice, 15%; April 1952, rice, 15%. The 1949 reduction is said to be for *grits*, and *rice* is not specifically mentioned. The usual Soviet practice is to include rice and legumes under the general heading *grits*, so the reduction is applied. The computed price corresponds to that cited for 1952 in Gurvits (1953) for *ris pervogo sorta* (rice, grade 1).

1954: This price is computed from the 1952 price and the following price reduction: April 1953, rice, 10%.

Comparability: The quotation for each year is for *grade 1 rice*. Although the grade is not indicated in the 1940 designation, the constancy of the price between 1937 and 1940 as reported in *MLR* indicates that the 1940 product is the same.

18. Wheat meal

1937: Wheat meal. The price shown was in effect throughout 1937, according to Trivanovitch and *UM*.

1940: Wheat meal. The price shown is reported in effect in July 1940 and January 1941, in *MLR*, February and May 1941.

Comparability: The designation is the same for each year.

19. Dried peas

1937: This price is the average of the prices of *gorohk krupn. stolovyi* (dried peas, table, large) — 2.50 rubles per kg — and of *gorokh stolovyi sredn. i melk.* (dried peas, table, medium and small) — 2.00 rubles per kg. The quotations are from *SRTS-36,* p. 26.

1928: Gorokh stolovyi (dried peas, table). This price is the approximate average of the prices in state and cooperative shops during the first 4 months of 1928 as reported in *ESBM.* The source does not give quotations for later dates.

Comparability: Since the size of the 1928 peas is not indicated, the average of the 1937 prices for *large peas* and for *small and medium peas* is used in the comparison. Comparability should be quite close.

20. Dried beans

1937: This price is the average of the 1936 prices of *fasol' belaia* (dried beans, white) — 4.20 rubles per kg — and *fasol' tsvetn. smes.* (dried beans, colored, mixed) — 3.70 rubles per kg. The quotations are from *SRTS-36,* p. 26.

1948: This price is the average of the prices of *dried beans, white* — 11.20 rubles per kg — and *dried beans, colored, mixed* — 10.00 rubles per kg. These prices are reported for January 1948 in *UM.*

1952: This price is computed from the 1948 price and the following price reductions: March 1949, grits, 10%; March 1950, peas and legumes, 20%; March 1951, peas and other legumes, 20%; April 1952, legumes, 15%.

The 1949 price reduction is said to be for *grits,* and *legumes* are not specifically mentioned. The usual Soviet practice is to include *legumes* under the general heading *grits,* so the reduction is applied. Apparently this is correct. Gurvits (1949) cites a post-March 1949 price of 10.00 rubles per kg for *fasol' belaia* (dried beans, white), approximately the same as the price for this date computed from the 1948 price for *dried beans, white* and the March 1949 reduction — 10.08 rubles per kg. Gurvits (1949), however, also cites a price for *fasol' smes'* (dried beans, mixed) of 5.40 rubles per kg; this is considerably lower than the 1949 price computed from my 1948 quotation for *dried beans, colored, mixed.* The reason for this difference is not known.

1954: This price is computed from the 1952 price and the following price reduction: April 1953, peas and other cereals and legumes, 10%.

Comparability: The 1937 and postwar quotations are averages of the prices of the same two types of beans and should be closely comparable.

21. Oats

1937: Oves (oats). The quotation is from *SRTS-36,* p. 20.

1928: Oves ruskii (Russian oats) and *oves kormovoi ruskii* (Russian fodder oats). This price is an average of the price in state shops from January to April 1928 and of the price in cooperative shops during November and December 1928 and early January 1929 as reported in *ESBM.* These are the only dates for which prices for this product are quoted in the source.

1948: Oves (oats). The quotation is from *PD-14-12-47.*

1952: This price is computed from the 1948 price and the following price reductions: March 1949, fodder grains, 20%; March 1950, oats, 22.7%; March 1951, oats, 15%; April 1952, oats, 15%. It is not entirely clear whether the 1949 price reduction is correctly applied to oats.

1954: This price is computed from the 1952 price and the following price reductions: April 1953, oats, 10%; April 1954, oats, 5%.

Comparability: The 1928 designation indicates the oats are *Russian* but presumably this is true of the oats priced in other years, simply described as *oats.*

22. Beef, average fed, grade 1

1937: Beef, second quality, for soup. This price is an annual average based on the following quotations: 7.60 rubles per kg in January, April, and July 1937; 8.00 rubles per kg in October 1937 and January 1938. The quotations are from Trivanovitch and *UM.* This commodity, it is believed, is *goviadina sr. upitannosti 1 sort* (beef, average fed, grade 1 cuts), listed at 7.60 rubles per kg in *SRTS-36,* p. 267.

1928: Goviadina parnaia 1 sort (beef, fresh, grade 1). This price is an average annual price based on the price prevailing in state and cooperative shops of 0.87 ruble per kg from January 1 to August 15, 1928 and 0.85 ruble per kg for the remainder of the year. The quotations are from *ESBM* and *ZA,* no. 52, 1928, p. 23.

1940: Beef, second quality, for soup or *beef, for soup.* This is an annual average price computed from the following quotations: January 1, 1940 — 9.00 rubles; January 24, 1940 — 12.00 rubles; April 10, 1940 — 16.00 rubles; July 1, 1940 and January 1, 1941 — 14.00 rubles per kg. The quotations are from *MLR,* May and August 1940; February and May 1941.

1948: Miaso goviazh'e sr. upitannosti, I s. (beef meat, average fed, grade 1 cuts). The quotation is from *PD-14-12-47.*

1952: This price is computed from the 1948 price and the following price reductions: March 1949, meat, 10%; March 1950, beef, average and above average fed, 24%; March 1951, beef, 15%; April 1952, beef, 15%.

1954: This price is computed from the 1952 price and the following price reduction: April 1953, beef, 15%. The computed price is the same as that indicated for this grade beef on the price lists posted in Moscow stores following the reduction of April 1953 *(UM).*

Comparability: Lacking information about grading practices in 1928, I assume that the 1928 beef, described only as *grade 1,* is comparable to the quality of beef priced for 1937 and all other years — *grade 1 cuts of average fed beef.* As indicated, the price of the latter in 1936 was 7.60 rubles per kg. At the same time *grade 1 cuts of above average fed beef* were 9.60 rubles per kg and *grade 1 cuts of below average fed beef* were 6.60 rubles per kg *(SRTS-36,* p. 267). For 1937 and 1940 the English designation reported by visitors is the same. For 1937 and the postwar years, the Russian designation is the same. Except possibly for 1928, the grade of beef priced in all years is the same.

The system of grading meat in the Soviet Union remained the same, it is believed, from September 1935 (or possibly earlier) until January 1, 1956. The quality of meat (other than pork) is indicated by how well fed the animal is, three degrees being common in both 1936 and the postwar years: "below average," "average," and "above average." The word "fed" is used here (at the suggestion of Dr. Naum Jasny) rather than "finish" because little real finishing is practiced in the Soviet Union. In addition, the cuts of meat are classified according to three or four grades, depending on the part of the carcass from which they are cut. First-grade cuts of beef account for 55% of the carcass and include the following: the rib, short loin, loin end, rump, round, and brisket. These data on the grading system are to be found in both a 1936 source — *SRTS-36,* p. 278 — and a 1948 source — D. D. Bakzevich, *Tovarovedenie pishchevykh produktov* (Moscow, 1948), p. 127. The grading system was changed on January 1, 1956; a revised scheme for grading the various parts of the carcass for beef is published in *SOVTORG,* no. 2,

1956, p. 40, and likely other changes were made also. Some visitors in Moscow at the time of the April 1953 price cut report that this was accompanied by a regrading of meat such as to result in a smaller price decline for the better cuts than specified in the price decree (Emmet Hughes, "A Perceptive Reporter in a Changing Russia," *Life,* February 8, 1954, p. 119; *UM*). In view of the evidence concerning the constancy of the meat grading system, it seems likely that these visitors were in error; however, it may be that the grades were not clearly indicated and the prices for each grade not strictly adhered to prior to the April 1953 decree. If this is the case and meat of a given grade was sold generally at the price for a higher grade prior to April 1953, my 1952 quotation is below the *de facto* price charged.

23. Pork

1937: Pork roast. This price is an annual average computed from the following observed quotations: 9.60 rubles per kg in January and April 1937; 10.60 rubles per kg in July 1937; 11.00 rubles per kg in October 1937 and January 1938 (Trivanovitch; *UM*). The pork priced is apparently equivalent to the Soviet described *svinina obrezn. saln. i p/saln I sort* (pork, trimmed, fat and semi-fat, grade 1 cuts). This is listed in *SRTS-36,* p. 269, at 9.60 rubles per kg in 1936. It may be, however, that the higher prices quoted from July 1937 on represent not an increase in the price of this grade of pork but the price of a higher grade of pork, for example, *svinina razrubochnaia neobrezn., I sort* (pork, lean, untrimmed, grade 1 cuts). This is listed in *SRTS-36,* p. 269, at 10.60 rubles per kg in 1936.

The term *razrubochnaia* is here translated as *lean* since *miasnaia razrubochnaia* is defined as having 2 to 5 cm of fat beneath the skin on the back, while *fat* (*sal'naia*) pork has over 7 cm of fat and *semi-fat* (*polusal'naia*) pork has from 5 to 7 cm of fat (NKVT, *Spravochnik tsen na miaso i miasoprodukty* (Moscow, 1936), p. 85).

1928: The designation for some dates is *svinina, I sort* (pork, grade 1), and for others, *svinina parnaia, I sort* (pork, fresh, grade 1). Both designations apparently relate to the same product. This price is the average price charged in cooperative shops, computed on the basis of monthly quotations for April 1928 through January 1929 in *ESBM*. The price in state shops was presumably about the same.

1940: Pork roast. This price is the average of the prices prevailing in July 1940 and January 1941, reported in *MLR,* May 1941, and *UM*.

1948: Fat pork (UM) or *pork (RES,* May 1950, p. 166). This price is reported for both January 1948 and January 1949 *(UM; RES,* May 1950, p. 166).

1952: This price is computed from the 1948 price and the following price reductions: March 1949, meat, 10%; March 1950, pork, 24%; March 1951, pork, 15%; April 1952, pork, 20%. The computed price — 23.70 rubles per kg — is somewhat below the price cited in Gurvits (1953) for *svinina sal'naia* (fat pork) — 25.20 rubles per kg — and above those cited for *svinina obreznaia polusal'naia* (pork, trimmed, semi-fat) — 19.70 rubles per kg — and *svinina sal'naia II sort* (pork, fat, grade 2 cuts) — 20.80 rubles per kg.

1954: Svinina sal'naia, I sort (pork, fat, grade 1 cuts). This price is that shown on the price lists posted in Moscow stores following the 15% reduction in the prices of pork and other meats in April 1953 *(UM)*. There were no reductions in meat prices in 1954. This price — 21.40 rubles per kg — is somewhat higher than the price of 20.15 rubles obtained by applying the annual price reductions to the 1948 price.

Comparability: 1928–37. Comparability of the quotations for these two years can be considered only approximate as the 1928 designation is so brief. Also it is not entirely clear whether all of the 1937 quotations relate to the same quality pork.

1937–40. The designation in the visitors' reports is the same for these two years and the quotations are probably comparable, although some variation may have taken place in the quality of pork priced at different dates.

1937–48–52–54. Comparability is only approximate between the quotation for 1937 and those for the postwar years. As indicated, it is not clear whether the quotations for all the dates in 1937 represent the same quality pork. Assuming that all 1937 quotations are for *pork, trimmed, fat and semi-fat, grade 1 cuts,* the postwar quotations appear to be for the same quality pork. But there is a possibility they relate to a higher quality pork. The postwar designation is simply *pork, fat, grade 1 cuts.* This differs from the 1937 designation above in excluding *semi-fat* pork and in not indicating whether the pork is *trimmed.* The *fat pork* priced is more expensive than *lean pork* in postwar years (Gurvits (1944) and (1953)), while in 1936 *untrimmed lean pork* was more expensive than *trimmed fat pork.* This may indicate that a change in price structure has taken place, or it may be that the postwar quotations are for *untrimmed fat pork.* This would probably be more expensive than either *trimmed fat pork* or *lean pork* under Soviet conditions. If this is the case, the rise in pork prices is somewhat overstated in my computations.

24. Mutton, average fed, grade 1

1937: Baranina srednei upitannosti, I sort (mutton, average fed, grade 1 cuts). The quotation is from *SRTS-36,* p. 268.

1928: Baranina svezhaia I sort (mutton, fresh, grade 1). This price is an estimated annual average price based on prices in state and cooperative shops for January through May 1928 and January 1929, as reported in *ESBM.*

1948: Baranina, average fed, first sort. The price was observed in November 1948 and in January 1949 (*UM*).

1952: This price is computed from the 1948 price and the following price reductions: March 1949, meat, 10%; March 1950, average and above-average fed mutton, 28%; March 1951, mutton, 15%; April 1952, mutton, 20%.

1954: Baranina srednaia, I sort (mutton, average, grade 1 cuts). The quotation is that shown on price lists posted in Moscow stores following the 15% reduction in mutton and other meat prices of April 1953 (*UM*). There were no reductions in meat prices in 1954. The price obtained from the official price list differs by only a few kopeks from the price obtained by applying the price reductions to my 1948 price.

Comparability: Lacking information about grading practices in 1928, I assume that the 1928 mutton, described only as *grade 1,* is comparable to the quality of mutton priced for 1937 and all other years, described as *average fed mutton, grade 1 cuts.*

25. Mutton

1937: Mutton. This price prevailed throughout 1937, according to *UM.*

1940: Mutton. This price is an annual average based on the following observed quotations: January 1, 1940, 8.00 rubles per kg; January 24, 1940, 14.00 rubles per kg; April 10, 1940, 18.00 rubles per kg; January 1, 1941, 14.00 rubles per kg. The quotations are from *MLR,* August 1940 and May 1941; *UM.*

Comparability: The designation is extremely brief. However, it is the same throughout the two years in the visitors' reports, and the quotations are probably comparable.

26. Mutton, above average fed, grade 1

1937: Baranina zhirnoi i vyshesrednei upitannosti, I sort (mutton, fat and above average fed, grade 1 cuts). The quotation is from *SRTS-36*, p. 268. The same price was in effect throughout 1937 (Trivanovitch; *MLR*, November 1939).

1948: Baranina, above average fed, first sort. The price was observed in January 1949 (*UM*). The same price was observed in January and November 1948 for *lamb* and *lamb or mutton, highest grade* (*RES*, May 1950, p. 166; *UM*).

1952: This price is computed from the 1948 price and the price reductions put into effect between 1948 and April 1952. These are the same as those affecting *average fed mutton*, listed above.

1954: Baranina, vyshe srednei, I sort (mutton, above average, grade 1 cuts). The price is that shown on the price list posted in Moscow meat stores following the 15% reduction in the prices of mutton and other meats in April 1953 (*UM*). There were no reductions in meat prices in 1954. This price — 14.10 rubles per kg — is somewhat higher than the price — 13.50 rubles per kg — obtained by applying the percentage price cuts to my 1948 price.

Comparability: The designation is the same for all years. The 1952 price computed from the 1948 price and the announced price reductions may err somewhat on the low side. As indicated, the 1954 price taken from an official price list was higher than would be obtained by applying the percentage price cuts to the 1948 price.

27. Chicken, grade 1

1937: Chicken, first quality. This price was observed at various dates throughout 1937 (Trivanovitch; *UM*).

1940: Chicken, first quality. This price was observed in January 1941. The source is *MLR*, May 1941.

1948: This price — 35.00 rubles per kg — is based on the following quotations: *Chicken*, 36.00 rubles per kg in January 1948 (*RES*, May 1950, p. 166); *chicken, dressed, highest*, 34.00 rubles per kg in November 1948 (*UM*); and *chicken, first grade*, 34.00 rubles per kg in January 1949 (*UM*). Gurvits (1949) lists *kury nepotroshennyi, I sort* (chicken, not drawn, grade 1) at 32.00 rubles per kg after the March 1949 price reduction. This is very close to my price, which would be 31.20 rubles per kg after the 1949 price reduction.

1952: This price is computed from the 1948 price and the following price reductions: March 1949, meat, 10%; March 1950, poultry, 24%; March 1951, poultry, 15%; April 1952, fowl, 15%. Although the 1949 decree did not specifically mention poultry, it is believed that the 10% reduction in price for "meat, sausage, and canned meat products" included poultry with meat. A price observed in the summer of 1952 for *chicken, dressed, I sort* (*UMA*) is very close to my computed price.

1954: This price is computed from the 1952 price and the following price reduction: April 1953, poultry, 15%.

Comparability: The quotation for each year is for *grade 1 chicken.* The prewar descriptions do not indicate whether the chicken is dressed and drawn, and as the postwar descriptions are not entirely consistent on this question, there may be some variation on this point.

28. Chicken, grade 2

1937: Kury, II sort (chicken, grade 2) (*SRTS-36*, p. 309) and *chicken, second quality* (Trivanovitch; *UM*). According to these sources, the same price was in effect in 1936 and throughout 1937.

1940: Chicken, second quality. The quotation is for January 1941, from *MLR,* May 1941.

1948: Chicken, second grade. The quotation is for January 1949, from *UM.* Gurvits (1949) lists *kury nepotroshennyi, II sort* (chicken, not drawn, grade 2) at 26.00 rubles per kg after the March 1949 price reduction; this is lower than my price, which would be 27.90 rubles per kg after the 1949 price reduction.

1952: This price is computed from the 1948 price and the price reductions through April 1952 shown above, under item 27. A price observed in the summer of 1952 for *chicken, dressed, II sort (UM)* is very close to my computed price.

1954: This price is computed from the 1952 price and the following price reduction: April 1953, poultry, 15%.

Comparability: The quotation for each year is for *grade 2 chicken.* The postwar quotations appear to be for *dressed* chicken, but the prewar designations do not indicate whether the chicken is dressed.

29. Goose, grade 2

1937: Geese, second quality. This price is an annual average based on the following observed quotations: January and April 1937 — 8.50 rubles per kg; July 1937 — 6.70 rubles per kg (Trivanovitch; *UM*).

1940: Geese, second quality. The quotation is for January 1941, from *MLR,* May 1941.

1948: Goose, second grade. This price — 25.00 rubles per kg — was observed in January 1949 *(UM).* Another source cited a range of 32.00 to 35.00 rubles per kg for *geese* in January 1948 *(UM).* It is assumed that this range relates to *first* and *highest* grade geese and that the January 1949 price specifically quoted for *second grade goose* was in effect throughout 1948.

1952: This price is computed from the 1948 price and the following price reductions: March 1949, meat, 10%; March 1950, poultry, 24%; March 1951, poultry, 15%; April 1952, geese, 20%. The computed price is close to the price observed in the summer of 1952 for *geese, second quality (UMA).*

1954: This price is computed from the 1952 price and the following price reduction: April 1953, poultry, 15%.

Comparability: The same grade of goose is priced in all years.

30. Duck, grade 1

See item 31.

31. Duck, grade 2

1937: Utki, I sort (duck, grade 1) was 11.00 rubles per kg and *utki, sort II* (duck, grade 2) was 8.50 rubles per kg in 1936, according to *SRTS-36,* pp. 309–310. *Duck,* apparently *grade 1,* was cited throughout 1937 at 11.00 rubles per kg in Trivanovitch and *UM.*

1940: Duck. Although the source does not state the grade, it is believed that the quotations relate to *grade 1,* as in the case of the 1937 observed quotations. The price shown is an average of the prices prevailing July 1, 1940 and January 1, 1941, reported in *MLR,* February and May 1941.

1948: Duck, second grade. The price was observed in January 1949 *(UM).*

1952: This price is computed from the 1948 price and the following price reductions: March 1949, meat, 10%; March 1950, poultry, 24%; March 1951, poultry, 15%; April 1952, ducks, 20%.

1954: This price is computed from the 1952 price and the following price reduction: April 1953, poultry, 15%.

Comparability: 1937–40. The quotation for 1940 appears to be for *grade 1* duck, and is compared with the 1937 price for *grade 1 duck.*

1937–48–52–54. The 1937 quotation for *grade 2 duck* is compared with postwar quotations for the same grade duck.

32. Turkey, grade 1

See item 33.

33. Turkey, grade 2

1937: Indeika, I sort (turkey, grade 1) was 13.00 rubles per kg and *indeika, II sort* (turkey, grade 2) was 10.50 rubles per kg in 1936, according to *SRTS-36*, p. 310. *Turkey* is cited at 13.00 rubles per kg during 1937 in Trivanovitch and *UM*. This was presumably *grade 1 turkey.*

1940: Turkey. The quotation is for January 1941, from *MLR*, May 1941. The quotation is apparently for *grade 1 turkey* as in the case of the 1937 observed prices.

1948: Turkey, first grade was 45.00 rubles per kg and *turkey, second grade* was 39.00 rubles per kg in January 1949, according to *UM*. A range of 45.00 to 48.00 rubles per kg for *turkey* is cited for January 1948 in another source (*UM*). It is assumed that this range relates to *first* and *highest grade turkey* and that the January 1949 prices specifically quoted for *first* and *second grade turkey* were in effect throughout 1948.

1952: These prices are computed from the 1948 prices and the following price reductions: March 1949, meat, 10%; March 1950, poultry, 24%; March 1951, poultry, 15%; April 1952, turkeys, 20%. The computed prices — 20.95 rubles per kg for *grade 1 turkey* and 18.15 rubles per kg for *grade 2 turkey* — are somewhat higher than the price of 17.50 rubles per kg observed for *turkey* in the summer of 1952 (*UMA*).

1954: These prices are computed from the 1952 prices and the following price reduction: April 1953, poultry, 15%.

Comparability: The comparison in each case is for the same grade or grades of turkey.

34. Rabbit

1937: Kroliki zhirn. i v/sredn. upitannosti (rabbit, fat and above average fed). The quotation is from *SRTS-36*, p. 269.

1948: Rabbit, first grade. The price was observed in January 1949 (*UM*).

1952: This price is computed from the 1948 price and the following price reductions: March 1949, meat, 10%; March 1950, rabbit, 30%; March 1951, poultry, 15%. The 1949 and 1951 price reductions for meat and poultry appear to be broad, across-the-board reductions, and it is assumed they applied to rabbit. The 1952 price reductions, on the other hand, were rather selective and, as rabbit was not mentioned, it is assumed there was no reduction in rabbit prices at that time.

The only quotation with which my computed price can be compared is for late 1950, when rabbits were observed at 10.00 to 11.00 rubles per kg (*UM*), considerably lower than the price I compute for the same time — a little over 15.00 rubles per kg.

1954: This price is computed from the 1952 price and the following price reductions: April 1953, meat, sausage, and poultry, 15%. It is assumed that this reduction applied to rabbit.

Comparability: The postwar *first grade* probably corresponds to the 1937 *fat and above average fed* rabbit, but I cannot be certain of this. There is some doubt as to whether the postwar price cuts for meat and poultry are properly applied to rabbit in cases when rabbit was not specifically mentioned; however, the fact that the only available observed quotation since 1948 is lower than my computed price for the same date seems to indicate that the reductions did affect rabbit, as I assume.

35. Bacon

1937: Bacon. This price was in effect throughout 1937, according to Trivanovitch and *UM.* The observed price — 16.00 rubles per kg — falls near the midpoint of the range of prices for bacon — 12.00 to 18.00 rubles per kg — listed in *SRTS-36,* pp. 292–293.

1940: Bacon. This price is an average of the prices in July 1940 and January 1941, reported in *MLR,* February and May 1941.

1948: Bacon. The price shown represents the midpoint of the range of prices — 50.00 to 68.00 rubles per kg — observed during 1948 by various visitors to the USSR (Walter Bedell Smith, *My Three Years in Moscow* (Philadelphia, 1950), p. 93; *UM*).

1952: This price is computed from the 1948 price and the following price reductions: March 1949, meat and sausage, 10%; March 1950, smoked meats, 27%; March 1951, pork, 15%; April 1952, pork, 15%.

1954: This price is computed from the 1952 price and the following price reduction: April 1953, pork, 15%.

Comparability: 1937–40. There is a fair degree of continuity in the visitors' reports over these years and, though the description is brief, the quotations for these two years are probably for the same quality bacon.

1937–48–52–54. The bacon priced in these years is probably reasonably comparable. The price used represents in each case about the midpoint of the range of bacon prices, and the spread between the lowest and highest price was similar in both 1937 and 1948.

36. Ham, smoked

1937: Ham, smoked. This price was in effect throughout 1937, according to Trivanovitch and *UM.*

1940: Ham, smoked. This price is an annual average based on the following quotations: January 1, 1940 — 18.00 rubles per kg; January 24, 1940 — 24.00 rubles per kg; April 10 and July 1, 1940 and January 1, 1941 — 27.00 rubles per kg. These quotations are from *MLR,* August 1940; February and May 1941; *UM.*

Comparability: The designation is the same in each year. Furthermore, the fact that the January 1, 1940 price is the same as the 1937 price suggests that the same quality ham was priced. Meat prices showed little change between 1937 and late January 1940.

37. Ham, smoked, average

1937: This price is the midpoint of the range of 12.00 to 18.00 rubles per kg listed for various types of *smoked ham* in *SRTS-36,* p. 291.

1948: This price is the midpoint of the range of prices — 48.00 to 70.00 rubles per kg — quoted for *ham* during 1948 (Smith, p. 93; *UM*).

1952: This price is computed from the 1948 price and the price reductions listed above, under item 35.

1954: This price is computed from the 1952 price and the following price reduction: April 1953, pork, 15%.

Comparability: The quotations are probably for roughly comparable types and grades of ham. The price in each case represents the midpoint of the range of ham prices, and the range is about the same in both 1937 and 1948.

38. Sausage, ordinary

1937: Sausage, ordinary. This price is an annual average computed from the following observed quotations: January and April 1937 — 8.00 rubles per kg; July and October 1937 and January 1938 — 10.00 rubles per kg. The quotations are from Trivanovitch and *UM*.

1940: Sausage, ordinary. This price is an annual average computed from the following quotations: January 1, 1940 — 10.00 rubles per kg; January 24, 1940 — 13.50 rubles per kg; April 10, 1940 through January 1, 1941 — 16.00 rubles per kg. The quotations are from *MLR*, May and August 1940; February and May 1941.

Comparability: The designation is the same for each year; and the fact that the January 1, 1940 price is the same as the price in the latter part of 1937 suggests that the same product was priced in both years.

39. Sausage, hamburger

1937. Sausage, hamburger. The quotation is from Trivanovitch and *UM*.

1940. Sausage, hamburger. This price is an annual average computed from the following quotations: January 1, 1940 — 16.00 rubles per kg; January 24, 1940 — 22.00 rubles per kg; April 10, 1940 — 26.00 rubles per kg; July 1, 1940 and January 1, 1941 — 23.00 rubles per kg. The quotations are from *MLR*, August 1940; February and May 1941; *UM*.

Comparability: The designation is the same in both years. The fact that the January 1, 1940 price is the same as the 1937 price suggests that the same quality product was priced in both years. However, the fluctuations in price during 1940 may indicate some variance in the quality priced after January 24.

40. Sausage, Moscow

1937: This price is the average of the 1936 prices of the following two sausages: (1) *letnye sorta kopchenykh (varenykh) kolbas, Moskovskaia* (summer type smoked (cooked) sausage, Moscow) — 20.00 rubles per kg; (2) *kolbasnye izdeliia, kopchenye (zimnie i letnie), Moskovskaia, I sort* (sausage products, smoked (summer and winter), Moscow, grade 1) — 27.00 rubles per kg (*SRTS-36*, pp. 288–290). Descriptions of these two sausages may be found in A. G. Konnikov and A. P. Bogatyrev, *Proizvodstvo kolbas i miasokopchenostei* (Moscow, 1948), pp. 50, 52–55, 57, 59–61. Scattered quotations for other types of sausage showed no price change during 1936 and 1937.

1948: Sausage, Moscow. This price was observed in January 1949 (*UM*).

1952: This price is computed from the 1948 price and the following price reductions: March 1949, sausage products, 10%; March 1950, sausage (*kolbasa*), 24%; March 1951, sausage, 15%; April 1952, sausage, 15%. The computed price — 40.50 rubles per kg — is somewhat lower than the 1952 price of 42.90 rubles cited in Gurvits (1953) for *kolbasa Moskovskaia tverdokopchenaia* (sausage, Moscow, hard smoked). This is probably a higher grade sausage than the one I price. The 1949 and 1952 sausage prices that can be compared in Gurvits (1949) and (1953) indicate that the announced price reductions were applied.

1954: This price is computed from the 1952 price and the following price reduction: April 1953, sausage (*kolbasa*), 15%.

Comparability: The 1948 source does not indicate which of two types of Moscow sausage was priced, so the comparison results in postwar price relatives which may err by about 17% in either direction. Nevertheless, quotations for several types of sausage in Gurvits (1949) and (1953) suggest that my price relatives for Moscow sausage are roughly in line with the movement of sausage prices generally.

41. Pike-perch, fresh, frozen, or salted

1937: This price is the midpoint of the 1936 prices of (a) *sudak krupnyi, parnoi i morozhenyi* (pike-perch, large, fresh and frozen), which was 3.80 rubles per kg, and (b) *sudak melkii i srednii, parnoi i morozhenyi* (pike-perch, small and medium, fresh and frozen), which was 3.00 rubles per kg. The quotations are from *SRTS-36*, pp. 314, 371, 379. The average 1937 prices were, it is believed, substantially the same as the 1936 prices, though there may have been a rise late in 1937.

1928: This price — 0.49 ruble per kg — is an average based on the April, July, August, and September 1928 prices in cooperative shops and the January 1929 prices in state and cooperative shops, as reported in *ESBM*. The quotations relate at different dates to three types of pike-perch, as follows: (a) *sudak svezhii* (pike-perch, fresh); (b) *sudak solenyi mernyi* (pike-perch, salted, large); (c) *sudak morozhenye* (pike-perch, frozen). The range of prices was from 0.38 ruble per kg for *salted large pike-perch* in August 1928 to 0.80 ruble per kg in cooperative shops and 0.85 ruble per kg in state shops for *frozen pike-perch* in January 1929.

Comparability: As indicated, the 1928 average price is based on quotations for different kinds of pike-perch at different dates — namely, *fresh pike-perch, salted pike-perch, large* and *frozen pike-perch*. The 1937 price is the midpoint of the range for different sizes of *fresh or frozen pike-perch*. However, the 1936 price of *salted pike-perch, large* falls within the range of prices for *fresh or frozen pike-perch* (*SRTS-36*, pp. 314, 371, 379). Thus the quotations for the two years appear reasonably comparable.

42. Pike-perch, frozen

1937: Pike-perch, frozen. This price is the annual average based on the following quotations: 3.20 rubles per kg in January, April, and July 1937; 3.70 rubles per kg in January 1938. The quotations are from Trivanovitch and *UM*.

1948: Ryba sudak svezhemorozhenyi, I sort (fish, pike-perch, fresh-frozen, grade 1). The quotation is from *PD-14-12-47*.

1952: This price is computed from the 1948 price and the following price reductions: March 1949, fish, 10%; March 1950, chilled and frozen pike-perch, 10.2%; March 1951, fish, 10%. The computed price is confirmed by an observed quotation for the summer of 1952 (*UMA*).

1954: This price is computed from the 1952 price and the following price reduction: April 1953, chilled, frozen, salted, and smoked fish, 10%.

Comparability: The 1937 quotation seems closely comparable to the postwar quotations, although there might be slight differences in the size or grade of fish.

43. Perch, frozen

1937: Perch, frozen. This price is the annual average based on the following quotations: January, April, and July 1937 — 3.50 rubles per kg; October 1937 and January 1938 — 3.80 rubles per kg. The quotations are from Trivanovitch and *UM*.

1940: Perch, frozen. The quotation is for January 1, 1941, from *MLR*, May 1941.

Comparability: The designation is the same in both years but it is rather brief and possibly the quotations relate to somewhat different qualities of perch.

44. Sturgeon, fresh or frozen

1937: Sturgeon, chilled. This price was observed in January, April, and July 1937 (Trivanovitch, *UM*). The observed price is the same as the 1936 price of *osert, mernyi, parnoi i morozhenyi* (osert sturgeon, large, fresh and frozen) cited in the price lists for most of the fishing trusts in K. V. Naimushin (comp.), *Preiskurant roznichnykh tsen na rybu i rybotovary* (Moscow, 1936), pp. 22, 23, 30, 52.

1940: Sturgeon, chilled. The quotation is for January 1, 1940, from *MLR*, May 1941.

1948: Osetrina, first grade. The quotation is for January 1949, from *UM*. It is assumed that this was the price for *fresh* or *frozen osert sturgeon,* and that another *osetrina* listed in the same source at 8.00 rubles per 200 gm was smoked or canned sturgeon, usually considerably more expensive.

1952: This price is computed from the 1948 price and the following price reductions: March 1949, fish, 10%; March 1950, sturgeon, 10%; March 1951, fish, 10%.

1954: This price is computed from the 1952 price and the following price reduction: April 1953, chilled, frozen, salted and smoked fish, 10%.

Comparability: 1937–40. The designation is the same in both years, but it is brief and somewhat different qualities or sizes of sturgeon may have been priced in the two years.

1937–48–52–54. The same species of sturgeon is priced at all these dates. Presumably the postwar *first grade* is approximately comparable to the 1937 *large* osert sturgeon, though there may be some quality differences.

45. Herring, salted, ordinary

1937: Sel'd' volgo-kaspiiskaia i kaspiiskaia, riadovaia, solenaia (herring, Volga-Caspian and Caspian, ordinary, salted). The quotation is from *SRTS-36*, pp. 334–335, and Naimushin, p. 20.

1928: Sel'di riadovye (herring, ordinary); *sel'd'* (herring); *sel'di astrakhanskie* (herring, Astrakhan); *sel'di riadovye astrahkanskie* (herring, ordinary, Astrakhan). Although the designation varies from month to month, it appears to relate to the same product throughout the year. This price is the annual average computed from monthly quotations of the price in cooperative shops cited in *ESBM*. It is assumed the price in state shops was about the same.

Comparability: It is assumed that the 1928 quotations are for salted herring, although the designations do not indicate this, as salted herring is a very common Russian food. Smoked herring was about 25% more expensive than salted herring and fresh or frozen herring was somewhat cheaper than salted herring in 1936 (*SRTS-36*, pp. 334–335), so there is some chance of an error in either direction. In other respects the designations are the same; the herring are from the same area (Astrakhan is on the Caspian) and both are described as *ordinary.* This apparently relates to the size of the fish.

46. Herring, salted, large

1937: Sel'd' volgo-kaspiiskaia; i kaspiiskaia; zalom; solenaia (herring, Caspian and Volga-Caspian, large, salted). The quotation is from Naimushin, p. 20. *Zalom* is here translated as "large" since, in one of its meanings, it is a South Russian word for the largest type of herring (*clupea pontica et clupea caspia*), according to *Slovar' russkogo iazyka* (Moscow, 1907).

1948: Sel'd' kaspiiskaia, bochkovogo posola krupnaia (herring, Caspian, salted, in barrels, large). The quotation is from *PD-14-12-47*.

1952: This price is computed from the 1948 price and the following price reductions: March 1949, fish, 10%; March 1950, Caspian herring, 10.1%; March 1951, herring, 10%.

1954: This price is computed from the 1952 price and the following price reduction: April 1953, herring, 10%.

Comparability: The 1937 herring priced is the most comparable of several herrings listed in the 1936 price handbook to the postwar herring priced, but difficulties in interpreting the terminology and classification system preclude absolute certainty as to comparability in this case.

47. Herring, salted

1937: Herring, salted. This price is the annual average based on the following quotations: January and April 1937 — 6.40 rubles per kg; July 1937 — 9.50 rubles per kg; October 1937 and January 1938 — 6.00 rubles per kg. The quotations are from Trivanovitch and *UM.*

1940: Herring, salted. This price is an average of the price of 8.00 rubles per kg observed in July 1940 and the price of 10.00 rubles per kg observed in January 1941. The quotations are from *MLR,* February and May 1941.

Comparability: Although the designation is the same in both years, it is very brief, and it may well be that different qualities or sizes of herring were priced at different dates.

48. Sturgeon, cured

1937: Sturgeon, cured (Balyk), first quality. This price was reported throughout 1937 in *UM.*

1940: Sturgeon, cured (Balyk), first quality. This price is an annual average computed from the following quotations: January 1940 — 30.00 rubles per kg; July 1940 — 45.00 rubles per kg; January 1941 — 40.00 rubles per kg. The quotations are from *MLR,* May 1940; February and May 1941.

1948: Balyk, smoked, first grade. The quotation is for January 1949, from *UM.*

1952: This price is computed from the 1948 price and the following price reductions: March 1949, fish, 10%; March 1950, cured filets (*balychnye izdeliia*) of salmon, lake salmon, and osert sturgeon, 30%; March 1951, fish, 10%.

1954: This price is computed from the 1952 price and the following price reduction: April 1953, chilled, frozen, salted and smoked fish, 10%.

Comparability: The 1937 and 1940 designations are the same and, in this case, the designations appear complete enough to assure comparability. The postwar item priced appears to be comparable also. The 1948 source did not specify that the *balyk* priced was sturgeon, but *balyk* apparently usually refers to sturgeon. It is defined as "cured filet of sturgeon, etc." in A. I. Smirnitskii (ed.), *Russko-angliiskii slovar'* (Moscow, 1949). In any case, the 1936 prices of two kinds of sturgeon *balyk* and of white salmon *balyk* were very similar (Naimushin, pp. 23, 30, 31, 56).

49. Caviar, black, granular

1937: Caviar, granulated. This price is an annual average based on observed quotations for 1937 in Trivanovitch and *UM.* The 1937 caviar priced is, it is believed, one of the following types of caviar: (1) *Ikra zernistaia, banochnaia, beluzh'ia i kaluzh'ia, I sort* (caviar, granular, of beluga and kaluga, in tins, grade 1); (2) *ikra zernistaia, banochnaia, osetrovaia i shipovaia, I sort* (caviar, granular, of osert and ship, in tins, grade 1); (3) *ikra sterliazh'ia zernistaia, banochnaia, parnaia, I sort* (caviar, granular, of sterlet, in tins, fresh, grade 1). These were the most expensive types of caviar; (1) and (3) were 40.00 rubles per kg and (2) was 36.00 rubles per kg in 1936, according to *SRTS-36*, p. 343, and Naimushin, p. 25.

1940: Caviar, granulated. The quotation is for July 1940 and January 1941, from *MLR,* February and May 1941; *UM.*

1948: Ikra beluzh'ia, kaluzh'ia, osetrovaia, sterliazh'ia, zernistaia, banochnaia, I sort (caviar of beluga, kaluga, osert, sterlet; granular, tinned, grade 1). The price established in December 1947 was 400 rubles per kg (*PD-14-12-47*). There was a 10% reduction in black caviar prices on April 10, 1948 (*Izvestiia,* April 10, 1948). The price shown is an average based on these data.

1952: This price is computed from the price effected April 10, 1948 and the following price reductions: March 1949, fish and fish products, 10%; March 1950, black caviar, 10%; March 1951, black and red caviar, 10%.

1954: This price is computed from the 1952 price and the following price reduction: April 1953, chilled, frozen, salted, and smoked fish, herring, and canned fish, 10%. This reduction is applied here on the assumption that caviar is included with "canned fish," but this may be in error.

Comparability: The quotations for all years appear to be for a comparable type and grade of caviar. As indicated, it is not entirely clear that there was a reduction in caviar prices between 1952 and 1954, as is assumed here.

50. Sugar, lump

1937: Sakhar rafinad kolotyi (sugar, refined, lump). The quotation is from *SRTS-36,* p. 139. The same price is cited throughout 1937 for *sugar, lump* in Trivanovitch and *UM.* The price apparently remained in effect until January 1940 (*UM; MLR,* May and August 1940).

1928: Sakhar rafinad kolotyi (sugar, refined, lump). The quotation is from *ESBM.*

1940: Sugar, lump. This price is the annual average based on the price of 4.10 rubles per kg from January 1 to January 24, and 5.50 rubles per kg for the rest of the year. The quotations are from *MLR,* May and August 1940; February and May 1941.

Comparability: The quotation for each year is for the same type of sugar.

51. Sugar, small lump

1937: Sakhar rafinad, melko-kolot. (sugar, refined, small lump). The quotation is from *SRTS-36,* p. 139. Presumably this price remained in effect until early 1940, as in the case of the other lump sugar priced (item 50).

1948: Sakhar rafinad melkokolotyi (sugar, refined, small lump). The quotation is from *PD-14-12-47.*

1952: This price is computed from the 1948 price and the following price reductions: March 1950, lump sugar, 12%; April 1952, granulated and lump sugar, 10%. The computed price is confirmed by a price observed in the summer of 1952 (*UMA*) and by Gurvits (1953).

1954: This price is computed from the 1948 price and the following price reduction: April 1953, granulated and lump sugar, 10%.

Comparability: The quotation for each year is for the same type of sugar.

52. Sugar, granulated

1937: Sakhar pesok (sugar, granulated). The quotation is from *SRTS-36,* p. 139. The same price is cited throughout 1937 for *sugar, granulated* in Trivanovitch and *UM.*

1928: Sakhar pesok (sugar, granulated). This price was in effect in both state and cooperative shops throughout 1928, according to *ESBM.*

1940: Sugar, granulated. This price is the annual average based on the price of 3.80 rubles per kg from January 1 to January 24, and 5.00 rubles per kg from January 24 through the end of 1940. The quotations are from *MLR*, May 1940; February and May 1941; *UM*.

1948: Sakhar pesok (sugar, granulated). The quotation is from *PD-14-12-47*.

1952: This price is computed from the 1948 price and the following price reductions: March 1950, granulated sugar, 15%; April 1952, granulated and lump sugar, 10%. The computed price is 5 kopeks below the price observed just prior to the 1953 price cut (*UMA*) and that cited by Gurvits (1953); this is a minor error in rounding.

1954: This price is computed from the 1952 price and the following price reduction: April 1953, granulated and lump sugar, 10%.

Comparability: The quotation for each year is for the same sugar.

53. Cocoa

1937: Cocoa of foreign origin or *cocoa.* This price is an annual average based on the price of 15.55 rubles per 250 gm from January through October 1937 and 14.75 rubles per 250 gm on January 1, 1938. The quotations are from Trivanovitch and *UM*.

1940: Cocoa of foreign origin. This is the annual average price computed from the following quotations: 15.55 rubles per 250 gm on January 1, 1940; 21.50 rubles per 250 gm on January 24, 1940; 18.06 rubles per 250 gm on January 1, 1941. The quotations are from *UM* and *MLR*, May 1940; May 1941.

1948: Cocoa. The price in December 1950 or January 1951 was reported to be 161.00 rubles per kg in *UM*. The 1948 price is computed from this quotation and the following price reduction: March 1950, powdered cocoa, 16.7%. The price computed for 1948 — 193.00 rubles per kg — is almost the same as that cited in Gurvits (1949) for *kakao Zolotyi iarlyk* (cocoa, Gold Label) — 192.00 rubles per kg.

1952: This price is computed from the quotation for late 1950 or early 1951 and the following price reduction: April 1952, cocoa, 15%. The March 1951 reduction of 10% in the prices of cocoa beverages (*kakao-napitki*) apparently did not apply to powdered cocoa. My computed price — 136.65 rubles per kg — is very close to the 1952 price of *kakao Zolotyi iarlyk* (cocoa, Gold Label), listed at 136.00 rubles per kg in Gurvits (1953).

1954: This price is computed from the 1952 price and the following price reductions: April 1953, cocoa, 20%; April 1954, cocoa, 15%.

Comparability: 1937–40. The designations in the visitors' reports are the same throughout both years, but there may be minor variations in the quality priced at different dates. The range of cocoa prices was rather narrow as far as can be determined from *SRTS-M-36*, pp. 95, 102, 107.

1937–48–52–54. The postwar quotations are apparently for *Gold Label cocoa.* In 1936, *Gold Label cocoa* was 16.10 rubles for 250 gm in urban areas of Moscow Oblast, excluding the city of Moscow, according to *SRTS-M-36*, p. 102. This is only 3.5% higher than the 1936 and 1937 price reported for *cocoa of foreign origin* in Moscow. The difference may indicate a difference in grade or brand of cocoa, a difference in packaging, or simply a differential between the price in Moscow city and the price in the rest of Moscow Oblast for the same cocoa. In any case, it seems clear that the quotations are for closely comparable qualities of cocoa. The 1937 cocoa priced was probably packaged cocoa since the quotation is for 250 gm (a standard cocoa package size), but the postwar quotations, cited per kg, may be for unpackaged cocoa. Packaged cocoa was about 6% more expensive than unpackaged cocoa in 1936 (*SRTS-M-36*, pp. 95, 102, 107).

54. Chocolate candy, best

1937: Chocolate candy, best. The quotation, effective throughout 1937, is from Trivanovitch and *UM*.

1940: Chocolate candy, best. This is an annual average based on the following quotations: January 1940 — 51.60 rubles per kg; July 1940 — 100.00 rubles per kg; January 1941 — 71.00 rubles per kg. The quotations are from *MLR,* May 1940; February and May 1941.

Comparability: The designation is the same in each year. The wide fluctuation in price during 1940 might suggest that somewhat different qualities of candy were priced at different dates during 1940, but this pattern of price movement appears to be typical of candy prices during 1940.

55. Bonbons

1937: Candy, bonbons, first quality or *candy, first quality.* This price is an annual average based on quarterly quotations in Trivanovitch and *UM*.

1940: Candy, bonbons, first quality. This price is an annual average computed from the following quotations: January 1, 1940 — 22.00 rubles per kg; January 24, 1940 — 27.00 rubles per kg; April 10, 1940 — 43.00 rubles per kg; July 1, 1940 — 42.00 rubles per kg; January 1, 1941 — 33.00 rubles per kg. The quotations are from *MLR,* May and August 1940; February and May 1941.

Comparability: The designation is the same in both years. It is possible there was some variation in the quality priced from date to date, but this does not seem significant in this case.

56. Honey

1937: Honey. This is an annual average based on the following quotations: January and April 1937 — 6.30 rubles per kg; July 1937 — 6.00 rubles per kg; October 1937 — 8.80 rubles per kg; January 1938 — 10.20 rubles per kg. The quotations are from Trivanovitch and *UM*.

1940: Honey. The quotation is for January 1, 1941, from *MLR,* May 1941.

Comparability: The designation is too brief to be certain of comparability, but it seems unlikely there was much variation in honey prices.

57. Hard candy

1937: Monpans'e "ledentsovoe" V/S (hard candy, "ledentsovoe," highest grade). The quotation is from *SRTS-M-36,* pp. 26, 88, 112. The quotation applies to urban areas of Moscow Oblast other than Moscow city in 1936. I assume the same price was in effect in Moscow city through 1937.

1948: This price is computed from the 1952 price and the following price reductions: March 1950, hard candy "ledentsovoe" and unwrapped caramels, 8%; April 1952, wrapped caramels, soft candies, chocolate, and other confectionery made with sugar, 10%.

1952: Monpans'e ledentsovoe vysshyi sort (hard candy, "ledentsovoe," highest grade). The quotation is from Gurvits (1953).

1954: This price is computed from the 1952 price and the following price reduction: April 1953, caramels, candy *(konfety),* chocolate, sweet biscuits, wafers, cakes, pastries, cookies, rusks, and other confectionery products, 10%.

Comparability: The designation is the same in each case. The 1937 quotation is for candy sold by weight, and probably this is true of the postwar quotations also. The 1937 quotation, as indicated, applies to urban areas of Moscow Oblast other than Moscow city, and the actual Moscow city price may have differed somewhat.

58. Soft candies

1937: Miagkie konfety: "pomada fruktovaia" (soft candy: "fruit paste"). The quotation is from *SRTS-M-36,* p. 114, and applies to urban areas of Moscow Oblast other than Moscow city in 1936. I assume the same price was in effect in Moscow city through 1937.

1948: Konfety "fruktovaia pomadka" (candy "fruit paste"). The quotation is from Gurvits (1949). Although this is cited as a 1949 price, the same price would have been in effect in 1948 as there were no changes in confectionery prices between December 1947 and March 1950.

1952: This price is computed from the 1948 price and the following price reductions: March 1950, soft candy, chocolate, fruit jellies, cookies, 20%; April 1952, wrapped caramels, soft candies, chocolate, and other confectionery made with sugar, 10%.

1954: This price is computed from the 1952 price and the following price reduction: April 1953, caramels, candy *(konfety)*, chocolate, sweet biscuits, wafers, cakes, pastries, cookies, rusks, and other confectionery products, 10%.

Comparability: The designation is the same in each case. Presumably the quotations are all for *grade 1* candy though this is not indicated in the designations. The 1937 quotation is for candy sold by weight, and this is probably true of the postwar quotations. The 1937 quotation, as indicated, applies to urban areas of Moscow Oblast other than Moscow city, and the actual Moscow city price may have differed somewhat.

59. Caramels, "Theatre"

1937: Karamel' "Teatral'naia" (caramels, "Theatre"). The quotation is from *SRTS-M-36,* p. 97. The price applies to urban areas of Moscow Oblast other than Moscow city in 1936. I assume the same price was in effect in Moscow city through 1937.

1948: Karamel' "Teatral'naia" (caramels, "Theatre"). The quotation is from Gurvits (1949). Although this is cited as a 1949 price, the same price would have been in effect in 1948 as there were no confectionery price changes between December 1947 and March 1950.

1952: This price is computed from the 1948 price and the following price reductions: March 1950, wrapped caramels not containing cocoa products, 11%; April 1952, wrapped caramels, soft candy, chocolate, and other confectionery made with sugar, 10%. From the brand name of the candies — "Theatre" — it seems probable the caramels are individually wrapped, and I apply the reductions for wrapped caramels. The reductions for *unwrapped caramels* were 8% in 1950 and 15% in 1952. I assume also that the caramels priced do not contain cocoa products; if this is in error there may have been no price reduction in 1950, or a reduction of 18 to 20%.

1954: This price is computed from the 1952 price and the following price reduction: April 1953, caramels, candy *(konfety)*, chocolate, sweet biscuits, wafers, cakes, pastries, cookies, rusks, and other confectionery products, 10%.

Comparability: The brand name is the same in all cases. Presumably the quotations are all for *grade 1 candy,* though this is not indicated in the designations. The 1937 quotation is for candy sold by weight, and this is probably true also of the postwar quotations. There are some doubts concerning the application of the postwar price reductions, and the computed 1952 and 1954 prices may err on this account. The 1937 quotation is for urban areas of Moscow Oblast other than Moscow city, and the actual Moscow city price may have differed somewhat.

60. Butter, sweet

1937: Maslo zhivotnoe parizhskoe, I sort (butter, Parisian, grade 1). The quotation is from *SRTS-36*, p. 469. The quality designated *grade 1* is actually the *third* of four grades listed in this source, the two higher grades being termed *extra* and *highest*. *Parisian butter* is made of *pasteurized sweet cream*, according to a 1924 encyclopedia, Vserossiiskii tsentral'nyi soiuz potrebitel'nykh obshchestv, *Torgovaia entsiklopediia* (vol. 4, 1924, pp. 349–350).

1928: The designation va.ies somewhat from date to date, as follows: *maslo slivochnoe svezhee* (fresh cream butter); *maslo slivochnoe svezhee, 1 sort* (fresh cream butter, grade 1); *maslo slivochnoe* (cream butter); *maslo slivochnoe sladkoe 1 sort* (cream butter, sweet, grade 1). These designations all relate, it is believed, to the same product — namely, *butter of unpasteurized sweet cream, grade 1.* Grade 1 was the *highest grade* at this time. This price is the annual average based on monthly quotations in *ESBM.*

Comparability: As indicated, the comparison here is between the 1928 *highest grade* (actually designated *grade 1*) *butter of unpasteurized sweet cream* and the 1937 *third highest grade* (actually designated *grade 1*) *butter of pasteurized sweet cream.* Although these products differ, their prices were the same in the 1928 price structure (*ZA*, no. 26, 1928, pp. 16–19).

61. Butter, rendered

1937: This is the average of the 1936 prices of (1) *maslo toplenoe ekstra* (butter, rendered, extra), which was 22.00 rubles per kg, and (2) *maslo toplenoe vysh. sort* (butter, rendered, highest grade), which was 18.50 rubles per kg. The quotations are from *SRTS-36*, p. 469.

1928: Maslo toplenoe, 1 sort (butter, rendered, grade 1). The designation *grade 1* did not accompany all the quotations but, it is believed, *grade 1* butter was priced at all dates. The price is computed from the monthly quotations in *ESBM.*

Comparability: The 1928 *grade 1*, it is believed, covers a range of qualities comparable to the two 1937 grades *extra* and *highest*. In 1928, rendered butter was classified according to three grades — *first, second,* and *third,* according to *ZA*, no. 26, 1928, pp. 16–19. In 1936, four grades were in use — *extra, highest, first,* and *second,* according to *SRTS-36*, p. 469. These same four grades were designated *highest, first, second,* and *third,* prior to a revision in nomenclature in July 1935 (*SRTS-35*, p. 482). Apparently when butter is produced in three grades, the best grade is 88 to 100 score (*ball*), while when butter is produced in four grades, the two best grades fall within the same range of 88 to 100 score (*ZA*, no. 26, 1928, pp. 16–19; D. A. Andrusevich, *Tovarovedenie promyshlennykh tovarov* (Moscow, 1948), p. 18).

62. Butter, grade 1

1937: Butter, first quality. This price was observed in April, July, and October 1937 and January 1938. The quotations are from Trivanovitch and *UM*. A slightly higher price reported in *UM* for January 1937 is assumed to have been for a higher quality butter.

1940: Butter, first quality. This price was apparently set on April 10, 1940 and remained in effect through the rest of the year, according to *MLR*, August 1940; February and May 1941. Before April, it is likely that the 1937 price was still in effect. However, this grade of butter was reported to be unavailable then (*MLR*, May and August 1940), and the nominal price is, therefore, not taken into account.

Comparability: The designation is the same in both years, and the products are probably comparable. However, the range of types and grades of butter is rather wide, and some error in comparability may have been made.

63. Butter, grade 2

1937: Butter, second quality. This price was observed in April, July, and October 1937 and January 1938. The quotations are from *UM* and Trivanovitch. A somewhat higher price reported in *UM* for January 1937 was, it is assumed, for a higher quality butter.

1940: Butter, second quality. This is an annual average price based on the following quotations: January 1, 1940 — 17.50 rubles per kg; July 1, 1940 and January 1, 1941 — 26.00 rubles per kg. The quotations are from *MLR,* August 1940; February and May 1941.

Comparability: The designation is the same in both years and the products are probably comparable. However, the range of types and grades of butter is rather wide and some error in comparability may have been made.

64. Butter (average of 7 kinds)

1937: This price is the unweighted average of the 1936 prices of seven kinds of butter (shown in the tabulation below) from *SRTS-36,* pp. 468–469. It is believed that these prices remained in effect throughout 1937.

1948: This price is the unweighted average of the 1948 prices of the same seven kinds of butter priced in 1937 (shown below). All these quotations were observed in January 1949 (*UM*); presumably they were in effect throughout 1948. The price of *maslo slivochnoe solenoe vysshego sorta* (creamery butter, salted, highest grade) is also given in *PD-14-12-47.*

1952: This price is computed from the 1948 price and the following price reductions: March 1949, creamery butter and rendered butter, 10%; March 1950, butter, 15%; March 1951, butter, 15%; April 1952, butter, 15%. The computed price is confirmed by observations in the summer of 1952 (*UMA*) and by butter prices cited in Gurvits (1953).

1954: This price is computed from the 1952 price and the following price reduction: April 1953, butter, 10%.

Comparability: The price compared in 1937 and 1948 is, in each case, the unweighted average of the prices of the same seven kinds and grades of butter, so comparability is assured. As the 1952 and 1954 prices are computed from the 1948 price and the annual price reductions, the quotations for these years should be equally comparable with the 1937 quotation.

The 1937 and 1948 prices of these seven butter products are shown in the accompanying tabulation, in rubles per kilogram:

Type and grade of butter	1937 price	1948 price
Salted, extra (*solenoe, ekstra*)	17.50	68.00
Salted, highest grade (*solenoe, v/sort*)	16.00	64.00
Sweet, extra (*ne solenoe, ekstra*)	20.00	70.00
Sweet, highest (*ne solenoe, v/sort*)	17.50	66.00
Sweet, first (*ne solenoe, I sort*)	16.50	62.00
Rendered, highest (*toplennoe, v/sort*)	18.50	72.00
Rendered, first (*toplennoe, I sort*)	16.50	68.00
Average	17.50	67.14

65. Sunflower oil

1937: Sunflower oil. This price is an annual average based on quarterly quotations in Trivanovitch and *UM.* The observed quotations relate, it is believed, to *maslo podsolnechnoe, rafinirovannoe, nerasfasovannoe* (sunflower oil, refined, in bulk) listed in *SRTS-36*, p. 474 at 13.50 rubles per kg in 1936. It is possible, however, that some of the observed quotations relate to *bottled* sunflower oil, which was one ruble more expensive than sunflower oil sold *in bulk* in 1936 (*SRTS-36*, p. 474).

1928: Maslo podsolnechnoe (sunflower oil). This price is an estimated annual average based mainly on quotations in *ESBM*. According to this source, the price in cooperative shops was 0.53 ruble per *kilogram* from January through June and 0.54 ruble per *kilogram* on July 1. For the rest of the year, the quotations are said to be expressed per *liter* and, except for September and October, the price cited is 0.48 ruble or 0.49 ruble per *liter*. For September and October the price is given as 0.55 ruble per *liter*, but it seems clear that this was actually the price per *kilogram*. It is assumed that the price of 0.55 ruble per kilogram was in effect from September through December. Another source, giving only quarterly quotations, cites sunflower oil at 0.48 ruble per *liter* in January, April, and July 1928, and 0.49 ruble per *liter* in October 1928 and January 1929 (Moskovskaia oblast', Statisticheskii otdel, *Moskva i Moskovskaia oblast' 1926/27–1928/29 gg.* (Moscow, 1930), p. 376).

1940: Sunflower oil. This price was observed in January and July 1940 and January 1941, as reported in *MLR,* May 1940; February and May 1941.

1948: Maslo podsolnechnoe, rafinirov., nerasfasovannoe (sunflower oil, refined, in bulk). The quotation is from *PD-14-12-47.*

1952: This price is computed from the 1948 price and the following price reductions: March 1950, vegetable oil, 10%; April 1952, vegetable oil, 20%. The computed price — 21.60 rubles per kg — is somewhat higher than the price of 20.90 rubles per kg observed just prior to the 1953 price cut (*UMA*) and also cited in Gurvits (1953) for both *refined* and *unrefined sunflower oil.*

1954: This price is computed from the 1952 price and the following price reductions: April 1953, vegetable oil, 10%; October 1, 1954, vegetable oil, 12½% (*Pravda,* August 14, 1954).

Comparability: It is assumed that the 1928 quotation is for *refined* sunflower oil, as are the quotations for other years. It is not known whether the 1928 sunflower oil was bottled or sold in bulk, though the latter seems more likely. The 1937 quotation is believed to be for sunflower oil sold in bulk, but one or two of the quarterly quotations from which the average is computed may relate to bottled sunflower oil. The postwar quotations are for sunflower oil sold *in bulk.* In 1936, refined sunflower oil was 0.50 ruble more expensive per kg than unrefined, and bottled sunflower oil was 1.00 ruble more expensive per kg than unbottled (*SRTS-36*, p. 474). In 1952, there was no difference in price between refined and unrefined sunflower oil, according to the Gurvits (1953) quotations.

66. Beef fat, rendered

1937: Goviahz'e toplenoe salo (beef fat, rendered). The 1936 price was 12.50 rubles per kg for *grade 1* and 11.00 rubles per kg for *grade 2,* according to *SRTS-36*, p. 305. The average of the *grade 1* and *grade 2* prices is used.

1928: Salo goviazhie toplenoe (beef fat, rendered). This price is an average calculated on the basis of the *ESBM* quotations for August, September, and October 1928 and January 1929.

Comparability: The grade of the 1928 beef fat is not indicated — possibly because this product was not graded in those days. Consequently, the 1937 *grade 1* and *grade 2* prices are averaged for the comparison.

67. Lard

1937: Salo-shpig (lard). The 1936 price range was 19.00 to 24.00 rubles per kg, according to *SRTS-36*, p. 306. The midpoint of the range is used.

1928: Salo svinoe solenoe; shpig (salted pork fat; lard). The price in January 1929 was 1.80 rubles per kg in state shops and 1.66 rubles per kg in cooperative shops, according to *ESBM*. The average of these two prices is used. It is assumed that this price was in effect throughout 1928.

Comparability: The 1928 and 1937 quotations probably relate to more or less comparable products.

68. Salt pork, fat

1937: Salt pork, fat. The quotation is for January 1937, from *UM*. The source indicates that the product was not available during much of 1937.

1940: Salt pork, fat. The quotation is for July 1940 and January 1941, from *MLR*, February and May 1941.

Comparability: The designation is the same for each year, and there is no reason to doubt that the quotations refer to the same quality of product.

69. Margarine

1937: Margarin stolovyi (margarine, table). The quotation is for 1936, from *SRTS-36*, p. 480. The same price was in effect throughout 1937, it is assumed.

1948: Table margarine. This price was observed in January 1949 (*UM*). The same price was probably in effect throughout 1948.

1952: This price is computed from the 1948 price and the following price reductions: March 1950, margarine, 35%; March 1951, margarine, 10%; April 1952, margarine, 15%.

1954: This price is computed from the 1952 price and the following price reduction: April 1953, margarine, 10%.

Comparability: The quotations appear to be for the same product, but the designations are brief and there may be minor quality differences.

70. Milk, fresh

1937: Milk, fresh. This price was in effect throughout 1937. The quotation is from Trivanovitch and *UM*.

1928: Moloko (milk). This price is an annual average based on quotations for six months of 1928 in *ESBM* and *Moskva i Moskovskaia guberniia; Statistiko-ekonomicheskii spravochnik 1923/24–1927/28 gg.* (Moscow, 1929), pp. 494–495. The available quotations indicate that a constant price was maintained during the off-season — October to April — and that the price fluctuated at a lower level during the rest of the year. In computing the annual average, the lower in-season price is weighted twice as heavily as the off-season price as a rough means of allowing for the greater quantities sold during the period of heavy supply.

1940: Milk, fresh. This price is an annual average based on the following quotations: January, April, and July 1940 — 2.10 rubles per liter; January 1941 — 2.30 rubles per liter. The quotations are from *MLR*, May and August 1940; February and May 1941.

1948: Moloko tselnoe (whole milk). This price is the top of the seasonal range of 3.00 to 4.00 rubles per liter established in December 1947 (*PD-14-12-47*). The lower price, which presumably should have been in effect from April 1 to October 1, was apparently in effect for only a short time, if at all, during 1948. Smith,

p. 93, reports the price of 4.00 rubles per liter in June, and the same price is cited for other dates in *UM*.

1952: This price is computed from the 1948 price and the following price reductions: March 1950, whole milk, 10%; March 1951, milk, 10%; April 1952, milk, 10%. The computed price is confirmed by Gurvits (1953) and by observations at various times between April 1952 and early 1955 (Hughes, p. 128; *New York Times,* February 26, 1955).

1954: The quotation is the same as for 1952 as there were no reductions in the price of milk between April 1952 and March 1955.

Comparability: The milk priced in each year is presumably comparable. It is believed that all quotations are for unpasteurized, unbottled milk. The 1952 and 1954 quotations tend to exaggerate the price rise from 1937 inasmuch as they do not take into account seasonal variations in price. As explained, there is evidence that the low seasonal price was not put into effect during 1948, and the top of the seasonal price range is used for 1948 in my index. The 1952 and 1954 quotations, computed from the 1948 price and the annual reductions, also represent the top of the seasonal range. However, there are indications that the low seasonal price was in effect during the season of heavier supply in 1952 and 1954 (Gurvits (1953); *MLR,* July 1953, p. 706; Madge, p. 232).

71. Sour cream (spring)

1937: Smetana I sort (sour cream, grade 1). The price was reduced from 8.00 to 6.50 rubles per kg on June 20, 1937, according to *ST,* June 20, 1937. The average of these two prices is used. This average should be roughly appropriate for the spring-summer period.

1928: Smetana I sort (sour cream, grade 1). The quotation is that effective in cooperative shops in April and May and on July 1, 1928, as reported in *ESBM.*

Comparability: The quotations both relate to *grade 1 sour cream* and should be comparable unless there were significant changes in grading standards between 1928 and 1937. The quotations relate to approximately the same period in each year, a period during the season of peak supply.

72. Sour cream

1937: Cream, sour. This price is an annual average based on quarterly quotations from Trivanovitch and *UM*. It is believed that the quotations are for *first grade* sour cream.

1940: Cream, sour. This price is an annual average based on quotations for January and July 1940 and January 1941, from *MLR,* May 1940; February and May 1941.

1948: Sour cream. This price is an estimated annual average price. On March 31, 1949, the price of sour cream was reduced from 30.00 to 25.00 rubles per kg (*New York Times,* April 1, 1949). This was apparently a seasonal reduction; the season at which milk products are sold at lower prices is April 1 to October 1 (G. L. Rubinshtein, *et al., Ekonomika sovetskoi torgovli* (Moscow, 1950), p. 480). It is assumed that the price was 30.00 rubles per kg during the fall-winter season and 25.00 rubles per kg during the spring-summer season in 1948 as well as in 1949. The price used — 26.50 rubles per kg — is nearer the low point of the range to allow for heavier sales during the spring-summer season. The sour cream priced is apparently *smetana, 30%-i zhirnosti 1-go sorta* (sour cream, 30% fat content, grade 1), listed at 25.00 rubles per kg in May 1949, in Gurvits (1949).

1952: This price is computed from the 1948 price and the following price reductions: March 1950, sour cream, 20%; March 1951, milk products, 10%; April 1952, milk products, 10%. The low seasonal price computed in the same way corresponds with that cited for July 1952 in Gurvits (1953) for *smetana 30%-i zhirnosti, 1-go sorta* (sour cream, 30% fat content, grade 1).

1954: The quotation is the same as for 1952, as there was no further price reduction after April 1952.

Comparability: Although the 1937 and 1940 designations do not indicate the grade of sour cream priced, it is believed that the quotations for these years, as well as for the postwar years, all refer to *grade 1* sour cream. An attempt is made to take seasonal variations into account in computing the average annual prices, but this can be done only roughly.

73. Cheese, Swiss-type

1937: Swiss-type cheese. This quotation, effective throughout 1937, is from Trivanovitch and *UM*. The observed 1937 price — 24.80 rubles per kg — is the same as the 1936 Moscow Oblast price of *syr Finlandskii importnyi, Shveitsarskii polnozh. v/s* (cheese, imported from Finland, Swiss, full fat content, highest grade). Domestic Swiss cheese, *syr Russko-shveitsarskii, polnozh., v/s* (cheese, Russian-Swiss, full fat content, highest grade) was about the same price, 25.00 rubles per kg (*SRTS-M-36,* pp. 74–76).

"Full fat content" means a fat content of 50% in the case of Swiss cheese, according to the description of Swiss cheese in Bakzevich, pp. 109ff.

1940: Cheese, Swiss; cheese, Swiss-type; or *cheese, best.* This price is the annual average based on the following quotations: January 1 and January 24, 1940 — 24.80 rubles per kg; July 1, 1940 and January 1, 1941 — 31.50 rubles per kg. The quotations are from *MLR,* May and August 1940; February and May 1941. In computing the average, it is assumed that the price rise took place on April 10, when a number of price rises were effected.

1948: This price is the average of the following two prices, observed in January, 1949: *Swiss cheese, 50%* — 76.00 rubles per kg, and *Swiss cheese* — 64.00 rubles per kg (*UM*).

1952: This price is computed from the 1948 price and the following price reductions: March 1949, cheese, 20%; March 1950, Swiss cheese, 20%; March 1951, cheese, 10%; April 1952, Swiss cheese, 20%. The price computed in this way is 33.20 rubles per kg. This falls between the following 1952 quotations from Soviet sources: (1) *Syr shveitsarskii 50 prots. zhirnosti, vysshii sort* (cheese, Swiss, 50% fat content, highest grade) — 36.90 rubles per kg (this price is computed from the post-March 1, 1949 price cited in Gurvits (1949) and the subsequent price reductions); and (2) *syr shveitsarskii 50-protsentnoi zhirnosti I sorta* (cheese, Swiss, 50% fat content, grade 1) — 32.20 rubles per kg (Gurvits (1953)).

1954: The quotation is the same as for 1952 as there were no further price reductions.

Comparability: The 1937 and 1940 quotations are probably for the same type and grade of cheese. The 1937 quotation appears to be for *50% fat content, highest grade Swiss cheese.* The postwar quotations are also for *50% fat content, Swiss cheese.* However, the 1952 and 1954 prices computed from incomplete 1948 data and the subsequent price reductions appear to be about 10% below the correct price for *highest grade* Swiss cheese of 50% fat content.

74. Cheese, Holland-type

1937: Holland-type cheese. This price is the annual average based on the price of 14.50 rubles per kg in January 1937, and 14.80 rubles per kg in April, July, and October 1937 and on January 1, 1938. The quotations are from Trivanovitch and *UM*.

1940: Cheese, Holland-type. This price is an average of the price of 23.50 rubles per kg in July 1940 and 25.00 rubles per kg in January 1941. The quotations are from *MLR*, February and May 1941. Probably a lower price was in effect until April 10, 1940. If so, my price is a little high for an annual average.

Comparability: The designation is the same in each year but there was a wide range in prices of Holland-type cheese (*SRTS-M-36*, pp. 74–76), and an error in comparability between the two years may have been made. The price rise between 1937 and 1940 shown in this case is considerably larger than in the case of the two other cheeses priced.

75. Cheese, American-type

1937: American-type cheese. This price is an annual average computed from the price of 21.00 rubles per kg in January, April, July, and October 1937 and 22.20 rubles per kg in January 1938. The quotations are from Trivanovitch and *UM*.

1940: Cheese, American-type, or *cheese, American.* This is an average computed from the following quotations: April 10, 1940 — 26.00 rubles per kg; July 1, 1940 — 29.00 rubles per kg; January 1, 1941 — 28.00 rubles per kg. The April 1940 quotation is said to be for *cheese, second quality,* but this is apparently *American-type cheese.* The quotations are from *MLR*, May and August 1940; February and May 1941. Probably a lower price was in effect before April 10, 1940; if so, my price is a little high for an annual average.

Comparability: The variation in the quotations from date to date in 1940 suggests that somewhat different grades of cheese may have been priced, but comparability between 1937 and 1940 is probably fairly close.

76. Eggs

1937: Eggs. This is the annual average price computed from the following quotations: January 1, 1937 — 6.50 rubles for ten; April 1, 1937 — 7.50 rubles for ten; July 1, 1937, October 1, 1937, and January 1, 1938 — 5.50 rubles for ten. The quotations are from Trivanovitch and *UM*. The April 1 quotation is higher than the price announced in *ST*, April 9, 1937 for *iaitsa II kategorii* (eggs, second category); it is assumed from this that the observed quotations are for *first category* or *first grade* eggs.

1928: This is the average annual price based on monthly quotations in *ESBM* and quarterly quotations in *Moskva i Moskovskaia guberniia 1923/24–1927/28 gg.,* pp. 494–495, and *Moskva i Moskovskaia oblast' 1926/27–1928/29 gg.,* p. 372. The monthly quotations generally refer to *iaitsa svezhie I sort* (eggs, fresh, grade 1), but for one date the quotation is for *iaitsa iz kholodil'nik* (cold storage eggs), and for some dates the designation is simply *iaitsa* (eggs).

1940: Eggs. This is the annual average price based on the following quotations: January and July 1940 — 8.50 rubles for ten; January 1941 — 7.50 rubles for ten. The quotations are from *MLR*, May 1940; February and May 1941.

1948: Iaitsa stolovye I kategorii (eggs, table, first category). A seasonal range of 12.00 to 16.00 rubles for ten eggs was established by *PD-14-12-47.* I use the top of this seasonal range as there is evidence that the lower prices were rarely, if ever, in effect during the season (*UM; New York Times,* April 1, 1949).

1952: This price is computed from the 1948 price and the following price reductions: March 1950, eggs, 15%; March 1951, eggs, 10%; April 1952, eggs, 15%.

1954: This price is computed from the 1952 price and the following price reduction: April 1953, eggs, 10%. Prices observed in the summer of 1954 confirm that the reductions were actually effected (*UMA*).

Comparability: The grade of egg priced in each year is, it is believed, comparable, but the evidence is not entirely clear. Seasonal price fluctuations are taken into account in the quotations for 1928, 1937, and 1940; though in the case of the latter year the annual average is based on quotations for only three dates. For the post-war years the upper limit of the seasonal price range is used. For 1948 this probably gives an approximately correct annual average as the lower seasonal prices were rarely in effect. Recent reports indicate that egg prices are actually lowered in April and raised in October (*UMA*); thus for 1954, and probably also for 1952, use of the top of the seasonal price range in the price index overstates somewhat the rise in price from 1937.

77. Potatoes

1937: Potatoes. The price of 0.40 ruble per kg is cited throughout 1937 in Trivanovitch and *UM*. The quotation is presumably for *old potatoes*, and also for new potatoes once they are being received in volume. A price of 0.50 ruble per kg announced in *ST*, August 5, 1937 was probably for new potatoes, and may well have represented a reduction from an earlier, higher price.

1928: Kartofel' (potatoes). This price is the average of the monthly quotations cited for cooperative shops in *ESBM*. The price in state shops is cited for only some months in this source. The state shop price appears to have been close to the cooperative shop price but may have averaged about one-half kopek higher.

1940: Potatoes. This is the annual average price based on the following quotations: January 1, 1940 — 0.50 ruble per kg; January 24, 1940 — 0.80 ruble per kg; April 10, 1940 — 1.20 rubles per kg; October 20, 1940 — 1.20 rubles per kg; October 21, 1940 through January 1, 1941 — 0.90 ruble per kg. The quotations are from *MLR*, May and August 1940 and May 1941; Prokopovicz, *Quarterly Bulletin of Soviet-Russian Economics*, no. 6, December 1940, p. 81; *Pravda*, October 21, 1940. The very high price of 8.00 rubles per kg is cited for July 1, 1940 in *MLR*, February 1941; this price, it is assumed, applies to early new potatoes and is not taken into account in computing the annual average price.

1948: Potatoes. The price of 1.00 ruble per kg was apparently in effect through-out 1948 (*UM; Moskovskii bol'shevik*, August 29, 1948; Ministerstvo prosve-shcheniia RSFSR, *Sbornik materialov dlia rabotnikov uchebno-proizvodstvennykh i podsobnykh khoziaistv* (Moscow, 1948), p. 96). A higher price — 2.00 to 4.00 rubles per kg — was reported in June in Smith, p. 93, but this seems clearly to relate to early new potatoes. The seasonal pattern of potato prices is made clear in one source which states that, after the 10% reduction in potato prices of March 1, 1950 *old potatoes* were 0.90 ruble per kg and *new potatoes (in season)* were 2.00 rubles per kg early in the season and were later 0.90 ruble per kg (*UM*).

1952: This price is computed from the 1948 price and the following price reduction: March 1950, potatoes, 10%. The computed price is confirmed by Gurvits (1953) and by several visitors' reports (Madge, p. 232; Eugène Zaleski, "Les fluctu-ations des prix de détail en Union Soviétique: Annexe méthodologique et statis-tique," *Conjoncture et Études économiques, Études spéciales*, no. 3, 1955, p. 77; *UM*).

1954: This price is an annual average computed from the following quotations: April 1, 1954 through October 31, 1954 — 0.45 ruble per kg; November 1, 1954 through February 28, 1955 — 0.60 ruble per kg; March 1 through March 31, 1955 — 0.80 ruble per kg. (1) In April 1953, prices of potatoes were cut by 50%, reducing the 1952 price to 0.45 ruble per kg. This price was observed at various times between April 1953 and August 1954 (*UM; New York Times*, March 11 and August 15, 1954; Hughes, p. 120). It is assumed this price remained in effect until the new price schedule announced in August 1954 came into effect. (2) The sea-sonal price schedule announced in *Pravda*, August 14, 1954 for *kartofel' pozdnii* (potatoes, late) is as follows: September 2 to October 31 — 0.45 ruble per kg; November 1 to February 28 — 0.60 ruble per kg; from March 1 — 0.80 ruble per kg.

The seasonal price schedule announced in August 1954 is for the *second price zone*. Moscow is in the *first price zone* for potatoes, according to Ministerstvo prosveshcheniia RSFSR, *Sbornik materialov dlia rabotnikov uchebno-proizvodstvennykh i podsobnykh khoziaistv*, p. 96, and G. M. Lasevich and A. G. Karelov, *Torgovye skidki na prodovol'stvennye i promyshlennye tovary* (Moscow, 1954), p. 11. However, it appears that the zone II prices announced in August 1954 were in effect in Moscow. The price observed in Moscow at the time of the announcement of the new seasonal price schedule was the same as the zone II low seasonal price in the schedule, and an observation in Moscow in February 1955 (*New York Times*, February 26, 1955) corresponds to the zone II price for that date.

Comparability: The quotations for all years appear to relate to old potatoes, or to new potatoes after they are available in volume. In all cases, it is believed, the quotations relate to first grade potatoes.

78. Cabbage, fresh (fall)

1937: Kapusta svezhaia (cabbage, fresh). This price — 0.30 ruble per kg — was established August 29, 1937 (*ST*, August 29, 1937) and was still in effect on January 1, 1938 (*UM*). This is the low-season price from late August through December. Cabbage prices declined during the year from a peak of 3.00 rubles per kg in early April to 0.40 ruble per kg in late July, and 0.30 ruble per kg at the end of August, according to periodic announcements in *ST*.

1928: Kapusta svezhaia (cabbage, fresh). This price is the approximate average of the prices in state and cooperative shops over the period September 1 through December 1, 1928, as reported in *ESBM* and *Moskva i Moskovskaia guberniia 1923/24–1927/28 gg.*, pp. 494–495. The *ESBM* monthly quotations indicate this as a period of plentiful supply and low prices.

1948: Cabbage, good quality. This price — 1.00 ruble per kg — was observed in November 1948 (*UM*). I assume this is representative of the price in effect during the height of the season. Other quotations are as follows: 8.00 rubles per kg in June (Smith, p. 93); 1.50 rubles per kg on August 6 (*Moskovskii bol'shevik*, August 6, 1948). The vegetable price list in Ministerstvo prosveshcheniia RSFSR, *Sbornik materialov dlia rabotnikov uchebno-proizvodstvennykh i podsobnykh khoziaistv*, p. 96, indicates a price of 1.50 rubles per kg in price zone I, which included Moscow; and Gurvits (1949) cites two prices — 1.00 and 1.50 rubles per kg — without explanation of the difference.

1952: This price is computed from the November 1948 price and the following price reduction: March 1950, cabbage, 14.7%.

1954: Kapusta pozdniaia svezhaia (cabbage, late, fresh). This price is an estimated average for the period September through December 1954. I estimate that the price was 0.65 ruble per kg in September and October, and 0.95 ruble per kg in November and December, on the basis of the following data: (1) In August 1954 a new seasonal price schedule was announced. For *price zone II* this was as follows: October 6 to 31 — 0.70 ruble per kg; November 1 to February 28 — 1.00 ruble per kg; from March 1 — 1.40 rubles per kg (*PD-14-8-54*). The new October price is the same as that which can be computed from the 1947 price in zone II — 1.60 rubles per kg (Ministerstvo prosveshcheniia RSFSR, *Sbornik materialov dlia rabotnikov uchebno-proizvodstvennykh i podsobnykh khoziaistv*, p. 96) and the two price reductions between 1947 and 1954. The reductions in cabbage prices were 14.7% in March 1950 and 50% in April 1953. In view of this correspondence, I assume that the price in effect in August 1954 at the time of the announcement of the new price schedule and until October 6 when the new schedule went into effect was the same as the new price set for October 6 to 31, that is, 0.70 ruble per kg in price zone II.

(2) Moscow is in *price zone I* in the case of vegetables, according to Lasevich and Karelov, p. 11. According to Ministerstvo prosveshcheniia RSFSR, *Sbornik materialov dlia rabotnikov uchebno-proizvodstvennykh i podsobnykh khoziaistv*, p. 96, the *zone I* price in 1947 was 1.50 rubles per kg. Applying the two percentage price reductions, I compute a price of 0.65 ruble per kg for the period from April 1953 until the new price schedule went into effect on October 6, 1954. This is 0.05 ruble per kg less than the zone II price apparently in effect at the same time. For each season I assume that the new seasonal price in zone I was 0.05 ruble cheaper per kg than the price in zone II. Two visitors' reports cite a Moscow price for cabbage of 0.65 ruble per kg during the period April 1, 1953 to April 1, 1954, but several observations of higher prices were also reported during this period (*UMA*).

Comparability: The quotations relate to approximately the same season in each year, and presumably the quality of cabbage available in season was roughly comparable in each year. One aspect of the question of comparability is the length of time during which cabbage was actually available at the low seasonal prices. The available data are too scanty to permit an analysis of this aspect.

79. Cabbage, fresh (July)

1937: Cabbage. The quotation is for July 1, 1937, from Trivanovitch.

1940: Cabbage. The quotation is for July 1, 1940, from *MLR*, February 1941. Cabbage was not available at other dates for which visitors' price reports are available.

Comparability: The quotations for each year refer to July 1. The quotations for a single date early in the season do not provide a very satisfactory basis for comparison. Judging from the course of cabbage prices in 1937, July is a month of particularly rapid price change. Between July 1 and July 29, 1937 the price of cabbage fell from 1.60 to 0.40 ruble per kg (Trivanovitch; *ST*, July 5, 11, 17, 23, and 29, 1937). Thus the comparison of the July 1 prices undoubtedly reflects not only the rise in the general level of prices but also differences in the timing of the increase in the flow of seasonal supplies, and even a few days might make a considerable difference.

80. Sauerkraut

1937: Sauerkraut (UM); kapusta kvashenaia (sauerkraut) (*ST*, August 29 and September 11, 1937). This price is an approximate annual average computed from the following quotations: January 1, 1937 — 0.40 ruble per kg; August 29, 1937 — 0.50 ruble per kg; September 11, 1937 — 0.40 ruble per kg; January 1, 1938 — 0.50 ruble per kg (*UM; ST*, August 29 and September 11, 1937).

1928: Kapusta kvashenaia (sauerkraut) or *kapusta kvashenaia rublenaia* (sauerkraut, chopped). These are apparently the same product. This price is an approximate annual average based on quotations for January, April, May, July, August, and December 1928, as reported in *ESBM* and *Moskva i Moskovskaia guberniia 1923/24–1927/28 gg.*, pp. 494–495.

1940: Sauerkraut. The quotation is for January 1, 1941, from *MLR*, May 1941. Sauerkraut was not available at other dates during 1940 for which visitors' reports are available.

Comparability: Presumably the sauerkraut priced in the three years was roughly comparable. The 1940 price is based on a quotation for only one date — January 1,

1940. The 1937 average annual price used, however, is the same as the average of the prices on January 1, 1937 and January 1, 1938; thus, in this case, January prices are in effect compared.

81. Cucumbers, fresh (August)

1937: Ogurtsy, I sort (cucumbers, grade 1). This is the price announced on August 11, 1937 in *ST* of that date. Other price quotations available for 1937 are expressed in terms of price per cucumber rather than per kilogram and cannot be compared with the available postwar quotations. An impression of the seasonal pattern of prices may be obtained from the movement of the price of nonstandard (*nestandartnye*) cucumbers, which was expressed in rubles per kilogram. This price declined from 6.00 rubles on April 1, to 1.80 rubles in June, and to 1.00 ruble toward the end of July (*ST*, April 1, June 17, July 23, 1937).

1948: Svezhie ogurtsy, I sort (fresh cucumbers, grade 1). This price was announced on August 6, 1948 in *Moskovskii bol'shevik* of that date. In June, cucumbers were 2.50 to 4.00 rubles per kg, according to Smith, p. 93.

1952: This price is computed from the August 1948 price and the following price reduction: March 1950, other vegetables, 10%.

1954: This price is computed from the 1952 price and the following price reduction: April 1953, fresh cabbage and other vegetables, 50%.

Comparability: The early August price used for each year was probably about the lowest price of the season. The designation is for *grade 1* cucumbers for both 1937 and 1948. This should be true also of the quotations for 1952 and 1954, inasmuch as these are computed from the 1948 price and the subsequent price reductions. Some doubts might be entertained as to whether cucumbers were included in the broad category "other vegetables" in the 1950 and 1953 price decrees, as is assumed here.

82. Cucumbers, fresh (July)

1937: Cucumbers, fresh. The quotation is for July 1, 1937, from Trivanovitch.

1940: Cucumbers, fresh. The quotation is for July 1, 1940, from *MLR*, February 1941. Cucumbers were not available at other dates for which visitors' reports are available.

Comparability: The quotation for each year refers to the same date — July 1 — but this is rather early in the season and the quotations may not be very representative of the change in in-season prices between the two years.

83. Cucumbers, pickled

1937: Cucumbers, pickled. This price is the average of the price on January 1, 1937 — 2.50 rubles per kg — and on January 1, 1938 — 3.00 rubles per kg. The quotations are from *UM*.

1940: Cucumbers, pickled. The quotation is for January 1, 1941, from *MLR*, May 1941.

Comparability: The designation is very brief but the quality of the product was probably roughly comparable. The quotations for both years are for January.

84. Cucumbers, salted

1937: Malosol'nye ogurtsy (fresh-salted cucumbers). This price was announced on August 11, 1937 in *ST* of that date. Presumably the quotation is for *grade 1* cucumbers.

1948: Malosol'nye ogurtsy, I sort (fresh-salted cucumbers, grade 1). This price was announced on August 6, 1948 in *Moskovskii bol'shevik* of that date.

1952: This price is computed from the August 1948 price and the following price reduction: March 1950, other salted, sour, and pickled vegetables, 15%.

1954: This price is computed from the 1952 price and the following price reduction: April 1953, fresh cabbage and other vegetables, 50%. It is not clear whether this price cut applies to *fresh-salted cucumbers.*

Comparability: The product priced appears to be comparable, and the quotation in each case is for the same month. As indicated, there is some doubt about whether the 50% price reduction of April 1953 applies, as is assumed.

85. Onions

1937: Onions. The available quotations are: January 1 and April 1, 1937 — 1.60 rubles per kg (*UM;* Trivanovitch); April 19, 1937 — 1.10 rubles per kg (*ST,* May 14, 1937); July 1, 1937—1.60 rubles per kg (Trivanovitch); October 1, 1937 and January 1, 1938 — 1.20 rubles per kg (*UM*). The annual average price computed from these quotations comes to about 1.40 rubles per kg. This is the price used in the computations. For purposes of comparison with 1928, the 1937 average for the period April to July also amounts to approximately 1.40 rubles per kg. And for purposes of comparison with 1940, the same price is considered as an average of the January 1937 and January 1938 prices.

1928: Luk repchatyi (bulb onions). This price is an average of the prices in state and cooperative shops in April, May, and July 1928, as reported in *ESBM.*

1940: Onions. This is the average of the price on January 1, 1940 — 1.50 rubles per kg — and that on January 1, 1941 — 3.00 rubles per kg. The quotations are from *MLR,* May 1940 and May 1941.

Comparability: The quality of onions priced is presumably roughly comparable in each year. The quotations relate to approximately the same period in each comparison: (1) for the 1928–37 comparison, the period is April to July; (2) for the 1937–40 comparison, the period is January.

86. Green onions

1937: Green onions (Trivanovitch; *UM*); *luk zhelenyi* (green onions) (*ST,* December 27, 1937). This price is an average of the prices on January 1, July 1, and December 27, 1937. The quotations are from *UM,* Trivanovitch, and *ST,* December 27, 1937.

1940: Green onions. This price is an average of the prices on January 1 and July 1, 1940 and January 1, 1941. The quotations are from *MLR,* May 1940; February and May 1941.

Comparability: The quality of the onions priced is presumably roughly comparable, and the price for each year is an average of the prices in the same three months.

87. Green onions (summer)

1937: Luk zhelenyi (green onions). This price was announced on July 5, 1937 in *ST* of that date. This, it is believed, was the lowest price during the year, and one in effect for several months.

1948: Luk zhelenyi s golovka (green onion with the bulb). This price was announced August 29, 1948 in *Moskovskii bol'shevik* of that date. It is assumed this was the lowest price of the year.

1952: This price is computed from the August 1948 price and the following price reduction: March 1950, other vegetables, 10%. Caution is in order with regard to this quotation (and consequently also that for 1954). Gurvits (1949) lists *luk repchatyi* (bulb onions) at 3.00 rubles per kg, while Gurvits (1953) lists *luk repchatyi* at 4.00 rubles per kg. This suggests that *onion* prices (and therefore perhaps also *green onion* prices) may have been raised between 1948 and 1952 rather than lowered.

1954: This price is computed from the 1952 price and the following price reduction: April 1953, fresh cabbage and other vegetables, 50%. The caution noted regarding the 1952 price should be taken into account here.

Comparability: The price used for each year represents, it is believed, the price at the height of the season. But, since only one quotation is available for 1948, I cannot be certain that this is the case of the 1948 price or of the 1952 and 1954 prices based on the 1948 quotation.

88. Beets (April)

See item 90.

89. Beets (January)

See item 90.

90. Beets (fall)

1937: Beets (*UM;* Trivanovitch); *svekly stolovye* (table beets) (*ST,* August 5, August 29, and December 27, 1937). The available 1937 quotations are as follows, in rubles per kilogram: January 1 and April 1 — 0.40 (*UM;* Trivanovitch); July 1 — 0.30 (*UM;* Trivanovitch); July 11 — 0.50 for *trimmed* beets (*ST,* July 11, 1937); August 5 — 0.35 (*ST,* August 5, 1937); August 29 — 0.26 (*ST,* August 29, 1937); October 1 — 0.26 (*UM*); December 27 — 0.75 for *hothouse* beets (*ST,* December 27, 1937); January 1, 1938 — 0.26 (*UM*).

In the comparison with 1928 (item 88), the price on April 1, 1937 — 0.40 ruble per kg — is used. In the comparison with 1940 (item 89), the average of the prices on January 1, 1937 and January 1, 1938 — 0.33 ruble per kg — is used. In the comparison with 1948 and subsequent years (item 90), the price established August 29, 1937 — 0.26 ruble per kg — is used. This price apparently remained in effect (except for hothouse beets) from August 29 through the end of 1937.

1928: Svekla (beets). This price is the average of the prices in state and co-operative shops in April and May, as reported in *ESBM.*

1940: Beets. This price is the average of the price on January 1, 1940 — 0.50 ruble per kg — and that on January 1, 1941 — 1.00 ruble per kg. The quotations are from *MLR,* May 1940 and May 1941.

1948: Svekla (beets). This price is the midpoint of the range — 0.80 to 1.00 ruble per kg — announced on August 29, 1948 in *Moskovskii bol'shevik* of that date.

Two Soviet sources which became available after the computations were made list *svekla* (beets) at 1.00 ruble per kg in 1947 and in 1949 (Ministerstvo prosveshcheniia RSFSR, *Sbornik materialov dlia rabotnikov uchebno-proizvo-dstvennykh i podsobnykh khoziaistv,* p. 96; Gurvits (1949). I should perhaps have used the upper limit of the August 1948 price range as the price of *grade 1* beets, rather than the midpoint of the range.

1952: This price is computed from the 1948 price and the following price reduction: March 1950, beets, 10%.

1954: Old crop beets (*New York Times,* August 15, 1954); *svekla pozdniaia, sort I* (beets, late, grade 1) (*Pravda,* August 14, 1954). This price is an average estimated for the period September through December 1954. (1) In mid-August 1954, Salisbury reported that *old crop beets* were 0.68 to 0.80 ruble per kg, depending on quality (*New York Times,* August 15, 1954). I assume the same prices remained in effect through September, that is, until the new seasonal price schedule went into effect. I use the top of the price range — 0.80 ruble per kg — as the price of *grade 1 beets*. (2) In October, the price was 0.45 ruble per kg, and in November and December, the price was 0.70 ruble per kg, according to the price schedule in *PD-14-8-54*. The prices in this schedule apply in *price zone II*, and also, it is believed, in Moscow. Moscow is in *price zone I*, but in the case of beets, there is apparently no difference between the zone I and zone II prices; this was true in 1947 at least, according to Ministerstvo prosveshcheniia RSFSR, *Sbornik materialov dlia rabotnikov uchebno-proizvodstvennykh i podsobnykh khoziaistv*, pp. 96–97.

Comparability: In each comparison of 1937 with one of the other years, the quotations relate to the same month or months. This should tend to ensure comparability with respect to seasonal fluctuations in price related to seasonal fluctuations in supply. The quotations used in the *1928–37* comparison and in the *1937–40* comparison are probably for a fairly standard grade of beet, though the designations are not detailed enough to be certain of this. With regard to the comparison between 1937 and the postwar years, the *1937* and *1954* quotations both relate to *grade 1 beets*. Although this is not indicated in the 1937 designation, the August quotation used in the comparison was announced in the Soviet press, and announced prices of this nature generally refer to *grade 1* products. As indicated above, the *1948* and *1952* quotations may be below the correct prices for *grade 1 beets*.

91. Carrots

1937: Carrots. This price is the average of the price on January 1, 1937 — 0.44 ruble per kg — and that on January 1, 1938 — 0.34 ruble per kg *(UM)*.

1940: Carrots. This price is the average of the price on January 1, 1940 — 0.50 ruble per kg — and on January 1, 1941 — 1.50 rubles per kg *(MLR, May 1940; May 1941).*

Comparability: The quotations for both years are for January and are probably for carrots of roughly comparable quality.

It should be mentioned that the price on July 1, 1940 was very high — 9.00 rubles per kg *(MLR, February 1941)*. Carrots must have been extremely scarce in the summer of 1940. The movement of the price of carrots suggests there was no such scarcity during 1937. The price on July 1, 1937 was 0.40 ruble per kg (Trivanovitch), and at the end of July was 0.60 ruble for an unspecified unit, with reductions following until mid-September *(ST, July 29, August 5, August 23, September 17, 1937)*.

92. Turnips

1937: Repy (turnips). This price is the average of the price established August 5, 1937 — 0.40 ruble per kg — and that established September 23 — 0.26 ruble per kg. The quotations are from *ST*, August 5 and September 23, 1937.

1948: Repa obreznaia (turnips, trimmed). This price is the midpoint of the range — 1.20 to 1.50 rubles per kg — announced August 29, 1948 in *Moskovskii bol'shevik* of that date.

1952: This price is computed from the 1948 price and the following price reduction: March 1950, other vegetables, 10%.

1954: This price is computed from the 1952 price and the following price reduction: April 1953, fresh cabbage and other vegetables, 50%.

Comparability: The price in each case represents, it is believed, about the seasonal low. The 1937 turnips are not designated as *trimmed;* if not trimmed, the purchaser would have obtained more edible turnips per kilogram in the postwar years than in 1937.

93. Tomatoes

1937: Pomidory (tomatoes). This price was announced August 29, 1937 in *ST* of that date. The quotation is undoubtedly for *grade 1 tomatoes*. There was a continuous decline in tomato prices from June 24, when the first hothouse tomatoes were 12.00 rubles per kg, until September 23, when tomatoes were 0.80 ruble per kg (*ST*, June 24 and September 23, 1937, and various dates between).

1948: Pomidory, sort I (tomatoes, grade 1). This price was announced August 29, 1948 in *Moskovskii bol'shevik* of that date.

1952: This price is computed from the 1948 price and the following price reduction: March 1950, other vegetables, 10%.

1954: This price is computed from the 1952 price and the following price reduction: April 1953, fresh cabbage and other vegetables, 50%.

Comparability: It is assumed that the late August price reflects about the same stage of the season in each year. If, however, the August 1948 price was the lowest price of the year (the fact that no further price reductions are known to have been announced might indicate this), then the 1937–48 price rise would be understated since tomato prices continued to decline after August in 1937.

The indicated price rise between 1937 and the postwar years is rather lower than for most foods, but this seems quite reasonable as, it is believed, the Russians have achieved considerable success in extending their tomato culture.

94. Pumpkin

1937: Tykva (pumpkin). This price is the average of the prices announced in *ST* between August 11 and September 11, 1937.

1948: Tykva (pumpkin). This price is the midpoint of the range — 0.60 to 0.80 ruble per kg — announced on August 29, 1948 in *Moskovskii bol'shevik.*

1952: This price is computed from the 1948 price and the following price reduction: March 1950, other vegetables, 10%. Application of this price reduction may be in error; the term in the decree was *ovoshchi,* while in Soviet terminology pumpkins are usually included with melons among *bakhchevye.*

1954: This price is computed from the 1952 price and the following price reduction: April 1953, fresh cabbage and other vegetables, 50%. Again, the term in the decree is *ovoshchi,* and the reduction may not be applicable to pumpkins.

Comparability: The price in each year is for about the same date and the product was presumably reasonably comparable. As indicated above, it is not clear whether the 1950 and 1953 price reductions applied to pumpkins, as I assume; if I am in error here, the 1952 and, especially, the 1954 prices used are too low.

95. Mushrooms, dried

1937: Mushrooms, dried. This price is that reported in effect on January 1, April 1, and July 1, 1937 in *UM* and Trivanovitch.

1940: Mushrooms, dried. This price is that reported for January 1, 1941 in *MLR,* May 1941.

Comparability: The products are presumably comparable. The available quotations suggest that the price of dried mushrooms does not fluctuate seasonally.

96. Mushrooms, pickled

1937: Mushrooms, pickled. This price is the average of the price on January 1, 1937 — 3.00 rubles per kg — and on January 1, 1938 — 3.50 rubles per kg. The quotations are from *UM.*

1940: Mushrooms, pickled. This price is that reported for January 1, 1941 in *MLR,* May 1941.

Comparability: The quotations are presumably for comparable products. The quotations in each case are for January so the comparison is not distorted by seasonal price fluctuations, if any.

97. Peas, canned

1937: Green peas, canned. The quotation is for January 1937, from *UM.* The peas priced are *highest grade,* it is believed. The reported price falls within the range for *highest grade peas, nos. 0, 1,* and *2* listed in a 1936 price handbook for canned goods, D. I. Kaplan (ed.), *Preiskurant otpusknykh i roznichnykh tsen na konservy* (Moscow, 1936), pp. 8–9.

1948: Peas, green, jar, highest sort. The quotation is for January 1949, from *UM.*

1952: This price is computed from the 1948 price and the following price reductions: March 1950, canned eggplant, pickles, and other canned vegetables, 20%; April 1952, canned cucumbers, peppers, green peas and tomatoes, and frozen vegetables, 20%.

1954: This price is computed from the 1952 price and the following price reduction: October 1, 1954, vegetable oil, canned vegetables, and fresh-frozen green peas, an average of 12.5% *(PD-14-8-54).* The extensive price reductions for vegetables in April 1953 apparently did not affect canned vegetables.

Comparability: The grade of canned peas priced in each year is the same, but as the number of the peas priced (presumably relating to the size of the peas) is not known for any year, there is some leeway for differences in quality. There was a 25% price differential between *no. 2 peas, highest grade* and *no. 0 peas, highest grade* in 1936, according to D. I. Kaplan, pp. 8–9.

98. Apples, fresh

1937: Apples. This is the average of the prices reported for January 1, April 1, and October 1, 1937, and January 1, 1938 in *UM* and Trivanovitch. A comparison of the observed quotation for October with prices of various types of apples announced in *ST* between July and September 1937 suggests that the prices used in this study are probably for apples of the so-called *group I. Group I* apples are the better quality Western European types of apples, according to Petrov, pp. 33–34.

1948: Iabloki 1 gruppa "Kandil," I sort (apples, group 1, "Kandil," grade 1). This price is the midpoint of the seasonal price range — 16.00 to 25.00 rubles per kg — established in December 1947 *(PD-14-12-47).* The midpoint of this range is clearly only a rough approximation to an annual average price, but not enough data are available to permit a more refined computation.

1952: This price is computed from the 1948 price and the following price reductions: March 1950, apples, 20%; April 1952, apples, 20%.

1954: Iabloki 1 gruppa, I sort (apples, group 1, grade 1). This is an annual average price estimated as follows: (1) The decree of August 14, 1954 establishes a seasonal price schedule for apples in zone II. A seasonal price schedule for zone III, which includes Moscow, is estimated from the zone II schedule and other data noted below. The seasonal schedules, in rubles per kilogram, for *group 1 apples* are as follows:

	Zone II	Zone III (estimated)
To October 15	3.90	5.10
October 15 to November 30	6.00	7.90
December 1 to January 31	6.50	8.50
From February 1	7.00	9.15

(2) The new low-season price in zone II corresponds to that computed from the low-season zone II price established in December 1947 — 12.00 rubles per kg — and the subsequent reductions in apple prices. These reductions were: March 1950, 20%; April 1952, 20%; April 1953, 50%. Applying these reductions to the low-season zone III price established in December 1947 — 16.00 rubles per kg — I compute a 1954 low-season price of 5.10 rubles per kg for zone III. I assume this was the low-season price established for zone III in August 1954. I assume further, though perhaps erroneously, that this price was in effect from April 1 through October 15, 1954. The decree does not specify the date at which the low-season price was to come into effect. (3) The zone III prices for other seasons are computed from the zone III low-season price and the ratios between the low-season price and the prices for other seasons in zone II as reported in the August 1954 price decree.

Comparability: It is believed that the 1937 quotations are for *group 1 apples, grade 1* as are the postwar quotations, but I cannot be certain of this.

99. Apples, fresh (January)

1937: Apples. This price is the average of that on January 1, 1937 — 6.40 rubles per kg — and on January 1, 1938 — 8.00 rubles per kg. The quotations are from *UM*.

1940: Apples. This price is the average of that on January 1, 1940 — 6.40 rubles per kg — and on January 1, 1941 — 10.00 rubles per kg. The quotations are from *MLR*, May 1940 and May 1941.

Comparability: The designation is too brief to be certain that all quotations relate to the same types of apples. In each case, the quotations are for January, and the comparison should not be distorted by seasonal price fluctuations.

100. Grapes, fresh

1937: Grapes. The quotation is for January 1, 1937, from *UM*.

1940: Grapes. The quotation is for January 1, 1941, from *MLR*, May 1941.

Comparability: The designations are too brief to be certain that exactly the same type and quality of grapes were priced in the two years. The quotation is for January in both years, and the comparison should not be distorted by seasonal fluctuations.

101. Apricots, canned

1937: Kompot fruktovyi v steklianykh bankakh; abrikosovyi (fruit compote in glass jars, apricot). This price is the average of the 1936 prices of *first grade* and *highest grade* apricots. The quotations are from D. I. Kaplan, p. 12.

1948: Apricots, canned. This price was observed in November 1948. The price was indicated to be the state store price for one liter (rather than 1,000 gm), but since the price in cooperative stores for 1,000 gm was the same (*UM*), it is assumed the quantity actually was 1,000 gm.

1952: This price is computed from the 1948 price and the following price reductions: March 1950, canned fruit, 30%; April 1952, canned fruit, 10%.

1954: This price is computed from the 1952 price and the following price reduction: April 1953, canned fruit, 25%.

Comparability: The grade of the postwar apricots priced is not known and is therefore compared with a 1937 average of the prices of *highest grade* and *grade 1;* some quality differences are likely here, but they are probably minor.

102. Apples, dried

1937: Dried apples. This price is the annual average based on quotations for January, April, July, and October 1937 and January 1938 in *UM* and Trivanovitch.
1948: Dried apples. The quotation is for January 1949, from *UM.*
1952: This price is computed from the 1948 price and the following price reductions: March 1950, dried fruits, 20%; April 1952, dried fruits, 20%.
1954: This price is computed from the 1952 price and the following price reduction: April 1953, dried fruits, 20%.
Comparability: Minor quality differences are possible here.

103. Prunes, dried

1937: Sukhofrukty; chernosliv sochinskii (dried fruits; prunes, Sochi). The quotation is for 1936, from *SRTS-M-36,* p. 125. Although the quotations in this source are applicable to Moscow Oblast excluding Moscow city, the same price is quoted for *dried prunes* in Moscow in April and July 1937 (Trivanovitch). A lower price (8.40 rubles per kg) is cited for *dried prunes* in January 1937 in *UM,* but this apparently relates to a lower quality prune, listed in *SRTS-M-36* at 8.40 rubles per kg.
1940: Dried prunes. The quotation is for January 1, 1941, from *MLR,* May 1941.
1948: Prunes, Sochi. The quotation is for January 1949, from *UM.*
1952: This price is computed from the 1948 price and the following price reductions: March 1950, dried fruits, 20%; April 1952, dried fruits, 20%. A price within 10 kopeks of the computed price was observed in the summer of 1952 for *prunes, 1 sort (UMA).*
1954: This price is computed from the 1952 price and the following price reduction: April 1953, dried fruits, 20%.
Comparability: The 1937 and postwar quotations are clearly for *Sochi prunes* and hence are comparable. The 1940 quotation is also for *Sochi prunes,* it is believed, but it is possible that this is incorrect and that the 1940 quotation should be compared with the lower of the 1937 quotations.

104. Raisins

1937: Raisins. This price is the annual average based on quotations for January, April, July, and October 1937 and January 1938, in *UM* and Trivanovitch.
1948: Raisins. This price was observed in November 1948 (*UM*).
1952: This price is computed from the 1948 price and the following price reductions: March 1950, dried fruits, 20%; April 1952, dried fruits, 20%.
1954: This price is computed from the 1952 price and the following price reduction: April 1953, dried fruits, 20%.
Comparability: The raisins priced in each year are presumed to be at least roughly comparable.

105. Mixed dried fruit

1937: Dried mixed fruits. This price is reported to have been in effect throughout 1937 in *UM* and Trivanovitch.
1948: Dry mixed compote. This price was reported in January 1949, in *UM.*
1952: This price is computed from the 1948 price and the following price reductions: March 1950, dried fruits, 20%; April 1952, dried fruits, 20%.
1954: This price is computed from the 1952 price and the following price reduction: April 1953, dried fruits, 20%.

Comparability: There may be some quality differences, for instance in the proportions of the various fruits contained in the mixture.

106. Salt, ground

1937: Sol' molotaia, no. 2 i no. 3 (salt, ground, no. 2 and no. 3). The quotation is from *SRTS-36,* p. 243. This price was established in September 1935 (*ibid.*) and, it is believed, remained in effect at least through 1937 and probably through 1940. *UM* and *MLR* cite a constant price for *salt* from October 1935 through January 1941. The price cited in these sources, however, is 0.05 ruble per kg. This price is lower than any listed in the 1936 price handbooks, where the lowest price for Moscow is 0.09 ruble per kg for *unground salt.* It has not been possible to explain this discrepancy.

1928: The designation was at some dates, *sol' stolovaia permskaia povarennaia* (salt, table, Permian, coarse grain), and at other dates, *sol' povarennaia dlia kukhn* (salt, coarse grain, for cooking). This price was in effect in both state and cooperative shops throughout 1928, according to the monthly quotations in *ESBM.*

1940: It is assumed that the 1937 price was still in effect, in view of the evidence cited above that the price of salt remained constant between September 1935 and January 1941.

1948: This price is an average of the prices of *sol' molotaia no. 2* (salt, ground, no. 2) — 1.60 rubles per kg — and that of *sol' molotaia no. 3* (salt, ground, no. 3) — 1.40 rubles per kg, established in December 1947. It is believed that these prices remained in effect throughout 1948.

1952: This price is computed from the 1948 price and the following price reductions: March 1949, salt, 30%; March 1950, ground salt, 40%; March 1951, salt, 21%; April 1952, salt, 30%.

1954: This price is computed from the 1952 price and the following price reductions: April 1953, salt, ground, unpackaged, 20%; April 1954, salt, ground, unpackaged, 20%.

Zaleski cites the following prices as observed in September 1954: *salt, ground, no. 2* — 0.80 ruble per kg; *salt, ground, no. 3* — 0.60 ruble per kg ("Annexe," p. 109). The prices computed for this date from the December 1947 prices and the subsequent announced price reductions come to 0.24 and 0.19 ruble per kg, respectively. It is possible, then, that the announced reductions were not actually effected, or that there were intervening unannounced price increases. An alternative possibility is that the prices cited by Zaleski are for packaged salt. The December 1947 price and the computed prices for 1952 and 1954 are almost certainly for unpackaged salt. Packaging may make a great difference in salt prices; in 1936, packaged salt was about three times as expensive as unpackaged salt (*SRTS-36,* p. 243; *SRTS-M-36,* p. 124).

Comparability: 1928–37. The 1928 and 1937 designations are apparently based on different schemes of classification of salt, and it is not certain which of several 1937 salts is most comparable to the item priced in 1928. It is assumed that the lowest priced *ground salt* (nos. 2 and 3) in 1937 is the salt most commonly used and most comparable to the 1928 product. This was 0.11 ruble per kg in 1937. The 1937 range of prices was 0.09 ruble per kg for *sol' nemolotaia* (salt, unground) to 0.14 ruble per kg for *sol' vyvarochnaia, sushenaia* (salt extracted by evaporation, dried), according to *SRTS-36,* p. 243. Salts packaged in cardboard boxes or cloth bags were much more expensive, but these prices do not seem relevant here.

1937–40. The description and price are the same in visitors' reports for these two years.

1937–48–52–54. The commodity designation is the same for both 1937 and 1948.

The same designation should apply to the 1952 and 1954 quotations computed from the 1948 price. However, as noted above, there is some doubt as to whether the prices actually in effect were as low as the prices computed for 1952 and 1954.

107. Tea

1937: Chernyi baikhovyi chai, pervyi sort no. 105: Gruzinskii; Kitaiskii (black "baikhovyi" tea, grade 1: no. 105 Georgian; Chinese). The quotation is from *SRTS-36,* p. 149. This price was established in June 1935 and, it is believed, remained in effect throughout 1937. Quotations for *tea* in *UM, MLR,* and Trivanovitch fluctuate somewhat over the period 1936–38, but it seems probable that different types or grades of tea were priced at different dates.

Baikhovyi stems from the same Chinese word as the English *bohea,* but in Soviet practice relates to all tea in loose or leaf form, as distinguished from pressed or brick tea.

1928: Chai tsentrosoiuza Kitaiskii no. 1 (tea, Central Union of Consumers' Cooperatives, Chinese, no. 1). This price is that reported monthly from August 1, 1928 through January 2, 1929 in *ESBM.* Quotations in this source for earlier dates relate to another kind of tea.

1940: It is assumed that the 1937 price for *black "baikhovyi" tea, grade 1: no. 105 Georgian* or *Chinese* remained in effect throughout 1940. In July 1940 and January 1941, the price for *tea, imported* cited in *MLR* (February and May 1941) is the same as that reported in effect in October 1937 and January 1938 in *UM.* This price — 40.00 rubles per 400 gm, or 100 rubles per kg — is apparently for a higher grade of tea; but presumably the prices of other teas also remained unchanged.

1948: Chai baikhovyi gruzinskii, I sort (tea, "baikhovyi," Georgian, grade 1). The quotation is from *PD-14-12-47.*

1952: This price is computed from the 1948 price and the following price reductions: March 1950, real tea, 10%; March 1951, tea, 10%; April 1952, tea, 20%.

1954: This price is computed from the 1952 price and the following price reductions: April 1953, tea, an average of 20%; April 1954, black "baikhovyi" tea, 10%. Some of the observed prices cited in Zaleski tend to confirm that the announced reductions were put into effect ("Annexe," p. 107).

Comparability: 1928–37. Both the 1928 and 1937 quotations relate to *Chinese tea, grade 1.* The 1928 designation does not specify that the tea is *black baikhovyi tea,* but presumably it is, as is the 1937 tea priced.

1937–40. As indicated, the evidence suggests that there was no change in tea prices between 1937 and 1940, and therefore no problem of comparability arises.

1937–48–52–54. The designations for 1937 and 1948 are very close and presumably relate to an identical product. Although the 1948 designation does not specify that the tea is black, it is assumed that this is the case, since black tea is the common tea in Russia. The number "105" in the 1937 designation seems to have no particular significance: only one *grade 1 Georgian tea* is listed in *SRTS-36,* and *grade 1 Georgian tea* is listed at the same price in *SRTS-M-36,* p. 119 without mention of the number. The 1952 and 1954 quotations computed from the 1948 quotation should be equally comparable.

108. Coffee

1937: This price is the average of the 1936 prices of the following two coffees: (1) *kofe natural'nyi; v zernakh zharenyi; "Mokko" i "Gvatemalla"; vesovoi* (coffee beans, roasted; "Mokko" and "Guatemala"; sold by weight) — 53.80 rubles per kg; and (2) *kofe natural'nyi; v zernakh zharenyi;* "*Santos,*" *vesovoi* (coffee beans, roasted; "Santos"; sold by weight — 48.20 rubles per kg (*SRTS-M-36*, p. 121). The prices quoted by *MLR*, Trivanovitch, and *UM* for *coffee, roasted* or *coffee, roasted, of foreign origin* fluctuate somewhat erratically between 1936 and 1938; it is believed that different grades or types were priced at different dates.

1948: Kofe natural'nyi zharenyi v zernakh, I sort (coffee, roasted, in the bean, grade 1). This price was established in December 1947 (*PD-14-12-47*); the same price was still in effect in January 1949 (*UM*).

1952: This price is computed from the 1948 price and the following price reductions: March 1951, coffee, 10%; April 1952, coffee, 15%. In March 1950 there was an 18% reduction in the prices of tea-, coffee-, and cocoa-beverages (*chainye, kofeinye i kakao-napitki*). In Soviet usage, this expression appears to mean beverages made of substitutes for tea, coffee, and cocoa; accordingly, I assume the reduction did not apply to real coffee. The computed price — 57.40 rubles per kg — is somewhat lower than the 1952 price of 59.00 rubles per kg cited in Gurvits (1953) for *kofe natural'nyi I-go sorta* (real coffee, grade 1); but some of the observed prices cited in Zaleski are very close to the computed price ("Annexe," p. 108).

1954: This price is computed from the 1952 price and the following price reductions: April 1953, coffee, 20%; April 1954, real coffee, cocoa, coffee-, tea-, and cocoa-beverages, an average of 15%.

Comparability: All quotations are for roasted coffee beans. The 1937 price is the average for two brands, but no brand is specified for the 1948 quotation. The grade of the 1937 coffee is not specified but is presumably first grade, as is the 1948 coffee. It is assumed that the 1948 coffee was sold by weight (as was the 1937 coffee priced) rather than packaged since the price was quoted for a kilogram and not for a smaller quantity. The 1952 and 1954 quotations computed from the 1948 quotation should be equally comparable.

109. Vodka, 40°

1937: Vodka, 40°. This price is reported throughout 1937 in *UM* and Trivanovitch. The price includes the bottle and cork, it is believed.

1928: Khlebnoe vino (vodka). This price was apparently in effect for about 10 months during 1928 and can thus be considered an approximate annual average. This is the price reported in *ESBM* for the four months August 1 through November 1, 1928. The December price was somewhat higher. Prices for earlier months are not reported in *ESBM*. The *TSU* retail price index for Moscow shows alcoholic beverage prices constant for the nine months from February through October 1928 and somewhat lower in January (*Moskva i Moskovskaia guberniia 1923/24–1927/28 gg.*, p. 491). It is assumed that this means the price of vodka remained constant over this period, although the index is based on the prices of both vodka and beer (*Dvizhenie tsen*, no. 13–14, 1927, pp. 34–35; *Statisticheskoe obozrenie*, no. 8, 1929, p. 117).

1940: Vodka, 40°. This price is reported for January and July 1940 and January 1941 in *UM*.

1948: Vodka, 40-gradusnaia (vodka, 40°). Following a 20% reduction in the prices of alcoholic beverages on April 10, 1948, the price was announced at 80.00 rubles per liter in *Pravda Ukrainy*, April 11, 1948. The price prior to April 10 can be computed at 100.00 rubles per liter. The average of these two prices, weighted by the length of time each was in effect, is used. The quotation is from a Ukraine newspaper, but vodka prices are uniform for the entire USSR, according to Lasevich and Karelov, p. 7.

1952: This price is computed from the April 10, 1948 price and the following price reductions: March 1949, vodka, 28%; March 1950, vodka, 16.7%; March 1951, vodka, 10%.

1954: This price is computed from the 1952 price and the following price reduction: April 1953, vodka, 11%.

Comparability: The quotations for all years relate to 40° vodka. The 1928 designation does not include the strength, but this is probably an indication that the strength was 40°. I am informed by former Soviet citizens that the standard strength of vodka in the late twenties was (and probably still is) 40°. Presumably if a stronger vodka were priced, the strength would be noted in the source. The 1937 and 1940 quotations apparently include the cost of the bottle and cork, but the quotations for other years may not.

110. Vodka, 50°

1937: Vodka, 50° s posudoi (vodka, 50°, including bottle). The quotation is from *SkTS-M-36,* p. 127. The quotation is for 1936, but there was apparently no change in vodka prices during 1936 and 1937. *Vodka 56°* is cited in *SRTS-M-36,* p. 127, and in *UM* and Trivanovitch at the same price throughout 1936 and 1937.

1948: Vodka, 50-gradusnaia (vodka, 50°). This price is an average of the prices in effect before April 10, 1948 — 80.50 rubles per ½ liter — and after April 10, 1948 — 60.00 rubles per ½ liter. These quotations are from *Pravda Ukrainy,* April 11, 1948. In computing the average, each price is weighted by the length of time it was in effect.

1952: This price is computed from the April 10, 1948 price and the following price reductions: March 1949, vodka, 28%; March 1950, vodka, 16.7%; March 1951, vodka, 10%.

1954: This price is computed from the 1952 price and the following price reduction: April 1953, vodka, 11%.

Comparability: The quotations for all years relate to *50° vodka.* The 1937 price includes the bottle, but it is not known whether this is the case of the postwar quotations.

111. Champagne, Soviet

1937: Champagne, Soviet or *champagne.* This price is an annual average based on the following quotations: 22.00 rubles per ⅘ liter bottle on January 1, April 1, and July 1, 1937; 18.00 rubles per ⅘ liter bottle on October 1, 1937 and January 1, 1938 (*UM;* Trivanovitch).

1940: Champagne, Soviet. This price was reported in effect on January 1 and July 1, 1940 and January 1, 1941, in *UM.*

1948: Champagne, ordinary. A price of 40.00 rubles per bottle was reported in January 1949, in *UM.* Making allowance for the average reduction of 20% in alcoholic beverage prices effected April 10, 1948, the pre-April 10 price is computed at 50.00 rubles per bottle, and the average for the year at 42.75 rubles per bottle.

1952: This price is computed from the April 10, 1948 price and the following price reduction: March 1950, Soviet champagne, 16.2%. A quotation for *Soviet champagne* in a visitor's report of early 1951 confirms the computed price (*UM*), although Michel Gordey, *France-Soir,* July 2–3, 1950 cites a somewhat lower price — 30.00 rubles per bottle — in the spring of 1950.

1954: This price is computed from the 1952 price and the following price reduction: April 1953, Soviet champagne, 15%.

Comparability: The size of the bottle is not known for the postwar years so there is a possibility of error here, unless champagne comes in only one size bottle. All quotations are for Soviet champagne, but there may be some quality differences. In the 1936 wholesale price list, only one brand of champagne is listed, but there was a differential in the wholesale price of about 25%, based on the sweetness of the wine (*SRTS-36*, p. 256).

112. Red wine, "Kagor"

1937: Red wine, Soviet "Kagor" or *red wine*. This price was in effect throughout 1937, according to *UM* and Trivanovitch.

1940: Red wine, Soviet "Kagor." This price was in effect throughout 1940, according to *UM*.

Comparability: The designation is the same, and in this case the designation is specific enough to be certain of comparability.

113. White wine, "Naporeuli"

1937: White wine, "Naporeuli" or *white wine*. This price is the average of the prices reported on January 1, April 1, July 1, and October 1, 1937 and January 1, 1938, in *UM* and Trivanovitch.

1940: White wine, "Naporeuli." This price prevailed throughout 1940, according to *UM*.

Comparability: The designation is the same, and in this case it is specific enough to be certain of comparability.

114. Port wine, Soviet

1937: Oporto, Soviet, or *oporto*. This price was in effect throughout 1937, according to Trivanovitch and *UM*.

1940: Oporto, Soviet. This price was in effect throughout 1940, according to *UM*.

Comparability: The designation is the same and the wines are probably comparable.

115. Calico, no. 6

1937: Sitets nabivn. krap no. 5, nono. tkanei: 06a, 6a, 6b; obyknovennyi krashen. i nabivka; 60–62 sm. (calico, printed, group no. 5; cloth nos. 06a, 6a, 6b; ordinary dye and print; 60 to 62 cm wide). The 1936 price was 3.65 rubles per meter (*RTS-M-36*, II:5). Calico prices were reduced by 10% on June 1, 1937 (*PD-28-4-37*). The average annual 1937 price shown is computed from these data.

1928: Sitets standart no. 6, seriia no. 5 (calico, standard no. 6, group no. 5). This price — 0.38 ruble per meter — is that prevailing in state and cooperative shops between October 1, 1928 and January 1, 1929, as reported in *ESBM*. In some cases, the price quoted was 0.375 ruble per meter but the round figure of 0.38 ruble is used. It is believed that this price was in effect throughout 1928. Quotations in the same bulletin for earlier months vary between 0.37, 0.375, and 0.38 ruble per meter; the variations may reflect slight variations in the type of calico priced from month to month (the commodity designation is less precise for the earlier months) or may simply be due to inconsistencies in rounding procedure. *Sitets no. 5* (calico, no. 5) is quoted at the same price — 0.375 ruble per meter — in January, April, July, and October 1928 in *Moskva i Moskovskaia guberniia 1923/24–1927/28 gg.*, pp. 494–495.

A more complete description of the item priced, *sitets standart no. 6, krap no. 5* (calico, standard no. 6, group no. 5) in *SMG-28*, p. 654, indicates that this material was 62 cm wide.

1948: Sitets nabivn. krap D, shir. 60–62 sm., artikul 6 (calico, printed, group D, 60 to 62 cm wide, article no. 6). The quotation is from *PD-14-12-47*.

1952: This price is computed from the 1948 price and the following price reduction: March 1950, cotton fabrics, 15%. The computed price is confirmed by an observed quotation in early 1953 (*UMA*).

1954: This price is computed from the 1952 price and the following price reductions: April 1953, calico, 15%; April 1954, calico, 15%.

Comparability: The 1928 *standard no. 6* and the 1948 *article no. 6* are presumably close equivalents of the 1937 *cloth nos. 06a, 6a,* and *6b.* Printed calico is divided into five groups (*krapy*) according to the complexity of the design (Andrusevich, p. 94). The group number is "5" in both the 1928 and 1937 designations. The group "D" in the 1948 designation is presumably the same thing, "D" being the fifth letter in the Russian alphabet. The 1937 quotation is for calico of *ordinary dye and print;* it is assumed that this is the case of the 1928 and postwar quotations also. In all cases, the quotation is for calico of the same width. The quotations for each year, then, appear to be for the same or very closely comparable materials.

116. Calico

1937: Calico. The price shown is an annual average based on the price of 3.75 rubles observed in January and April, and the price of 3.32 rubles per meter observed in July (*UM*; Trivanovitch). The latter price, it is assumed, was in effect from June 1, when a 10% reduction in price was effected, through the end of the year.

1940: Calico. The price shown is an average of the price observed in July 1939 — 3.50 rubles per meter — and that observed in July 1940 and January 1941 — 7.50 rubles per meter. The quotations are from *MLR,* November 1939; February and May 1941.

Comparability: The designation is very brief, and I cannot be certain of comparability. The range of calico prices in 1936 was rather wide, from 2.70 to 4.70 rubles per meter (*RTS-M-36,* II:5–7); however, as the 1937 price is near the middle of the range, the maximum possible error is probably not over 30%.

117. Sateen

1937: Satin nabivn. i gl. krash. temnyi; nono. 72 i 572; 61.5–63.5 sm.; obyknovennyi krashen i nabivka (sateen, printed and plain colors, dark; nos. 72 and 572; 61.5 to 63.5 cm; ordinary dye and print). *RTS-M-36,* II:10 lists this at 5.35 rubles per meter. There was a 7% reduction in sateen prices on June 1, 1937.

1928: Satin gladko-krashen, temn. st. 72 (sateen, plain colors, dark, standard no. 72). This price is cited in *ESBM* for the period August 1928 through December 1929. It is assumed the same price was in effect during the first part of the year as well. This material was *61 centimeters wide,* according to the description given in *SMG-28,* p. 656.

Comparability: The quotations for both years appear to be for the same sateen.

118. Sateen, mercerized

1937: The quotation represents the midpoint of the range of prices for *cotton sateen* (*satin*) specifically identified as being *mercerized* (*merserizovannyi*) and as being *60 to 63 centimeters wide,* and *special dye or print* (*prochnoe krashen. i nabivka*). The 1936 range for all items falling under this general description in *RTS-M-36,* II:10–11, 32, was 6.00 to 7.40 rubles per meter. The midpoint of this range — 6.70 rubles per meter — is taken as the price in effect until June 1, 1937, when sateen prices were reduced by 7%.

1948: Satin "ekstra" merserizovannyi; shir. 60–63 sm., artikul 144 (sateen, "extra" mercerized, 60 to 63 cm wide; article no. 144). The quotation is from *PD-14-12-47*.

1952: This price is computed from the 1948 price and the following price reduction: March 1950, cotton fabrics, 15%.

1954: This price is computed from the 1952 price and the following price reductions: April 1953, sateen, 15%; April 1954, calico, sateen, and other cotton fabrics, on the average, 15%.

Comparability: The quotations for all years are for essentially comparable sateens, though there may be some minor quality differences between the 1937 and the postwar products. It is assumed that the postwar fabric, described in the 1948 designation as "extra," is more comparable to the 1937 *special dye or print* than to the *ordinary dye or print*.

119. Satinette

1937: Satinette. The quotation was observed in January and April 1937 (*UM*; Trivanovitch).

1940: Satinette. The price shown is the average of that observed in July 1939 — 7.50 rubles per meter — and that observed in July 1940 and January 1941 — 14.50 rubles per meter. The quotations are from *MLR*, November 1939; February and May 1941.

Comparability: The designation is brief and errors of comparability may be involved here.

120. Sheeting, cotton, no. 49

1937: Biaz' prostyn., otbel'n., no. 49a, 125–128 sm. (muslin sheeting, bleached, no. 49a, 125 to 128 cm). The price shown is the 1937 average annual price, computed from the 1936 quotation of 7.50 rubles per meter, in *RTS-M-36*, II:8, and the 5% reduction in prices of bleached muslin on June 1, 1937.

1928: Biaz' otbel'n. prostaia, standart no. 49, 130 sm. (muslin, bleached, plain, standard no. 49, 130 cm). The wholesale price of this material was 0.81 ruble per meter, according to *SMG-28*, p. 655. The retail price shown in the table is computed on the assumption that the retail trade markup in Moscow was 11%. The maximum permissible retail margin for textiles sold in state and cooperative shops in urban areas of Moscow Province was established at 13.5% of the wholesale price in February 1927 (*SMG-28*, p. 16). The actual margin in effect in Moscow city during 1928 seems to have been about 11%. All but one of the ten or so textile items for which both the wholesale prices and the Moscow retail prices are available indicate a margin of 10 to 12% between the wholesale and the retail price.

The 1928 fabric is probably a *sheeting*, although not specifically identified as such, for materials of this type in wide widths are considered as sheeting (Andrusevich, p. 99).

Comparability: The 1928 *biaz' no. 49* is presumably about the same quality as the 1937 *biaz' no. 49a*, and the two materials are approximately the same width.

121. Sheeting, cotton

1937: Biaz' prostyn. otbel'n., no. 50a, 149–153 sm. (muslin sheeting, bleached, no. 50a, 149 to 153 cm). This 1937 average price is computed from the 1936 quotation of 10.00 rubles per meter in *RTS-M-36*, II:8, and the 5% reduction in prices of bleached muslin on June 1, 1937.

1948: Sheeting, cotton, about 60 inches wide, medium heavy, stock no. 59. A visitor's report cites this at 29.40 rubles per meter in June 1950 (*UM*). The 1948 price is computed from this 1950 price and the following price reduction: March 1950, cotton fabrics, 15%.

1952: Sheeting, cotton, about 60 inches wide, medium heavy, stock no. 59. The price shown is that observed in June 1950 (*UM*). No further reductions in cotton textile prices were effected until April 1953.

1954: This price is computed from the 1952 price and the following price reductions: April 1953, calico, sateen, muslin, and other cotton fabrics, 15%; April 1954, calico, sateen, and other cotton fabrics, on the average 15%. (Note that here the "other" excludes some fabrics specifically mentioned separately in the decree.)

Comparability: The same width sheeting is compared — 60 inches equals about 152 centimeters. There may be some quality differences, but the range of qualities of cotton sheeting produced may not be great.

122. Madapolam

1937: Madapolam otb., no. 9a, 75–78 sm. (madapolam, bleached, no. 9a, 75 to 78 cm). This 1937 average price is computed from the 1936 quotation of 4.00 rubles per meter in *RTS-M-36*, II:9, and the 8% reduction in the price of madapolam on June 1, 1937.

1928: Madapolam otbel'n., st. 9 (madapolam, bleached, standard no. 9). The quotation is for the months August 1928 through January 1929 as reported in *ESBM*. It is believed this price was in effect for the entire year 1928. This material was *78 centimeters wide,* according to *SMG-28*, p. 655.

Comparability: The 1928 madapolam *no. 9* is presumably the same or very close to the 1937 madapolam *no. 9a,* and the materials are about the same width.

123. Moleskin

1937: Moleskin, gl. krashen., obyknovenni krashen., no. 220a, 61–63 sm. (moleskin, plain colored, ordinary dye, no. 220a, 61 to 63 cm). The quotation is for 1936 from *RTS-M-36*, II:16. There was apparently no change in the price of moleskin during 1937.

1928: Moleskin (moleskin). The quotation is that reported in *ESBM* for April, May, and July 1928 and January 1929. It is believed the same price was in effect throughout 1928.

The item for which *ESBM* reports the retail price is apparently *moleskin, gladko-krashen., standart 220, 62 sm.* (moleskin, plain colored, standard no. 220, 62 cm). This item is listed in *SMG-28*, p. 660, at a wholesale price of 0.585 ruble per meter. The retail price cited in *ESBM* — 0.65 ruble per meter — would mean a retail margin of about 11%, which appears to be consistent with other data on the size of the retail margin in Moscow. (See item 120.)

Comparability: The 1928 *moleskin standard no. 220* is presumably the same as, or very close to, the 1937 *moleskin no. 220a,* and the materials seem comparable in other respects.

124. Woolen, part wool broadcloth

1937: Tonko-sukonye tkani: sukno b/o A, 136 sm. (fine woolen fabrics: broadcloth, cotton warp A, 136 cm). The quotation is from *RTS-M-36*, II:56. This price was in effect throughout 1937, it is believed.

1928: Tonkosukonnye izdeliia, polusherstianye, na bumazhnoi osnove: sukno A, 133 sm. (fine woolen fabrics, part wool, cotton warp, broadcloth A, 133 cm). The price shown is computed from the wholesale price — 3.50 rubles per meter — cited in *SMG-28*, p. 670, and a retail margin of 11%. As indicated above, this was apparently the retail margin in effect in Moscow during 1928 for textiles.

Comparability: The 1928 and 1937 designations are the same, except that the 1937 material is a few centimeters wider.

125. Woolen, pure wool plush velour

1937: Tonkosukonnye tkani: drap veliur ch./sh., 142 sm. (fine woolen fabrics: plush velour, pure wool, 142 cm). The quotation is from *RTS-M-36*, II:56. The same price was in effect throughout 1937, it is believed.

1928: Tonkosukonnye izdeliia, chisto-sherstianye: drap veliur melanzh, 142 sm. (fine woolen fabrics, pure wool: plush velour, mixture, 142 cm). The price shown is computed by adding 11% to the wholesale price — 15.00 rubles per meter — cited in *SMG-28*, p. 671. As indicated above, it is believed that the retail margin for textiles in Moscow was 11%. The term *melanzh* (mixture) apparently means that the cloth is made of yarn formed by blending previously dyed fibers (Andrusevich, p. 89).

Comparability: The 1928 and 1937 designations are almost identical. In both years, the fabric priced was the most expensive listed in the official price handbooks (along with a few others at the same prices).

126. Woolen, pure wool "Boston"

1937: Tonko-sukonye tkani; kostiumnye: triko Boston ch/sh, 135 sm. (fine woolen fabrics; suitings: tricot Boston, pure wool, 135 cm). The quotation is from *RTS-M-36*, II:55. The price was established in July 1936, and apparently remained in effect through 1937.

1948: Boston chistosherstianoi art. no. 125, 136 sm. (Boston, pure wool, article 125, 136 cm). The quotation is from *PD-14-12-47*.

1952: This price is computed from the 1948 price and the following price reductions: March 1949, wool fabrics, 10%; March 1950, pure wool fine woolen fabrics, 12%.

1954: This price is computed from the 1952 price and the following price reduction: April 1953, worsted, fine and other wool and part wool fabrics, 5%.

Comparability: The 1937 fabric is listed under suit materials; the postwar Boston no. 125 is, it is known, used in coats (see item 146) but perhaps also in suits, as is Boston no. 124 (see item 142). Probably there are some differences in quality, but it is believed the fabrics are rather closely comparable. There is, however, a slight possibility of a considerable error. The only two domestically produced Bostons listed in the 1936 source are the one priced at 120 rubles per meter used in the comparison and one at 70 rubles per meter (*RTS-M-36*, II:51, 63). This lower priced fabric seems too cheap in relation to the total range of wool fabric prices for comparison with the postwar fabric priced; however, I might be in error here. Imported Bostons ranged in 1936 from 120 to 200 rubles per meter, with one at 70 rubles per meter (*RTS-M-36*, II:57–63). Prices of imported fabrics are not considered in the comparison on the grounds that it is most unlikely that the few fabrics priced in the December 1947 decree would include an imported fabric.

127. Worsted, part wool

1937: Kamvol'nye tkani; platel'nye: artikul no. 17, kl. 104 sm. (worsted fabrics; for dresses: article no. 17, checked, 104 cm). The quotation is from *RTS-M-36*, II:54. The same price was in effect throughout 1937, it is believed.

1928: Kamvol'nye izdeliia, polu-sherstianye platel'nye: 17 gladk. i ris., 104 sm. (worsted fabrics, part wool, for dresses: no. 17, plain or figured, 104 cm). The price shown is computed by adding 11% to the wholesale price — 2.00 rubles per meter — cited in *SMG-28*, p. 675.

Comparability: Although this is not indicated in the designation, the 1937 fabric is probably part wool like the 1928 fabric, since it is the lowest priced worsted dress goods listed in the 1936 price handbook. The article number and width of the 1928 and 1937 fabrics are the same.

128. Worsted, pure wool

1937: Kamvol'nye tkani; platel'nye: Rekord, 106 sm. (worsted fabrics; for dresses: "Rekord," 106 cm). The quotation is from *RTS-M-36*, II:54. This price remained in effect throughout 1937, it is believed.

1928: Tkan "Rekord" platel'n. chisto shersti (dress fabric, "Rekord" pure wool). The quotation is that reported for August 1928 through January 1929 in *ESBM*. It is assumed this price was in effect earlier in 1928 as well. The material priced is *worsted, 106 cm wide,* according to *SMG-28*, p. 675.

Comparability: These fabrics have the same brand name — "Rekord" — and are presumably entirely comparable. The 1937 designation does not indicate that the material is pure wool, but the similarity of the brand name to the 1928 pure wool fabric and the high price of this fabric compared to the price of the part wool worsted dress fabric described immediately above indicate the 1937 material is most likely pure wool.

129. Wool and cotton mixture

1937: Mixed wool and cotton cloth for trousers. The price shown is the average of that on January 1, 1937 — 65.00 rubles per meter — and that on April 1, 1937 — 70.00 rubles per meter, as reported in *UM* and Trivanovitch.

1940: Mixed wool and cotton cloth. The price shown is an average of that observed in Moscow in July 1939 — 75.00 rubles per meter (*MLR*, November 1939) — and that observed in Kuibyshev in January 1942 — 94.00 rubles per meter (*UM*). The price of 120.00 rubles per meter was reported for July 1940 and January 1941 in *MLR*, February and May 1941. This price is so much higher than the July 1939 price and also than the 1942 price that I must assume a different, and higher quality fabric was priced in July 1940 and January 1941 than at the other dates.

Comparability: The commodity designation is the same in both years but the wide fluctuations in the quotations for 1939, 1940, and 1942 suggest different qualities were priced at different dates. It is believed that the estimated 1940 price is probably for a material fairly comparable to that priced in 1937 but I cannot be sure.

130. Coarse wool baize, solid color

1937: Grubo-sukonnaia gruppa; baika pol/krashen, 142 sm. (coarse woolens group; baize, solid color, 142 cm). The price shown is a 1937 annual average computed from the following data: (1) the 1936 wholesale price of 30.00 rubles per meter (*RTS-36*, p. 14); (2) the retail margin of 4.5% effective in Moscow (*RTS-M-36*, II:53); (3) the 10% reduction in the prices of coarse woolen cloth effected on June 1, 1937.

1928: Grubosherstnye, izdeliia, chisto-sherstianye: baika I s. p/krash., 142 sm. (coarse wool fabrics, pure wool: baize, grade 1, solid color, 142 cm). The price shown is computed from the wholesale price — 5.00 rubles per meter — cited in *SMG-28*, pp. 673–674, and the 11% retail trade margin.

Comparability: These fabrics appear to be comparable. However, the 1937 baize might be only *part wool* while the 1928 material is *pure wool*. Although the 1937 item is not identified specifically as *grade 1* as is the 1928 item, the quotations in the price handbooks are generally for *grade 1* products unless otherwise noted.

131. Coarse wool baize, mixture

1937: Grubo-sukonnaia gruppa; baika melanzh, 142 sm. (coarse woolens group; baize, mixture, 142 cm). The price shown is a 1937 annual average computed from the following data: (1) the 1936 wholesale price of 37.00 rubles per meter (*RTS-36*, pp. 14–15); (2) the retail trade margin of 4.5% effective in Moscow (*RTS-M-36*, II:53); (3) the 10% reduction in the prices of coarse woolen cloth effected on June 1, 1937.

1948: Sherst' baika melanzh, shir. 142 sm., artikul 384 (wool baize, mixture, 142 cm wide, article no. 384). The quotation is from *PD-14-12-47*.

1952: This price is computed from the 1948 price and the following price reductions: March 1949, wool fabrics, 10%; March 1950, coarse woolen fabrics, 24%.

1954: This price is computed from the 1952 price and the following price reduction: April 1953, worsted, fine, and other wool and part wool fabrics, 5%.

Comparability: The quotations appear to be for the same material.

132. Sheeting, linen

1937: L'nianye tovary: polotno beloe prostynnoe, 138 sm. (linen goods: plain weave linen sheeting, white, 138 cm). The price shown is the midpoint of the 1936 range of prices for this type of material — 10.00 to 16.50 rubles per meter — cited in *RTS-M-36*, II:43. There was apparently no change in linen sheeting prices in 1937, although the prices of linen sheets and some linen fabrics were reduced by 5 to 10% in June 1937.

1928: Polotno l'nianoe beloe, 138 sm. (plain weave linen, white, 138 cm). The wholesale prices of this type of material ranged from 1.41 rubles to 2.26 rubles per meter, according to *SMG-28*, p. 680. The midpoint of the wholesale price range is increased by 11% to obtain the estimated Moscow retail price. Although the designation does not specify this, the width of the material indicates it is *sheeting* (Andrusevich, p. 99).

Comparability: The range of prices for this type and width of material was quite similar in the two years, so use of the midpoints of the 1928 and 1937 price ranges should assure fairly close comparability.

133. Sheeting, part linen

1937: Polotno beloe polul'nianoe, 136 sm., sort 9 (plain weave, white part-linen, 136 cm, grade or type 9) and *polotno beloe polul'nianoe, 140 sm., sort 16* (plain weave, white part-linen, 140 cm, grade or type 16). These fabrics are both listed at the same price, and appear to be the only white part-linen sheetings in *RTS-M-36*, II:42. Again, the width of the material indicates it is *sheeting*. There was apparently no change in the price of these fabrics during 1937, although some linen fabric prices were reduced in June 1937.

1928: Polul'nianye tkani; polotnianye prostyn. beloe, no. 9, 140 sm. (part-linen fabrics; plain weave sheeting, white, no. 9, 140 cm). The price shown is computed from the wholesale price — 1.50 rubles per meter — cited in *SMG-28*, p. 686, and the 11% retail trade margin.

1948: Sheeting, white, half-linen, excellent quality, 133 cm wide. The quotation is for November 1948 from *UM*.

1952: This price is computed from the 1948 price and the following price reduction: March 1950, linen fabrics, 15%.

1954: This price is computed from the 1952 price and the following price reduction: April 1953, linen fabrics, 8%.

Comparability: 1928–1937. These sheetings appear comparable. Although the

1928 *no. 9* sheeting is a few centimeters wider than the 1937 *no. 9* sheeting, the other 1937 sheeting at the same price is the same width as the 1928 material.

1937–48–52–54. The quotations are probably for rather closely comparable sheetings, although the postwar fabric is a few centimeters narrower than the 1937 fabric.

134. Rayon crepe de Chine

1937: Krep-de-shin; iskustven. shelk krugom (crepe de Chine, entirely of synthetic silk). All materials of this description in various widths between 88 and 104 cm are listed at the same price — 30.00 rubles per meter — in *RTS-M-36*, II:72. There was, it is believed, no change in the price of silk or synthetic silk during 1937.

1948: Synthetic crepe de Chine prints, 1 meter wide. The price shown is the midpoint of the range — 72.00 to 95.00 rubles per meter — reported for November 1948, in *UM*.

1952: This price is computed from the 1948 price and the following price reductions: March 1949, silk fabrics, 10%; March 1950, part silk and artificial silk fabrics, 12%. The March 1949 reduction is probably applicable to both synthetic and natural silk fabrics as these are generally lumped together in Soviet statistics under the heading "silk fabrics."

1954: This price is the same as the 1952 price as there were no further reductions in synthetic silk fabric prices.

Comparability: Comparability in this case can be only approximate as the range of qualities was apparently considerably wider in the postwar years than in 1937.

135. Silk crepe de Chine no. 5

1937: Chistoshelkovaia gruppa; krep-de-shin, artikul 5, 92 sm. (pure silk group; crepe de Chine, article no. 5, 92 cm). *RTS-M-36*, II:67–68, lists this item at 50.00 rubles per meter and indicates that an additional charge of 3.00 to 6.00 rubles per meter was made if the fabric was *printed.* I add the midpoint of the surcharge for printing to the price for the unprinted material. There was apparently no change in silk fabric prices during 1937.

1948: Krep-de-shin chistoshelkovyi nabivnoi v 1, 2, 3 tsveta A, shir. 92–94 sm., artikul 5 (crepe de Chine, pure silk, printed in 1, 2, or 3 colors "A," 92 to 94 cm wide, article no. 5). The quotation is from *PD-14-12-47.*

1952: This price is computed from the 1948 price and the following price reduction: March 1949, silk fabrics, 10%.

1954: This price is computed from the 1952 price and the following price reductions: April 1953, natural silk fabrics, 15%; April 1954, natural silk fabrics, on the average 10%. Prices observed in Moscow in March 1954 for *pure silk crepes de Chine* correspond quite closely to my computed price for the same period (*New York Times*, March 4, 1954).

Comparability: The quotations are for materials of the same type and width and with the same article number.

136. Silk crepe de Chine

1937: Crepe de Chine. The price shown is an annual average computed from the following quotations: January and April 1937 — 54.00 rubles per meter; July 1937 — 63.00 rubles per meter (*UM*; Trivanovitch). The high price of the material indicates it is *pure silk.*

1940: Crepe de Chine. This price was observed both in July 1939 and in January 1942 (*MLR*, November 1939; *UM*). It is assumed that this price was in effect throughout 1940 as well. Higher prices — 120.00 and 114.00 rubles per meter — are cited for January and July 1940 in *MLR*, May 1940 and February 1941; but it seems likely these were for a better quality silk.

Comparability: The designations are so brief that comparability can be only approximate. Also, there is some question about the meaning of the various quotations for 1940.

137. Shirt, cotton

1937: Shirt, cotton. The price shown is the 1937 annual average based on the following observed quotations: January and April 1937 — 40.00 rubles each; July 1937 — 38.70 rubles each. These quotations are from *UM* and Trivanovitch.

1940: Shirt, cotton. The price shown is the average of the price observed in July 1939 — 65.00 rubles each (*MLR*, November 1939) — and that observed in January 1942 — 76.00 rubles each (*UM*). I assume the price observed in January 1942 was that effected in mid-1940. Higher prices — 123.00 and 105.00 rubles — are cited for July 1940 and January 1941 in *MLR*, February and May 1941. Again it seems likely these higher prices were for a higher quality product.

Comparability: The designation is extremely brief and the series of observed prices show considerably more fluctuation over the period from late 1935 through 1942 than would be expected if the same quality item were priced at each date.

138. Shirt, cotton zephyr

1937: Sorochki muzhskie "Fantazi" s dvoinymi manzhetami, iz zefira gladko-krashennogo, pestrotkannogo, art. 133, 134, 134-a; gruppa tkanei: 213 (shirts, men's, "Fantasy" with double cuffs, of plain colored or checked zephyr, article nos. 133, 134, 134-a; cloth group: 213). This product is listed among the *higher quality garments.* The 1936 price was 44.00 rubles each, according to *NKVT, Preiskurant roznichnykh tsen na shveinye izdeliia* (Moscow, 1936), p. 37. There was a 5% reduction in the prices of higher quality men's and women's shirts and underwear (*bel'e*) on July 1, 1937.

1948: This price is computed from the 1952 price and the following price reduction: March 1950, coats, suits, dresses, linen (*bel'e* — that is, underwear and outerwear such as shirts) and other garments of cotton fabrics, 13%.

1952: This is the midpoint of the prices of the following two shirts: (1) *shirt, cotton, art. 463–212, sort 1 Fantasia, style 792, collar attached, French cuffs, bone supports in collar, colored, of zephyr 221* — 73.50 rubles, (2) *shirt, cotton, almost same, art. 465–212* — 81.50 rubles. The quotations are reported in *UMA* as in effect in Moscow prior to the price cut of April 1953.

1954: This price is computed from the 1952 price and the following price reductions: April 1953, dresses, blouses, linen (*bel'e*) and other garments of cotton fabrics, an average of 14%; April 1954, dresses, blouses, linen (*bel'e*) and other garments of cotton fabrics other than summer weight cottons, an average of 10%.

Comparability: The shirts are similar in that they are both "Fantasy" style (this means simply that the collar is attached, according to Andrusevich, p. 113) and have *French* or *double cuffs.* Also they are of comparable fabrics. The second part of the article numbers in the 1952 designation — nos. 463–212 and 465–212 — indicates that these are of fabrics in *fabric group 212;* this is very close to the fabric group of the 1937 shirt priced — *group 213.*

In Soviet practice, the first part of the article number of a garment relates to type of garment, style, et cetera, and the second part of the article number indicates the group of fabrics of which the garment is made. The fabric group is based on the price of the fabric, all fabrics of a given type (cotton, wool, et cetera) falling in the same price range being in the same group. (G. B. Gubenko, *Kontrol' kachestva shveinykh tovarov* (Kiev, 1950), p. 56; Andrusevich, pp. 108ff.; D. Ia. Zamkovskii, *Kachestvennaia priemka shveinykh izdelii* (Moscow, 1951), pp. 121–125.)

Zefir 133, one of the fabrics of the 1937 shirt, was 6.50 rubles per meter in 1936 (*RTS-M-36,* II:13). The fabrics of the postwar shirt in *fabric group 212* cost 16.55 to 17.84 rubles per meter of the same width in 1952 (Zamkovskii, p. 123). This seems in line with the rise in cotton fabric prices generally. It is believed that the system of classifying cotton fabrics into groups remained the same over the period from 1936 to the present, although there have apparently been some changes in the system of grouping wool fabrics.

As indicated, the 1937 shirt priced is listed among the *higher quality garments* (*shveinye izdeliia povyshennogo kachestva*) as distinguished from mass-produced or *lower quality garments* (*shveinye izdeliia massovogo poshiva*). Higher quality shirts at that time appear to have been about 50% more expensive than lower quality shirts of the same general description and material. Apparently the classification of garments into two general quality groups is no longer in use; at least no reference to such a distinction has been noted in postwar sources. The postwar shirt price used in the comparison is not among the lowest shirt price quotations available. Probably it is at least roughly similar to the 1937 shirt priced in general quality.

139. Cotton dress

1937: Plat'ia khlopchatobumazhnye; fason: 1-ia slozhnost'; gruppa tkani: 210 (dress, cotton; style: 1st degree of complexity; fabric group 210). The price of this dress is estimated from the price of a dress of this designation but of material in fabric group no. 212. The latter was 48.00 rubles in 1936, according to *NKVT, Preiskurant roznichnykh tsen na shveinye izdeliia,* p. 23. According to the same source, the same dress of fabrics in cloth group 213–214 was 5.00 rubles more expensive than the dress of fabrics in fabric group 212; I assume that dresses of fabrics in fabric group 210 were 5.00 rubles cheaper. This dress is listed among *higher quality garments,* but there was very little difference in price between these and the mass-produced dresses of the same fabrics when the dresses were of the simpler styles. In July 1937 there was a reduction of 7% in the prices of men's and women's garments.

1948: This price is computed from the 1952 price and the following price reduction: March 1950, coats, suits, dresses, linen, and other garments of cotton fabrics, 13%.

1952: This price is computed from the 1954 price and the following price reductions: April 1953, dresses, blouses, linen, and other garments of cotton fabrics, an average of 14%; April 1954, dresses, blouses, linen, and other garments of cotton fabrics other than summer weight cottons, an average of 10%.

1954: Woman's cotton dress, model no. 193–0210, fason (style) 206, material 309; dress hung straight from shoulders without fit and with belt to tie around at waist. The quotation is for January 1955, from *UMA.* The dress is described as cotton. The model number shows that the fabric of the dress is in *fabric group 0210.* This indicates linen fabrics in the (1951–52) price range 13.81 to 15.28 rubles per meter; however, as *cotton* fabrics in the same price range are classified as *fabric group 210* (Zamkovskii, p. 123), I assume the dress priced is of *cotton* in *fabric group 210.*

Comparability: The postwar dress hanging straight from the shoulders without fit would appear to be the *simplest style* and in this respect comparable to the 1937 dress with a style of the *first* (least) *degree of complexity.* The dresses are of comparable material also, both the postwar and prewar dresses, it is believed, being made of *cotton in fabric group 210.* However, it was necessary to estimate the 1937 price from the price of dresses of somewhat higher quality fabrics, and an error may have been made here. Also, the 1954 designation is not entirely clear as to whether the dress is of cotton or linen; however, as indicated above, it is probably of cotton in fabric group 210. Even if it is of linen in fabric group 0210, fabrics in both these groups fall within the same price range; presumably the price of a comparable dress of either fabric would be the same.

140. Cotton blouse

1937: Bluzki zhenskie khlopchato-bumazhnye; iz zefira 133: gruppa tkanei: 113; 1 slozhn. (blouses, women's cotton; of zephyr 133; cloth group 113; style of first degree of complexity). This blouse is of the common mass-produced quality and is the lowest priced blouse listed in *NKVT, Preiskurant roznichnykh tsen na shveinye izdeliia,* p. 4. It is believed the price established in 1936 was in effect throughout 1937.

1948: Soviet produced cotton blouses, lowest priced. This price was observed by Edmund Stevens in 1949 (*Christian Science Monitor,* October 27, 1949). The same price would have been in effect during 1948.

1952: This price is computed from the 1948 price and the following price reductions: March 1950, coats, suits, dresses, linen, and other garments of cotton fabrics, 13%.

1954: This price is computed from the 1952 price and the following price reductions: April 1953, dresses, blouses, linen, and other garments of cotton fabrics, an average of 14%; April 1954, an assumed reduction of 12.5%. As I do not know whether the material of the blouse priced is summer weight, I take the average of the 15% reduction for dresses, blouses, et cetera, of summer weight cotton dress fabrics and the 10% reduction for dresses, blouses, et cetera, of other cotton fabrics.

Comparability: As indicated in the 1937 and 1948 descriptions, the blouse in each case is the lowest priced one for which any quotation was found. The 1948 designation is meager, but the blouses are probably roughly comparable in quality.

141. Trousers, part wool

1937: Bruiki sherstianye muzhskie s manzhetami, iz kamvol'noi tkani 747, gruppa tkani 16 (trousers, wool, men's, with cuffs, of worsted no. 747, cloth group no. 16). This item is listed among the mass-produced garments (*shveinye izdeliia massovogo poshiva*). The quotation is from *NKVT, Preiskurant roznichnykh tsen na shveinye izdeliia,* p. 3. The price was established in July 1936 and, it is believed, was not changed during 1937.

1928: Bruiki iz sukna b/O s. A (trousers of cotton-warp broadcloth, grade A). The price shown is the average of the price in state shops — 7.00 rubles per pair — and the price in cooperative shops — 7.78 rubles per pair — as reported for August 1928 through January 1929 in *ESBM.* It is assumed the prices were the same throughout 1928.

Comparability: The basis for comparison is the similarity of the 1936 prices of the fabrics of which the trousers are made. In 1936, the retail price of the fabric of the 1937 trousers — *worsted no. 747* — was the same as the price of *part-wool broadcloth A* (*RTS-M-36,* II:54–56); and, as indicated, the 1928 trousers were made of *cotton-warp broadcloth A.*

It seems most likely that the 1928 trousers are comparable to the *mass-produced quality* 1937 trousers priced, which were 75.00 rubles a pair rather than to the *higher quality* trousers of the same material, which were 115.00 rubles a pair (*NKVT, Preiskurant roznichnykh tsen na shveinye izdeliia,* p. 11); but this may be in error.

142. Suit, wool, fabric group 46

1937: Kostiumy muzhskie sherstianye na khlopchatobumazhnoi podkladke, dvoiki (pidzhak i bruiki); fasony: 1-ia, 2-ia, 3-ia i 4-ia slozhnost', odnobortnyi i dvuknbortnyi (men's suits, wool with cotton lining, two-piece (coat and trousers); styles: 1st, 2d, 3d, and 4th degrees of complexity, single-breasted and double-breasted). Suits of this description of *triko kamvol'noe* (worsted tricot) *nos. 1090* and *1238, fabric group no. 37–40* were 355.00 rubles each; and the same suits but of *koverkot* (covertcloth) *no. 975, fabric group no. 51* were 460.00 rubles each in 1936, according to *NKVT, Preiskurant roznichnykh tsen na shveinye izdeliia,* p. 10. I take the approximate average of the prices of these two suits — 410 rubles each — to represent the price of suits of fabrics in *fabric group 46.* These suits are listed among the *higher quality garments.* These were about 65% more expensive than *mass-produced suits* of the same fabrics. There was a 7% reduction in the prices of higher quality men's and women's garments on July 1, 1937.

1948: Kostium muzhskoi sherstianoi dvoika, odnobortnyi, iz bostona 124, art. 12–46 (man's suit, wool, two-piece, single-breasted, of Boston 124, article no. 12–46). The quotation is from *PD-14-12-47.*

1952: This price is computed from the 1948 price and the following price reductions: March 1949, coats, suits, dresses, and other garments of wool fabrics, 12%; March 1950, coats, suits, dresses, and other garments of worsted fabrics and pure wool fine fabrics, 10%.

1954: This price is the same as the 1952 price as there have been no reductions in wool suit prices since March 1950.

Comparability: The basis for comparison here is the similarity of the group number of the fabrics of which the suits are made — *fabric group 46.* This is indicated in the 1948 designation by the second part of the article number — 12–46. On this ground, and also in view of the relative position of the prices of these suits in relation to the total range of suit prices in each year, it is believed that the suits priced are fairly closely comparable. However, there are possibilities of substantial errors. (1) There were apparently some changes in the system of classifying wool fabrics into fabric groups between 1936 and 1948. I do not know the nature of these changes as I have no details on the system prevailing in 1936. Obviously if the changes were substantial, the fabric group number is not a sound basis for comparison. In 1936, the fabrics in *group 46* must have been about 70 rubles per meter; those of the suits priced designated as being in *group 37–40* were 60 rubles per meter and those in *group 51* were 80 rubles per meter (*RTS-M-36,* II:54–55). In 1952, fabrics in *group 46* were 358 to 473 rubles per meter (Zamkovskii, p. 121). This is a considerably greater rise in price than appears to have been true of textiles generally. If changes in the fabric group numbering system were substantial and affected the group in question, I may on this ground overstate the price rise by up to 50%.

(2) The 1937 suit priced is a *higher quality suit,* and these were more expensive than *mass produced suits* of the same fabrics, generally by around 60%. The 1948 suit priced may be more comparable to the 1936 *mass-produced* quality than to the *higher quality* suits: (a) The fact that this suit is listed in the price decree of December 1947 suggests it is the more commonly consumed quality of pure wool suit rather than a specially high quality; (b) *A two-piece, single-breasted suit of Boston 125* (probably very similar to the Boston 124 of the 1948 suit used in

the comparison) is reported to have been 1654.50 rubles in 1954 (*UMA*), or about 50% more expensive than the suit priced in the comparison. On grounds of quality of construction, then, I may understate the price rise by as much as 50%. Although substantial errors are possible, they are of an offsetting nature and, on balance, the suits priced are probably reasonably comparable.

143. Suit, wool

1937: Suit, men's, Soviet wool cloth or *men's suit of Soviet cloth.* The quotation is for January and April 1937, from *UM* and Trivanovitch.

1940: Suit, men's, Soviet wool cloth. The price shown — 900 rubles — is reported to have been in effect in Moscow in July 1939 (*MLR*, November 1939) and in Kuibyshev in January 1942 (*UM*). It is assumed that the same price was in effect throughout 1940. The item was not available in Moscow in July 1940 and is reported to have been 1,130 rubles in Moscow in January 1941 (*UM; MLR,* May 1941). I assume that this latter quotation actually represents a somewhat better quality suit, or perhaps includes an extra charge for a central Moscow store, though this may be in error.

Comparability: The sources of both the 1937 and 1940 quotations distinguish this suit from both a lower and a higher quality suit, so the likelihood of the quotations being for a comparable quality garment is greater than is the case for many observed quotations. This middle-priced suit was chosen for the comparison as the quotations show less erratic fluctuations over the years than those for the cheaper and more expensive suits. Still, there is margin for error, and also some uncertainty about the course of suit prices during 1940.

144. Overcoat, common quality

1937: Overcoat, common quality. The price shown is the annual average based on the following observed prices: January and April — 300 rubles; July — 334.50 rubles. The quotations are from *UM* and Trivanovitch.

1940: Overcoat, common quality. The price shown — 460 rubles — was observed in July 1939 (*MLR*, November 1939). Inasmuch as a very similar price — 450 rubles — was reported in Kuibyshev in January 1942 (*UM*), I assume the July 1939 price was in effect throughout 1940. Considerably higher prices are reported for July 1940 — 999.20 rubles — and January 1941 — 725.00 rubles — in *MLR,* February and May 1941; again I assume that these latter quotations are for higher quality coats, though this may be in error.

Comparability: The sources of the quotations for both years distinguish this coat from two better quality coats, and this should increase the chances that the quotations are actually for comparable quality coats. However, the quotations for all three coats priced in the sources show unusually erratic behavior and comparability is somewhat questionable.

145. Overcoat, women's

1937: This price is the midpoint of the range of prices for *pal'to sherstianoe, zhenskoe, iz triko kamvol'nye nono. 747, 1322, 1038, 757, 977, 1189, 1067* (coat, wool, women's, of worsted tricot nos. 747, 1322, 1038, 757, 977, 1189, 1067). The least expensive of these coats is described as *pal'to sherstianoe letnee, na polushelkovoi podkladke do niza, fasony 1-ia i 2-ia slozhnost'; triko kamvol'noe art. 747, 1322; gruppa tkani 25–28* (coat, wool, summer, full-length part-silk lining, styles of first and second complexity; worsted tricot nos. 747, 1322, cloth group 25–28). The most expensive is described as *pal'to zimnee zhenskoe na polushelkovoi podkladke s vatoi, fason 3-ia i 4-ia slozhnost'; triko kamvol'noe art. 757, 977, 1069, 1067, 1189, 1038; gruppa tkani 29–32* (coat, winter, women's, part-silk lining with padding, styles of 3d and 4th complexity; worsted tricot nos. 757, 977, 1069, 1067, 1189, 1038; cloth group 29–32). The quotations are for coats classified as *higher quality garments*.

The 1936 range of prices for the coats described above was 285.00 to 365.00 rubles each (*NKVT, Preiskurant roznichnykh tsen na shveinye izdeliia,* pp. 11–14). The midpoint of this range — 325.00 rubles — is reduced to 314.00 rubles to take account of the 7% reduction in the prices of ready-made higher quality garments effected July 1, 1937.

1948: Woman's coat, "Cheviot." The price was 732.00 rubles shortly after the March 1949 reduction of 12% in the prices of coats, suits, dresses, and other garments of wool fabrics (*UM*). The 1948 price is computed from the 1949 price and the March 1949 reduction.

1952: This price is computed from the 1949 price and the following price reduction: March 1950, coats, suits, dresses, and other garments of part wool fine woolen fabrics, 20%.

1954: This price is the same as the 1952 price as there were no further reductions in prices of wool coats.

Comparability: The basis for comparison here is the similarity of the 1936 prices of the fabrics of which the coats priced are made. *Cheviots (shevioty),* the fabric of the 1948 coat, ranged from 30.00 to 50.00 rubles per meter in 1936, while the *worsted tricots* of which the coats priced for 1937 are made ranged from 35.00 to 55.00 rubles per meter (*RTS-M-36,* II:54–55, 59, 61). It might be mentioned that most of the cheviots listed in this source are made on a cotton warp; this is probably true also of the fabrics of the 1937 coats priced, the fiber content of which is not indicated.

The designation of the coat priced for 1948 and subsequent years contains no details beyond the type of material, and the quotations can be only roughly comparable. Even for coats of cheviot, there is apparently a wide price range. Gurvits (1953) cites the following 1952 prices for *pal'to zimnee zhenskoe* (coat, winter, women's): (1) *iz sheviota progress* (of cheviot "Progress") 268.00 rubles; (2) *iz sheviota ekstra* (of cheviot "Extra") 616.00 rubles; and (3) *iz sheviota Moskovskogo G. 62* (of cheviot "Moscow G. 62") 607.00 rubles. The *cheviot "Progress"* was 35.00 rubles per meter in 1936 (*RTS-M-36,* II:55), that is, at the low end of the cheviot price range; but the other cheviots are not listed in the 1936 price book. My computed price — 586.00 rubles — is considerably higher than the first item cited in Gurvits (1953), but fairly close to his other two quotations.

146. Overcoat, better

1937: Pal'to zimnee zhenskoe, na polushelkovoi podkladke s vatoi, iz fule nord chernoe, gruppa tkani 76 (winter coat, woman's, part-silk lining with padding, of black northern "fule," fabric group 76). Coats of this description of styles of the 1st and 2d degree of complexity were 585 rubles each and of styles of the 3d and 4th degrees of complexity were 610 rubles each in 1936, according to *NKVT, Preiskurant roznichnykh tsen na shveinye izdeliia,* p. 12. The coats are listed as *higher quality* garments. The 1937 price is computed from the midpoint of this price range and the reduction of 7% in the prices of men's and women's garments effected July 1, 1937.

1948: Woman's overcoat, "Boston." This is reported to have been 1,476 rubles after the March 1949 price reduction, in *UM.* The 1948 price is computed from this quotation and the following price reduction: March 1949, coats, suits, dresses, and other garments of wool fabrics, 12%.

1952: This price is computed from the 1949 price cited above and the following price reduction: March 1950, coats, suits, dresses, and other garments of wool worsted and pure wool fine fabrics, 10%.

1954: This price is the same as the 1952 price as there were no further reductions in the prices of wool coats. The computed price — 1,328 rubles — is very close to that quoted in Gurvits (1953) for *pal'to zhenskoe zimnee iz Bostona 125* (coat, women's, winter, of Boston 125) — 1,283 rubles.

Comparability: The basis for comparison in this case is the fabric of the coats. The fabric of the 1937 coats was 130.00 rubles per meter in 1936 (*RTS-M-36*, II:56). This is the closest to the price of *Boston,* which was 120 rubles per meter (see item 126), of any of the fabrics of coats for which quotations are available. The 1948 designation indicates the coat was of *Boston* and the Gurvits (1953) quotation for 1952 indicates this was probably *Boston 125* or a closely comparable Boston. Under item 126 I argue that the 1936 *Boston* at 120.00 rubles is comparable to the postwar *Boston 125;* however, see also the doubts expressed there. If this is correct, the coats priced should be rather closely comparable with regard to fabric. This may, however, be in error. The 1936 coat fabric is in fabric group 76 but the *Boston* of the postwar coat is in a fabric group between no. 45 and no. 48. This can be deduced from Zamkovskii and the article numbers of various garments made of Boston. As indicated above, there have been some changes in the fabric group numbering system. But if these changes were not very significant, it is possible that my comparison here understates the price rise of the coat on the grounds of the fabric.

The postwar quotation is among the highest available for women's winter coats without fur and likely it is comparable to the 1936 *higher quality* coats priced. There may be differences in style, lining, and other features.

147. Blouse, silk

1937: Bluzki shelkovye, gruppa tkanei 517–520 (blouses, silk, cloth groups 517 to 520). The 1936 price range was 69.00 to 99.00 rubles each, the difference depending on the complexity of the pattern (*NKVT, Preiskurant roznichnykh tsen na shveinye izdeliia,* pp. 32–34). The midpoint of these prices — 84.00 rubles — is reduced to 81.00 rubles to account for the 7% reduction in prices of higher quality men's and women's garments of July 1, 1937.

1948: Woman's silk blouse no. 118/518. This price was observed in January 1949 (*UM*).

1952: This price is computed from the 1948 price and the following price reduction: March 1949, dresses, shirts, blouses, and other garments of silk fabrics, 15%.

1954: This price is computed from the 1952 price and the following price reductions: April 1953, dresses, blouses, and other garments of natural silk fabrics, 12%; April 1954, dresses, blouses, linen (*bel'e*), and other garments of natural silk fabrics, on the average 7%.

Comparability: The second part of the 1948 garment number — *118/518* — indicates that it is made of group "518" material; this falls within the range of cloth groups of the 1937 blouses priced — 517 to 520. Thus, unless there has been a change in the numbering system, the blouses compared are made of the same quality material. The complexity of the style of the blouse priced for 1948 and subsequent years is not known; the 1936 average price used is the midpoint of the prices for blouses of the first and the fourth degrees of complexity.

148. Necktie, rayon

1937: Necktie, rayon. The price shown is an annual average based on the quotation of 15.00 rubles each in January and April, and 14.10 rubles each in July 1937 (*UM;* Trivanovitch).

1940: Necktie, rayon. The price shown was observed in July 1939, July 1940, and January 1941, according to *MLR,* November 1939; February and May 1941.

Comparability: The designation is brief, and the quotations may be for only roughly comparable ties.

149. Hat, felt

1937: Hat, felt. The price shown is an annual average based on the quotations of 45.00 rubles in January and April and 40.00 rubles in July 1937 (*UM;* Trivanovitch).

1940: Hat, felt. The price shown is an average of the price of 40.00 rubles observed in July 1939 and assumed to be in effect for the first half of 1940, and the price of 44.00 rubles observed in July 1940 and January 1941 (*MLR,* November 1939; February and May 1941).

1948: Men's hats, felt. The price shown is the midpoint of the range of prices — 100.00 to 150.00 rubles — reported for November 1948, in *UM.*

1952: This price is computed from the 1948 price and the following price reductions: March 1949, headgear (hats and caps), 15%; March 1950, felt, beaver and wool hats, berets and caps (*kolpaki*), 10%.

1954: This price is computed from the 1952 price and the following price reduction: April 1953, hats, berets, and caps, 15%.

Comparability: The designations are very brief, but the hats priced are probably roughly comparable.

150. Hat, fur

1937: Fur cap, astrakhan. This price was observed in January, April, and July 1937 (*UM;* Trivanovitch).

1940: Fur cap, astrakhan. The quotation is for January 1942, from *UM.* A much higher price — 505 rubles — is cited for January 1941 in *MLR,* May 1941. However, inasmuch as the 1942 price is the same as the 1937 price, it is assumed that the same price was in effect throughout 1940 and that the January 1941 quotation is not for a comparable hat.

1948: The price shown is the average of the following two quotations for November 1948, from *UM: fur hat with flaps, standard caracul* (1) *black* — 600.00 rubles; (2) *dark grey and rust brown, best quality* — 850.00 rubles.

1952: This price is computed from the 1948 price and the following price reductions: March 1949, fur, 10%; March 1950, fur collars and caps, 10%.

1954: This price is computed from the 1952 price and the following price reduction: April 1953, fur goods and skins, 7%. The computed price — 546.00 rubles — is considerably higher than the price cited by Clifton Daniel for the *smartest Persian lamb shapka* — 429.00 rubles ("How To Dress for the Russians," *New York Times Magazine,* August 28, 1955, p. 72). The difference may be the result of the difference in the fur or other qualities of the hats priced; and possibly the price reductions for fur hats were larger than the average reductions for fur products.

Comparability: 1937–40. It is assumed that the hat priced in January 1942 is comparable to the hat priced in 1937; however, it may be that the higher price reported for January 1941 is actually for a hat more closely comparable to that priced in 1937. If so, the 1940 price is very much too low.

1937–48–52–54. The 1948 hat is described as *caracul,* but probably *karakul* is meant. *Karakul* is the same as *astrakhan,* the fur of the 1937 hat. The color and quality of the hat priced for 1937 is not known; hence it is compared with the average of the prices of the two hats priced for 1948 and subsequent years.

151. Stockings, cotton

1937: Chulki zhenskie, khl.-bum., artikul 8 (stockings, women's, cotton, article no. 8). The price shown is computed from the wholesale price of 1.65 rubles per pair and the retail trade markup for Moscow of 6.5% of the wholesale price (*RTS-36,* pp. 17, 34). The wholesale price is cited also in Moskovskii oblastnoi otdel vnutrennei torgovli, *Preiskurant roznichnykh tsen na trikotazhnye izdeliia po Moskovskoi oblasti* (Moscow, 1936), p. 29, and in *Preiskuranty snizhennykh s 1 iiulia 1937 g. otpusknykh tsen na promyshlennye tovary* (Kursk, June 1937), p. 3. The fact that the wholesale price in the latter source is still listed at the 1936 price is taken to indicate there was no reduction in the retail price of this item in June 1937.

1948: Chulki zhenskie khlopchatobumazhnye, artikul 8 (stockings, women's, cotton, article no. 8). The quotation is from *PD-14-12-47.*

1952: This price is computed from the 1948 price and the following price reduction: March 1950, cotton, silk, and wool stockings and socks, 15%.

1954: This price is computed from the 1952 price and the following price reductions: April 1953, stockings and socks, on the average 20%; April 1954, cotton stockings and socks, on the average 20%.

Comparability: The 1937 and 1948 commodity designations and article numbers are the same, and the item priced is presumably the same in all years.

152. Socks, cotton, plain

1937: The price shown represents the midpoint of the range of prices for the following socks: *noski muzhskie gladkie n/piatk; khl.-bum. 24/2; artikul 61, 64, 65, 66, 67, 69* (socks, men's, plain, low; cotton no. 24/2; article nos. 61, 64, 65, 66, 67, 69). The wholesale price range for these socks established in August 1935 was 1.50 to 2.10 rubles per pair, according to Moskovskii gorodskoi otdel vnutrennei torgovli, *Preiskurant edinykh otpusknykh tsen na trikotazhnye izdeliia* (Moscow, 1936), pp. 35, 38; Moskovskii oblastnoi otdel vnutrennei torgovli, *Preiskurant roznichnykh tsen na trikotazhnye izdeliia po Moskovskoi oblasti,* pp. 5, 30; *RTS-36,* pp. 18, 34. After the price reduction of July 1, 1937 the wholesale price range for these socks was 1.30 to 1.95 rubles per pair, according to *Preiskuranty snizhennykh s 1 iiulia 1937 g. otpusknykh tsen na promyshlennye tovary,* pp. 3–4. The average 1937 Moscow retail price is computed from the midpoints of these wholesale price ranges and the retail trade margin for Moscow city of 6.5%.

1928: Noski bum. mash. (socks, cotton, machine-made). The price shown is that cited for April, May, and July 1928 and January 1929 in *ESBM.* It is assumed the price was the same throughout the year.

Comparability: The 1928 designation is very brief, but it seems likely that the 1928 quotation is for a plain, inexpensive, and commonly consumed sock. Accordingly, it is compared with the midpoint of the 1937 range of prices for plain socks of the lowest count yarn listed in the handbooks. Most of the socks listed are of this yarn, and likely they are the most commonly worn type of sock. Comparability is probably fairly close.

153. Socks, cotton

1937: Socks, cotton. The price shown is the annual average based on the quotation of 2.75 rubles per pair in January and April, and 2.40 rubles per pair in July 1937 (*UM;* Trivanovitch).

1940: Socks, cotton. The price shown is the average of that in January 1940 — 3.60 rubles a pair — and that in January 1942 — 3.75 rubles a pair, as reported in *MLR,* November 1939, and *UM.* It is assumed that the price of 5.00 rubles a pair reported for July 1940 and January 1941 in *MLR,* February and May 1941, is for a higher quality sock.

Comparability: The designation is brief and only rough comparability could be expected. Also, there is doubt again about the level of the 1940 price.

154. Socks, cotton, cheapest

1937: Noski muzhskie, khl./bum. 24, artikul 64 (socks, men's, of cotton yarn no. 24, article no. 64). This price is the 1937 average based on the Moscow retail price of 1.60 rubles a pair until July 1, 1937 and 1.39 rubles a pair for the rest of the year. These prices are computed from the wholesale prices and the Moscow city retail trade margin of 6.5% for hosiery (*RTS-36,* p. 17). The wholesale price was 1.50 rubles a pair from August 1935 until July 1, 1937 when the wholesale price was reduced to 1.30 rubles a pair (*RTS-36,* pp. 17, 35; Moskovskii gorodskoi otdel vnutrennei torgovli, *Preiskurant edinykh otpusknykh tsen na trikotazhnye izdeliia,* p.35; *Preiskuranty snizhennykh s 1 iiulia 1937 g. otpusknykh tsen na promyshlennye tovary,* p. 3).

1948: Chaussettes coton. The price was 4.65 rubles a pair after the March 1950 price reductions, according to Gordey, *France-Soir,* July 2–3, 1950. The 1948 price is computed from this quotation and the following price reduction: March 1950, cotton, silk, and wool stockings and socks, 15%.

1952: Chaussettes coton. This price is that reported by Gordey as in effect after the price reduction of March 1950. There were no further reductions in hosiery prices until 1953.

1954: This price is computed from the 1952 price and the following price reductions: April 1953, stockings and socks, an average of 20%; April 1954, cotton stockings and socks, an average of 20%.

Comparability: The sock priced for 1937 is the cheapest listed in the various 1936 and 1937 price handbooks, and the postwar sock is the cheapest for which any price quotation is available; they are presumably comparable.

155. Socks, rayon

1937: Socks, rayon. This price is the 1937 annual average based on the price of 7.00 rubles a pair in January and April and 6.15 rubles a pair in July 1937 (*UM;* Trivanovitch).

1940: Socks, rayon. This price is reported as having been in effect in Moscow in July 1939 (*MLR,* November 1939) and in Kuibyshev in January 1942 (*UM*). It is assumed that the same price was in effect throughout 1940. The price of 10.00 rubles per pair cited for July 1940 and January 1941 in *MLR,* February and May 1941, is apparently for a higher quality sock.

Comparability: The designations are very brief and comparability can only be approximate. Also, there is again doubt as to the course of prices during 1940.

156. Socks, rayon, no. 86

1937: Noski muzhskie risunchatye, khl.-bum. viskoz, artikul 86 (socks, men's, figured, cotton and viscose rayon, article no. 86). The wholesale price was 5.40

rubles per pair in 1936 (*RTS-36*, p. 35) and until July 1, 1937 when the wholesale price was reduced to 4.91 rubles a pair (*Preiskuranty snizhennykh s 1 iiulia 1937 g. otpusknykh tsen na promyshlennye tovary*, p. 30). The annual average 1937 Moscow retail price is computed from these wholesale quotations and the Moscow retail trade margin of 6.5%.

1948: Noski muzhskie risunchatye s viskosoi, artikul 86 (socks, men's, figured, part viscose rayon, article no. 86). The quotation is from *PD-14-12-47*.

1952: This price is computed from the 1948 price and the following price reductions: March 1949, silk stockings and socks, 15%; March 1950, cotton, silk, and wool stockings and socks, 15%. It is assumed, as in the case of fabrics, that the term "silk" here covers artificial as well as natural silks.

1954: This price is computed from the 1952 price and the following price reductions: April 1953, stockings and socks, an average of 20%; April 1954, silk and other (other than cotton or kapron, which were listed separately) stockings and socks, an average of 10%.

Comparability: The commodity designation and article number are the same in each year.

157. Cowhide boots, one-piece upper

1937: Sapogi muzhskie ialovye vytiazhnye, obyk. i form.; dereviannoshpil'kovye; stand.; chern. (boots, men's, cowhide, one-piece upper, ordinary and military; pegged sole; standard quality; black). The 1936 price was 140.00 rubles per pair, according to *RTS-M-36*, I:49. The 1937 price shown takes into account the 5% reduction in the prices of standard quality leather-soled shoes of June 1, 1937.

1928: The designation varies somewhat at different dates, as follows: *sapogi kozhanye ialovochnye prostye* (boots, cowhide leather, plain); *sapogi ialovye* (boots, cowhide); *sapogi ialovye vytiazhnye* (boots, cowhide, one-piece upper); *sapogi ialovye vyt. 12 vershk.* (boots, cowhide, one-piece upper, 12 vershok or 53.3 cm high). All designations add that the boots are *machine made*. It is believed that all quotations for the year relate to the same item. The price shown is that which prevailed throughout the year in state shops, as reported in *ESBM*. The price in cooperative shops for similar boots produced by handicraft artisans was 19.00 rubles per pair throughout the year, considerably higher than the price of machine-made boots in state shops.

Comparability: The 1928 boot for which quotations were published monthly is presumably more comparable to the 1937 *standard quality* boot than to the more expensive qualities — *special order footwear* (*obuvi osobogo zakaza*) or *model footwear* (*model'nye obuvi*). The boots priced appear to be quite closely comparable. There may be differences in the manner of attaching the sole or in the height of the boot, but these appear to be minor enough to have little effect on the prices.

158. Cowhide boots

1937: Sapogi ialovye prikroinye; obyk. i form., der. shp.; stand., chern. (cowhide boots, "prikroinye"; ordinary and military; pegged sole; standard, black). *Prikroinye* means that the boot upper is made of two pieces — (a) the vamp and (b) the top and heel — sewn together (Andrusevich, p. 146). These boots are listed in the section on shoes with *leather soles*. The 1936 price was 110.00 rubles per pair, according to *RTS-M-36*, I:49. There was a 5% reduction in the prices of standard quality leather-soled shoes on June 1, 1937.

1940: Iuftovaia obuv'; sapogi prikroinye obyknovennye, bez podnariada, s tekstil'noi podlkeikoi, vintovye i derevianno-shpilechnye; muzhskie; na kozhanoi podoshve; ialovaia iuft', art. 2306 Ch Iu (juft footwear; boots, "prikroinye," ordinary, vamp unlined; tops lined with cloth; screwed or pegged sole; men's; leather soles; black cowhide juft; article 2306 Ch Iu). The quotation is from a list of retail shoe prices established July 5, 1940 in Ministerstvo torgovli SSSR, *Sbornik normativov i spravochnykh materialov dlia shveinykh i obuvnykh predpriiatii dlia predpriiatii sistemy Glavvoentorg* (Moscow, 1947), p. 237. The price prior to July 5 may have been lower but, lacking definite information on this, I assume the price established July 5 to have been in effect throughout 1940.

Comparability: So far as can be determined from the designations, the boots priced are comparable in all major respects. However, there is some question concerning the comparability of the price lists from which the quotations are taken.

(1) The 1937 price is based on a quotation in a 1936 price list applicable to Moscow, while the 1940 quotation is from a price list applicable to the entire USSR *except* Moscow, Leningrad, Kiev, and Minsk. In 1936 the average USSR price was only about 1% higher than the Moscow price. This can be computed from the regional retail trade margins in effect at that time, given in *RTS-36*, p. 91. We do not have information on the relationship of Moscow shoe prices to prices in the rest of the USSR in 1940. However, the small difference between the Moscow and the average USSR price in 1937 means that the comparison of the Moscow 1937 price with the 1940 price for the USSR except Moscow and three other cities is representative of the movement of shoe prices outside of Moscow, at least. Probably this is fairly representative of the movement of Moscow prices as well.

(2) The 1940 price list relates only to shoes produced by cooperative and local industry and in factories administered by various institutions, including Glavvoentorg. Glavvoentorg is the organization in charge of retail shops for military personnel. Thus the bulk of the shoe output, that of state operated factories, is not covered. The 1936 quotation used in the present comparison applies to shoes produced in state operated factories. This is true of most of the quotations in the 1936 price list, though some quotations relate to the output of cooperatives, and some apparently relate to the particular type of shoe described, regardless of where produced.

There is some evidence that price differentials have existed between the products of state industry and those of local or cooperative industry, sometimes even for identical products. This may not have been very widespread in the case of shoes. In 1936, the prices established for shoes produced in state industry were made applicable also to the output of local and cooperative industry, and a separate price list was promulgated only for items produced by local and cooperative industry which were not included in the price list for state industry, presumably because not produced in state factories (*NKMP, Preiskurant edinykh otpusknykh tsen na obuv' proizvodstva gosudarstvennykh predpriiatii kozhevnnoi promyshlennosti Narkommestproma RSFSR* (Moscow, 1936), p. 3). It is not known whether there was a differential in 1940 between the retail prices of shoes produced in state factories and those covered in the available price list. It seems unlikely there could have been much of a price differential for shoes of exactly the same quality and type. The main doubt here would seem to lie in the possibility that the available 1940 quotations are for shoes differing in general quality of workmanship and materials from those included in the 1936 price list. The commodity designations in the price lists might not reveal such basic quality differences.

159. Leather boots, black

1937: Botinki muzhskie iz vyrostka, opoika, rosshevro ili dogshevro, shevro; standartnye; vintovogo ili derevianno-shpilechnogo metod krepleniia na kozhanoi podoshve, chernye, artikul 2000, 2100, 2200 (men's boots, of young calf, calf, *glacé* horse, dogskin, or kid; standard quality; screwed or pegged leather soles, black, articles 2000, 2100, 2200). A price of 100.00 rubles per pair was established in August 1936, according to *RTS-M-36*, I:90. There was a reduction of 5% in the prices of standard grade leather-soled shoes on June 1, 1937.

1928: Botinki khromovye muzhskie (chrome leather boots, men's). The price was 8.75 rubles a pair in state shops and 9.05 rubles a pair in cooperative shops, according to the quotations in *ESBM* for April through December 1928. It is assumed the same prices were in effect during the first quarter of 1928 also. The average of the state and cooperative shop prices is used.

The item priced is probably closely similar to the following shoe listed in *SMG-28*, p. 604: *botinki vintovye, proshivnye (zakrytaia vyrezka) i derev. shpil'-kov.: khromovogo opoika, otreznaia soiuzka, na shnurkakh, polotnianaia podkladka* (boots, soles screwed, sewn with concealed seam, or pegged; chrome calf, split vamp, laced, linen lining). This boot is almost certainly *black;* prices for *colored* (presumably including brown) boots were higher. This item is listed in a price list for the trust *Moskozh* at 8.90 rubles a pair. It is believed that this is a Moscow retail price.

A few words concerning the *Moskozh* and other official 1928 shoe price lists seem in order here, and should be kept in mind in connection with other comparisons making use of these. *EMG-28* contains two leather shoe price lists: (1) a list of wholesale and retail prices for machine-made shoes produced in state and co-operative factories and in mixed private-state companies with capital supplied predominantly by the state (pp. 6–13); (2) a list for *Moskozh* (pp. 630ff.). This latter gives no indication as to whether the prices listed are wholesale or retail. A comparison of these price lists indicates that the *Moskozh* price list is probably a retail price list for shoes sold through the *Moskozh* trust, and therefore a Moscow retail price list. The *Moskozh* prices are generally about 10% above the whole-sale prices in the general wholesale-retail price list. This seems a reasonable trade margin for Moscow. The maximum retail trade margin for shoes was 20% for all urban areas of the USSR, and local trade organs were instructed to set prices as low as possible, according to a law of April 5, 1927 (*ZA*, no. 20–21, 1927, pp. 17–20). Furthermore, the *Moskozh* prices correspond fairly well with the Moscow retail prices cited in *ESBM*.

Comparability: The boots priced are, it is believed, closely comparable. It is assumed that the 1928 quotation from *ESBM* is for a boot comparable in general quality to the 1937 *standard quality*. Beyond this, minor differences in style, leather and construction would have little effect on the price relative. The 1937 quotation is applicable to almost all *men's black chrome leather standard quality boots*. At that time, no price differential was made for variations in style, for different varieties of chrome leather, or even for welted soles as opposed to soles attached in other ways (*RTS-M-36*, I:43, 46, 47, 90). In 1928 differences in style and in type of chrome leather were reflected in price differentials, though such differentials were rather minor. Welted boots and shoes, however, were consider-ably more expensive than those with screwed, sewn, or pegged soles in 1928 (*SMG-28*, pp. 6–12, 603–606). No welted boot is listed in *SMG-28* with even a wholesale price as low as the retail price cited in *ESBM* and used in the present comparison; it is clear, then, that the 1928 quotation is for a boot with sole attached by some method other than welting. This comparison, then, represents the change in price of boots with other than welted soles.

160. Leather boots, welted

1937: Botinki zhenskie na kozhanoi podoshve; zhestkii nosok, tekstil'naia podkladka, na shnurkakh, dlina berts 20–21 sm. i 25–26 sm.; kozhanye bertsy iz vyrostka, opoika, barana i dogshevro; rant.; chern.; stand.; no. 2044 (boots, women's, leather soles: hard toe, cloth lining, laced, height of upper 20 to 21 or 25 to 26 cm; leather upper of calf, young calf, sheep, or dogskin; welted; black; standard quality; article no. 2044). The price was 75.00 rubles per pair in 1936, according to *RTS-M-36*, I:50. There was a 5% price reduction in the prices of standard quality leather-soled footwear on June 1, 1937.

1928: Obuv' damskaia; botinki rantovye s kozhanymi ili dereviannymi poliro-vannymi kablukami: khromovogo opoika, otreznaia soiuzka, na shnurkakh, polotnia-naia podkladka (ladies' shoes; welted boots with leather or polished wood heels; chrome calf, split vamp, laced, linen lining). Boots of this description *20 to 21 cm high* were 10.80 rubles per pair while those *25 to 26 cm high* were 12.20 rubles per pair, according to the *Moskozh* price list in *SMG-28*, p. 605. The average of these two prices is used. (See the note on the *Moskozh* price list under item 159 above.)

Comparability: These boots appear to be closely comparable. It is assumed again that the 1928 quotation is for a boot generally similar in quality to the 1937 *standard quality*. Like the 1937 boot, the 1928 boot is almost certainly *black*, although this is not stated in the description.

161. Leather boots, brown

1937: Botinki, kozhanye bertsy, iz opoika i vyrostka, barana, dogshevro i shevro, na kozhanoi podoshve, vint., korichn., stand.: otreznaia soiuzka, artikul 2000; kroia Derbi, artikul 2100; tsel'naia soiuzka, artikul 2200 (boots, leather uppers, young calf, calf, sheep, dogskin or kid, leather soles, screwed, brown, standard quality: split vamp, article 2000; "Derby" style, article 2100; one-piece vamp, article 2200). The 1936 price of these boots was 105 rubles a pair, according to *RTS-M-36*, II:43, 47. On June 1, 1937 there was a reduction of 5% in the prices of standard quality shoes with leather soles.

1948: This price is computed from the 1952 price and the following price reduction: March 1950, leather shoes, 15%.

1952: Botinki muzhskie korichnevye art. 3006 (boots, men's, brown, article 3006). The quotation is from Gurvits (1953). The article number indicates that these are *laced boots of all styles, leather uppers, pegged, screwed, or glued leather soles* (Ministerstvo torgovli SSSR, *Sbornik normativov i spravochnykh materialov dlia shveinykh i obuvnykh predpriiatii*, pp. 258–260).

1954: This price is computed from the 1952 price and the following price reductions: April 1953, leather shoes (with leather soles), 8%; April 1954, leather shoes, 7%

Comparability: The 1952 designation does not indicate the leather of which the boots are made, but the 1936 price covers boots of several of the most common leathers and probably the postwar boots are of one of these leathers. In all other important respects, the boots priced are comparable.

162. Leather boots, composition soles

1937: Khromovaia obuv': botinki muzhskie iz vyrostka, opoika, dogshevro, shevreta i shevro na shnurkakh ili na rezinkakh; otreznaia ili tselaia soiuzka ili kroia "derbi," zhestkii nosok, nakladnoi zadnik, tekstil'naia podkladka, kozhanye bertsy, chernye na podoshve iz plastkozhi, rantovye s otkrytym rissom, artikul 2005, 2105, 2205, 2605, 2705 (chrome leather shoes: men's boots of calf, young calf, dogskin, sheepskin, and kid, laced or with elastic; split or one-piece vamp or "Derby" style, hard toe, overlaid counter, fabric lining, leather uppers, black, composition soles, welted with exposed seam, article numbers 2005, 2105, 2205, 2605, 2705). It is not clear whether all article numbers listed refer to this particular shoe. The 1936 price was 60.00 rubles a pair, according to *RTS-M-36*, I:76.

On June 1, 1937 there was a reduction of 8% in the prices of standard quality shoes with rubber soles. It is assumed that this applies also to shoes with composition soles. Shoes with rubber and composition soles are listed together, separately from shoes with leather soles in *RTS-M-36*.

1948: This price is computed from the 1952 price and the following price reduction: March 1950, leather shoes, 15%.

1952: Botinki muzhskie shevro chernye art. 3002 (boots, men's, black kid, article number 3002). The quotation is from Gurvits (1953). The article number indicates that these are *laced boots of all styles*, with *leather uppers, composition or sponge rubber (mikroporistaia rezina) soles, attached by welting or modifications of welting* (Ministerstvo torgovli SSSR, *Sbornik normativov i spravochnykh materialov dlia shveinykh i obuvnykh predpriiatii*, pp. 258–60).

1954: This price is computed from the 1952 price and the following price reductions: April 1953, leather shoes with rubber soles, 10%; April 1954, leather shoes, 7%.

Comparability: These boots are comparable in all important respects. The difference between the 1937 and 1952 article numbers apparently reflects a change in numbering system rather than differences in the style, type, or quality of the boots.

163. Leather oxfords, women's

1937: Polubotinki zhenskie na kozhanoi podoshve; otreznaia soiuzka, zhestkii nosok, kozhanaia podkladka v chasti zadnika, na shnurkakh, iz vyrostka, opoika, barana i dogshevro; rant., chern., art. 3044, stand. (oxfords, women's, leather-soled; split vamp, hard toe, leather heel lining, laced, of young calf, calf, sheep, or dogskin; welted, black, article no. 3044, standard quality). (The source actually says the shoes are brown, but in the context, this is clearly an error and the shoes are black.) The price in 1936 was 65.00 rubles per pair, according to *RTS-M-36*, I:50. There was a 5% reduction in the prices of standard quality leather-soled footwear on June 1, 1937.

1928: P/botinki damskie rantovye s kozhan. ili dereviannymi polirovannymi kablukami: khromovogo opoika, otreznaia soiuzka, na shnurkakh, s kozhanoi podkladkoi (oxfords, ladies', welted, with leather or polished wood heels: chrome calf, split vamp, laced, leather lining). The quotation is from the *Moskozh* price list in *SMG-28*, p. 605. (See the note on this price list under item 159 above.) The shoes are presumably *black*. This is not stated, but the price for *colored* (presumably including brown) shoes of the same designation was considerably higher.

Comparability: These appear to be closely comparable shoes.

164. Leather shoes, children's

1937: Obuv' kozhanaia na kozhanoi podoshve detskaia; razmery ot No. 27 po No. 30 ili ot No. 1 po No. 4: polubotinki na shnurkakh, otreznaia soiuzka, s nakladnym i bez nakladnogo zadniki, zhestkii nosok, kozhanaia podkladka vokrug piatki, verkh iz vyrostka, opoika, shevro, rosshevro, dogshevro i shevret; vint., chern., stand., artikul 3070, 3076 (leather footwear with leather soles, children's; sizes 27 to 30 or 1 to 4: oxfords, laced, split vamp, with or without overlaid counter, hard toe, leather heel lining, upper of calf, young calf, kid, horse, dogskin, or sheep; screwed soles, black, standard, article nos. 3070, 3076). The 1936 price was 25.00 rubles per pair, according to *RTS-M-36*, I:69. There was an 8% reduction in the prices of children's shoes on June 1, 1937.

1928: Detskaia obuv' razmery ot No. 27 po No. 30; polubotinki khromovogo opoika ili shevretovye, otreznaia soiuzka, na shnurkakh, polotnianaia podkladka, vintovye (children's shoes, sizes 27 to 30; oxfords of chrome leather calf or sheep, split vamp, laced, linen lining, screwed soles). The shoes priced are probably *black*. *Colored* shoes (probably including brown) are listed at a higher price. The quotation is from the *Moskozh* price list in *SMG-28*, p. 606. (See the discussion of this price list under item 159 above.)

Comparability: These shoes are comparable except that the 1937 shoe has a leather heel lining while the quotation mentions only a linen lining for the 1928 shoes. This seems a minor detail in view of the close similarity of the shoes in other respects.

165. Leather shoes, men's, no. 4004

1937: Muzhskaia kozhanaia obuv': polubotinki, otreznaia soiuzka, zhestkii nosok, na shnurkakh, s nakladnym i bez nakladnogo zadnika, iz opoika, vyrostka, barana, dogshevro i shevro, na kozhanoi podoshve, rant., chern., stand., art. 3004 (men's leather shoes: oxfords, split vamp, hard toe, laced, with or without an overlaid counter, of calf, young calf, sheep, dogskin or kid, leather soles, welted, black, standard, article no. 3004). The same price applied also to two other styles of the same shoe — *"Derby" style, article no. 3104* and *one-piece vamp style, article no. 3204*. The price established in April 1936 was 85.00 rubles, according to *RTS-M-36*, I:44–47. There was a 5% reduction in the prices of standard quality leather-soled shoes on June 1, 1937.

1940: Khromovaia obuv': polubotinki muzhskie vsekh vidov kroia, rantovye na kozhanoi podoshve; chernye shevro, artikul 4004 Ch. Sh. (chrome leather shoes: men's oxfords of all styles, welted leather soles; black kid, article no. 4004 ChSh). The quotation is from Ministerstvo torgovli SSSR, *Sbornik normativov i spravochnykh materialov dlia shveinykh i obuvnykh predpriiatii*, p. 239. The price is that established July 5, 1940.

Comparability: The designations are similar in all respects. The article number is 3004 in 1937 and 4004 in 1940. Apparently there was a change in the numbering system between these dates. A 1948 source indicates that the first digit "3" in a shoe article number indicates boots (*botinki*) and that the first digit "4" indicates oxfords (*polubotinki*) (Andrusevich, p. 150); however, the 1937 shoe is stated to be an *oxford* like the 1940 shoe.

The remarks indicating some doubts as to the comparability of the 1937 and 1940 price lists from which the quotations are taken (see item 158) should be kept in mind. These doubts are of somewhat less concern in the present case, however, than in some of the other 1937–40 comparisons. The 1937 quotation used here is stated to apply to a number of named factories, including the Gorky and Kim Unions of producer cooperatives. As indicated above, the 1940 price list applies to shoes produced in cooperative and local industry, et cetera, but not to shoes produced in factories operated by the state.

166. Leather shoes, women's

1937: Tufli na kozhanoi podoshve: tufli iz opoika, shevreta, shevro i dogshevro; nisk., vensk. i frants. kabl; AGO, chern., stand.: s 1 remnem, art. 4146, 4046; to zhe, s otdelkoi, art. 4346, 4246; to zhe, figurnogo kroia, art. 4546, 4446; s 2 remniami gladkie, art. 5146, 5046; to zhe, s otdelkoi; art. 5346, 5246, 5546, 5446, 6046, 6146, 6246 (leather-soled slippers: slippers of calf, sheep, kid, or dogskin; low, Viennese or French heels; soles attached by "AGO" method; black, standard: with one strap, article nos. 4146, 4046; the same, with trimming, article nos. 4346, 4246; the same, figured style, article nos. 4546, 4446; with two straps, plain, article nos. 5146, 5046; the same, with trimming, article nos. 5346, 5246, 5546, 5446, 6046, 6146, 6246). The price established in April 1936 was 70.00 rubles per pair, according to *RTS-M-36*, I:51. There was a 5% reduction in the prices of standard quality leather-soled shoes on June 1, 1937.

1940: The price shown is the midpoint of the range of prices for the following shoes: *polubotinki, tufli i lodochki zhenskie na srednikh i vysokikh kablukakh, khromovye, chernye:*

> *gladkie, dereviannoshpilechnye ili kleevye na kozhanoi podoshve:*

artikul 4146 ChSh	80.00
artikul 4146 ChL	70.00
artikul 4146 ChN ChB	60.00

> *s otdelkoi, dereviannoshpilechnye ili kleevye na kozhanoi podoshve:*

artikul 4346 ChSh	90.00
artikul 4346 ChL	80.00
artikul 4346 ChN ChB	70.00

> *figurnogo kroia, kleevye na kozhanoi podoshve:*

artikul 4546 ChSh	105.00
artikul 4546 ChL	95.00
artikul 4546 ChN ChB	85.00

(Oxfords, slippers, and pumps, women's, medium or high heels, chrome leather, black: plain, pegged or glued leather soles: article nos. 4146 ChSh, 4146 ChL, 4146 ChN ChB; with trimming, pegged or glued leather soles: article nos. 4346 ChSh, 4346 ChL, 4346 ChN ChB; figured style, glued leather soles, article nos. 4546 ChSh, 4546 ChL, 4546 ChN ChB). The "Ch" in all the article numbers indicates the shoes are *black*. "Sh" indicates the shoes are of *kid*. "L" indicates the shoes are of *smooth leather,* calf or chrome horse with a smooth surface. "N" indicates the shoes are of *grained leather,* calf or chrome horse with a grained surface or pigskin. "B" indicates the shoes are of *sheep* or *suede-finished calf or kid (veliur).* The shoes are *standard quality.* The quotations are from Ministerstvo torgovli SSSR, *Sbornik normativov i spravochnykh materialov dlia shveinykh i obuvnykh predpriiatii,* pp. 243–244, 260. Again, the price used is that established on July 5, 1940.

Comparability: The single 1937 price apparently applies to the entire group of shoes for which there was a considerable price range in 1940. The midpoint of the 1940 range should be reasonably comparable to the 1937 quotation. The 1937 designation indicates the soles are attached by the "AGO" method while the 1940 soles are glued or pegged. This is a relatively minor difference; where shoes are listed in the 1936 price list with either AGO, sewn, glued, or pegged soles, no price differential is shown. (See *RTS-M-36,* I:66ff., and 74ff.)

The doubts regarding the comparability of the 1936 and 1940 price lists from which the quotations are taken, discussed under item 158, are applicable in this case. The 1937 quotation applies to all state factories while the 1940 quotation is for factories run by cooperative and local industry.

167. Leather shoes, men's

1937: Polubotinki s nakladnym i bez nakladnogo zadnika iz opoika, vyrostka, barana, dogshevro i shevro na kozhanoi podoshve, vint., korichn., stand.: otreznaia soiuzka, artikul 3000; kroia Derbi, artikul 3100; tselaia soiuzka, artikul 3200 (oxfords with or without overlaid counter of calf, young calf, sheep, dogskin, or kid, leather soles, screwed, brown, standard quality: split vamp, article 3000; "Derby" style, article 3100; one-piece vamp, article 3200). These shoes were 90 rubles per pair in 1936, according to *RTS-M-36,* I:44, 48. On June 1, 1937, there was a 5% reduction in the prices of standard quality leather shoes with leather soles.

1948: This price is computed from the 1952 price and the following price reduction: March 1950, leather shoes, 15%.

1952: Polubotinki muzhskie shevro korichnevye art. 4206 (oxfords, men's, kid, brown, article 4206). The quotation is from Gurvits (1953). The article number indicates that these are *men's oxfords of smooth leather with trimming, pegged, screwed, or glued leather soles* (Ministerstvo torgovli SSSR, *Sbornik normativov i spravochnykh materialov dlia shveinykh i obuvnykh predpriiatii*, pp. 258–260).

1954: This price is computed from the 1952 price and the following price reductions: April 1953, leather shoes (with leather soles), 8%; April 1954, leather shoes, 7%.

Comparability: These shoes appear comparable in all important respects except that the postwar shoe may have a little extra trimming not on the 1937 shoe.

168. Leather shoes, rubber soles

1937: Khromovaia obuv': polubotinki muzhskie, na shnurkakh, otreznaia ili tselaia soiuzka ili kroia "derbi"; vintovye i dereviannoshpil'kovye, proshivnye, kleevye; iz svinogo khroma i khroma s iskusstvennym litsom, chernye, na rezinovoi podoshve; artikul 3001, 3101, 3201, 3003–3007, 3103–3107, 3203–3207 (chrome leather shoes: men's oxfords, laced, split vamp, one-piece vamp, or "Derby" style; soles screwed, pegged, sewn, or glued; of chrome pigskin or artificially grained chrome leather, black, rubber soles, article nos. 3001, 3101, 3201, 3003 to 3007, 3103 to 3107, 3203 to 3207). It is not clear whether all the article numbers listed refer to the shoe priced. The 1936 price was 37.00 rubles per pair, according to *RTS-M-36*, I:78. There was an 8% reduction in the prices of standard quality rubber-soled shoes on June 1, 1937.

1940: Khromovaia obuv': polubotinki muzhskie vsekh vidov kroia; kleevye na podoshve iz obyknovennoi reziny, artikul 4007 ChN ili proshivnye na podoshve iz obyknovennoi reziny, artikul 4003 ChN; chernye nakatnye (chrome leather shoes: men's oxfords of all styles; glued soles of ordinary rubber, article no. 4007 ChN or sewn soles of ordinary rubber, article no. 4003 ChN; black grained leather — that is, calf or chrome horse with a grained surface or chrome pigskin). The quotation is from Ministerstvo torgovli SSSR, *Sbornik normativov i spravochnykh materialov dlia shveinykh i obuvnykh predpriiatii*, p. 239. Again the price is that established July 5, 1940.

Comparability: The designations are comparable. The source in each case indicates that the quotations are for standard quality shoes, though this is not included in the individual designations.

The doubts regarding the comparability of the 1936 and 1940 price lists from which the quotations are taken, discussed above under item 158, are applicable in this case. The portion of the 1936 price list from which the 1937 quotation is taken does not indicate the type of shoe factories to which the prices apply. Perhaps in this case the quotation applies to all shoes answering the designation, regardless of where produced. As indicated, the 1940 quotation applies to the output of local and cooperative shoe factories.

169. Sandals

1937: Sandali muzhskie iz iufti s odnim remnem, rantovye, korichn., art. 7004, standart. (men's sandals of juft with one strap, welted; brown, article no. 7004, standard). The 1936 price was 40.00 rubles per pair, according to *RTS-M-36*,

I:49. There was a 5% reduction in the prices of standard quality leather-soled shoes on June 1, 1937.

1928: Sandali muzhskie, tsvetnogo vyrostka, polukozhnika ili iufti, s 1 remnem (men's sandals, colored calf, goat or juft, with one strap). The wholesale price was 3.69 rubles per pair, the maximum retail price was 4.43 rubles per pair, and the *Moskozh* or Moscow retail price was 4.05 rubles per pair, according to *SMG-28*, pp. 7, 604. The Moscow retail price is used in the comparison.

Comparability: These sandals appear closely comparable, although the 1928 sandal may not have a welted sole while the 1937 sandal does.

170. Canvas shoes, leather soles

1937: Polubotinki muzhskie iz parusiny, repsa i tkani, gladkie i kombinirovannye s kozhei, na kozhanoi podoshve; rant.; tsvetn., standart., artikul 3604 i 3304 (men's oxfords of canvas, rep or cloth, plain or combined with leather, leather-soled, welted; colored, standard, article nos. 3604 and 3304). The 1936 price was 45.00 rubles per pair, according to *RTS-M-36*, I:48–49. There was a 5% reduction in the prices of standard grade leather-soled shoes, assumed to be applicable here, on June 1, 1937.

1928: Polubotinki parusinovye, muzhskie, otresnaia soiuzka, na shnurkakh, kozhanaia podkladka, rantovye, tsvetnye (canvas oxfords, men's, split vamp, laced, leather lining, welted, colored). The wholesale price was 7.40 rubles per pair and the maximum retail price was 8.88 rubles per pair, according to *SMG-28*, p. 7. The Moscow retail price, it is assumed, was about 10% above the wholesale price, or 8.15 rubles per pair.

Comparability: These shoes seem closely comparable. Although the designation does not indicate it, the 1928 shoe is probably leather-soled, as is the 1937 shoe. The 1937 price applies to shoes with uppers of all cloth or of cloth and leather while the 1928 shoe upper appears to be all cloth but is leather-lined.

171. Cloth and leather shoes

1937: Polubotinki zhenskie na shnurkakh kombinirovannye: soiuzka i bertsy iz bashmachnoi tkani, repsa, kirzy i dr. tkanei, a noski, zadniki, zadnie naruzhnye remni i nadblochniki iz kozhi (khrom, shevro); prosh. i kleenye na rezin. podoshve; tsvetnye, artikul 3343 (oxfords, women's, laced, combined: vamp and uppers of shoe cloth, rep, "Kirza" and other fabrics, but toe-cap, counter, back outside binding and eyelet binding of leather (chrome, kid); sewn or glued on rubber soles; colored, article 3343). The price in 1936 was 32.00 rubles per pair, according to *RTS-M-36*, I:81. On June 1, 1937 there was an 8% reduction in the prices of standard quality shoes with rubber soles.

1948: Women's brown wing-tip oxfords, 1½" heel, apparently imitation leather with possibly real leather toe-cap and binding, thin rubber soles, number marked in shoe 4947 TsRKh 213666. These shoes are part of a collection of Soviet clothes brought from Russia to the United States by Mrs. Alan G. Kirk, wife of the Ambassador to the USSR at the time, and exhibited by Bonwit Teller. The above description is based on an inspection of the shoes by the author. The article number *4947* indicates that these are *women's oxfords, slippers or pumps of combined cloth and leather with medium or high heels, glued rubber soles.* The letters "Ts" indicate the shoes are *colored* (brown in the case of leather, or all colors but black and white in the case of cloth). The meaning of the letter "R" is not clear but it probably indicates the kind of fabric. The letters "Kh" indicate that the leather part of the shoe is *chrome leather.* The numbers "213666" marked in the shoe apparently are not part of the article number in the usual sense. These shoes were

56.75 rubles per pair, according to a Bonwit Teller press release of March 24, 1952. This price was in effect when the shoes were purchased sometime in 1950 or 1951, almost certainly after the price cut of March 1950. The 1948 price is computed from this price and the following price reductions: March 1949, cloth and cloth-and-leather shoes, 15%; March 1950, cloth and cloth-and-leather shoes, 20%.

1952: This is the same as the 1950 price cited above as there were no further price reductions until April 1953.

1954: This price is computed from the 1952 price and the following price reductions: April 1953, shoes of leather substitutes, cloth and cloth-and-leather shoes with rubber soles, 20%; April 1954, cloth and cloth-and-leather shoes, an average of 20%.

Comparability: These shoes appear closely comparable in all important respects.

172. Rubbers

1937: Galoshi melkie, rezinovye, muzhskie, vsekh artikulov (overshoes, low, rubber, men's, all article numbers). A price of 22.00 rubles per pair was established in August 1936, according to *RTS-M-36,* I:84. *Men's rubber overshoes,* obviously the same item, are reported at 22.00 rubles per pair before the price reduction of June 1, 1937, and at 18.70 rubles per pair after this reduction, in Trivanovitch and *UM.* The average annual price is computed from these quotations.

1928: Galoshi muzhskie No. 10 (overshoes, men's, no. 10) and *galoshi muzhskie 1 sort* (overshoes, men's, grade 1). The price shown is that reported in *ESBM* for April through December 1928. It is assumed the same price was in effect prior to April also. The item priced is apparently the same as the item described in *SMG-28,* p. 5 as *galoshi muzhskie, art. 110* (overshoes, men's, article no. 110). This source lists the price as 3.60 rubles per pair, slightly higher than the *ESBM* quotation for Moscow of 3.55 rubles per pair.

1940: Man's rubber overshoes, or *overshoes, rubbers, men's.* This is an estimated annual average 1940 price. The price in July 1939 was 19.65 rubles per pair, according to *MLR,* November 1939. It is assumed this price remained in effect until July 1940. The price was reported to be 22.00 rubles per pair in July 1940 and 33.00 rubles per pair in January 1941 in *MLR,* February and May 1941.

1948: Galoshi rezinovye muzhskie obyknovennye artikul 110 (overshoes, rubber, men's, ordinary style, article no. 110). The quotation is from *PD-14-12-47.* The same price is cited for *men's rubbers* in January 1949, in *UM.*

1952: This price is computed from the 1948 price and the following price reduction: March 1950, men's and women's rubber footwear, 10%.

1954: This price is computed from the 1952 price and the following price reductions: April 1953, overshoes (*galoshi*) and other rubber footwear, 15%; April 1954, overshoes (*galoshi*), boots (*boty, sapogi*) and other rubber footwear, an average of 12%.

Comparability: The quotations are comparable rubbers for all years, with the possible exception of 1940 (see below). The identity of the 1928 and 1948 article number — "110" — suggests the same type and style rubber has been produced over the entire period. (One of the 1928 sources gives the article number as "110." The other gives the number as "10"; however, the first digit "1" in the number "110" simply indicates that the rubbers are *men's,* and both 1928 sources indicate the quotation is for *men's* rubbers.) The 1937 designation does not specify a particular article number but indicates the quotation is for all article numbers relating to the rubbers described. Also the 1937 designation indicates the rubbers are *low.* The 1948 article number indicates the rubbers are *low rubbers, without a tongue,* according to an illustration in N. A. Arkhangel'skii (ed.), *Tovarovedenie promysh-*

lennykh tovarov (Moscow, 1947), II:51. This is no doubt true of the 1928 rubbers also.

With regard to 1940, the designation is too brief to be certain that all three quotations used in computing the average price are for the same rubbers, though they probably are. Also, use of the July 1939 price as representing the price in effect during the first half of 1940 may result in an error in the annual average.

173. Valenki

1937: Valenki, muzhskie obyknovennye, tonkie i dvoinye, utiazhelennye, natural'nogo tsveta, razmer 26–32 sm.; fabrik "Krasnyi Tekstil'shchik," im. Razumova, "Smychka" i dr. (valenki, men's, ordinary height; thin, double or heavy weight; natural color, size 26 to 32 cm; produced in "Krasnyi Tekstil'shchik," "Razumov," "Smychka," and other factories). This price was established in August 1936, according to *RTS-M-36*, I:88. There was apparently no price change during 1937.

1928: Valianaia obuv': sapogi dvoinye; natural'nye serye obyknovennye; muzhskie; razmer 29 sm (felt footwear: boots, double; natural grey, ordinary height; men's; size 29 cm). The quotation is from a price list for the Union of Producers' Cooperatives (*Vsekopromsoiuz*) and applies to footwear of the Nizhegorod raion, in *SMG-28*, p. 607. This price list is a retail price list, it is believed, comparable to that for *Moskozh*, discussed under item 159.

1948: Valenki muzhskie nekrashenye, artikul 0129N (valenki, men's, natural color, article no. 0129N). The quotation is from *PD-14-12-47*. A more detailed description of these boots can be worked out from data on the meaning of the article numbering system given in Andrusevich, p. 157, as follows: *valenki grubosherstnye obyknovennye, s obyknovennym golenishchem, muzhskie, razmer 29, nekrashenye* (valenki, coarse wool felt of ordinary weight (that is, neither thin nor heavy and probably equivalent to the weight described above as "double"), ordinary height, men's, size 29, natural color).

1952: This price is computed from the 1948 price and the following price reduction: March 1950, felt footwear, 25%. Approximately the same price for very similar valenki was reported in March 1952 in *UMA*.

1954: This price is computed from the 1952 price and the following price reduction: April 1953, felt footwear (*obuv' valianaia*), 5%.

Comparability: 1928–37. The 1928 boots priced appear to be the most comparable of those listed in the source to the 1937 boots. They are comparable in height, thickness of material, and size, and both are undyed or natural. The 1928 boots priced, however, are described as *valianaia sapogi* and may not be entirely comparable to the 1937 *valenki*. There does not appear to have been much difference between prices of sapogi and valenki in 1928, but the price list in *SMG-28* is difficult to interpret and I cannot be certain of this. Also, other difficulties in interpreting the 1928 price list mean some reservations must be made regarding comparability. One of these uncertainties lies in the fact that the prices are cited by producing area, without indication as to whether the prices reflect quality differences or simply regional price differentials.

1937–48–52–54. The 1937 and 1948 descriptions are similar. In both years, the valenki compared appear to be among the lower priced ones: (1) A 1936 valenki of the same description but produced in two other named factories was 90.00 rubles. The prices of valenki went up to 115.00 rubles per pair, according to *RTS-M-36*, I:88. (2) Men's valenki were reported by various sources to range up to 480.00 rubles per pair during 1948. One source reported in January 1949 that the 195.00-ruble valenki mentioned in the December 1947 decree were not available while higher priced valenki were on the market (*UM*).

174. Cotton thread, 6-strand

1937: Khlopchato-bumazhnye nitki 6-ti slozhenii, matovye i appretirovannye, 200 iard., belye i chernye (cotton thread, 6-strand, mat or glazed, 200 yards, white or black). The quotation apparently applies to threads of *no. 10 to no. 80*. The quotation is from *RTS-M-36*, I:38.

1928: Nitki matov. belye na katushkakh 200 iard no. 30–40 "Medved" (thread, mat white, 200-yard spools, no. 30 to 40, "Medved" brand). This price is the average of the monthly quotations for state and cooperative shops reported in *ESBM*. "Medved" brand thread is a 6-strand thread, according to the designation in a wholesale price list in *SMG-28*, p. 667.

Comparability: The quotations are for comparable types of thread.

175. Cotton thread, 3-strand

1937: Khlopchatobumazhnye nitki trekh slozhenii: Ramgreb 1-i sort, glantsevye i matovye, chernyi etiket; 200 m; belye i chernye (cotton thread, 3-strand; "Ramgreb" grade 1, glossy or mat, black label; 200 meters; black and white). The quotation is from *RTS-M-36*, I:37 and *RTS-36*, p. 150. The price was established in April 1935 and, it is believed, remained in effect through 1937.

1948: Nitki khlopchatobumazhnye na katushkakh, belye i chernye (cotton thread on spools, white and black). The price established by *PD-14-12-47* was 1.75 rubles per spool. Late in 1948 *thread, black and white, cotton* was reported to be 1.90 rubles per spool (*UM*). It is assumed this was the same thread, and the average of the two quotations is taken as an approximate average annual price.

1952: This price is computed from the 1948 price and the following price reductions: March 1949, thread, 15%; March 1950, thread and thread products, 20%. A somewhat lower price — 1.20 rubles per spool of 200 meters — was reported in early 1953 for *cotton thread, no. 40, highest grade* and *no. 30, grade I* (*UMA*).

1954: This price is computed from the 1952 price and the following price reductions: April 1953, thread and thread products, 10%; April 1954, thread and thread products, on the average, 15%.

Comparability: The 1948 description does not indicate the grade of thread, the number of strands, or even the size of the spool, but (1) presumably *first grade* was the grade priced in the 1947 decree; (2) common sewing thread is usually 3-strand, at least in America, and 3-strand thread is the kind for which the greatest number of prices are listed in the retail section of the 1936 price list; (3) the ordinary postwar spool size appears to be 200 meters. A postwar commodity handbook states that cotton thread is wound on spools of 200 meters and for the sewing industry on spools up to 5,000 meters (Andrusevich, p. 184). On these grounds, the 1937 thread selected is believed to be comparable to the postwar thread priced.

176. Silk thread

1937: Shelkovye nitki shveinye na katushkakh, no. 8, 100 m (silk sewing thread on spools, no. 8, 100 meters). The quotation is from *RTS-M-36*, I:42; II:76. The price was established in August 1936 and, it is believed, remained in effect through 1937.

1948: Thread, black and white, spool, silk. The quotation is for November 1948, from *UM*.

1952: This price is computed from the 1948 price and the 1949 and 1950 reductions in the prices of thread listed under cotton thread, (item 175).

1954: This price is computed from the 1952 price and the 1953 and 1954 reductions in the prices of thread listed under cotton thread (item 175).

Comparability: It is assumed that the thread priced in 1948 and subsequent years is comparable to the 1937 *no. 8 silk thread.* This, it is believed, is the common type of sewing thread. It is the only type of silk thread listed in the main 1936 retail price list; however, a supplementary price list includes also a *no. 20* thread at about twice the price of the *no. 8* thread. Silk sewing thread is ordinarily sold in 100-meter spools, according to Andrusevich, p. 184; thus the size of the postwar spool priced is presumably the same as the 1937 size spool. The 1937 source makes no distinction between black and white thread on the one hand, and colored thread on the other, while the postwar price is for black and white thread only.

177. Dress pattern

1937: The price shown is the average of the following: *women's dress patterns —* 0.50 ruble each, and *children's dress patterns —* 0.35 ruble each. The patterns were for spring and summer fashions. The quotations are from *ST*, April 2, 1937, p. 4.

1948: The price shown is the average of the following: *dress patterns, women's —* 6.00 rubles each, and *dress patterns, children's —* 4.50 rubles each. The quotations are for November 1948, from *UM.*

1952: This price is the same as the 1948 price. None of the postwar price decrees specifically mentions dress patterns, and these do not appear to be included in any group for which price reductions are mentioned. Accordingly, I assume there was no change in price, but this may be in error.

1954: This price is the 1952 price reduced by 15%. I assume there was a reduction in April 1954 of 15%, the same reduction that applied to thread. This is rather arbitrary, but it is intended to take account of the probability that there was some reduction in the prices of such items as dress patterns between 1948 and 1954, even though such items cannot be identified among the products and groups of products for which price reductions have been listed in the price decrees.

Comparability: It seems unlikely there was much of a spread of prices for dress patterns, and the items priced are probably reasonably comparable. The postwar price relatives — over 1200 in 1948 and 1952 — are greater than for any other product priced; this may reflect a desire to discourage home sewing. As indicated, there is some doubt as to whether any of the price reductions since 1948 have applied to dress patterns, and there is a possibility of error in the 1952 and 1954 quotations.

178. Straightedge razor

1937: This is the midpoint of the range of prices for *britvy parikmakherskie* (razors, barbers' or straightedge) produced by the RSFSR People's Commissariat of Local Industry. The least expensive is described as: *britvy parikmakherskie obyknovennye, 72 x 18 mm s dereviannoi ruchkoi* (straightedge razors, ordinary, 72 x 18 mm, wooden handle); the most expensive as: *britvy parikmakherskie uzkie, 72 x 14 mm so vstavnoi ruchkoi* (straightedge razors, narrow, 72 x 14 mm, detachable handle). Prices established July 1, 1937 ranged from 5.05 to 16.10 rubles each, according to *Preiskuranty snizhennykh s 1 iiulia 1937 g. otpusknykh tsen na promyshlennye tovary,* p. 51. The midpoint of this range is used. It is increased by 5% to allow for the fact that the July 1937 prices were those established following the average reduction of 10% in the prices of *galentereia* (haberdashery and notions) on July 1, 1937. Razors, it is believed, are included in the *galentereia* group, and it is assumed the average price reduction is applicable.

1948: A *straightedge razor* was 23.00 rubles in the summer of 1948, according to *UM*; and *straightedge razors, plastic handles* were 30.00, 40.00, and 75.00 rubles each in November 1948, according to *UM*. The midpoint of this entire range is used.

1952: This price is computed from the 1948 price and the following price reductions: March 1949, metal haberdashery and notions, 10%; March 1950, jewelry and metal haberdashery and notions, 15%. It is not clear whether these reductions applied to razors, as assumed.

1954: This price is computed from the 1952 price and the following price reduction: April 1953, metal haberdashery and notions, 10%. It is not clear whether this reduction applied to razors, as assumed.

Comparability: The range of prices is so similar for the two years, 1937 and 1948, that it seems safe to assume that the comparison made of the midpoints of the ranges is valid. There seems to have been some substitution of plastics for some of the older materials used in the razor handles; all but one of the 1948 razors are described as having plastic handles while the 1937 razors had handles of wood, bone, and jet as well as celluloid. However, there seems no reason to believe that the utility of the razors would have been significantly changed by this substitution.

As indicated, there is some doubt about whether the postwar price reductions for the group *metal haberdashery and notions* applied to razors, as assumed here.

179. Razor blades

1937: Lezviia dlia bezopasnykh britv iz importnoi stali (razor blades for safety razors, imported steel). *Grade 1 (sort I)* blades were 0.29 ruble each and *grade 2 (sort II)* were 0.26 ruble each in 1936, according to *RTS-M-36,* I:7. The average of these prices is used. There was an average reduction of 10% in the prices of haberdashery and notions on July 1, 1937, which, it is assumed, applied to razor blades.

1948: Razor blades. The quotation is for the summer of 1948, from *UM.*

1952: This price is computed from the 1948 price and the following price reductions: March 1949, metal haberdashery and notions, 10%; March 1950, jewelry and metal haberdashery and notions, 15%. It is not clear whether these reductions applied in fact to razor blades. After the March 1950 price reduction, *razor blades* were reported to be 0.30 to 0.40 ruble each (*UM, UMA*). The high price was for *extra grade* blades, while the lower prices (0.30 and 0.36 ruble) are for blades designated only by brand and not by grade (*UMA*). The computed price thus corresponds to the low end of the price range in effect in 1952.

1954: This price is computed from the 1952 price and the following price reduction: April 1953, metal haberdashery and notions, 10%. Again, it is not clear whether this reduction is applicable to razor blades.

Comparability: The 1952 quotation appears to be for a grade of razor blades comparable to either the 1937 *grade 1* or *grade 2,* and thus reasonably comparable to the 1937 average price of these two grades. There is some doubt as to whether the postwar price reductions for the group *metal haberdashery and notions* apply to razor blades, as is assumed here. If they did in fact apply, the 1948 and 1954 quotations are also reasonably comparable to that for 1937. If these reductions did not apply, the 1948 quotation is probably for a higher grade of blade than the 1937 quotation, and the 1954 quotation is too low.

180. Household soap, 50% fat content

1937: Khoziaistvennoe mylo mramornoe 50% zhirnosti (household soap, marbled, 50% fat content). The quotation is from *RTS-M-36,* I:28. This price was established in May 1936. Apparently household soap prices did not change until 1941 (*MLR,* November 1939; May 1941).

1928: Mylo mramornoe (marbled soap). At various dates the designation was *mylo mramornoe goriachei varki* (marbled soap, produced by boiling process) or *mylo iadrovye* (grained soap). These are presumably descriptions of the same soap. The quotation was the same throughout 1928. The quotation is from *ESBM*.

Comparability: The *50% fat content* 1937 soap priced is the only one described as *marbled* and is probably comparable to the 1928 *marbled* soap. The fat content of the 1928 soap is not indicated so there is some doubt as to comparability. The 1937 price range was from 2.30 rubles per kg for *second grade 40% fat content soap* to 4.60 rubles per kg for *highest grade, 72% fat content soap* (*RTS-M-36,* I:28).

181. Household soap, 60% fat content

1937: Tverdoe khoziaistvennoe mylo, vysshii sort 60% zhirnosti (solid household soap, highest grade, 60% fat content). The quotation is from *RTS-M-36,* I:28. The price was established in May 1936. The same price is cited for *laundry soap* from October 1936 through January 1, 1941 in *UM*; Trivanovitch; and *MLR,* May 1941.

1940: Laundry soap. The quotation is from *MLR,* May 1940; February and May 1941.

1948: Mylo khoziaistvennoe vyssh. sort 60% (household soap, highest grade, 60%). The quotation is from *PD-14-12-47.*

1952: This price is computed from the 1948 price and the following price reductions: March 1950, household soap, 40%; March 1951, household and toilet soap, 15%.

1954: This price is computed from the 1952 price and the following price reductions: April 1953, household soap, 15%; April 1954, household soap, an average of 15%.

Comparability: The designation is the same for all years.

182. Glycerine soap

1937: Glycerine soap. This is an average annual price computed from the following observed quotations: January and April 1937 — 1.70 rubles per cake; July and October 1937 and January 1938 — 1.55 rubles per cake. The quotations are from *UM* and Trivanovitch. The price change occurred on June 1, 1937, according to *PD-28-4-37.*

1940: Glycerine soap. This price is an average computed from the following observed quotations: January 1940 — 1.60 rubles per cake; July 1940 and January 1941 — 2.20 rubles per cake. The quotations are from *MLR,* May 1940; February and May 1941. It is assumed the price change took place July 1, 1940.

Comparability: The soaps priced are probably comparable. In 1936 there was a range of prices of glycerine soaps of 1.35 to 2.15 rubles per 100 gm, according to *RTS-M-36,* I:30–35. There is then some room for error in the comparison. However, the observed prices move as one would expect them to, and very likely the same grade soap is priced at each date.

183. Toilet soap, "Family"

1937: Mylo tualetnoe, pervyi sort 70%, "Semeinoe," poluoval'noe, otkrytoe (toilet soap, grade 1, 70% fat content, "Family," semi-oval, unwrapped). The average 1937 price is computed from the following data: (1) The price was set at 1.80 rubles per 200-gm cake or 0.90 ruble per 100-gm cake in May 1936, according to *RTS-M-36,* I:31, 35 and *RTS-36,* pp. 166, 169, 171, 173. (2) This price was reduced to 1.45 rubles per 200-gm cake (or 0.73 ruble per 100-gm cake) on June 1, 1937, according to *ST,* May 22, 1937.

1948: Mylo tualetnoe, Semeinoe (toilet soap, Family). The price of 4.00 rubles per 100-gm cake was established in *PD-14-12-47*. The average 1948 price is computed from this quotation and the following price reduction: April 1948, "perfume-cosmetic" products (*parfiumerno-kosmeticheskie tovary*), 10%. This category refers to perfumes, toiletries, and cosmetics, but just what products are included is not entirely clear. I assume that toilet soap falls under this heading, but this may be in error.

1952: This price is computed from the April 10, 1948 price and the following price reductions: March 1950, toilet soap, 50%; March 1951, household and toilet soap, 15%. In March 1949 there was a 20% reduction in the prices of "perfume products" (*parfiumernye izdeliia*); I assume this did not affect toilet soap prices, but the coverage of this category is not clear and I may be in error.

1954: This price is computed from the 1952 price and the following price reductions: April 1953, toilet soap, 20%; April 1954, toilet soap, an average of 20%.

Comparability: The same brand of soap is priced in each year. The 1948 designation does not indicate the fat content of the soap, but since the brand is the same, it is likely the fat content is the same for all years also. As indicated, some errors may have been made in applying the postwar price reductions.

184. Toothpaste, "Sanit"

1937: Zubnaia pasta "Sanit" (toothpaste, "Sanit"). The price was 3.00 rubles per tube prior to June 1, 1937 and 2.50 rubles per tube after that date, according to an advertisement in *ST,* June 6, 1937.

1948: Toothpaste, "Sanit," about 100-gm tube. In July 1950 the price was reported to be 2.43 rubles per tube, in *UM.* The 1948 price is computed from this price and the following price reductions: March 1950, "perfume-cosmetic products" other than perfumes, Eau de Cologne, and certain surprise packages, 25%; March 1949, "perfume products," 20%; April 1948, "perfume-cosmetic products," 10%.

1952: This price is computed from the July 1950 price and the following price reduction: March 1951, perfume, Eau de Cologne, surprise packages, and other "perfume-cosmetic products," 15%.

1954: This price is computed from the 1952 price and the following price reductions: April 1953, perfume, Eau de Cologne, and other "perfume-cosmetic products," 10%; April 1954, perfume, Eau de Cologne, and other "perfume-cosmetic products," an average of 10%.

Comparability: The same brand of toothpaste is priced in all years. The size of the 1937 tube is not known, and there is room for discrepancy here, though the fact that the 1937 advertisement did not indicate the size of the tube may be an indication that this brand comes in only one size tube. There is some doubt about the postwar prices, all computed from a quotation for July 1950. It is assumed in the computations that all the postwar reductions in the prices of *perfume-cosmetic products* or *perfume products* apply to toothpaste. Toothpaste, it is believed, is generally included in this category. The decree of April 28, 1937, for instance, lists a price reduction for the group "perfume goods (Eau de Cologne, tooth powder, perfume, vaseline, and others)." Even so, the postwar group price reductions may not always have been applicable to toothpaste, and the actual reductions in toothpaste prices may have differed from the average group price reductions.

185. Toothbrush

1937: Zubnaia schetka (toothbrush). This is presumably a child's toothbrush. This item, with a 1938 price of 0.84 ruble, is listed among the items which might be included in a combination of toilet and *galentereia* articles in a gift package for children in *Voprosy sovetskoi torgovli*, no. 8–9, 1938, pp. 58–59. The 1937 average price shown is computed from the 1938 price and the 10% reduction in *galentereia* prices effected July 1, 1937.

1948: Toothbrush, plastic handle, second-rate pig bristles. Prices in November 1948 were 3.30 and 8.00 rubles each, according to *UM*. The lower price is used in the comparison. The average 1948 price is computed from this quotation and the following price reduction: April 1948, several plastic consumer goods, 20%.

1952: This price is computed from the April 1948 price and the following price reduction: March 1949, plastic and celluloid products (dishes, home appliances (*bytovye pribory*) and other), 20%. It is assumed that the following price reductions did not affect toothbrushes: March 1950, plastic products, 20%; March 1951, plastic products, 10%. In both these cases, plastic products are listed under the general heading *household goods* (*tovary khoziaistvennogo obykhoda*), which presumably does not include toothbrushes. My assumptions may be in error, however.

1954: This price is computed from the 1952 price and the following price reductions: April 1953, toothbrushes, clothes brushes, and other brushes, an average of 20%; April 1954, medicines and other sanitary and hygienic supplies, an average of 15%.

Comparability: Comparability can be only rough in this case. Probably the inexpensive 1948 toothbrush is more comparable than the expensive one to the 1937 toothbrush, since the latter is a child's toothbrush. However, the 1948 price range is wide, and there is a possibility of a fairly large error. More or less arbitrary assumptions had to be made regarding the applicability of the postwar price cuts to toothbrushes, and the 1952 and 1954 computed prices are by no means firm.

186. Absorbent cotton

1937: This price is the average of the prices of the following: *vata gigroskopicheskaia* (absorbent cotton) — 0.75 ruble per 50 gm, and *vata gigroskopicheskaia-sterilizov* (absorbent cotton, sterilized) — 0.80 ruble per 50 gm. The quotations are from *RTS-36*, p. 209.

1948: Cotton wool. The quotation is for January 1951, from *UM*. The same price was in effect in 1948, it is believed. There was a reduction of 20% in the price of *vata* (wadding or cotton wool) in March 1950; but this appears to apply only to the wadding used to line clothing and not to medicinal cotton. The quotation is clearly for medicinal cotton, as it is listed in the source among medicines and toilet articles.

1952: This price is the same as the 1948 price. There were apparently no price changes until 1953.

1954: This price is computed from the 1952 price and the following price reductions: April 1953, medicines and other sanitary and hygienic supplies, an average of 15%; April 1954, medicines and other sanitary and hygienic supplies, an average of 15%.

Comparability: It is not known whether the postwar quotations are for *sterilized* cotton, so they are compared with the 1937 average of the prices of *sterilized* and *unsterilized* cotton. On the basis of the 1937 price differential, this means an error of about 3.5% in either direction is likely.

187. Gauze bandage

1937: Bint beloi marli, 14sm x 7m (bandage, white gauze, 14 cm by 7 m). The quotation is from *RTS-36*, p. 201.

1948: Bandages, 7 meters long by 14 cm wide. The quotation is for January 1951, from *UM*. There is no evidence of any price changes in such items between 1948 and 1951.

1952: This price is the same as the 1948 price. There were apparently no price changes until 1953.

1954: This price is computed from the 1952 price and the following price reductions: April 1953, medicines and other sanitary and hygienic supplies, an average of 15%; April 1954, medicines and other sanitary and hygienic supplies, an average of 15%.

Comparability: The bandages priced are of the same size and presumably of the same material, although the 1948 source does not specify the material.

188. Thermometer

1937: Termometr maksimal'n. (thermometer, maximum). The quotation is from a price list for medicines, et cetera, in *RTS-36,* p. 210.

1948: Clinical thermometer. The quotation is for January 1951, from *UM.* There is no evidence of any price changes in such items between 1948 and 1951.

1952: This price is the same as the 1948 price. There were apparently no price reductions until 1953.

1954: This price is computed from the 1952 price and the following price reductions: April 1953, medicines and other sanitary and hygienic supplies, an average of 15%; April 1954, medicines and other sanitary and hygienic supplies, an average of 15%.

Comparability: The description in each case is so brief that there is no way of knowing how closely comparable the thermometers priced are.

189. Castor oil capsules

1937: Kastorovoe maslo v kapsuliakh, kor. (castor oil in capsules, box). The quotation is from *RTS-36,* p. 207.

1948: Castor oil, 8 capsules of 0.5 gm. The quotation is for January 1951, from *UM.* The same price was in effect in 1948, it is believed.

1952: This price is the same as the 1948 price. There were apparently no price reductions until 1953.

1954: This price is computed from the 1952 price and the following price reductions: April 1953, medicines and other sanitary and hygienic supplies, an average of 15%; April 1954, medicines and other sanitary and hygienic supplies, an average of 15%.

Comparability: The 1937 source does not indicate the number of capsules to the box; it is assumed this was the same number as in the case of the postwar quotations. If this assumption is correct, there was no change in castor oil prices between 1937 and 1953. Scattered data suggest that medicine prices remained fairly constant over this period; and apparently aspirin was cheaper in 1953 than in 1937 (*RTS-36,* p. 207; *UMA*).

190. Tea kettle, brass, 3.5-liter

1937: Chainiki latunnye nikelirovannye, Tul'skogo patronnogo zavoda, emk. 3.5 litr. (tea kettles, nickel-plated brass, Tula cartridge factory, 3.5-liter capacity). The quotation is from *RTS-M-36,* I:100.

1928: Chainiki obyknovennye, latunnye nikelirovannye no. 3, 178 x 140 mm., emkost' 3.5 litr; 1.44 kg. (tea kettles, ordinary, nickel-plated brass, no. 3, 178mm x 140mm, 3.5-liter capacity; 1.44 kg). The 1928 price shown is computed as follows: (1) The wholesale price was 3.10 rubles per kg plus 0.50 ruble per piece for nickel-plating, according to *SMG-28,* pp. 518–519. For this kettle, which weighs 1.44 kg, the wholesale price is then: 1.44 x 3.10 rubles + 0.50 ruble = 4.96 rubles per kettle. (2) The retail price is computed by increasing this wholesale price by 18%. This is the maximum retail margin in price zone I, which included Moscow, established by a decree of April 15, 1927 for many kinds of metal housewares, according to *SMG-28*, pp. 39–40. Brassware, however, is not specifically mentioned in the decree, and the retail margin used here may be incorrect.

Comparability: Both quotations are for nickel-plated brass tea kettles of the same capacity, but there may be some quality differences.

191. Tea kettle, brass

1937: This price is the midpoint of the range of prices of *chainiki latunnye nikelirovannye, Tul'skogo patronnogo zavoda* (tea kettles, nickel-plated brass, Tula cartridge factory) of 2.5- to 7.5-liter capacity — 35.00 to 65.00 rubles each. The quotations are from *RTS-M-36*, I:100.

1948: Plain nickel teapot, medium size. The quotation is for November 1949, from *UM*. It is believed the price was the same in 1948.

A somewhat higher quotation is available, but this is presumably for a larger tea kettle. An advertisement in *Sovetskaia Belorossiia* of April 19, 1950 offers *nickel-plated brass tea kettles* for 130.00 rubles postpaid. This price would have been about 153.00 rubles in 1948, prior to the 15% reduction in the prices of brass utensils in March 1950.

1952: This price is computed from the 1948 price and the following price reduction: March 1950, brass utensils, 15%. There was a 10% reduction in prices of *metal housewares (knives, forks, spoons, and others)* in March 1949; this appears not to include utensils such as tea kettles and pots and pans.

1954: This price is computed from the 1952 price and the following price reduction: April 1953, primary alloy aluminum, enameled iron, galvanized, enameled cast-iron, brass, stainless steel, and electroplated utensils, 10%.

Comparability: The 1937 price used is the midpoint of the prices of all sizes of teapots listed in the source and hence should be at least roughly comparable to the postwar quotation for a tea kettle described in 1948 as medium-sized.

192. Pan, aluminum, 22-cm

1937: Kastriuli aliuminevye s 2 ruch. s kryshkami, diametr. 22 sm. (aluminum pans, with 2 handles and lid, 22 cm in diameter). The quotation is from *RTS-M-36*, I:103.

1928: Kastriulia alliuminevaia 22 s. (aluminum pan, 22 cm). Quotations for August 1928 through January 1929 in *ESBM* give the price in cooperative shops at 2.40 rubles each and the price in state shops at 2.49 rubles or 2.50 rubles each. The average of the state and cooperative shop prices is used.

Comparability: The pans compared are of the same diameter but may differ in various other respects.

193. Pan, aluminum, 18-cm

1937: Kastriuli aliuminevye s 2 ruchkami s kryshkami, 18 x 13 (aluminum pans, with 2 handles and lid, 18 x 13). The quotation is from *RTS-M-36*, I:95. It is clear from the context that the "18" in the phrase "18 x 13" indicates that the diameter of the pan is 18 cm; it is assumed that the "13" indicates a height of 13 cm. On this assumption, the capacity of the pan can be calculated at about 3.3 liters, or almost 3.5 quarts. The price was established in June 1936 and, it is believed, remained in effect through 1937.

1948: Three- to four-quart pan and lid, aluminum ware, unpolished and thin-looking. The price range in November 1948 was 25.00 to 30.00 rubles each, according to *UM*. The midpoint of this range is used.

1952: This price is computed from the 1948 price and the price reduction of

March 1950. The price reduction was 15% for utensils of primary alloy aluminum and 30% for utensils of secondary alloy aluminum. Not knowing which grade aluminum the pan priced is made of, I apply a reduction of 22.5%, the average of the percentage reductions for the two grades.

1954: This price is computed from the 1952 price and the following price reduction: April 1953, primary alloy aluminum, enameled iron, galvanized, enameled cast-iron, brass, stainless steel, and electroplated utensils, 10%. It is not clear whether the reduction for utensils of primary alloy aluminum is applicable to the pan priced, as is assumed.

Comparability: As indicated, it is believed that the 1937 pan priced had a capacity of about *3.5 quarts* and is thus comparable to the 1948 pan described as of *3- to 4-quart capacity.* There seems to have been little or no difference in price between one-handled and two-handled pans in 1936, so the fact that the number of handles is not indicated in the 1948 description is of no importance. The quality or weight of the aluminum is not specified and may not be entirely comparable. The postwar price reductions varied with the quality of aluminum, and some errors, probably minor, may have been made in computing the 1952 and 1954 prices.

194. Wash basin, aluminum

1937: Tasy dlia umyvaniia, aliuminevye, no. 105/45 (wash basins, aluminum, no. 105/45). It is believed that the second part of the article number indicates the basin has a circumference of 45 cm. The quotation is from *RTS-M-36*, I:94.

1948: Medium wash basin, aluminum. The price shown is the average of two prices observed in November 1948 — 29.00 and 35.00 rubles each. The quotations are from *UM*.

1952: This price is computed from the 1948 price and the price reduction of March 1950. As in the case of the aluminum pan (item 193), I apply a reduction of 22.5%, the average of the percentage price reductions for utensils of primary alloy and secondary alloy aluminum.

1954: This price is computed from the 1952 price and the following price reduction: April 1953, primary alloy aluminum, enameled iron, galvanized, enameled cast-iron, brass, stainless steel, and electroplated utensils, 10%. It is not clear whether the reduction for utensils of primary alloy aluminum is applicable to the wash basin priced, as is assumed.

Comparability: The 1948 *medium sized* wash basins are probably comparable in size to the 1937 *45-cm* basin. Wash basins are made in sizes of 40 to 55 cm, according to Andrusevich, p. 73 (the statement was made in connection with enameled ironware but is presumably applicable to aluminumware also), and the 45-cm one would seem to be about *medium* sized. The designations are too brief to determine comparability in other respects. The quality of the aluminum is not indicated for either year. Lacking knowledge on this point, the postwar price cuts for utensils of specified types of aluminum had to be applied rather arbitrarily, and some errors, probably minor, may have been made in computing the 1952 and 1954 prices.

195. Wash basin, enameled iron

1937: Zhelezno-emalirovannaia posuda: tasy umyval'n. glubokie, 38 sm. (enameled iron utensils: wash basin, deep, 38 cm). The quotation is from *RTS-M-36*, I:99.

1928: Emalirovannaia zheleznaia posuda: miski i tazy umyval'n., glubokie, 38 sm. (enameled iron utensils: wash basins, deep, 38 cm). The wholesale price was

1.10 rubles each, and the maximum retail trade margin in the Moscow price zone was 18% of the wholesale price, according to *SMG-28*, pp. 39–40, 77–79.

Comparability: The quotations are for basins of the same size and general characteristics, but there may be some quality differences. As indicated, the 1928 price is computed by applying the maximum retail margin to the wholesale price; the actual retail price may have been somewhat lower.

196. Cast-iron pot

1937: Zhelezno-emalirovannaia posuda: chuguny tsel'nye (gorshki), indeks 522, art. 14, 20 sm. (enameled iron utensils: pot cast in one piece (cast-iron pot), index 522, article no. 14, 20 cm in diameter). The quotation is from *RTS-M-36*, I:97.

1928: Emalirovannaia zheleznaia posuda: chuguny tsel'nye no. 30, 20 sm. (enameled iron utensils: pot cast in one piece, no. 30, 20 cm in diameter). The wholesale price was 1.15 rubles each, and the maximum retail margin for the price zone including Moscow was 18% of the wholesale price, according to *SMG-28*, pp. 39–40, 78.

Comparability: These pots are of the same material, type and size, but the model article numbers differ and there may be some small differences in quality. As indicated, the 1928 price is computed by applying the maximum legal retail margin to the wholesale price; the actual retail price may have been somewhat below the maximum.

197. Frying pan, enameled iron

1937: Zhelezno-emalirovannaia posuda: skovorody ploskie s ruchkami, indeks 507, artikul 6, 18 sm. (enameled iron utensils: frying pans, flat, with handles, index 507, article no. 6, 18 cm). The quotation is from *RTS-M-36*, I:97.

1928: Emalirovannaia zheleznaia posuda: skovorodki ploskie s ruchkoi, no. figur 13, razmer 18 sm. (enameled iron utensils: frying pans, flat with handle, shape no. 13, 18 cm). The wholesale price was 0.47 ruble each, and the maximum retail margin for the zone including Moscow was 18% of the wholesale price, according to *SMG-28*, pp. 39–40, 76–77.

Comparability: The quotations are for frying pans of the same size and general characteristics, but there may be some quality differences. As indicated, the 1928 price is computed by applying the maximum legal retail margin to the wholesale price; the actual retail price may have been somewhat lower.

198. Tea cup, enameled iron

1937: Zhelezno-emalirovannaia posuda: chashki chainye, indeks 518, 8 ili 9 sm. (enameled iron utensils: tea cup, index 518, 8 or 9 cm). The quotation is from *RTS-M-36*, I:97.

1928: Emalirovannaia zheleznaia posuda: chainye chashki, vypuklye, vysokie, no. 22 (enameled iron utensils: tea cup, rounded, deep, no. 22). The price used is the average of the prices of the *8-cm cup* — 0.28 ruble each — and the *9-cm cup* — 0.32 ruble each. These retail prices are computed from the wholesale prices and the maximum retail margin of 18%, given in *SMG-28*, pp. 39–40, 77–78.

Comparability: The quotations are for cups of the same size and general characteristics. The 1928 price, computed by applying the maximum retail margin to the wholesale price, may be somewhat above the actual retail price.

199. Pail, galvanized iron

1937: Otsinkovannaia posuda: vedro tsilindr. (galvanized iron utensils: cylindrical pail). This price is the midpoint of the range — 5.00 to 6.40 rubles each — cited in *RTS-M-36*, I:101–102.

1928: Vedro zheleznoe (iron pail). According to *ESBM*, the price in January 1929 was 1.05 rubles in state shops and 1.11 rubles in cooperative shops. The average of these two prices is used. The item priced is probably the same as the item described in *SMG-28*, p. 521 as follows: *posuda otsinkovannaia: vedro tsilindr.* (galvanized iron utensils: cylindrical pail). The wholesale price of this pail was 0.95 ruble each, and the maximum retail price — applying the maximum margin of 18% — would be 1.12 rubles. This is close to the actual prices quoted in *ESBM*.

Comparability: The quotations appear to be for roughly comparable pails.

200. Primus stove

1937: Primus latun. s gorelkoi (primus stove, brass, with burner). The quotation is from *RTS-M-36*, I:106.

1928: Latunnaia posuda i predmety domashnego obykhoda: primusa s chugunnoi reshetkoi (brass utensils and household appliances: primus stove with cast-iron grate). The price shown is computed from the wholesale price, cited in *SMG-28*, p. 524, at 6.50 rubles each, and the maximum retail margin of 18%.

1948: Primus stove, polished brass, with burner. Sovetskaia Belorossiia, April 19, 1950 advertised this item at 86.00 rubles. The average 1948 price is computed from this quotation and the following price reductions: March 1950, meat grinders, kerosene stoves, primus stoves, and spare parts, 20%; April 1948, primus stoves, kerosene stoves, and electric hot plates, 10%.

1952: This price is computed from the quotation for April 1950 and the following price reduction: March 1951, meat grinders, kerosene stoves, primus stoves, and spare parts, 10%.

1954: This price is computed from the 1952 price and the following price reduction: April 1953, hardware, meat grinders, kerosene stoves, lamps, lanterns, and other metal housewares, 10%. Although primus stoves are not specifically mentioned here, it is assumed, perhaps erroneously, that the price cut is applicable to them.

Comparability: Primus stoves are rather standardized, simple products, and the quotations are probably for closely comparable stoves. All are of brass. Although it is not specified, the 1928 quotation presumably includes the burner, as do the quotations for other years.

The 1937 and 1928 quotations are Moscow prices. Although the postwar quotations are taken from a Belorussian source, prices of primus stoves are probably uniform for the entire USSR.

201. Samovar

1937: The quotation applies to both of the following: (1) *samovary latun. No. 3 bankoi 666 mm* (samovars, brass, no. 3, jar-shaped, 666 mm); (2) *samovary nikel. No. 3 bankoi 622 mm* (samovars, nickel-plated, no. 3, jar-shaped, 622 mm). The quotations are from *RTS-M-36*, I:106.

1928: Samovary obykn. fasona, kryshka bankoi latun 15 v. 21.5 st.; razmer 660 mm; emkost' 5.18 l.; ves 5.53 kg (samovars, ordinary style, lid, jar-shaped, brass, 15 vershok (1 vershok = 4.445 cm), 21.5 glasses; circumference 660 mm; capacity 5.18 liters; weight 5.53 kg). *SMG-28*, p. 517, lists the wholesale price at 3.00 rubles per kg, which comes to 16.59 rubles for this samovar which weighs 5.53 kg. I assume the maximum retail price margin of 18% applicable to many metal housewares to be applicable also to samovars, though these are not mentioned in the decree setting forth retail trade margins (*SMG-28*, pp. 39–40).

1948: Plain nickel samovar, 3.622 liters. The quotation is for November 1949, from *UM*. The same price was in effect during 1948, it is believed. The source was probably mistaken in describing the samovar as having a capacity of 3.622 liters; the "622" may indicate a circumference of 622 mm, a standard size samovar. According to a 1947 handbook, A. K. Mel'kinov, *Posudo-khoziaistvennye tovary* (Moscow, 1947), p. 42, the only sizes in which samovars were made at the time were 622 mm, 666 mm, and 711 mm in circumference; these also are the only sizes listed in *RTS-M-36*. The "3" in the designation I assume means *article no. 3*, though it might alternatively relate to capacity or some other feature. I assume further that the adjective *plain* means the samovar was *jar-shaped* or *straight-sided* (*bankoi*) as distinguished from wine-glass-shaped (*riumkoi*).

1952: This price is computed from the 1948 price and the following price reduction: March 1950, brass samovars, 20%. The computed price corresponds with that reported in early 1953 for *samovar, lowest priced, 5-liter, no. 3, plain,* in *UMA*.

1954: This price is computed from the 1952 price and the following price reduction: April 1953, primary alloy aluminum, enameled iron, galvanized, enameled cast-iron, brass, stainless steel, and electroplated utensils, 10%. It is assumed that samovars are included here under the heading *utensils* (*posuda*) of *brass,* but this may be incorrect.

Comparability: 1928–37. The 1937 brass samovar with a circumference of 666 mm (article (1) above) appears to be closely comparable to the 1928 samovar priced.

1937–48–52–54. If all the assumptions made about the meaning of the 1948 designation are correct, the postwar quotations are for a samovar closely comparable to the 1937 *nickel-plated, no. 3, jar-shaped samovar with a circumference of 622 mm* (article (2) above). Although these assumptions are fairly strenuous, some confidence in their validity may be gained from the agreement of the price computed for 1952 with a price reported for a samovar fairly well matching the 1937 designation. If the assumption that the postwar quotation is for a samovar with a circumference of *622 mm* is correct, but the assumption that it is *jar-shaped* is incorrect, the postwar price relatives are probably too low. *Byzantine* (*Visant.* — possibly another term for wine-glass-shaped) *samovars, nickel-plated, 622 mm* were 130.00 and 165.00 rubles each in 1937 (*RTS-M-36*, I:106), compared with the samovar costing 105.00 rubles used in the comparison.

202. Samovar, 711-mm

1937: Samovary nikel. no. 3 bankoi, 711 mm (samovars, nickel-plated, no. 3, jar-shaped, 711-mm). The quotation is from *RTS-M-36*, I:106.

1948: Samovar, nickel-plated brass, jar-shaped, 6-liter. This quotation is from an advertisement of the Tashkent branch of the Soviet Mail Order House in *Pravda Vostoka,* January 21, 1950. Samovar prices were apparently not changed between December 1947 and March 1950, but it is possible that there were changes in the charge for handling and postage included in the advertised price. The mail order price advertised in *Pravda Vostoka* is applicable anywhere in the Soviet Union but might be somewhat higher than the price of the same samovar purchased in a Moscow store.

1952: This price is computed from the January 1950 price and the following price reduction: March 1950, brass samovars, 20%.

1954: This price is computed from the 1952 price and the following price reduction: April 1953, primary alloy aluminum, enameled iron, galvanized, enameled cast-iron, brass, stainless steel, and electroplated utensils, 10%. It is assumed that samovars are included in this category, but this may be incorrect.

Comparability: 1937 and 1948 designations are similar except that the size is expressed in terms of the circumference in the 1937 designation and in terms of capacity in the 1948 designation. The 1937 samovar with a circumference of 711 mm is comparable in size to the postwar samovar with a capacity of 6 liters, it is believed. The relationship between circumference and capacity indicated in *SMG-28*, p. 517 for jar-shaped samovars is as follows: 560 mm: 3.32 liters; 660 mm: 5.18 liters; 730 mm: 7.43 liters. As indicated under item 201, the only sizes in which samovars were made in 1947 and 1936 were 622 mm, 666 mm, and 711 mm.

203. Kerosene lamp

1937: Lampy "Stennik" no. 43, bez gorelki (kerosene lamps, "Wall" no. 43, without burner). The quotation is from *RTS-M-36*, I:106.

1928: Lampy stenniki no. 43, bez gorelok, razmer 10 lin. (kerosene lamps, wall, no. 43, without burner, size 10 lines). According to *SMG-28*, p. 524, the wholesale price of this lamp was 0.60 ruble each, *without reflector (reflektor)* and 0.75 ruble each *with reflector.* The average of these two wholesale prices is raised by 18% to obtain an estimated retail price. It is assumed that this maximum retail margin applies to kerosene lamps although they are not specifically mentioned among the metal housewares to which the maximum retail margin of 18% is applicable in *SMG-28*, p. 39.

The size of kerosene lamps and lamp chimneys is based on the width of the wick, expressed in "lines," according to Andrusevich, pp. 45, 76. One line (*liniia*) equals 2.5 mm.

Comparability: The lamps priced are of the same type and article number. The size of the 1937 wick is not mentioned, but it may well be the same size as the 1928 wick. The 1937 description does not indicate whether the reflector is included in the price cited for the lamp; accordingly, the average of the 1928 prices including and excluding the reflector is used.

204. Lamp chimney

1937: The price shown is the estimated average retail price of the following two lamp chimneys: *steklo dlia lamp ploskogo goreniia, OST 1442, Berlinskogo fasona, dlia gorelok razmer 7 lin.:* (1) *otoplen. s kleim. I sort;* (2) *zabelen. s kleim. I i II sort* (chimney for lamps with flat wicks, OST standard 1442, Berlin style, for burners size 7 lines: (1) fired designs, grade I; (2) frosted designs, grade I or II). The wholesale price of (1) was 8.50 rubles per 100 and the wholesale price of (2) was 7.00 rubles per 100, according to *RTS-36*, p. 201. The retail trade margin in Moscow was 35% of the wholesale price, according to *RTS-M-36*, I:110. The average of the two wholesale prices is increased by 35% to obtain the retail price used in the comparison.

1928: Steklo lampovoe 7 lin. (lamp chimney, 7 lines). The quotation is from *ESBM,* for January 1929. The same price, it is assumed, was in effect throughout 1928.

Comparability: The lamp chimneys priced are for lamps of the same size wick. Although it is not stated in the 1928 designation, the 1928 chimney is almost certainly for a flat-wicked lamp, as is the 1937 chimney. Beyond this there may well be some differences in quality.

205. Electric light bulb

1937: This price is the midpoint of the range of prices of *electric light bulbs of 10 to 50 watts* coming under the following description: *elektricheskie lampy nakalivaniia vakuumnye s metallicheskoi vol'framovoi nit'iu dlia napriazheniia 110, 120 i 127 vol't* (electric light bulbs, vacuum incandescent, tungsten metal filament, for 110, 120, and 127 volts). The 1936 prices ranged from 0.63 to 0.82

ruble each, depending on the wattage, the shape, and whether frosted or clear. The least expensive is *grusheobraznye: v prozrachn. kolbe moshchnost'iu 10–15–25 vatt* (pear-shaped, transparent bulb of 10, 15, or 25 watts); the most expensive is *sharoobraznye: v matirovannoi kolbe moshchn. 40–50 vatt* (ball-shaped: frosted bulb, 40 to 50 watts). The quotations are from *RTS-M-36*, II:106. The midpoint of this 1936 price range is used in the comparison. It is adjusted to an average 1937 price by taking into account the reduction of 8% in the prices of electric light bulbs on June 1, 1937.

1948: The quotation is for both of the following *electric light bulbs:* (1) *40 watt, 120 volt, filament and evacuation good;* (2) *25 watt, 120 volt, zinc based socket poorly soldered.* The quotations are for November 1948, from *UM*.

1952: This price is computed from the 1948 price and the following price reductions: March 1949, electrical housewares (electric tea kettles, electric hot plates, electric irons, and others), 10%; March 1950, electric light bulbs, 11%. The application of the March 1949 reduction to light bulbs may be incorrect.

1954: This price is computed from the 1952 price and the following price reductions: April 1953, electric light bulbs, 25%; April 1954, electric light bulbs, electric heaters, washing machines, and vacuum cleaners, 10%.

Comparability: The postwar quotations are for bulbs falling within the range of wattage and are of the same voltage as the 1937 bulbs but the lack of other descriptive details about the postwar bulbs precludes any further narrowing of the comparison.

206. Electric hot plate

1937: Elektro-plitki, otkrytye, "Kr. Maiak," "Iabep" (electric hot plates, open element, "Kr. Maiak" and "Iabep" brands). The quotation is from *RTS-M-36*, II:109.

1948: Hot plates, ordinary. In January 1949, the price of this was 30.00 rubles, according to *UM*. The average 1948 price is calculated from this quotation for January 1949 and the following price reduction: April 1948, primus stoves, kerosene stoves, and electric hot plates, 10%. The description of this hot plate as *ordinary* is taken to mean an *open element hot plate* of the simplest kind. The same source reports these other January 1949 prices: *concealed element hot plate* — 50.00 rubles and *large hot plate* — 54.00 rubles.

1952: This price is computed from the April 1948 price and the following price reductions: March 1949, electrical housewares (electric tea kettles, electric hot plates, electric irons, and others), 10%; March 1950, other electrical housewares, 20%.

1954: This price is computed from the 1952 price and the following price reduction: April 1953, electric household appliances, electrical fixtures, and other electrical products, 15%.

Comparability: As indicated above, the 1948 *ordinary hot plate* appears to be an *open element hot plate* as is the 1937 item priced. This kind of hot plate seems to have been the least expensive type on the market in both the prewar and postwar years; presumably any advances in design, et cetera, made over this period were incorporated in the more complicated and more expensive types.

207. Electric iron

1937: This price applies to six of the eight *elektro-utiugi* (electric irons) listed in *RTS-M-36*, II:109: (1) *"Elektrik" 2.5 kl., artikul 9031;* (2) *Khemz 2.5 kl.;* (3) *"Elektrozavoda" 2.5 kl.;* (4) *"Mortrest" 2.5 kl.;* (5) *"Aviokhim";* (6) *"Iabep" 2.8 kl.* The brand names apparently relate to the producing factory. The *2.5 kl* or *2.8 kl* presumably indicate the weight of the irons in kilograms, although *kg* and not *kl* is the usual abbreviation for kilogram. The price of the above six irons was 23.00 rubles each; and two other irons are listed in the source at 26.00 and 28.75 rubles each.

1948: Electric iron. The quotation is for January 1949, from *UM*. This appears to be about the lowest priced iron. Another unpublished source reports a range of 60.00 to 100.00 rubles each for *electric irons* in January 1951; calculating back to 1948 on the basis of price reductions in March 1949 and March 1950, the 1948 range would be about 90.00 to 150.00 rubles. One lower quotation is available — 68.40 rubles in November 1949 (*UM*) or 76.00 rubles in 1948 — but this is said to be for a *second grade iron*. Presumably the quotation used is for a *first grade iron*.

1952: This price is computed from the 1948 price and the following price reductions: March 1949, electrical housewares (electric tea kettles, electric hot plates, electric irons, and others), 10%; March 1950, electric irons, 25%.

1954: This price is computed from the 1952 price and the following price reduction: April 1953, electrical household appliances, electrical fixtures, and other electrical products, 15%. In March 1954, the *cheapest electric iron* was reported to be 40.00 rubles by Harrison Salisbury, *New York Times,* March 25, 1954. This is considerably below the 1954 price computed for the electric iron priced in the index — 51.65 rubles — but rather near the price which can be computed for the *second grade iron,* which was 76.00 rubles in 1948 and would be 43.60 rubles in 1954.

Comparability: The designations are so brief as to give little basis for judging the degree of comparability. However, the prices compared appear to be for about the least expensive first grade irons and the products may be roughly comparable.

208. Sewing machine

1937: Shveinye mashiny ruchnye, 1-go klassa (sewing machines, hand-operated, first class). The 1936 wholesale price was 178.00 rubles and the retail trade margin was 9.85%, according to *RTS-36,* p. 204. The 1936 retail price is then calculated at 195.50 rubles. Local governments were entitled to set an additional markup to cover transportation costs (*RTS-36,* p. 204) but it is assumed no such additional charge was made in Moscow as the Moscow price list mentions only the regular 9.85% markup (*RTS-M-36,* II:101). This may be incorrect but transportation costs, if added, would probably have been small, as the sewing machine industry, it is believed, is centered close to Moscow. The 1937 average retail price is computed from the 1936 retail price and the price reduction of June 1, 1937. *PD-28-4-37* specified an average reduction of 10% in sewing machine prices; the actual reduction for *hand-operated sewing machines* is stated to have been 20.00 rubles in *ST,* June 1, 1937.

First class sewing machines have a *central shuttle* or bobbin (*tsentral'nyi chelnok*) and *second class* machines have an *oscillating shuttle* (*kachaiushchiisia chelnok*), according to *Voprosy sovetskoi torgovli,* no. 1–2, 1938, p. 66.

1948: Shveinye mashiny (sewing machines). The average 1948 price shown is based on the statement in *Pravda Ukrainy,* April 11, 1948 that the price was 1,000 rubles before the price reduction of April 10, 1948 and 900 rubles after this reduction. The price of 900 rubles was still in effect in Moscow in January 1949, according to *UM*. The quotation, it is believed, is for *shveinye mashiny semeinye, ruchnye, tsentral'noshpul'nye* (sewing machines, domestic, hand-operated, central bobbin). Machines of this description were advertised at 965 rubles postpaid by the Soviet Mail Order House in *Sovetskaia Belorossiia,* October 26, 1949. This price is somewhat higher than the post-April 10, 1948 price used — 900 rubles. The difference is probably explained by freight and handling charges included in the mail order price. Mail order prices are apparently the same over the entire Soviet Union and presumably include a freight charge based on average transportation costs. Freight and postal charges were increased in the fall of 1948 (*New York Herald Tribune,* October 24, 1948) — that is, after the date of the *Pravda Ukrainy* quotation and before the date of the *Sovetskaia Belorossiia* advertisement. An alternative possibility, however, is that the 900-ruble machine priced for the index is a *second class* machine, rather than a *first class* machine, as I assume.

1952: This price is computed from the April 1948 price and the following price reductions: March 1950, sewing machines and parts, 20%; March 1951, sewing machines and parts, 10%.

1954: This price is computed from the 1952 price and the following price reduction: April 1953, sewing machines, 10%.

Comparability: The 1937 and postwar quotations are for *hand-operated sewing machines.* The designations are brief but there has been little if any change in sewing machines over this period, it is believed. (See Tom Whitney, *New York Times,* September 29, 1953.) The 1937 quotation is for *class 1* or *central bobbin* machines and it is believed this is true of the postwar quotations also. However, they may be for *class 2* or *oscillating shuttle* machines, and if this is the case, the postwar price relatives are roughly 10% too low.

209. *Pravda*

1937, 1928, 1940, 1948, 1952, 1954: Pravda (Truth), the daily newspaper of the Communist Party of the USSR. The price is printed on each issue.

Comparability: The size and format of *Pravda* were approximately the same in all years.

210. *Bol'shevik*

1937, 1928, 1940, 1948, 1952: Bol'shevik, the bimonthly journal of the Central Committee of the CPSU(B). The price is printed on each issue.

1954: The price shown is the 1952 price. It is intended to represent the price which probably would have been charged for *Bol'shevik* had this journal been published in 1954. In October 1952 *Bol'shevik* was superseded by *Kommunist,* which is larger and more expensive.

Comparability: The size and format of *Bol'shevik* remained about the same from 1928 until October 1952, when it was superseded by *Kommunist.* The issues of *Bol'shevik* examined contained 96 to 104 pages in 1929, 96 pages in 1937 and 1940, 72 to 96 pages in 1948, and 80 to 88 pages in 1952. Although *Kommunist* is somewhat thicker (128 pages) and more expensive than *Bol'shevik,* there was no change in size or price (1.80 rubles) between 1952 and 1954. Accordingly, as indicated, I use the 1952 price of *Bol'shevik* for 1954 also.

211. *Ogonek*

1937: Ogonek (The Spark), a popular illustrated weekly. The usual number of pages is 43 to 44, but one issue contains 22 pages. Some colored illustrations are included. The price — 0.50 ruble per issue — is printed on most issues. A few issues were marked 0.75 ruble, but this may be only in cases when two issues are combined in one or for other special issues.

1928: The issues examined contain 22 pages. The periodical is printed on newspaper-type paper and contains black and white but no colored illustrations. The price is printed on each issue. The price shown is stated to be for Moscow Province and railroad stations; perhaps a higher price was charged elsewhere.

1940: The quotation is taken from an issue for 1939; however, the same price, it is believed, was in effect through 1940. The author was not able to examine 1940 issues.

1948: Most issues contain 32 pages. Some colored illustrations are included. The cover is usually a black and white photograph. The price is printed on each issue.

1952: Most issues contain 32 pages. There are more colored illustrations than in issues for earlier years and the cover is usually a colored photograph. The price is printed on each issue.

1954: Most issues contain 32 pages. The appearance and number of colored illustrations are about the same as in 1952. The price is printed on each issue.

Comparability: Over the years there has been an improvement in quality of paper and in the number and quality of colored illustrations. In 1937, the number of pages was greater than in either 1928 or the postwar years.

212. *Planovoe khoziaistvo*

1937, 1928, 1940, 1948, 1952, 1954: Planovoe khoziaistvo (Planned Economy), a journal published by Gosplan. The journal was published monthly through 1940 and 6 times a year in 1948 and later years. The price is printed on each issue. This is a paper-covered journal. In 1928 a hard-covered edition was also published at 0.50 rubles more per issue.

Comparability: There was a substantial decrease in the number of pages over the period, from 317 to 352 pages in 1928, to 178 to 200 pages in 1937, 128 pages in 1940, and 96 pages in 1948, 1952, and 1954. The size and quality of the paper and cover and the general appearance have shown little change over the entire period.

213. *Lenin Collection*

1937: Institut Marksa-Engel'sa-Lenina pri TSK VKP (*b*) (Marx-Engels-Lenin Institute under the Central Committee of the Communist Party (Bolshevik), *Leninskii sbornik* (Lenin Collection), vol. XXX, 1937. This volume contains 330 pages and one illustration. The price is printed in the book.

1928: Ibid., vol. VII, 1928. This volume contains 374 pages and two illustrations. The number of pages and price of this volume are indicated in an advertisement in the back of vol. X of the same series.

1940: It is assumed that a volume of the same *Leninskii sbornik* (Lenin Collection) published in 1940 would have been 6.00 rubles. Volume XXXV, published in 1945, was 6.00 rubles. Volumes of a similar work, the 4th edition of *V. I. Lenin Sochinenie* (V. I. Lenin's Works), published in 1941, 1946, and 1948 were all 6.50 rubles.

1948: It is assumed that a volume of the same *Leninskii sbornik* published in 1948 would have been 6.00 rubles. This is the price of vol. XXXV, published in 1945. As indicated, volumes of the 4th edition of *V. I. Lenin Sochinenie* published in 1941, 1946, and 1948 were all the same price.

1952: This price is computed from the 1948 price and the following price reduction: April 1952, books, including textbooks, an average of 18%. The actual price reductions varied from 10% to 40%, depending upon the type of book and whether published by central or local publishing houses, according to *Izvestiia,* April 6, 1952. The reduction for political, social, and economic works published by central publishing houses was 10% (*ibid.*). This would be the correct percentage reduction for the *Leninskii sbornik* or similar works; however, inasmuch as the few books priced are intended to represent all books, I apply the average 18% price reduction to all books priced in the index.

1954: This is the same as the 1952 price as there were no further reductions in book prices.

Comparability: The 1928 and 1937 quotations are for volumes of the same series and of about the same number of pages. The quotations for 1940 and the postwar years are extrapolations of the price assumed to be charged for the same series based on the 1945 price of a volume of the same work and the 1941, 1946, and 1948 prices of volumes of a similar series, and the price cut effected in April 1952. As indicated, in the interest of representativeness, I apply the April 1952 average reduction in book prices of 18% rather than the 10% reduction applicable to works of this nature.

214. *Pushkin Works*

1937: Akademiia nauk SSSR (USSR Academy of Sciences), *Pushkin — polnoe sobranie sochinenii* (Pushkin — Complete Works), vols. I and IV, 1937. Vol. I contains 531 pages and vol. IV contains 484 pages. The price is printed on the back of each volume.

1940: Ibid., vol. VIII, book 1, 1940 and vol. IX, 1940. These volumes contain 619 and 462 pages. The price is printed on the back of each volume.

1948: Ibid., vol. III, book 1, 1948; vol. VIII, book 1, 1948; and vol. XV, 1948. These volumes contain 634, 494, and 391 pages, respectively. The price is printed on the back of each volume.

1952: This price is computed from the 1948 price and the following price reduction: April 1952, books, including textbooks, an average of 18%. The average reduction is applied for reasons mentioned under item 213, although the actual reduction for works of imaginative literature published by central publishing houses was 10%, according to *Izvestiia,* April 6, 1952.

1954: This is the same as the 1952 price as there were no further price reductions.

Comparability: The books compared are different volumes in the same series and are printed and bound in the same way. The number of pages varies somewhat from volume to volume but this apparently does not affect the price.

215. Book on Turgenev

1937: M. K. Kleman, *Ivan Sergeevich Turgenev; ocherk zhizni i torchestva* (Ivan Serge Turgenev; An Essay on His Life and Work), Gos. izd-vo khudozh. lit-ry (State Publishing House for Belles Lettres), Leningrad, 1936, 224 pages. The price is printed on the back of the book. This is a 1936 price but there seems to have been no significant change in book prices between 1936 and 1937.

1928: Leonid Grossman, *Sobranie sochinenii v piati tomakh, Tom III Turgenev; etudy v Turgeneve — Teatr Turgeneva* (Complete Works (in five volumes, vol. III), Turgenev; Studies of Turgenev — Turgenev's Theatre); Kn-vo "Sovremennye problemy," N. A. Stolliar (Publisher "Contemporary Problems," N. A. Stolliar), Moscow, 1928, 255 pages. The price is printed on the book.

Comparability: Both are small, cardboard-covered books of approximately the same quality and size. There are fewer pages in the 1937 book, but these are a little larger than the pages of the 1928 book.

216. Novel

1937: Viacheslav Shishkov, *Straniki* (The Wanderers), *izdanie tret'e pererabotannoe avtorom* (3d ed., rev. by the author), Gos. izd-vo khudozh. lit-ry (State

Publishing House for Belles Lettres), Leningrad, 1936, 454 pages. The price is marked on the back of the book. The book was published in 1936, but there seems to have been little if any change in book prices between 1936 and 1937.

1928: Fedor Gladkov, *Sobranie sochinenii, Tom II, desiatoe izdanie prosmotren-noe avtorom, Tsement, roman* (Works, vol. II, 10th ed. rev. by the author, Cement, novel), *"Zemlia i fabrika"* ("Earth and Factory"), Moscow-Leningrad, 1927, 317 pages. The price is marked on the back of the book. The book was published in 1927, but the price is probably fairly typical of 1928 prices as well.

Comparability: Both novels have hard covers. The 1928 novel contains fewer pages than the 1937 novel, but the pages of the 1928 book are somewhat larger and the general quality of the 1928 binding is a little better than in the case of the 1937 book. On balance, the novels priced seem comparable.

217. The Quiet Don

1937: M. Sholokov, *Tikhi Don, kniga tret'ia,* illustratsii S. G. Korol'kova (The Quiet Don. Book Three, illustrated by S. G. Koral'kov), Gos. izd-vo khudozh. lit-ry (State Publishing House for Belles Lettres), Moscow, 1937, 423 pages. The price is printed on the back of the book.

1940: This is the same as the 1937 price. No precisely comparable novel was found for 1940, but an examination of a number of novels printed in 1937 and 1940 suggests there was no change in the price of novels.

1948: M. Sholokov, *Tikhi Don, kniga tret'ia i chetvertaia* (The Quiet Don, Books Three and Four), Gos. izd-vo khudozh. lit-ry (State Publishing House for Belles Lettres), Leningrad, 1949, 803 pages. The price is marked on the back of the book.

1952: This price is computed from the 1948 price and the following price reduction: April 1952, books, including textbooks, an average of 18%. The reduction applicable to imaginative literature published by central publishing houses was 10%, according to *Izvestiia,* April 6, 1952. However, for reasons given above (item 213), the average price reduction of 18% is applied.

1954: This is the same as the 1952 price, as there were no further reductions in book prices.

Comparability: As indicated, I assume the 1937 price was applicable to novels of similar quality in 1940, and no further comment on comparability between these two years is in order. The 1937 edition priced contains only one book of the novel and has about half as many pages as the two-book 1948 edition. On the other hand, the pages of the 1937 edition are somewhat larger, and the 1937 edition contains full-page illustrations while the 1948 book contains only a few vignettes. In other respects the 1937 and 1948 books are similar in appearance and quality. As indicated, the 1952 and 1954 price is computed on the basis of the 1952 average price reduction rather than the specific reduction for this kind of book.

218. Pamphlet, 32 pages

1937: N. Evreinov, *O svoeobraznom krizise Profsoiuzov i ob ikh novykh zada-chakh* (On the Peculiar Crisis of the Trade Unions and Their Current Tasks), November 1936, 32 pages, edition of 75,000 copies. The price is printed on the pamphlet.

1928: D. Shvartsman, *Novyi sposob ustanovleniia zarabotnaia platy* (The New Method of Establishing Wage Rates), Gos. izd-vo (State Publishing House), Moscow, 1928, 32 pages. This item with its price — 0.10 ruble — is listed in the bibliography section of *Voprosy truda,* no. 5, 1928, p. 151. Pamphlets of 32 pages listed in this and other 1928 issues of *Voprosy truda* ranged from 0.05 to 0.20 ruble each, but the most common price was 0.10 ruble.

1948: A. P. Klimov, *Sovetskaia potrebitel'skaia kooperatsiia* (Soviet Consumer Cooperative Societies), Izd-vo "Pravda" (Published by *Pravda*), Moscow, 1948, 32 pages, edition of 100,000 copies. The price is printed on the pamphlet. This pamphlet is one of an extensive series of verbatim reports of public lectures issued under the auspices of *Vsesoiuznoe obshchestvo po rasprostraneniiu politicheskikh i nauchnykh znanii* (All-Union Society for the Dissemination of Political and Scientific Knowledge), all sold at the same price.

1952: This price is computed from the 1948 price and the following price reduction: April 1952, books, including textbooks, an average of 18%. Presumably the reduction applies to pamphlets. For reasons mentioned above, the average reduction of 18% is applied, rather than the reduction of 10% applicable to political, social, and economic works published in central publishing houses, indicated in *Izvestiia*, April 6, 1952.

1954: This price is the same as the 1952 price, as there were no further price reductions.

Comparability: The pamphlets are of the same size and are directed to about the same size and type of audience.

219. Pamphlet, 48 pages

1937: A. Khamadan, *Iaponiia na putiakh k bol'shoi voine* (Japan on the Road to a Major War), Sotsekgiz (State Publishing House of Social Sciences and Economics), Moscow, 1936, 48 pages. The price is printed on the pamphlet.

1940: A. Vyshinskii, *Konstitutsionnye printsipy Sovetskogo gosudarstva* (Constitutional Principles of the Soviet State), Gos. izd-vo polit. lit-ry (State Publishing House for Political Literature), Moscow, 1940, 48 pages. The price is printed on the pamphlet.

Comparability: These pamphlets are of the same size; they are similar in quality and in the type of audience to which they are addressed.

220. Phonograph PT-3

1937: Patefon PT-3 (phonograph PT-3). The average 1937 price is based on a statement in *ST*, June 1, 1937, that this phonograph would be 58.00 rubles cheaper after the 15% price reduction of June 1, 1937. From this it is calculated that the pre-June 1 price was 387.00 rubles (58 is 15% of 387) and that the post-June 1 price was 329.00 rubles. Other evidence indicates that this calculation gives a correct post-June 1 price, or one that may be a few rubles high. Several prices within the narrow range of 319 to 329 rubles for this phonograph are cited in a letter to the editor complaining about the variation in price within one city (Odessa) after the June price reduction, in *ST*, June 22, 1937.

The PT-3 is a hand-crank portable phonograph in a wooden case with leatherette finish, measuring 415mm x 290mm x 165mm, according to *Spravochnaia kniga po kul'ttovaram* (Moscow, 1954), p. 237.

1948: Patefon model' PT-3 (phonograph, model PT-3). The average 1948 price is computed from the price of 900.00 rubles established in December 1947 and the reduction of 20% in the prices of phonographs of April 10, 1948.

1952: This price is computed from the April 10, 1948 price and the following price reductions: March 1949, phonographs, 30%; March 1950, phonographs and parts, accordions, and baian accordions, 25%.

1954: This price is the same as the 1952 price as there were no further reductions.

Comparability: The commodity designation and model number are the same, and it seems unlikely that there were any changes in the phonograph between 1937 and 1954.

221. Baian accordion

1937: Trekhriadnaia khromaticheskaia garmonika sistemy "Baian"; s Moskovskim raspolozheniem klaviatury, 52 klapana pravoi ruki (4¼ oktavy) s gotovym ak- kompanementom; dlia akkompanementa 100 basov v 5 riadov (three-set chromatic scale accordion, Baian system; Moscow arrangement of the keyboard, 52 right-hand keys (4¼ octaves), with ready accompaniment; for the accompaniment 100 bass notes in 5 sets). Further descriptive details, not relevant to the comparison, are given in the source — *RTS-36*, p. 218.

The price is estimated as follows: (1) The 1936 wholesale price was 1,250.00 rubles for the instrument and 23.00 rubles for the case, and the retail trade margin was 16%, according to *RTS-36*, pp. 218, 223. This brings the 1936 retail price of instrument and case to 1,477.00 rubles. (2) Since transport costs were added at cost, an arbitrary addition of 5% of the retail price is made, bringing the total 1936 retail price to 1,550.00 rubles. (3) The average 1937 price is computed from the 1936 price and the reduction effected July 1, 1937. According to *PD-28-4-37*, musical instrument prices were to be reduced an average of 10 to 15%, but *ST*, June 30, 1937, indicates the actual reduction for baian accordions was 5 to 7%. I assume the reduction was 6%.

1948: Baiani s futliarami, 52 x 100, proizvodstva promarteli "Kirovskaia garmonika" (baian accordions with case, 52 x 100, produced by the Kirov Accordion Producers Cooperative). This was advertised in *Sovetskaia Belorossiia*, October 26, 1949 at 3,050 rubles postpaid. The average 1948 price is computed from this October 1949 quotation and the following price reductions: March 1949, pianos, accordions, baian accordions, and concertinas, 20%; April 1948, baian accordions, 10%.

1952: This price is computed from the October 1949 quotation and the following price reduction: March 1950, phonographs and parts, accordions and baian accordions, 25%.

1954: This price is computed from the 1952 price and the following price reduction: April 1953, musical instruments, an average of 10%.

Comparability: It seems clear that the *52 x 100* of the 1948 designation indicates *52 treble and 100 bass notes* and that the 1937 and postwar accordions are comparable in this respect. The price includes a case in both years, and is the price delivered to the consumer. However, the postwar price is a Belorussian price, and the amount included in the 1937 price for transportation costs may be incorrect.

For both 1937 and 1948 a quotation is available for a lower priced baian accordion with 52 treble and 100 bass notes. The 1937 item is described as identical to the instrument priced except that it is smaller, being of portable size (*portativnogo razmera*). Its price was roughly two-thirds of the price of the instrument priced (*RTS-36*, p. 218). The only difference indicated in the 1949 source between the instrument priced in the index and the less expensive one is that the latter is a product of the RKKA factory while the former is a product of the Kirov Accordion Producers Cooperative. It is assumed that the less expensive instrument with a 1949 price about two-thirds of the price of the instrument used in the comparison was a portable instrument like the less expensive 1937 accordion, and that the comparison made is correct, aside from possible minor differences in quality. This, however, may be in error.

222. Piano

1937: This is an average of the prices of the following three pianos. The prices shown below are retail prices, excluding transport costs, computed from the whole-sale prices and the retail trade margin of 16%. (1) *pianino kabinetnoe, model' IX B, cherno-polirovannoe, s metallicheskoi ramoi i perekrestnymi strunami, 7 oktav* (upright piano, cabinet, model IX B, black finish, metal frame, cross-strung, 7 octaves) — 1,740 rubles. (2) *pianino kabinetnoe, model' IX SH, cherno-polirivannoe, s metallicheskoi pantsyrnoi ramoi, perekrestnymi strunami, odinarnoi repetitsionnoi mekhanikoi, 7 oktav* (upright piano, cabinet, model IX SH, black finish, metal reinforced frame, cross-strung, single repeat mechanism, 7 octaves) — 1,856 rubles; (3) *pianino kabinetnoe, model' Muztrest, cherno-polirovannoe, s metalicheskoi ramoi, noveishei konstruktsii, perekrestnymi strunami i repetitsion-nym mekhanizmom, 7 oktav* (upright piano, cabinet, model "Music Trust," black finish, metal frame, newest construction, cross-strung, repeat mechanism, 7 octaves) — 1,972 rubles. The quotations are from *RTS-36*, pp. 217, 223. To allow for trans-portation costs, not included in the retail prices shown above, I increase the average price by about 8%. The prices of some musical instruments were re-duced on July 1, 1937 (*PD-28-4-37*) but, it is believed, piano prices were not affected.

1948: Piano droit (Gordey); *piano, upright, small* (*UM*); *piano* (*pianino Krasnyi Oktyabr*), *upright type, black finish* (*UM*). Gordey, in *France-Soir,* July 2–3, 1950, reports the price was 5,850 rubles in the spring of 1950. Prior to the reduction of 10% in piano prices of March 1, 1950, this price would be 6,500 rubles. This is the price cited in the two unpublished reports for the period March 1, 1949 to March 1, 1950. The 1948 price is computed from this price and the following price reduction: March 1949, pianos, accordions, baian accordions, and concertinas, 20%.

1952: Piano droit. This price is the one cited by Gordey for the spring of 1950. There were no further price reductions until April 1953.

1954: This price is computed from the 1952 price and the following price reduc-tion: April 1953, musical instruments, an average of 10%. The computed price — 5,265 rubles — falls within the range reported in early 1954 for *upright pianos* of 3,500 to 5,400 rubles by Marshall MacDuffie, "Russia Uncensored," *Collier's,* March 5, 1954, p. 98.

Comparability: Since one of the postwar sources describes the piano priced as small, this is compared with the three 1937 *cabinet-type, 7-octave pianos.* The only other upright piano listed in the 1936 handbook is a *salon* or *concert* (*salonnoe*) *piano of 7¼ octaves.* It should be noted that the addition of about 8% to the 1937 list prices to cover transportation charges is rather arbitrary. The postwar prices presumably include such transportation charges, at least to the Moscow store.

223. Bicycle

1937: Muzhskie velosipedy dorozhnye, s polirovannymi sharikovymi putiami, shlifovannymi konusami, val'tsovannoi bol'shoi zubchatka, s nikelirovannymi obo-dami i lakirovannymi shchitkami, s tsep'iu s soprotivleniem razryvu ne menee 650 kg., s konusnym i gaechnym kliuchami, s nasosom i sumkoi, linovannye (men's bicycles, road, with polished ball-bearing action, ground cones, milled large gear wheel, nickel-plated rims, lacquered fenders, chain with a tensile strength of not less than 650 kg, with cone and nut wrenches, pump and tool case, lined). The same bicycle but with a bell, first-aid kit, oiler, and nipple-wrench (or nickel-wrench; the sources differ), and screwdriver was 10 rubles more expensive. The quotation is from *RTS-36*, p. 205 and *RTS-M-36*, I:6. The price was established in July 1935 and, it is believed, remained in effect through 1937. There was a reduction in the prices of "sports goods (fishing and hunting gear, balls, chess and checker sets, and others)" on June 1, 1937; bicycles seem important enough to have been specifically mentioned if the reduction was intended to apply to them, and it is assumed it was not.

1948: Velosipedy (bicycles). The average 1948 price is computed from the statement in *Pravda Ukrainy,* April 11, 1948, that these were 1,400 rubles each before and 1,120 rubles each after the 20% price reduction of April 10, 1948. It is assumed that the quotation is for a standard men's bicycle with few accessories.

The price used — 1,120 rubles after April 10, 1948 — may be compared with other available quotations. The following quotations are for the period April 10, 1948 to March 1, 1949; in some cases the price for this period has been computed from a quotation for a later date and the relevant annual price reductions: *Bicycles of many makes and designs* — 900 to 2,500 rubles (Edmund Stevens in *Christian Science Monitor,* October 27, 1949); *Bicyclette pour hommes, 3 vitesses* — 1,173 rubles (Gordey in *France-Soir,* July 2–3, 1950); *Velosipedy Khar'kovskogo zavoda, uluchshenye, dorozhnye, muzhskie "V-17"* (Bicycles, Kharkov factory, improved road, men's, "V-17") — 1,341 rubles (advertisement in *Sovetskaia Belorossia,* October 26, 1949); *Man's bicycle* — about 1,120 rubles *(UM).* The latter — which agrees with the quotation used in the index — is the lowest price specifically cited for a man's bicycle. The lower prices are perhaps for children's bicycles, and the higher prices are presumably for better quality bicycles (and in some cases for women's bicycles, which are somewhat more expensive than men's of the same quality).

1952: This price is computed from the April 1948 price and the following price reductions: March 1949, bicycles, 20%; March 1950, bicycles and parts, 20%; March 1951, bicycles, motorcycles, and parts, 10%. The computed price — 645 rubles — is below the range cited for the same period for *men's standard (not racer) model bicycles* of 724 to 761 rubles, in *UMA.*

1954: This price is computed from the 1952 price and the following price reduction: April 1953, bicycles and parts, 10%.

Comparability: The nature of the source of the 1948 quotation and the fact that the postwar quotation falls at the low end of a rather wide price range indicate that the postwar bicycle priced is probably a standard men's bicycle with few or no accessories or extra features. It should be at least roughly comparable to the 1937 bicycle priced, it is believed.

The 1937 price is for bicycles produced in state enterprises, as is presumably the postwar price. It should be pointed out, however, that bicycles produced by producer cooperatives were more expensive in 1937. An order of November 1935 indicates that retail prices of cooperative produced bicycles might exceed the established prices for state produced bicycles of similar quality by as much as 30% (*RTS-M-36,* I:7). This obviously would make a considerable difference if cooperatives produced bicycles in significant quantities; it is believed they did not.

224. Camera, FED

1937: Fotapparaty sistemy FED (cameras, FED system). This price represents the midpoint of two prices — 704 and 881 rubles — cited for this camera in a letter of complaint about the variance in price in *ST,* June 15, 1937. The FED camera is a portable camera of the Leica type, according to Arkhangel'skii, II:221.

1948: Fotoapparat "FED-1" (camera, FED-1). The quotation is from *PD-14-12-47.* The same price is reported in *UM* in January 1949 for a FED *3.5 lens camera,* described as similar to the Leica 3.5.

1952: This price is computed from the 1948 price and the following price reductions: March 1949, cameras and binoculars, 10%; March 1950, cameras and other photographic supplies, 20%. The computed price — 792 rubles — is considerably below the price of 890 rubles reported for *camera, FED* in late 1952 or early 1953 in *UMA*.

1954: This price is computed from the 1952 price and the following price reduction: April 1954, cameras, an average of 10%.

Comparability: The same camera is priced in all years but there may have been some changes in model. It is not known which of the two 1937 quotations was the correct legal price; as indicated, the midpoint of the two prices cited is used. The price computed for 1952 is below that reported in a visitor's report; perhaps not all of the postwar reductions in camera prices affected the FED camera, as assumed.

225. Pencil, "Union"

1937: Karandashi chernye I sort, "Soiuz" shestigrannyi; no. 1 miagkii, no. 2 sr. tverd., no. 3 tverdyi, no. 4 ochen' tverd. (lead pencils, grade 1, "Union" hexagonal; no. 1 soft, no. 2 medium hard, no. 3 hard, no. 4 very hard). The quotation is from *RTS-M-36*, II:102. This is a 1936 price. It is assumed that the 5% reduction in the prices of school supplies effected July 1, 1937 was not applied to such inexpensive items, and that the 1936 price was in effect throughout 1937.

1928: Karandash prostoi chern. (pencil, plain, lead). The quotation is for state and cooperative shops in January 1929, as reported is *ESBM*. This is apparently one of the *"Soiuz"* ("Union") brand pencils listed at 3.20 to 4.00 rubles per gross wholesale in *SMG-28*, pp. 37, 577, 585. At the maximum retail margin for pencils of 20% in Moscow (*ibid.*, p. 37), any of these wholesale prices would amount to about 0.03 ruble per pencil at retail.

Comparability: Both the 1928 and 1937 quotations are, it is believed, for the same brand and type of pencil.

226. Pencil

1937: This is the average price of a group of *karandashi chernye 1-i sort* (pencils, black, grade 1) priced at 0.05 and 0.07 ruble apiece. The following pencils were 0.07 ruble: *"Soiuz" shestigrannyi no. 1 miagkii; no. 2 sr. tverd.; no. 3 tverdyi; no. 4 ochen' tver.* ("Union," hexagonal, no. 1 soft; no. 2 medium hard; no. 3 hard, and no. 4 very hard); *"Shkol'nyi" kruglyi i shestigrannyi no. 1; no. 2; no. 3* ("School," round and hexagonal, nos. 1, 2, and 3). The following were 0.05 ruble: *karandash shestigrannyi i kruglyi nono. 233, 234, 235, 260 i 1926* (pencil, hexagonal and round, nos. 233, 234, 235, 260, and 1926). Four other pencils are listed at 0.10 ruble, but since one of them is described as a drawing pencil and one is called "Rembrandt" it is assumed that all the 0.10-ruble pencils were drawing pencils. The quotations are from *RTS-M-36*, II:102. The 5% reduction in prices of school supplies of July 1, 1937 presumably did not apply to such inexpensive items.

1948: Lead pencils. The quotation is for November 1948, from *UM*.

1952: This is the same as the 1948 price as there were no reductions in pencil prices between 1948 and April 1953.

1954: This price is computed from the 1952 price and the following price reductions: April 1953, pencils, pens, and other writing and drawing supplies, 15%; April 1954, pencils, pens, and other writing and drawing materials and office supplies, 15%.

Comparability: The postwar designation is too brief to be certain, but the quotations are probably for closely comparable pencils.

227. Pen holder

1937: Ruchki uchenicheskie (pen holders, students'). The 1936 price range was 0.12 to 0.15 ruble each, according to *RTS-M-36*, II:103. The only difference indicated in the source among the three pen holders listed relates to the producing factory. The midpoint of the 1936 price range — 0.135 ruble — is reduced to 0.13 ruble to take account of the 5% reduction in prices of school supplies effected July 1, 1937.

1948: Pen. (This is clearly a *pen holder;* the source also lists *pen nibs.*) The quotation is for late 1950, from *UM.* The same price, it is believed, was in effect in 1948.

1952: This is the same as the 1948 or 1950 price cited above; there were no reductions in prices of pen holders until April 1953.

1953: This is computed from the 1952 price and the following price reductions: April 1953, pencils, pens (*per'ia, ruchki*), and other writing and drawing materials, 15%; April 1954, pencils, pens (*per'ia, ruchki*), and other writing and drawing materials and office supplies, 15%.

Comparability: The descriptions are too brief to be certain of the degree of comparability here.

228. Pen point

1937: Per'ia, 1-i sort (pen points, grade 1). The price shown — 0.02 ruble each — is that of three of the four pen points listed in *RTS-M-36*, II:103; the fourth pen point listed was 0.03 ruble. There was a 5% reduction in the prices of school supplies on July 1, 1937, but presumably this was not applied to a 2-kopek item.

1948: Pen nibs. The quotation is for late 1950, from *UM.* The same price, it is believed, was in effect during 1948.

1952: This is the same as the 1948 and 1950 price cited above. There were no reductions in prices of pen points until April 1953.

1954: This price is computed from the 1952 price and the following price reductions: April 1953, pencils, pens (*per'ia, ruchki*), and other writing and drawing materials, 15%; April 1954, pencils, pens (*per'ia, ruchki*), and other writing and drawing materials and office supplies, 15%.

Comparability: The postwar quotation is probably for a pen point comparable to one of the three 1937 pen points priced though there is a possibility it is more comparable to the 1937 3-kopek pen point.

229. Paint set

1937: Akvarel'nye kraski v tubakh No. 2 i maslianye kraski v tubakh No. 3; nabor 10 tsvetov v karton. kor. (water colors in no. 2 tubes or oil paints in no. 3 tubes; set of 10 colors in cardboard box). This is listed at 2.30 rubles per set in *RTS-M-36*, II:104. There was an average reduction of 5% in the prices of school supplies on July 1, 1937. This presumably applied to the paint sets priced, which are listed among school supplies in the source.

1928: The quotation is for either oil or water colors, as follows: (1) *kraski maslianye i etiudnye, v kart. kor., nabor 10 tonov, No. 2300.10 i No. 2305.10* (oil and sketch paints, in cardboard box, set of 10 colors, nos. 2300.10 and 2305.10); (2) *kraski akvarel'nye v tubakh, v kart. kor., nabor 10 tonov, No. 2310.10 i No.*

2315.10 (water colors in tubes, in cardboard box, set of 10 colors, Nos. 2310.10 and 2315.10). It is clear from the context of the price list that the *oil paints* are in size *no. 3 tubes* and the *water colors* in size *no. 2 tubes*. The quotation is from *SMG-28*, p. 706.

Comparability: The designation is the same in each year and is fairly detailed, so comparability is assured.

230. Kerosene

1937: Kerosin (kerosene). This price is given for the urban parts of price zone II, which includes Moscow and most of the rest of the USSR, in *RTS-36*, p. 228. The same price is cited for *kerosene* throughout 1937 in *UM* and Trivanovitch.

1928: This price is cited for both state and cooperative shops throughout 1928 in *ESBM*.

1940: This price is cited for January and July 1940 and January 1, 1941 in *MLR*, May 1940; February and May 1941.

1948: The quotation is from *PD-14-12-47*.

1952: This price is computed from the 1948 price and the following price reductions: March 1950, kerosene, 10%; March 1951, kerosene, 22%.

1954: This price is computed from the 1952 price and the following price reductions: April 1953, kerosene, 25%; April 1954, kerosene for lighting, 38%. These reductions bring the post-April 1, 1954 price to exactly the 1940 level. This is in accord with a statement of Mikoyan's in *Pravda*, April 27, 1954.

Comparability: The product is presumably comparable. None of the price lists make any reference to different grades of kerosene. However, a 1948 commodity handbook indicates there are two grades of kerosene for lighting (Andrusevich, p. 25) and it may be that in recent years a distinction in grades has been made, which is reflected in retail prices. Nevertheless, the quotations used presumably relate to the most commonly used grade, which has likely been of the same quality throughout the period.

231. Matches

See item 232.

232. Matches

1937: Spichki (matches). The price established in December 1932 was 0.03 ruble per box (*korobka*); in December 1935, without changing the price per *box,* a price of 0.25 ruble per *package of 10 boxes* (*pachka 10 korobok*) was introduced, according to *RTS-36*, p. 178. As of June 1, 1937, the price was reduced from 0.03 to 0.02 ruble per *box* (*PD-28-4-37*). It is assumed that the price per *package of 10 boxes* was reduced correspondingly. The 1937 quotations in *UM* for a box of matches correspond with the above prices.

1928: Spichki (matches) or *spichki svedskie* (Swedish matches). This price is reported in effect in all types of retail outlets from January 1 through July 1, 1928 and again in January 1929 in *ESBM*. The source does not price matches at other dates, but presumably the price was in effect throughout the year. The unit priced, designated *pachka*, is a *package of 10 boxes*, it is believed.

1940: Matches. This price is an average of the following quotations: January 1, 1940 and January 1, 1941 — 0.05 ruble per *box;* July 1, 1940 — 0.03 ruble per *box*. The quotations are from *MLR*, May 1940; February and May 1941.

1948: Spichki (matches). The quotation is for a *box* (*korobka*) of matches, from *PD-14-12-47*.

1952: This price is computed from the 1948 price per box and the following price reductions: March 1950, matches, 25%; March 1951, matches, 20%. The computed price is confirmed by a report for early 1953 (*UMA*).

1954: This price is computed from the 1952 price and the following price reductions: April 1953, matches, 17%; April 1954, matches, 20%.

Comparability: 1928–37. The comparison between 1928 and 1937 is based on the price of a *package of 10 boxes* as (a) this is the unit priced in *ESBM* — probably because it was the standard unit sold in 1928, and (b) the price per box was somewhat less when purchased in a package of 10 boxes than when purchased separately in 1937, but probably not in later years. The standard number of matches in a box in 1937 was 52 (see below); it is not known whether this was the same in 1928.

Some of the 1928 quotations, and possibly all, are for Swedish matches, while presumably the 1937 matches are Soviet produced. The extent to which Soviet matches were made the butt of jokes of Americans visiting Russia in the 1930's suggests that the 1937 matches may have been of a lower quality than the 1928 matches.

1937–40–48–52–54. The comparison between 1937 and later years is based on the price per *box* of matches. The same number of matches — 52 — were supposedly included in a box in all of these years, according to statements in *ST*, March 22, 1937 and V. I. Sheinman, *Bakaleinye tovary; spravochnoe posobie* (Moscow, 1946), p. 92. It should be mentioned that the 1937 statement was in a letter to the editor complaining about usually getting less than the standard number of matches in a box; it is not known whether the situation was any better in later years. Presumably the matches are of comparable quality.

233. Cigarettes, grade 3

1937: Papirosy, 3 sorta (cigarettes, grade 3). The quotation is from *RTS-36*, p. 161. Twenty-one different brands of this grade of cigarette are listed at the same price.

1928: Papirosy 2 sort A (cigarettes, grade 2 A). This price was established by a law of May 7, 1927 (*ZA*, no. 27–28, 1927, p. 21), and remained in effect until August 10, 1929 (*ZA*, no. 45, 1929, p. 20; no. 59, 1929, p. 9). The same price is cited throughout 1928 in *ESBM*. The *ESBM* designations vary as follows: *papirosy 2 sorta* (cigarettes, grade 2); *papirosy 2 sorta A* (cigarettes, grade 2 A); *papirosy 4 sorta A — byvshii 2-oi sort* (cigarettes, grade 4 A — formerly grade 2); *papirosy sort 4* (cigarettes, grade 4). These designations all relate to the same product. There was a change of grading nomenclature during 1928, under which *grade 2 A* cigarettes were renamed *grade 4* cigarettes. This is indicated in one of the *ESBM* designations — *cigarettes grade 4 A, formerly grade 2* — and also in a law of October 19, 1929. This lists the following item: *papirosy sorta 2 A (4 s.)* (cigarettes grade 2 A (grade 4)), along with other grades expressed both in terms of the old and the new nomenclature (*ZA*, no. 59, 1929, p. 9).

Comparability: The 1937 *grade 3* cigarettes are, it is believed, comparable to the 1928 *grade 2 A* or *grade 4* cigarettes. There were numerous changes in the nomenclature of the various grades of cigarettes between 1927 and 1937, apparently without changes in quality, and sometimes without any change in price. Following the laws through this period, the changes of nomenclature for the cigarettes priced appear to be as follows: (1) May 1927 until sometime during 1928: *grade 2 A;*

(2) 1928 and 1929: *grade 2 A* and *grade 4* both in use; (3) March 1930 to March 1932: *grade 4;* (4) March 1932 to July 1933: *3 sort (sushchestv. 4 s.)* (grade 3 (essentially grade 4)); (5) July 1933 to January 1935: *vnutrenn. r. 3 sort* (domestic market, grade 3); (6) January 1935 to, probably, the present: *3 sort* (grade 3). The sources are as follows: *ZA,* no. 27–28, 1927, p. 21; no. 45, 1929, p. 20; no. 59, 1929, p. 9; *Zakanodatel'stvo i rasporiazheniia po torgovle,* no. 14, 1930, p. 11; no. 56, 1930, p. 15; *SRTS-35,* pp. 465–468; *RTS-36,* pp. 156–162. If my interpretation of the laws and other data is correct, the 1937 and 1928 cigarettes are the same quality; if not, there is a possibility of a fairly substantial error.

234. Cigarettes, "Metro"

1937: Papirosy 1 sort "V," "Metro," 1/25 pachka (cigarettes, grade 1 "C," "Metro," pack of 25). The quotation is from *RTS–36,* p. 160. There was a reduction in the prices of higher grade cigarettes (*papirosy vysshikh sortov*) on June 1, 1937, but presumably this did not apply to the grade of cigarettes priced.

1948: "Metro" cigarettes. In January 1949 the price was reported in *UM* to be 2.00 rubles per box of 20, which is the same as 2.50 rubles per box of 25. The average 1948 price is computed from this 1949 quotation and the following price reduction: April 10, 1948, cigarettes, cigars and cigarillos, 10%.

1952: This price is computed from the April 1948 price and the following price reductions: March 1949, tobacco products, 10%; March 1950, cigarettes, cigarillos, tobacco, and makhorka, 20%; March 1951, cigarettes, cigarillos, and tobacco, 10%.

1954: This price is computed from the 1952 price and the following price reduction: April 1953, cigarettes of grades other than highest, cigarillos, and tobacco, 5%.

Comparability: The brand of cigarettes priced is the same and, although the grade is not indicated in the 1948 designation, it is believed that all "Metro" brand cigarettes are *grade 1 "C"* — at least this was the case in 1936.

235. Cigarettes, "Pushki"

1937: Cigarettes, "Pushki." This price is computed from the price prevailing until June 1, 1937 of 2.50 rubles per pack of 25 and the price after that date of 2.25 rubles per pack. The quotations are from *UM* and Trivanovitch. The same item is described as *papirosy V/sort no. 4, Pushki* (cigarettes, highest grade no. 4, "Pushki") in *RTS-36,* p. 158. The price reduction of June 1 was 10% for highest grade cigarettes, according to *PD-28-5-37.*

1940: Cigarettes, "Pushki." This price is cited throughout 1940 in *UM* and in *MLR,* May 1940.

Comparability: The same brand of cigarette is priced in both years.

236. Cigarettes, "Deli"

1937: Cigarettes, "Deli." The price was 3.00 rubles per pack of 25 until June 1, 1937 when it was reduced to 2.70 rubles per pack. The quotations are from *UM* and Trivanovitch. The price reduction of June 1 was 10% for highest grade cigarettes. The cigarettes priced are listed as *papirosy V/sort no. 3, Deli* (cigarettes, highest grade no. 3, "Deli") in *RTS-36,* p. 158.

1940: Cigarettes, "Deli." This price is cited throughout 1940 in *UM* and in *MLR,* May 1940.

Comparability: The same brand of cigarette is priced in both years.

237. Cigarettes, "Kazbek"

1937: Papirosy v/sort no. 3, "Kazbek," 1/25 kor. (cigarettes, highest grade no. 3, "Kazbek," box of 25). This price is computed from the 1936 price — 3.60 rubles — cited in *RTS-36,* p. 158, and the 10% reduction in the prices of highest grade cigarettes of June 1, 1937.

1948: Papirosy "Kazbek" vyssh. sorta no. 3, 25 sht. korobka (cigarettes "Kazbek," highest grade no. 3, box of 25 pieces). *PD–14–12–47* sets the price at 6.30 rubles per box. There was a 10% reduction in prices of cigarettes, cigars, and cigarillos on April 10, 1948. The price of *Kazbek cigarettes,* however, was reduced only to 6.00 rubles per pack, according to *UM.*

1952: This price is computed from the April 1948 price and the following price reductions: March 1950, tobacco products, 10%; March 1951, cigarettes, cigarillos, and tobacco, 10%.

1954: This price is computed from the 1952 price and the following price reduction: April 1953, highest grade cigarettes, 10%. The computed price is confirmed by a visitor's report of early 1955 *(UMA).*

Comparability: The brand and grade are the same for all years.

238. Cigarettes, "Allegro"

1937: Cigarettes, "Allegro." The price was 5.00 rubles per pack of 25 up to June 1, 1937 and 4.50 rubles after June 1, 1937, according to *UM.* The price reduction of June 1 was 10% for highest grade cigarettes. These cigarettes are listed as *papirosy V/sort No. 2, "Allegro"* (cigarettes, highest grade no. 2, "Allegro") in *RTS-36,* p. 157.

1940: Cigarettes, "Allegro." This price is cited throughout 1940, in *UM* and in *MLR,* May 1940.

Comparability: The same brand of cigarette is priced in both years.

239. Tobacco, grade 2

1937: Pipe tobacco, "Sphinx" *(UM); tabak trubochnyi, Sfinks* (pipe tobacco, "Sphinx") *(RTS-M-36,* p. 132); *tabak trubochnyi, 2 sort* (pipe tobacco, grade 2) — several brands of this grade are listed *(RTS-36,* p. 162). All designations apply to tobacco which was 5.00 rubles per 100 gm in 1936. The same price was in effect throughout 1937 for *pipe tobacco, Sphinx,* according to *UM,* and probably also for the other tobaccos listed above.

1928: Tabak 2 sort (tobacco, grade 2). The quotation is from *ESBM.* This item is apparently the same as (or at least its price was the same as the price of) *kuritel'nyi tabak, 2 sort A* (smoking tobacco, grade 2 A); this can be deduced from laws indicating the percentage price increase and the new absolute price effective August 1, 1929 in *ZA,* no. 45, 1929, p. 20; no. 59, pp. 11–12.

1940: Pipe tobacco, "Sphynx." This price was in effect in January 1940 and January 1941, according to *MLR,* May 1940 and *UM.*

Comparability: 1928–37. The 1928 tobacco is *kuritel'nyi tabak,* which presumably means *smoking tobacco for cigarettes,* while the 1937 tobacco is *pipe tobacco.* This is of little significance as there seems to have been little or no price difference between smoking and pipe tobacco of the same grade in 1937. The 1928 quotation is for *grade 2 A* while the 1937 quotation is simply for *grade 2.* The difference between these grades is probably minor and the tobacco priced is probably closely comparable. A note of caution is in order here in light of the many changes in grading nomenclature of cigarettes over this period. No evidence has been found indicating significant changes in grading nomenclature of tobacco, but it is possible that there were some changes.

    1937–40. The same brand of tobacco is priced in both years.

240. Tobacco, grade 1

    1937: Tabak trubochnyi 1 sort Zolot. Runo (pipe tobacco, grade 1, Golden Fleece). The quotation is from *RTS-36,* p. 162. As *Sphinx tobacco* (item 239) showed no price change during 1937, this is probably the case of *Golden Fleece* tobacco as well.

    1948: Smoking tobacco, "Golden Fleece." The quotation is for January 1949, from *UM.* Tobacco prices were not affected by the price reduction of April 1948.

    1952: This price is computed from the 1948 price and the following price reductions: March 1949, tobacco products, 10%; March 1950, cigarettes, cigarillos, tobacco, and makhorka, 20%; March 1951, cigarettes, cigarillos, and tobacco, 10%.

    1954: This price is computed from the 1952 price and the following price reduction: April 1953, cigarettes other than highest grade, cigarillos, and tobacco, 5%.

    Comparability: The quotations are for the same brand of tobacco. It is believed that the postwar product is *pipe tobacco;* that the 1948 designation of the product as *smoking tobacco* was meant to distinguish this from chewing tobacco rather than to make the finer Soviet distinction between *kuritel'nyi tabak* (smoking tobacco for cigarettes) and *trubochnyi tabak* (pipe tobacco). *Golden Fleece* is listed only as a pipe tobacco in the 1936 source. In any case, as indicated above, there was little or no difference between the prices of *cigarette* and *pipe* tobaccos of the same grade in 1936.

241. Makhorka

    1937: This is the average of the prices of the following two makhorkas: *makhorka obyknovennaia kuritel'naia* (makhorka, ordinary smoking) — 0.35 ruble per 50-gm package — and *makhorka vysshego kachestva* (makhorka, highest grade) — 0.40 ruble per 50-gm package. The quotations are from *RTS-36,* p. 162. Makhorka is a low-grade, coarse, strong tobacco high in nicotine content (Lazar Volin, *A Survey of Soviet Russian Agriculture,* Agriculture Monograph 5, U.S. Department of Agriculture (Washington, 1951), p. 148).

    1928: Makhorka v pachkakh Ranenburgskaia (makhorka in packages, Ranenburg) was 0.06 ruble for 50 gm from January to April 1928; *makhorka kuritel'naia* (smoking makhorka) was 0.07 ruble per 50 gm in August and September 1928 and 0.065 ruble from October on, according to the monthly quotations in *ESBM.* The average of these quotations is used. It is not clear whether the quotations are for different types of makhorka or whether they are for the same makhorka but indicate price changes during the year.

    1948: Makhorka. In late 1950, the price was 0.85 ruble per 50 gm, according to *UM.* The 1948 price is computed from this quotation and the following price reductions: March 1950, cigarettes, cigarillos, tobacco and makhorka, 20%; March 1949, tobacco products, 10%. Presumably the March 1949 reduction applies to makhorka as assumed, but this is not entirely certain.

    1952: This price is computed from the quotation for late 1950 cited above and the following price reduction: March 1951, makhorka, 15%.

    1954: This price is computed from the 1952 price and the following price reduction: April 1953, makhorka, 10%.

    Comparability: The quotations are probably for closely but perhaps not precisely comparable qualities of makhorka.

242. Makhorka, highest grade

1937: Makhorka tobacco. This price was in effect throughout 1937, according to quotations in *UM* and Trivanovitch. It corresponds to the price of *makhorka, highest grade* listed in *RTS-36*, p. 162 (see item 241).

1940: Makhorka tobacco. This price was in effect in January 1940 and in January 1941, according to *MLR*, May 1940 and *UM*.

Comparability: Probably the quotations are for the same grade of makhorka.

243. Rent

1928–1954: The rental rate compared is that paid for standard accommodations by a wage earner or salaried employee earning the average wage. For each year the rent is computed from the average monthly wage of wage earners and salaried employees and the formula established by law for calculating rentals for government housing. The rent law, promulgated in June 1926 and revised somewhat in May 1928, has remained essentially unchanged since then. The law is set forth in convenient form in V. P. Maslakov, *et al., Finansirovanie zhilishchno-kommunal'nogo khoziaistva* (Moscow, 1948), pp. 115–123; and, in more detail, in T. D. Aleksecv (comp.), *Zhilishchnye zakony* (Moscow, 1947).

According to the law, the rent paid by each tenant varies with (1) the basic rental rate for the city; (2) the location, conveniences, and condition of the apartment building and individual room or apartment; (3) the social class of the tenant; (4) the wage of the tenant; (5) the number of dependents of the tenant.

The basic rental rate for standard quality accommodations for cities of over 40,000 population is 0.35 to 0.44 ruble per square meter per month, and for cities of under 40,000 the minimum is 0.30 ruble per square meter per month. Within this range the rate is established locally for each city. The basic rate in Moscow has been 0.44 ruble per square meter per month since 1926, at least (N. I. Bronshtein, *Oplata zhilykh pomeshchenii* (Moscow, 1928), p. 77). I take the average basic rental for the USSR to have been 0.38 ruble per square meter per month over the entire period.

Deductions from or additions to the basic rental rate are made for variance from the general standards of accommodation for the city. That is, if there is no running water in the apartment house, there is a deduction of 10%; if there is hot water in the apartment, there is an addition of 5%; for rooms through which strangers have to pass, there is a deduction of 30%; for rooms with no outside source of light, a deduction of 75% is made. The minimum rent is 0.055 ruble per square meter per month. I compute the rent for standard quality accommodations and hence ignore such additions and deductions.

The basic rent applies to a tenant who is a wage earner or salaried employee (or falls within certain other social categories) and who earns 145 to 154 rubles per month. For persons earning less than this, there is a deduction from the basic rent, varying with his earnings and the number of his dependents. For persons earning more than this, an additional rental of 0.033 ruble per square meter per month is charged for each full 10 rubles of monthly wage above 145 rubles. There is, however, an upper limit of 1.32 rubles per square meter per month, regardless of the earnings of the tenant. Rent for a wage earner or salaried employee earning the average wage in the USSR can then be calculated from the following formula, where R is the monthly rental in rubles per square meter and W is the average monthly ruble wage of wage earners and salaried employees:

$$R = 0.38 + [0.033] [(W - 145)/10].$$

The average monthly wage of all wage earners and salaried employees was as follows:

Year	Rubles
1928	59
1937	253
1940	338
1948	583
1952	666
1954	696

(See Table 13.)

The years 1937 and 1940, it will be observed, are the only years to which the formula actually applies. Rent for these years is computed according to the above formula. With a basic rental rate of 0.38 ruble per square meter per month, the maximum rental is reached with a wage of 435 rubles or more a month. For the years from 1948 through 1954, the maximum rental of 1.32 rubles per square meter per month is applicable.

In 1928, the average wage was below 145 rubles a month, and the formula does not apply. According to the scale established in a decree of 1926, which, it is believed, remained in effect until September 1, 1928, wage earners and salaried employees with a monthly wage of 51 to 60 rubles paid 45% less than the basic rental rate (Biulleten' finansovogo i khoziaistvennogo zakonodatel'stva, no. 36, 1926, pp. 1423–1425). Rent for the period January 1 to September 1, 1928 is computed as $(1 - 0.45)$ (0.38) rubles $= 0.21$ rubles per square meter per month. From September 1, 1928 a tenant earning a wage of 50 to 60 rubles a month and having two dependents paid 75% of the basic rental rate, according to Zhilishchnoe zakonodatel'stvo . . . za 1928 g. (Moscow, 1929), pp. 295, 329. Thus, for the 4 months September 1 through December 31, 1928, average rent is calculated as (0.75) 0.38 ruble $= 0.285$ ruble per square meter per month. The average for the year comes to 0.235 ruble per square meter per month, rounded to 0.24 ruble.

Comparability: The rental rates used are comparable in that for each year the rent is that which would be paid for standard quality accommodations by a wage earner or salaried employee earning the average wage at the time. Certain comments relevant to comparability should be made, however. (1) The quality of accommodation I refer to as "standard" may well have changed over the period, but perhaps not significantly enough to affect the index. (2) It will be noted that the existence of a maximum rent means that after a certain level of wages is reached, the additions to or deductions from the basic rent become inapplicable and the same rent is paid for all quality housing. Up through 1940 a tenant in better than average housing earning the average wage would have paid somewhat more than the average rent figure used, and a tenant in below average housing earning the average wage would have paid less than the rent figure used. For a person earning the average wage, rent for the worst quality housing — that for which the minimum basic rent is 0.055 ruble per square meter per month — would have been as follows: 1928 — 0.055 ruble; 1937 — 0.385 ruble; 1940 — 0.68 ruble; 1948 on — 1.32 rubles.

(3) As indicated, I assume the same average USSR basic rental rate for the entire period 1928 through 1954. The Moscow rate has remained the same over this entire period and this is probably true of most cities, but it is quite likely there were increases in the basic rental rate of some of the newer and faster growing cities, in particular those whose population grew from under 40,000, in which the minimum basic rent of 0.30 ruble per square meter per month applies, to over 40,000, in which the minimum rate of 0.35 ruble per square meter per month

applies. If there was an increase in the average USSR basic rental rate between 1928 and 1940, the index from the time of the change through 1954 overstates to that extent the rise in rent; but an increase in the average basic rental rate occurring after 1940 would not affect the index inasmuch as the maximum rent would apply in any case for years from 1948 on.

244. Electricity

1937: The quotation is from Zhilishchnoe upravlenie Mossoveta, *Domovoe khoziaistvo; sbornik postanovlenii i instruktsii* (Moscow, 1938), pp. 93–94. The rate is for Moscow; it is believed the same rate was in effect in Leningrad.

1928: The quotation is from Leningradskoe ob"edinenie gosudarstvennykh elektricheskikh stantsii "Elektrotok," *Statisticheskii spravochnik, 1913–1928 gg.* (Leningrad, 1929), pp. 100ff. The rate is for lighting private apartments in Leningrad; the same rate was in effect in Moscow, it is believed.

1940: This rate is computed from the 1937 rate, which was apparently still in effect in early 1940, and a 25% rate increase ordered in a decree of April 10, 1940 (B. B. Veselovskii, *Kurs ekonomiki i planirovaniia kommunal'nogo khoziaistva* (Moscow, 1945), p. 346). It is assumed that the increase was effected as of April 1, 1940. The rate computed for the period following the increase — 0.25 ruble per kw-hr — is confirmed as in effect in Leningrad on January 1, 1941 in Leningradskaia oblastnaia planovaia kommissia, *Spravochnik tsen na stroitel'nye materialy, oborudovanie i transport,* no. 34, 1941, p. 575.

1948: The rate in Moscow was 0.25 ruble per kw-hr until August 16, 1948, according to *UM.* As of August 16, 1948 a rate of 0.40 ruble per kw-hr was established for all areas of the USSR except those where the rate previously had exceeded the new rate; in such areas, the old rate remained in effect (Maslakov, *et al.,* pp. 89–90). The 1948 average rate is computed from these Moscow rates.

1952: This is the rate established in August 1948. V. P. Maslakov, *Kommunal'nye tarify v SSSR* (Moscow, 1951), still indicates a rate of 0.40 ruble per kw-hr. Zaleski, "Annexe," p. 141, cites visitors' reports confirming this rate in April and May 1952 and in February 1953.

1954: This is the rate established in August 1948. No evidence has been found indicating a change in rates since that date.

Comparability: The item priced — 1 kw-hr of electric power — is the same in all years.

245. Water

1937: The quotation is from Zhilishchnoe upravlenie Mossoveta, *Domovoe khoziaistvo; sbornik postanovlenii i instruktsii,* p. 81. Actually this source cites a rate of 0.15 ruble per 100 *veder* or 0.128 ruble per cubic meter. Apparently the 0.128 ruble is a misprint for 0.122 ruble per cubic meter. (a) Dividing 1.23 cubic meters (100 *veder* = 1.23 cubic meters) by 0.15 ruble gives 0.122 ruble per cubic meter. (b) The 1928 source (see next paragraph) cites a rate of 0.15 ruble per 100 veder or 0.122 ruble per cubic meter. The quotation is for Moscow.

1928: The quotation is from *Kommunal'noe khoziaistvo,* no. 7–8, 1929, pp. 73, 76–77. This is the rate for Moscow and Leningrad. Rates varied considerably at this time. In 1925/26 the rate in 26 cities ranged from 0.03 ruble to 0.81 ruble per cubic meter, according to *Kommunal'noe khoziaistvo,* no. 9–10, 1929, p. 18.

1940: This rate was established for Moscow in late 1939 or January 1940, according to Maslakov (1951), pp. 81, 98.

1948: The rate established for Moscow in late 1939 or January 1940 remained in effect at least through 1951, according to Maslakov (1951), p. 98. There was still a considerable variance in water rates. Maslakov (1951), p. 99, indicates the range in 1950 was from 0.40 ruble per cubic meter in Moscow and Leningrad to 1.00 ruble per cubic meter in the Tadzhik SSR.

1952, 1954: It is assumed that the 1948 rate remained in effect through 1954 as no evidence has been found indicating a change in rate.

Comparability: The item priced — one cubic meter of water — is the same in each year.

246. Tram ride

1937: Vsia Moskva 1936 gives the 1936 Moscow rate as 0.10 ruble for the first station (two half-stations) and 0.05 ruble for each additional half-station. Inasmuch as the rate for most other years is a flat rate per ride regardless of distance, a single rate for 1937 is required. The rate for three half-stations — 0.15 ruble — is used in the index. The reason for selecting the rate for three half-stations is that the 1928 rate for three half-stations is the closest of the 1928 per-station rates to the single rate per ride established in 1929. (See below.) Presumably three half-stations was considered about the average length ride in 1929, and possibly this was more or less true in 1937 as well, though we have no evidence on this point. The 1936 rate was probably in effect in 1937.

1928: The 1928 Moscow rate varied with the distance, from 0.08 ruble for two half-stations, 0.11 ruble for three half-stations, 0.14 ruble for four half-stations, up to 0.28 ruble for eight half-stations. The rates are from *Kommunal'noe khoziaistvo*, no. 19–20, 1929, pp. 36–37. The rate adopted for the index is that for three half-stations — 0.11 ruble. This is about the same as the uniform rate per ride regardless of distance, established in Moscow in October 1929, 0.10 ruble per ride (*ibid.*).

1940: This is a flat rate per ride. I do not have specific 1940 rates but assume, from the following data, that this rate was in effect in Moscow and Leningrad in 1940. According to Maslakov (1951), p. 53, in June 1943 a uniform rate per ride of 0.20 ruble was established in cities other than Moscow and Leningrad, while in these cities the former rate of 0.15 ruble per ride was maintained. Thus this rate was in effect in Moscow and Leningrad immediately prior to June 1943, and probably also in 1940.

1948: As of August 16, 1948 a uniform rate for the entire USSR of 0.30 ruble per ride was established, according to Maslakov, *et al.* (1948), p. 89. Prior to this date the rate in Moscow was still at the 1940 level — 0.15 ruble per ride — while rates in certain other cities varied from 0.15 to 0.30 ruble per ride (*ibid.*). It is assumed that the average USSR rate before August 16, 1948 was 0.17 ruble per ride — that is, the same as my estimated 1944 average USSR rate. (See appendix D.)

1952, 1954: The rate established in August 1948 remained in effect through 1954. The same rate is reported for April 1952 in P. J. D. Wiles and T. Schulz, "Earnings and Living Standards in Moscow," *Bulletin of the Oxford University Institute of Statistics*, 14:326 (1952). Zaleski, "Annexe," p. 144, cites a rate of 0.40 ruble a ride in February 1953, but the rate of 0.30 ruble a ride is cited for Moscow in visitors' reports of early 1953 and January 1955 (*UMA*).

Comparability: 1928–1937. The rate for both these years is for three half-stations and is comparable, unless there were major changes in the distances between stations.

1937–1940. Both rates are for Moscow. The 1940 rate is a flat rate per ride while the 1937 rate is that for three half-stations. It is assumed that this is about the average length of ride, but to the extent that I am in error here the comparison is inexact.

1937–1948. (1) The 1937 rate is a Moscow rate while the 1948 rate is intended to represent the average USSR rate. (2) The 1948 rate is a flat rate per ride while the 1937 rate is that for three half-stations.

1937–1952–1954. (1) The 1937 rate is the Moscow rate while the 1952 and 1954 rates are for the entire USSR, including Moscow. (2) Again, the 1952–54 rate is a flat rate per ride while the 1937 rate is that for three half-stations.

247. Railroad fare, Moscow-Leningrad

The rate for all years is the *one-way fare* from *Moscow to Leningrad* on an *ordinary passenger train, hard car, with reserved berth.* The sources are as follows:

1937: The quotation is from Narodnyi komissariat putei soobshcheniia SSSR, *Ofitsial'nyi ukazatel' zheleznodorozhnykh, vodnykh i drugikh passazhirskikh soobshchenii zimnee dvizhenie 1937–38 g.* (Moscow, 1937), p. 84. This is the fare for winter travel, but the rate for summer travel was the same, according to a letter from James Blackman.

1928: The quotation is from Narodnyi komissariat putei soobshcheniia SSSR, *Ofitsial'nyi ukazatel' zheleznodorozhnykh, parokhodnykh i drugikh passazhirskikh soobshchenii zimnee dvizhenie 1927/28 g.* (2d ed., Moscow, 1927), p. 5.

1948: This is an average 1948 rate computed from the following: (1) From April 15, 1942 until August 16, 1948, the rate was 76.15 rubles, according to Ministerstvo putei soobshcheniia SSSR, *Ofitsial'nyi ukazatel' passazhirskikh soobshchenii leto 1948 goda* (Moscow, 1948), pp. 86, 531. (2) On August 16, 1948, the rate was raised to 87.20 rubles, according to Ministerstvo putei soobshcheniia SSSR, *Ofitsial'nyi ukazatel' passazhirskikh soobshchenii leto 1950 g.* (Moscow, 1950), pp. 84, 587.

1952, 1954: This is the rate established in August 1948. In the absence of any evidence of changes in railroad fares, I assume it remained in effect through 1954.

Comparability: As indicated, the rate for all years is for a trip between the same two cities in the same class of accommodations. Undoubtedly there have been some changes in the quality of service in the same class of accommodations, but these may not be very significant and, in any case, it is impossible to take them into account. The 1937 and 1928 rates are from the winter rate books while the postwar quotations are from the summer rate books. While some seasonal difference in rates might be expected in the Soviet Union, James Blackman informs me there was no difference between the winter and summer rates in 1937.

248. Railroad fare

1937: The rate shown is the average revenue per passenger-kilometer. The source is L. Ia. Volf'son, *et al., Ekonomika transporta* (Moscow, 1941), p. 653.

1940: The rate shown is the average revenue per passenger-kilometer. The figure is estimated by James Blackman and Holland Hunter from data in N. G. Vinnichenko, *Finansirovanie zheleznykh dorog* (1st ed., Moscow, 1948), p. 46; (2d ed., Moscow, 1951), p. 148; S. A. Beliunov, *et al., Planirovanie na zheleznodorozhnom transporte* (Moscow, 1946), p. 137; (Moscow, 1948), p. 77.

Comparability: Since it was impossible to locate a railroad passenger rate book for 1940, it is necessary to base the comparison on average revenue per passenger-kilometer. This may reflect changes in the composition of passenger traffic as well as changes in the fare for a trip of the same distance in comparable accommodations.

249. Movie

1937: This price — 1.00 ruble — is the lowest admission charged at the Moscow motion picture theatre Forum, and the lowest price in 24 of the 43 motion picture theatres listed in the source. The Forum was the largest motion picture house.

The total range of prices was 0.50 to 5.00 rubles. The quotations are from *Vsia Moskva 1936*, pp. 467–468, the 1936 Moscow telephone directory. The same prices were in effect during 1937, it is believed.

1928: This price — 0.30 ruble — is the lowest admission price at the Moscow motion picture theatre Forum, and in 18 other of the 49 motion picture theatres listed in the source. The Forum was the second largest movie house listed. The total range of prices was from 0.20 to 1.75 rubles. The quotations are from *Vsia Moskva 1927*, p. 396. The 1927 prices were in effect during 1928, it is believed.

1948: This price is the low end of the range of 3.00 to 6.00 rubles reported in Moscow in late 1950, in *UM*. It is assumed the same prices were in effect in 1948.

1952: This price is the low end of the range of 3.00 to 6.00 rubles reported in Moscow in April 1952 in Wiles and Schulz, p. 326. A range of 2.00 to 6.00 rubles is cited for May 1952 in Zaleski, "Annexe," p. 146. My low price of 3.00 rubles may then be somewhat on the high side; however, the 1928 and 1937 quotations represent the most typical low price and not the very lowest price, and the 1952 price used in the index is perhaps most comparable.

1954: This price is the low end of the range of prices for evening performances in neighborhood theatres as observed in December 1953. The source is a visitor's report cited in *ibid.*, p. 146. The range of prices indicated in this visitor's report was as follows: 1.50 to 3.00 rubles for matinees in neighborhood theatres, 2.00 to 4.00 rubles for evening performances in neighborhood theatres, and up to 6.00 rubles in deluxe theatres. Other but less precise quotations from visitors' reports for late 1953 and 1954 (*ibid.*) range from 0.50 to 5.00 rubles.

Comparability: The 1928 and 1937 quotations are for similar seats in the same motion picture house and, in addition, are very typical prices for the cheaper seats. The postwar quotations are less specific and may not be entirely comparable to the 1937 quotation. There are too few quotations to be certain of the course of movie ticket prices during the years since 1948, but the available evidence suggests prices were probably fairly constant between 1948 and 1952 and that there was a decline between 1952 and 1954.

250. Trousers made to order

1937: Bruiki, gladkii fason, karman szadi i dlia chasov, bez shelka (trousers, plain style, back and watch pockets, without silk). The price is for making the garment only, and excludes the cost of the material and findings. It apparently applies to wool trousers, as a deduction is made for garments made of cotton. The price used is the midpoint of the range of prices for making these trousers in Moscow *first* and *second category made-to-order clothing workshops* (*masterskie*) — 17.00 to 18.00 rubles. The quotation is from *RTS-M-36*, II:88, 100.

1940: Bruiki sherstianye bez manzhet ili kavaleriiskie, s chasovym i zadnim karmanami, gruppa fasonov no. 1 (wool trousers, without cuffs or cavalry style, with back and watch pockets, of style group no. 1). The price is for making the garment and excludes the material but includes findings. The price used is the midpoint of the range of prices for making clothes in *made-to-order clothing workshops* — 35.00 to 45.00 rubles. The difference here depends on the cost of the material used; no distinction is made between class of workshop. The prices are applicable to the entire USSR. The quotation is from Ministerstvo torgovli SSSR, *Sbornik normativov i spravochnykh materialov dlia shveinykh i obuvnykh predpriiatii*, pp. 205–206. The price was established in January 1939, and, as the source was published in 1947, must have remained in effect through 1940 and after.

Comparability: The trousers appear to be closely comparable. The 1937 price excludes, while the 1940 price includes, the cost of findings. However, for a plain pair of trousers, the buttons and other findings could not make much difference in the price. In fact, the 1940 price list indicates that no deduction is to be made from the price when the customer supplies his own findings in the case of trousers, although deductions are made when the customer supplies the findings for various other, more complicated garments. The 1937 price is for Moscow and the 1940 price is for the entire USSR. Thus the indicated price change is applicable to Moscow but perhaps not to the entire USSR.

251. Coat made to order

1937: This is the midpoint of the range of 56.00 to 99.00 rubles for making a man's coat in Moscow made-to-order clothing workshops (*masterskie*) of the first and second categories. The price excludes material and findings. The source is *RTS-M-36*, II:88–89.

1948: This is the midpoint of the range of 210.00 to 310.00 rubles charged for making a coat in Moscow made-to-order workshops (*masterskie*). The quotation is from *Trud*, July 31, 1948.

1952: This price is computed from the 1948 price and the following price reductions: March 1949, clothing made to order in ateliers (*atel'e*) and workshops (*masterskie*), 20%; March 1950, clothing made to order in second category ateliers and in workshops, 15%.

1954: This is the same as the 1952 price. No reductions were announced after 1950.

Comparability: The price ranges compared probably relate to a reasonably comparable range of qualities, but the postwar description is too brief to be certain here. All quotations relate to coats made in the *workshops* rather than in the *ateliers,* which are more expensive and emphasize high-style garments.

252. Haircut

1937: Haircut. The quotation is for 1937 or 1938. The source is John Maynard, "Conditions of the Urban Worker, Moscow and London," *Political Quarterly,* 13:325–326 (July-September 1942).

1952: Haircut. The quotation is for January 1951; it is assumed the same price remained in effect through 1952. The quotation is from Frank Rounds, Jr., *A Window on Red Square* (Cambridge, Mass., 1953), p. 14.

1954: Haircut. The quotation is from MacDuffie, p. 101, and apparently relates to late 1953 or early 1954.

Comparability: The quotations appear to be comparable.

253. Shave

1937: A *shave.* The quotation is from Maynard, pp. 325–326, and is for 1937 or 1938.

1952: A *shave.* The quotation is for January 1951, from *UM.* It is assumed the same price remained in effect through 1952.

1954: It is assumed there was a 25% reduction in the price of a shave between 1952 and 1954, as was the case for haircuts.

Comparability: The quotations appear to be comparable. As indicated, in the absence of a quotation for 1954, I assume that the price of a shave declined between 1952 and 1954 by the same percentage as the price of a haircut; this may be in error.

254. Average hourly wage

All years: This is the index number of average hourly earnings of nonagricultural wage earners and salaried employees from Table 14.

APPENDIX B

NOTES TO TABLE 4: THE WEIGHTS

In this appendix I describe the sources for and the methods of computing the major category and group weights for the price index shown in Table 4 and the subgroup and representative commodity weights. The latter are shown in Table B-1. The 1928 weights are described in section 1. The estimation of the major category weights is explained first (section 1A), then the group and representative commodity weights for foods (section 1B), for manufactured consumer goods (section 1C), and for services (section 1D). The weights for all other years — 1937, 1940, 1948, 1952, and 1954 — are described in section 2. These years are treated together because the data underlying the weights for each of these years are similar in nature and, for the most part, are from the same source. The major category weights are dealt with first in section 2A. The group weights for foods and for manufactured consumer goods for 1937, 1940, 1948, and 1954 are discussed in section 2B. A separate section (2C) is devoted to the 1952 group weights for foods and manufactured consumer goods as these had to be estimated separately. The derivation of the subgroup and representative commodity weights for each group of foods and manufactured goods is described in section 2D. Finally, in section 2E, the service weights, both group and representative commodity, for 1937, 1940, 1948, 1952, and 1954 are explained.

I. THE 1928 WEIGHTS

The 1928 weights represent the pattern of urban worker expenditures. They are based on a Soviet study of the incomes and expenditures of urban wage-earner families. The data are presented in terms of average expenditure per household per quarter so it is possible to add the averages for four quarters to obtain an annual average. The weights are computed from the budgets for the fourth quarter of 1927 and the first three quarters of 1928, reported in *Statistika truda*, no. 5–6, 1928, pp. 16–20; no. 1, 1929, pp. 18–19; no. 5–6, 1929, pp. 22–27. In the following discussion I shall refer to these sources as "the 1927/28 budget study."

This budget study provides data of the following kinds: (1) A breakdown by fairly broad category of total income and outlays per household. The breakdown of outlays in Table B-2 shows the annual average expenditures, computed from the original source by adding the average expenditures for each quarter. (2) A very detailed breakdown of expenditures on food per person — or, more precisely, per conventional adult. (3) Fairly detailed breakdowns of expenditures per person on (a) clothing, textiles, and shoes; (b) alcoholic beverages and tobacco; and (c) household furnishings.

A. *Major Category Weights*

The 1928 major category weights in Table 4 are based mainly on Table B-2. In determining the breakdown among food, manufactured consumer goods, and services, all items of expenditure falling within any of these categories are considered, even though some of these items are not explicitly represented in my price index. As has been said, the price index is intended to measure the movement of prices of all consumer goods. It is not intended to include the cost of private houses or of the construction of private houses. Logically, my weights should be based on data excluding investment in private housing. Actually, in estimating the major category weights, expenditures on building materials are included in the total weight for manufactured consumer goods, and payments for construction labor are (probably) included in the weight for services. This is simply an expedient. For one thing, there are no firm data providing a basis for estimating such expenditures. The estimates for 1928 are only of the crudest sort and for later years no estimate could be made. Also, the proportion of total expenditures involved is small enough to constitute only a minor source of error.

Some of the outlay categories in Table B-2 cover expenditures on both goods and services, and the total must be allocated between goods and services, sometimes rather arbitrarily. This undoubtedly leads to some error in the major category weights, but the error is probably small.

(1) *Food.* The weight for food is the sum of the outlay categories "food" and "alcoholic beverages" shown in Table B-2.

(2) *Manufactured consumer goods.* The weight for manufactured goods consists of the following items from Table B-2. (a) 10% of the category "rent, utilities, construction and repair, and other expenditures on housing," assumed, arbitrarily, to represent purchases of commodities, mainly building materials. (b) "Wood and kerosene." (c) "Tobacco, cigarettes, and matches." (d) 92.4% of "clothing." The remainder represents repairs of clothing and clothing made to order, according to the breakdown of expenditures per person on clothing in the 1927/28 budget study. (e) Two-thirds of the sum of the three categories "laundry and soap," "hygiene," and "medical care." This is an arbitrary division. (f) 97% of "household articles and home decorating." The remainder of this category represents repairs to household articles, according to the breakdown of expenditures per person on household articles in the 1927/28 budget study. (g) 70% of "cultural and educational expenditures." This is an arbitrary division. (h) 36% of "other expenditures." This is the proportion of this category remaining after deducting estimated expenditures on transportation and communication services. (i) "Unknown expenditures."

(3) *Services.* The weight for services is made up of the following items from Table B-2: (a) 90% of the category "rent, utilities, construction and repair, and other expenditures on housing." As indicated above, the other 10% of this group is assumed to represent purchases of building materials and other goods. (b) 7.6% of "clothing," representing repairs of clothing and clothing made to order. (c) One-third of the sum of the three categories "laundry and soap," "hygiene," and "medical care." (d) 3% of "household articles and home decorating," representing repairs of household articles. (e) 30% of "cultural and educational expenditures." (f) "Rest homes, sanatoriums, and other expenditures on vacations." (g) 64% of "other expenditures." This latter is taken to represent expenditures on transportation and communications, for which no figure is given in the source. The basis for this estimate for transportation and communications is explained below in section 1D. It should be said here, though, that the estimate is rather rough and may be a source of error in the allocation of total expenditures between goods and services.

B. *Food Weights, Group and Representative Commodity*

The food group weights as well as the representative commodity weights are based directly on the breakdown of expenditures on foods as given in the 1927/28 budget study. In this study expenditures are indicated separately for fifty foods or groups of foods. The data are presented in such detail that very little adaptation of them was required. My explanation of the derivation of the weights can then be limited to the following comments:

TABLE B-1

Representative Commodity Weights for Cost-of-Living Index Numbers, USSR, 1928–54
(in percent of group)

Group and subgroup	1928–37 Price index number Representative commodity	1928 Weight	1937 Weight	1937–40 Price index number Representative commodity	1937 Weight	1940 Weight	1937–48–52–54 Price index numbers Representative commodity	1937 Weight	1948 Weight	1952 Weight	1954 Weight
Grain products and legumes											
Flour	Rye flour	6.2	4.6	Wheat flour, 72%	6.9	4.1	Rye flour	4.6	5.1	5.5	6.0
	Whole wheat flour	19.8	4.6	Wheat flour, 30%	6.9	4.1	Wheat flour, 85%	4.6	5.1	5.5	6.0
	Wheat flour, 30%	19.8	4.6				Wheat flour, 72%	4.6	5.1	5.5	6.0
Bread and bakery products	Rye bread	10.8	21.2	Rye bread	21.3	22.4	Rye bread	21.2	14.4	13.9	13.4
	Wheat bread, 80 to 85%	34.2	57.5	Wheat bread, 96%	34.6	36.5	Wheat bread, 85%	39.4	28.7	27.8	26.9
				Wheat bread, 85%	17.3	18.3	Wheat bread, 72%	15.7	21.5	20.8	20.2
				French loaf, 30%	5.5	5.8	French loaf, 72%	2.4	7.2	7.0	6.7
Macaroni products	Macaroni	2.1	1.8	—	—	—	Macaroni	1.8	4.4	5.2	5.8
Grits and legumes	Buckwheat grits	2.1	1.7	Buckwheat grits	1.7	1.9	Buckwheat grits	1.7	2.5	2.6	2.6
	Millet grits	2.1	2.6	Millet grits	2.4	3.1	Millet grits	2.6	4.0	4.1	4.2
	Rice	2.1	1.1	Rice	1.7	1.9	Rice	1.1	1.6	1.6	1.7
	Dried peas	0.4	0.2	Wheat meal	1.7	1.9	Dried beans	0.2	0.3	0.3	0.4
	Oats	0.4	0.1				Oats	0.1	0.1	0.1	0.1
		100.0	100.0		100.0	100.0		100.0	100.0	100.0	100.0
Meat and poultry											
Meat	Pork	17.4	50.0	Pork	22.7	25.7	Pork	22.7	20.1	23.5	27.4
	Beef, average fed, grade 1	49.8	37.0	Beef, average fed, grade 1	16.9	19.1	Beef, average fed, grade 1	16.9	14.9	17.5	20.4
	Mutton, average fed, grade 1	32.8	13.0	Mutton	5.8	6.5	Mutton, average fed, grade 1	4.4	3.8	4.5	5.2
							Mutton, above average fed	1.5	1.3	1.5	1.7
Poultry	—			Chicken, grade 1	0.6	0.7	Chicken, grade 1	0.4	0.4	0.4	0.5
				Chicken, grade 2	0.6	0.7	Chicken, grade 2	0.4	0.4	0.4	0.5
				Goose, grade 2	0.6	0.7	Goose, grade 2	0.4	0.4	0.4	0.5
				Duck, grade 1	0.6	0.7	Duck, grade 1	0.4	0.4	0.4	0.5
				Turkey, grade 1	0.6	0.7	Turkey, grade 1	0.4	0.4	0.4	0.5
							Turkey, grade 2	0.4	0.4	0.4	0.5
							Rabbit	0.4	0.4	0.4	0.5
Sausage and smoked meat	—			Bacon	7.7	6.8	Bacon	7.7	8.6	7.5	6.3
				Ham	7.7	6.8	Ham	7.7	8.6	7.5	6.3
				Sausage, ordinary	18.1	15.8	Sausage, Moscow	36.2	40.1	35.0	29.2
				Sausage, hamburger	18.1	15.8					
		100.0	100.0		100.0	100.0		99.9	100.2	99.8	100.0

Left variant

Group	Subgroup	Item	%	%
Fish	Herring	Herring, salted, frozen	36.0	26.0
		Pike-perch, fresh, or salted	64.0	74.0
	Other fish		100.0	100.0
Sugar and confectionery	Sugar	Sugar, lump	50.0	50.0
		Sugar, granulated	50.0	50.0
	Confectionery	—	—	—
			100.0	100.0
Fats	Butter	Butter, sweet	29.9	28.7
		Butter, rendered	29.9	28.7
	Vegetable oil	Sunflower oil	14.9	24.6
	Other fats	Beef fat, rendered	11.9	9.0
		Lard	13.4	9.0
			100.0	100.0
Milk and milk products		Milk, fresh	88.0	82.0
		Sour cream	12.0	18.0
			100.0	100.0
Eggs	Eggs	Eggs	100.0	100.0
Vegetables and fruit	Potatoes	Potatoes	60.5	44.0
	Other vegetables	Cabbage	11.3	15.1
		Sauerkraut	14.5	7.3
		Onions	8.1	22.4
		Beets	5.6	11.2
	Fruit	—	—	—
			100.0	100.0

Middle variant

Group	Item	I	II
Fish	Herring, salted	40.0	
	Perch, frozen	24.0	
	Sturgeon, fresh or frozen	24.0	
	Sturgeon, cured	10.8	
	Caviar, black, granular	1.2	
		100.0	
Sugar	Sugar, lump	21.6	
	Sugar, granulated	21.6	
	Cocoa	14.2	
	Chocolate candy, best	14.2	
	Bonbons	14.2	
	Honey	14.2	
		100.0	
Fats	Butter, grade 1	28.2	
	Butter, grade 2	28.2	
	Sunflower oil	30.6	
	Salt pork, fat	13.0	
		100.0	
Milk	Milk, fresh	70.0	
	Sour cream	15.0	
	Cheese, Swiss-type	5.0	
	Cheese, Holland-type	5.0	
	Cheese, American-type	5.0	
		100.0	
Eggs	Eggs	100.0	
Vegetables	Potatoes	25.0	31.0
	Cabbage	5.8	6.2
	Sauerkraut	2.9	3.1
	Cucumbers, fresh	5.8	6.2
	Cucumbers, pickled	2.9	3.1
	Onions	4.3	4.7
	Green onions	4.7	4.7
	Carrots	2.2	2.4
	Beets	2.2	2.4
	Mushrooms, dried	0.8	0.9
	Mushrooms, pickled	0.8	0.9
Fruit	Apples, fresh	21.5	17.2
	Grapes, fresh	10.7	8.6
	Prunes, dried	10.7	8.6
		99.9	100.0

Right variant

Group	Item	I	II	III	IV
Fish	Herring, salted	26.0	29.5	36.5	43.5
	Pike-perch, fresh, frozen	29.6	28.2	25.4	22.6
	Sturgeon, fresh or frozen	29.6	28.2	25.4	22.6
	Sturgeon, cured	13.3	12.7	11.4	10.2
	Caviar, black, granular	1.5	1.4	1.3	1.1
		100.0	100.0	100.0	100.0
Sugar	Sugar, lump	25.0	22.7	25.4	26.0
	Sugar, granulated	25.0	22.7	25.4	26.0
	Cocoa	12.5	13.6	12.3	12.0
	Hard candy	12.5	13.6	12.3	12.0
	Soft candies	12.5	13.6	12.3	12.0
	Caramels, "Theatre"	12.5	13.6	12.3	12.0
		100.0	99.8	100.0	100.0
Fats	Butter (average of 7 kinds)	57.4	59.0	47.0	47.0
	Sunflower oil	24.6	23.0	28.0	28.0
	Margarine	18.0	18.0	25.0	25.0
		100.0	100.0	100.0	100.0
Milk	Milk, fresh	70.0	65.0	65.0	65.0
	Sour cream	15.0	14.0	14.0	14.0
	Cheese, Swiss-type	15.0	21.0	21.0	21.0
		100.0	100.0	100.0	100.0
Eggs	Eggs	100.0	100.0	100.0	100.0
Vegetables	Potatoes	25.0	24.5	20.7	16.0
	Cabbage	6.5	6.9	7.1	7.2
	Cucumbers, fresh	4.0	4.2	4.3	4.3
	Cucumbers, salted	2.6	2.7	2.8	2.8
	Green onions	6.5	6.9	7.1	7.1
	Beets	1.7	1.7	1.8	1.8
	Turnips	1.7	1.7	1.8	1.8
	Tomatoes	3.2	3.4	3.5	3.5
	Pumpkin	7.1	5.8	6.2	6.9
	Peas, canned	5.8	9.2	9.5	9.5
Fruit	Apples, fresh	21.5	17.5	18.6	20.7
	Apples, dried	2.6	1.9	2.1	2.3
	Prunes, dried	2.6	1.9	2.1	2.3
	Raisins	2.6	1.9	2.1	2.3
	Mixed dried fruit	2.6	1.9	2.1	2.3
	Apricots, canned	4.0	7.8	8.2	9.2
		100.0	100.0	100.0	100.0

Note: The dash (—) indicates that the group or subgroup is not represented.

TABLE B-1 (Continued)

Representative Commodity Weights for Cost-of-Living Index Numbers, USSR, 1928-54
(in percent of group)

Group and subgroup	1928-37 Price index number			1937-40 Price index number			1937-48-52-54 Price index numbers				
	Representative commodity	1928 Weight	1937 Weight	Representative commodity	1937 Weight	1940 Weight	Representative commodity	1937 Weight	1948 Weight	1952 Weight	1954 Weight
Salt	Salt	100.0	100.0	Salt	100.0	100.0	Salt	100.0	100.0	100.0	100.0
Tea and coffee	Tea	100.0	100.0	Tea	100.0	100.0	Tea	90.0	90.0	90.0	90.0
							Coffee	10.0	10.0	10.0	10.0
		100.0	100.0		100.0	100.0		100.0	100.0	100.0	100.0
Alcoholic beverages Vodka	Vodka, 40°	100.0	100.0	Vodka, 40°	66.7	66.7	Vodka, 40°	33.3	33.3	33.3	33.3
							Vodka, 50°	33.3	33.3	33.3	33.3
Other alcoholic beverages	—		—	Champagne, Soviet	8.3	8.3	Champagne, Soviet	33.3	33.3	33.3	33.3
				Red wine	8.3	8.3					
				White wine	8.3	8.3					
				Port wine	8.3	8.3					
		100.0	100.0		99.9	99.9		99.9	99.9	99.9	99.9
Textiles Cotton	Calico	16.1	15.4	Calico	37.0	36.0	Calico	23.0	20.7	21.4	18.7
	Sateen	16.1	15.4	Satinette	37.0	36.0	Sateen	23.0	20.7	21.4	18.7
	Sheeting, cotton	16.1	15.4				Sheeting, cotton	23.0	20.7	21.4	18.7
	Madapolam	16.1	15.4								
	Moleskin	16.1	15.4								
Wool	Woolen, part wool broadcloth	5.2	5.8	Wool and cotton mixture	15.0	18.0	Woolen, pure wool "Boston"	10.5	17.6	13.1	14.5
	Woolen, pure wool plush velour	0.6	0.6				Coarse wool baize	3.5	5.9	4.4	4.8
	Worsted, part wool	5.2	5.8								
	Worsted, pure wool	0.6	0.6								
	Coarse wool baize	4.5	3.2								
Linen	Sheeting, linen	1.6	3.5	—	—	—	Sheeting, part linen	6.4	3.6	2.5	1.8
	Sheeting, part linen	1.6	3.5								
Silk and rayon	—			Silk crepe de Chine	11.0	10.0	Silk crepe de Chine	1.9	3.2	4.7	6.8
							Rayon crepe de Chine	9.5	7.6	11.1	16.0
		100.0	100.0		100.0	100.0		100.0	100.0	100.0	100.0
Garments Cotton	—			Shirt, cotton	48.0	48.0	Shirt, cotton	24.0	23.0	23.0	23.0
							Cotton dress	12.0	11.0	11.0	11.0
							Cotton blouse	12.0	11.0	11.0	11.0
Wool	Trousers, part wool	100.0	100.0	Suit, wool	19.0	19.0	Suit, wool	19.0	22.0	22.0	22.0
				Overcoat, common quality	17.0	17.0	Overcoat, women's	11.0	13.0	13.0	13.0
							Overcoat, better	6.0	7.0	7.0	7.0

Group / Subgroup	Item	%	Item	%	%	Item	%	%	%	%	%
Silk and rayon	—	—	Necktie, rayon	1.0	1.0	Blouse, silk	1.0	3.0	3.0	3.0	3.0
Headwear	—	—	Hat, felt	7.5	7.5	Hat, felt	7.5	5.0	5.0	5.0	5.0
Fur	—	—	Hat, fur	7.5	7.5	Hat, fur	7.5	5.0	5.0	5.0	5.0
		100.0		100.0	100.0		100.0	100.0	100.0	100.0	100.0
Knitwear	Socks, cotton	100.0	Socks, cotton	90.0	90.0	Socks, cotton	45.0	40.0	40.0	40.0	40.0
			Socks, rayon	10.0	10.0	Stockings, cotton	45.0	40.0	40.0	40.0	40.0
						Socks, rayon	10.0	20.0	20.0	20.0	20.0
		100.0		100.0	100.0		100.0	100.0	100.0	100.0	100.0
Shoes											
Leather	Cowhide boots	13.7	Cowhide boots	19.7	20.6	Leather boots, brown	21.2	18.1	19.2	19.2	21.2
	Leather boots, black	8.6	Leather shoes, men's, no. 4004	19.7	20.6	Leather boots, composition soles	21.2	18.1	19.2	19.2	21.2
	Leather boots, welted	8.6	Leather shoes, women's	19.7	20.6	Leather shoes, men's	21.2	18.1	19.2	19.2	21.2
	Leather oxfords, women's	8.6	Leather shoes, rubber soles	19.7	20.6						
	Leather shoes, children's	8.6									
	Sandals	6.8									
Cloth and leather combined	Canvas shoes, leather soles	13.7	—	—	—	Cloth and leather shoes	8.5	9.8	10.2	10.2	8.5
Rubber	Rubbers	13.2	Rubbers	21.2	17.6	Rubbers	19.5	23.7	21.7	21.7	19.5
Felt	Valenki	18.4	—	—	—	Valenki	8.5	12.2	10.5	10.5	8.5
		100.2		100.0	100.0		100.1	100.0	100.0	100.0	100.1
Haberdashery and notions	Cotton thread, 6-strand	100.0	—	—	—	Cotton thread, 3-strand	37.0	37.0	37.0	37.0	37.0
						Silk thread	6.0	6.0	6.0	6.0	6.0
						Dress pattern	2.0	2.0	2.0	2.0	2.0
						Straightedge razor	27.5	27.5	27.5	27.5	27.5
						Razor blades	27.5	27.5	27.5	27.5	27.5
		100.0					100.0	100.0	100.0	100.0	100.0
Soap, drugs, etc.											
Household soap	Household soap, 50% fat	100.0	Household soap, 60% fat	69.0	66.0	Household soap, 60% fat	30.0	43.0	43.0	43.0	43.0
			Glycerine soap	31.0	34.0	Toilet soap, "Family"	13.5	13.5	13.5	13.5	13.5
Toilet soap	—	—	—	—	—	Toothpaste, "Sanit"	20.0	15.0	15.0	15.0	15.0
Toiletries	—	—	—	—	—	Toothbrush	12.5	8.5	8.5	8.5	8.5
Drugs, etc.	—	—	—	—	—	Absorbent cotton	6.0	5.0	5.0	5.0	5.0
						Gauze bandage	6.0	5.0	5.0	5.0	5.0
						Thermometer	6.0	5.0	5.0	5.0	5.0
						Castor oil capsules	6.0	5.0	5.0	5.0	5.0
		100.0		100.0	100.0		100.0	100.0	100.0	100.0	100.0
Housewares											
Metal utensils	Tea kettle, brass	5.2	—	—	—	Tea kettle, brass	18.2	16.0	16.0	16.0	16.0
	Pan, aluminum, 22-cm	5.2				Pan, aluminum, 18-cm	18.2	16.0	16.0	16.0	16.0
	Wash basin, enameled iron	5.2				Wash basin, aluminum	18.2	16.0	16.0	16.0	16.0
	Cast-iron pot	5.2									
	Frying pan, enameled iron	5.2									
	Tea cup, enameled iron	5.2									
	Pail, galvanized iron	5.2									

Note: The dash (—) indicates that the group or subgroup is not represented.

TABLE B-1 (Continued)

Representative Commodity Weights for Cost-of-Living Index Numbers, USSR, 1928-54
(in percent of group)

Group and subgroup	1928-37 Price index number			1937-40 Price index number			1937-48-52-54 Price index numbers				
	Representative commodity	1928 Weight	1937 Weight	Representative commodity	1937 Weight	1940 Weight	Representative commodity	1937 Weight	1948 Weight	1952 Weight	1954 Weight
Housewares (Continued), Electrical	—	—	—				Electric light bulb	13.6	9.0	9.0	9.0
							Electric hot plate	2.3	9.0	9.0	9.0
							Electric iron	2.3	9.0	9.0	9.0
Other housewares	Primus stove	15.6	10.6				Primus stove	6.8	5.0	5.0	5.0
	Samovar	15.6	10.6				Samovar	2.3	1.0	1.0	1.0
	Kerosene lamp	15.6	10.6				Samovar, 711-mm	2.3	1.0	1.0	1.0
	Lamp chimney	16.9	13.6				Sewing machine	15.8	18.0	18.0	18.0
		100.1	100.0					100.0	100.0	100.0	100.0
Reading matter Newspaper	*Pravda*	48.5	49.0	*Pravda*	49.0	49.0	*Pravda*	49.0	49.0	49.0	49.0
Periodicals	*Bol'shevik*	8.1	8.2	*Bol'shevik*	8.2	8.2	*Bol'shevik*	8.2	8.2	8.2	8.2
	Ogonek	8.1	8.2	*Ogonek*	8.2	8.2	*Ogonek*	8.2	8.2	8.2	8.2
	Planovoe khoziaistvo	8.1	8.2	*Planovoe khoziaistvo*	8.2	8.2	*Planovoe khoziaistvo*	8.2	8.2	8.2	8.2
Books and pamphlets	*Lenin Collection*	6.8	6.6	*Lenin Collection*	6.6	6.6	*Lenin Collection*	6.6	6.6	6.6	6.6
	Book on Turgenev	6.8	6.6	*Pushkin Works*	6.6	6.6	*Pushkin Works*	6.6	6.6	6.6	6.6
	Novel	6.8	6.6	*The Quiet Don*	6.6	6.6	*The Quiet Don*	6.6	6.6	6.6	6.6
	Pamphlet, 32 pages	6.8	6.6	Pamphlet, 48 pages	6.6	6.6	Pamphlet, 32 pages	6.6	6.6	6.6	6.6
		100.0	100.0		100.0	100.0		100.0	100.0	100.0	100.0
Cultural and sports goods	Pencil	50.0	50.0	—	—	—	Phonograph PT-3	15.0	18.0	18.0	18.0
	Paint set	50.0	50.0				Baian accordion	10.0	7.0	7.0	7.0
		100.0	100.0				Piano	3.0	4.0	4.0	4.0
							Bicycle	20.0	20.0	28.0	34.0
							Camera, FED	10.0	12.0	10.0	7.0
							Pencil	14.0	13.0	11.0	10.0
							Pen holder	14.0	13.0	11.0	10.0
							Pen point	14.0	13.0	11.0	10.0
								100.0	100.0	100.0	100.0
Kerosene and matches	Kerosene	75.0	75.0	Kerosene	75.0	75.0	Kerosene	75.0	55.0	58.0	62.0
	Matches	25.0	25.0	Matches	25.0	25.0	Matches	25.0	45.0	42.0	38.0
		100.0	100.0		100.0	100.0		100.0	100.0	100.0	100.0
Tobacco products	Cigarettes, grade 3	80.5	82.0	Cigarettes, "Pushki"	35.0	35.0	Cigarettes, "Metro"	52.0	52.0	52.0	52.0
				Cigarettes, "Deli"	35.0	35.0	Cigarettes, "Kazbek"	30.0	30.0	30.0	30.0
				Cigarettes, "Allegro"	12.0	12.0					
	Tobacco, grade 2	2.8	2.0	Tobacco, grade 2	2.0	2.0	Tobacco, grade 1	2.0	2.0	2.0	2.0
	Makhorka	16.7	16.0	Makhorka, highest grade	16.0	16.0	Makhorka	16.0	16.0	16.0	16.0
		100.0	100.0		100.0	100.0		100.0	100.0	100.0	100.0

Services				
Rent	Rent	25.3	13.4	
Utilities	Electricity	8.8	4.8	
	Water	6.0	1.8	
Transportation and communications	Tram ride	6.7	16.3	
	Railroad fare	15.6	30.2	
Entertainment	Movie	7.0	10.5	
Clothing made and repaired	—	...	...	
Personal services	—	...	...	
Other services	Average hourly wage	30.6	23.0	
		100.0	100.0	

Rent	15.0	16.4	
Electricity	5.4	5.2	
Water	2.0	5.7	
Tram ride	18.2	13.3	
Railroad fare	33.7	34.8	
Movie	—	—	
Trousers made to order	6.7	8.6	
	...	...	
Average hourly wage	19.0	16.0	
	100.0	100.0	

Rent	13.4	13.0	11.5	11.0
Electricity	4.8	4.8	8.5	9.0
Water	1.8	4.2	4.5	4.5
Tram ride	16.3	8.0	12.5	13.5
Railroad fare	30.2	33.5	25.0	25.0
Movie	10.5	13.5	15.0	14.0
Coat made to order	6.0	6.0	6.0	6.0
Haircut	2.0	...	2.0	2.0
Shave	2.0	...	2.0	2.0
Average hourly wage	13.0	17.0	13.0	13.0
	100.0	100.0	100.0	100.0

Note: The dash (—) indicates that the group or subgroup is not represented. The sign (...) indicates that the item is represented under "Other services."

TABLE B-2

Expenditures of Soviet Wage-Earner Families in 1927/28

	Rubles per family per year
1. Rent, utilities, construction and repair, and other expenditures on housing	100.84
2. Wood and kerosene	56.37
3. Food	552.76
4. Alcoholic beverages	41.26
5. Tobacco, cigarettes, and matches	16.53
6. Clothing	249.81
7. Laundry and soap	10.16
8. Hygiene	5.84
9. Medical care	3.77
10. Household articles and home decorating	53.17
11. Cultural and educational expenditures	28.91
12. Rest homes, sanatoriums, and other expenditures on vacations	19.23
13. Social and political expenditures	29.28
14. Religion	.57
15. Expenditures on own economy	.98
16. Purchases of government bonds	9.17
17. Debt payments, payments for commercial credit, payments on account	17.45
18. Other expenditures	66.01
19. Unknown expenditures	2.12
Total expenditures	1,264.13

The only items given in the source but not classified in any of my group weights are "nuts and sunflower seeds" and "other foods," amounting together to 1.3% of total expenditures on food. As indicated in the text, my price index is a representative index. Accordingly, in computing the weight for a given group, I include expenditures on all subgroups falling within that group even when no representative of the subgroup is priced. Thus, the weight for *meat and poultry* includes expenditures on poultry and sausage though no poultry or sausage products are priced in the 1928–37 index. The weight for *sugar and confectionery* includes expenditures on confectionery even though no confectionery products are priced. The weight for *vegetables and fruit* includes expenditures on fruit even though no fruits are priced.

The group weight for *tea and coffee* includes expenditures on substitutes for tea and coffee. It is not known whether this is so of the weight for *tea and coffee* for 1937 and later years.

Within the *grain products and legumes* group, the weight for all *wheat flour* is divided equally between the two wheat flour products priced — *whole wheat flour* and *wheat flour, 30%*. The budget study gives separate figures for "whole wheat flour" and "(other) wheat flour," showing whole wheat flour to represent a rather small share of the total purchases of wheat flour. However, the *wheat flour of 30% extraction* priced is too fine a flour to be considered a representative of all purchases of wheat flour other than whole wheat flour. Most flour purchased would be of 75% or 80% extraction, qualities falling between the two flours priced. Thus equal weights for the two wheat flours priced seem reasonable.

C. *Manufactured Goods Weights, Group and Representative Commodity*

(1) *Textiles, garments, knitwear, haberdashery and notions, shoes.* The total for these five groups is the expenditure category "clothing" in Table B-2. I first reduce this total by 7.6%, the amount spent on repairs of clothing and clothing made to order. The amount spent on the making and repairing of clothing and also the breakdown of total expenditures on clothing among the five groups — textiles, garments, knitwear, haberdashery and notions, and shoes — are computed from the tables showing quarterly expenditures per person on textiles and clothing in the 1927/28 budget study.

Expenditures on *textiles* are broken down in the source by types of cloth — cotton, wool, linen, and silk. In Table B-1, the more detailed breakdowns of the weights within these subgroups are fairly arbitrary. No breakdowns of the *garments* and *knitwear* groups are required as only one item in each group is priced.

The *haberdashery and notions* group covers expenditures on cotton and other wadding, yarn, and leather goods other than shoes. The coverage may be less complete than the coverage of the weight for this group for 1937 and later years. No breakdown of this group is required as only one item in the group is priced.

The representative commodity weights for *shoes* are based on the breakdown in the tables of expenditures on clothing in the 1927/28 budget study.

(2) *Soap, drugs, etc.* The weight for this group amounts to about two-thirds of the total family expenditures on the three categories in Table B-2 "laundry and soap," "hygiene," and "medical care," the other third of these expenditures being allocated to services. The division here between goods and services is rather arbitrary. No further breakdown of the group is required as only one representative product is priced.

(3) *Housewares.* The weight for this group is 56% of the outlay category "household articles and home decorating" in Table B-2. Furniture and bedding, accounting for 41% of expenditures in this category, are excluded as they are not priced and are not covered in the weight for housewares for 1937 and later years. Repairs to household articles, accounting for 3% of expenditures in this category, are included among services. These figures are computed from the quarterly data on expenditures per person on household articles in the 1927/28 budget study.

The budget study provides a partial breakdown of expenditures on various types of household articles. However, this breakdown does not correspond with the items I price, and the division of the group weight into representative commodity weights had to be made on a rule-of-thumb basis.

(4) *Reading matter; cultural and sports goods.* The combined weight for these two groups is 70% of the outlay category "cultural and educational expenditures" in Table B-2; the remainder of expenditures in this category is allocated to services. The division between goods and services again had to be made on a rule-of-thumb basis. Of the weight for the two groups, 60% is assigned to *reading matter* and 40% to *cultural and sports goods.* According to the "November" budget study for November 1925, reported in *Statistika truda,* no. 1–2, 1927, p. 14, newspapers and journals accounted for about half of total expenditures on reading matter and cultural and sports goods. Allowing for books as well, the weight of 60% for all reading matter seems reasonable.

The representative commodity weights for *reading matter* are fairly arbitrary. For all years, *newspapers* are given a weight of about half the total, on the assumption that Soviet citizens buy newspapers regularly but rely more on libraries for periodical literature and books. *Books and pamphlets* should have a weight of one-sixth of the group weight, according to the derivation of the group weight (see above). But this latter is so rough I prefer simply to divide the remaining half of the group weight equally between *periodicals* and *books and pamphlets*.

In the *cultural and sports goods* group only two items are priced, and neither seems obviously more important than the other; accordingly, the weight is divided equally between them.

(5) *Kerosene and matches*. The weight for *kerosene* is 10% of the outlay category "wood and kerosene" in Table B-2. This is based on urban wage-earner expenditures in the "continuous" budget study for 1926 in *Statistika truda*, no. 11–12, 1927, p. 21. The weight for *matches* is set at 10% of the outlay category "cigarettes, tobacco, and matches" on the basis of the 1927/28 budget study.

(6) *Tobacco products*. The weight for the group is 90% of the outlay category "tobacco, cigarettes, and matches" in Table B-2, the other 10% being for matches. The breakdown between cigarettes, tobacco, and makhorka is based on the breakdown of expenditures per person in the 1927/28 budget study.

D. *Service Weights, Group and Representative Commodity*

(1) *Rent*. Rent is taken to be 52.5% of the outlay category "rent, utilities, construction and repair, and other expenditures on housing" in Table B-2 after deducting the 10% of this category assumed to be spent for building materials. This is based on the breakdown of expenditures of wage-earner families on housing in 1926, in the "continuous" budget study for 1926, reported in *Statistika truda*, no. 11-12, 1927, p. 20.

(2) *Utilities*. The weights are again based on the 1926 budget study. The weight for the group is 31% of the outlay category "rent, utilities, construction and repair, and other expenditures on housing" in Table B-2, after deducting the 10% of this category assumed to be spent on building materials. According to the 1926 budget study, central heating, electricity, and water accounted for 22.5% of this total; to this is added 8.5% of the total, about one-third of the subcategory "construction, repair, and other expenditures on housing" (after deducting estimated purchases of building materials) to allow for other utilities. The weight for *electricity* is 60% and for *water* 40% of the group weight. This is based on the relative importance of these two utilities in the 1926 budget study.

(3) *Transportation and communications*. No figure for expenditures on transportation is given in the 1927/28 budget study. Presumably such expenditures are included in the category "other expenditures" in Table B-2. The weight for transportation and communications is a rough estimate based on the following: Total railroad passenger revenue in 1928 was 327 million rubles, according to an unpublished memo of James Blackman. This figure, of course, includes railroad travel by the rural population and possibly official travel, but it does not cover urban transportation in trams and buses, or communications. A figure of something like 275 million rubles seems roughly reasonable for all urban expenditures on personal travel and communications. On a per family basis, for about 6.5 million urban families, this amounts to about 42 rubles or 22.3% of average family expenditures on services. The total urban population in 1928 was 28.4 million persons. The average size of the urban families covered in the 1927/28 budget study was 4.3 persons. If this was typical of the urban population generally, there were about 6.5 million urban families.

Railroad transportation is given a weight of 70% and *local urban transportation* (tram ride) a weight of 30% of the group weight. The division of the weight, though more or less arbitrary, is based in part on the weights for 1937 and the fact that there was a larger increase in the value of railroad than of urban transportation between 1928 and 1937.

(4) *Entertainment*. The weight for this group is made up of 30% of the outlay

category "cultural and educational expenditures" plus about one-fifth of the outlay category "rest homes, sanatoriums, and other expenditures on vacations" in Table B-2. Presumably the latter include some expenditures on entertainment during vacations but how much can only be a guess.

(5) *Other services.* This group is not intended to include all services not included in the above groups but rather services in which labor constitutes a relatively large share of the cost. It will be recalled that the "price" corresponding to this weight is the average hourly wage. A partial breakdown of the weight for this group is shown in Table B-6. The weight is computed as the sum of the following items: (a) Clothing made to order and clothing repairs (7.6% of the outlay category "clothing" in Table B-2) plus repairs to household goods (3% of the outlay category "household articles and home decorating" in Table B-2). These repair items amount to 11% of the total weight for services. (b) Medical care and such services as laundries, barbers, and public baths, amounting to one-third of outlays on "laundry and soap," "hygiene," and "medical care" in Table B-2. This subgroup accounts for 3.6% of all services. (c) Two-thirds of expenditures on the "rent, utilities, etc." subcategory "construction and repair and other expenditures on housing" after deducting estimated purchases of building materials. This is intended to represent payments for domestic help and various other household services. Probably the figure includes some payments for construction labor, though conceptually these are not covered in my cost-of-living index. This subgroup amounts to about 8% of all services. (d) 80% of expenditures on "rest homes, sanatoriums, and other expenditures on vacations" in Table B-2. This amounts to about 8% of the total weight for services.

2. THE 1937, 1940, 1948, 1952, AND 1954 WEIGHTS

For these years the major category weights are intended to reflect the distribution of urban worker expenditures among the three major categories — foods, manufactured goods, and services. The further breakdowns of the total weight for food and of the total weight for manufactured goods, however, are based on the structure of total retail sales in state and cooperative shops and restaurants. Data on urban worker budgets, or even on the structure of urban retail sales, are not available for these years. The weights for services are intended to reflect urban worker expenditures, but they are rather rough estimates.

A. *Major Category Weights*

(1) *Foods vs. manufactured goods.* The breakdown represents the estimated distribution, between foods and manufactured goods, of urban workers' purchases of commodities in state and cooperative shops. The proportion of the worker budget spent on food would, of course, be considerably higher if purchases on the collective farm market were considered. Purchases on the collective farm market are taken into account in the cost-of-living index in the adjustment factor for collective farm market prices, rather than in the weights used in computing the index of official prices. No explicit attempt is made to deduct expenditures on building materials from total expenditures on manufactured consumer goods in determining the food–manufactured goods breakdown of expenditures. Logically this should be done, as the cost-of-living index is not intended to cover the cost of private building. However, there seems no basis for estimating the share of building materials in urban worker expenditures. The figures on the share of building materials in total retail sales in state and cooperative shops, shown in Table B-4, are not very revealing inasmuch as the main purchasers of building materials are institutions (including collective farms) and rural households. In any

case, urban worker expenditures on building materials must be small enough to result in only a small error in the weights.

The elements in the calculation of the food–manufactured goods breakdown are shown in Table B-3. The figures on the share of food in total retail sales in state and cooperative shops and restaurants shown in column (1) of Table B-3 are from *Sovtorgstat-56*,* p. 39. For 1952 and 1954 the figures designated "actual" are from this source. The adjusted figures allow for a change in the definition of retail sales which occurred in 1951. In that year the definition of retail sales was extended to cover certain transactions not previously included. The most important of these were certain services such as clothing made to order from the customer's own material and repairs of clothing and household goods. Also newly included was the sale of houses (N. Riauzov and N. Titel'baum, *Statistika sovetskoi torgovli* (Moscow, 1951), pp. 72ff.). There seems no basis for making a firm estimate of the value of trade involved in this change in definition. I assume, following Wiles in *Bulletin of the Oxford University Institute of Statistics,* 16:382 (1954), that the items added may have amounted to about 2% of total retail sales in 1952 and 1954. None of the items newly counted as retail sales is a food. Accordingly, for consistency with earlier years, 2% of total sales is deducted from sales of manufactured consumer goods and the share of food in the total is adjusted upward.

TABLE B-3

Share of Food in Retail Sales and Urban Worker Purchases

Year	Food as percent of all commodities		
	In total state and cooperative sales	In urban state and cooperative sales	In urban worker purchases
	(1)	(2)	(3)
1937	63.1	65.7	69
1940	63.1	66.0	69
1948	64.4	—	71
1952			
Actual	57.3	60.1	—
Adjusted	58.5	—	64
1954			
Actual	54.8	57.6	—
Adjusted	56.0	—	62

Note: The dash (—) indicates that data were not available.

The figures in column (2) of Table B-3 showing the share of food in urban sales in state and cooperative shops and restaurants are derived as follows:

(a) *1937:* Urban retail sales in state and cooperative shops and restaurants were 86.6 billion rubles in 1937, of which 8.4 billion rubles represent restaurant sales of foods and 78.2 billion rubles represent sales in shops (*Narkhoz,* p. 201; *Sovtorgstat-56,* p. 23). According to Shnirlin, *PKh,* no. 2, 1938, pp. 102ff., sales of foods accounted for 62% of total retail sales in urban state and cooperative shops, excluding restaurant sales. Thus urban sales of foods in shops were 48.5 billion rubles (0.62 x 78.2 billion rubles) and in restaurants 8.4 billion rubles, a total of 56.9 billion rubles or 65.7% of all urban state and cooperative retail sales.

(b) *1940, 1952, 1954:* For these years the figures in column (2) of Table B-3 represent the share of food in retail sales in all state shops and restaurants and in

* See the list of abbreviations at the end of the volume.

cooperative shops and restaurants other than consumer cooperatives. They are computed by deducting sales in consumer cooperatives of foods and of manufactured goods from total state and cooperative retail sales. The data on total state and cooperative retail sales and on consumer cooperative retail sales, including the food–manufactured goods breakdowns, are from *Sovtorgstat-56*, pp. 27, 39, 62. The consumer cooperatives carry on the bulk of the rural retail trade and conduct very little trade in urban areas. Thus sales in state and cooperative shops and restaurants other than the consumer cooperatives should be a fairly close approximation to urban sales. Interestingly, the share of food in sales other than in consumer cooperatives is about 5% greater than the share of food in all state and cooperative retail sales in all of these three years. This is true also of 1950. In 1937, the share of food in urban state and cooperative sales was a bit over 4% greater than in all state and cooperative sales.

For the cost-of-living index, the share of food in urban worker purchases of commodities, shown in column (3) of Table B-3, is estimated at about 10% greater than the share of food in total state and cooperative retail sales for all years from 1937 on. This is a rough means of allowing for purchases in urban shops by the rural population. Such purchases are fairly significant and fall much more heavily on manufactured goods than on foods.

(2) *Commodities vs. services.* The weights in this case represent the estimated distribution between goods and services of urban worker expenditures on commodities in all markets and on services.

(a) *1937:* Urban household expenditures on money rent, utilities, and miscellaneous services are estimated to be 80% of total household outlays on these categories. Total household outlays on money rent, utilities, and miscellaneous services in 1937 were 15.9 billion rubles, according to Abram Bergson, *Soviet National Income and Product in 1937* (New York, 1953), p. 110. Urban household outlays on these categories would then be 12.7 billion rubles or 12.0% of the total of urban retail sales to households plus urban expenditures on services. Total urban retail sales to households — that is, total retail sales to households in urban state and cooperative shops and on the collective farm market — were 92.9 billion rubles in 1937 (Table 12).

(b) *1940–54:* The weights for these years for services are crude guesses. They are based partly on a comparison of the change in the value of urban retail sales in state and cooperative shops with an approximate index of the change in value of services consumed. This index of the change in value of services is very rough, being based on the change in volume and in price of only a limited number of services. It is derived in the process of estimating the service group and representative commodity weights for these years from the 1937 weights and the change in price and volume of six services.

B. *Group Weights, Commodities, 1937, 1940, 1948, 1954*

The commodity group weights in Table 4, as well as the weights for many subgroups, are based on the breakdown by commodity group of total retail sales in state and cooperative shops and restaurants. *Sovtorgstat-56*, pp. 44–47, gives this breakdown in considerable detail for the years 1937, 1940, 1950, and 1954. (Data for 1928 and 1955 are also given but are not required for my purpose.) This breakdown is reproduced in Table B-4. The weights for 1937, 1940, 1950, and 1954 are computed directly from this table. Certain adaptations of the data in the table were necessary and are noted below. The 1950 group weights are used as if they were given-year weights for 1948; but the major category weights for 1948 are based on 1948 data. The weights for 1952 are estimated from those for 1950 and 1954 and certain other data. This computation will be described subsequently.

Generally the *Sovtorgstat-56* breakdown of sales is arranged to suit my needs rather well, especially in the case of the food groups, and relatively little re-arrangement of the material was required. In computing the group weights the following adaptations of the data in Table B-4 are made:

(1) *Food group weights.* Sales of "canned goods" are allocated to the weights for *meat and poultry, fish,* and *vegetables and fruit* according to the distribution of canned goods among these three food groups in Table B-4. For 1937 and 1940 no breakdown of canned goods by types of foods canned is given in the source and I use the 1950 distribution.

The weight for *tea and coffee* for each year is the sale of "tea" as given in the source plus 0.1% of total food sales taken from sales of "other foods." The latter category specifically includes coffee. This is fairly arbitrary, but the total weight that could possibly be assigned to coffee is too small to attempt a more refined adjustment. It is not clear whether the weight for *tea and coffee* includes tea and coffee substitutes for 1937 and later years, as is the case of the 1928 weight for this group.

TABLE B-4

Commodity Structure of Retail Sales in State and Cooperative
Shops and Restaurants, USSR, 1937, 1940, 1950, and 1954
(percent of total sales)

Commodity	1937	1940	1950	1954
Foods				
Bread and bakery products	17.1	17.2	12.6	8.2
Flour, grits, and macaroni products	4.6	3.5	5.0	4.0
Flour	(3.0)	(1.7)	(2.7)	(2.2)
Grits and legumes	} (1.6)	(1.3)	(1.5)	(1.1)
Macaroni products		(0.5)	(0.8)	(0.7)
Meat, poultry, and sausage	5.0	6.1	4.5	4.4
Meat and poultry	(2.4)	(3.3)	(1.9)	(2.4)
Sausage products	(2.6)	(2.8)	(2.6)	(2.0)
Fish and herring	2.1	1.8	2.0	1.8
Fish	(1.6)	(1.1)	(1.4)	(1.0)
Herring	(0.5)	(0.7)	(0.6)	(0.8)
Sugar	4.6	2.8	3.8	5.1
Confectionery	4.6	3.7	4.6	4.7
Fats	3.4	3.3	4.3	4.1
Butter	(2.0)	(1.9)	(2.5)	(1.9)
Vegetable oil	(0.8)	(1.0)	(1.0)	(1.2)
Other fats	(0.6)	(0.4)	(0.8)	(1.0)
Milk and milk products, including cheese	1.1	1.2	1.1	1.4
Cheese	—	—	—	(0.3)
Eggs	0.4	0.6	0.4	0.3
Potatoes	0.8	1.0	0.6	0.3
Other vegetables	0.8	1.0	0.7	0.6
Fruit and melons	1.3	1.0	0.8	0.8
Salt	0.2	0.2	0.5	0.2
Tea	0.6	0.5	0.6	0.5
Alcoholic and nonalcoholic beverages	11.5	12.4	12.8	14.1
Canned goods	0.6	0.5	0.8	1.1
Meat	—	—	(0.1)	(0.3)
Fish	—	—	(0.3)	(0.4)
Vegetables and fruit	—	—	(0.4)	(0.4)
Other foods (coffee, spices, vitamins, mushrooms, soy products, etc.)	3.0	3.6	1.9	1.8
Restaurant markup	1.4	2.7	1.4	1.4
All foods	63.1	63.1	58.4	54.8

TABLE B-4 (Continued)

Commodity	1937	1940	1950	1954
Nonfoods				
Textiles	6.5	6.4	11.0	10.5
Cotton	(4.5)	(4.3)	(6.8)	(5.9)
Wool	(0.9)	(1.1)	(2.6)	(2.0)
Silk	(0.7)	(0.6)	(1.2)	(2.4)
Linen	(0.4)	(0.4)	(0.4)	(0.2)
Garments, hats and fur	5.6	6.6	6.5	8.3
Garments	—	(5.6)	(6.1)	(7.5)
Fur and fur clothing	—	(0.5) } (0.4)		(0.4)
Hats	—	(0.5)		(0.4)
Knitwear and hosiery	1.9	2.1	2.2	2.8
Knitwear	(1.0)	(1.3)	(1.3)	(1.8)
Hosiery	(0.9)	(0.8)	(0.9)	(1.0)
Shoes	4.0	3.6	5.0	5.0
Leather	} (3.2)	} (2.8)	} (3.2)	(3.2)
Cloth and combined				(0.4)
Felt		(0.2)	(0.6)	(0.4)
Rubber	(0.8)	(0.6)	(1.2)	(1.0)
Haberdashery and thread	1.7	1.8	1.8	2.0
Haberdashery	(1.6)	(1.6)	(1.5)	(1.7)
Thread	(0.1)	(0.2)	(0.3)	(0.3)
Household soap	0.7	0.6	0.8	0.6
Toilet soap and toiletries	1.5	1.6	0.9	0.7
Toilet soap	(0.3)	(0.3)	(0.3)	(0.2)
Toiletries	(1.2)	(1.3)	(0.6)	(0.5)
Metal utensils	1.2	1.2	0.7	0.9
Glass and china utensils	0.5	0.3	0.4	0.4
Cultural goods	3.8	3.1	2.8	3.4
Printed matter	(1.2)	(1.1)	(0.9)	(0.9)
Notebooks, paper, and office supplies	(0.8)	(0.7)	(0.6)	(0.6)
Bicycles and motorcycles		(0.1)	} (0.3)	(0.4)
Sports goods		(0.2)		(0.3)
Radios	} (1.8)	(0.1)	} (0.4)	(0.4)
Musical goods		(0.3)		(0.2)
Toys		(0.3)	(0.2)	(0.3)
Other cultural goods		(0.3)	(0.4)	(0.3)
Kerosene	0.6	0.6	0.4	0.3
Matches	0.2	0.2	0.3	0.2
Tobacco and makhorka	2.9	2.9	2.8	2.3
Furniture and metal beds	0.9	1.1	0.6	1.3
Other nonfoods	4.9	4.8	5.4	6.5
Window glass	—	(0.1)	(0.9)	(0.1)
Building materials	—	(0.2)	—	(1.6)
All nonfoods	36.9	36.9	41.6	45.2
All commodities	100.0	100.0	100.0	100.0

Note: The dash (—) indicates that data were not available.

The weight for *alcoholic beverages* is taken for all years to be 73% of sales of "alcoholic and nonalcoholic beverages" as shown in Table B-4. "Nonalcoholic beverages" here apparently means bottled soft drinks; tea and coffee are included elsewhere in the table and canned juices are almost certainly classified with canned goods. This percentage figure is based on data for 1937.

Sales of vodka only were planned to be 5.6% of all state and cooperative retail sales in 1937, according to Zberzhkovskii, *SOVTORG*, no. 2, 1937, pp. 19–20. Sales of alcoholic beverages other than vodka, it is believed, would amount to about half the value of sales of vodka, making sales of all alcoholic beverages 1.5 times sales of vodka or 8.4% of all retail sales. The ratio of vodka sales to sales of other alcoholic beverages of about two to one is based on the following information: (a) The 1927 wage-earner budget study in *Statistika truda,* no. 5–6, 1928, p. 22, indicates that expenditures on vodka were somewhat less than twice expenditures on other alcoholic beverages. (b) A very rough calculation of the value at retail prices of the various types of alcoholic beverages produced in 1937 suggests that the value of vodka was about 2.5 times the value of other alcoholic beverages.

Sales of all alcoholic beverages of 8.4% of total retail sales in 1937 means that sales of alcoholic beverages were about 73% of 1937 sales under the category "alcoholic and nonalcoholic beverages" in Table B-4. This same percentage is used in computing the weight for alcoholic beverages from Table B-4 for all other years. The volume of sales of nonalcoholic beverages has probably risen more than the volume of sales of alcoholic beverages over this whole period, but the prices of alcoholic beverages have risen much more than prices of nonalcoholic beverages.

In computing the food group weights the following groups in the original breakdown in Table B-4 are excluded: "nonalcoholic beverages," most of "other foods," and the "restaurant markup." The food groups considered in my index represent about 90% of all sales of food, excluding the restaurant markup.

(2) *Manufactured goods group weights.* The weight for *soap, drugs, etc.* for each year consists of sales of "household soap," "toilet soap and toiletries," and 0.1% of all sales. This latter is to allow for sales of drugs, which, it is believed, are not included in the Soviet category "toiletries" (*parfumeriia*). This is an arbitrary adjustment but the weight would be so small in any case that further refinement is not justified.

The weight for *housewares* consists of sales of "metal utensils" and "glass and china utensils" from Table B-4 plus a more or less arbitrary additional amount from "other nonfoods" to allow for such items as electric light bulbs and appliances and sewing machines. For 1937, 1940, and 1950, the amount added on this account is 0.3% of total sales; for 1954, it is 0.4% of total sales. This allows housewares other than metal utensils and glass and china utensils a steadily increasing proportion of the weight for all housewares — from 15% in 1937 to 24% in 1954. This group does not cover furniture.

In computing the group weights for manufactured goods, the following groups in the original breakdown shown in Table B-4 are excluded: "furniture and metal beds" and most of "other nonfoods." The included groups amount to 84 to 86.5% of all sales of manufactured goods. For 1940, however, inasmuch as some groups could not be represented by price quotations, the groups actually included in the index represent only 70% of all sales of manufactured goods.

C. *Group Weights, Commodities, 1952*

The 1952 group weights are estimated from the 1950 and 1954 weights and data on the changes in the value of sales of the various commodity groups over the period 1950 to 1954. In the process of estimating the 1952 group weights, three sets of computations were made, as follows: (1) a set of 1952 weights computed by averaging the weights for 1950 and 1954; (2) a set of 1952 weights computed from the 1950 weights and the change in value of sales of the various commodity groups between 1950 and 1952; (3) a set of 1952 weights computed from the 1954 weights and the change in value of sales of the various commodity groups between 1952 and 1954.

For most commodity groups the change in value of sales between 1950 and 1952 and between 1952 and 1954 can be estimated from the index of change in volume of sales by commodity group in *Sovtorgstat-56,* p. 11, and the index of official retail prices by commodity group in *Sovtorgstat-56,* p. 131. This information was supplemented by reports of the annual changes in the volume of sales of certain commodity groups in the annual plan fulfillment reports and price data in the annual price decrees.

All three sets of computations lead to similar results. The food group weights actually used are those computed from the 1954 weights and the change in value of sales by commodity group between 1952 and 1954. Data on the changes in value of sales between 1952 and 1954 are more complete than for the period 1950–52. For two food groups — *salt* and *alcoholic beverages* — no estimate of the change in value of sales could be made. For these groups, the average of the 1950 and 1954 weights are used.

The group weights for manufactured goods used are computed as averages of (1) the weights computed from the 1950 weights and the 1950–52 changes in value of sales and (2) the weights computed from the 1954 weights and the 1952–54 changes in value of sales. In the case of groups for which no estimate of the change in value of sales could be made — *haberdashery and notions, housewares, cultural and sports goods, kerosene and matches* — the average of the 1950 and 1954 weights is used.

The 1952 group weights are subject to error, but probably any errors are rather small. One would in any case not expect any very substantial change in the pattern of sales in a two-year period, and I do have firm data on the pattern of sales in 1950 and 1954 and also rather complete data on changes in sales between these years. Information on the commodity structure of retail sales in 1952 has since been published (TSU, *Narodnoe khoziaistvo SSSR v 1958 g.,* pp. 722–733); in general this tends to confirm the estimated weights.

D. *Subgroup and Representative Commodity Weights, 1937, 1940, 1948, 1954*

(1) *Grain products and legumes.* The weights for the subgroups — *bread, flour, grits and legumes, macaroni products* — are from the breakdown of retail sales in state and cooperative shops in *Sovtorgstat-56,* shown in Table B-4. For 1937 the source does not separate grits and legumes from macaroni products; I assume about one-quarter of the total to be for macaroni products, as was the case in 1940. For 1952, the averages of the 1950 and 1954 subgroup weights are used.

(a) *Flour:* The subgroup weight is divided equally among the two or three flours priced in each set of weights. Data on the types of flour sold as flour are not available. For the mid-thirties a rough breakdown of the retail value of all flour produced can be estimated from data on 1935 flour output and 1936 retail flour prices. However, the amount of flour sold at retail is such a small part of the total that there seems no reason to assume that the breakdown of sales of flour follows the same pattern as the output of flour.

(b) *Bread:* For 1937 and 1940, *rye bread* is given a weight of 27% and *wheat bread* a weight of 73% of the total bread weight. For the postwar years, *rye bread* is given a weight of 20% and *wheat bread* a weight of 80%. In 1936, wheat bread accounted for 73.3% of the output of the breadbaking industry (Shnirlin in *PKh,* no. 5, 1938, p. 86) and wheat bread accounted for 73.9% of the bread purchases of urban wage earner families (*Za industrializatsiiu,* April 23, 1937). The share of wheat bread was larger, it is believed, in the postwar years.

Among *wheat breads,* the 1937 and 1940 weights are based roughly on the 1935 output of the various kinds of wheat flour by the state milling industry, as reported in TSUNKHU, *Mukomol'no-krupianaia promyshlennost' SSSR* (Moscow, 1937), p. 16. The 1935 flour output figures are weighted by the 1937 retail flour prices in price zone III, from *SRTS-36*, pp. 28–29. This computation results in the following breakdown of flour output at approximate retail values: 96% extraction flour, 57.0%; 85% extraction flour, 25.5%; 72 to 75% extraction flour, 17.5%. The 72 to 75% extraction flour includes the so-called "10% flour" and "30% flour"; these are the first grades obtained when wheat flour is extracted at a rate of 72 to 75% and divided into two or three grades. (See *SRTS-36*, pp. 28–29; V. I. Petrov, *Tovarovedenie prodovol'stvennykh tovarov* (Moscow, 1947), p. 16.) This distribution is taken as a rough guide to the relative importance of the various types of bread in urban worker purchases in 1937 and 1940.

For the 1937–40 price index number, the 1937 and 1940 weights for wheat bread are the same. The wheat breads priced for this index number and the weights are as follows:

Bread of 96% extraction flour	60%
Bread of 85% extraction flour	30
French loaf of 30% extraction flour	10
	100

The bread of 30% extraction flour is of higher quality than is usually consumed. Accordingly, the weight for the French loaf of 30% extraction flour is somewhat less than the weight that would apply to all bread of 72% and lower extraction rates, and the weights for the two breads of coarser flour are increased correspondingly.

For the postwar years, the wheat breads priced and the 1937 and postwar weights are as follows:

	1937 weights	Postwar weights
Bread of 85% extraction flour	67%	50%
Bread of 72% extraction flour	27	37
French loaf of 72% extraction flour	6	13
	100	100

As no whole wheat (96% extraction flour) bread is priced, I let the bread of 85% extraction flour partially represent whole wheat bread. Accordingly, the 1937 weight for bread of 85% extraction flour is greater and that for the two breads of 72% extraction smaller than their relative shares in the value of flour output estimated above. The weights for the postwar years allow for a relative increase in the consumption of bread of 72% extraction flour which has taken place. According to *PKh*, no. 5, 1954, p. 37, wheat bread of 72% extraction flour is the main type consumed in the postwar period, while the main type consumed in prewar years was bread of 85% extraction flour. This would suggest that the postwar weight for bread of 85% extraction flour should be smaller than that for bread of 72% extraction flour. But it is believed that the statement refers only to bread made of the so-called "graded flours" — those extracted at a rate of 85% or less. Kaganovich reported in *Pravda*, April 27, 1954, that whole-grain flour (rye and wheat) accounted for 60% of total output. And, as indicated, the bread of 85% extraction flour is intended to represent in part whole wheat bread. As between the two breads of 72% extraction flour, the division is intended to reflect the fact that ordinary bread sold by weight is much more common than loaf bread but that there has been an increase in the sales of loaf bread and rolls in relation to bread sold by weight (*Pravda*, October 30, 1953).

(c) *Grits, rice, and legumes:* The breakdown of this subgroup into representative commodity weights is the same for all years. The breakdown is based on the

1935 output of the various products as given in TSUNKHU, *Mukomol'no-kru-pianaia promyshlennost' SSSR*, p. 16, weighted by the 1936 prices of the different kinds of grits, et cetera. The prices are from *SRTS-36*, p. 26.

(2) *Meat and poultry*. The division between *sausage products* (which include smoked meat) and other *meat and poultry* is given in Table B-4. For 1952, the average of the 1950 and 1954 subgroup weights is used.

(a) *Meat and poultry, fresh:* The breakdown of this subgroup into representative commodity weights for all years is based on data on the types of meat produced in 1937 and the 1936 retail prices. Of the 1937 output of meat and meat products by enterprises under the People's Commissariat of the Meat and Milk Industry — the main source of meat entering retail trade — 40.9% was sausage and smoked meat, 24.7% was pork and 3.0% was poultry, according to Gosplan, *Tretii piatiletnii plan razvitiia narodnogo khoziaistva Soiuza SSR (1938–42 gg.)* (Moscow, 1939), p. 61. This distribution is used for the volume weights for pork and poultry (assumed to include rabbit). The breakdown of the remainder of the subgroup weight between beef and mutton is based on figures on the total output of meat (including meat consumed on the farm), showing that the output of beef and veal was about three times that of mutton and goat (Gosplan, *Tretii piatiletnii plan*, p. 82). This gives the following breakdown of physical volume: pork, 42%; beef, 40%; mutton, 13%; poultry and rabbit, 5%. (The figures on the output of meat by types in TSU, *Promyshlennost' SSSR; Statisticheskii sbornik* (Moscow, 1957), p. 378 (which became available after these computations were made) indicate substantial errors in my meat weights. In particular, beef is seriously underweighted and pork is overweighted. This means the rise in average meat prices is somewhat overstated as pork prices rose more than beef prices throughout the period. However, the effect on the cost-of-living index numbers is probably negligible.) These physical output figures are weighted by the 1936 zone IV retail price of first grade cuts of the average fed grade of the meat in question and the most typical poultry price. The prices used per kilogram are: pork, 9.60 rubles; beef, 7.60 rubles; mutton, 7.60 rubles; and poultry, 10.00 rubles. These quotations are from *SRTS-36*, pp. 267–269, 309–310.

Where two grades of mutton are priced, I give three-quarters of the weight to the average-fed grade and one-quarter to the above average-fed quality. The weight for poultry and rabbit is divided equally among all the items priced in this subgroup.

(b) *Sausage and smoked meat:* Sausage is much more important in the Soviet diet than bacon or smoked ham and, for all years, I allocate 70% of the subgroup weight to *sausage*, 15% to *bacon*, and 15% to *smoked ham*.

(3) *Fish*. The weight for *herring* is given in Table B-4. The breakdown of the weight for fish other than herring is the same for all years. It is estimated on the basis of scattered physical output data for 1934, 1936, and 1941 (planned) from Zberzhkovskii, *SOVTORG*, no. 2, 1937, p. 15; TSUNKHU, *Socialist Construction in the USSR* (Moscow, 1936), p. 219; and *Gosudarstvennyi plan na 1941 g.*, p. 165. It is assumed that the physical quantities represent adequately the retail values of the various types of fish. The range of fish prices is rather large, but there is much overlapping among groups and on the average there may not have been difference among the prices of the various subgroups. The subgroups in question are fresh and frozen fish, smoked fish, and caviar. One clear exception is caviar, which is considerably more expensive, but a large part of the caviar is exported so no adjustment for its high price is made.

(4) *Sugar and confectionery*. The breakdown of the group weight between sugar and confectionery is from Table B-4. The subgroup weight for sugar is divided equally between the two types of sugar priced. It seems impossible to

determine from Soviet statistics how much of each type of sugar was sold, or even produced. While figures are available for output of granulated sugar (*sakhar pesok* — actually whitened but unrefined sugar) and for refined lump sugar (*sakhar refinad*), some double counting is involved since granulated sugar is the raw material for the refined lump sugar. In any case, the prices of granulated and lump sugar moved closely together throughout the period.

The subgroup weight for confectionery is divided equally among the four confectionery items priced. No data were found which would permit a more refined breakdown.

(5) *Fats.* The breakdown among butter, vegetable oil, and other fats is from Table B-4. For 1952, the average of the 1950 and 1954 weights is used. Where more than one product falling within one of these subgroups is priced, the subgroup weight is divided equally among them.

(6) *Milk and milk products.*

(a) *1937* and *1940:* For these years, *milk* is assigned a weight of 70% of the group and *sour cream* and *cheese* each 15% of the group. This is a fairly arbitrary division. Cheese must have accounted for a smaller proportion of sales of this group in these years than in 1954, and fresh milk must be by far the most important product in the group.

(b) *1948, 1952, 1954: Cheese* sales accounted for 21% of sales in this group in 1954, according to Table B-4. The same weight is used for 1948 and 1952. The relationship between the two other products — *milk* and *sour cream* — is assumed to be about the same as in the prewar period.

(7) *Eggs.* Only one representative commodity is priced.

(8) *Vegetables and fruit.*

(a) *Subgroup weights:* The weight for *potatoes* is the share "potatoes" were in total sales, from Table B-4. The weight for *other vegetables* is the share indicated for "vegetables" in Table B-4 plus part of the share of "canned fruit and vegetables." The weight for *fruit* is the share indicated for "fruit and melons" plus part of the share of "canned fruit and vegetables," as given in Table B-4. The distribution of the total for canned fruit and vegetables as between vegetables and fruit is fairly arbitrary. Following Soviet classification procedure, pumpkins and squash are included with fruits rather than with other vegetables in computing the weights.

In the price index for 1928–37 no fruits are priced. The 1937 group weight for vegetables and fruit is the sum of the weights for potatoes, and other vegetables and fruit, including canned vegetables and fruit. The total group weight is divided between potatoes and other vegetables (including canned vegetables) according to their relative importance in total sales.

(b) *Representative commodity weights, vegetables other than potatoes:*

1. *1937:* The weights for this subgroup are based mainly on the planned delivery of vegetables to the state in 1937, weighted by approximate average annual 1937 retail prices. These data are shown in Table B-5. The figures on planned deliveries are from *SOVTORG,* no. 5, 1937, p. 28. A breakdown of actual deliveries in 1937 is not available though it is known that total deliveries were less than planned (Gosplan, *Tretii piatiletnii plan,* p. 232). The planned delivery figures refer only to centralized procurements and may not be very representative of the pattern of total procurements of vegetables. The retail prices shown are intended as rough approximations to the annual average prices for the entire USSR. They are based on the price quotations in appendix A and other scattered data. The approximate retail value is obtained by multiplying the planned deliveries by the approximate retail price.

The weights used, shown in the final column of Table B-5, are based on the

TABLE B-5

Representative Commodity Weights for Vegetables, 1937

Commodity	Planned deliveries (thousand tons)	Retail price (rubles per kg)	Approximate retail value (million rubles)	Weight (percent of group)
	(1)	(2)	(3)	(4)
Cabbage	584	0.30	175	25.0
Onions	122	1.40	171	25.0
Cucumbers	198	0.90	178	25.0
Table roots	291	0.33	96	12.5
Tomatoes	405	1.20	486	12.5
Totals	1600		1106	100.0

approximate retail value of planned deliveries, except in the case of tomatoes. The figure for tomatoes seems incredibly high. Fresh tomatoes are available only for a very short season in most of the USSR while cabbage, onions, and table roots are the staple vegetables and are available most of the year. It may be that fairly large quantities of tomatoes are canned. But even so, it seems the plan for deliveries of tomatoes must have been unrealistic. More or less arbitrarily, I set the weight for tomatoes equal to that for table roots.

The above data form the basis for the 1937 weights but must be adapted to the specific vegetables priced in each index. For the 1928–37 price index the above weights are adjusted to exclude tomatoes and cucumbers, which are not priced. In the 1937–40 price index, tomatoes are not priced but mushrooms are. Probably these are less important than tomatoes. I assign a weight of 5% to mushrooms and allocate the remaining 95% of the subgroup weight among cabbage, onions, cucumbers, and table roots according to the relationship among these products in the weights shown in Table B-5.

For the price index for 1937–48–52–54, the above weights are used for all but *canned peas* and *pumpkin*. As indicated above, pumpkin is classified with fruit. *Canned peas* are taken to represent all canned vegetables and a separate weight for canned vegetables is computed at 18% of the total weight for vegetables other than potatoes. This weight for canned vegetables is the amount taken from the category "canned goods" and added to the category "vegetables" (other than potatoes) as given in Table B-4. For 1937, canned goods are not broken down according to types of foods canned in Table B-4; I assume that half of the sales of canned goods were vegetables and fruit in 1937, as was the case in 1950, and that 60% of these were sales of canned vegetables.

More detailed breakdowns — for example, that of the weight for cabbage into weights for fresh cabbages and for sauerkraut — are made on a rule-of-thumb basis.

2. *1940:* The 1937 weights are used.

3. *1948, 1952, 1954:* Canned vegetables are estimated to have accounted for about 25% of all sales of vegetables other than potatoes in both 1950 and 1954, from the data in Table B-4. This is the weight assigned to *canned peas*. For the remaining vegetables, the same breakdown is used as in the case of the 1937 weights. The structure of obligatory deliveries of vegetables planned for 1953 (as reported in *Pravda*, September 29, 1953) does not differ greatly from that for 1937 shown above.

(c) *Representative commodity weights, fruit:*

1. *1937: Fresh and canned fruits* are given a weight of 75% and *dried fruits*

a weight of 25% of the total weight for fruit. This division is based on budget expenditures of urban workers in 1926 and 1927, as reported in *Statistika truda,* no. 11–12, 1927, p. 19 and no. 5–6, 1928, p. 19. Data for the 1930's are not available. For the 1937–40 price index, apples are assigned two-thirds of the weight for fresh and canned fruit or 50% of the total weight for fruit; fresh *grapes* are assigned the remainder of the weight for fresh and canned fruit or 25% of the total weight for fruit; and *dried prunes* are assigned the 25% representing dried fruit.

For the 1937–48–52–54 price index, *dried fruits* are given a weight of 25% of the total for fruit and melons. (Actually, the figure of 24.2% is used; this results from rounding the weight for each representative item to the nearest 0.1% of the group weight.) This is divided equally among the four *dried fruits* priced. *Canned apricots,* representing all canned fruits, are assigned a weight of 9% of the total weight for fruit. This is computed from the amount taken from the category "canned goods" and added to the category "fruit" in Table B-4 in deriving the total weight for fruit. In this it is assumed that half the sales of canned goods were sales of canned vegetables and fruit and that 40% of these were sales of canned fruit. The rest of the subgroup weight applies to fresh fruit and melons; it is divided between *fresh apples* and *pumpkin* in the ratio of 3 to 1. Apples are the one fruit available the year round and must be by far the most important single fruit.

2. *1940:* The 1937 weights are used.

3. *1948, 1952, 1954:* The weights within this subgroup are the same for these three years. For both 1950 and 1954 the weight for *canned apricots,* representing all canned fruit, is computed from Table B-4 at 20% of all sales of fruit. I assume here that half the sales of canned vegetables and fruits were sales of canned fruits. The same weight is used for 1952. In view of the increase in canned fruit, I set the weight for *dried fruit* at 20%, lower than in 1937. The remaining 60% of the subgroup weight is divided between *fresh apples* and *pumpkin* in the ratio of 3 to 1, as in the case of the 1937 weights.

(9) *Salt.* Only one representative commodity is priced.

(10) *Tea and coffee.* In the 1928–37 and 1937–40 price index numbers only tea is priced. *Tea* and *coffee* are both priced in the index for 1937–48–52–54. Tea is by far the more important of these two beverages, and I assign 90% of the group weight to *tea* and 10% to *coffee* for all years.

(11) *Alcoholic beverages.* As indicated above, in computing the 1937 group weight for alcoholic beverages it was assumed that sales of *vodka* accounted for two-thirds and sales of *other alcoholic beverages* for one-third of all sales of alcoholic beverages. Some evidence suggesting this distribution for 1928 and 1937 was cited above. I use these weights for 1937 and the same weights for 1940 and the postwar years. Production of vodka has increased less over this period than production of wine and beer, but prices of vodka have increased much more than prices of other alcoholic beverages. On balance, the share of vodka in the total value of purchases of alcoholic beverages may not have changed very much. Where two vodka products are priced, the weight for vodka is divided equally between them; where several items under *other alcoholic beverages* are priced, they are given equal weights.

(12) *Textiles.* The subgroup weights for *cotton, wool, silk,* and *linen* fabrics are computed from Table B-4 for 1937, 1940, 1950, and 1954. For 1952 the subgroup weights are derived in computing weights from the 1950 and 1954 weights and the changes in value of sales of cotton, wool, and silk fabrics over the years 1950 to 1954. The further breakdowns are as follows:

(a) *Cotton fabrics.* In all cases the weight for this subgroup is divided equally among the various representative cotton fabrics priced. Each of the items priced in a given price index represents a distinct group of cotton fabrics, as these are classified in Soviet practice. At any rate this is true except in the case of the fabrics priced for the 1928–37 index; here *sheeting* and *madapolam* both fall into the same group. On the basis of the quantities of each of the main groups of cotton fabrics produced in 1936 and planned for 1937 and for 1941, and taking into consideration the relative prices in 1937, it appears that the groups represented in the index should have approximately equal weights. The production data are from Gosplan, *Narodno-khoziaistvennyi plan SSSR na 1937 g.,* p. 98, and *Gosudarstvennyi plan na 1941 g.,* pp. 157–159; the retail prices are from *RTS-M-36,* II:5–34.

(b) *Wool fabrics.* This subgroup covers part-wool fabrics and wool substitutes as well as pure wool fabrics. And, in fact, pure wool fabrics are but a small proportion of the total. In the 1928–37 price index, the items priced are good representatives of the main types of wool cloth produced in the USSR. The breakdown of the 1937 subgroup weight among these products is based mainly on a breakdown of wool textile output by types as planned for 1941 in *Gosudarstvennyi plan na 1941 g.,* pp. 160–161. This indicates that coarse woolens were to constitute 27% of total output; considering the lower prices, I give the *coarse wool baize* a weight of 20% of the wool subgroup weight. The remainder of the weight is divided equally between woolen and worsted, although actually the 1941 plan called for a larger output of woolen than of worsted. According to the 1941 plan breakdown, which is not entirely complete, pure wool fabrics were to be less than 4.5% of the planned 1941 output of woolens and worsteds. Allowing for the higher prices of the pure woolen fabrics, I give the *pure wool woolen* a weight of 10% of the weight for woolens and the *pure wool worsted* a weight of 10% of the weight for worsteds.

In the 1937–40 price index only one wool fabric is priced. In the index for 1937–48–52–54, the two items priced are not particularly good representatives of the kinds of wool fabrics produced. For all years, I give the *wool Boston* 75% and the *coarse wool baize* 25% of the subgroup weight.

(c) *Linen fabrics.* In the 1928–37 price index a *pure linen* and a *part-linen* fabric are priced; the weight is arbitrarily divided equally between them.

(d) *Silk fabrics.* This group covers rayon and other artificial silks and mixtures of silk with other fibers as well as pure silk. In the 1937–48–52–54 index both a pure silk and a rayon fabric are priced. For 1937, I assume more or less arbitrarily that pure silk amounted to 10% of the value of sales of this group. In view of the increase in the output of pure silk in recent years, I raise the weight for pure silk to 30% of the group for 1948, 1952, and 1954.

(13) *Garments.*

(a) *1937:* The subdivision here is very rough. It is based in part on data on the number of the various types of garments produced in 1937, from A. K. Il'inskii, "Shveinaia promyshlennost' v tret'em piatiletii," *Legkaia promyshlennost,* no. 6, 1939, p. 36, and on relative prices from NKVT, *Preiskurant roznichnykh tsen na shveinye izdeliia* (Moscow, 1936). The weight for the *felt hat* (taken to represent all *headwear*) and for the *fur hat* (taken to represent all *fur garments*) are the 1940 weights for these two subgroups as shown in Table B-4.

(b) *1940:* The weights are the same as those for 1937.

(c) *1948, 1952, 1954:* The weights for *headwear* and *fur garments* are those shown for 1954 in Table B-4. For the rest, the weights for these three postwar years are based on the 1937 weights but with somewhat greater weights for wool and silk garments and somewhat smaller weights for cotton garments than for 1937. This is intended to reflect the relatively greater increase in the output of wool, silk, and rayon fabrics than of cotton.

(14) *Knitwear.*

(a) *1937, 1940:* For both years, about 10% of the group weight is assigned to rayon socks and the remainder to cotton hosiery. This is based on a statement in *SOVTORG,* no. 5, 1937, p. 39 that 88.5% of the yarn used in the state knitting industry was to be cotton in 1937.

(b) *1948, 1952, 1954:* For these years, in view of the relative increase in the production of rayon and other artificial silks, I set the weight for rayon socks at 20% of the total and that for the two cotton hosiery items at 40% each.

(15) *Shoes.*

(a) *1937:* The weight for rubbers — 19.5% of the group weight — is from the breakdown between rubber shoes and all other shoes in Table B-4. The other shoes are not broken down into types for 1937 in this source. Since the weight for rubber shoes is the same for 1937 as for 1954, I use the 1954 breakdown to obtain the 1937 weights for the subgroups *all leather shoes; cloth and combined cloth-and-leather shoes;* and *felt footwear.* The weight for *leather* shoes is divided equally among the representative all-leather shoes priced.

(b) *1940:* The breakdown between *leather shoes* and *rubber shoes* is computed from Table B-4. The weight for leather shoes includes cloth and cloth-and-leather shoes although no such shoes are priced. Felt shoes, not being priced, are ignored in computing the weights. The weight for leather shoes is divided equally among the representative leather shoes priced.

(c) *1948, 1952:* The weights for *rubber shoes* and *felt shoes* are computed from Table B-4. It is assumed for both years that all-leather shoes accounted for 85% of the sales of leather, cloth, and cloth-leather combined shoes. According to the breakdown in Table B-4 for 1954, all-leather shoes were 88% of sales of leather, cloth, and cloth-and-leather combined shoes in 1954. Aside from changes in production, about which I have no information, changes in the price structure would mean that all-leather shoes should have a somewhat smaller weight in relation to cloth and cloth-and-leather shoes in 1948 and 1952 than in 1954. The shoe price structure remained the same between 1950 and 1952, but the price cuts of April 1953 and April 1954 reduced the prices of all-leather shoes by only about 15% while the prices of cloth and cloth-and-leather shoes were cut by about one-third. Within the all-leather shoe subgroup, equal weights are assigned to the representative shoes priced.

(d) *1954:* The subgroup weights are computed from the breakdown in Table B-4. Within the all-leather shoe subgroup, equal weights are assigned to each of the all-leather shoes priced.

(16) *Haberdashery and notions.* The breakdown is arbitrary. Although a breakdown between *thread* and other products in this group is given in Table B-4, it did not seem advisable to base the weight for thread on this. The other items which could be priced in this group are not representative enough of the group as a whole to warrant assigning them the weight for everything but thread.

(17) *Soap, drugs, etc.*

(a) *1937, 1940:* In the 1937–40 price index, only *household soap* and *toilet soap* are priced. The weights for each year are based on the relationship of sales of household soap to sales of toilet soap shown in Table B-4.

(b) *1937, 1948, 1952, 1954:* As indicated above, the group weight is computed as the sum of the following items from Table B-4: "household soap," "toilet soap," "toiletries," plus 0.1% of total retail sales. The computation gives directly the weights for *household soap* and for *toilet soap.* The weights here for 1950 and 1952 are so close to those for 1954 that I use the 1954 weights for all these years. The remainder of the weight, covering toiletries and drugs, is arbitrarily divided among the other representative items priced.

(18) *Housewares.*

(a) *1937:* The breakdown is quite rough. It is based in part on the percentage distribution of retail sales of specialized housewares shops in the third quarter of 1936, from A. Briukhanov, "Roznitsa Soiuzmetizstroitorg v 1936 g.," *SOVTORG,* no. 1, 1937, p. 44 and scattered data on production of the various items from Gosplan, *Narodno-khoziaistvennyi plan na 1937 g.;* Gosplan, *Tretii piatiletnii plan;* and *Gosudarstvennyi plan na 1941 g.;* and on their prices from *RTS-36* and *RTS-M-36.* The *metal utensils* items are weighted equally for lack of any information suggesting more appropriate weights.

(b) *1948, 1952,* and *1954:* The same breakdown is used for all three years. Again the breakdown is rough. To allow for the probable shifts in consumption within this group, the weights for electrical products and sewing machines are larger and the weights for metal utensils, primus stoves, and samovars smaller than for 1937.

(19) *Reading matter.* The weights are fairly arbitrary. They are the same for all years, including 1928. *Newspapers* are given a weight of about half the total, on the assumption that Soviet citizens buy newspapers regularly but rely more on libraries for periodicals and books. About one-quarter of the weight is assigned to *periodicals* and one-quarter to *books and pamphlets.*

(20) *Cultural and sports goods.*

(a) *1937 weights for 1928–37 price index:* Only two items are priced and neither seems obviously more important than the other; accordingly, the weight is divided equally between them.

(b) *1937, 1948, 1952, 1954:* The weights are based on the breakdown shown in Table B-4. For 1952, the weights are taken as averages of those for 1950 and 1954. The weights for 1937, 1950, and 1954 are computed from the data in Table B-4 as follows: The category "notebooks, paper, and office supplies" in Table B-4 is divided equally among the three representative commodities: *pencil, pen, pen point.* The two categories "bicycles and motorcycles" and "sports goods" in Table B-4 are the weight for the *bicycle.* The two categories "radios" and "musical goods" in Table B-4 are divided among the three musical instruments priced — *gramophone, accordion,* and *piano* — more or less arbitrarily. Half of the category "other cultural goods" in Table B-4 is assigned as weight for the *camera.* For 1937 the breakdown in Table B-4 is incomplete. I use the amount shown for 1937 under the category "notebooks, paper, and office supplies" as weight for the *pencil, pen holder,* and *pen point* and divide the remainder of the 1937 weight according to the distribution among the other categories in 1940.

(21) *Kerosene and matches.* The weights are computed from the data in Table B-4.

(22) *Tobacco products.*

(a) *1937:* The breakdown between tobacco products (cigarettes and pipe tobacco) and makhorka is estimated from the following output and price data: Production of cigarettes was 102 billion pieces in 1937, according to Gosplan, *Tretii piatiletnii plan,* pp. 209–210. About 95% of output was to be allocated to the retail market, according to L. E. Hubbard, *Soviet Trade and Distribution* (London, 1938), p. 107, or, in round figures, 95 billion cigarettes. I estimate the average retail price was about 1.00 ruble per 25 cigarettes. This is the price of *second grade "A"* cigarettes, listed in *RTS-36,* p. 160. Data on the quantities of the various grades of cigarettes produced in 1934 and planned for 1941 (TSUNKHU, *Socialist Construction in the USSR,* p. 221; *Gosudarstvennyi plan na 1941 g.,* p.

167) suggest that this price may be roughly equivalent to the average price of all cigarettes in 1937. Retail sales of 95 billion cigarettes at 1.00 ruble per 25 or 0.04 ruble each amounts to 3.8 billion rubles. Production of makhorka in 1937 was 5,343 thousand cases, according to "Osnovnye pokazateli itogov vypolneniia vtorogo piatiletnego plana SSSR," *PKh*, no. 5, 1939, p. 161. The average retail price is estimated at 0.36 ruble per 50-gm package, or 144 rubles per case. The price of *ordinary makhorka* was 0.35 ruble and of *higher quality makhorka* was 0.40 ruble per 50-gm package; and in remote and mountainous regions, the prices were 0.05 ruble higher (*RTS-36*, p. 162). The price per case is indicated to be 400 times the price per 50-gm package in *SRTS-35*, p. 461. This gives a value of total output of 770 million rubles, of which I assume 700 million rubles represents retail sales. On this computation, then, the retail value of cigarette and makhorka sales totals 4,500 million rubles, of which cigarettes account for 3,800 million rubles, or 84% and makhorka for 700 million rubles, or 16%. This is the breakdown I use.

In light of the fact — not known at the time the above computation was made — that retail sales of tobacco and makhorka amounted to only 3.6 billion rubles in 1937 (*Sovtorgstat-56*, p. 42), the above estimates leading to total sales of 4.5 billion rubles must be in error. The most likely source of error appears to be in the valuation of cigarette output. The cigarette output figure actually includes cigarette tobacco sold in tobacco form to be rolled by the consumer, expressed in terms of cigarettes. Thus, using the price of finished cigarettes to value output overstates the value of sales of cigarettes and cigarette tobacco, and the over-valuation might be large if a significant part of total output is actually loose cigarette tobacco. If this surmise is correct, I probably overweight cigarettes in relation to makhorka. However, even if all the error lies in the computation of cigarette sales, the weight for makhorka would only be increased from the 16% I use as weight to 19% of the total for the group; that is, makhorka sales of 0.7 billion ruble are 19% of total retail sales of tobacco and makhorka of 3.6 billion rubles.

The weight for *cigarettes* is considered to include *pipe tobacco*, and to some extent, this may compensate for the probable overweighting of cigarettes. The weight for *pipe tobacco* is very small as pipe smoking is not very common in the Soviet Union. Among the cigarettes priced, the lower grades are given relatively larger weights.

(b) *1940, 1948, 1952, 1954:* The 1937 weights are used.

E. Service Weights, 1937, 1940, 1948, 1952, and 1954

The weights for the index of rent and service prices are shown in Table B-6 for 1937, 1940, 1948, 1952, and 1954. For convenience the weights for 1928 are shown also. The weights shown in Table B-6 are the weights as computed for all types of services priced in any year even though in a given year one or more of the services may not be priced. These differ in some cases from the weights shown in Table B-1, as the latter are the weights as recomputed to apply to the list of service items actually priced. In particular: In the 1928–37 price index no items representing *clothing made and repaired* or *personal care* are priced and the weights computed for these two subgroups are assigned to the category *other services,* in the case of both the 1928 and the 1937 weights. The "price" corresponding to the category *other services,* it will be recalled, is the average wage. The two excluded categories can presumably be represented fairly well by the average wage. In the 1937–40 price index number, no item representing *entertainment* is priced. In this case, the weight for entertainment is deducted from the total and the weights for the other items are recomputed to equal 100, excluding entertainment for 1937 and 1940. This procedure is adopted here as there seems no

TABLE B-6

Weights for Rent and Service Price Index Numbers, USSR, 1928–54
(percent of total)

Service	1928	1937	1940	1948	1952	1954
Rent	25.3	13.4	15.3	13.0	11.5	11.0
Utilities						
Electricity	8.8	4.8	4.9	4.8	8.5	9.0
Water	6.0	1.8	5.3	4.2	4.5	4.5
Transportation and communications						
Tram	6.7	16.3	12.4	8.0	12.5	13.5
Railroad travel	15.6	30.2	32.5	33.5	25.0	25.0
Entertainment						
Movie	7.0	10.5	6.6	13.5	15.0	14.0
Clothing made and repaired	11.0	6.0	8.0	6.0	6.0	6.0
Personal care						
Haircut	1.8	2.0	1.5	2.0	2.0	2.0
Shave	1.8	2.0	1.5	2.0	2.0	2.0
Other services	16.0	13.0	12.0	13.0	13.0	13.0
Totals	100.0	100.0	100.0	100.0	100.0	100.0

reason to assume that changes in the price of entertainment can be represented by changes in the average wage. In the 1937–40 and 1937–48 price index numbers, no items under *personal care* are priced, and the weight is assigned to *other services* for the same reason as in the case of the 1928–37 index.

(1) *1937:* The 1937 weights are based mainly on the expenditures of the urban population on services in 1935 shown in Table B-7.

TABLE B-7

Urban Expenditures on Services, USSR, 1935

Service	Million rubles	Percent
Rent	700	13.4
Utilities	343	6.6
Transportation and communications	2,428	46.6
Culture and entertainment	536	10.4
Personal services	1,200	23.0
Totals	5,207	100.0

Urban expenditures on rent are estimated as follows. Interpolating between the 191 million square meters of urban dwelling space in 1932 and the 221 million square meters of urban dwelling space in 1937 (Timothy Sosnovy, *The Housing Problem in the Soviet Union* (New York, 1954), p. 89), I estimate roughly that total urban dwelling space in 1935 was 209 million square meters. Of this, about 55%, or 115 million square meters, would have been owned by the government and rented. The average rent is computed at 6.12 rubles per square meter per year (0.51 ruble per square meter per month) on the basis of the rental formula described in appendix A and the 1935 average money wage of all wage earners and salaried employees of 2,269 rubles per year (H. Schwartz, *Russia's Soviet Economy* (New York, 1950), p. 460). Total money rent for 115 million square meters at 6.12 rubles per square meter per year comes to 703.8 million rubles, which is rounded to 700 million rubles.

The other figures in Table B-7 are from U. Cherniavskii and S. Krivetskii,

"Pokupatel'nye fondy naseleniia i roznichnyi tovarooborot," *PKh,* no. 6, 1936, pp. 111–112. This source gives total urban expenditures on rent and utilities as 1,043 million rubles; deducting rent of 700 million rubles leaves 343 million rubles for utilities. Expenditures on personal services (*bytovye raskhody*) by the entire population are estimated by Cherniavskii and Krivetskii at 1.5 billion rubles. I assume 80% of this, or 1.2 billion rubles, were urban expenditures.

Cherniavskii and Krivetskii are quite convincing in their attempt to provide complete data but evince a definite awareness of the shortcomings of the data on expenditures on services. Probably some expenditures are omitted so that even for 1935 the breakdown is not accurate. One wonders, in particular, whether transportation and communications are overweighted. Presumably, data available to the authors on the revenues of the transportation system and the postoffice, et cetera, were complete while there might well be gaps in the data on municipally provided services, and an evaluation of expenditures on the many services provided by cooperatives and individuals could hardly be much more than an informed estimate. It may be, too, that some services which I might classify as entertainment are included in the estimate for personal services; if so, my weight for entertainment is too low.

Using this 1935 breakdown as the basis for weights for 1937, as I do, must involve further errors. Two indicators of changes in the value of services provided — urban money rent and railroad passenger revenue — move closely enough over the period 1935 to 1937 to suggest that the relationship between at least these two important subgroups probably did not change much.

An alternative set of weights for 1937 was computed from the 1928 weights and the change between 1928 and 1937 in volume and price of a limited number of services — rent, electricity, water, railroad transportation, urban transportation, and entertainment. This computation leads to a significantly smaller weight for transportation in relation to those for the other five enumerated services than the weights based on the 1935 data, but the two computations lead to a fairly similar distribution among the other five enumerated services. This is a reason, in addition to that mentioned above, for thinking my weight for transportation is perhaps on the high side. One difficulty in using the weights based on those for 1928 is the absence of information on services other than the six for which data on both volume and price changes are available. On balance, it seemed preferable to use the 1935 data as a basis for the 1937 weights. In any case, several earlier calculations of the service price index suggest that within fairly wide limits, differences in weighting do not make much difference in the results.

(a) *Utilities.* The division of the weight for utilities between *water* and *electricity* is based on the 1928 weights for these two items and the change in volume and price of the two services between 1928 and 1937. The urban average daily use of water in 1937 was 332 per cent of that in 1928, according to *BSE, SSSR,* column 1005, and V. P. Maslakov, *Kommunal'nye tarify v SSSR* (Moscow, 1951), p. 11. As there was no change in the price of water, the 1937 index of the value of water service is 332 (1928 = 100). The consumption of electric power for municipal and household needs in urban areas in 1937 was 521% of that in 1928, according to Lynn Turgeon, *Prices of Industrial Electric Power in the Soviet Union, 1928 to 1950,* The RAND Corporation, RM-1244, April 27, 1954, p. 6. This differs slightly from the index in Maslakov (1951), p. 10. The 1937 price relative for electricity is 111 (1928 = 100), as can be computed from Table A-1. This gives a 1937 index of the value of electric service provided of 578 (1928 = 100).

(b) *Transportation and communications.* Some crude computations based on data on railroad passenger revenue and the number of passengers carried in trams and other urban means of transport are the basis for the division of the weight here between *railroad travel* and the *tram ride*. The former is given 65% and the latter 35% of the subgroup weight.

(c) *Personal service.* The subdivision of this weight is rather arbitrary. It seems probable that clothing repairs and (particularly) clothing made to order were relatively less important and that barber shop and related services were relatively somewhat more important in 1937 than in 1928.

(2) *1940, 1948,* 1952, *1954:* The service weights for each of these years are computed from the 1937 weights and the estimated change in value of the various services between 1937 and the year in question. Some measure of the change in value of the services provided can be estimated for the following six services — housing, electricity, water, railroad transportation, urban transportation, and entertainment. The measures for railroad transport and entertainment relate to the entire USSR while those for the other services are for urban areas only. As there is no basis for estimating the change in value of the numerous other services, I have to resort to fairly arbitrary estimates for these.

The procedure in computing the weights is as follows: The 1937 weight for each of the six items for which I have an index of the value of change is multiplied by the index of the change in value of that service between 1937 and 1940 (or other given year). The results, divided through by the total, give the 1940 (or other year) percentage distribution among these six items. The weights so computed are, of course, rounded. In the case of the 1952 and 1954 weights, some adjustments are made in the weights computed from the 1937 weights to take into account the results of a computation for 1952 based on the 1928 weights and the changes in the value of the six services between 1928 and 1952. I assume, rather arbitrarily, for all years that the six services on which I have data accounted for 77% of all expenditures on services, as was the case in 1937. The distribution of the remaining 23% of the total weight is also taken arbitrarily to be the same in 1948, 1952, and 1954 as in 1937. For 1940 I assign a relatively larger weight to *clothing made and repaired* and relatively smaller weights to the two groups *personal care* and *other services* than for 1937. In view of the shortages of ready-made clothing reported in the shops in that year, it seems quite likely there was an increase in expenditures on clothing made to order.

The estimated changes in volume, price, and value of the six services used in computing the weights for 1940, 1948, 1952, and 1954 are shown in Table B-8. Data for 1944 are shown also, as these are of some interest. The price relatives in this table are from Table 3. The price index for urban transportation refers to the price of a tram ride. The price index for entertainment refers to the price of a movie ticket. The index of value is computed by multiplying the index of physical volume by the price index. The estimates of the index numbers of volume are explained below.

(a) *Urban housing.* This is an index of the physical volume of the total urban housing stock. The absolute figures underlying this index for 1937, 1940, 1944, and 1948 are from Abram Bergson and Hans Heymann, Jr., *Soviet National Income and Product, 1940–1948* (New York, 1954), p. 132; those for 1952 and 1954 are preliminary figures from *SNIP-49-55.*

(b) *Electricity.* The index of physical volume here refers to the consumption of electric power for municipal and household needs (*kommunal'no-bytovye nuzhdy*) in urban areas. The figures probably include power used in street lighting and possibly other municipal services as well as private household consumption. The figures for 1937 and 1940 are from Turgeon (1954), p. 6. These differ slightly from the index in Maslakov (1951), p. 10. The index for 1944 is assumed to be slightly below that for 1945, which is computed at 121. This is computed from the 1950 figure and the statement in Maslakov (1951), p. 17 that 1950 consumption was 171% of that in 1945. An index of 206 for 1950 is computed from an estimate of John Hardt's that 11.4% of total power generated went to municipal services in that year (letter of March 16, 1955) and total power generated in 1950 from Turgeon (1954), p. 2. The 1948 index is an interpolation between that for 1947 and that for 1950. The 1947 figure used here is computed from that for 1945 and the statement in Maslakov (1951), p. 17 that consumption in 1947 was 22% greater than in 1945. The index for 1952 is an interpolation between that for 1950 and that for 1954. The index for 1954 is computed from that for 1940 and the following statement from *Elektricheskie stantsii,* no. 1, 1955, p. 1: "The supply of electric energy for the needs of the municipal economy and the household needs of the population increased over three times in comparison with the prewar period." The comparison here, it is believed, is between 1940 and 1954.

TABLE B-8

Change in Volume, Price, and Value of Selected Services, USSR, 1937–54
(1937 = 100)

Services	1940	1944	1948	1952	1954
Urban housing					
Volume[a]	127	96	133	158	173
Rent	142	175[b]	186	186	186
Value	180	168[b]	247	294	322
Electricity, urban					
Volume	131	119	167	298	392
Price	120	125	155	200	200
Value	157	149	259	596	784
Water, urban					
Volume	144	123	184	239	271
Price	328	328	328	328	328
Value	472	403	604	784	889
Railroad travel					
Volume	108	73	82	119	142
Price	153	216	228	248	248
Value	165	158	187	295	352
Urban transport					
Volume	117	56	91	143	186
Price	100	113	147	200	200
Value	117	63	134	286	372
Entertainment					
Volume	101	70	113	154	266
Price	—	—	300	300	200
Value	(100)[c]	(80)[c]	339	462	532

[a] These figures differ slightly from those underlying the urban per capita housing space figures in Table 27; the latter are based on more recent figures.
[b] The 1944 rent index was revised, after these computations were made, to 169 (appendix D, section 3). This reduces the 1944 value index to 162.
[c] Because entertainment could not be priced for 1940 and 1944 the index numbers of value are only crude guesses for these years and are therefore shown in parentheses.
Note: The dash (—) indicates that data were not available.

(c) *Water.* The index of the physical volume of water in Table B-8 refers to the urban average daily use of water, but it is possible that for some years the index relates to the total volume of water supplied during the year for municipal needs. The 1937 and 1940 figures are from *BSE, SSSR,* column 1005 and Maslakov (1951), p. 11. The 1944 figure is a rough interpolation between the index for 1942 of 67% of 1940 and an index for 1945 of "almost the prewar level" from Maslakov (1951), pp. 12-13. I assume the index in 1945 was 139. The 1948 figure is interpolated between the figures for 1947 and 1950. These latter are computed from the 1945 index and the index in Maslakov (1951), p. 17 indicating consumption in 1947 was 123% of 1945 and in 1950 was 150% of 1945. The figures for 1952 and 1954 are interpolated between that for 1950 and that for 1955. The municipal supply of water in 1955 was 141% of that in 1950, according to *PKh*, no. 1, 1956, p. 88. It is not clear whether this refers to average daily use or total annual supply.

(d) *Railroad travel.* The index of physical volume of railroad travel is based on the number of passenger-kilometers. The figures for 1937, 1940, and 1944 are from James H. Blackman, "Transportation" in A. Bergson (ed.), *Soviet Economic Growth* (Evanston, 1953), p. 154. The 1944 index shown is actually Blackman's figure for 1945. The 1940 figure is also given in *Narkhoz*, p. 177. The 1948 figure is an estimate of Holland Hunter's, based on data which became available after publication of the Blackman study (Hunter letter of August 12, 1955). The 1952 index is also from Hunter's letter of August 12, 1955; this was directly implied in a Soviet source. The 1954 figure is from *Narkhoz*, p. 177.

(e) *Urban transport.* The index of the physical volume of urban transport shown in Table B-8 for the years 1937, 1940, and 1944 is based on the number of passengers carried in trams and trolleybuses. The 1944 index is actually that for 1945. For 1948, 1952, and 1954, autobus passengers are also taken into account. The data on the number of passengers carried in trams and trolleybuses are given in Table B-9. *1937:* Tram passengers carried are computed at 5,609 million from the

TABLE B-9

Tram and Trolleybus Passengers Carried per Year, USSR, 1937–54

Year	Million	Index, 1937 = 100
1937	5,732	100
1940	6,691	117
1945	3,190	56
1948	4,639	81
1952	6,060	106
1954	6,720	117

1928 figure of 1,640 million in Gosplan, *Summary of the Fulfillment of the First Five Year Plan for the Development of the National Economy of the USSR*, p. 288 and the index of the volume of tram passengers in *BSE, SSSR*, column 1005. Trolleybus passengers are computed at 123 million from the 1940 figure, and the index showing the number of passengers carried in 1937 was 35.8% of the number carried in 1940 in *BSE, SSSR*, column 1005. *1940:* Tram passengers are computed at 6,347 million from the 1928 figure and the index in *BSE, SSSR*, column 1005. Trolleybus passengers are assumed to be 344 million, 84% of the figure planned for 1941 (*Gosudarstvennyi plan na 1941 g.*, p. 602); the number of tram passengers carried in 1940, as computed here, was 84% of the number planned for 1941. *1945:* The figure is computed from the figures for 1950 and the index in Maslakov (1951), p. 17 showing that in 1950, the volume of tram passenger traffic was 158% and the volume of trolleybus passengers was 312% of that in 1945. In 1950, urban tramways carried over 4.8 billion passengers and trolleybuses carried about 600 million passengers. These figures from Maslakov (1951), pp. 93–94, are taken to refer to 1950 although the source does not indicate the year. *1948:* This figure is an interpolation between those for 1947 and 1949. The latter are calculated from data in Maslakov (1951), pp. 17–18. *1952* and *1954:* The figures are interpolated between those for 1950 and 1955. In 1955, the number of passengers carried in trams was 22% greater and the number carried in trolleybuses was twice as great as in 1950, according to *PKh*, no. 1, 1956, p. 88.

In view of the large increase in autobus traffic it seemed in order to make an allowance for this in the index number for the postwar years. I therefore construct an index number for 1948, 1952, and 1954 with 1940 as the base year, which takes into account autobus as well as tram and trolleybus traffic. This is linked to the index number based on tram and trolleybus passengers only, with 1937 as base year. The autobus passenger figures are based on the absolute number of autobus passengers carried in 1950 and an index number of the number of autobus passenger-kilometers traveled. In 1950, over 1.5 billion passengers were carried in autobuses of the Republic Ministries of Auto Transport, according to Maslakov (1951), p. 95. (*Narkhoz*, p. 183, gives a 1950 figure of 1,053 million passengers carried in autobuses of the USSR Ministry of Auto Transport and Highways. The Maslakov figure, which I use, is apparently more inclusive, though even this does not include passengers carried in autobuses of various ministries, enterprises, and institutions.) The 1940 and 1954 figures are computed from the 1950 figure of 1.5 billion passengers carried and the index number of passenger-kilometers traveled in autobuses of the USSR Ministry of Auto Transport and Highways, from *Narkhoz*, p. 183. This index is as follows: 1940, 100; 1950, 152; and 1954, 414. The index in the same source of the number of passengers carried is higher, but the index of passenger-kilometers traveled is a better measure for present purposes. The 1948 figure is an estimate, and the 1952 figure is an interpolation between those for 1950 and 1954.

(f) *Entertainment.* The index of the physical volume of entertainment is based on the number of theatres and motion picture houses or projectors for the years 1937 and 1940 and on motion picture attendance for subsequent years. The two index numbers are linked at 1940. Obviously the number of theatres and projectors is hardly a satisfactory basis for measuring even the consumption of theatre and motion picture entertainment, much less all other forms of entertainment. The motion picture attendance figures, on the other hand, clearly are a measure of the consumption of motion picture entertainment, which must be at least the single largest entertainment service and possibly a very large component of total expenditures on entertainment. In 1950, for instance, 1,144 million persons attended motion pictures, while attendance at theatres and circuses was only 89 million persons. These figures are from TSU, *Kul'turnoe stroitel'stvo SSSR*, pp. 297, 314, and *Narkhoz*, p. 238.

The figures underlying the index on the number of theatres and motion picture projectors are from TSU, *Kul'turnoe stroitel'stvo SSSR*, pp. 293, 300. Figures on motion picture attendance are given in *Narkhoz*, p. 238, for 1940, 1945, 1950, and 1955. For 1944 the 1945 figure is used. For 1948, it is assumed that attendance was 87% of that in 1950; attendance at theatres in 1948 was 87% of that in 1950, according to the figures in TSU, *Kul'turnoe stroitel'stvo SSSR*, p. 293. The 1952 figure is computed from that for 1950 and the following: Motion picture attendance in 1951 was 12% greater than in 1950, according to the 1951 Plan Fulfillment Report (*Pravda*, January 29, 1952); it is assumed attendance in 1952 was 5% greater than in 1951 on the basis of the 5% increase in motion picture projectors reported in the 1952 Plan Fulfillment Report (*Pravda*, January 23, 1953). For 1954 it is assumed attendance was 7.5% less than in 1955 (for which the attendance is known) on the basis of the 7.5% increase in the number of projectors between 1954 and 1955 reported in the 1955 Plan Fulfillment Report (*Pravda*, January 30, 1956).

For 1940 and 1944 no motion picture or other form of entertainment could be priced. The index numbers of the value of entertainment services for these two years, shown in Table B-8 in parentheses, represent crude guesses.

APPENDIX C

SOVIET STATISTICS ON THE COLLECTIVE FARM MARKET

As I rely heavily on the Soviet index of collective farm market prices for the period since 1940 and make various other uses of Soviet statistics on the collective farm market in the computations, it seems in order to describe insofar as possible the Soviet methods of collecting data on the collective farm market and of collating them into price and volume index numbers, and to point out the serious limitations of such index numbers.

At present, three index numbers of collective farm market prices are in use in the Soviet Union: (1) An index number of collective farm market prices in 71 large cities. (2) An index number of collective farm market prices in what I shall refer to as the "complete sample" of cities. The complete sample currently covers 251 cities but, as will be pointed out below, the size of the sample has varied over the years. (3) An index number of prices on all urban collective farm markets in the USSR.

Corresponding to the three price index numbers there are three index numbers of the volume of sales on the collective farm market. The price index numbers for the 71 cities and the entire USSR and volume data for the 71 cities, the complete sample of 251 cities, and the entire USSR were published in 1956 in *Sovtorgstat-56*, pp. 179–185. Prior to the publication of this source only scattered statements about the movement of collective farm market prices and sales during the postwar years were published, and usually no indication was given as to the coverage of the statement. Among the three indexes computed, it is the index number of collective farm market prices in all urban markets in which we are interested. Unfortunately, this appears to be the least reliable of the available series.

Soviet data on the collective farm market are much less reliable than their data on sales and prices in the state and cooperative trade systems. This is hardly surprising since the state itself sets the official prices while prices on the collective farm markets fluctuate in accordance with local conditions of supply and demand. The bulk of sales on the collective farm market is made by millions of individuals — members of collective farms, independent peasants, and workers with gardens — who keep no records. The raw price and quantity data for the Soviet index numbers are for the most part the estimates of recording clerks stationed at the market place. Presumably, many of the recording clerks are really expert at this kind of estimating, but there is obviously room for much error in the raw data.

The volume of sales of each important product is estimated by an expert at the market place each day trading takes place. This is largely a matter of appraisal by eye of the quantities brought in and of the amounts left unsold at the end of the day. Supplementary and probably more accurate data on meat, milk, and livestock are obtained from the quality control stations through which these products must pass at many markets. Records of the sales by the collective farms are available to the authorities, but the collective farms account for only a fraction of total collective farm market sales. (Their share was 14.8% in 1940, 13.4% in 1950, and 9% in 1955, according to *SOVTORG*, no. 11, 1956, p. 9.)

Reports on the volume of sales are limited to a sample of towns and to a sample of products. In 1933, the base year for most published prewar collective farm market index numbers, the sample covered only ten cities and 11 to 15 products. By 1937 the sample had been increased to 160 cities and it included 175 cities in 1939. (See J. F. Karcz, *Soviet Agricultural Marketings and Prices, 1928–1954,* The RAND Corporation, RM-1930, July 2, 1957, appendix B, section IV, and the references cited there.) During the war years the sample fell to 36 cities (John T. Whitman, "The *Kolkhoz* Market," *Soviet Studies,* 7:385 (1956)) but had increased to 200 by 1946 (N. Riauzov and N. Titel'baum, *Kurs torgovoi statistiki* (Moscow, 1947), p. 128). The present sample covers 251 cities and 73 products (A. I. Gozulov, *Ekonomicheskaia statistika* (Moscow, 1953), p. 353).

The raw price data are also estimates of experts at the market place. The reported prices are supposed to be "representative" prices and the recording clerks are instructed to report the price prevailing during the hour of briskest trade. Where there is more than one market in a given town, the local authorities are to estimate the average price for the town. The number of towns in the sample for price reporting has generally been larger than that for volume data. Thus, in 1935, when volume data were reported for 100 cities, price data were reported for 158 cities and 600 *raion* centers (Karcz, The RAND Corporation, RM-1930, appendix B, section IV). In 1938, the sample was 160 cities and 600 *raion* centers. At that time, for the 160 cities, prices of 50 products were reported once a month and prices of 15 products were reported three times a month; for the 600 *raion* centers, prices were reported once monthly, probably for fewer products than in the case of the monthly reports for the 160 cities (*PKh,* no. 3, 1938, p. 175). Later in 1938 the sample was increased to cover 200 cities and 800 *raion* centers (Iu. Pisarev, N. Riauzov, and N. Titel'baum, *Kurs torgovoi statistiki* (Moscow, 1938), p. 111; M. V. Tenenbaum and N. Riauzov, *Torgovo-kooperativnaia statistika* (Moscow, 1939), p. 204). The sample seems to have declined by 1940; for comparisons of the postwar years with 1940, the sample for price statistics is apparently 136 cities. During the war the sample undoubtedly declined as was the case for volume statistics. At present, the sample is 251 cities for which the prices of 73 products are reported once a month and the prices of a smaller number of products are reported three times a month; in addition, prices are reported once a month for fifteen products in all *raion* centers (Gozulov, p. 357).

The volume of sales in all the sample cities is presumably computed by adding the volume of sales of each commodity in each city. The procedure would be the same for the smaller sample of large cities. The volume of sales on all urban collective farm markets in the country is an estimate, based in part on the data for the sample cities. The first step here is to extend the data for the sample cities to the entire urban USSR. This is done by multiplying the volume of sales per inhabitant in each city in the sample by the total urban population which that sample city is supposed to represent. Human population weights are used for sales of food products, but in the case of feed the weights are based on the number of livestock in the various cities. The method of weighting has apparently varied. A 1938 source (Pisarev, Riauzov, and Titel'baum, p. 114) says that the population represented by a given sample city is based on the geographic location and the size of the city. A 1939 source (Tenenbaum and Riauzov, pp. 169–170), however, indicates that it is only the size of the city (large, medium, or small) which is the basis for representation. A 1951 source (N. S. Margolin, *Balans denezhnykh dokhodov i raskhodov naseleniia,* p. 86) mentions only the geographic location of the sample city as the basis for extending the data for the sample cities to the entire urban USSR.

All accounts agree that the estimates obtained in this way from the sample data are not accurate and must be carefully checked against and adjusted on the basis of data on agricultural output, on procurements, on consumption as indicated in studies of urban worker budgets, and on market sales as indicated in budgets of collective farmers, et cetera. It is clear, then, that the published figures are estimates and probably quite rough ones.

The index of collective farm market prices for the cities in the sample is computed by weighting the price in each sample city by the volume of sales of that product in that city in the given year (Riauzov and Titel'baum (1947), pp. 149–150). The procedure is the same in the case of the smaller sample of large cities. As described in the statistical manuals, the price index number is computed according to a given-year weighted aggregative formula (Riauzov and Titel'baum (1947), p. 150; TSU, *Slovar'-spravochnik po sotsial'no-ekonomicheskoi statistike* (Moscow, 1944), p. 178). Probably the index numbers are computed on a year-to-year basis and then chained for comparisons over periods of longer than one year.

It is not clear how the problem of changes in the size of the sample is handled. There is some reason to believe that comparisons are made on the basis of data only for cities which are included in the sample in both years compared. *Sovtorgstat-56*, for instance, shows a price index number comparing the postwar years 1950–55 with 1940 for the 71 large cities; these cities, it is believed, are common to the sample in both 1940 and the postwar years. But the index number for the complete sample of 251 towns shown in this source relates only to the period from 1950 on. Comparisons between 1940 and the postwar years in other sources are based on data for 136 cities. See Table C-3 and the sources cited there and Riauzov and Titel'baum (1947), pp. 149–150. For the entire urban USSR, however, a price index number with 1940 as base year is given in *Sovtorgstat-56*.

How the index number of prices on all urban collective farm markets in the USSR is computed is not explained in the Soviet statistical texts. One step must be extending the price index numbers for the sample towns to the entire urban USSR. From the account of how the urban USSR index number of the volume of sales is computed, we might deduce that the price of a given product in a sample city is weighted by the volume of sales that city is supposed to represent, this latter having been estimated from the per capita sales in the sample city and the urban population which the sample city represents. In addition to the price data for the cities in the sample, the price data for the *raion* centers presumably enter into the computation. Volume data are not reported for the *raion* centers and it is not known how the *raion* center prices are weighted. The weights may be based on the volume of sales per capita in the very few small towns included in the regular sample. If so, this means that so far as quantity weights are concerned, a very large part of total sales is represented in the index number by a very small sample. In the case of the nation-wide index number of urban collective farm market prices, changes in the size of the sample are apparently not considered as limiting the periods which can be compared. The price index number for all urban collective farm market trade published in *Sovtorgstat-56* compares the postwar years with 1940. It is possible, though, that some adjustments are made in the index number for changes in the size of the sample. And presumably adjustments are also made on the basis of other types of nation-wide data, as in the case of the volume index.

So far as the value of sales on the collective farm market in current prices is concerned, this is computed from the data on the physical volume of sales and on average prices. Accordingly, the figures for total collective farm market sales at current market prices are even less accurate estimates than the figures on volume of sales and on prices (Riauzov and Titel'baum (1947), p. 130).

The price and volume index numbers and the figures on the value of sales for collective farm market trade are, then, based in the first place on data for a limited sample of cities and products. The raw data themselves are estimates and

undoubtedly subject to many shortcomings. Beyond this, the sample is not representative of all urban collective farm markets. This will be discussed in more detail
below. The computations based on the data for the sample are then adjusted on
the basis of other types of economic data in an attempt to derive estimates applicable to all urban collective farm markets. Little is known about the nature
of these adjustments or how adequately they compensate for the numerous shortcomings of the sample data. It is clear, however, that the figures for the urban
collective farm market are only estimates, and probably rather rough estimates
at that.

The complete sample for both price and volume data (excluding the *raion* centers
for which only price data are reported) has for some time included most of the
large cities, all republic, krai, and oblast capitals, and a few remote small towns
and workers' settlements. Since 1938 (except for the war years) over half the
urban population has lived in the towns included in the sample (Whitman, p. 385).
Sales on the collective farm markets in the 251 cities in the present sample accounted for almost 40% of all urban collective farm market sales in 1950 and for
just under 56% of all urban collective farm market sales in 1956, according to
data in *Sovtorgstat-56*, pp. 19, 188. For a "sample" this is a fairly large proportion
of either population or sales. However, by Soviet admission, the sample is not
representative. The following statement by Iu. Shnirlin in *SOVTORG*, no. 6, 1956,
pp. 10–11, is revealing: "Statistical observation of sales on the collective farm
market is carried on in 251 of the total of 3,938 cities and workers' settlements.
It is true that more than half of the urban population lives in cities where collective
farm market trade is observed. Nevertheless, data on sales in the 251 cities are
not typical of the other cities and, consequently, cannot reflect the situation on all
markets in the country, let alone all urban collective farm market trade. The fact
is that (the sample) includes all the large cities — Moscow, Leningrad, republic
capitals, krai and oblast centers; there are far fewer medium-sized cities, and very
few small ones. The population in the small towns (in the sample) constitutes
approximately 2% of the total population of small towns and workers' settlements."
Similar statements are to be found in Tenenbaum and Riauzov, pp. 69–70, and
N. Riauzov and N. Titel'baum, *Statistika sovetskoi torgovli* (Moscow, 1951), pp.
140–141.

While the larger towns dominate the sample, sales in the small towns account
for a large share of the total. Furthermore, there are significant differences between the large city markets and those in medium and small towns. Market prices
in the small towns are generally lower than in the large cities. During the 1930's
market prices in small towns were sometimes as much as 50% lower than the
corresponding prices in the nearest large city (TSUNKHU, *Kolkhoznaia i individual'no-krestianskaia torgovlia* (Moscow, 1936), p. 204; *Problemy ekonomiki*,
no. 3, 1940, p. 94). And in October 1954, the average prices of six important
products in *raion* centers ranged from 77 to 94% of the corresponding average
prices in republic capitals and oblast centers (*SOVTORG*, no. 9, 1956, p. 13).

In the small towns, local conditions of supply and demand dominate the market,
and the market conditions must differ from those in the larger cities. The small
town is the main, and in most cases the only, free market for the surplus produce
of the surrounding countryside. And the surrounding countryside is usually the
only source of supply for the small town free market. In season, supplies must be
plentiful relative to demand. Demand must be relatively light as many small-
townspeople have their own garden and perhaps a cow or some chickens. Out of
season, there may be hardly any trade at all. Thus, not only are the in-season
prices likely to be low relative to those in larger cities but also, since most trade

TABLE C-1

Soviet Index Numbers of Collective Farm Market Prices,
71 Large Cities and Urban USSR, 1950, 1954, and 1955
(1940 = 100)

	1950		1954		1955	
	71 Cities	Urban USSR	71 Cities	Urban USSR	71 Cities	Urban USSR
All commodities	98	104	110	107	114	111
Grain	108	128	79	109	82	114
Potatoes	69	77	96	109	86	105
Other vegetables	95	132	126	134	126	138
Fruit	110	113	133	143	128	138
Meat[a]	102	93	103	105	118	114
Milk and milk products	96	92	104	110	107	113
Eggs	110	104	102	101	108	99

[a] The figures for the 71 cities are for "meat products" while those for the urban USSR are for "meat and fat."
They may not be entirely comparable.
Source: *Sovtorgstat-56*, pp. 182–183.

takes place in season, the average annual prices (weighted by the volume of trade) are likely also to be much lower than in the large cities.

In the large cities, on the other hand, the city population produces very little of its own food and must depend on the state shops and the collective farm market. Produce is brought to the market from greater distances, both because transportation is easier into the large towns and because higher prices are more of an incentive to the farmers to bring their produce in. In the largest cities, at least, the state makes an effort to encourage shipments from distant areas and to maintain a more even flow of produce over the year. Seasonal fluctuations in supplies must be more moderate than in the small towns but, at the same time, more of the trade must be conducted at high, off-season prices.

An impression of the differences in market price and quantity movements as shown in the index numbers for the sample cities and for the entire urban USSR may be obtained by examining Tables C-1 through C-4. Table C-1 shows the index numbers of collective farm market prices in the 71 large cities and in the

TABLE C-2

Prices of Beef and Potatoes on the Collective Farm Market, Moscow,
71 Cities, and Urban USSR, 1947–55
(1940 = 100)

	1947	1950	1953	1954	1955
Beef					
Moscow	401	116	122	125	134
71 Cities	—	99	—	119	131
Urban USSR	—	100	—	116	127
Potatoes					
Moscow	377	92	77	131	192
71 Cities	—	69	—	⎰96	⎰86
Urban USSR	—	77	—	109	105

Note: The dash (—) indicates that data were not available.
Sources: *SOVTORG*, no. 9, 1956, p. 16; *Sovtorgstat-56*, pp. 182–183. The Moscow prices are those prevailing on
September 25; the other prices are annual averages.

TABLE C-3

Volume of Sales on the Collective Farm Market, 71 Large Cities, 136 Cities,
and Urban USSR, 1950
(1940 = 100)

Commodity	71 Cities[a]	136 Cities	Urban USSR[a]
All commodities	148	150[b]	163
Grain	121	—	406
Flour	238	—	—
Grain and flour	—	171[c]	—
Potatoes	259	243[c]; 245[d]	295
Other vegetables	157	150[c]	105
Fruit	196	179[c]	141
Vegetable oil	191	185[c]	—
Meat	129	126[d]	114
Milk and milk products	135	—	116
Milk	111	171[c]	—
Butter	170	164[c]; 180[d]	—

[a] *Sovtorgstat-56*, pp. 180–181.
[b] *Voprosy ekonomiki*, no. 8, 1953, p. 129, states: "In 1950 the total volume of shipments to the collective farm market was almost one and one-half times the pre-war level." It is assumed that this statement refers to the 136 cities, but it may be a rounded figure for the 71 large cities.
[c] V. Sokolov and R. Nazarov, *Sovetskaia torgovlia v poslevoennyi period* (Moscow, 1954), pp. 78, 84. Except in the case of grain and flour, the figures are for shipments to the market rather than sales.
[d] M. M. Lifits (ed.), *Ekonomika sovetskoi torgovli* (Moscow, 1955), p. 285. The figures appear to refer to the 136 sample cities, but the source is not explicit on this point.
Note: The dash (—) indicates that data were not available.

entire urban USSR for 1950, 1954, and 1955 with 1940 as base. The two sets of price index numbers are fairly similar except in the case of grain and, in 1950, vegetables. Table C-2 shows 1940-based relatives of the free market prices of beef and potatoes in Moscow, the 71 large cities, and the entire urban USSR during the postwar years. The difference is striking in the case of potatoes.

Changes between 1940 and 1950 in the volume of sales of the main products

TABLE C-4

Volume of Sales on the Collective Farm Market, 71 Large Cities, 251 Cities,
and Urban USSR, 1954 and 1955
(1950 = 100)

	1954			1955		
	71 Cities	251 Cities	Urban USSR	71 Cities	251 Cities	Urban USSR
All commodities	128	124	100	137	—	103
Grain	319	235	84	331	250	72
Potatoes	135	136	101	153	154	100
Other vegetables	166	172	125	183	182	126
Fruit	171	171	109	200	199	123
Vegetable oil	62	68	—	82	84	—
Meat[a]	86	92	97	84	91	100
Milk and milk products	96	—	101	109	—	115
Milk	102	105	—	123	128	—
Butter	69	69	—	72	70	—
Eggs	321	292	225	348	311	230

[a] The designation of this group is "meat products" for the 71 cities, "meat and poultry" for the 251 cities, and "meat and fat" for the urban USSR; the figures may not be entirely comparable.
Note: The dash (—) indicates that data were not available.
Sources: *Sovtorgstat-56*, pp. 180–181; 185–187; M. M. Lifits (ed.), *Ekonomika sovetskoi torgovli* (Moscow, 1955), pp. 285–286; *SOVTORG*, no. 4, 1955, p. 3.

traded on the collective farm market in the 71 large cities, in the sample of 136 cities, and in the entire urban USSR are shown in Table C-3. Similarly, Table C-4 shows changes from 1950 to 1954 and 1955 for the 71 large cities, the sample of 251 cities, and the entire urban USSR. For the two samples, the data in both tables show a fairly similar pattern except in the case of grain products. Probably the 71 large cities dominate the complete sample generally, but as more grain is sold in the smaller cities, their influence would be heavy in this case. For the entire urban USSR, however, the volume of sales shows significant differences in movement from that in the two samples. The adjustments made in the index for the sample cities to extend the index to the entire USSR must be substantial. Probably the urban USSR index number gives a picture for the entire urban USSR which is much closer to reality than the index number for the sample cities; but it is a more or less rough estimate and undoubtedly subject to considerable error.

APPENDIX D

INDEX NUMBERS OF OFFICIAL RETAIL PRICES IN MOSCOW IN 1944

As indicated in the text, the cost-of-living index number for 1944 is a rough estimate and is not comparable in method to the index numbers for other years. In this appendix I explain the sources for and methods of computing the various price index numbers which form the basis of the 1944 cost-of-living index number. These are: the index number of ration prices (section 1), the index number of prices in commercial shops (section 2), and the index number of service prices (section 3).

I. RATION PRICES

The index number of ration prices in 1944 is computed by linking to the index number of official prices for 1937–40 an estimate of the change in prices between 1940 and 1944. The 1937–40 link here is that computed on the basis of 1937 weights. I classify the 1937–44 price index number as a 1937-weighted index number in the tables in the text. It will be obvious, however, that because of the linking procedure this is not a true Laspeyres index number. The structure of ration prices in 1944 was very similar to the structure of official prices in 1940. Because of this, it seems unlikely that a true Laspeyres index number would differ much from one computed by linking at the year 1940 as I do. For lack of data on both prices and quantities in 1944, it is impossible to present any approximation to a Paasche-type index for 1944.

The change in prices between 1940 and 1944 is estimated in two stages. (1) The level of retail prices in state and cooperative shops prevailing when rationing was introduced in July 1941 is estimated to be about 3% above the level of official prices during the year 1940. More specifically, this appears to be the difference between average 1940 prices and January 1941 prices. There was apparently little change in prices between January and July 1941. An index number was computed of the change in official prices between 1937 and January 1941, using 1937 weights. The 1941 quotations for the most part are prices observed in Moscow in January 1941. The source for these quotations is *MLR*, May 1941. Some quotations observed in Kuibyshev in January 1942, from unpublished materials, were also used. With few exceptions, the commodities priced are the same as those priced in the index number for 1937–40. The resulting price index number for January 1941 was 3% higher than the corresponding price index number for the year 1940. (This is based on computations which, for 1940, have since been revised. The revisions were not carried through for the index number for January 1941. The difference between the two index numbers would probably not be affected by the revisions.)

My estimate here accords with Soviet data. In *Narkhoz*, p. 210, two sets of retail price index numbers for the years 1950 to 1955 are presented, one with average annual 1940 prices as base and one with prices at the end of 1940 as base. The former index number for any given year is 2½ to 3% higher than the latter index number. This would imply that average prices for the entire year 1940 were almost 3% lower than prices at the end of 1940.

The index number of official prices in 1940, using 1937 weights, is 132 (1937 =

100). This is raised by 3% to obtain the index number of official prices in 1941 of 136.

(2) Between the introduction of rationing in 1941 and 1944, it is estimated there was an increase of roughly 5% in the prices of rationed goods. The index number of official prices in 1941, computed above at 136, is raised by 5% to obtain the index number of ration prices in 1944 of 143 (1937 = 100).

Most Soviet statements claim that ration prices were maintained at a constant level during the war (N. Voznesenskii, *Voennaia ekonomika SSSR* (Moscow, 1948), p. 128; M. M. Lifits, *Sovetskaia torgovlia* (Moscow, 1948), p. 104). There is evidence, however, that prices of alcoholic beverages, tobacco products, and reading matter were raised, seemingly substantially. This is discussed below. Aside from these price rises, the Soviet claim that ration prices remained unchanged is substantiated by observers' reports. For foods, there are fairly numerous observed quotations for 1944, mostly from *UM*, which closely correspond to the prices prevailing in January 1941. For manufactured consumer goods, there are fewer available quotations, and these are harder to judge because of difficulties of quality comparability; but no clear evidence of any significant change in prices of manufactured goods has come to hand. The effect of those price increases which are known to have occurred appears to mean an average increase in prices of rationed goods of very roughly 5%.

By Soviet admission, ration prices of tobacco products and alcoholic beverages were raised in 1943. (See Voznesenskii, p. 128; G. L. Rubinshtein, *et al.*, *Ekonomika sovetskoi torgovli* (Moscow, 1950), pp. 106–107.) Presumably the full effect of the rise in these prices is not reflected in Voznesenskii's index number of ration prices in 1943 — 100.5% of 1940 (*Voennaia ekonomika SSSR*, p. 128). Specific price quotations for alcoholic beverages and tobacco products in 1944 are not available. But there is evidence that the price rise was substantial. Henry C. Cassidy reports in *Moscow Dateline, 1941–1943* (Boston, 1943), p. 321, that the state twice doubled the price of vodka. And, according to Lifits (1948), p. 114, the prices of tobacco products established in December 1947 were the same as the ration prices in effect immediately prior to the price reform. These prices were over twice the 1940 prices. The ration prices in effect in 1944 may have been below those in effect just before the 1947 price reform, but were probably considerably above the 1940 level.

Prices of reading matter almost doubled between 1940 and 1944. With 1937 as base, and using 1937 weights, the index number of prices of reading matter in 1940 is 108 (see Table 5). A comparable index number computed for 1944 comes to 210. Notes on the 1944 price quotations used in computing this index number are presented below. These should be compared with the corresponding 1937 quotations in Table A-1 and the 1937 notes on the quotations in appendix A. For convenience, the items are numbered to correspond with the numbering in Table A-1 and appendix A.

209. *Pravda.* 0.20 ruble per issue. The price is printed on each issue.

210. *Bol'shevik.* 0.70 ruble per issue. The issues examined contain 64 to 80 pages. The price is printed on each issue.

211. *Ogonek.* 1.00 ruble per issue. The price is printed on each issue.

212. *Planovoe khoziaistvo.* 3.00 rubles per issue. The price is printed on each issue.

216. *Novel*

1937: N. Ostrovskii, *Rozhdennye burei* (Children of the Storm), Sovetskii pisatel', Moscow, 1937, 207 pages. The price, printed on the back of the book, was 3.00 rubles, in paper cover.

1944: Konstantin Simonov, *Dni i nochi* (Days and Nights), Sovetskii pisatel',

Moscow, 1944, 220 pages. The price, printed on the back of the book, was 11.00 rubles. This is a paper-bound book.

Comparability: Both novels are paper-bound, contain approximately the same number of pages, and appear generally similar in quality.

219. *Pamphlet, 48 pages.* 0.60 ruble per copy. A. Vishinskii, *Sovetskoe gosudarstvo v otechestvennoi voine* (The Soviet Government During the Patriotic War), Moscow, 1944, 48 pages. The price is printed on the back of the pamphlet.

2. COMMERCIAL SHOP PRICES

It is assumed that the 1937–44 index number of prices on the collective farm market — estimated at 2200 in chapter VI — is a reasonably good measure also of the degree to which prices in commercial shops in 1944 exceeded official prices in 1937. This is fairly arbitrary, but there is scattered evidence for Moscow's tending to support the assumption. In any case, sales in commercial shops in 1944 amounted to only 6 billion rubles; this is only 5% of total retail sales in state and cooperative shops and about 7% of urban retail sales in state and cooperative shops. Thus, a very large error in my index number of commercial shop prices would have little effect on the cost-of-living index number.

In principle, commercial shop trade was supposed to exert a downward influence on market prices, and commercial shop prices were supposed to be below market prices. In Moscow, according to observers' reports, the opening of the commercial shops in April 1944 did lead to a reduction in collective farm market prices. This was followed by some reduction in commercial shop prices and a further reduction, perhaps partly seasonal, in market prices. This may well have been true of other parts of the country also, though I have no evidence on this. Scattered quotations for Moscow for the period April through the summer of 1944 indicate that food prices in commercial shops and on the collective farm market were roughly the same. Price quotations and comments on the market in Moscow in 1944 are mainly from the following sources: Harry Schwartz, "Prices in the Soviet War Economy," *American Economic Review,* 36:872–882 (December 1946); Irving B. Kravis and Joseph Mintzes, "The Soviet Union: Trends in Prices, Rations, and Wages," *MLR,* 65:28–35 (July 1947); Harrison Salisbury, *Russia on the Way* (New York, 1946), pp. 75–79; Richard E. Lauterbach, *These Are the Russians* (New York, 1945), p. 37; Edgar Snow, *People on Our Side* (New York, 1944), p. 167; *Washington Post,* August 20, 1944; *UM.*

My index number of commercial shop prices implies that prices in commercial shops averaged over 15 times the ration prices. Within a fairly wide margin for error, this seems plausible. Available quotations of commercial shop prices of foods in Moscow suggest that these may have been as high as 25 times the ration prices during the first few months of operation of the commercial shops, that is, from April through July. There is evidence that commercial shop prices declined from the very high level initially established. Also, the volume of sales in commercial shops increased toward the end of the year. Thus the average gap between commercial and ration prices for the entire period April through December must have been considerably smaller than during the spring and early summer. And for the country as a whole, the gap was probably smaller than for Moscow.

3. SERVICE PRICES

The index number of service prices in 1944 is 170 (1937 = 100). This is computed with 1937 weights in the same manner as the service price index numbers for other years. *Entertainment* could not be priced and is not represented in the 1944 service price index number. No items falling in the category *personal care* could be priced for 1944, and it is assumed that these, as well as the category "other services," are represented by the average hourly wage. Data on the changes between 1937 and 1944 in price, volume, and value of six important services are shown in Table B-8.

Notes on the 1944 service price quotations are presented below. These should be compared with corresponding quotations for 1937 in Table A-1 and the notes on the 1937 quotations in appendix A. The following items are numbered to correspond with the numbering in Table A-1 and appendix A.

243. *Rent.* 1.20 rubles per square meter per month. This is computed according to the official Soviet rental formula (see appendix A) and the estimated 1944 average wage excluding earnings for overtime work. Rental rates are based on earnings exclusive of overtime pay, according to V. P. Maslakov, *et al., Finansirovanie zhilishchno-kommunal'nogo khoziaistva* (Moscow, 1948), p. 119. As overtime work was so extensive in 1944, it seems in order to adjust the average wage figure to exclude overtime earnings, but this can be done only roughly. Average earnings of all wage earners and salaried employees in 1944 were 5,270 rubles a year or 439 rubles a month (Table 13); it is assumed that 90% of this, or about 395 rubles a month, represents earnings exclusive of pay for overtime work.

Overtime pay probably amounted to something like 20% of the total earnings of wage earners in industry, where overtime was extensive, but more likely to around 10% on the average for all wage earners and salaried employees. For industrial wage earners my estimate is based on the following rather crude calculations: (1) In industry, 265.4 days were actually worked during the year 1934 and 266.3 days were actually worked during 1935. In 1934, the days not worked were accounted for as follows: vacations, 14.3 days; free days and holidays, 65.8 days; illness, et cetera, 17.7 days; full day stoppages, 1.8 days (TSUNKHU, *Trud v SSSR* (Moscow, 1935), p. 142; 1936, p. 78). In 1944, I assume, the number of days worked was 24 more than in 1935 or a total of 290 days. This allows 14 days for the wartime cancellation of regular vacations (Decree of June 26, 1941, *Vedomosti Verkhovnogo soveta SSSR,* no. 30, 1941; V. Gsovski, *Soviet Civil Law* (Ann Arbor, 1948), vol. I, p. 827; S. Schwarz, *Labor in the Soviet Union* (New York, 1951), pp. 299–300) and 10 days for the canceling of some holidays, reduction in absenteeism and stoppages, et cetera (see Voznesenskii, p. 114). With the normal work day of 8 hours in effect in 1944, 290 days worked amounts to a total of 2,320 hours a year, or an average of 44.6 hours a week of normal work excluding overtime. (2) The total hours, including overtime, worked by industrial workers in 1944 is estimated at 52 hours a week by Abram Bergson, *The Real National Income of Soviet Russia Since 1928* (Cambridge, Mass., 1961). Thus, overtime work averaged 7.4 hours a week for industrial workers. (3) Overtime work was generally paid at the rate of 150% of the straight-time rate (Decree of June 26, 1941, *Vedomosti Verkhovnogo soveta SSSR,* no. 30, 1941; Gsovski, *Soviet Civil Law,* I:827; Schwarz, p. 300). On this basis, for the 52 hours actually worked the industrial worker was paid for 44.6 hours at the straight-time rate and for 7.4 hours at 1.5 times the straight-time rate, or for a total at the straight-time rate of 55.7 hours. Of this, payment for 44.6 hours, or 80% of the total, represents pay for work during normal hours, and 20% represents overtime pay.

Comparability: See the discussion in appendix A.

244. *Electricity.* 0.25 ruble per kw-hr. This is a Moscow rate, probably in effect also in Leningrad and possibly in some other cities. It was established in April 1940 (see appendix A, item 244, 1940) and remained in effect until August 16, 1948. Evidence that this rate was in effect in Moscow in 1944 is contained in an example in D. P. Proferansov (ed.), *Zhilishchnoe khoziaistvo* (Moscow, 1945), p. 93.

Comparability: The item priced — one kilowatt-hour of electric power — is the same as for 1937 and other years.

245. *Water.* 0.40 ruble per cubic meter. This rate was established for Moscow in late 1939 or January 1940 and remained in effect at least through 1951, according to V. P. Maslakov, *Kommunal'nye tarify v SSSR* (Moscow, 1951), pp. 81, 98.

Comparability: The item priced — one cubic meter of water — is the same as for 1937 and other years.

246. *Tram ride.* 0.17 ruble per ride. This is an estimated rate intended to reflect the change in average USSR rates between 1940 and 1944. As indicated in appendix A, the 1940 rate in Moscow and Leningrad was, it is believed, 0.15 ruble per ride, the same as the estimated 1937 rate in these cities. The Moscow (and probably also Leningrad) rate remained the same until August 1948. However, according to Maslakov (1951), p. 82, the average tram rate in the RSFSR in 1943 was 113.0% of 1940 and in 1945 was 112.8% of 1940. The table containing these figures is described as indicating average realized wholesale tariffs, but presumably in the case of tram transport the retail fare is the one presented. It is assumed that in 1944 the average tram fare was 113% of that in 1940. The 1940 Moscow rate (0.15 ruble per ride) is multiplied by 1.13 to obtain the 1944 fare.

Comparability: The 1937 rate is a Moscow rate while the 1944 rate is intended to represent the average USSR rate. As indicated, it is computed from the 1940 Moscow rate and the average USSR increase in rates between 1940 and 1944. There was no change in the Moscow rate between 1937 and 1944. The 1944 rate is a flat fare per ride while the 1937 rate is that for three half-stations. It is assumed this is the average length of ride, but to the extent that I am in error here the comparison is inexact.

247. *Railroad fare, Moscow-Leningrad.* 76.15 rubles for one-way ticket, *Moscow to Leningrad, ordinary passenger train, hard car, reserved berth.* The quotation is from Ministerstvo putei soobshcheniia SSSR, *Ofitsial'nyi ukazatel' passazhirskikh soobshchenii leto 1948 goda* (Moscow, 1948), p. 86. This source is a 1948 rate book, but it is indicated (p. 531) that the rates were established on April 15, 1942. Hence they were in effect during 1944.

Comparability: The quotation is comparable to that for 1937 and other years, aside from possible minor changes in quality of service in the same class and type of accommodations.

250. *Trousers made to order.* 40.00 rubles. Designation, price, source and comparability as for 1940. See appendix A, item 250, 1940.

254. *Average hourly wage.* 120% of 1937. This is the index number of average hourly wages of nonagricultural wage earners and salaried employees from Table 14.

APPENDIX E

INDEX NUMBERS OF RETAIL PRICES IN ALL SOVIET MARKETS

The retail price index numbers presented in the body of this work refer to prices paid by urban workers in the USSR. For purposes of deflating total retail sales to households, I have also computed retail price index numbers applicable to all retail sales in all areas of the Soviet Union. These are shown in Table E-1.

TABLE E-1

Index Numbers of Official Retail Prices, Collective Farm Market Prices, and Average Retail Prices, All USSR, 1928–54
(1937 = 100)

Year	Official prices		Collective farm market prices	Average prices, all retail markets	
	1937 weights	Given-year weights		1937 weights	Given-year weights
	(1)	(2)	(3)	(4)	(5)
1928	—	—	—	16.8	11.5
1937	100	100	100	100	100
1940	132	126	200	138	132
1944a	(161)	—	(2200)	(200)	—
1948	333	300	350	335	305
1952	216	198	208	215	199
1954	180	170	214	183	173

a The 1944 index numbers are shown in parentheses as they are less reliable than those for other years.
Note: The dash (—) indicates that data were not computed.

For each year except 1928 and 1944 I compute two index numbers of official prices prevailing in all retail sales in state and cooperative shops, one based on 1937 weights and the other based on given-year weights. For 1944 I compute only a 1937-weighted index number of official prices prevailing in all retail sales in state and cooperative shops. These are shown in columns (1) and (2) of Table E-1. In column (3) I show the index number of prices on the collective farm market from Table 9. These are applicable to all collective farm market sales to households. Finally, in columns (4) and (5) of Table E-1 I show two alternative index numbers of average USSR prices in all retail markets. These are computed for 1928 as well as for the other years. My computations for 1937, 1940, 1948, 1952, and 1954 are described immediately below. The computations for 1928 and 1944 are somewhat more complicated and will be treated in separate sections.

I. 1937, 1940, 1948, 1952, 1954

Average USSR official prices. For these years, the index numbers of average USSR official prices, applicable to total sales in state and cooperative shops, are computed from the index numbers of Moscow official prices of all foods and of all manufactured consumer goods in Table 5. These two major category price index numbers are weighted according to the relative shares of foods and of manufactured consumer goods in total retail sales in state and cooperative shops. The ratios of the weights, food to manufactured goods, are as follows: 1937, 63.1:36.9; 1940, 63.1:36.9; 1948, 64.4:35.6; 1952, 58.5:41.5; 1954, 56.0:44.0. (See Table B-3, column (1).) Thus the index number of average USSR official prices differs in each case from the corresponding urban worker (Moscow) official retail price index number only with respect to the major category weights. It will be recalled that for the years from 1937 on (a) the group and representative commodity weights used in computing the cost-of-living index numbers are actually based on the structure of total retail sales in state and cooperative shops and (b) the changes in official Moscow prices can be taken as representative of the changes in average USSR official prices. Thus, the simple computation should give a quite accurate measure of the change in average retail prices in all sales in state and cooperative shops for these years.

The index numbers for 1952 and 1954 shown in Table E-1 have been put on a calendar-year basis.

Average prices in all Soviet retail markets. The index numbers of average prices in all Soviet retail markets for 1940, 1948, 1952, and 1954 are computed from the index numbers of average official prices and the index number of collective farm market prices. The price index number for each type of market is weighted according to the relative share of that market in the volume of sales in the year in question. The value at current prices of total retail sales to households in state and cooperative shops and on the collective farm market in each year covered in this study is shown in Table E-2. To obtain the volume weights it is necessary

TABLE E-2

Retail Sales to Households, USSR, 1928–54
(billion rubles, at current prices)

Year	In state and cooperative shops	On the collective farm market	Totals
1928	—	—	12.1
1937	110	16	126
1940	160	26	186
1944	111	30	141
1948	283	34	317
1952	350	51	401
1954	426	49	475

Note: The dash (—) indicates that data were not computed.
Sources: Abram Bergson, Hans Heymann, Jr., and Oleg Hoeffding, *Soviet National Income and Product, 1928–1948: Revised Data*, The RAND Corporation, RM-2544, November 15, 1960; Oleg Hoeffding and Nancy Nimitz, *Soviet National Income and Product, 1949–1955*, The RAND Corporation, RM-2101, April 6, 1959.

to revalue sales on the collective farm market in terms of the official retail prices of the year in question. For this, I use the ratio of collective farm market prices to official prices of foods from Table 11. Expressed in terms of the official prices, the share of the collective farm market in total retail sales to households (that is, the weight for the index number of collective farm market prices) is as follows: 9.1% in 1940; 9.6% in 1948; 11.6% in 1952; and 7.8% in 1954. In 1937, as has been said, collective farm market prices were, it is believed, at about the same level as prices in official outlets and no adjustment for 1937 collective farm market prices is necessary.

2. 1928

Because of the different institutional arrangements for marketing in 1928 as well as the different nature of the available information, my computations for 1928 do not quite parallel those for other years. I do not, for instance, compute an index number of average USSR official prices. The series of price index numbers computed for 1928, culminating in index numbers of average retail prices in all markets, are shown in Table E-3.

(1) The index numbers of official Moscow prices of (a) foods and (b) manufactured consumer goods shown in Table E-3 are from Table 5. In computing

TABLE E-3

Retail Price Index Numbers, USSR, 1928
(1937 = 100)

	1937 Weights	1928 Weights
1. Official prices, Moscow		
a. Food	13.3	11.2
b. Manufactured goods	23.7	14.3
c. All commodities	17.1	12.4
2. Official prices, urban USSR, all commodities	16.1	11.5
3. Average prices, all markets, urban USSR, all commodities	18.7	13.1
4. Average prices, all markets, rural USSR, all commodities	14.0	9.8
5. Average prices, all markets, all USSR, all commodities	16.8	11.5

(c), the index numbers of official Moscow prices of all commodities, the 1937 weights for foods and manufactured goods are based on the 1937 breakdown between these two major categories of total retail sales in state and cooperative shops, as is the case of the 1937 weights used in the computations for other years. The 1928 weights for foods and manufactured consumer goods are intended to represent the breakdown between these two major categories of total retail sales to households, including sales in private shops and cash sales to households in intravillage trade. The 1928 weight for food is 57% and for manufactured goods 43% in this computation. The derivation of these 1928 weights is explained later.

The group and representative commodity weights underlying these computations are the same as those employed in computing the cost-of-living index numbers. The 1937 group and representative commodity weights are, as has been said, based on the structure of total retail sales in state and cooperative shops. The 1928 group and representative commodity weights are based on urban worker expenditures in all markets. This is clearly not an entirely appropriate basis for weights for a price index number relating to all (rural and urban) retail sales. Unfortunately, there are no adequate data relating to the structure of total retail sales to households. (The breakdown by commodity group of total retail sales in state and cooperative shops in 1928 in *Sovtorgstat-56*, pp. 44–47, is of little help as a guide to the structure of total retail sales to households for consumption because of (a) the inclusion of sales to institutions and sales of producer goods to households and (b) the exclusion of sales to households in private shops, on the urban free market and on the village markets.) This is a limitation — but perhaps not too serious a one — on the validity of the 1928-weighted index number of average USSR prices in all retail markets. As has been said, in an earlier set of computations I attempted to adapt the urban worker budget weights to represent more closely the structure of total retail sales to households, but the price index number for 1928–37 computed on the basis of these weights differed by less than 2% from that computed on the basis of the original urban worker budget weights.

(2) The index numbers of official retail prices in the entire urban USSR take into account the estimated difference between the rise in Moscow official prices and the rise in average urban official prices between 1928 and 1937. See chapter VI, section 1.

(3) The index numbers of average retail prices in all markets in the urban USSR take into account prices prevailing in private shops in 1928. The adjustment is based on the estimated gap between official prices and average prices in all urban markets in 1928, as set forth in chapter VI, section 2. No adjustment is required for 1937 as there was little or no gap between official and collective farm market prices in that year.

(4) The purchasing power of the ruble in the villages was 135% of that in the towns in 1928, according to Gosplan, *Piatiletnii plan narodno-khoziaistvennogo stroitel'stva SSSR*, vol. II, part 2, p. 12. This implies that the rural price level was about 75% of the urban price level. In the absence of other data on rural prices in 1928, I take this statement at face value (though not without reservations). Each index number of average prices in all rural markets is computed as 75% of the corresponding index number of average prices in all urban markets. In 1937, rural prices of many manufactured consumer goods were somewhat higher than urban prices, but for all commodities together, the rural price level must have exceeded the urban by only a few percent (see Janet Chapman, *The Regional Structure of Soviet Retail Prices*, The RAND Corporation, RM-425, July 20, 1950, pp. 26–28); not enough to take into account, particularly in light of the magnitude and crudity of the allowance for 1928 rural prices.

(5) The 1928 index numbers of average retail prices in all markets in the entire USSR are computed from the index numbers of average prices in all urban retail markets and the index numbers of average prices in all rural retail markets. In the computation, I give the urban retail price index number a weight of 60% and the rural retail price index number a weight of 40%. These weights are based on the estimated distribution of total retail sales to households between urban and rural households in 1928. This estimate is explained below.

Urban-rural distribution of retail sales in 1928. As shown in Table E-4, I estimate that urban households accounted for 60% and rural households for 40% of total

TABLE E-4

Urban-Rural Distribution of Retail Sales to Households for Consumption, USSR, 1928
(million rubles)

	Urban	Rural	Totals
1. Sales of industrial goods and extravillage sales of agricultural products	6,783	3,656	10,439
2. Intravillage sales of agricultural products	0	1,000	1,000
3. Restaurant sales	564	94	658
4. Totals	7,347	4,750	12,097
5. Percentage breakdown of total	60.7	39.3	100.0

retail sales to households for consumption in 1928. The figures for total retail sales to households in Table E-4 are from Oleg Hoeffding, *Soviet National Income and Product in 1928* (New York, 1954), pp. 115–116, as subsequently revised to exclude sales of building materials in A. Bergson, H. Heymann, Jr., and O. Hoeffding, *Soviet National Income and Product, 1928–1948: Revised Data*, The RAND Corporation, RM-2544, November 15, 1960. The distribution of total sales as between urban and rural households is based largely on data on the incomes and outlays of the urban and farm populations in Gosplan, *Kontrol'nye tsifry narodnogo khoziaistva SSSR na 1929/30 g.* (Moscow, 1930), pp. 478-481. Rural households in this connection comprise essentially farm households; rural households with urban type budgets are classified in the source with urban households.

(1) Sales of industrial goods to households for consumption totaled 6,647 million rubles in 1928, it can be computed from the figures for 1927/28 and 1928/29 in Gosplan, *Kontrol'nye tsifry 1929/30 g.*, pp. 565–566. Of this I assume 45%, or 2,991 million rubles, were purchased by urban households and 55%, or 3,656 million rubles, were purchased by rural households. According to the tables on the incomes and expenditures of the population in Gosplan, *Kontrol'nye tsifry 1928/29 g.*, p. 445, and *Kontrol'nye tsifry 1929/30 g.*, pp. 478–481, urban purchases of industrial goods amounted to about 40% and rural purchases to about 60% of the combined urban and rural expenditures on industrial products. These figures presumably include purchases of producer goods by households, which amounted to about 26% of total sales of industrial products to households in 1927/28 and 1928/29 (Gosplan, *Kontrol'nye tsifry 1929/30 g.*, pp. 565–566). As most of the purchases of producer goods must have been made by rural households, their share of total purchases of industrial products for consumption must have been less than 60%; I assume it was 55%.

The remainder of the total under item (1) in Table E-4 represents extravillage sales of agricultural products to households, amounting to 3,792 million rubles. From the data in Gosplan, *Kontrol'nye tsifry 1929/30 g.*, pp. 478–481, 566, it is apparent that all extravillage sales of agricultural products to households were considered as urban. This is assumed to be the case in deriving my urban-rural distribution of retail sales to households. However, as will be noted, it is believed that rural households must have purchased some agricultural products in extravillage trade (for example, from the consumer cooperatives) and, at some sacrifice of consistency, I allow for this in the breakdown of retail sales as between foods and manufactured consumer goods below.

(2) All intravillage sales of agricultural products to households are, by definition, to rural households.

(3) One-seventh of sales in state and cooperative restaurants were rural in 1928, according to TSUNKHU, *Sotsialisticheskoe stroitel'stvo v SSSR* (Moscow, 1936), p. 608. I assume this ratio is applicable to total restaurant sales.

Major category weights for all retail sales in 1928. Of total retail sales to households in 1928, it is estimated that 57% represented sales of foods and 43% sales of manufactured consumer goods. I assume that retail sales of foods to urban households were 4.4 billion rubles or 60% of the total, the same percentage as shown in the 1927/28 urban wage earner budget study. For sales to rural households, rough computations explained below suggest that 53%, or 2.5 billion rubles, were sales of foods. Adding urban and rural figures, foods accounted for 6.9 billion rubles, or 57% of retail sales to households, which totaled 12.1 billion rubles.

The breakdown of rural sales is based largely on the data in Table E-5 on the money expenditures of farm households. The figures on total expenditures shown are weighted average annual money expenditures per farm household in the Russian, Belorussian, and Ukrainian Republics in 1928, from L. Litoshenko, "Sezonnost' oborota krest'ianskikh khoziaistv," *Statisticheskoe obozrenie*, no. 2, 1929, p. 4. These figures multiplied by the total number of farms in the USSR at

TABLE E-5

Average Annual Money Expenditures per Farm Household, USSR, 1928

	Total expenditures (rubles)	Consumption expenditures	
		(rubles)	(percent of total)
Agricultural products			
Grain	12.92	6.46	3.2
Flour and grits	27.38	27.38	13.5
Livestock	37.50	18.75	9.2
Unspecified	40.41	20.20	10.0
Total agricultural products	118.21	72.79	35.9
Industrial products			
Farm implements	19.70	0	0
Other	175.28	130.00	64.1
Total industrial products	194.98	130.00	64.1
Totals	313.19	202.79	100.0

the time — 25 million (there were 22.5 million farms in the republics covered in the Litoshenko figures) — agree fairly well with the figures on total rural expenditures on agricultural and industrial products in the rural income–outlay balances in Gosplan, *Kontrol'nye tsifry 1929/30 g.*, pp. 480–481. Accordingly, it seems reasonable to base the estimates of the pattern of retail sales to rural households on these data. The figures on total farm household expenditudes include purchases of producer goods which are excluded in the estimates of expenditures for consumption, also shown in Table E-5. Following a suggestion of Oleg Hoeffding, expenditures for consumption are computed on the assumption that one-half the total expenditures on grain, livestock, and unspecified agricultural products and one-third of the total expenditures on industrial goods were for productive purposes.

From the figures on outlays for consumption it is still necessary to estimate the distribution between foods and nonfoods. I allocate 30% of the expenditures for consumption on industrial products, which include processed foods and alcoholic beverages, to foods. In 1927/28, food products and alcoholic beverages (included with foods in my computations) accounted for 26% of rural expenditures on industrial goods, according to P. Gladilin, "Priobretenie promyshlennykh tovarov sel'-skim naseleniem SSSR v 1927/28 g.," *Statisticheskoe obozrenie*, no. 6, 1930, p. 64. I assume further that about 5% of rural expenditures on agricultural products were purchases of nonfoods. According to these calculations, of total rural expenditures for consumption, 34% was for agricultural foods and 19% for industrial foods — a total of 53% for foods of all kinds — and 2% was for nonfood agricultural products and 45% for nonfood industrial products — a total of 47% for nonfoods.

My computations for 1928 are crude and may be subject to error. Although there is (relative to later years) a fair amount of material relevant to the problem for this period, it does not seem possible to reconcile at all points the Soviet data on household budgets, on the incomes and outlays of the population, and on retail sales. In this connection, it should be mentioned that the computation underlying the weights for foods and manufactured goods based largely on budget data is not entirely consistent with the computation underlying the urban-rural distribution of retail sales to households shown in Table E-4, which is based on data on incomes and outlays of the population and on retail sales. In particular, the food–manufactured goods breakdown assumes larger purchases of agricultural products and smaller purchases of industrial consumer goods by rural households than the figures in Table E-4. It is not clear where the errors lie, but probably they are not significant enough to affect the results.

3. 1944

Official prices. The index number of official retail prices in all sales in state and cooperative shops in 1944 shown in column (1) of Table E-1 is a weighted average of three index numbers of official retail prices: (1) the index number of ration prices — 143 (see appendix D); (2) the index number of prices prevailing in commercial shops — 2200 (see appendix D); (3) an index number of retail prices in effect for sales of certain manufactured consumer goods in rural areas — 330.

The distribution of retail sales in the various types of state and cooperative shops in 1944 is shown below, valued first at the actual prices prevailing in the various types of outlets and then as revalued at ration prices, in billion rubles:

	At actual prices	At ration prices
Sales at ration prices		
Urban	77.7	77.7
Rural	15.0	15.0
Total	92.7	92.7
Sales in commercial shops	6.0	0.4
Rural sales subject to higher prices	12.3	5.3
Total	111.0	98.4

Sales to urban households, I estimate, totaled 83.7 billion rubles, about 75% of retail sales to households in all state and cooperative outlets, valued at actual prices. (Urban retail sales were 74% of total retail sales in state and cooperative shops in 1945, according to *Sovtorgstat-56*, p. 21.) Of the urban total, 6 billion rubles represent sales in commercial shops (*Sovetskaia torgovlia za tridtsat' let* (Moscow, 1947), p. 129). The share of total rural sales that was subject to the special rural prices, I set at 45% of total retail sales to rural households. This is a crude guess which cannot be checked as there seems to be no information on the proportion of rural sales which were made at the special higher prices.

Special rural prices. Before describing how the index number of special rural prices of manufactured consumer goods is computed, it may be helpful to explain the need for a special index number of rural prices. Most Soviet sources discussing the system of official prices prevailing during the war refer only to ration prices and prices in commercial shops, and rural wartime prices are seldom mentioned. That a special set of rural prices was established for at least some manufactured consumer goods, however, is made clear in the following three references. L. Maizenberg, in *Tsenoobrazovanie v narodnom khoziaistve SSSR* (Moscow, 1953), p. 232, says that at the end of the war the following types of (official) prices existed for one and the same commodity: (1) ration prices; (2) "somewhat higher" prices of manufactured goods sold without ration coupons in rural areas in exchange for sales of agricultural products by the rural population; and (3) "high" commercial shop prices. According to M. M. Lifits, *Sovetskaia torgovlia* (Moscow, 1948), p. 114, the official prices established in December 1947 for manufactured consumer goods sold in rural areas were the same as those existing prior to the December 1947 price reform, which had been established in April 1942. Specific mention of an increase in the rural price of kerosene in April 1942 to a level "considerably higher" than the urban ration price is to be found in A. K. Suchkov,

Gosudarstvennye dokhody SSSR (Moscow, 1949), p. 109. No mention has been found of special rural prices of foods, and presumably the ration prices prevailing in urban shops applied also to rural sales of foods. Tobacco products and reading matter, it is believed, were sold at the same prices in urban and rural areas. It is not very clear, however, just which groups of manufactured consumer goods were subject to the higher rural prices.

In computing the index number of rural prices of manufactured consumer goods, I assume that Lifits' statement that the rural prices established in April 1942 were the same as those announced in December 1947 can be taken at face value, and that they prevailed also during 1944. On this assumption, I base the index number of 1944 rural prices mainly on the group price index numbers for the relevant commodity groups for the period 1937–48. For the most part, the 1948 prices are those established in December 1947. For textiles, garments, knitwear, and shoes I use the 1937–48 group price index numbers computed with 1937 weights (see Table 5). However, inasmuch as these 1937–48 group price index numbers are based on Moscow prices, I make an adjustment for the difference between Moscow and rural prices. For these types of commodities, rural prices in 1937 were roughly 5% higher than Moscow prices while in 1948 rural prices were about 10% higher than urban (or Moscow) prices. Average rural prices of these goods then rose by about 5% more than Moscow prices; accordingly, I increase the 1937–48 price index numbers for these groups by 5% to represent the increase in rural prices between 1937 and 1944. For the two groups "haberdashery and notions" and "soap, drugs, etc." I use the 1937-weighted 1937–48 price index numbers without adjustment as there was no urban-rural price differential for these products in 1948 and only a slight urban-rural differential in the price of one of the products (household soap) in 1937. For matches, the 1937 price — which was uniform for the entire country — is compared with the 1944 price observed in urban ration shops; this latter is the same as the price announced in December 1947 for the entire country and is probably the same as the 1944 rural price. For kerosene, the 1937 price of 0.66 ruble per liter prevailing in rural areas in the main price zone (*RTS-36*, p. 228) is compared with the December 1947 rural price of 2.50 rubles per liter (*PD*-14-12-47).

These group price index numbers are weighted according to the 1937 weights for these groups based on the structure of total sales in state and cooperative shops. These may not be very appropriate for rural sales alone, but the entire computation is so rough that working out rural weights for this purpose can hardly be justified.

Average prices, all retail markets. The 1944 index number of average prices in all retail markets is computed from the index number of average official prices and the index number of prices on the collective farm market. Collective farm market sales in 1944 totaled 30 billion rubles at market prices. When sales in all types of retail outlets in 1944 are revalued at ration prices, the 1944 weight for the collective farm market is 1.9% of total retail sales to households.

APPENDIX F

SOVIET SOCIAL INSURANCE

In section 1 the main types of Soviet social insurance benefits are described. Section 2 comprises the notes to Table 17.

I. MAIN TYPES OF SOVIET SOCIAL INSURANCE BENEFITS

Temporary disability insurance. For illness or other temporary disability, the 1922 Labor Code provided in principle that the worker was to be compensated for the full amount of wages lost during his illness or disability. This principle has in the main been applied throughout the period studied with the important exception that, since 1931, the worker must have been employed in the same enterprise for a certain number of years to be eligible for compensation equal to his full pay. For less than the required number of years of employment in the same enterprise, insurance benefits are less than the worker's full pay. From 1931 until, it is believed, 1938, the worker had to have worked a total of three years of which at least two years were in his last place of employment to be eligible for insurance compensation equal to his full pay. From 1938 until August 9, 1948 the requirement was six years in the same enterprise, and from August 1948 until 1955 the requirement was eight years in the same enterprise[1] (S. Schwarz, *Labor in the Soviet Union* (New York, 1951), pp. 310–317; N. N. Rovinskii, *Gosudarstvennyi biudzhet SSSR* (Moscow, 1951), p. 299). Some exceptions are apparently made; workers in the metallurgical, chemical, and certain other important industries were entitled to sick benefits equal to 100% of their wages if they had worked one year or more in the same enterprise, according to *Social Insurance in the USSR* (Moscow, 1953), p. 8. In the case of young workers, the length of employment requirement is reduced or not applied. And there are provisions for taking into account certain types of justifiable transfers of jobs as well as military service in reckoning the length of continuous employment. (See Lief Björk, *Wages, Prices and Social Legislation in the Soviet Union* (London, 1953), pp. 119–122.) Nonunion members, it should be noted, receive only half the benefits to which union members are entitled.

There have at times been limits to the maximum sick benefits that could be paid but these were so high in relation to the average wage of the time that they could have had little effect. The maximum sick benefits payable in 1928 were 120 to 180 rubles per month, depending on the wage zone (Schwarz, p. 310) when the average monthly wage of all wage earners and salaried employees was under 59 rubles a month. The August 1948 legislation provided for a maximum sick benefit of 160 rubles a day, about 4,000 rubles a month (Rovinskii, p. 299) as compared with the 1948 average wage of not quite 585 rubles a month.

Maternity insurance. Social insurance grants during maternity leave, a form of temporary disability insurance, are subject to special regulations. The length of maternity leave during which social insurance compensation is paid is the aspect which has changed most. In 1928 maternity leave totaled sixteen weeks (eight

---

[1] Since 1955 the maximum sick benefit rate has been 90% of the wage and to obtain this the worker has to have been employed twelve or more years on the same job. Gliksman, "Recent Trends in Soviet Labor Policy," *MLR,* July 1956, p. 774.

weeks preceding and eight weeks following childbirth) for manual workers and twelve weeks for nonmanual workers. In 1937, the period was sixteen weeks for all categories of workers. The length of maternity leave was cut to a total of nine weeks at the end of 1938 and then in July 1944 increased to a total of eleven weeks, with an extra two weeks in case of abnormal delivery or multiple births (Schwarz, pp. 317–320).[2]

To be eligible for maternity benefits the insured had to have been employed at least six months during the year preceding maternity leave in 1928; this period was increased to seven months in 1938. As in the case of temporary disability insurance, the general principle is that compensation should be equal to the full wages of the insured. Since 1931, compensation equal to 100% of wages has been dependent upon a certain length of employment in the same enterprise (two to three years), but these requirements are less stringent than in the case of general temporary disability benefits (Schwarz, p. 319).

In addition to the maternity insurance proper, the social insurance system provides certain additional benefits at the birth of a child to families in which either the mother or father comes under the social insurance system, if their incomes do not exceed a certain amount — a lump sum payment for a layette and nine monthly payments to nursing mothers. These benefits, although not by nature a form of insurance, may be included in the figures on social insurance grants.

Disability insurance. Workers who have partially or wholly lost their ability to work for a prolonged period are in most cases entitled to a disablement pension. The provisions regarding pensions for workers whose disability resulted from their work — industrial accidents and occupational disease — are understandably considerably more generous than those regarding pensions for disability arising from other causes. In cases of work-connected disability, there is no requirement as to length of employment before becoming eligible for compensation. During most of the period studied, disabled workers have been classified according to the following three groups: group I, persons who have completely lost their ability to work and need special daily care; group II, persons who have completely lost their ability to work but do not need special care; group III, persons unable to work regularly at their former occupation but capable of performing irregular work or work in another less skilled or less arduous occupation. The degree of disablement is determined in each case by a special medical commission.

The nominal rates of pensions for job-connected disability have been, apparently throughout the period studied, 100% of the former wage for those in disability group I, 75% of the former wage for those in disability group II, and 50% of the former wage for those in disability group III. The term "nominal" rate is used, however, because the maximum wage on which pensions are calculated is 300 rubles a month. This limit was established in 1932 and remained the general limit until 1956 (*Pravda*, July 12, 1956). Thus, aside from some exceptions which increased the maximum pension for certain favored groups, the maximum pension actually was 150 to 300 rubles (depending upon degree of disability) regardless of the earnings of the insured. This maximum was increased to 210 to 360 rubles a month in September 1946 when the pensions of all nonworking pensioners living in urban areas were increased by 60 rubles a month as a cost-of-living adjustment (*Pravda*, September 16, 1946).

The effect of this limitation can be readily seen if we calculate the pension to which a person would have been entitled whose earnings during the year he became

[2] In 1956 maternity leave was extended to the 1928 level, sixteen weeks (*Pravda*, March 27, 1956).

disabled were equal to the average wage of all wage earners and salaried employees and whose disablement put him in disability group I. Such a person would have received a pension equal to 100% of his former wage if he became disabled in 1928 or 1937, 89% of his former wage if he became disabled in 1940, 68% of his former wage in 1944, 62% in 1948, 54% in 1952, and 52% in 1954.[3]

In the case of disablement through accident or disease not connected with the insured's employment — general disability — pensions are also payable but the pensions are generally smaller and there are length of employment requirements which must be met to be eligible for a pension. In 1928, to be eligible for a general disability pension, a worker had to have been employed one to eight years, depending on his age at the onset of disability. According to the regulations in effect from 1932 to the end of 1938, to be eligible for a general disability pension, underground workers and workers in other hazardous occupations had to have worked one to six years, other manual workers had to have worked two to eight years, and nonmanual workers two to twelve years, depending on the age at onset of the disability. Since 1938, underground workers and workers in other hazardous occupations must have been employed at the same enterprise for one to fourteen years, all other men workers for three to twenty years, and all other women workers from two to fifteen years (Schwarz, pp. 325–327; Rovinskii, p. 300).

The rate of the general disability pension in 1928 was a straight 67% of former earnings for group I disability, about 45% of former earnings for group II disability, and 33% of former earnings for group III disability. The maximum income for calculating benefits was set in July 1928 at 180 to 225 rubles a month, depending on the wage zone — an amount well over twice the average wage at the time (Schwarz, pp. 322–323). Legislation of 1932 maintained about these same rates as basic nominal rates but provided for increases in the percentage rate which varied according to the category of worker and length of his employment beyond the minimum required to be eligible for a pension. Three categories of workers were distinguished: category 1, underground workers and workers in other hazardous occupations; category 2, workers in a number of specified important industries; category 3, all other workers. (The 1932 law actually stipulated four categories; category 4 comprised all nonmanual workers not engaged in direct production, and nonmanual workers engaged in direct production were classified in category 3. The discrimination against nonmanual workers was ended in July 1937. See S. Schwarz, pp. 325–326.) For group I disability, a worker who met the eligibility requirements and was in category 1 would receive a pension equal to 69% of his former earnings but could receive as much as 100% of his former earnings if he had worked 18 years or more; a worker in category 3 would receive 67% of his former earnings but could receive as much as 80% of his former pay if he had worked at least 31 years (Schwarz, pp. 325–326; A. S. Krasnopol'skii, *Osnovnye printsipy sovetskogo gosudarstvennogo sotsial'nogo strakhovaniia* (Moscow, 1951), p. 105). The requirements as to length of employment for the maximum pension rates refer to total employment, but it is also required that at least two years be at the last place of employment.

As in the case of job-connected disability, the maximum wage on which the pension could be computed was 300 rubles a month from 1932 until 1956, again probably with some exceptions. General disability pensions also were increased

---

[3] The pension rates established in 1956 provide for a job-connected disability pension which would amount to something like 77 to 84% of former earnings for a worker becoming disabled in 1957 whose earnings in 1957 equaled the average wage. This is computed from the Law on State Pensions of July 14, 1956 (*Pravda,* July 15, 1956) and an assumed average 1957 monthly wage of 750 rubles.

by 60 rubles a month in September 1946. A person earning the average wage who became disabled in 1928 through a general cause and was in disability group I would have received a pension amounting to 67% of his former pay. Although the nominal rate for group I general disability pensions has been 67 to 100% of former earnings since 1932, a person earning the average wage and becoming disabled in 1937 would have received this rate but the actual rate has been lower since then; the rates can be computed at approximately 59 to 89% in 1940, 46 to 68% in 1944, 45 to 62% in 1948, 39 to 54% in 1952, and 37 to 52% in 1954.[4]

Survivors' insurance. Throughout the period studied the family of a deceased insured worker has been entitled to benefits to cover the burial of the insured and to a pension. Pensions are granted only to family members who were dependent on the insured and who are unable to work, that is, children, old people, the disabled, and a family member caring for children under eight years of age. Survivors' insurance is closely linked to disability insurance. Survivors are entitled to a pension if the deceased provider was entitled to a job-connected or general disability pension or would have become eligible for such through the accident or disease which caused his death. The rate of pension is 50 to 125% of the pension to which the deceased would have been entitled under group II disability, depending upon the number of surviving dependents. (See Krasnopol'skii, p. 121; Schwarz, pp. 328–329. Rovinskii, p. 302, puts the percentage at 50 to 100% of the appropriate group II disability pension.)

Old-age insurance. Old-age insurance was established somewhat more slowly than other forms of workers' insurance, and in 1928 provision for old-age insurance had been made only for wage earners in the textile industry. By 1932, most categories of wage earners and salaried employees were covered and in mid-1937 old-age insurance was extended to all wage earners and salaried employees without exception (Schwarz, pp. 329–330). To qualify for an old-age pension men must have reached the age of 60 and show an employment record of 25 years, while women must be 55 and have an employment record of 20 years. This has been the requirement throughout the period studied. For workers in underground and other dangerous occupations, however, the qualifying age and length of employment are less. The nominal rate of the old-age pension from 1932 until 1956 was 60% of the former wage for category 1 workers (those in underground and other hazardous employment), 55% of the former wage for category 2 workers (those in certain important industries), and 50% of the former wage for category 3 workers (all other workers). However, as in the case of disability pensions, the maximum wage on which the pension was calculated was 300 rubles a month. Thus, the effective maximum pension was 150 to 180 rubles a month until September 1946, when it was raised to 210 to 240 rubles a month by the cost-of-living increase allowed to all pensioners. This remained the general norm applicable to the bulk of workers until July 1956, but beginning in 1947 old-age pensions were increased for basic categories of workers in leading branches of the economy to 50% of their wage and for leading officials of a number of ministries to 65% of their former salary, with no limit on the size of the pension (*Pravda,* July 12, 1956). A worker retiring in 1928 would have received no pension, unless he had been employed in the textile industry. A worker earning the average wage and retiring in 1937 would have received an old-age pension amounting to 50 to 60% of his former pay. Because of the maximum the actual percentage rates

---

[4] The general disability pension rates established in 1956 provide for a group I disability pension of something like 60 to 72% of the former wage for a person becoming disabled in 1957 and earning the average wage, assuming a 1957 average wage of 750 rubles a month (*Pravda,* July 15, 1956).

have declined so that a worker earning the average wage and retiring in 1954 would have received an old-age pension equal to only 30 to 34% of his former wage. Persons eligible for an old-age pension are entitled to receive it even if they continue to work. Until 1938 there was a limit on the total of earnings plus pension while from 1938 to 1956 the full old-age pension was paid regardless of other earnings.[5]

From the above account of the provisions of the Soviet social insurance system over the period studied, it will be evident that there has been a general decline in the benefits available to the Soviet worker when measured as a percentage of his wage. Interestingly, it is the benefits to those no longer able to work — the disabled and the aged — and the dependents of deceased workers which have shown the greatest decline. Benefits to those only temporarily absent from the labor force have on the whole been maintained at a rate which about makes up for the full amount of pay lost. Even here, though, the requirements as to length of service to be eligible for compensation equal to full pay have been stiffened over the period, and the length of maternity leave during which a woman is entitled to receive compensation was shortened.

2. NOTES TO TABLE 17

The sources for and methods of estimating the amounts of total social insurance grants and pensions paid, shown in Table 17, are explained here.

1928: The figures are computed from data in Oleg Hoeffding, *Soviet National Income and Product in 1928* (New York, 1954), pp. 111–113. The total of 676 million rubles is made up of the following items: (1) Unemployment compensation of 131 million rubles, of which 107 million rubles was paid by the social insurance system or from the state and local government budgets and 24 million rubles was paid by trade unions from funds contributed by employers. (2) Temporary disability grants paid by the social insurance system of 326 million rubles. (3) Pensions paid from social insurance funds of 219 million rubles.

1937 through 1948: For this period the data on grants and pensions are incomplete and there are difficulties in interpreting the available data. One major difficulty arises from the fact that social insurance grants and social insurance pensions to working pensioners are paid directly by the social insurance system but pensions to retired insured workers are paid by the social assistance program. In 1937, pensions to retired pensioners were financed from general funds of the government budget (R. W. Davies, *The Development of the Soviet Budgetary System* (Cambridge, England, 1958), p. 254). Since 1939, pensions to retired insured pensioners disbursed through the social assistance program have been financed with funds supplied by the social insurance system (Davies, pp. 264–266). The problem is further complicated by the fact that Soviet sources are not always explicit as to whether the figures given for outlays of the social insurance system are gross or net of transfers to the social assistance program. Further, outlays of the social insurance system including transfers to social assistance are generally somewhat smaller than revenues of the social insurance system. Presumably, the surplus is transferred to general funds of the state budget. But for the postwar years some sources cite figures for social insurance expenditures which are apparently gross of such transfers as well as of the transfers to the social assistance program.

[5] The law of July 14, 1956, provides for old-age pensions ranging from 100% of former wages if the former wage was 350 rubles a month or less to 50% of the former wage if this was over 1,000 rubles a month, with a minimum pension of 300 rubles and a maximum of 1,200 rubles a month (*Pravda,* July 15, 1956).

The data underlying my estimates for 1937 through 1948 are shown in Table F-1. The sources and methods are as follows:

P 1937: Davies, p. 254.

1937: Line 1: Abram Bergson and Hans Heymann, Jr., *Soviet National Income and Product, 1940–1948* (New York, 1954), p. 22. Line 2: K. N. Plotnikov, *Biudzhet sotsialisticheskogo gosudarstva* (Moscow, 1948), p. 219. Lines 3b, 3c, 3d: Payments of grants and pensions by the social insurance system are assumed to have

TABLE F-1

Social Insurance Revenues, Expenditures, Grants and Pensions,
and Social Assistance Expenditures, 1937–49
(billion rubles)

	P 1937	1937	P 1940	1940	1944	1948	P 1949
1. Social insurance revenues	5.3	6.6	9.1	8.5	9.0	16.2	17.5
2. Social insurance expenditures	5.0	5.2	7.8	—	—	14.4	16.6
3. Social insurance expenditures other than payments to social assistance							
a. Total	—	—	5.8	5.0	3.7	8.7	11.8
b. On grants	2.9	2.9	2.8	2.4	2.0	—	5.8
c. On pensions	0.2	0.2	0.7	0.6	—	—	—
d. On grants and pensions	3.1	3.1	3.5	3.0	—	—	—
4. Pensions							
a. From outside social insurance budget (i.e., in addition to amount in (3c))	—	1.4	2.0	1.8	—	—	—
b. Total (3c) plus (4a)	—	1.6	2.7	2.4	3.2	—	7.2
5. Total social insurance grants and pensions (sum of (3b) and (4b) *or* sum of (3d) and (4a))	—	4.5	5.5	4.8	5.2	11.8	13.0
6. Social assistance expenditures	—	2.2	—	3.1	15.8	18.4	21.4

Notes: The dash (—) indicates that data were not available. The "P" indicates planned figures.

been as planned. Line 4a: Estimated by interpolation from the pensions paid to retired insured workers of 1.25 billion rubles in 1936 (Davies, p. 254), and 1.8 billion rubles in 1940 (see below). Line 6: Plotnikov, p. 146.

P 1940: Davies, p. 254. The figure of 2.0 billion rubles in line 4a represents planned transfers from the revenues of the social insurance system to the government budget for pensions to retired workers. It is assumed that this is the total amount planned for pensions to retired workers insured under the social insurance system.

1940: Line 1: Bergson and Heymann, p. 22. Lines 3a and 6: Plotnikov, p. 329. Lines 3b, 3c, 3d, and 4a: It is assumed the plan was fulfilled by approximately the same percentage as the plan for total revenues.[6]

1944: Line 1: Bergson and Heymann, p. 22. Lines 3a and 6: Plotnikov, p. 329. Line 3b: It is assumed that temporary disability and maternity grants amounted to about the same percentage of the wage bill in 1944 as in 1940, that is, about

[6] Information which became available after these computations were made indicate the 1940 estimates are low. Grants and pensions totaled 5.2 billion rubles in 1940, of which 2.6 billion rubles were for grants and 2.6 billion rubles were for pensions. Of the latter, 2.0 billion rubles represent payments under the social assistance program from funds of the social insurance system (*TSU, Narodnoe khoziaistvo SSSR v 1958 g.,* pp. 900, 906).

1.8%. With long wartime hours and canceled vacations, sickness may have increased, but probably fewer women had babies. The full civilian wage bill in 1944 was 146 billion rubles, but this figure is reduced by about 10% before computing social insurance grants to allow for payment for overtime as overtime earnings are not taken into account in computing social insurance grants and pensions. Roughly 10% of the wage bill probably represents payment for overtime work in 1944 (see appendix D). Line 4b: I rather arbitrarily assume that pensions to working and nonworking pensioners insured under the social insurance system amounted to about 20% of total expenditures under the social assistance program. According to the planned data for 1949 shown in Table F-1, pensions to working and nonworking insured pensioners were to be about one-third of total planned expenditures on social assistance. In 1944 presumably a smaller share of social assistance expenditures went to workers' pensions and a larger share to military pensions and grants.

1948: Line 1: Bergson and Heymann, p. 22. Line 2: A. G. Zverev, *O gosudarstvennom biudzhete SSSR na 1949 g.* (Moscow, 1949), p. 20. Lines 3a and 6: Zverev, *Planovoe khoziaistvo*, no. 2, 1949, p. 48. Plotnikov, *Finansy i kredit SSSR*, no. 10, 1953, p. 21, gives a figure of 9.8 billion rubles for social insurance expenditures other than payments to social assistance. Line 5: It is assumed that 73% of the total revenues of the social insurance system went to social insurance grants and pensions to working and retired pensioners. This is based on the planned data for 1949 shown in Table F-1, which provides that 74% of total social insurance revenues go to grants and pensions. Similar data for 1950 show planned grants and pensions were to be 78% of total social insurance revenues (Krasnopol'skii, *Osnovnye printsipy sovetskogo gosudarstvennogo sotsial'nogo strakhovaniia*, pp. 57–58, 102; Krasnopol'skii, *Sovetskoe gosudarstvo i pravo*, no. 6, 1951, as translated in *Current Digest of the Soviet Press*, 3:4 (December 29, 1951)).

P 1949: Line 1: Lief Björk, *Wages, Prices and Social Legislation in the Soviet Union* (London, 1953), p. 97. Lines 2 and 6: Zverev, *O gosudarstvennom biudzhete na 1949 g.*, p. 20. Krasnopol'skii, *Osnovnye printsipy sovetskogo gosudarstvennogo sotsial'nogo strakhovaniia*, p. 56, gives a figure of 17.5 billion rubles as the total social insurance budget, or total expenditures planned for 1949; but apparently this is the broadest concept and is the same as total revenues. Line 3a: Zverev, *Planovoe khoziaistvo*, no. 2, 1949, p. 48. Lines 3b and 4b: Krasnopol'skii, *Osnovnye printsipy sovetskogo gosudarstvennogo sotsial'nogo strakhovaniia*, p. 102.

1952 and 1954: The figures for these years in Table 17 are from Oleg Hoeffding and Nancy Nimitz, *Soviet National Income and Product, 1949–1955*, The RAND Corporation, RM-2101, April 6, 1959, p. 166. They were estimated by interpolation on the basis of the planned percentage of total social insurance expenditures going to grants and pensions in 1950 (78%) and in 1956 (88%). These estimates seem reasonable in light of the figures for 1950, 1953, and 1955 in *TSU, Narodnoe khoziaistvo SSSR v 1958 g.* (Moscow, 1959), pp. 899–900, 903–906.

ABBREVIATIONS

BSE, SSSR   *Bol'shaia sovetskaia entsiklopediia: SSSR* (Great Soviet Encyclopedia: USSR), unnumbered supplementary volume on USSR (Moscow, 1948).

CPSU(B)   Communist Party of the Soviet Union (Bolshevik).

ESBM   Statisticheskii otdel Moskovskogo soveta (Statistical Department of the Moscow Soviet), *Ezhemesiachnyi statisticheskii biulleten' po gorodu Moskve i Moskovskoi gubernii* (Monthly Statistical Bulletin for Moscow City and Moscow Province), Moscow.

Gosplan   Gosudarstvennaia planovaia komissiia (State Planning Commission).

MLR   *Monthly Labor Review.*

Narkhoz   TSU, *Narodnoe khoziaistvo SSSR* (The National Economy of the USSR) (Moscow, 1956).

NKMP   Narodnyi komissariat mestnoi promyshlennosti RSFSR (RSFSR People's Commissariat of Local Industry).

NKVT   Narodnyi komissariat vnutrennei torgovli SSSR (USSR People's Commissariat of Domestic Trade).

PD   Price decree.

PKh   *Planovoe khoziaistvo* (Planned Economy), Moscow.

RES   *Review of Economics and Statistics.*

RTS-36   Nozhkina, Z. L., *et al.* (comps.), *Otpusknye i roznichnye tseny i torgovye nakidki na promtovary* (Wholesale and Retail Prices and Trade Margins for Manufactured Goods) (Moscow, 1936).

RTS-M-36   Moskovskii gorodskoi otdel vnutrennei torgovli (Moscow City Department of Domestic Trade), *Spravochnik roznichnykh tsen i torgovykh nakidok na promyshlennye tovary po g. Moskve* (Handbook of Retail Prices and Trade Margins for Manufactured Goods for Moscow City) (2 vols., Moscow, 1936).

SMG-28   Sereda, S. P., *et al.* (eds.), *Universal'nyi spravochnik tsen* (Universal Price Handbook) (Moscow, 1928).

SNIP-49-55   Hoeffding, Oleg, and Nancy Nimitz, *Soviet National Income and Product, 1949–1955.* The RAND Corporation, RM-2101, April 6, 1959.

SOVTORG   *Sovetskaia torgovlia* (Soviet Trade), Moscow. Monthly journal.

Sovtorgstat-56   TSU, *Sovetskaia torgovlia; Statisticheskii sbornik* (Soviet Trade; Statistical Handbook) (Moscow, 1956).

SRTS-35   *Sbornik otpusknykh tsen na tovary pishchevoi promyshlennosti* (Collection of Wholesale Prices of Products of the Food Industry) (Moscow, 1935).

SRTS-36   Nozhkina, Z. L., *et al.* (comps.), *Sbornik otpusknykh i roznichnykh tsen i torgovykh nakidok na prodovol'stvennye tovary* (Collection of Wholesale and Retail Prices and Trade Margins for Food Products) (Moscow, 1936).

SRTS-M-36   Moskovskii oblastnoi otdel vnutrennei torgovli (Moscow Oblast Department of Domestic Trade), *Spravochnik roznichnykh tsen na prodovol'stvennye tovary po Moskovskoi oblasti* (Handbook of Retail Prices of Food Products for Moscow Oblast) (Moscow, 1936).

ST   *Sovetskaia torgovlia* (Soviet Trade), Moscow. Daily newspaper.

TSU   Tsentral'noe statisticheskoe upravlenie SSSR (Central Statistical Administration of the USSR).

TSUNKHU   Tsentral'noe upravlenie narodno-khoziaistvennogo ucheta (Central Administration of National Economic Accounting).

UM   Unpublished materials.

UMA   Unpublished materials consulted after original computations were completed.

ZA   *Zakonodatel'stvo i administrativnye rasporiazheniia po vneshnei i vnutrennei torgovle* (Legislation and Administrative Orders on Foreign and Domestic Trade), Moscow.

BIBLIOGRAPHY

(WITH TRANSLATIONS OF RUSSIAN TITLES)

Akademiia nauk SSSR, Institut ekonomiki (USSR Academy of Sciences, Economic Institute), *Politicheskaia ekonomiia* (Political Economy) (Moscow, 1954; 1955).

—— *Sovetskaia sotsialisticheskaia ekonomika, 1917–1957 gg.* (The Soviet Socialist Economy, 1917–1957) (Moscow, 1957).

Alekseev, T. D. (comp.), *Zhilishchnye zakony* (Housing Laws) (Moscow, 1947).

Aliutin, F., "Rol' potrebitel'skoi kooperatsii" (The Role of the Consumer Cooperatives), *Izvestiia Akademii nauk SSSR, otdelenie ekonomiki i prava* (News of the USSR Academy of Sciences, Division of Economics and Law), no. 1, 1949, pp. 13–33.

Allais, M., "L'Économie Soviétique est-elle efficiente?" *Nouvelle Revue de L'Économie Contemporaine,* no. 10, October 1950, pp. 4–12.

—— "Productivités, niveaux de vie et rythmes de croissance comparés, en Russie Soviétique, aux États-Unis et en France, 1880–1955," Communication devant L'Académie des Sciences Morales et Politiques, April 30, 1955 (photo offset).

Allen, R. G. D., "The Economic Theory of Index Numbers," *Economica,* n.s., 16:197–203 (August 1949).

Andrusevich, D. A., *Tovarovedenie promyshlennykh tovarov* (The Science of Manufactured Commodities) (Moscow, 1948).

Arkhangel'skii, N. A. (ed.), *Tovarovedenie promyshlennykh tovarov* (The Science of Manufactured Commodities) (2 vols., Moscow, 1947).

Bakzevich, D. D., *Tovarovedenie pishchevykh produktov* (The Science of Food Products) (Moscow, 1948).

Baran, Paul, "Currency Reform in the USSR," *Harvard Business Review,* 26:194–206 (March 1948).

Barker, G. R., *Some Problems of Incentives and Labour Productivity in Soviet Industry* (Oxford, 1955).

Baykov, Alexander, *The Development of the Soviet Economic System* (New York, 1947).

—— "Internal Trade During the War and Its Postwar Development," *Bulletins on Soviet Economic Development,* no. 4, September 1950, pp. 1–9.

Beliunov, S. A., *et al., Planirovanie na zheleznodorozhnom transporte* (Planning in Railroad Transport) (Moscow, 1946; 1948).

Bennett, M. K., "International Disparities in Consumption Levels," *American Economic Review,* 41:632–649 (1951).

Bergson, Abram, "On Inequality of Incomes in the USSR," *American Slavic and East European Review,* 10:95–99 (1951).

—— "A Problem in Soviet Statistics," *Review of Economic Statistics,* 29:234–242 (November 1947).

—— *The Real National Income of Soviet Russia Since 1928* (Cambridge, Mass., 1961).

—— *Soviet National Income and Product in 1937* (New York, 1953).

—— *The Structure of Soviet Wages* (Cambridge, Mass., 1946).

—— and Hans Heymann, Jr., *Soviet National Income and Product, 1940–1948* (New York, 1954).

———— Hans Heymann, Jr., and Oleg Hoeffding, *Soviet National Income and Product, 1928–1948: Revised Data,* The RAND Corporation, RM-2544, November 15, 1960.

Biulleten' finansovogo i khoziaistvennogo zakonodatel'stva (Bulletin of Financial and Economic Legislation), Moscow.

Björk, Lief, *Wages, Prices and Social Legislation in the Soviet Union,* trans. from the Swedish by M. A. Michael (London, 1953).

Blackman, James H., "Transportation," in A. Bergson (ed.), *Soviet Economic Growth* (Evanston, 1953), pp. 126–162.

Bol'shaia sovetskaia entsiklopediia (Great Soviet Encyclopedia). The first edition was published in 30 volumes from 1935–47. (An unnumbered volume, *Bol'shaia sovetskaia entsiklopediia: SSSR,* was published as a supplement in 1948). The second edition was published in 51 volumes from 1949–58; in this edition, vol. 50 (1957) is on the USSR.

Bol'shaia sovetskaia entsiklopediia: SSSR (Great Soviet Encyclopedia: USSR). Unnumbered supplementary volume on the USSR dated 1948.

Bol'shevik (now called *Kommunist*), Moscow.

Briukhanov, A., "Roznitsa Soiuzmetizstroitorg v 1936 g." (Retail Trade of the Union for Marketing Metal Products and Construction Materials in 1936), *Sovetskaia torgovlia,* no. 1, 1937, pp. 42–53.

Bronshtein, N. I., *Oplata zhilykh pomeshchenii; deistvuiushchie uzakonenie tsentral'nykh organov vlasti, Moskovskogo i Leningradskogo sovetov, sudebnaia praktika Verkhsuda i Mosgubsuda* (The Payment of Rent; Current Legislation of the Central Organs of Power, the Moscow and Leningrad Soviets and Judicial Practice of the Supreme Court and the Moscow Province Court) (Moscow, 1928).

Brown, Emily C., "The Soviet Labor Market," *Industrial and Labor Relations Review,* 10:179–200 (1957).

Burmistrov, D. V. (ed.), *Spravochnik nalogovogo rabotnika* (Handbook for the Tax Worker) (Moscow, 1951).

Cassidy, Henry C., *Moscow Dateline 1941–1943* (Boston, 1943).

Chapman, Janet G., "Consumption," in Abram Bergson and Simon Kuznets (eds.), *Economic Trends in the Soviet Union* (Cambridge, Mass., 1963), pp. 235–282.

———— "Real Wages in the Soviet Union, 1928–52," *Review of Economics and Statistics,* 36:134–156 (May 1954).

———— *The Regional Structure of Soviet Retail Prices,* The RAND Corporation, RM-425, July 20, 1950 (also on file as Master's essay, Columbia University).

Cherniavskii, U., and S. Krivetskii, "Pokupatel'nye fondy naseleniia i roznichnyi tovarooborot" (The Purchasing Power of the Population and Retail Turnover), *Planovoe khoziaistvo,* no. 6, 1936.

Current Digest of the Soviet Press, Ann Arbor.

Dadugin, A. P., and P. G. Kagarlitskii, *Organizatsiia i tekhnika kolkhoznoi-bazarnoi torgovli* (Organization and Techniques of Collective Farm Market Trade) (Moscow, 1949).

Daniel, Clifton, "How To Dress for the Russians," *New York Times Magazine,* August 28, 1955, p. 72.

Davies, R. W., *The Development of the Soviet Budgetary System* (Cambridge, England, 1958).

Dobb, Maurice, "A Comment on Soviet Statistics," *Review of Economics and Statistics,* 30:34–38 (1948).

Dvizhenie tsen (The Movement of Prices), Moscow.

Eason, Warren, "Population and Labor Force," in A. Bergson (ed.), *Soviet Economic Growth* (Evanston, 1953), pp. 101–125.

—— "Soviet Manpower: The Population and Labor Force of the USSR" (unpublished Ph.D. dissertation, Department of Economics, Columbia University, 1959).

—— "The Soviet Population Today," *Foreign Affairs,* July 1959, pp. 598–606.

Eidel'man, M., "O metodologii ischisleniia indeksa real'noi zarabotnoi platy" (On the Method of Calculating the Index Number of Real Wages), *Vestnik statistiki* (Journal of Statistics), no. 3, 1956, pp. 33–46.

Elektricheskie stantsii (Electric Stations), Moscow.

Elvin, G. H., "Earnings and Living Standards in Moscow: A Comment," *Bulletin of the Oxford University Institute of Statistics,* 15:309–314 (September 1953).

Figurnov, S. P., "Chto poluchaiut rabochie i sluzhashchie SSSR sverkh zarabotnoi platy" (What the Wage Earners and Salaried Employees of the USSR Receive above Their Wages), *V pomoshch' politicheskomu samoobrazovaniiu* (In Aid of Political Self-education), no. 9, 1959, pp. 76–81.

—— "K voprosu o metodologii ischisleniia real'nykh dokhodov i real'noi zarabotnoi platy trudiashchikhsia SSSR" (On the Question of the Method of Calculating the Real Income and Real Wages of the Workers of the USSR), *Trud i zarabotnaia plata* (Labor and Wages), no. 12, 1959, pp. 44–48.

—— "Osnovnye formy povysheniia real'noi zarabotnoi platy v SSSR" (The Main Forms of Raising Real Wages in the USSR), *Sotsialisticheskii trud* (Socialist Labor), no. 5, 1959, pp. 50–56.

—— *Real'naia zarabotnaia plata i pod"em material'nogo blagosostoianiia trudiashchikhsia v SSSR* (Real Wages and the Rise in the Material Welfare of the Workers in the USSR) (Moscow, 1960).

Finansy i kredit SSSR (Finances and Credit in the USSR), Moscow.

Finansy i sotsialisticheskoe stroitel'stvo (Finances and Socialist Construction) (Moscow, 1957).

Frisch, Ragnar, "Annual Survey of General Economic Theory: The Problem of Index Numbers," *Econometrica,* 4:1–38 (January 1936).

Furth, J. Herbert, "Indicators of Inflation in Western Europe, 1952–55," *Review of Economics and Statistics,* 38:335–338 (1956).

Galenson, Walter, "Industrial Training in the Soviet Union," *Industrial and Labor Relations Review,* 9:562–576 (1956).

Gerschenkron, Alexander, "Comments on Naum Jasny's 'Soviet Statistics'," *Review of Economics and Statistics,* 32:250–251 (1950).

—— *A Dollar Index of Soviet Machinery Output, 1927/28 to 1937,* The RAND Corporation, R-197, April 6, 1951.

Gilbert, Milton, and Irving B. Kravis, *An International Comparison of National Products and the Purchasing Power of Currencies: A Study of the United States, the United Kingdom, France, Germany, and Italy,* Organization of European Economic Communities (OEEC) (Paris, 1954).

Gladilin, P., "Priobretenie promyshlennykh tovarov sel'skim naseleniem SSSR v 1927/28 g." (Purchases of Industrial Products by the Rural Population of the USSR in 1927/28), *Statisticheskoe obozrenie,* no. 6, 1930.

Gliksman, J. G., "Recent Trends in Soviet Labor Policy," *Monthly Labor Review,* July 1956, pp. 767–775.

Gogol', B. I. (ed.), *Sorok let sovetskoi torgovli* (Forty Years of Soviet Trade) (Moscow, 1957).

Gordey, Michel, Series of articles in the Paris *France-Soir,* July 1950.

Gosplan, *Kontrol'nye tsifry narodnogo khoziaistva SSSR na 1928/29 god* (Control Figures for the National Economy of the USSR for 1928/29) (Moscow, 1929).

—— *Kontrol'nye tsifry narodnogo khoziaistva SSSR na 1929/30 god* (Control Figures for the National Economy of the USSR for 1929/30) (Moscow, 1930).

—— *Narodno-khoziaistvennyi plan na 1936 god* (National Economic Plan for 1936) (2d ed., Moscow, 1936).

—— *Narodno-khoziaistvennyi plan SSSR na 1937 god* (National Economic Plan of the USSR for 1937) (Moscow, 1937).

—— *Piatiletnii plan narodno-khoziaistvennogo stroitel'stva SSSR* (Five Year Plan for National Economic Construction in the USSR) (3 vols., Moscow, 1930).

—— *The Soviet Union Looks Ahead: The Five Year Plan for Economic Construction* (New York, 1929).

—— *Summary of the Fulfillment of the First Five Year Plan for the Development of the National Economy of the USSR* (Moscow, 1933).

—— *Tretii piatiletnii plan razvitiia narodnogo khoziaistva Soiuza SSR (1938–42 gg.)* (proekt) (Third Five Year Plan for the Development of the National Economy of the USSR, 1938–42. Draft) (Moscow, 1939).

Gosudarstvennyi plan razvitiia narodnogo khoziaistva SSSR na 1941 god (State Plan for the Development of the National Economy of the USSR in 1941). A classified appendix to a decree of the Council of People's Commissars and the Central Committee of the Communist Party, January 17, 1941. American Council of Learned Societies. Reprints: Russian Series no. 30, Baltimore, n.d.

Gozulov, A. I., *Ekonomicheskaia statistika* (Economic Statistics) (Moscow, 1953).

Grossman, Gregory, "Soviet Agriculture Since Stalin," *Annals of the American Academy of Political and Social Science,* 303:62–74 (January 1956).

Gsovski, Vladimir, "Elements of Soviet Labor Law," *Monthly Labor Review,* March 1951, pp. 257–262; April 1951, pp. 385–390.

—— *Soviet Civil Law* (2 vols., Ann Arbor, 1948; 1949).

Gubenko, G. B., *Kontrol' kachestva shveinykh tovarov* (Control of the Quality of Garments) (Kiev, 1950).

Gurevitch, S., "Soviet Rural Stores," *USSR Information Bulletin* (Soviet Embassy, Washington, July 1948).

Gurvits, L. Kh., *Torgovye vychisleniia* (Trade Calculation) (Moscow, 1949).

—— *Torgovye vychisleniia* (Trade Calculation) (2d ed., Moscow, 1953).

Harris, Seymour, Colin Clark, Alexander Gerschenkron, Paul Baran, Abram Bergson, and A. Yugov, "Appraisals of Russian Economic Statistics," *Review of Economic Statistics,* 29:213–246 (1947).

Hicks, J. R., "The Valuation of Social Income," *Economica,* n.s., 7:105–124 (May 1940).

Hoeffding, Oleg, *Soviet National Income and Product in 1928* (New York, 1954).

—— and Nancy Nimitz, *Soviet National Income and Product, 1949–1955,* The RAND Corporation, RM-2101, April 6, 1959. (References are to preliminary drafts of this study.)

Holzman, Franklyn D., "An Estimate of the Tax Element in Soviet Bonds," *American Economic Review,* 47:390–396 (1957).

—— *Soviet Taxation* (Cambridge, Mass., 1955).

Hubbard, L. E., *Soviet Trade and Distribution* (London, 1938).

Hughes, Emmet, "A Perceptive Reporter in a Changing Russia," *Life,* February 8, 1954, pp. 114–131.

Ignatov, I. D., "Razvitie kolkhoznoi torgovli" (The Development of Collective Farm Market Trade), in B. I. Gogol' (ed.), *Sorok let sovetskoi torgovli* (Forty Years of Soviet Trade) (Moscow, 1957), pp. 108–134.

Il'inskii, A. K., "Shveinaia promyshlennost' v tret'em piatiletii" (The Garment Industry in the Third Five Year Plan), *Legkaia promyshlennost* (Light Industry), no. 6, 1939.

International Labour Review, International Labour Office, Geneva.

Ioffe, Ia. A. (comp.), *SSSR i kapitalisticheskie strany* (The USSR and the Capitalist Countries) (Moscow, 1939).

Izvestiia (News), Moscow.

Jasny, Naum, "Prospects for Soviet Farm Output and Labor," *Review of Economics and Statistics*, 36:212–219 (1954).

―――― *The Socialized Agriculture of the USSR* (Stanford, 1949).

―――― *The Soviet Economy During the Plan Era* (Stanford, 1951).

―――― *The Soviet 1956 Statistical Handbook: A Commentary* (East Lansing, 1957).

―――― *The Soviet Price System* (Stanford, 1951).

―――― "Soviet Statistics," *Review of Economics and Statistics*, 32:92–99 (1950).

Joint Economic Committee, U.S. Congress, *Comparisons of the United States and Soviet Economies* (3 parts, Washington, 1959).

Kaplan, D. I. (ed.), *Preiskurant otpusknykh i roznichnykh tsen na konservy* (Price List of Wholesale and Retail Prices of Canned Goods) (Moscow, 1936).

Kaplan, N. M., and R. H. Moorsteen, "An Index of Soviet Industrial Output," *American Economic Review*, 50:295–318 (1960).

―――― *Indexes of Soviet Industrial Output*, The RAND Corporation, RM-2495, May 13, 1960.

Kaplan, N. M., and Eleanor Wainstein, *An Addendum to Previous USSR-US Retail Price Comparisons*, The RAND Corporation, RM-1906, May 13, 1957.

―――― *A Comparison of Soviet and American Retail Prices in 1950*, The RAND Corporation, RM-1692-1, May 1, 1956, rev. October 3, 1956.

Karcz, J. F., *Soviet Agricultural Marketings and Prices, 1928–1954*, The RAND Corporation, RM-1930, July 2, 1957.

Klimov, A. P., *Sovetskaia potrebitel'skaia kooperatsiia* (Soviet Consumer Cooperative Societies) (Moscow, 1948).

Kommunal'noe khoziaistvo (Municipal Economy), Moscow.

Kommunist (formerly *Bol'shevik*), Moscow.

Kommunisticheskaia akademiia, Institut ekonomiki (Communist Academy, Economics Institute), *Ekonomika sovetskoi torgovli* (The Economics of Soviet Trade) (Moscow, 1933).

Konnikov, A. G., and A. P. Bogatyrev, *Proizvodstvo kolbas i miasokopchenostei* (The Production of Sausage and Smoked Meat Products) (Moscow, 1948).

Krasnopol'skii, A. S., *Osnovnye printsipy sovetskogo gosudarstvennogo sotsial'nogo strakhovaniia* (The Basic Principles of Soviet State Social Insurance) (Moscow, 1951).

Kravis, Irving B., and Joseph Mintzes, "Food Prices in the Soviet Union, 1936–50," *Review of Economics and Statistics*, 32:164–168 (May 1950).

―――― "The Soviet Union: Trends in Prices, Rations, and Wages," *Monthly Labor Review*, 65:28–35 (July 1947).

Kuznetsov, G. I. (ed.), *Sbornik otpusknykh i roznichnykh tsen i torgovykh nakidok na prodovol'stvennye tovary* (Collection of Wholesale and Retail Prices and Trade Margins on Food Products) (Moscow, 1936).

Lasevich, G. M., and A. G. Karelov, *Torgovye skidki na prodovol'stvennye i promyshlennye tovary* (Trade Margins for Food and Manufactured Commodities) (Moscow, 1954).

Lauterbach, Richard E., *These Are the Russians* (New York, 1945).

Leningradskaia oblastnaia planovaia komissiia (Leningrad Oblast Planning Commission), *Spravochnik tsen na stroitel'nye materialy, oborudovanie i transport* (Handbook of Prices of Building Materials, Equipment and Transport), no. 34, Leningrad, 1941.

Leningradskoe ob"edinenie gosudarstvennykh elektricheskikh stantsii "Elektrotok" (Leningrad Union of State Electrical Stations "Elektrotok"), *Statisticheskii spravochnik, 1913–1928 gg.* (Statistical Handbook, 1913–1928) (Leningrad, 1929).

Lifits, M. M., (ed.), *Ekonomika sovetskoi torgovli* (The Economics of Soviet Trade) (Moscow, 1955).

—— *Sovetskaia torgovlia* (Soviet Trade) (Moscow, 1948).

Litoshenko, L., "Sezonnost' oborota krest'ianskikh khoziaistv" (Seasonal Fluctuations in the Turnover of Peasant Farms), *Statisticheskoe obozrenie,* no. 2, 1929.

Lorimer, Frank, *The Population of the Soviet Union* (Geneva, 1946).

MacDuffie, Marshall, "Russia Uncensored," *Collier's,* March 5, 1954, pp. 90–101.

Madge, Charles, "Notes on the Standard of Living in Moscow, April 1952," *Soviet Studies,* 4:229–236 (January 1953).

Maizenberg, L., "O tsenoobrazovanii v sovetskoi ekonomike" (On Price Formation in the Soviet Economy), *Planovoe khoziaistvo,* no. 6, 1945, pp. 57–69.

—— *Tsenoobrazovanie v narodnom khoziaistve SSSR* (Price Formation in the USSR) (Moscow, 1953).

—— "Voprosy tsenoobrazovaniia" (Problems of Price Formation), *Planovoe khoziaistvo,* no. 5, 1939, pp. 18–37.

Malkis, A. I., *Potreblenie i spros v SSSR* (Consumption and Demand in the USSR) (Moscow, 1935).

Margolin, N. S., *Balans denezhnykh dokhodov i raskhodov naseleniia* (The Balance of Money Incomes and Expenditures of the Population) (Moscow, 1951).

—— *Voprosy balansa denezhnykh dokhodov i raskhodov naseleniia* (Problems of the Balance of Money Incomes and Expenditures of the Population) (Moscow, 1939).

Maslakov, V. P., *Kommunal'nye tarify v SSSR* (Municipal Service Rates in the USSR) (Moscow, 1951).

—— *et al., Finansirovanie zhilishchno-kommunal'nogo khoziaistva* (Financing Housing and the Municipal Economy) (Moscow, 1948).

Maynard, John, "Conditions of the Urban Worker, Moscow and London," *Political Quarterly,* 13:321–327 (1942).

Mazel', L., "Ob urovne tsen na gorodskikh kolkhoznykh rynkakh" (On the Level of Prices on the Urban Collective Farm Markets), *Sovetskaia torgovlia,* no. 9, 1956, pp. 11–17.

Medynskii, E. N., *Narodnoe obrazovanie v SSSR* (Public Education in the USSR) (Moscow, 1952).

Mel'kinov, A. K., *Posudo-khoziaistvennye tovary* (Household Utensils) (Moscow, 1947).

Ministerstvo prosveshcheniia RSFSR (RSFSR Ministry of Education), *Sbornik materialov dlia rabotnikov uchebno-proizvodstvennykh i podsobnykh khoziaistv uchrezhdenii Ministerstva prosveshcheniia RSFSR* (Collection of Materials for Workers in the Training and Subsidiary Farms of Institutions of the Ministry of Education of the RSFSR) (Moscow, 1948).

Ministerstvo putei soobshcheniia SSSR (USSR Ministry of Transportation), *Ofitsial'nyi ukazatel' passazhirskikh soobshchenii leto 1948 goda* (Official Guide for Passenger Transportation for the Summer of 1948) (Moscow, 1948).

—— *Ofitsial'nyi ukazatel' passazhirskikh soobshchenii leto 1950 g.* (Official Guide for Passenger Transportation for the Summer of 1950) (Moscow, 1950).

Ministerstvo torgovli SSSR, Sektor torgovykh kadrov i zarabotnoi platy (USSR Ministry of Trade, Section for Trade Personnel and Wages), *Sbornik normativov i spravochnykh materialov dlia shveinykh i obuvnykh predpriiatii dlia predpriiatii sistemy Glavvoentorg* (Collection of Norms and Reference Materials for Garment and Shoe Enterprises for Establishments of the Chief

Administration of Trade Establishments Serving the Armed Forces) (Moscow, 1947).

Ministerstvo vneshnei torgovli SSSR (USSR Ministry of Foreign Trade), *Vneshniaia torgovlia SSSR za 1956 god* (The Foreign Trade of the USSR in 1956) (Moscow, 1958).

Molotov, V., "The Third Five Year Plan," in *The Land of Socialism Today and Tomorrow* (Moscow, 1939), pp. 101–157.

Monthly Labor Review, U.S. Bureau of Labor Statistics.

Moskovskaia oblast', Statisticheskii otdel (Moscow Oblast, Statistical Department), *Moskva i Moskovskaia oblast' 1926/27–1928/29 gg.* (Moscow and Moscow Oblast 1926/27–1928/29) (Moscow, 1930).

Moskovskii bol'shevik (Moscow Bolshevik), Moscow.

Moskovskii gorodskoi otdel vnutrennei torgovli (Moscow City Department of Domestic Trade), *Preiskurant edinykh otpusknykh tsen na trikotazhnye izdeliia* (Price List of Uniform Wholesale Prices of Knitwear) (Moscow, 1936).

—— *Spravochnik roznichnykh tsen i torgovykh nakidok na promyshlennye tovary po g. Moskve* (Handbook of Retail Prices and Trade Margins for Manufactured Goods for Moscow City) (2 vols., Moscow, 1936).

Moskovskii oblastnoi otdel vnutrennei torgovli (Moscow Oblast Department of Domestic Trade), *Preiskurant roznichnykh tsen na trikotazhnye izdeliia po Moskovskoi oblasti* (Price List of Retail Prices of Knitwear for Moscow Oblast) (Moscow, 1936).

—— *Spravochnik roznichnykh tsen na prodovol'stvennye tovary po Moskovskoi oblasti* (Handbook of Retail Prices of Food Products for Moscow Oblast) (Moscow, 1936).

Moskva i Moskovskaia guberniia; Statistiko-ekonomicheskii spravochnik 1923/24–1927/28 gg. (Moscow and Moscow Province; Statistical Economic Handbook, 1923/24–1927/28) (Moscow, 1929).

Mudgett, Bruce D., *Index Numbers* (New York, 1951).

Mudrik, M., "Kapitalisticheskaia torgovlia v gorodakh SSSR v 1927/28 g." (Capitalist Trade in Cities of the USSR in 1927/28), *Statisticheskoe obozrenie*, no. 11, 1929.

Naimushin, K. V. (comp.), *Preiskurant roznichnykh tsen na rybu i rybotovary* (Price List of Retail Prices of Fish and Fish Products) (Moscow, 1936).

Narodnyi komissariat finansov SSSR (USSR People's Commissariat of Finances), *Instruktsiia Narodnogo komissariata finansov SSSR o poriadke provedeniia podokhodnogo naloga s chastnykh lits* (Instructions of the USSR People's Commissariat of Finances on the Procedure for Applying the Income Tax on Private Persons) (Moscow, 1936).

Narodnyi komissariat mestnoi promyshlennosti RSFSR (RSFSR People's Commissariat of Local Industry), *Preiskurant edinykh otpusknykh tsen na obuv' proizvodstva gosudarstvennykh predpriiatii kozhevennoi promyshlennosti Narkommestproma RSFSR* (Price List of Uniform Wholesale Prices of Shoes Produced in State Enterprises of the Leather Industry under the RSFSR People's Commissariat of Local Industry) (Moscow, 1936).

Narodnyi komissariat putei soobshcheniia SSSR (USSR People's Commissariat of Transportation), *Ofitsial'nyi ukazatel' zheleznodorozhnykh, parokhodnykh i drugikh passazhirskikh soobshchenii zimnee dvizhenie 1927/28 g.* (Official Guide for Railway, Steamship, and Other Passenger Transportation for the Winter of 1927/28) (2d ed., Moscow, 1927).

—— *Ofitsial'nyi ukazatel' zheleznodorozhnykh, vodnykh i drugikh passazhirskikh soobshchenii zimnee dvizhenie 1937–38 g.* (Official Guide for Railway, Water, and Other Passenger Transportation for the Winter of 1937–38) (Moscow, 1937).

Nash, Edmund, "Purchasing Power of Soviet Workers, 1953," *Monthly Labor Review*, 76:705–708 (July 1953).

Nauchno-issledovatel'skii institut truda Gosudarstvennogo komiteta Soveta ministrov SSSR po voprosam truda i zarabotnoi platy (Scientific-Research Institute of Labor of the State Committee of the USSR Council of Ministers for Questions of Labor and Wages), *Voprosy truda v SSSR* (Questions of Labor in the USSR) (Moscow, 1958).

New York Herald Tribune.

New York Times.

NKVT, *Preiskurant roznichnykh tsen na shveinye izdeliia dlia vsekh magazinov vsekh torguiushchikh organizatsii gorodov: Moskva, Leningrad, Kiev, Minsk* (Price List of Retail Garment Prices for all Shops of all Trade Organizations of Moscow, Leningrad, Kiev, and Minsk) (Moscow, 1936).

———— *Spravochnik tsen na miaso i miasoprodukty* (Handbook of Prices of Meat and Meat Products) (Moscow, 1936).

Nove, A., "The Purchasing Power of the Soviet Ruble," *Bulletin of the Oxford University Institute of Statistics*, 20:187–204 (1958).

Novyi zakon po podokhodnomu nalogu (New Law on the Income Tax) (Moscow, 1928).

Nozhkina, Z. L., et al. (comps.), *Otpusknye i roznichnye tseny i torgovye nakidki na promtovary* (Wholesale and Retail Prices and Trade Margins for Manufactured Goods) (Moscow, 1936).

———— *Sbornik otpusknykh i roznichnykh tsen i torgovykh nakidok na prodovol'-stvennye tovary* (Collection of Wholesale and Retail Prices and Trade Margins for Food Products) (Moscow, 1936).

Nutter, G. Warren, "Industrial Growth in the Soviet Union," *American Economic Review*, 48:398–411 (1958).

"Osnovnye pokazateli itogov vypolneniia vtorogo piatiletnego plana SSSR." (Main Indicators of the Results of the Fulfillment of the Second Five Year Plan of the USSR), *Planovoe khoziaistvo*, no. 5, 1939.

Partigul, S., "Demand and Supply under Socialism," *Voprosy ekonomiki*, no. 10, 1959 (trans. in *Problems of Economics*, 2:10–14, 29 (February 1960)).

Pasternak, Boris, *Doctor Zhivago* (New York, 1958).

Petrov, V. I., *Tovarovedenie prodovol'stvennykh tovarov* (The Science of Food Commodities) (Moscow, 1947).

Pisarev, Iu., N. Riauzov, and N. Titel'baum, *Kurs torgovoi statistiki* (Course on Trade Statistics) (Moscow, 1938).

Planovoe khoziaistvo (Planned Economy), Moscow.

Plotnikov, K. N., *Biudzhet sotsialisticheskogo gosudarstva* (The Budget of the Soviet Government) (Moscow, 1948).

Plyshevskii, B. P., *Raspredelenie natsional'nogo dokhoda v SSSR* (The Distribution of National Income in the USSR) (Moscow, 1960).

Postavka tovarov v sisteme sovetskoi torgovli; sbornik vazhneishikh postanovlenii, instruktsii i prikazov (The Distribution of Commodities in the Soviet Trade System; Collection of the Most Important Decrees, Instructions and Orders) (Moscow, 1947).

Pravda (Truth), Moscow.

Pravda Ukrainy (Ukraine Truth), Kiev.

Pravda Vostoka (Truth of the East), Tashkent.

Preiskuranty snizhennykh s 1 iiulia 1937 g. otpusknykh tsen na promyshlennye tovary (Price Lists of Wholesale Prices of Manufactured Goods Reduced as of July 1, 1937), *Prilozhenie k torgovomu biulleteniu No. 6 Kurskogo oblast-nogo otdela vnutrennei torgovli* (Supplement to Trade Bulletin No. 6 of the Kursk Oblast Department of Domestic Trade) (Kursk, June 1937).

Problemy ekonomiki (Problems of Economics), Moscow.

Proferansov, D. P. (ed.), *Zhilishchnoe khoziaistvo; sbornik vazhneishikh postanovlenii po eksploatatsii zhilogo doma* (The Housing Economy; Collection of the Most Important Decrees on the Utilization of Houses) (Moscow, 1945).

Prokopovicz, S. N., *Russlands Volkswirtschaft unter den Sowjets* (Zurich, 1944).

—— (ed.), *Quarterly Bulletin of Soviet-Russian Economics* (Trans. from the Russian) (Geneva, 1939 to 1941).

Riauzov, N., and N. Titel'baum, *Kurs torgovoi statistiki* (Course on Trade Statistics) (Moscow, 1947).

—— *Statistika sovetskoi torgovli* (Statistics of Soviet Trade) (Moscow, 1951).

Rice, Stuart, Harry Schwartz, Frank Lorimer, A. Gerschenkron, Lazar Volin, and Abram Bergson, "Reliability and Usability of Soviet Statistics," *The American Statistician*, April-May 1953, pp. 8–21; June-July 1953, pp. 8–16.

Romeuf, Jean, *Le Niveau de Vie en U.R.S.S.* (Paris, 1954).

Rounds, Frank, Jr., *A Window on Red Square* (Cambridge, Mass., 1953).

Rovinskii, N. N., *Gosudarstvennyi biudzhet SSSR* (The Government Budget of the USSR) (Moscow, 1951).

Rubinshtein, G. L., *et al.*, *Ekonomika sovetskoi torgovli* (The Economics of Soviet Trade) (Moscow, 1950).

Salisbury, Harrison, *Russia on the Way* (New York, 1946).

Samuelson, Paul A., *Foundations of Economic Analysis* (Cambridge, Mass., 1947).

Sbornik otpusknykh tsen na tovary pishchevoi promyshlennosti (Collection of Wholesale Prices of Products of the Food Industry) (Moscow, 1935).

Schwartz, Harry, "A Critique of 'Appraisals of Russian Economic Statistics'," *Review of Economics and Statistics*, 30:38–41 (1948).

—— "Prices in the Soviet War Economy," *American Economic Review*, 36:872–882 (December 1946).

—— *Russia's Soviet Economy* (New York, 1950; 1954).

—— and Maurice Dobb, "Further Appraisals of Russian Economic Statistics," *Review of Economics and Statistics*, 30:34–41 (1948).

Schwarz, Solomon, *Labor in the Soviet Union* (New York, 1951).

Serebriakov, S. V., *Organizatsiia i tekhnika sovetskoi torgovli* (The Organization and Technique of Soviet Trade) (Moscow, 1949).

Sereda, S. P., *et al.* (eds.), *Universal'nyi spravochnik tsen* (Universal Price Handbook) (Moscow, 1928).

Shavrin, V. A., *Gosudarstvennyi biudzhet SSSR* (The Government Budget of the USSR) (3d ed., Moscow, 1951).

Sheinman, V. I., *Bakaleinye tovary; spravochnoe posobie* (Grocery Products; Reference Text) (Moscow, 1946).

Shestaia sessiia verkhovnogo soveta SSSR, 29 marta-4 apreliia 1940 g.; Stenograficheskii otchet (Sixth Session of the Supreme Soviet of the USSR, March 29-April 4, 1940; Verbatim Report) (Moscow, 1940).

Shkundin, Z. I., *Obiazatel'stvo postavki tovarov v sovetskom prave* (The Obligation To Deliver Commodities in Soviet Law) (Moscow, 1948).

"Sistema detsentralizovannykh indeksov roznichnykh tsen *TSU*" (The System of the *TSU* Decentralized Index Numbers of Retail Prices), *Statisticheskoe obozrenie*, no. 8, 1929, pp. 115–120.

Sivolap, I. K., *Pod"em pishchevoi promyshlennosti SSSR v poslevoennoi Stalinskoi piatiletke* (Development of the Food Industry During the Postwar Stalin Five Year Plan) (Moscow, 1950).

Slovar' russkogo iazyka (Dictionary of the Russian Language) (Moscow, 1907).

Smirnitskii, A. I. (ed.), *Russko-angliiskii slovar'* (Russian-English Dictionary) (Moscow, 1949).

Smith, Walter Bedell, *My Three Years in Moscow* (Philadelphia, 1950).

Snow, Edgar, *People on Our Side* (New York, 1944).

Sobranie postanovlenii i rasporiazhenii pravitel'stva SSSR (Collection of the Laws and Decrees of the Government of the USSR), Moscow.

Sobranie zakonov i rasporiazhenii SSSR (Collection of the Laws and Decrees of the USSR), Moscow.

Social Insurance in the USSR (Moscow, 1953).

Sokolov, V., and R. Nazarov, *Sovetskaia torgovlia v poslevoennyi period* (Soviet Trade in the Postwar Period) (Moscow, 1954).

Sosnovy, Timothy, *The Housing Problem in the Soviet Union* (Studies on the USSR no. 8) (New York, 1954).

Sovetskaia Belorossiia (Soviet Belorussia), Minsk.

Sovetskaia Rossiia (Soviet Russia), Moscow.

Sovetskaia torgovlia (Soviet Trade), Moscow. Daily newspaper.

Sovetskaia torgovlia (Soviet Trade), Moscow. Monthly journal.

Sovetskaia torgovlia za tridtsat' let (Soviet Trade During Thirty Years) (Moscow, 1947).

Spravochnaia kniga po kul'ttovaram (Reference Handbook on Cultural Goods) (Moscow, 1954).

Spravochnik direktora prodovol'stvennogo magazina (Handbook for the Food Store Manager) (Moscow, 1949).

Stalin, J. V., *Sochineniia* (Works), vol. XII (Moscow, 1949).

Statistical Abstract of the United States: 1959 (Washington, 1959).

Statisticheskii otdel Moskovskogo soveta (Statistical Department of the Moscow Soviet), *Ezhemesiachnyi statisticheskii biulleten' po gorodu Moskve i Moskovskoi gubernii* (Monthly Statistical Bulletin for Moscow City and Moscow Province), Moscow.

Statisticheskoe obozrenie (Statistical Review), Moscow.

Statistika truda (Labor Statistics), Moscow.

Stevens, Edmund, Series of articles in the *Christian Science Monitor,* October 18, 1949–February 9, 1950.

Suchkov, A. K., *Dokhody gosudarstvennogo biudzheta SSSR* (Revenues of the Government Budget of the USSR) (Moscow, 1945).

—— *Gosudarstvennye dokhody SSSR* (Government Revenues in the USSR) (Moscow, 1949).

Sukharev, A. M., *Kurs promyshlennoi statistiki* (Course on Industrial Statistics) (Moscow, 1959).

Survey of Current Business, U.S. Department of Commerce.

Tenenbaum, M. V., and N. Riauzov, *Torgovo-kooperativnaia statistika* (Trade and Cooperative Statistics) (Moscow, 1939).

Trivanovitch, Vaso, "Purchasing Power of Wages in the Soviet Union," National Industrial Conference Board, *Conference Board Bulletin,* 12:25–28 (March 7, 1938).

Trud (Labor), Moscow.

TSU, *Dostizheniia sovetskoi vlasti za sorok let v tsifrakh* (The Achievements of Soviet Power over Forty Years in Figures) (Moscow, 1957).

—————— *Kul'turnoe stroitel'stvo SSSR; Statisticheskii sbornik* (Cultural Construction in the USSR; Statistical Handbook) (Moscow, 1956).

—————— *Narodnoe khoziaistvo SSSR* (The National Economy of the USSR) (Moscow, 1956).

—————— *Narodnoe khoziaistvo SSSR v 1956 g.* (The National Economy of the USSR in 1956) (Moscow, 1957).

—————— *Narodnoe khoziaistvo SSSR v 1958 g.* (The National Economy of the USSR in 1958) (Moscow, 1959).

—————— *Narodnoe khoziaistvo SSSR v 1959 g.* (The National Economy of the USSR in 1959) (Moscow, 1960).

—————— *Promyshlennost' SSSR; Statisticheskii sbornik* (USSR Industry; Statistical Handbook) (Moscow, 1957).

—————— *Slovar'-spravochnik po sotsial'no-ekonomicheskoi statistike* (Dictionary-Handbook of Social and Economic Statistics) (Moscow, 1944).

—————— *Sovetskaia torgovlia; Statisticheskii sbornik* (Soviet Trade; Statistical Handbook) (Moscow, 1956).

TSUNKHU, *Kolkhoznaia i individual'no-krestianskaia torgovlia* (Collective Farm and Independent Peasant Trade) (Moscow, 1936).

—————— *Mukomol'no-krupianaia promyshlennost' SSSR* (The Flour and Groats Industry of the USSR) (Moscow, 1937).

—————— *Narodnoe khoziaistvo SSSR* (The National Economy of the USSR) (Moscow, 1932).

—————— *Socialist Construction in the USSR* (English trans.) (Moscow, 1936).

—————— *Sotsialisticheskoe stroitel'stvo v SSSR* (Socialist Construction in the USSR) (Moscow, 1936).

—————— *Sotsialisticheskoe stroitel'stvo SSSR, 1933–1938 gg.* (Socialist Construction in the USSR, 1933–1938) (Moscow, 1939).

—————— *Trud v SSSR* (Labor in the USSR) (Moscow, 1935; 1936).

Tsverevitinov, F. V., *Tovarovedenie pishchevykh produktov* (The Science of Food Products) (4 vols., Moscow, 1949).

Turgeon, Lynn, "On the Reliability of Soviet Statistics," *Review of Economics and Statistics*, 34:75–76 (1952).

—————— *Prices of Industrial Electric Power in the Soviet Union, 1928 to 1950*, The RAND Corporation, RM-1244, April 27, 1954.

Ulmer, Melville J., *The Economic Theory of Cost-of-Living Index Numbers* (New York, 1949).

U.S. Department of Health, Education and Welfare, *Education in the USSR*, Bulletin 1957, no. 14 (Washington, 1957).

—————— *Report of United States Public Health Mission to the Union of Soviet Socialist Republics, August 13–September 14, 1957* (Washington, 1959).

Vankevich, V. P., *Khlebo-bulochnye tovary* (Bread and Bakery Products) (2d rev. ed., Moscow, 1948).

Vedomosti Verkhovnogo soveta SSSR (Gazette of the Supreme Soviet of the USSR), Moscow.

Veitzer, I., "Sovetskaia politika tsen" (Soviet Price Policy), *Pravda*, August 7, 1937, pp. 2–3.

Veselovskii, B. B., *Kurs ekonomiki i planirovaniia kommunal'nogo khoziaistva* (Course on the Economics and Planning of the Municipal Economy) (Moscow, 1945).

Vinnichenko, N. G., *Finansirovanie zheleznykh dorog* (Financing the Railroads) (1st ed., Moscow, 1948; 2d ed., Moscow, 1951).

Vinogradov, V. I., and Ia. A. Kaminskii, *Organizatsiia i tekhnika sovetskoi torgovli* (The Organization and Technique of Soviet Trade) (Moscow, 1954).

Volf'son, L. Ia., *et al.*, *Ekonomika transporta* (The Economics of Transportation) (Moscow, 1941).

Volin, Lazar, *A Survey of Soviet Russian Agriculture*, Agriculture Monograph 5, U.S. Department of Agriculture (Washington, 1951).

Voprosy ekonomiki (Problems of Economics), Moscow.

Voprosy sovetskoi torgovli (Problems of Soviet Trade), Moscow.

Voprosy truda (Problems of Labor), Moscow.

Voznesenskii, N., *Voennaia ekonomika SSSR v period otechestvennoi voiny* (The War Economy of the USSR in the Period of the Great Patriotic War) (Moscow, 1948).

Vserossiiskii tsentral'nyi soiuz potrebitel'nykh obshchestv (All-Russian Central Union of Consumer Societies), *Torgovaia entsiklopediia* (Trade Encyclopedia) (Moscow, 1924).

Vsia Moskva 1927 (All-Moscow 1927), Moscow. (This is the Moscow telephone directory.)

Vsia Moskva 1936 (All-Moscow 1936), Moscow.

Ware, Henry H., "The Function and Formation of Commodity Prices in the USSR," *Bulletins on Soviet Economic Development*, no. 4, September 1950, pp. 21–31.

Washington Post.

Whitman, John T., "The *Kolkhoz* Market," *Soviet Studies*, 7:384–408 (1956).

Wiles, P. J. D., "Average Wages in USSR," *Bulletin of the Oxford University Institute of Statistics*, 15:327–339 (1953).

——— "Retail Trade, Retail Prices and Real Wages in USSR," *Bulletin of the Oxford University Institute of Statistics*, 16:373–392 (1954).

——— and T. Schulz, "Earnings and Living Standards in Moscow," *Bulletin of the Oxford University Institute of Statistics*, 14:309–326 (1952); 15:315–326 (1953).

Winnick, Louis, *American Housing and Its Use; The Demand for Shelter Space* (Census Monograph Series, New York, 1957).

Yanowitch, Murray, "Changes in the Soviet Money Wage Level Since 1940," *American Slavic and East European Review*, 14:195–223 (April 1955).

——— "Trends in Soviet Occupational Wage Differentials" (unpublished Ph.D. dissertation, Department of Economics, Columbia University, 1960).

Za industrializatsiiu (For Industrialization), Moscow.

Zakonodatel'stvo i administrativnye rasporiazheniia po vneshnei i vnutrennei torgovle (Legislation and Administrative Orders on Foreign and Domestic Trade), Moscow.

Zakonodatel'stvo i rasporiazheniia po torgovle (Legislation and Orders on Trade), Moscow.

Zaleski, Eugène, "Les fluctuations des prix de détail en Union Soviétique," *Études et Conjoncture*, no. 4, April 1955, pp. 329–384.

——— "Les fluctuations des prix de détail en Union Soviétique; Annexe méthodologique et statistique," *Conjoncture et Études économiques, Études spéciales*, no. 3, 1955 (mimeographed).

Zamkovskii, D. Ia., *Kachestvennaia priemka shveinykh izdelii* (Verification of Garment Quality) (Moscow, 1951).

Zhilishchnoe upravlenie Mossoveta (The Housing Administration of the Moscow Soviet), *Domovoe khoziaistvo; sbornik postanovlenii i instruktsii* (The Housing Economy; Collection of Decrees and Instructions) (Moscow, 1938).

Zhilishchnoe zakonodatel'stvo; spravochnik postanovlenii i rasporiazhenii tsentral'noi i mestnoi vlasti s prilozheniem sudebnoi praktiki za 1928 g. (Housing Legislation; Handbook of Decrees and Orders of Central and Local Authorities with a Supplement on Judicial Practice for 1928) (Moscow, 1929).

Zverev, A. G., *O gosudarstvennom biudzhete SSSR na 1949 god* (On the USSR Government Budget for 1949) (Moscow, 1949).

INDEX

The letter t preceding a page number indicates tabular material; the letter n following a page number indicates a footnote.

SELECTED RAND BOOKS

Arrow, Kenneth J., and Marvin Hoffenberg. *A Time Series Analysis of Interindustry Demands*. Amsterdam: North-Holland Publishing Company, 1959.

Bergson, Abram. *The Real National Income of Soviet Russia Since 1928*. Cambridge, Mass.: Harvard University Press, 1961.

Bergson, Abram, and Hans Heymann, Jr. *Soviet National Income and Product, 1940–48*. New York: Columbia University Press, 1954.

Buchheim, Robert W., and the Staff of The RAND Corporation. *Space Handbook: Astronautics and Its Applications*. New York: Random House, Inc., 1959.

Dinerstein, H. S. *War and the Soviet Union: Nuclear Weapons and the Revolution in Soviet Military and Political Thinking*. New York: Frederick A. Praeger Inc., 1959.

Dinerstein, H. S., and Leon Gouré. *Two Studies in Soviet Controls: Communism and the Russian Peasant; Moscow in Crisis*. Glencoe, Ill.: The Free Press, 1955.

Dorfman, Robert, Paul A. Samuelson, and Robert M. Solow. *Linear Programming and Economic Analysis*. New York: McGraw-Hill Book Company, Inc., 1958.

Fainsod, Merle. *Smolensk under Soviet Rule*. Cambridge, Mass.: Harvard University Press, 1958.

Gale, David. *The Theory of Linear Economic Models*. New York: McGraw-Hill Book Company, Inc., 1960.

Galenson, Walter. *Labor Productivity in Soviet and American Industry*. New York: Columbia University Press, 1955.

Garthoff, Raymond L. *Soviet Military Doctrine*. Glencoe, Ill.: The Free Press, 1953.

Gouré, Leon. *Civil Defense in the Soviet Union*. Berkeley and Los Angeles: University of California Press, 1962.

Gouré, Leon. *The Siege of Leningrad, 1941–1943*. Stanford, Calif.: Stanford University Press, 1962.

Hitch, Charles J., and Roland McKean. *The Economics of Defense in the Nuclear Age*. Cambridge, Mass.: Harvard University Press, 1960.

Hoeffding, Oleg. *Soviet National Income and Product in 1928*. New York: Columbia University Press, 1954.

Johnstone, William C. *Burma's Foreign Policy: A Study in Neutralism*. Cambridge, Mass.: Harvard University Press, 1963.

Kramish, Arnold. *Atomic Energy in the Soviet Union*. Stanford, Calif.: Stanford University Press, 1959.

Krieger, F. J., *Behind the Sputniks: A Survey of Soviet Space Science*. Washington, D.C.: Public Affairs Press, 1958.

Leites, Nathan. *The Operational Code of the Politburo*. New York: McGraw-Hill Book Company, Inc., 1951.

Leites, Nathan. *A Study of Bolshevism*. Glencoe, Ill.: The Free Press, 1953.

Leites, Nathan, and Elsa Bernaut. *Ritual of Liquidation: The Case of the Moscow Trials*. Glencoe, Ill.: The Free Press, 1954.

Lubell, Harold. *Middle East Oil Crises and Western Europe's Energy Supplies.* Baltimore, Maryland: The Johns Hopkins Press, 1963.

Mead, Margaret. *Soviet Attitudes toward Authority: An Interdisciplinary Approach to Problems of Soviet Character.* New York: McGraw-Hill Book Company, Inc., 1951.

Moorsteen, Richard. *Prices and Production of Machinery in the Soviet Union, 1928–1958.* Cambridge, Mass.: Harvard University Press, 1962.

Rush, Myron. *The Rise of Khrushchev.* Washington, D.C.: Public Affairs Press, 1958.

Scitovsky, Tibor, Edward Shaw, and Lorie Tarshis. *Mobilizing Resources for War: The Economic Alternatives.* New York: McGraw-Hill Book Company, Inc., 1951.

Selznick, Philip. *The Organizational Weapon: A Study of Bolshevik Strategy and Tactics.* New York: McGraw-Hill Book Company, Inc., 1952.

Sokolovskii, V. D. *Soviet Military Strategy.* Translated and annotated by H. S. Dinerstein, L. Gouré, and T. W. Wolfe. Englewood Cliffs, N.J.: Prentice-Hall, Inc., 1963.

Trager, Frank N. (ed.). *Marxism in Southeast Asia: A Study of Four Countries.* Stanford, Calif.: Stanford University Press, 1959.

Wolf, Charles, Jr. *Foreign Aid: Theory and Practice in Southern Asia.* Princeton, N.J.: Princeton University Press, 1960.